CW00664958

BIBLICAL CRITICISM IN EARLY MODERN EUROPE

Mediaeval western theologians considered the Johannine comma (1 John 5:7–8) the clearest biblical evidence for the Trinity. When Erasmus failed to find the comma in the Greek manuscripts he used for his New Testament edition, he omitted it. Accused of promoting Antitrinitarian heresy, Erasmus included the comma in his third edition (1522) after seeing it in a Greek codex from England, even though he doubted the manuscript's authenticity. The resulting disputes, involving leading theologians, philologists and controversialists, such as Luther, Calvin, Sozzini, Milton, Newton, Bentley, Gibbon and Porson, touched not simply on philological questions but also on matters of doctrine, morality, social order and toleration. While the spuriousness of the Johannine comma was established by 1900, it has again assumed iconic status in recent attempts to defend biblical inerrancy among the Christian Right. A social history of the Johannine comma thus provides significant insights into the recent Culture Wars.

GRANTLEY MCDONALD is a postdoctoral fellow at the Universität Wien, and leader of the research project 'The court chapel of Maximilian I: between art and politics'. His research has been distinguished with prizes from the Australian Academy of the Humanities (Canberra) and the Praemium Erasmianum Foundation (Amsterdam). His recent work has focused on print, religious radicalism and censorship.

BIBLICAL CRITICISM IN EARLY MODERN EUROPE

Erasmus, the Johannine Comma and Trinitarian Debate

GRANTLEY MCDONALD

Universität Wien

CAMBRIDGE UNIVERSITY PRESS

CAMBRIDGE
UNIVERSITY PRESS

One Liberty Plaza, 20th Floor, New York, NY 10006, USA

Cambridge University Press is part of the University of Cambridge.

It furthers the University's mission by disseminating knowledge in the pursuit of
education, learning and research at the highest international levels of excellence.

www.cambridge.org
Information on this title: www.cambridge.org/9781107125360

© Grantley McDonald 2016

First published 2016

Printed in the United States of America by Sheridan Books, Inc.

A catalog record for this publication is available from the British Library.

Library of Congress Cataloging in Publication Data
Names: McDonald, Grantley, author.
Title: Biblical criticism in early modern Europe : Erasmus,
the Johannine comma and Trinitarian debate / Grantley McDonald.
Description: New York : Cambridge University Press, 2016. |
Includes bibliographical references and index.
Identifiers: LCCN 2015042174 | ISBN 9781107125360 (hardback)
Subjects: LCSH: Bible – Criticism, interpretation, etc. – Europe – History. |
Erasmus, Desiderius, –1536. | Bible. John, 1st, V, 7–8 – Criticism, Textual. |
Trinity – History of doctrines.
Classification: LCC BS500.M345 2016 | DDC 224/.940486–dc23
LC record available at http://lccn.loc.gov/2015042174

ISBN 978-1-107-12536-0 Hardback

For
Henk Jan de Jonge
sine quo non

I know not a Passage in all the New Testament so contested
as this.

Edmund Calamy, 1719

It is rather a danger to religion than an advantage to make it now
lean upon a bruised reed. There cannot be better service done to
the truth than to purge it of things spurious.

Isaac Newton, 1690

To use a weak argument in behalf of a good cause, can only tend
to infuse a suspicion of the cause itself into the minds of all who
see the weakness of the argument. Such a procedure is scarcely a
remove short of pious fraud.

Richard Porson, 1790

Contents

Figures

Foreword

Outside the domain of critical scholarship, textual criticism is generally regarded as the highly technical and dull pastime of a small minority of scholars who bury themselves in dusty corners, without external connection or relevance to living issues.

Grantley McDonald's study of Erasmus and the textual and theological problems surrounding the 'Johannine comma' (1 John 5:7–8) gives the lie to that assumption. In a fascinating study of Erasmus' response to the disputed Johannine text, McDonald traces the remarkable history of debate in the centuries that followed. This history is intimately intertwined with doctrinal debates on the Trinity, becoming particularly acute with the rise of Unitarianism. It is also strangely interconnected with Erasmus' own initial rejection of the comma and his later inclusion of it in a further edition of the Greek New Testament – subsequent generations using this ambiguity to support radically different conclusions.

The book tells an engrossing story of acrimonious debate in which text-critical issues become the basis of hardening and opposing views on central theological issues. Beneath this story lies the wider cultural issue of the place of tolerance and diversity within society, and the often rival claims of science and religion.

Today, the Johannine comma is widely dismissed by New Testament scholars as a later interpolation in the text of 1 John. This is true of mainstream scholarship across the theological and denominational spectrum, regardless of the approach to Trinitarian theology and despite the question of whether, and to what extent, the doctrine of the Trinity emerges from the pages of the New Testament. Nonetheless, the basic issues of interpretation are still pertinent. Does a single image of God emerge from the multiple portraits in the Bible? How is Christian doctrine to be elucidated in dialogue with the diverse writings of Scripture?

Equally pertinent in today's world – not only within but also beyond the bounds of the Judaeo-Christian tradition – is the ever-present question of how to interpret sacred texts. Protecting treasured texts from the kind of investigative study that is brought to bear on any literary text can lead to a fundamentalism where questioning by the reader is prohibited and official interpretations alone are permitted.

McDonald's study in reception history, with its lucid prose, its scholarly precision and its engaging style, tells an engrossing tale that makes for lively, thoughtful and challenging reading.

Dorothy A. Lee
Trinity College
University of Divinity
Melbourne

Acknowledgements

I rang the bell at Lambeth Palace Library and stamped my feet with anticipation. I was working on sixteenth-century Platonism, and at last I was to get my hands on the rare work *Tractatus aliquot Christianae religionis* by Johann Sommer, who set out to demonstrate that several Christian doctrines had been stolen from Plato. As I followed Sommer straight into the heart of the Antitrinitarian debates of the sixteenth century, I noticed with fascination that a number of his arguments depended on text-critical issues, such as the authenticity of the Johannine comma. Researching further, I found several stimulating articles on early modern biblical philology by Henk Jan de Jonge. I wrote to Prof. de Jonge with some questions, and before long he had put off his retirement to supervise me as a PhD candidate at the University of Leiden. Without his keen eye, critical intelligence, uncompromising standards and generosity, this book would never have been written, and it is presented to him in gratitude. I also thank the members of my examination committee – Jan Krans, Johannes Magliano-Tromp, Hans Trapman, Ernestine van der Wall, Jürgen Zangenberg and especially the eagle-eyed Miekske van Poll-van de Lisdonk – who all improved the result. As I reworked the text for publication, Andrew Turner, Henk Jan de Jonge, Keith Elliott, Mordechai Feingold and Johannes Brandl kindly read the draft and saved me from some mistakes, and Teunis van Lopik drew my attention to several sources I had missed the first time around. Laura Morris, Alexandra Poreda and Kanimozhi Ramamurthy were efficient and helpful midwives at CUP. To all of them, and to the anonymous readers for the Press, I say thank you.

My heartfelt thanks go also to the many friends and colleagues who gave their support, time, assistance and advice: Elizabethanne Boran, Massimo Ceresa, the late Patrick Collinson, Elisabeth Gieselbrecht, Royston Gustavson, Dieter Harlfinger, Rob Iliffe, Martin Heide, Leofranc Holford-Strevens, Jeffrey Kurtzman, Barbara Crostini Lappin, Dorothy Lee, Andrea Lindmayr-Brandl, Andrew McKenzie-McHarg, Scott

Mandelbrote, Vivian Nutton, Sandy Paul, Leigh Penman, Jac Perrin, Julian Reid, Joshua Rifkin, Erika Rummel, Gian Piero Siliquini, Stephen Snobelen, Mark Statham, Josef Struber, Naomi van Loo, Klaus Wachtel, Timothy Wengert and Piotr Wilczek.

My thanks are also due to the Centre d'Études Supérieures de la Renaissance (Université François-Rabelais de Tours), Le Studium (CNRS Orléans), KU Leuven, Trinity College Dublin and the Universität Salzburg for institutional support while I was writing this study. Thanks also go to the many libraries which allowed me access to their invaluable collections of rare books or provided scans: Universiteitsbibliotheek, Amsterdam; Bibliothèque municipale, Avranches; Öffentliche Bibliothek der Universität, Basel; Library of Corpus Christi College, Cambridge; Library of Gonville and Caius College, Cambridge; Library of Trinity College, Cambridge; University Library, Cambridge; Library of Trinity College, Dublin; Marsh's Library, Dublin; The National Archives, Kew; Universiteitsbibliotheek, Leiden; Universitätsbibliothek, Leipzig; Universiteitsbibliotheek and Maurits Sabbe Bibliotheek, KU Leuven; British Library, London; Lambeth Palace Library, London; Bayerische Staatsbibliothek, Munich; Universitätsbibliothek, LMU Munich; Bodleian Library, Oxford; Library of Corpus Christi College, Oxford; Library of Magdalen College, Oxford; Library of New College, Oxford; Bibliothèque nationale de France, Paris; Biblioteca Apostolica Vaticana, Rome; Stiftsbibliothek St Peter, Salzburg; Württembergische Landesbibliothek, Stuttgart; Herzog August Bibliothek, Wolfenbüttel; Biblioteka Uniwersytecka, Wrocław; Zentralbibliothek, Zürich.

My thanks also go to the Praemium Erasmianum Foundation, which unexpectedly distinguished this dissertation with a generous research prize.

And thanks to my family, near and far, who have patiently kept hold of one end of the string while I set off into the labyrinth in search of monsters.

Abbreviations

ASD.	*Opera Omnia Desiderii Erasmi.* Amsterdam: North Holland/Elsevier, 1969–2008; Leiden: Brill, 2009–.
ASD VI-4.	*Epistolae Apostolicae (secunda pars) et Apocalypsis Iohannis.* Ed Andrew J. Brown. Leiden: Brill, 2012.
ASD VI-8.	*Annotationes in Novum Testamentum, 1–2 Cor.* Ed. Miekske L. van Poll-van de Lisdonk. Amsterdam: North Holland/Elsevier, 2003.
ASD VI-10.	*Annotationes in Novum Testamentum, 1. Tim.–Ap. Ioh.* Ed. Miekske L. van Poll-van de Lisdonk. Leiden: Brill, 2014.
ASD IX-2.	*Apologia respondens ad ea quae Iacobus Lopis Stunica taxaverat in prima duntaxat Novi Testamenti aeditione.* Ed. Henk Jan de Jonge. Amsterdam: North Holland, 1983.
ASD IX-4.	*Apologia qua respondet duabus invectivis Eduardi Lei; Responsio ad annotationes Eduardi Lei; Manifesta Mendacia.* Ed. Erika Rummel. *Responsio ad disputationem cuiusdam Phimostomi de divortio.* Ed. Edwin Rabbie. Amsterdam: North Holland/Elsevier, 2003.
BAV.	Vatican City, Biblioteca Apostolica Vaticana.
BL.	London, British Library.
BnF.	Paris, Bibliothèque nationale de France.
BSB.	Munich, Bayerische Staatsbibliothek.
CCCM.	*Corpus Christianorum. Continuatio Mediaevalis.* 285 vols. Turnhout: Brepols, 1971–2014.
CCSL.	*Corpus Christianorum. Series Latina.* 176 vols. Turnhout: Brepols, 1953–2014.
CE.	*Contemporaries of Erasmus: A Biographical Register of the Renaissance and Reformation.* Ed. Peter

	G. Bietenholz and Thomas B. Deutscher. 3 vols. Toronto: Toronto University Press, 1985–1987.
Correspondence.	*The Correspondence of Erasmus.* Trans. R. A. B. Mynors and D. F. S. Thompson, annotat. Wallace K. Ferguson and Peter G. Bietenholz. 11 vols. Toronto: Toronto University Press, 1974–1994.
CSEL.	*Corpus scriptorum ecclesiasticorum latinorum.* 96 vols. Vienna: Tempsky, 1866–.
CR.	*Corpus Reformatorum.* Ed. Karl Gottlieb Bretschneider *et al.* 101 vols. Halle, Braunschweig and Zürich: [various publishers], 1834–1959.
CW.	*Collected Works of Erasmus.* Toronto: Toronto University Press, 1974–.
DM.	Thomas Herbert Darlow and Horace Frederick Moule. *Historical Catalogue of the Printed Editions of the Holy Scripture in the Library of the British and Foreign Bible Society.* 2 vols. London: Bible House, 1903–1911.
GA.	Gregory-Aland manuscript numbers, given according to Aland *et al.*, *Kurzgefaßte Liste der griechischen Handschriften des Neuen Testaments.* 2nd ed. Berlin: De Gruyter, 1994.
LB.	Desiderius Erasmus, *Opera Omnia.* Ed. Jean Le Clerc. 10 vols. Leiden: Van der Aa, 1703–1706.
MGH.	*Monumenta Germaniae Historica.* Hannover: Hahn; Weimar: Böhlau; Stuttgart: Hiersemann, 1826–.
ODNB.	*Oxford Dictionary of National Biography.* Ed. H. C. G. Matthew and Brian Howard Harrison. 60 vols. Oxford: Oxford University Press, 2004.
OER.	*The Oxford Encyclopedia of the Reformation.* Ed. Hans J. Hillebrand. Oxford: Oxford University Press, 1996.
Omnia Opera.	Desiderius Erasmus, *Omnia Opera.* 9 vols. Basel: Froben, 1538–1540.
Opus Epist.	*Opus Epistolarum Des. Erasmi Roterodami.* Ed. Percy S. Allen, H. M. Allen and H. W. Garrod. 12 vols. Oxford: Oxford University Press, 1906–1958.
PG.	*Patrologiae cursus completus. Series Graeca.* Ed. Jacques-Paul Migne. 161 vols. Paris: Seu Petit-Montrouge, 1857–1866.

PL.	*Patrologiae cursus completus. Series Latina.* Ed. Jacques-Paul Migne. 221 vols. Paris: Garnier, 1844–1905.
Text und Textwert.	*Text und Textwert der griechischen Handschriften des Neuen Testaments.* Ed. Kurt Aland *et al.* Berlin: De Gruyter, 1987–2013. Numbers given in brackets after a biblical citation refer to a *Teststelle* and *Lesart* assigned by *Text und Textwert.*
Vetus Latina.	Catalogue numbers for manuscripts of the Vetus Latina, given according to Bonifatius Fischer, *Verzeichnis der Sigel für Handschriften und Kirchenschriftsteller.* Freiburg: Herder, 1949.
WA.	Martin Luther, *Werke. Kritische Gesamtausgabe.* Weimar: Böhlau, 1883–. I *Schriften* (58 vols), 1883–1983 [*WA*]; II *Tischreden* (6 vols), 1912–1921 [*TR*]; III *Die deutsche Bibel* (12 vols), 1906–1961 [*DB*]; IV *Briefe* (18 vols), 1930–1985 [*Br*].

Unless otherwise stated, biblical citations in English are taken from the New Revised Standard Version, copyright © 1989 the Division of Christian Education of the National Council of the Churches of Christ in the United States of America. Used by permission. All rights reserved. All other translations, except where specifically noted, are my own. When citing early modern English texts, I silently expand abbreviations (y^e, y^t, wch and so on). Years are given as beginning on 1 January.

Introduction
The birth of the Trinity

Perhaps the most characteristic of Christian doctrines is that of the Holy Trinity, one godhead in three persons: Father, incarnate Son and Holy Spirit. This doctrine developed out of attempts to understand the relationships between God; Jesus, whom the Christian Scriptures designate as 'Son of God'; and the Holy Spirit, whom the Scriptures sometimes describe as sent by God, at other times as given by Christ – and all this within the context of monotheism. I say this doctrine *developed*, since it is not expressed unambiguously in the writings which the early Christians accepted as Scripture. Over time it was implied from several episodes in the New Testament, such as the baptism of Christ: 'And just as he was coming up out of the water, he saw the heavens torn apart and the Spirit descending like a dove on him. And a voice came from heaven, "You are my Son, the Beloved; with you I am well pleased"' (Mk 1:10–11, cf. Ps 2:7). But this episode gave rise to differences of interpretation. Some early Christians concluded that God adopted Jesus as his Son when he was baptised. Other episodes that mention God, Jesus and the Holy Spirit gave rise to similar disagreement. For example, at the end of his earthly ministry, Jesus was said to have commissioned his disciples with these words: 'Go therefore and make disciples of all nations, baptising them in the name of the Father and of the Son and of the Holy Spirit' (Mt 28:19). But some early Christians pointed out that this formulation does not necessarily imply that the Father, Son and Holy Spirit are one, or even equal. It is true that Jesus says in the fourth gospel that he and his Father are one (Jn 10:30), but what exactly does that mean, especially considering that Jesus also says in the same gospel that the Father is greater than he (Jn 14:28)? When Paul bade 'the grace of the Lord Jesus Christ, the love of God, and the communion of the Holy Spirit' be with the church at Corinth (2 Cor 13:13), it is easy to assume from a post-Nicene perspective that he was referring to the Trinity. But Paul's phraseology might lead a post-Nicene reader to wonder whether Paul implies here that Jesus is not God, or that the Holy Spirit is not God, or simply to doubt whether Paul understood the doctrine of the Trinity. The existence of divergent conclusions in the early church over the theological implications of these passages is sufficient evidence that they are not self-evident, despite what we might assume from our post-Nicene perspective. Nevertheless, on the basis of such passages, several varieties of a doctrine of the Trinity were proposed and defended in vigorous and often acrimonious debate, as the early church attempted to make sense of the witness of Scripture and the tradition of its interpretation.

The ways early Christians made sense of the stories and the texts received from other believers varied widely, and changed over time in reaction to different circumstances and conflicts between rival interpretations. If we want to understand how Christians in the first few centuries came to hold the beliefs they did, we need to forget later doctrinal formulations – or at least suspend them – and acknowledge the strangeness and primeval variety of their ideas. We must also remember that the terms 'orthodoxy' and 'heresy' are not absolute, but relational and subjective. What one person considers perfectly orthodox may be execrable heresy to another. Moreover, there is no reason to assume that those branded as heretics by those who held a different view perversely set out to give a false account of the faith and of the world. People defend their religious beliefs when they believe that they are right, not when they believe they are wrong. And even if some 'heretics' provided an inadequate theological account of Scripture, it should also be acknowledged that they sometimes emphasised or preserved important details neglected by their 'orthodox' opponents.[1]

Christology, the attempt to define and understand the nature and role of Christ, precedes any attempt to articulate a theory of the Trinity, both conceptually and historically. In the gospels, Jesus receives a number of titles from the Hebrew Scriptures, and the way readers understood these titles partly determined the way they conceived Jesus' mission, and even his nature. In Mt 27:42, Mk 15:32, Jn 1:49 and Jn 12:13, Jesus is called 'King of Israel'. In the canonical gospels and Acts, Jesus is called 'Son of God' more than two dozen times. These titles are related, since 'Son of God' was a royal title given to those who represented God, such as David

---

[1] Eusebius' conception of a monolithic, originary Christian orthodoxy from which 'heretical' groups fell away was challenged by Bauer 1934 (English trans. 1971). Bauer's thesis has been challenged and modified in several ways, but his essential argument remains valid; further, see Harrington 1980; Ehrman 1993; Wiles 1996, 1–2.

or Solomon (2 Sam 7:14; Ps 2:7). Did these titles mean merely that Jesus' followers hoped he would become king of a free Israel? Did they imply that Jesus was God? Or something else still? Some maintained that Jesus was a human, albeit one through whom God had chosen specially to proclaim his power. Others insisted that Jesus was in some sense one with God. This latter position is represented by the Johannine Epistles and the theologically sophisticated fourth gospel, in which Jesus is identified as the Word who was in the beginning with God (Jn 1:1).

Some early Christian thinkers, notably the Alexandrian presbyter Arius (*c.* 256–*c.* 335), appealed to the triple witness of Scripture, tradition and reason to propose a different understanding of the relationship between God and Jesus. Arius acknowledged that God is one, alone unbegotten, everlasting, without beginning, true, immortal, wise and sovereign. Jesus was created by the Father out of nothing, before the rest of creation (cf. Prov 8:22–23). There was thus a time when Jesus did not yet exist. Since Jesus is part of creation, he cannot be part of the deity, but is subordinate to the Father. Although Jesus is not identical with the one God, the Father, he is nevertheless our Lord, through whom all things, including humans, exist (1 Cor 8:6). When Jesus describes himself as one with the Father (Jn 10:30, 17:11, 17:22), he is referring to a unity of will, not of essence. Jesus carries out the work given to him by the Father (Jn 5:30, 17:4), and is called Lord because of his faithfulness to the Father's will (Phil 2:5–11; Heb 1:8–9). He is thus subordinate to the Father, not equal. But Arian Christology encounters a problem here: it is difficult to reconcile the notion that the Word existed before Jesus' birth with the belief that Jesus was adopted as Son of God.[2]

By contrast, the ancestors of the orthodox position described Jesus as coeternal and coequal with the Father. The way that Jesus' nature was understood had further implications for the way believers conceived of the Holy Spirit. Dominant strands in Christianity came to agree that God the Father, Jesus and the Holy Spirit are equal in essence and power. At the first council of Nicaea (325) and the council of Constantinople (381), the eternal equality of the Father and the Son was enshrined in credal form.[3] (While the equality of the Holy Spirit with the other two persons is not stated explicitly in the Nicene formulation, it is more or less implicit.) Belief in the equality of the Father and the Son thus became

---

[2] Wiles 1996, 10–17.
[3] The text of both versions is given in Denzinger 2001, 62–64, §§ 125–126 (Nicaea); 83–85, § 150 (Constantinople).

normative for orthodox Christian belief. The orthodox believed that
ideas such as adoptionism (espoused by Theodotus, Artemon and Paul of
Samosata) and subordinationism (Origen, Arius and many others) injured
Jesus' dignity as the Christ, the anointed one of God. For orthodox apologists, such as Athanasius, such ideas also raised the suspicion of idolatry,
for if Jesus was created, then worshipping him would mean worshipping
the creation rather than the creator. Moreover, if Jesus was merely a creature, he could have no power to save us. Raising a creature to the status
of the divine also endangered the strict monotheism that followed from
Christianity's Jewish origins. Some believed that conceiving of Jesus as
ontologically separate from God created problems for his role as mediator.
Distinguishing Jesus from God would suggest that God is too lofty, or too
idle, to take an interest in our salvation. Moreover, if Jesus was appointed
as our Saviour, then he was created for us, rather than we for God.[4] Many
heterodox ideas were espoused during the Middle Ages, yet with the gradual acceptance of the Nicene formulation of the Trinity and its restatement at Constantinople, the arch-heresy of Arius disappeared – with a
few isolated exceptions – for the best part of a thousand years.

Historically, the most explicit Scriptural expression of the consubstantial Trinity – that is, of the Father, the Son and the Spirit as a Trinity
united in essence – has been seen in a neatly balanced pair of verses in the
fifth chapter of the first letter of John:

> [7] For there are three that bear record [in heaven, the Father, the Word, and
> the Holy Ghost: and these three are one. [8] And there are three that bear
> witness in earth], the Spirit, and the Water, and the Blood, and these three
> agree in one. (1 Jn 5:7–8; Authorised Version, 1611; brackets added).

> [7] Ὅτι τρεῖς εἰσιν οἱ μαρτυροῦντες [ἐν τῷ οὐρανῷ, ὁ Πατήρ, ὁ Λόγος,
> καὶ τὸ ἅγιον Πνεῦμα· καὶ οὗτοι οἱ τρεῖς ἕν εἰσι. [8] Καὶ τρεῖς εἰσιν οἱ
> μαρτυροῦντες ἐν τῇ γῇ], τὸ πνεῦμα, καὶ τὸ ὕδωρ, καὶ τὸ αἷμα· καὶ οἱ
> τρεῖς εἰς τὸ ἕν εἰσιν. (1 Jn 5:7–8, as given in the 1633 Leiden edition, which
> presents the *textus receptus*; brackets added).

But as we shall see, the textual history of these two verses is problematic. To begin with, the passage from 'in heaven' (ἐν τῷ οὐρανῷ) in
v. 7 to 'in earth' (ἐν τῇ γῇ) in v. 8 does not occur in any extant Greek
bible older than the fourteenth century. These missing words, indicated
above with brackets, are known collectively as the 'Johannine comma'
or *Comma Johanneum*. (*Comma* here means not a mark of punctuation,

4 Wiles 1996, 7–8.

but a clause or sentence.)[5] Indeed, the reading of the comma given in the *textus receptus* is not found in *any* Greek manuscript except a handful copied from printed editions between the sixteenth and eighteenth centuries. The comma is also absent from the earliest Latin bibles, such as *Codex Fuldensis* (copied by Victor, bishop of Capua, in the 540s), and many others well into the Middle Ages.[6] The first extant bibles containing the Johannine comma are Latin manuscripts copied in Spain during the seventh century: some fragments in Munich (BSB Clm 6436, the 'Freising fragments' = Vetus Latina 64) and a palimpsest in León (Archivo catedralicio ms 15 = Vetus Latina 67). These two fragmentary sources are closely related, and represent – at least in the Catholic Epistles – a Vetus Latina text resembling that used in the Spanish liturgy.[7] The introduction of the comma evidently confused some scribes, and in an eighth-century New Testament from Reichenau, the heavenly witnesses have supplanted the earthly ones entirely.[8] An eighth-century New Testament from Luxeuil shows that the text was already unstable, displaying the 'comparative' reading of the comma ('there are three witnesses on earth ... *just as* there are three witnesses in heaven ...') attested until about the twelfth century.[9] However, the comma did not appear with any regularity in Latin bibles before the ninth century, and is even lacking from Latin bibles copied as late as the fifteenth century. Moreover, the readings of the comma in these early Latin bibles – where it occurs – are inconsistent and unstable, which suggests that the textual ground upon which they rest is less firm than for the surrounding verses, which do not display the same degree of variation. Yet as long as the Orthodox world remained virtually separate from the Catholic West, and as long as knowledge of Greek in the West remained relatively rare, this textual difference raised only occasional comment.

[5] The first appearance of the term *comma Iohanneum* seems to be in Kortholt 1686, 87: 'Observa etiam porro, non in solis Graecis exemplaribus quibusdam comma, de quo agimus, Johanneum desiderari, (quod quidem Bellarminus lectori audet persuadere) sed etiam in aliquibus codicibus vetustissimis mss. editionis vulgatae Latinae.' The term is attested sporadically over the next century: Wolf 1741, 5:311–313; Masch 1778–1790, 1:199: 'Textus graecus ex Erasmica tertia est exscriptus, hinc comma Johanneum hic exhibetur [...].' Cf. also Masch 1778–1790, 1:198, 247, 248. Other words and phrases used to describe the passage include *particula* (Lefèvre d'Étaples 1527, *31, 61–62; Erasmus, *ASD* IX-4:326; Erasmus 1532, 182; Naogeorgus 1544, 128r–v; Sozzini 1614, 423), *membrum* (Bullinger 1549, 103), *versus* (Mariana 1609, 73; Roger 1713, 99; Maran 1746, 161), *versiculus* (Bèze 1556, 318; Polanus von Polansdorff 1609, 1406; Crell 1680, 19), *dictum Johanneum* (Kettner 1713), *pericope* (Roger 1713, 120), and *clausula* (Maran 1746, 161).

[6] Fulda, Hochschul- und Landesbibliothek ms Bonifatius 1, Gregory-Aland ms F, prerecensional text; see Fischer 1985, 57–66. For a fuller discussion of the manuscript attestation of the comma and the ways it was used (or not used) by the early fathers, see McDonald 2011.

[7] De Bruyne 1921, 67; Ayuso 1947–1948, 57; Fischer 1985, 70, 77–78; Gryson 1999–2004, 1:98–99.

[8] Karlsruhe, Badische Landesbibliothek Codex Augiensis CCXXII, 55r.

[9] Wolfenbüttel, Herzog August Bibliothek ms Weissenburgensis 99, 117v.

In 1516, Erasmus of Rotterdam (*c.* 1466–1536), the greatest textual scholar of his generation, published an edition of the New Testament containing a humanistic revision of the Latin Vulgate and a parallel Greek text to support his revisions.[10] Since the Johannine comma was absent from all the Greek manuscripts Erasmus consulted, he did not include it in his text. He was immediately censured for this decision by critics, notably the Englishman Edward Lee and the Spaniard Diego Lopez de Zúñiga (better known under his Latin name, Stunica). Erasmus defended his choice by pointing out that he had merely recorded the readings in the Greek manuscripts available to him. Lee argued that since the comma is the most explicit Scriptural reference to the Father, Son and Holy Spirit as a Trinity, its omission could hardly be interpreted as a neutral editorial decision. He even accused Erasmus of promoting the long-dormant error of Arius. This charge had no basis in fact, and Erasmus was naturally keen to shake it off. During this acrimonious debate, Erasmus was presented with a Greek manuscript from England which contained the disputed passage in its body text. On the strength of this one textual witness, Erasmus included the comma in his next edition of the New Testament to avoid further criticism. However, in the accompanying annotation on the passage he suggested that the text presented in this 'British codex' had been altered to conform to the Vulgate.[11]

Erasmus' ambivalent decision to include the comma within the text while questioning its textual legitimacy in the *Annotationes* prompted vigorous debate, becoming one of the hinges on which wide-ranging social debates in early modern Europe turned. Many of these debates were associated with the revival, real or imagined, of the ideas of Arius. In his important monograph on Arius (1987), Rowan Williams highlighted the difficulty of defining Arianism in late antiquity, and noted that the picture of Arius and of his followers bequeathed to the later church was derived from the polemical constructions of Athanasius. Arianism is no less difficult to define in the early modern period. The term could be used in a strict sense to distinguish Arius' ideas from the orthodox doctrine of the Trinity on one side and from alternatives such as Sabellianism or Socinianism on the other. It was also used in a looser sense to indicate a sceptical stance towards the orthodox formulation of the Trinity and a critical attitude towards its Scriptural basis. It could also be used in a looser sense still, as a catch-all term, for any heterodox conception of God.

---

[10] De Jonge 1984b. On the date of the Latin translation, see A. J. Brown 1984; de Jonge 1988a, 1988b.
[11] A translation of Erasmus' annotations on this passage is given in the appendix.

The debate over the Johannine comma was not simply a matter of a few words here or there. It touched a raw hermeneutical nerve. Much more than Roman Catholic theologians, the Protestant reformers emphasised the importance of Scripture as the sole source and rule of doctrine. While Roman Catholics could rely on the church's teaching office as repository and conduit of traditions of interpretation where the Scripture was not entirely clear, Protestants were obliged to determine exactly what Scripture says in order to develop and justify their doctrines. In the absence of a body like the Inquisition to define doctrine and enforce conformity, the Protestant churches shattered into a broken mosaic of sparring groups. Radical understandings of Scripture and doctrines such as baptism or the Trinity often accompanied social ideas feared as potentially subversive by those who bore state power. When drawn into broader discussions about the Trinity, the debate over the Johannine comma invariably assumed a wider social significance.

The Italian lawyer and theologian Fausto Sozzini was the most prominent of several sixteenth-century thinkers who rejected the traditional account of the Trinity. Sozzini also developed distinctive ideas on human nature, will and responsibility, as well as the duties of the individual to the state. After his followers, the Socinians, were expelled from Poland, many ended up in the more tolerant Netherlands, and some moved on from there to England. Many churchmen in England, both Anglican and Nonconformist, feared that Socinianism would promote a laxity of doctrine which would lead inexorably to a chic liberalism or even worse. John Edwards (1695) asserted that 'in the very *Socinian* Doctrine it self there seems to be an *Atheistick* Tang'.[12] Many also considered Socinianism a threat to the unity of a nation recently reunited under a Protestant flag. In 1693, William Sherlock, dean of St Paul's London, warned that 'these Disputes about the Trinity make sport for Papists'. Should they continue, he admonished, 'we shall certainly be conquered by France'.[13] By the nineteenth century, British Unitarians (heirs both to the continental Socinians and to native traditions of dissent) resented the fact that they were still liable to punishment – or at least stigmatisation and social exclusion – because of their beliefs.[14] Many other minority religious groups in Britain, most notably Roman Catholics, shared this sense of disenfranchisement.

---

[12] John Edwards 1695, 64.
[13] Sherlock 1690, 23.
[14] Unitarians distinguished themselves from Socinians, particularly on the issue of the worship due to Jesus (see Kell 1830), but such distinctions had as much to do with theological niceties as with the desire to avoid further persecution and legal discrimination.

When Socinians and Unitarians used the philological advances won by pious critics like John Mill to advance their theology and its attendant attitudes towards society, the worst fears of conservative commentators seemed to be realised.

By the late seventeenth century, the authenticity of the Johannine comma had become an issue on which any educated person could be expected to have an opinion, and tempers ran high on both sides. According to Isaac Newton (1690), the comma was 'in every bodies mouth'.[15] For Thomas Long (1703), the comma was 'one of the plainest Proofs of the Trinity, which is the first and most fundamental Article of the Christian Religion', and anyone who doubted its genuineness was 'a greater Friend to the *Socinians* and *Arians*, than to the Church of *England* and her Articles'.[16] The comma was discussed in sermons and public lectures. With the spread of Enlightenment scepticism in the eighteenth century, traditional Christian doctrine, including the Nicene formulation of the Trinity, came increasingly under the spotlight. These tensions reached a head when Edward Gibbon dismissed the Johannine comma as an interpolation in the third volume of his *History of the Decline and Fall of the Roman Empire* (1781). Gibbon was attacked by the clergyman George Travis, whose misdirected defence of orthodoxy was in turn exploded by the philologists Richard Porson and Herbert Marsh. The work of these men represented the culmination of Erasmus' attempt to understand the documents of Christianity in their historical, literary and linguistic context. But ever since Erasmus' time, fears had been voiced that impious investigation into the text of Scripture would lead to a scepticism and disbelief that could only undermine doctrine and faith. Literary and theological journals were deluged with essays attacking or defending the comma with varying degrees of competence, from the fatuous to the vertiginously erudite. The heat generated by this debate is difficult to appreciate until one leafs through the smart journals like the *Journal Britannique*, the *Gentleman's Magazine*, and *The Eclectic Review* from the 1750s through to the 1830s. Fascination with the Johannine comma, minutely dissected by dozens of learned critics and untold thousands of lay commentators, became a cultural phenomenon. Popular attitudes displayed what sociologists call an 'informational cascade' (or informally the 'bandwagon effect'), in which individuals opt to follow group tendencies, even ignoring their

---

[15] Newton 1959–1977, 3:90.
[16] Long 1703, 44, 47.

own information, and even when the choice is incorrect.[17] The mythology surrounding Erasmus' inclusion of the comma in the third edition of his Greek text became a weapon easily deployed in interdenominational polemic. As late as 1887, during the modernist debate within the Roman Catholic church, Jean-Pierre Paulin Martin could assert that the status of the comma was 'a burning question, one of those by which one can sometimes judge a man's tendencies'.[18]

By the middle of the twentieth century, scholarly debate had led to a consensus: the comma was an interpolation, with no right to be included in the Greek text. The issue was solemnly declared dead and buried. But the comma is an unquiet corpse, and has been clamouring for exhumation for some time now. The revival of the Christian right, especially in Evangelical circles, has reanimated the debate over the comma as part of a wider defence of the *textus receptus*. Attention to this issue on the Internet shows that the Johannine comma has again become a hot-button issue, since it seems to pose questions concerning the accuracy and reliability of Scripture, and raises suspicions of ecclesiastical conspiracy, anxieties stoked by recent popular fiction. As a result of an informational cascade amongst non-scholarly believers, the divide between academic consensus and lay conviction is growing. In a poll taken on the website puritanboard. com, nearly half the respondents replied that they believe the comma to be a genuine part of Scripture.[19] Some conservative churches and religious organisations explicitly defend the comma as genuine Scripture.[20] Many of those who defend the comma are convinced that textual and historical criticism of the bible compromises the integrity of Christianity by chipping away at its foundations, minutely but persistently. Some are led by such suspicions to dismiss and even revile academic biblical studies, in order to justify their rejection of scholarly criticism of the *textus receptus*. But adherence to the *textus receptus* and translations based upon it, notably the Authorised Version, is not simply a textual or literary preference. It frequently underlies a conservative social and moral program. In recent decades, some who hold such views have attempted to influence

---

[17] Bikhchandani et al. 1992.
[18] J.-P. P. Martin 1887, 98.
[19] www.puritanboard.com/showthread.php/37481-Johannine-Comma/ (accessed 1 January 2016).
[20] The 2006 *Report of the Religion and Morals Committee of the Free Church of Scotland*, 17, criticises the omission of the comma from the English Standard Version; http://www.fpchurch.org .uk/wp-content/uploads/2014/06/Religion-Morals-Report-2006.pdf. See also G. W. and D. E. Anderson, 'Why 1 John 5.7–8 is in the bible', www.tbsbibles.org/pdf_information/40-1.pdf (accessed 1 January 2016).

public education policy, such as the teaching of evolution in schools, and the regulation of sexual and reproductive issues, such as the availability of abortion and the legality of same-sex relationships. In the last few decades, the Johannine comma, one of the clearest instances of a conflict between academic critics and biblical conservatives, has thus regained its power to raise considerable passions.

Whenever the Johannine comma is discussed, Erasmus inevitably appears as a central player. He was responsible not only for formulating the basis of the familiar Greek wording of the comma and including it in the text form which would dominate the scene from the early sixteenth to the late nineteenth centuries, but also for questioning the authority of his only manuscript source for the verse. The story of his decision to include the comma has often been altered in the telling. Some variants in this narrative seem innocuous enough, but they frequently conceal further motives. According to a popular legend still recounted widely, Erasmus promised to restore the comma to his published text if a single Greek manuscript could be found in support of the reading, and challenged his adversary Edward Lee to produce such a manuscript. When such a manuscript was produced, Erasmus is alleged to have honoured his promise by including the comma in the third edition of his Greek New Testament (1522a). This myth, however appealing, suggests misleading conclusions about Erasmus' character and his editorial standards. More significantly, it implies that he ultimately came to be convinced of the authenticity of the comma. In 1980, Henk Jan de Jonge roasted this old chestnut, showing that there is no evidence that Erasmus ever made such a promise, and that the story grew from a careless misreading of Erasmus' published reply to Lee. However, like all good stories which are not true but really ought to be, the myth of Erasmus' promise to Lee refuses to go away, and is still cited in scholarly and popular literature on biblical criticism.[21] Even more important than Erasmus' contribution to the story of the comma was his development of an approach to Scriptural study that was both respectful and objective. Building on foundations laid by Lorenzo Valla, Erasmus was one of the first scholars to appreciate that the text of Scripture is dynamic, subject to corruption through impersonal physical processes as well as deliberate intervention. He also realised that Christian doctrine is not a lapidary whole, but has been subject to

---

[21] De Jonge 1980b, cites many nineteenth- and twentieth-century authorities who cite the myth; see also *ASD* IX-2:12, 259; Rummel 1986, 132–133.

negotiation and change through history as various groups jockeyed for power and influence.

An examination of the interpretation of a single disputed verse in the New Testament may seem a forbidding prospect. But the Johannine comma is a keyhole that allows us to peer straight into the heart of the violent struggles over the understanding of the Trinity that took place from the sixteenth to the nineteenth centuries. It also provides a guiding thread that permits us to see connections between diverse thinkers and writers. Moreover, a detailed examination of this textual problem permits us to observe the variety of responses to a fundamental question: what is essential to Christianity, and what is incidental? Many early Christians considered Jesus' divinity less important than the existence and sovereignty of God, or obedience to the two great commandments. Since at least the late Middle Ages, Roman Catholics have considered the seven sacraments central to Christianity. This attitude predisposed some Catholic interpreters to see in the three earthly witnesses of water, Spirit and blood a veiled reference to the sacraments of baptism and eucharist. For Luther, the relative importance of Scripture over tradition was more pressing than it was to his Roman Catholic opponents, and the quest for literal accuracy in the biblical text became a typically (though not exclusively) Protestant obsession. In Erasmus' New Testament, Luther found a firm basis for his insistence on the authority of Scripture, and he followed Erasmus in rejecting the comma. Later Lutherans were torn between the instinct to remain true to Luther's rejection of the comma, and the desire to use it against Antitrinitarians. To Socinians, the doctrine of the Trinity was not an original element of Christian belief, and could be jettisoned without damaging the core of the faith. Socinian discussions thus tend to downplay the doctrinal significance of the verse. Many modern-day evangelicals consider the defence of the *textus receptus*, including details such as the comma, as a matter of the utmost importance, while Christians of other traditions find this priority puzzling. Observing the changing fortunes of the Johannine comma provides a kaleidoscope of different perspectives on what has been considered indispensible to Christianity, and what is negotiable.

Many aspects of the disputes over the comma have been examined before, notably by August Bludau, Henk Jan de Jonge, Robert Coogan, Cecilia Asso and Joseph M. Levine, who nevertheless remarked in 1999: 'The long story of the Johannine comma between Erasmus and

Gibbon remains to be told.'[22] While we shall take some modest steps towards
filling this gap, we shall even go a little further. First, we shall investigate
the production of Codex Montfortianus, the Greek manuscript from which
Erasmus took his reading of the Johannine comma, suggesting a number of
new conclusions based on a detailed examination of the manuscript. Second,
we shall suggest how Erasmus came to inspect this manuscript. Third, we
shall examine the mythology surrounding Erasmus' inclusion of the comma
within his text. Fourth, we shall sketch a social history of the debate, ana-
lysing how arguments for and against the authenticity of the comma have
been deployed in religious disputes through time. Such a social history of the
debate shows that philology is not an abstruse scholarly exercise, but exists in
a symbiotic relationship with larger religious and social issues. Fifth, we conclude from recent contests over the authenticity of the comma show that the
early modern critique of traditional beliefs of the authorship and inspiration
of the Scriptures did not bring about a universal and unchallenged shift of
'episteme' (to use Foucault's term). Rather, it marked a fork in the road. One
path was followed by those who insisted on the providential preservation of
Scripture. The other was taken by those who believe that Scripture, whatever
its source, is subject to the same processes of transmission as any other text.
(Suffice it to say that these two positions have rather different claims to verifiability.) The story that emerges from these disagreements is not a jubilant
narrative of progress from ignorance to enlightenment, of superstition to true
knowledge. It is a story of constantly competing claims, in which outcomes
are rarely clear, and motives often obscure. And we shall see that the disputed
authenticity of the Johannine comma has frequently acted as a lightning rod
for anxieties caused by the pressures of religious and social difference.

---

[22] Levine 1999, 157.

CHAPTER I

Erasmus

This chapter has a number of purposes. It outlines the production of Erasmus' New Testament and its relationship to the Complutensian bible, a rival project from the University of Alcalá. It investigates the resistance to Erasmus' edition from churchmen in England (Henry Standish and Edward Lee), Spain (Stunica and the commission of Valladolid), France (Noël Béda) and Italy (Alberto Pio da Carpi). It examines the source of Erasmus' Greek text for the Johannine comma, the so-called Codex Montfortianus, and suggests how he came to see it.

All along we shall observe a number of presuppositions, sometimes unspoken, sometimes spoken very loudly. First is the conviction that textual purity was equal to doctrinal and even moral purity. Second is the ambiguous claim, made frequently by New Testament scholars, that their philological work was based on the 'faithfulness of the Greek codices' (*ad fidem Graecorum codicum*) rather than on the decadent Vulgate. This apparently straightforward claim was counterbalanced by the survival of the Roman prejudice that 'Greek faithfulness' (*Graeca fides*) was no faith at all, and by long-standing tensions between the Roman Catholic and Greek Orthodox Churches.[1] The Greek New Testament and the Latin Vulgate would thus continue to exist in a fratricidal standoff for the entire period considered in this book.

1. The Complutensian bible and the politics of sacred philology

During the fifteenth and sixteenth centuries, humanist scholars in Western Europe sought to recover ancient texts for their own time. This impulse took many forms, from uncovering, copying and publishing long-forgotten manuscripts in monastic libraries to restoring the integrity

---

[1] Frick 1995, 139–140.

of more familiar texts through ever more sophisticated tools of philological and textual criticism. The desire to restore the pristine form of a given
text also led to the rejection of mediaeval Latin translations and the prep-
aration of new ones based on a more reliable original text and on a better
knowledge of the original and target languages.

Among the ancient texts revised by humanists were the books of
Scripture themselves. The first plan to publish the bible in Hebrew and
Greek was initiated in 1502 by cardinal Francisco de Ximénez de Cisneros
(1436–1517), who assembled valuable manuscripts to be edited by a group
of scholars at the University of Alcalá de Henares (Lat. *Complutum*).[2]
The bible produced by this committee contained not merely the text of
the Vulgate. The four Old Testament volumes also include the Hebrew
text, the Septuagint, the Targum (with Latin translation) as well as 'primitive' versions of the Hebrew and Targum. The New Testament volume
contains both the Vulgate and the Greek. A final volume presents grammatical and lexical aids. The printing of the first volume, containing the
New Testament, was finished on 10 January 1514, and the remaining five
volumes were completed on 10 July 1517, but when Ximénez died on 8
November the same year, the printed gatherings had still not been divided
into volumes for binding and sale.

There is something striking about the financial arrangements for the
Complutensian bible. It cost more than 50,000 ducats to produce. The
600 copies were sold for six and a half ducats each. Even if all the copies
were sold all full price, the project could not hope to recover even 8 per
cent of what it had cost. Clearly, some other kind of value played a major
part in the calculations. Each step in the production of an early printed
book, from author to reader, was determined by a number of transactions
at which value was exchanged. Although several stages in the production
and consumption of a printed book involved the exchange of money, the
exchange was often in less tangible elements, such as the creation of reputational value for the stakeholders (author, patron, printer, purchaser,
collector), or the acquisition of the right to possess and use the book.[3] The
huge discrepancy between the initial investment in the Complutensian
Polyglot and the projected profit shows that this project must have been
intended to capture other kinds of intangible value, such as the creation
of a reputation for scholarly or spiritual excellence. Such intangible value

[2] See Delitzsch 1871; Lyell 1919; Bataillon 1937; Jerry H. Bentley 1983, 70–111; Metzger and Ehrman 2005, 137–142; Elliott 2009c, 232–234.
[3] Gustavson 2010, esp. 186–188.

could also lead to financial value, for example from greater enrolments at Alcalá, or increased patronage.

While the project advanced in Alcalá, Erasmus was gathering materials for his own edition of the New Testament. He based his Greek text principally on manuscripts containing the Byzantine text. Although this text type is the best represented statistically in the manuscripts, it is the most recent and least authoritative text type. Erasmus' choice to use the Byzantine text would have long-lasting consequences for the development of New Testament criticism. Erasmus deduced that the Latin Vulgate was not all the work of Jerome, a church father he held in great respect, but was a composite of makeshift efforts made over time by fallible humans. He denied that his revision of the Vulgate constituted a threat to the church, which had never officially authorised the Vulgate as its official text or invested it with any particular claim to accuracy. He did not wish to deny that the authors of Scripture were divinely inspired, but to insist that the Holy Spirit perched on the shoulder of every subsequent scribe and translator was asking too much. In short, Erasmus insisted that he was not undermining Scripture, but restoring it. Philology was not the sole basis of correct interpretation, but it was its necessary precondition, as Jerome and Augustine had also believed. He was not making any theological claims for his work as 'grammarian', simply laying the groundwork for others to do so. And in all things he submitted his private judgement to the teaching authority of the Church.

In August 1514, Erasmus met the Basel printer Johannes Froben and entered into negotiations to publish his edition of the New Testament with the accompanying *Annotationes*. Froben obtained an imperial privilege to prevent others from producing a reprint for four years within the Holy Roman Empire, or from importing pirated copies printed outside the empire. Froben's preface – probably written by Erasmus or one of the other editors in the shop, such as Oecolampadius, Beatus Rhenanus or one of the Amerbach brothers – emphasises the piety and scholarly integrity of the enterprise, and condemns the unscrupulous practices of other printers, content to turn out corrupt texts as long as they could make a profit.[4] The dedication to Leo X promised a revival of Christianity through a text purified of the errors of the centuries, a completion of the task Jerome never completed. Erasmus insisted that determining the literal meaning of the text in its original language was the necessary first step

---

[4] Erasmus 1516, aaIv. Further, see Pabel 2005, 218–219. On Froben's abilities as a scholar and his relations with humanists, see Hilgert 1971.

before any allegorical interpretation or theological work could begin.[5] In private, Erasmus admitted that the first edition, which emerged from the press in late February 1516, was full of editorial and printing errors caused by the haste with which it was put together, 'not so much issued as thrown headlong from the press.'[6] Erasmus' opponents seized upon these faults as evidence of his lack of qualification for the task.

Despite its shortcomings, Erasmus' edition captured much of the projected market of the Complutensian Polyglot. It had many attractive features, including an accompanying volume of detailed textual annotations. The iconoclastic style of Erasmus' annotations and his opposition to the scholastic establishment lent his work a progressive, even radical, appeal. Erasmus' continual revisions gave subsequent editions the appearance of ever greater degrees of accuracy and completeness. By the time the Complutensian Polyglot was finally published, Erasmus' edition had enjoyed a four-year head start in establishing 'brand awareness'. Since it included only the New Testament, it was more compact and cheaper than the Spanish edition. By cutting into the projected market of the Complutensian bible, Erasmus' New Testament had reduced its power to capture value for a number of the stakeholders. But in time, circumstances would provide an opportunity for some of this value to be recovered.

2. English opposition to Erasmus: Edward Lee

Although Erasmus had a number of powerful supporters in England, including Thomas More, William Warham, archbishop of Canterbury, and John Colet, dean of St Paul's London, not everyone there was equally enthusiastic about his sacred philology. In 1520–1521, Henry Standish, minister provincial of the Conventual Franciscans, preached against Erasmus' translation of the opening of John's gospel as *In principio erat sermo* (Erasmus argued that *sermo* more accurately expressed the active and creative power of God's word than the *verbum* enshrined in the Vulgate, and was used by the earliest Latin theologians, Tertullian and Cyprian).[7] Standish also accused Erasmus of denying the general resurrection.[8]

---

[5] On Erasmus' Scriptural hermeneutics, see Payne 1969–1970.

[6] Erasmus to Willibald Pirckheimer, Leuven, 2 November 1517, *Epist.* 998 (*Opus Epist.* 3:117; *Correspondence* 5:167).

[7] See Boyle 1977; Coogan 1992, 84–88; *ASD* VI-2:13, n. 1,1. On Standish, see *ASD* IX-2:10. Levine 1999, 44, misattributed to Henry Standish *Whether it is expedient that the Scripture should be in English* (1554); the author was actually John Standish.

[8] Erasmus, *Epist.* 1126, 1127A, 1196 (*Correspondence* 8:7–17, 19–23, 193); *Annotationes* to 1 Cor 15:51, *Opera omnia* 6:518–519; *LB* 6:724F-725A; *ASD* VI-8:310–312. See also J. R. Harris 1887,

A more tenacious critic was Edward Lee (*c.* 1482–1544), a young English theologian who would subsequently climb the greasy pole of ecclesiastical preferment to become archbishop of York.[9] Lee claimed that Erasmus had invited him to comment on his New Testament, but then dismissed the resulting criticisms as trifling, inane or mistaken. Lee took umbrage at Erasmus' ill-disguised scorn and the way he mocked Lee's efforts before others. A rift opened between the two men, which soon turned to open hostility, antagonism and mutual recriminations.[10] Lee published his own *Annotationes* on Erasmus' *Annotationes* in early 1520, despite Erasmus' best efforts to prevent their coming to light. Erasmus suggested that Lee was motivated more by a desire for self-aggrandisement than concern for the integrity of the biblical text. Lee could not object that Erasmus had dared print the Greek Scriptures, for Aldus had done the same in 1518, and Lee was not pursuing him. He could not object that Erasmus had demonstrated that the Greek text varies from the Latin Vulgate, for Valla had shown the same thing. He could not object that Erasmus alone had dared to translate the Greek text, for Jacques Lefèvre d'Étaples had done this before Erasmus. What was worse, Lee had the presumption to pick holes in an edition showered with superlatives by Pope Leo himself.[11]

The issue came to a head over the Johannine comma. Erasmus had declined to include the comma in his 1516 and 1519 editions, explaining his choice with a brief explanation – a little too brief, considering the theological importance with which the passage had become invested – that the passage was not found in the Greek manuscript text.[12] Erasmus was aware of the importance attached to this verse in fifteenth- and sixteenth-century apologetic. He may have expected opposition to his excision of the comma, for he quoted it in his devotional *Brief method for attaining true theology* (*Ratio seu methodus compendio perveniendi ad veram*

50–51; Robertson and Plummer 1914, 376–377; J. H. Bentley 1978, 317–318; van Poll-van de Lisdonk 2000.

[9] See Coogan 1992, esp. 101–113; Asso 1993, esp. 82–87, 179–184.

[10] Further, see Rummel 1989, 1:95–120; Coogan 1992, 20–23; *ASD* IX-4:1–18. On Erasmus' character, see Minnich and Meissner 1978, still suggestive despite the dated Freudian analysis.

[11] Erasmus' dedication of his edition to the pope was apparently intended in part to silence those who had initially criticised him for undertaking the task without papal mandate; further, see Rummel 1989, 1:17–18.

[12] Erasmus 1516, 618: '*Tres sunt qui testimonium dant in coelo*.) In graeco codice tantum hoc reperio de testimonio triplici: ὅτι τρεῖς εἰσιν οἱ μαρτυροῦντες, τὸ πνεῦμα καὶ τὸ ὕδωρ, καὶ τὸ αἷμα id est quoniam tres sunt qui testificantur, spiritus, & aqua, & sanguis. *Et hi tres unum sunt*.) Hi redundant. Neque est, unum, sed in unum, εἰς τὸ αὐτό id est siue in idem.' Asso 1993, 83 and 179, stated incorrectly that Erasmus included the comma in the Latin text of his 1516 New Testament but deleted it in the 1519 edition.

theologiam, 1519) to support his argument that all believers are in union with God, and share in the unity of the godhead itself. Indeed, his wording of the comma in the *Methodus* (complete with his signature translation of *sermo* instead of *verbum*) resembles that which appeared subsequently in his 1521 monoglot Latin New Testament and in the 1522 diglot.[13]

Lee devoted a long comment (*Annotation* XXV) to the comma. He quoted the prologue to the Catholic Epistles to show that this passage had been 'adulterated by heretics'. For Lee, this prologue showed that the evidence of any single manuscript is of dubious value. 'The Christian reader ought to ponder whether it is right to believe that what is in the Greek manuscripts possesses oracular status.' Lee would not have been surprised if Erasmus had found his reading in a carelessly selected copy corrupted by a heretic, and simply accepted its text without checking it against other manuscripts. Such indolence when dealing with sacred texts, Lee charged, was impiety. Lee pointed out that Lorenzo Valla had inspected seven manuscripts, and never made any comment about the comma. (This point was almost certainly designed to get under Erasmus' skin, for it was he who had rediscovered Valla's annotations on the New Testament at Leuven, and however much he protested his own independence, he certainly considered Valla an important predecessor.)[14] But then Lee came to the point: he was afraid that if the Arians were to reappear, seeking to diminish Christ's divinity, Erasmus' edition would be music to their ears. Lee, like many of his contemporaries, considered the comma as the single most important witness to the Trinity in all Scripture. He considered other verses central to Christology, such as Jn 10:30 ('the Father and I are one'), an insufficient foundation for a theology of the Trinity, because they do not mention the Holy Spirit. 'But as soon as you have produced *this* verse,' Lee exulted, 'the mouth of the heretic is stopped, such that he dare not hiss one syllable more. On this point you will win, without any contest. There is no corner for him to hide.'[15]

Erasmus was incensed. In a published reply, he retorted with justifiable indignation that he had drawn attention to the comma because the words were not found in his Greek manuscripts.[16] Lee had thrown Valla's failure to mention this textual difficulty in Erasmus' face. Erasmus conceded that Valla did not mention this passage, but this may have been the result of inattention or mistake. Valla was not immune to error. Erasmus

[13] Erasmus 1519c, 110; Erasmus 1933, 258–259; Erasmus 1521a, 475. Cf. Semler 1764, 49.
[14] Rummel 1986, 13–15.
[15] E. Lee 1520b, 200–201.
[16] Erasmus 1520, 260 [280]–295; *ASD* IX-4:323–335; *CW* 72:403–419.

categorically rejected Lee's suggestion that Valla 'concealed' the imperfections of his Greek texts by supplying whatever they lacked from the Latin, lest he should diminish the authority of his Greek texts. Moreover, Valla constantly criticised the Latin Vulgate. Why would he want to make his Greek text conform to a version he considered less than perfect? Perhaps Valla's Greek manuscripts did contain the comma. What then? Since Erasmus had not seen the manuscripts from which Valla worked, he refused to apologise for differing from Valla on this point. Was it impiety not to have seen all the manuscripts in the world? In any case, Erasmus claimed to have inspected more manuscripts than Valla ever did. (In fact Erasmus was bluffing here. His text of the Catholic Epistles was as yet based only on three manuscripts: GA 1, 2815 and 2816.)[17] Had he found one Greek manuscript with the comma, he certainly would have added the missing phrase from that one textual witness, but since that had not happened, he had no choice but to indicate that the comma was absent from the Greek manuscripts available to him.

Lee had accused Erasmus of following the Greek manuscripts as an oracle, but Erasmus replied that this was not the case. In fact, since all manuscript copies of the New Testament contain variants, none can be claimed as absolutely reliable, much less as an oracle. And what else was Erasmus

[17] P.-Y. Brandt 1998, 121–122; *ASD* VI-3:1–12; Krans 2006, 335–336; and *ASD* VI-4:1–6, 484, identify the manuscripts used by Erasmus. For the first edition he consulted the following manuscripts: GA 1[eap] (used for proofreading and annotations); GA 2[e] (printer's copy); GA 817[e] (proofreading and annotations [Theophylact]); GA 2814[rKt] (the second volume of GA 1, borrowed from Reuchlin); GA 2815[ap] (the second volume of GA 2; used for printer's copy and corrections, and as principal source for Acts, Heb 12:18–13:25, Catholic Epistles); GA 2816[ap] (used for corrections; Estienne used the first volume as his γ' [= GA 4[e]]); GA 2817[pt] (printer's copy, used for corrections and annotations). Since Erasmus counted manuscripts comprising multiple volumes as a single manuscript, his claim to have used five manuscripts at Basel (a claim questioned by Krans 2006, 335 n. 1) is correct. Erasmus also drew on notes taken from manuscripts he had examined in England, and his edition consequently contains readings taken from GA 69 (text and annotations; see *ASD* VI-3:10–11) and 2105[pt] (annotations [Theophylact; not noted by Brandt]). For the 1519 edition, Erasmus integrated some corrections from GA 3[eap] and a manuscript of the Gospels from St Agnes at Zwolle; see *ASD* IX-2:191, note to line 461; and Erasmus, *Epist.* 504, 516. For the 1522 edition, Erasmus added material from the Aldine edition and Montfortianus (GA 61[eapr]). The 1527 edition integrated variants from the Complutensian edition. In the 1535 edition of the *Annotations*, Erasmus recorded variants from codex Vaticanus (GA B/03), supplied to him by Juan Ginés de Sepúlveda, in a letter sent in 1533: see the annotations on Mk 1:1, Lk 10:1, Lk 23:46, and Acts 27:16 (Erasmus 1535b, 113, 187, 216, 331). Erasmus found the agreements between the readings in GA 03 and the Latin Vulgate suspicious, though in the case of Mk 1:1 he thought that Vaticanus had the correct reading. See also his comments on Vaticanus in 1535a, β3v; and the commentary in Semler 1764, 75–76. In his *Apologia to Stunica*, Erasmus mentions having used manuscripts in England, Brabant and Basel; on these manuscripts (one Greek, one Latin), see *ASD* IX-4:55, note to line 855; and 327, note to line 250. Tregelles, in Horne 1856, 4:108–111; Rummel 1986, 35–42, 195; Elliott 2009c, 244.

to do with the texts available to him? If the pope were hypothetically to entrust Lee with the task of translating the manuscripts of the Greek New Testament in the Vatican, would Lee thunder against the pope's manuscripts, or dare to insert words not present in them? Such conduct would only draw upon him the justified accusation of untrustworthiness. Erasmus had not set himself up as judge over the Greek manuscripts, merely as their translator.

One element of Lee's attack especially annoyed Erasmus: the slanderous suggestion that he had only consulted *one* Greek manuscript, an accusation aimed at calling his philological competence and editorial diligence into question. If Lee could produce a Greek manuscript containing the comma, and could prove that Erasmus had had access to this manuscript, then he might have cause to make accusations of indolence.[18] Regarding Lee's accusation that Erasmus concealed evidence from his readers, all he had done was to present the evidence from the Greek manuscripts available to him. Even if one of Erasmus' manuscripts did contain the comma, why would Lee assume that Erasmus had hidden the fact from his readers, rather than that he had inadvertently omitted it through inattention? Such accusations of deceit and turpitude said more about the accuser than the accused. In any case, why would Erasmus conceal or intentionally omit textual evidence that could be used to refute heretics? And what good would it do Erasmus to falsify the evidence of the Greek manuscripts when anyone able to read Greek could easily check the manuscripts?

Erasmus also dealt with Lee's citation of the prologue to the Catholic Epistles.[19] This prologue was generally ascribed to Jerome until the seventeenth century, when John Selden, Christoph Sand and Richard Simon argued that it is a pseudonymous forgery.[20] Erasmus never openly questioned the authenticity of the prologue, though he excluded it from his edition of Jerome's works.[21] In his response to Lee, Erasmus dealt with the arguments presented in the prologue as if they had been put forward by Jerome. He even made the text work for his own ends. First, Erasmus pointed out that even Jerome was not always consistent, and sometimes approved of readings he had criticised elsewhere. Jerome called into doubt

---

[18] *ASD* IX-4:326. Cf. *LB* 9:277AB; *CW* 72:408. Bainton 1970, 169–170, 354 n. 21, and de Jonge 1980b, 385–386, identify this passage as the origin of the myth of Erasmus' promise. De Jonge, in *ASD* IX-2:189, points out a parallel in Erasmus' *Apology to Stunica*.

[19] Ed. in Wordsworth, White and Sparks 1889–1954, 3.2:230–231 (cf. *PL* 29:825–832). The relevant section of the prologue is translated in the appendix below, 317.

[20] Selden 1653, 2:136; Sand 1669, 383; Simon 1689a, 206–211; Simon 1689b, 2:4–11; Bludau 1904b; Bludau 1921, 16.

[21] *ASD* IX-2:255.

and obelised much that the church taught without harm, such as the stories in the Old Testament Apocrypha, and liturgical texts such as the Song of the Three Young Men (Dan 3:52–87). Erasmus suggested archly that those who disagreed with Jerome's judgement on those passages should suspect his conclusions about the comma. In any case, Erasmus noted that Lee had misread the prologue, which simply pointed out that variations between rival Latin translations of the Catholic Epistles had led to confusion and uncertainty. Moreover, Erasmus pointed out that Jerome complains in the prologue that he had been criticised for changing the readings of the Latin bible as they were commonly accepted in his time. In other words, Jerome's Vulgate did *not* reflect the Scriptural text most familiar in the late fourth century. In fact, the prologue provided evidence that the Latin translations most widely read in the late fourth century gave a reading in 1 Jn 5:7–8 which corresponded to that found in the Greek manuscripts familiar to Erasmus; in other words, they also excluded the comma. And lest Lee should convince himself that it was only heretics who excluded the comma from their texts, Erasmus cited two orthodox fathers, Cyril and Bede, who both quoted a large section of 1 Jn 5, yet omitted the comma.[22]

Potentially the most damaging accusation that Lee brought against Erasmus was that he had omitted the comma through a desire to promote Arianism. Erasmus felt he could afford to scoff at this suggestion, since Arianism was long suppressed. 'Who then are these heretics Lee tells me about? To be sure, people who survive only in name. That scared little man is afraid of their ghosts when there is really no need.'[23] Even if these long-dead Arians should come back to life, Erasmus asked, why would they be silenced and backed into a corner by this one passage, as Lee had maintained? There are many passages in Scripture that apologists might use more effectively to defend the doctrine of the Trinity.[24] The Arians might dispose of Jerome's testimony, since they were erudite and familiar with the Scriptures. If for this reason only, Erasmus almost regretted that the books of the Arians had been destroyed. When faced with Jesus' statement that 'I and the Father are one' (Jn 10:30), would Arians be forced to admit that the Son is of one essence with the Father? Might they not argue that this unity was one of agreement rather than one of essence? To support this interpretation, they could cite Jesus' prayer: 'May they be

---

[22] See, for example, Cyril, *Thesaurus, assertio* 34, *PG* 75:616; Bede, *Super epistolas catholicas expositio, ad* 1 Jn 5:7–8, *CCSL* 121:321–322, ll. 84–111 (cf. *PL* 93:114); see *ASD* IX-4:325. Erasmus was familiar with the idea that the text of 1 Jn (e.g. 1 Jn 4:2–3) had been adulterated by heretics, although he did not believe it; see Erasmus 1535b, 768.

[23] Erasmus 1520, 288; *ASD* IX-4:329.

[24] Erasmus 1520, 285; *ASD* IX-4:326.

one, as we are one' (Jn 17:22). (Erasmus almost certainly knew Thomas Aquinas' condemnation of Joachim of Fiore's similar interpretation of these passages.)[25] When expounding this and similar passages, defenders of the Trinity were obliged to show that the writers of Scripture spoke not merely of a unity of witness, will or function, but used the word 'one' to refer to a substance identical both in species and also in number, a *uniquely singular* substance. Not even Augustine had managed successfully to explain how this could be.[26] Just as the Arians managed to work their way around Jn 17:22, they would get around the comma with equal ease. It is obvious, they would say, that the Spirit, water and blood can only be one in testimony, not in essence. The Father, Word and Holy Spirit are one in the same way, with the Father attesting to the Son, the Son teaching what he has received from the Father and the Spirit instilling in the Apostles what he has received from the Son. Lee's confidence in the power of the comma to silence the Arians was thus misplaced. And if the Arians found a particular passage in Scripture uncongenial, they would corrupt it anyway. But to fear that the entire Scripture would collapse if one passage was found to be corrupt opened oneself up to an even greater danger, since the Scriptures are full of textual snags. Not even the heretics would be bold enough to make judgements about the trustworthiness of the Scripture as a whole because of one corrupt passage. Erasmus insisted that he had put forward these arguments not because he wanted to encourage Arianism, but simply because he wanted to show that Lee's slanders were baseless. To ward off any possible accusation of heresy, Erasmus explicitly declared his orthodox belief that 'the Son is of the same essence with the Father, as the church believes and proclaims.'[27]

Despite his bluster, Erasmus was clearly worried that the stink of Arianism might harm the reception of his New Testament. And when Arians did reappear later in the sixteenth century, they found in Erasmus' New Testament and *Annotationes* a goldmine of arguments, just as Lee had feared.

3.   Spanish opposition to Erasmus: Jacobus Stunica

In the summer of 1520, Jacobus Stunica († 1531), one of the editors of the Complutensian edition, published a systematic critique of Erasmus'

---

[25] Aquinas 1881, 3:450–451.
[26] Augustine, *Adversus Maximinum* III.22, *PL* 42:794–795.
[27] Erasmus 1520, 287; *ASD* IX-4:328.

text.[28] Stunica's antipathy towards Erasmus was probably kindled by the fact that the Dutchman had released two editions of the New Testament before the Complutensian New Testament, printed and lying ready to be bound for six years, could be published. But not all the blame for these circumstances could be placed at Erasmus' feet. A cluster of factors had delayed the publication of the Complutensian bible. First, Ximénez was dead, and no one had yet applied formally to the pope to request permission to publish. Three years had passed since the last volume was printed, so Leo X took matters into his own hands, addressing a brief on 22 March 1520 to Francisco Ruiz, bishop of Ávila and Francisco de Mendoza, archdeacon of Pedroche. This letter suggests that Ximénez' executors disagreed over the price at which the bibles were to be sold. Clearly, the disparity between the cost of the edition and its potential to generate both cash and reputational value had become an issue, probably as a result of the appearance of Erasmus' editions in 1516 and 1519, and the Aldine edition in 1518. Leo broke the deadlock by commanding the men to fix a price and to sell the bibles without further delay.[29]

The timing of Leo's brief suggests that the appearance of Erasmus' edition had contributed to the delay in the publication of the Complutensian bible.[30] Leo was surely aware of the imperial privilege protecting Erasmus' edition from being reprinted for four years. Since the election of Charles V as Holy Roman Emperor in June 1519, the protection afforded by Froben's privilege extended to Spain as well. Even if the Complutensian bible was not actually a reprint of Erasmus' edition, it would have looked bad for the pope to consent to a publication that *seemed* like it infringed on Froben's privilege. Moreover, Erasmus had dedicated the 1516 edition of his New Testament to Leo. To consent prematurely to the publication of a similar work that trod on the heels of an earlier papal dedication would have looked even worse. The fact that Leo's order to publish came a mere three weeks after Froben's privilege expired is probably no coincidence.

[28] There is no evidence for the oft-repeated claim, made for example by Scrivener 1894b, 2:405, that Stunica was the editor-in-chief of the project; see Bataillon 1937, 43; and de Jonge in *ASD* IX-2:14–17.

[29] K. Aland and B. Aland 1995, 3–4, write: 'The final volume of the polyglot was completed on 10 July 1517, shortly before the death of Ximénes, but publication of the whole work was delayed until 22 March 1520, when papal authorization for its issuance was finally granted (after the manuscripts loaned from the Vatican library had been returned to Rome).' This account gives the impression that the pope withheld permission pending the return of the manuscripts, but it is clear from the pope's brief, printed on ₳8v of the first volume of the Old Testament, that the final initiative for the publication of the Bible came from Leo himself.

[30] Elliott 2009c, 231.

The delayed publication of the Complutensian Polyglot had the unexpected benefit of allowing corrections in response to controversial details
of Erasmus' text. Michael Screech's examination of the typography of the
Complutensian New Testament has provided fascinating insights into the
final stages of its production. As Screech noted, several bifolia are cancels (reprinted sheets), including the bifolium KK2/5, the sheet on which
the comma occurs. There is good reason to suppose that the comma
was part of the body text before the cancels were reprinted. In order to
make the Greek text more manageable for those with little knowledge
of the language, the Complutensian edition uses superscript letters to
cross-reference each Greek word against the corresponding word in the
parallel Latin text. The fact that the sequence of these superscript letters
runs unbroken from fol. KK2v (a cancel) to fol. KK3r (not a cancel) suggests that the comma was part of the text in the first impression. When
the editors at Alcalá saw that Erasmus had omitted the comma, they evidently felt compelled to justify its appearance in their edition. Bifolium
KK2/5 was therefore reprinted with a long note concerning the comma
shoehorned into the margins of fol. KK2v.[31] The new marginal note,
drawn from Thomas Aquinas' commentary on the condemnation of
Joachim of Fiore's position on the Trinity at the Fourth Lateran Council,
has two functions. First, it gives an authoritative theological justification
for the omission of the phrase καὶ οἱ τρεῖς εἰς τὸ ἕν εἰσιν at the end of
v. 8 in the Complutensian edition. More importantly, it shows, on the
authority of Aquinas himself, that Erasmus' omission of the comma from
his edition and his inclusion of the last phrase of v. 8 betrayed a hint of
Arianism.

Several details support the suggestion that bifolium KK2/5 was reprinted
in response to Erasmus' edition. First, the long marginal annotation on
the comma does not appear in the manuscript notes made by the editors
at Alcalá while they were establishing the text for publication.[32] Second,
the ornamental woodcut capital *I* on fol. KK5v shows more wear than the
same woodcut on fol. KK4r (particularly evident on the frame and the
forehead of the saint), which suggests that it was printed later. Third, this
is the only example in the entire Complutensian New Testament of such
a long note – so long in fact that it has to loop into the lower margin. It
is also one of only two marginal notes that deals directly with matters of

---

[31] Reeve and Screech 1990, XXI, reproduce KK2r–v of the Complutensian New Testament.
[32] J. H. Bentley 1980, tentatively ascribed these notes (Madrid, Universidad Complutense, Archivo
Historico Universitario, ms 117–Z-1) to the editors Demetrius Ducas and Elio Antonio de Nebrija.

doctrine, the other being at 1 Cor 15:51, another passage that had drawn Erasmus into hot water.

Screech attributed the reprinting of bifolium KK2/5 to sinister motives: 'behind the austere text of the Complutensian Polyglot lay tensions between scholarly integrity and the arrogance of power. And somebody was prepared to betray the reader's trust, quietly giving at times readings in the Greek which never had [...] any valid manuscript authority behind them.'[33] Yet this revision may equally be interpreted as an expedient designed to recapture value expected from the Complutensian bible by Ximénez, the editors, and the University of Alcalá, value compromised by the appearance of Erasmus' edition. Stunica's criticisms likewise served to undermine the reputational value of Erasmus' edition by casting his orthodoxy and scholarly competence into doubt. And since the beginnings of the Lutheran debate in 1517, a reputation for orthodoxy had been at a premium.

Arnald Guillén de Brocar, the printer of the Complutensian bible, printed Stunica's critique of Erasmus' edition in mid-1520.[34] In his annotation on the comma, Stunica defended the reading from the Latin Vulgate as it was commonly found in the late Middle Ages, and contrasted this with the shorter Greek text. Stunica cited the Greek text of 1 Jn 5:8 – one typographical error aside – as it appeared in Erasmus' 1516 edition, not as it is given in the Complutensian bible. Stunica's position was clear: 'One should know that in this passage the manuscripts of the Greeks are quite clearly corrupt, but that ours,' that is, those of the Latin Vulgate, 'contain the truth, as they were translated in the earliest times.' To support his argument he cited the notorious prologue to the Catholic Epistles.[35]

Erasmus wrote a response to Stunica's work between June and September 1521, and it appeared in early October. This initial volley initiated a series of thirteen attacks and counterattacks between Stunica and Sancho Carranza on one side, and Erasmus on the other.[36] Some material in Erasmus' first defence against Stunica is adapted from the defence against Lee, and parts would also be included in the revised *Annotationes* accompanying Erasmus' 1522 edition of the New Testament. Erasmus therefore kept his remarks brief. At five places, Stunica gave readings from a manuscript Apostolos from Rhodes, then housed in the university library at Alcalá, which he believed was more authoritative than Erasmus'

---

[33] Reeve and Screech 1990, XXII–XXIII.
[34] See *ASD* IX-2:15–22.
[35] Stunica 1520, K2r.
[36] See *ASD* IX-2:17–47, on the course of this exchange.

manuscript sources. Two of Stunica's four annotations on 1 Jn record variants from the Rhodian codex, but on the comma this codex was clearly
silent.[37] 'Though my dear Stunica so often boasts of his Rhodian codex,
to which he attributes such authority, he has strangely not adduced it as
an oracle here, especially since it almost agrees with our [Latin] codices
so well that it might seem to be a 'Lesbian straight-edge' [that is, one that
bends to fit the needs of the occasion].'[38] Erasmus taunted Stunica with
this unfortunate circumstance: 'And now where is that Rhodian codex of
yours slumbering all the while?'[39] If Stunica could not cite a single Greek
manuscript to support the reading of the comma in the Complutensian
bible, that could only mean one thing: it did not rest on *any* manuscript
authority, but had simply been translated from Latin. For his own part,
Erasmus claimed sententiously – and not entirely truthfully – that he did
not emend the readings in his Greek codices, but merely reported their
contents.

While the prologue to the Catholic Epistles claimed that the comma
had been omitted by unfaithful translators, Erasmus pointed out that
when the orthodox Cyril of Alexandria cited 1 Jn 5, he also omitted the
comma, a passage he almost certainly would have cited in his disputes
with the Arians if he had known it.[40] The implication is clear: if the
comma was present in the Greek New Testament current in the fourth or
fifth century, as the prologue to the Catholic Epistles claims, why was it
apparently unknown to Cyril? Erasmus also added new information about
his ongoing investigations. In August 1521, he inspected two old manuscripts (probably Latin bibles) in the library at St Donatian in Bruges, and
found that both lacked the comma. In June 1521, Paolo Bombace wrote to
inform Erasmus that the comma was lacking from 'an extremely old codex
in the Vatican library' (BAV ms Vat. gr. 1209 = GA ms B/03).[41] Given this

---

[37] Stunica 1520, gives five readings from the Codex Rhodiensis (Wettstein Paul 50 = Apostolos 52), at
   Jn 3:16, 2 Cor 2:3, Jas 1:22, 2 Pt 2:2, and 1 Jn 5:20. On the basis of these readings, Rhodiensis cannot
   be identified with any extant manuscript. Erasmus later cited the reading from Rhodiensis in his
   Annotations on 2 Cor 2:3, not mentioning Stunica by name but heaping Ximénez with exaggerated
   praises. Here Erasmus also suggests that readings in Rhodiensis were altered to make them conform more closely to the readings of the Latin Vulgate. Further, see *ASD* VI-8:342–345; Delitzsch
   1871, 30–32.
[38] *ASD* IX-2:258, repeated in 1522 *Annotationes*.
[39] *ASD* IX-2:252.
[40] Cyril, *Thesaurus, assertio* 34, *PG* 75:616.
[41] Paolo Bombace to Erasmus, *Epist.* 1213, 18 June 1521 (*Opus Epist.* 4:530; *Correspondence* 8:248); de
   Jonge 1980b, 389; Coogan 1992, 107.

evidence, Erasmus concluded that the prologue attributed to Jerome may not have given a true picture of the facts.

Although Stunica did not explicitly raise the spectre of Arianism in his 1520 critique, Erasmus sensed that he had implied it by citing the prologue of the Catholic Epistles. Erasmus made a pre-emptive strike by summarising his arguments against Lee. He claimed piously that the purpose of reading Scripture is not to build speculative systems, but to become more like God. He went further, arguing that biblical texts were virtually powerless to prove anything when arguing against heretics: 'I for one do not see how the view rejected by the Arians can be upheld except with the help of speculative reasoning. But finally, since this entire passage is obscure, it does not have much power to refute heretics.'[42]

But Erasmus kept the biggest surprise until last, a stunning revelation which he related with wry, even sarcastic humour:

> However – lest I should keep *anything* hidden – there has been found in England a single Greek manuscript in which occurs what is lacking in the commonly accepted texts. It is written as follows: Ὅτι τρεῖς εἰσιν οἱ μαρτυροῦντες ἐν τῷ οὐρανῷ, πατήρ, λόγος καὶ πνεῦμα, καὶ οὗτοι οἱ τρεῖς ἕν εἰσιν. Καὶ τρεῖς εἰσιν μαρτυροῦντες ἐν τῇ γῇ, πνεῦμα, ὕδωρ, καὶ αἷμα. Εἰ τὴν μαρτυρίαν τῶν ἀνθρώπων, etc, although I am not sure if it is by accident that the phrase 'and these three are unto one', which is found in our Greek manuscripts, is not repeated at this point [that is, in v. 8]. I therefore restored from this British codex what was said to be lacking in our editions, lest anyone should have any cause to blame me unjustly. However, I suspect that this codex was adapted to agree with the manuscripts of the Latins.[43]

The 'British codex' Erasmus consulted has been identified as Codex Montfortianus (GA 61[eapr]), housed in the library of Trinity College Dublin since the seventeenth century. However, the reading reported in the *Apology to Stunica* (and absorbed into the 1522 *Annotationes*) differs from that in Montfortianus in three details: in v. 7, it omits ἅγιον after πνεῦμα, and gives εἰσιν instead of εἰσι, a minor variant arising from the moveable *v*; and in v. 8, it omits οἱ before μαρτυροῦντες (Figure 1.1). These discrepancies can probably be attributed to the haste with which the *Apology to*

---

[42] *ASD* IX-2:258–259 (with commentary), repeated in 1522 *Annotationes*; translation in the appendix. Further, see Asso 1993, 179–180.

[43] *ASD* IX-2:258, repeated in 1522 *Annotationes*. It should be noted that Erasmus' phrase *quod in vulgatis deest* does not refer to the Latin Vulgate, which usually contains the comma, but either to the Greek Vulgate (i.e. the Byzantine text) or the editions that Erasmus had already published.

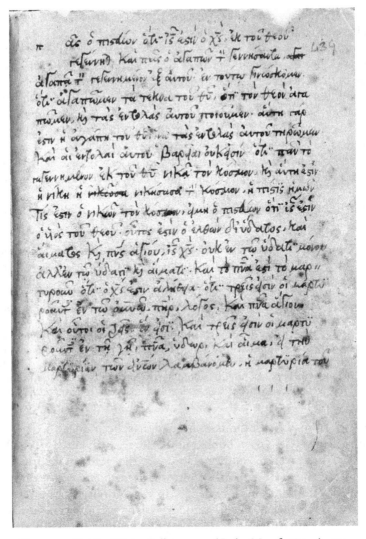

Figure 1.1. Dublin, Trinity College ms 30 (Codex Montfortianus), 439r.
Reproduced by kind permission of the Board of Trinity College, Dublin.

Stunica was written, or to compositor's errors. These apparent transcriptional errors in the *Apology* are repeated in Erasmus' description of the British codex in his 1522 annotations on the passage, which draw a good deal on the *Apology*.

4. Erasmus' reading of the comma

Although Erasmus was convinced that the criticisms of Lee and Stunica were ultimately futile, they gave him sufficient reason to believe that the reception of his edition might be damaged by their accusations of heresy, and that any suspicion about his orthodoxy would hamper the propagation of the pious *philosophia Christi* he outlined in the *Paraclesis*. In order to remove anything by which he might be accused further of Arianism, and to maintain the integrity – and market value – of his edition, Erasmus decided to commit the lesser evil of including the reading of the comma from Codex Montfortianus in the text of his Greek New Testament, despite his suspicion that it had been adapted to the Latin Vulgate.[44] There are differences between the reading of 1 Jn 5:7–8a (ὅτι ... αἷμα) given in the *Apology* (and later repeated in the *Annotationes*) and that given in the body text of the 1522 New Testament. This suggests that Erasmus rechecked Montfortianus while establishing the reading of the comma for the 1522 edition, which reads as follows:

Ὅτι τρεῖς εἰσιν οἱ μαρτυροῦντες ἐν τῷ οὐρανῷ, πατήρ, λόγος, καὶ πνεῦμα ἅγιον, καὶ οὗτοι οἱ τρεῖς ἕν εἰσι. καὶ τρεῖς εἰσιν οἱ μαρτυροῦντες ἐν τῇ γῇ, πνεῦμα, καὶ ὕδωρ, καὶ αἷμα, καὶ οἱ τρεῖς εἰς τὸ ἕν εἰσιν.

This reading differs from that in Montfortianus in two details, both in v. 8. Both discrepancies evidently arose out of Erasmus' attempts to harmonise the reading in his new source with that in his earlier editions. In the transcription of the British codex given in Erasmus' *Apology* and *Annotationes*, there is no καὶ before ὕδωρ in v. 8. For the body text of the 1522 New Testament edition, Erasmus added a καὶ before ὕδωρ, following the manuscripts upon which he had based his 1516 text. Likewise, Erasmus spliced in the concluding clause of v. 8 (καὶ οἱ τρεῖς εἰς τὸ ἕν εἰσιν) from his 1516 edition (repeated unaltered in the 1519 edition). This latter alteration was not without significance. Aquinas mistakenly believed that this clause was an Arian interpolation, and it is consequently omitted from many Latin manuscripts copied after Aquinas' day. The absence of this clause from the Greek text of Montfortianus and the Complutensian edition strongly suggests that they both follow the Latin reading of the comma as it was altered by western scribes following Aquinas. Aside from the two elements taken over from his 1516 text (the addition of καὶ and καὶ οἱ τρεῖς εἰς τὸ ἕν εἰσιν in v. 8), the reading of the comma in Erasmus' 1522

---

[44] On Erasmus' attitude to *mendacium, simulatio* and *prudentia*, see Trapman 2002.

edition is thus identical to that in Montfortianus. There is therefore good reason to conclude that the British codex used by Erasmus was indeed Montfortianus.[45]

The Greek reading in Erasmus' 1522 edition corresponds to a revised reading in his Latin translation, which appeared even a little earlier, in a Latin monoglot edition published by Froben in June 1521:

> Quoniam tres sunt qui testimonium dant in coelo, pater, sermo, & spiritus sanctus: & hi tres unum sunt. Et tres sunt qui testimonium dant in terra, spiritus, & aqua, & sanguis: & hi tres unum sunt.[46]

This detail suggests that Erasmus inspected Montfortianus by the middle of 1521 at the latest.

Erasmus' suspicions about Montfortianus arose from his belief that it had been 'adapted' to conform to the Vulgate. He often made this accusation if a particular Greek manuscript varied significantly from the Byzantine text with which he was familiar.[47] However, in the case of Montfortianus, his suspicions were well founded. The highest concentration of scribal interventions in Montfortianus is in 1 Jn 5. In this single chapter, the scribe departed from the reading in his parent manuscript (Oxford, Lincoln College ms gr. 82, GA 326[apt]) in five instances to make the resulting Greek text conform more closely to the Latin Vulgate. In 1 Jn 5:6, GA 326 gives ὅτι τὸ πνεῦμα ἐστιν ἡ ἀλήθεια ('for the Spirit is the truth'), while Montfortianus has ὅτι ὁ Χριστός ἐστιν ἀλήθεια ('that Christ is the truth'). This reading is found in no other extant Greek manuscript, though it corresponds to the variant *quoniam Christus est veritas*, attested in the Latin Vulgate as early as Codex Fuldensis.[48] This variant changes the sense significantly, turning the ὅτι-clause from an affirmation that the Spirit is identifiable with the truth into an indirect statement reporting the content of the Spirit's testimony. The suspicion of alteration is strengthened by the unidiomatic omission of ἡ before ἀλήθεια. In Montfortianus, the article is also missing before πατήρ, λόγος and

---

45 Supporters of the authenticity of the comma, from D. Martin 1721 to Maynard 1995, point to Erasmus' first account of the 'British codex' to suggest that Codex Montfortianus and the British codex are not the same book, apparently with the intention of multiplying the manuscript evidence for the comma.

46 Erasmus 1522a, 517v [=X3v]. On the 1521 Latin edition, see *ASD* IX-2:259.

47 De Jonge 1980b, 387.

48 This variant in the Latin text apparently arose from an optical confusion of the abbreviated *nomina sacra* S̄P̄S̄ (*Spiritus*) and X̄P̄S̄ (*Christus*). This mistake is easy to imagine in Latin; confusion between Π̄Ν̄Ᾱ (Πνεῦμα) and Χ̄Ρ̄Σ̄ (Χριστός) in a Greek text would be more difficult to explain. Bruns 1778, 259; 'Inspector', 1816, 502; 'Crito Cantabrigiensis', 1827, 26; Horne 1856, 4:215; Westcott 1892, 183–184.

πνεῦμα ἅγιον in 1 Jn 5:7, and before πνεῦμα, ὕδωρ and αἷμα in v. 8. This grammatical irregularity raises the suspicion that the scribe simply translated both verses inexpertly from Latin, which has no articles. In 1 Jn 5:9, Montfortianus departs from GA 326 by giving ὅτι instead of ἦν, which reflects the Vulgate reading *quoniam*. In 1 Jn 5:12, GA 326 gives ὁ ἔχων τὸν υἱόν, while Montfortianus gives the fuller reading ὁ ἔχων τὸν υἱὸν τοῦ Θεοῦ, which corresponds to the Vulgate reading *qui habet filium Dei*.[49] In 1 Jn 5:20, GA 326 gives the indicative ἐσμεν, while Montfortianus gives the subjunctive ὦμεν, which corresponds with the subjunctive *simus* in the Latin Vulgate.[50] In 1 Jn 5:8 Montfortianus also transmits the unique reading ἐν τῇ γῇ ('on the earth'). This is apparently a translation of the Latin Vulgate reading *in terra*. The rendering of this phrase in the Complutensian edition (ἐπὶ τῆς γῆς) is more idiomatic, though it does not reflect the reading in any known Greek manuscript, and was presumably translated from Latin as well.[51] The occurrence in one chapter of so many unfamiliar and in some cases unidiomatic readings may have made Erasmus wary of using the British manuscript more than he had to. However, the codex did offer Erasmus a way out of his difficulties with Lee and Stunica, and accordingly he adopted its reading of the comma for his 1522 text. He even deleted the article τὸ before πνεῦμα, ὕδωρ and αἷμα in 1 Jn 5:8, which he had given in his 1516/1519 text on the basis of the manuscript Basel, UB ms A. N. IV. 4 (GA 2815ᵃᵖ).[52]

Erasmus' suspicions about Montfortianus may have led him to conclude that it was of little further value as a witness to the Greek text. Ever since Lorenzo Valla had unmasked the *Donation of Constantine*, humanist philologists prided themselves on their ability to detect textual anomalies. Erasmus himself questioned the identity of the author who called himself Dionysius the Areopagite, and diligently separated the wheat of Seneca's real correspondence from the tares of mediaeval pseudepigrapha. But the pruning hook of philological criticism can easily be hammered into the forger's stylus, and not even Erasmus was immune from temptation. The presence in the ancient translations or quotations of details not present in the known form of the Greek text can reflect variants present in early Greek manuscripts which have since perished without further trace. The probability that such details reflect an early form of the Greek

---

[49] This variant is found in GA 61, 104, 180, 206, 429, 467, 522, 614, 630, 876, 1127, 1292, 1490, 1505, 1611, 1799, 1831, 1832, 1838, 1846, 2138, 2147, 2200, 2243, 2412, 2544, 2652; *ECM* 4:354.

[50] This variant is only found in GA 61, 323, 2544; *ECM* 4:365. Cf. Griesbach 1794, 14; *ASD* VI-4:70.

[51] The phrase ἐν τῇ γῇ also occurs at Lk 12:51, but after the verb δοῦναι.

[52] *ASD* VI-4:484.

text increases when such details appear in more than one ancient translation or in multiple independent citations. At Acts 9:5, the Harclean Syriac
version (which Erasmus could not read) and the Latin Vulgate add the
following words: '"It is hard for you to kick against the goads." And he,
trembling and astonished, said, "Lord, what will you have me to do?" And
the Lord said to him [...].' Erasmus wanted to retain these words, swayed
by their presence in the Latin Vulgate, so he translated them into Greek
from the Latin, borrowing material where necessary from Acts 22:10 and
Acts 26:14, duly noting in his *Annotationes* that these words were not
found in the Greek codices he had consulted (GA 1, 2815, 2816).[53] He
made similar changes to his Greek text at Mt 14:12 and Mk 1:16 to make
it conform more closely to the Latin Vulgate.[54] More boldly, he translated
Rev 22:16c–21 from Latin, since his only Greek manuscript of Revelation
(GA 2814^{rKt} [*olim* GA 1], which he consulted at Basel) was defective at the
end. In the *Annotationes* to this passage, he indicated how he had arrived
at these readings, though he minimised the extent of his intervention.[55]
None of these alterations aroused any comment from Lee, presumably
because Erasmus had 'corrected' the Greek to make it conform to the
Vulgate. More problematically, Erasmus' fourth edition of the works of
Cyprian (1530) includes the treatise *De duplici martyrio*, which Erasmus
wrote himself to promote his conviction that the daily martyrdom of the
everyday Christian is equal to the more conspicuous self-sacrifice of the
traditional martyr.[56] To Erasmus, the idea of 'adapting' sacred texts was
thus nothing new. He had done it himself.

Given the incomplete evidence, it is impossible to know why the scribe
of Montfortianus altered his Greek text in so many places to conform
to the Latin Vulgate. At several points throughout the manuscript, this
scribe added variant readings from Erasmus' 1516 New Testament in the
margins. These variant readings are written in a slightly different ink and
with different pens from that used for the body text, which may suggest
that they were added later, perhaps days, perhaps years. It is clear that the

[53] Erasmus 1516, 385: '*Durum est tibi*.) In graecis codicibus id non additur hoc loco, cum mox sequa-
tur surge, sed aliquanto inferius, cum narratur haec res.' Cf. Bruce 1988, 182; Heide 2006, 51–53.

[54] Elliott 2009c, 234.

[55] Erasmus 1516, 625: 'Quanquam in calce huius libri, nonnulla verba repperi apud nostros [*i.e.* in
the Latin Vulgate], quae aberant in Graecis exemplaribus, ea tamen ex Latinis adiecimus.' Cf. *ASD*
IX-4:55, 278. See Heide 2006, 101–111; commentary in *ASD* VI-4:667–670.

[56] Erasmus 1530, 508–527; in the list of contents (b3v), Erasmus describes the work thus: 'Liber unus
De duplici martyrio ad Fortunatum, quem in uetustissima bibliotheca repertum adiecimus: uti-
nam liceat & caetera huius uiri salutifera scripta peruestigare.' Further, see *Opus Epist.* 4:24; Seidel
Menchi 1978; Grafton 1990, 43–45; Kraye 1990, 44–48; Hallyn 1999.

scribe had access to Erasmus' 1516 edition before relinquishing possession of the manuscript. It is less certain whether he copied it in direct reaction to Erasmus' work. Samuel Prideaux Tregelles (1844) spoke for many when he expressed his suspicion that the manuscript 'was written out for the purpose of producing a MS. which should contain 1 John 5.7 in Greek.'[57] However, this conclusion is too confident. Had the manuscript been written at Lee's command to force Erasmus' hand, one would expect it to contain more readings that supported Lee's many other criticisms of Erasmus' *editio princeps*. Tregelles' conclusion also implies an accusation of forgery, and proving such an accusation would require establishing that the scribe possessed a requisite degree of *mens rea*. But any competent scribe paid constant attention to the textual integrity of the documents he copied, weighing each word to decide whether his archetype required emendation. The scribe of Montfortianus might have believed that he was innocently restoring a genuine part of the text that had inadvertently been lost through the imperfections of the scribal process.[58] Andrew J. Brown has argued that the scribe perhaps 'held a favourable view of the Vulgate text, which led him to make occasional changes which, in his opinion, helped to improve the Greek wording.'[59] Until the manuscript can be dated more precisely than the current estimate (*c.* 1500–1520), it is difficult to know for certain whether the scribe intended to influence Erasmus' editorial choices.[60] But that a recent Greek manuscript containing the comma – one of only two in the world – should have appeared in the homeland of Erasmus' critic Lee, and should have been presented to Erasmus at the moment when it might make a difference, can certainly be described as a remarkable coincidence.

[57] Tregelles 1844, xxvi.

[58] In comparison it is useful to consider the unusual fourteenth-century diglot (Latin/Greek) New Testament manuscript GA 629[ap]. The Greek text in this manuscript has been altered in hundreds of places to conform more closely to the Latin, to the extent of providing the Johannine comma in both languages, but this manuscript should probably not be considered a forgery, since there is no evidence that these alterations were made for deceptive purposes.

[59] *ASD* VI-4:36–37. Here Brown also writes: 'If the purpose of those other pro-Vulgate readings was also to deceive Erasmus, it could be asked why they were not brought to his attention, as he makes no reference to them and seems to have remained unaware of their existence.' However, Erasmus admitted that he considered the manuscript to be suspect, and that he only adopted its reading of the comma to silence his critics. It would not have been in his interests to adopt further readings from a manuscript he considered recent and textually inferior. If he thought the manuscript was of any value, he could have used it elsewhere, for example to improve the Greek text of the end of Revelation.

[60] For a description of the manuscript, a provisional dating and an identification of its manuscript sources, see McDonald 2011.

For the 1527 edition of the New Testament, Erasmus tinkered further with the reading of the comma, adding the article before each noun or noun-phrase in v. 7 (ὁ πατήρ, ὁ λόγος, καὶ τὸ πνεῦμα ἅγιον), probably influenced by the reading in the Complutensian edition, which he had seen in the meantime. Curiously, he did not add the articles before πνεῦμα, ὕδωρ, or αἷμα in v. 8 in the 1527 edition, nor in that of 1535; they were only added in Robert Estienne's 1550 *editio regia*. The reading of the comma in the Complutensian bible is different from that found in the two late mediaeval Greek New Testament manuscripts containing the comma (GA 629, which Erasmus had not seen, and Montfortianus), and Erasmus suspected that it too had simply been translated into Greek from the Latin Vulgate.[61] The additions Erasmus made to the 1527 edition of the *Annotationes* on the comma show a little confusion. Comparing the reading in the Complutensian edition with that from his British codex, he claimed that the manuscript had contained the phrase καὶ οἱ τρεῖς εἰς τὸ ἕν εἰσι at the end of v. 8. In the intervening years, his memory of the British codex must have become hazy. He apparently remembered that he had used the British codex as the basis for his reading of the comma, but forgot that he had spliced the phrase καὶ οἱ τρεῖς εἰς τὸ ἕν εἰσιν into v. 8 from his 1516/1519 text.[62] Erasmus thus published three different readings of the comma in the successive editions of his New Testament (1516/1519, 1522, 1527/1535). Only the first – the one that omits the comma – accurately reflects the reading of any one manuscript source.

In summary: the reading of the comma in Montfortianus is clearly translated from the Latin Vulgate. Erasmus' third edition of the Greek New Testament (1522) integrated the comma from Codex Montfortianus. In 1 Jn 5:8b, Erasmus included two details absent from Montfortianus but present in the Greek manuscripts on which he had established his initial reading of the passage. When preparing his 1527 edition, Erasmus adapted his reading of the comma to make it conform more closely to that found in the Complutensian edition, thus hoping to remove every cause for his critics to accuse him of fomenting Arianism. It is impossible to determine the motives of the scribe of Montfortianus with confidence, and difficult

---

[61] The comma, as given in the Greek text of the Complutensian Bible, reads: 'ὅτι τρεῖς εἰσίν οἱ μαρτυροῦντες εν τω ουρανώ, ὁ πατήρ και ὁ λόγος και τό ἅγιον πνεύμα, και οἱ τρεῖς εἰς τό εν εἰσί. και τρεῖς εἰσίν οἱ μαρτυρούντες επί τῆς γης· τό πνεύμα και τό ύδωρ και τό αίμα.' The parallel Latin text reads: 'quoniam tres sunt qui testimonium dant in caelo pater verbum et spiritus sanctus et hi tres unum sunt. et tres sunt qui testimonium dant in terra spiritus et aqua et sanguis.' On the unusual accentuation of the Greek in the Complutensian Polyglot, see J. Lee 2005.

[62] Heide 2006, 62–65.

to know whether he copied the manuscript before or after he had seen
Erasmus' *editio princeps*.

5. John Clement and Codex Montfortianus

Thus far the story is well known. But two questions have never been
answered adequately: where did Codex Montfortianus come from? And if
Erasmus inspected Montfortianus while he was living in Leuven, how did
he come to see it? Codex Montfortianus contains several marks attesting
to its provenance, and these permit us to venture some conclusions.

A few points about Montfortianus may be noted here. Some of its parent manuscripts are now in England, and Erasmus referred to the book as
a British codex.[63] These factors suggest that Montfortianus was probably
copied in England. The manuscript probably cannot have been copied
before the end of the fifteenth century, since one of its presumed parent
manuscripts dates from this time. This conclusion is consistent with the
evidence of the watermarks, similar to those found in paper produced at
Genoa in around 1516 (Briquet 5258). The consistency of the watermarks
throughout the codex suggests that it was conceived as a unit, and not
produced over decades, as some have suggested. The presence of variant
readings copied by the text scribe from Erasmus' 1516 New Testament into
the margins of Revelation shows that the book was still in the scribe's
possession when Erasmus' edition appeared. Details may suggest that the
manuscript was written in some haste: the roughness and irregularity of
the handwriting, and the lack of gilding, illumination or real decoration
apart from the *kephalaia*, which are sometimes entered in the margins in
red. The scribe was almost certainly a Franciscan, for twice on 198v is written the inscription ἰησοῦς μαρία φράγκισκος (Jesus, Mary, Francis), a
formula often found in Franciscan manuscripts, albeit usually in Latin.
On the bottom of 12v is an ownership mark: *sū thome clemētis olim
fratris froyke* ('I belong to Thomas Clement, formerly to Friar Froyke')
(Figure 1.2). This note is in the hand of the physician John Clement
(*c.* 1490–1572), the father of Thomas Clement, who made comparable
marks in several manuscripts before distributing them to his children.[64]

---

[63] Oxford, New College ms 68 (GA 58ᵉ); Oxford, Lincoln College ms gr. 82 (GA 326ᵃᵖᵗ); see *ASD*
VI-4:76–80, 103–104.

[64] Further on Clement, see Hamilton 1904–1906; Lechat 1914; Guilday 1914; Wenkebach 1925, esp. 54;
Mercati 1926, esp. 84; Reed 1926; Emden 1974, 121–122; Merriam 1988; *CE* 1:310–311; Coates 1999,
142–144; Mayer and Walters 2008, 137–138; McDonald 2013. I am currently working on a biography of Clement which will present much new documentary material.

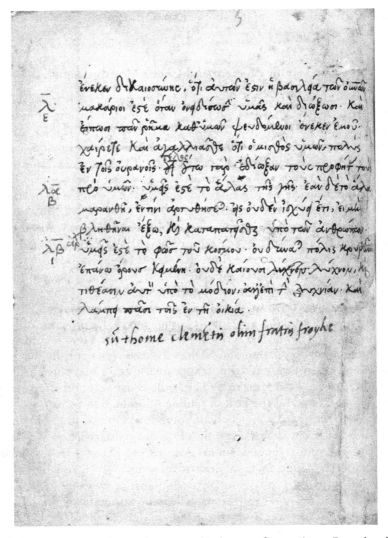

Figure 1.2. Dublin, Trinity College ms 30 (Codex Montfortianus), 12v. Reproduced
by kind permission of the Board of Trinity College, Dublin.

John Clement entered Thomas More's household in about 1514 as a
student-ward and tutor to More's children. In 1515 he accompanied More
on a diplomatic mission to Flanders, where he met Erasmus. By 1516
Clement had made such progress that he could teach Greek to John Colet,

dean of St Paul's.[65] In early 1520, he left Oxford definitively to deepen his studies of Greek at Leuven.[66] There he studied and boarded in the house of Erasmus' friend Juan Luis Vives.[67] Clement also spent time socialising with Erasmus, who was impressed by the young man's intelligence.[68] Erasmus left for Basel on 28 October 1521. Clement visited him there around Easter 1522, on his way to begin his medical studies in Italy, and brought him letters from More.[69] If we want to know how Erasmus could have seen Montfortianus, we need look no further than John Clement, a member of Erasmus' Leuven circle at precisely the time he was preparing his third edition of the New Testament.

6. Frater Froyke

The 'frater Froyke' from whom Clement acquired the manuscript is more mysterious. To begin, there has been a persistent confusion about his name. The description of the manuscript in the London Polyglot (1657), written either by James Ussher or Brian Walton, states that Montfortianus was once the property of 'brother Froy the Franciscan' (*fratris Froy Franciscani*).[70] Walton's report was subsequently adopted by Hottinger (1664), Mill (1707), Le Long (1709) and Wettstein (1730).[71] Barrett (1801) got a little closer with the orthography 'Froyhe', the form under which the one-time owner of this codex has generally been known ever since.[72] On the basis of Barrett's orthography, James Rendel Harris suggested (1887) that 'frater Froyhe' was William Roye, a member of the Observant Franciscan house in Greenwich with reported links to the

---

[65] Fowler 1893, 88–89, 369, 371; McConica 1986, 1–68, at 21, 26, 67–68.

[66] More to Erasmus (March/April 1520), *Epist.* 1087 (*Opus Epist.* 4:232; *Correspondence* 7:254).

[67] De Vocht 1934, 4; De Vocht 1951–1955, 2:43, 358–359, 404; McConica 1986, 26; Tournoy *et al.* 1993, 16.

[68] Erasmus to Burbank (Leuven, 1.9.[1520]), *Epist.* 1138 (*Opus Epist.* 4:334; *Correspondence* 8:38–39).

[69] Vives to Erasmus (Leuven, 19 January 1522), *Epist.* 1256 (*Opus Epist.* 5:11; *Correspondence* 9:17); Vives to Erasmus (Bruges, 1 April 1522), *Epist.* 1271 (*Opus Epist.* 5:40; *Correspondence* 9:56).

[70] Walton 1657, 6:1 (in section *Variantes lectiones Graecae Novi Testamenti*): 'Novum Testamentum quod olim fuit fratris Froy Franciscani, postea Thomae Clementis, deinde Guilielmi Clerk [*sic*], & nuper Thomae Montfortii, S. T. D. Cantabrig. In Evangeliis habet utraque κεφάλαια tum ordinaria cum Eusebiana cum στίχων numero.' The original description in the draft, Oxford, Bodleian Library ms Auct. T. 5, 15r, reads: 'D. Novum Testamentum, recentiore manu descriptum: quod olim fuerat [*add. in margine*: Franciscani, ut colligo ex verbis illic ab eo adscriptis, Ἰησοῦς Μαρία Φράγκισκος.] fratris Froyheˢ, posteà Thomae Clementis, deinde Guilielmi Chark, et nunc Thomae Montfortii, Sᵃᵉ Theologiae Doctoris. In Evangelijs habet utraque κεφάλαια (tùm ordinaria tùm Eusebiana) cum στίχων numero.' Cf. *ASD* VI-2:43–44.

[71] Hottinger 1664, 129; Mill 1707, cxlviii; Le Long 1709a, 1:672; Wettstein 1730, 52.

[72] Barrett 1801, Appendix:2.

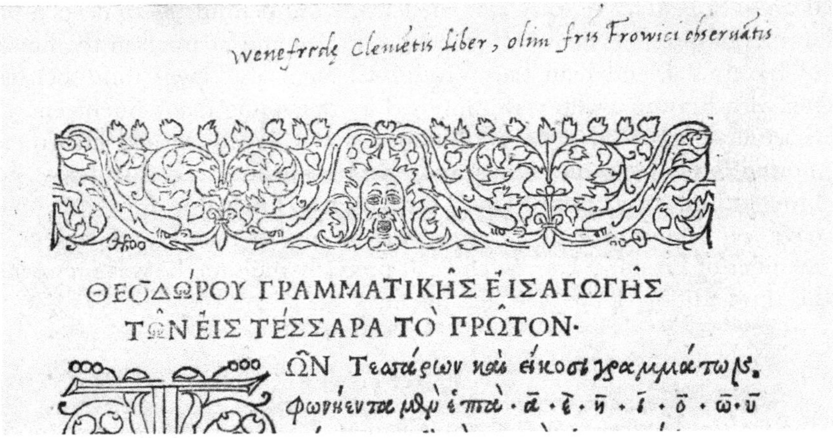
wenefrede clemētis liber, olim frīs Frowici obseruātis

ΘΕΟΔΩΡΟΥ ΓΡΑΜΜΑΤΙΚΗΣ ΕΙΣΑΓΩΓΗΣ
ΤΩΝ ΕΙΣ ΤΕΣΣΑΡΑ ΤΟ ΠΡΩΤΟΝ.
ΩΝ Τεσσάρων καὶ εἴκοσι γραμμάτων.
φωνήεντα μὲν ἑπτά· α· ε· η· ι· ο· ω· υ

Figure 1.3. Theodore of Gaza, *In hoc volumine haec insunt. Introductivae grammatices libri quatuor* (Venice: Aldus, 1495), α2r.
Private collection. Reproduced by kind permission.

house in Cambridge, a man who would later earn notoriety as assistant to William Tyndale and author of a number of religious satires and translations of Protestant literature.[73] Harris's plausible hypothesis has been widely accepted.[74]

However, important new evidence has undermined this identification. The name of the friar in John Clement's inscription is 'Froyke', not 'Froyhe'. An extant copy of the Aldine edition of Theodore of Gaza's Greek grammar (1495) bears a comparable *ex libris* marking on the recto of the second page: *Wenefredę Clementis Liber, olim fratris Frowici obseruantis* ('Property of Winifred Clement, formerly of brother Frowyk the Observant')[75] (Figure 1.3). Like all her siblings, Winifred Clement (1527–1553) had received instruction in Greek from both her parents, probably using this copy of Theodore's grammar.[76] Her epitaph, formerly

[73] J. R. Harris 1887, 46–53.

[74] For example by Scrivener 1894b, 200; Nestle 1901, 86; Bludau 1902b, 173; *ASD* IX-2:259; Coogan 1992, 101; Metzger and Ehrman 2005, 146.

[75] Sotheby's 1988, nº 35; Sotheby's 2005, 80. The provenance of the book is as follows: Frowyk – John Clement – Winifred Clement – unknown – Jesuit library in Brussels (1643) – Louise Françoise de La Baume Le Blanc de La Vallière (1783) – George John, Earl Spencer – John Rylands Library, Manchester – unknown – present owner, whom I thank for allowing me to inspect the book.

[76] Bishop Foxe mandated this textbook in the statutes for Corpus Christi College, so Clement will have used it while teaching there; Fowler 1893, 38. On the education of John Clement's children, see Sander 1571, 710: 'Omnes tum Graece Latineque docuit.'

in St Peter's church in Leuven, describes her as 'knowledgeable in the Latin language, and quite outstanding in Greek'.[77] Given the similarities to the inscription in Montfortianus, there can be little doubt that 'frater Frowicus' and 'frater Froyke' are the same man.

Francis Frowyk (also documented as Frowik, Frowike, Frowyc, Frwick, Frowicus, Froickus, Frowycus) was an Observant Franciscan of the Greenwich house. He was probably a member of the illustrious Frowyk family that had provided many members of parliament, judges and lord mayors of London.[78] Beside possible connections between More and the Frowyks through the legal profession, there were also local links. The More family seat was Gobions, in North Mymms.[79] The Frowyk seat was only three miles away, in South Mimms.[80] Francis Frowyk's date of birth is unknown. Even his given name is uncertain; Francis may be his professed name. He was ordained as acolyte on 15 February 1505, deacon on 28 March 1506, and priest on 26 February 1507.[81] Subsequently promoted to the rank of minister provincial of the Observant Franciscans in England, Frowyk attended the historic general meeting of the order at Rome in 1517 at which Leo X proclaimed the Bull of Union. He returned with instructions from Leo X to Henry VIII regarding the procedure for future elections of ministers general.[82] On his way back from Rome, Frowyk stopped at Leuven in late August 1517, and showed Erasmus some of the Greek editions

---

[77] Transcr. in Bang 1907, 248.

[78] See Norman Doe, 'Frowyk [Frowicke, Frowyke], Sir Thomas', in *ODNB*.

[79] Ives 1983, 469–470.

[80] Cass 1877; Ives 1983, 463–464; Roffey 2007, 171.

[81] London Guildhall Library ms 9531/8, 90v (ordination as acolyte by the bishop of Gallipoli, at St Mary Without Bishopsgate); 93r (ordination as deacon by John Bell, bishop of Mayo, at St Bartholomew's Hospital, London); 96r (ordination as priest). Cf. Davis 2000; *ASD* VI-4:46 n. 45–46.

[82] Leo X to Henry VIII, Rome, 16 June 1517, Kew, National Archives SP 1/15, 177r; English digest in Brewer 1862–1908, 2:1077, n° 3370. Silvestro de' Gigli, bishop of Worcester, to Henry VIII, Rome, 17 June 1517, Kew, National Archives SP 1/15, 180r–v, briefly reported the outcome of the decisions at the Rome meeting of the Franciscan order, mentioning that 'Reuerendus Pater Religiosus et Modestissimus vir frater Franciscus Frwick [*sic*] istius Inclitissimę Prouincię Anglicę Prouincialis' would give a fuller explanation upon his return. English digest in Brewer 1862–1908, 2:1078, n° 3374. The only record of the year of Frowyk's death may be unreliable: see the letter introducing a series of sermons preached in 1517 in Longland, c. 1528–1532, M1r (54r): 'Siquidem undecim plus minus abhinc annis ab inuictissimo rege nostro Christianissimoque Fidei defensore Henrico huius nominis octauo (Coleto Froickoque iam ante relatis in numerum sanctorum patrum) designatus sum ut coram sua maiestate, aulęque sue splendidissima corona, contiones haberem singulis quadragenarij ieiunij sextis ferijs.' The distance of eleven years mentioned would place this preface in 1528. Longland says Colet and Frowyk were already dead by this time, but he was mistaken; Colet died in 1519, and Frowyk visited Erasmus in the summer of 1517. A *terminus ante quem* for the printing of the edition is provided by the date of the latest sermon in the collection, 27 November 1527 (35r). See also Lupton 1909, 91; W. A. Jackson et al. 1986, 3:289; McDonald 2011, 108; *ASD* VI-4:50 n. 57.

recently produced by Aldus: Strabo's *De situ orbis* (November 1516), Pindar with scholia (January 1513), and Gregory of Nazianzus' *Orationes lectis-simae XVI* (April 1516). Frowyk also brought news of Greek editions still in press when he left Italy: the edition of the entire Greek bible, which Aldus and Asulanus would publish in February 1518 with a dedication to Erasmus himself, and Plutarch's *Lives*, which Giunta published at Florence on 27 August 1517.[83] To judge from the books Frowyk showed or reported to Erasmus, he was interested in biblical philology and at least reasonably competent in Greek. If Frowyk had showed Montfortianus to Erasmus during his visit in August 1517, Erasmus probably would have mentioned it in his correspondence with Tunstall, if not in his responses to Lee (April/May 1520) rather than waiting until his *Apology to Stunica*, written between June and September 1521, after Clement had arrived in Leuven.

The identity of the scribe of Montfortianus is unclear. Without a sample of Frowyk's Greek hand, it is impossible to identify him as the scribe. There was at least one other Greek scholar amongst the Franciscans in England: Richard Brinkley (BTh 1489 Cantab., DTh 1492 Cantab., DD 1524 Oxon., † 1526), who lived in the Cambridge house from 1489 at the latest, and served as Conventual minister provincial of England from 1518 to 1526.[84] A. G. Little (1943) suggested that Brinkley may have been involved in the production of Montfortianus.[85] However, Brinkley can be ruled out as the scribe, for a short extant sample of his Greek hand does not match that in Montfortianus.[86] Lee could have copied out the manuscript, but he did not return to England until September 1520, after Clement had

[83] Erasmus, *Epist.* 642, in *Opus Epist.* 3:63–64, dated 30 August [1517]: 'S. D., eruditissime Tunstalle. Aceruum voluptatum his litteris tibi adfero: quem nobis optimus ille Frowicus Roma reuersus offudit. Asulanus vtrunque Testamentum excudit Graece, Opera Nazianzeni nobis ostendit. Excusus est Strabo Graecus, Vitae Plutarchi, Pindarus cum commentariis, aliaque permulta quae in praesentia non succurrunt.' *Correspondence* 5:91, mistranslates the present tense *excudit* as perfect: 'Asulanus has printed both Old and New Testaments in Greek.' However, the printing was not complete until the following February. Erasmus was aware that the edition was still being printed, as is evident from his *Epist.* 643 (*Opus Epist.* 3:65), dated 31 August [1517], in which he repeats the same news to Tunstall; Allen suggested in his notes that Erasmus sent this letter with a different courier. It is possible that Frowyk himself delivered *Epist.* 642 to Tunstall.
[84] Bateson 1903, 1:4, 21, 46, 48, 49; Little 1943, 205; J. R. H. Moorman 1952, 155–156; Emden 1963, 103. Moorman, drawing on Little, states that Brinkley 'was Provincial Minister, possibly of the Observants as well as of the Conventuals, from 1518 to 1526'. However, K. D. Brown 1986, 250, 294, records that Henry Chadworth is recorded as provincial minister of the English Observants in September 1518. See London, Guildhall ms 9531/9, 187r. Chadworth was subsequently sent by Henry VIII as an emissary to Scotland; London, BL ms Cotton Caligula B II 333, Dacre to Wolsey, 22 October 1519; summary in Brewer 1862–1908, 3.1:168. See also *ASD* VI-4:49.
[85] Little 1943, 141–142.
[86] GA 59[e]. At the end of the Gospels, in Greek characters (Ρ Βρηνκελει Διδαϲκολωϲ [*sic*, intended as equivalent to *magister*]). Cf. J. R. Harris 1887, 19.

reached Leuven.[87] It is also unlikely that Clement copied Montfortianus. The surviving samples of his Greek hand do not match that in the manuscript.[88] Moreover, it would be strange for him to pretend to his son that he had acquired the book from Frowyk if he had copied it himself. Finally, the hand does not match that of either of the two known native Greek scribes active in England in the later fifteenth century, Emmanuel of Constantinople and Johannes Serbopoulos.[89]

7. Running with the hares, hunting with the hounds: Erasmus' contradictory attitude towards the comma

Even after Erasmus had expressed his doubts about the comma in the *Annotationes* to his 1522 edition of the New Testament, he still employed it when it suited his purposes. In 1523 he published his *Paraphrases of all the Apostolic Epistles*, a Latin translation that runs seamlessly into theological commentary. In the paraphrase of 1 Jn, Erasmus included the comma without hesitation, interpreting the heavenly witnesses as testifying to Christ's divinity, and the earthly witnesses as testifying to his humanity. Erasmus avoided mentioning the consubstantiality of the persons of the Trinity, and stated merely that they are united in witness.[90]

---

[87] Brown, *ASD* VI-4:40, refers to a letter, dated 6 December 1520 (*Ep.* 1165, *Opus Epist.* 4:395), in which Erasmus expressed his suspicion to Capito that Edward Lee (now back in England) and Polydore Vergil were hatching some plan. Brown comments: 'This could seem to raise the question of whether the production of codex 61 was planned by Edward Lee in collusion with Polydore Vergil.' On this basis, Brown suggests that Polydore Vergil 'could have provided one of the exemplars followed by codex 61, or that he had some connexion with providing the paper on which the manuscript was written [...]'.

[88] John Clement to Frans Cranevelt, Bruges, December 1521, Leuven, KU Centraalbibliotheek ms B96/*LCB* 94, 119r; transcription in IJsewijn et al. 1995, 3–4.

[89] On Emmanuel, see Gamillscheg and Harlfinger 1981, 1:77–78; Dionisotti 1988, 30, 36–38; Gamillscheg and Harlfinger 1989, 1:72. On Serbopoulos, see Gamillscheg and Harlfinger 1981, 1:106–107; Dionisotti 1988, 30–31, 36–38; Gamillscheg and Harlfinger 1989, 1:103–104.

[90] Erasmus 1523a, I15v–6r: 'Tres sunt enim in coelo, qui testimonium praebent Christo: pater, sermo, & spiritus: pater, qui semel atque iterum uoce coelitus emissa, palàm testatus est hunc esse filium suum egregie charum, in quo nihil offenderet: sermo, qui tot miraculis aeditis, qui moriens ac resurgens declarauit se uerum esse Christum, deum pariter atque hominem, dei & hominum conciliatorem: spiritus sanctus, qui in baptizati caput descendit, qui post resurrectionem delapsus est in discipulos. Atque horum trium summus est consensus: pater est autor, filius nuncius, spiritus sug [I16r] gestor. Tria sunt item in terris, quae attestantur Christum: spiritus humanus, quem posuit in cruce: aqua, & sanguis, qui fluxit è latere mortui. Et hi tres testes consentiunt. Illi declarant deum, hi testantur hominem fuisse. Testimonium perhibuit & Ioannes. Quod si testimonium hominum recipimus, aequum est ut plus apud nos habeat ponderis testimonium dei. Manifestum est enim dei patris testimonium: Hic est filius meus dilectus, in eo complacitum est mihi, ipsum audite. Quid dici potuit apertius aut plenius?'

Edward Lee, sent to France by Henry VIII on a diplomatic mission, continued to stir up trouble for Erasmus. Amongst those he won over was Noël Béda, syndic of the faculty of theology at the Sorbonne and former rector of the Collège de Montaigu, where Erasmus himself had studied in 1496. In 1526, Béda published a critique of Erasmus' *Paraphrases*, and encouraged the Paris faculty to condemn the work. In the paraphrases of Jn 10:30, Erasmus had placed the following words in the mouth of Jesus: 'We are two, but we two bear the same testimony and have the same judgement. And from us two there is one who, if he were alone, would still have an irrefutable judgement' (*Duo sumus, sed duorum idem est testimonium, idem iudicium. Sed ex his duobus unus est, qui si solus esset, tamen esset illius irrefutabile iudicium*). Béda asserted that Erasmus' interpolation undermined the essential unity of the Father and the Son.[91]

In his published refutation of Béda's work, Erasmus denied that he had ever written or thought such an error. But if it was heresy to maintain that the Father and the Son are two, then John's statement that there are *three* that bear witness in heaven should likewise be condemned. Erasmus maintained that in all his writings, he had always confessed the Trinity to be three persons and one essence. To suggest otherwise was impudent misrepresentation.[92] Erasmus knew that a condemnation from the Paris faculty would be damaging, and he naturally used all possible resources in his own defence, but to use the comma to defend his own orthodoxy was a little unscrupulous.

In 1525, Edward Lee was sent on a diplomatic mission to Spain. Erasmus worried that his old enemy was sowing seeds of opposition within the religious orders there, whom he had alienated with his pungent criticisms of monastic life, morals and learning. Erasmus' correspondence from 1526 and 1527 contains dark references to plots spearheaded by well-placed clerics like García de Loaysa, the emperor's confessor.[93] In the summer of 1527, the Spanish Inquisition, acting on instructions from Clement VII, called a conference of theologians at Valladolid to examine the orthodoxy of Erasmus' theological writings. A preliminary list of charges accused Erasmus of attacking the Trinity; the divinity, dignity and glory of Christ; the divinity of the Holy Spirit; the Inquisition; the seven sacraments; the authority of the Scriptures; the power of the church, councils and orthodox fathers; the honour of Mary; the authority of pope and council alike;

---

[91] Béda 1526, 262v. Further, see Rummel 1986, 124–125, 209–210.
[92] Erasmus 1527c, 7v (*LB* 9:446BC); Erasmus 1527d, 153v–154v (*LB* 9:632B–633A).
[93] Rummel 1989, 2:83–86.

the ceremonies of the church; the custom of fasting and refraining from certain foods; celibacy; scholastic theology; indulgences; veneration of the saints, relics and images; pilgrimages; the right of the church in temporal affairs; free will; and the torments of hell.[94]

Under the rubric that Erasmus had argued 'against the sacrosanct Trinity of God' was the more specific accusation that 'Erasmus, in his *Annotationes* on 1 Jn 5, continually defends corrupt manuscripts, rages against St Jerome, and argues the case of the Arians, setting up defences for them.' Erasmus had allegedly attacked the comma 'with inexorable warfare', had rejected all evidence in favour of its authenticity, and had dared to call Jerome 'violent on many occasions, shameless, often changeable, and self-contradictory'. In his work *On how to pray (De modo orandi)*, he had maintained that we cannot affirm anything in religion except what is expressly stated in the Scriptures. He had moreover asserted that what is rejected by the Arians can only be demonstrated through reason. In his defence against Lee, he had allegedly said many improper things about the Father and the Son: that the Father is the origin of his own being, which is from none other; that the Son participates in the divine essence; and that he did not detract the status 'originary principle' from the Son simply by attributing more of this quality to the Father.[95]

The inquisitors framed their articles in scholastic fashion, but by removing sentences and the ideas they expressed from their context, they often distorted Erasmus' meaning. For example, Erasmus had said in his defence against Stunica (in a passage reused in the *Annotations* of 1522) that since the Arians were not likely to be convinced by the comma, what they denied could only be taught through logical demonstration. This sentence, when quoted out of context, could have been interpreted as referring to anything and everything the Arians might deny. Accordingly, some delegates criticised the way in which the charges against Erasmus were framed. Antonio de Alcaraz suggested that since there are many things the Arians might deny, the question should have been phrased more carefully. Alcaraz, bishop Santiago Cabrero, Sancho Carranza de Miranda, Miguel Gómez, Pedro de Lerma and Martín de Samunde stated that while Erasmus' comments about Jerome may have displayed arrogance and

---

[94] Madrid, Archivo Historico Nacional, Sección de la Inquisición Legajo 4426, n° 27, ed. in Beltrán de Heredia 1970–1973, 6:16–120, from which all citations here are made. A facsimile of the accusations, but not the responses, is in Avilés 1980, 17–50. I made particular use of the commentary in Avilés 1980, 72–83; Gilly 1985, 283–284; Rummel 1989, 2:81–105; and Homza 1997, esp. 86–93, 111.

[95] Madrid, Archivo Historico Nacional, Sección de la Inquisición Legajo 4426, n° 27, facsimiles in Avilés 1980, 20–21; text also in Erasmus 1528, 27; Beltrán de Heredia 1970–1973, 6:17–18.

irreverence, they did not constitute an attack on the Trinity, and should not have been included amongst Erasmus' alleged denials of this doctrine. Samunde suggested facetiously that it was not the Inquisition's job to censure Erasmus for attacking Jerome's dignity – this task was best left to his confessor. Some respondents, familiar with Erasmus' work, pointed out that a judgement of his orthodoxy required a more complete view of his work than had been dished up in the inquisitors' articles to the conference. Pedro de Ciria and Fernando Matatigui noted that these articles distorted the general tenor of Erasmus' position so badly as to make him sound like a Lutheran. Miguel Carrasco pointed out that Erasmus' great respect for Jerome, impugned by the inquisitors' articles, was evident from the preface to his edition of the saint's writings. To accuse him of despising Jerome because of a passing remark went against the grain of his work as a whole.

The twenty-nine delegates met at Valladolid on 27 June 1527. Most commented on Erasmus' treatment of the comma, with the exception of Pedro Chico, who gave no written response, and Antonio Rodríguez de la Fuente, who followed the judgement of Pedro de Lerma. The delegates' written judgements represent a broad range of orthodox responses to Erasmus' biblical philology. Some of the respondents were open to Erasmus' historical, humanistic style of exegesis. Others considered Erasmus' work as a threat to academic theological study. Erasmus had remarked in his annotations on 1 Jn 5:7 that his readers should devote themselves to the studies of piety in order to become more like God, rather than torture themselves with abstract speculations about the distinction between the persons of the Trinity. While some delegates considered this exhortation to piety and sanctity praiseworthy, others treated it as an insidious attack on the project of scholastic theology. Erika Rummel has identified certain tendencies in the responses: the delegates from Salamanca tended to condemn Erasmus, while those from Alcalá showed a more positive attitude to his work, perhaps surprisingly given the dispute over the Complutensian bible. While Franciscans and Dominicans tended to be hostile, Benedictines tended to be more indulgent. Several suggested that Erasmus' refusal to employ traditional theological language had sometimes led him into infelicitous and even potentially heterodox formulations.[96]

Many of the written assessments of Erasmus' annotations on the comma touched upon the question of the Scriptural canon. Most delegates

[96] Rummel 1989, 2:90–92.

considered that the crucial issue was whether the comma was part of the received canon of the church, which derives its authority not from the readings found in this or that manuscript, but from ecclesiastical tradition. For most of the delegates, the question under debate was thus not the philological value of particular readings, or even whether the comma was written by the author of 1 Jn, but the integrity of the canon of Scripture as it had been handed down by the church. Gil López de Béjar maintained that the comma was 'part of the sacred canon, because it appears that the church has manifestly received it'. While Béjar seemed to put the cart before the horse – after all, the church could not have received the comma if it were not found in at least some manuscripts – he was drawing on the notion that the church represents the authoritative repository and conduit of extra-Scriptural traditions. Drawing on Jn 21:25, Alonso de Córdoba noted that the Scriptures themselves confess that they do not contain every detail pertaining to the faith. Some matters thus derive their authority exclusively from the tradition of the church. Juan de Quintana, confessor to the emperor, distinguished between the authorship of the books of Scripture and their canonicity. But since the comma was indeed part of the Scriptures received and transmitted by the Roman Catholic Church, Quintana considered it wrong to doubt either that the comma was written by John, or that it was part of the body of the sacred canon. By contrast, Alonso de Virués and Cabrero argued that usage was not a sufficient criterion of canonicity. It was true that popes and councils had cited the comma, but they were simply following the biblical text current in their day. Carranza was one of the few who realised that the distinction between canon and manuscript attestation was crucial to any discussion of Erasmus' orthodoxy. While Carranza believed that the comma was part of the canon of Scripture, he (like his colleague Luis Coronel) considered that Erasmus had not erred in his annotation, since he merely reported the absence of the comma from his Greek manuscripts. Moreover, Carranza pointed out that Erasmus proved his willingness to submit to ecclesiastical tradition by restoring the passage in his third edition. By contrast, Pedro Ciruelo and Córdoba maintained that it was wrong to deny or even doubt that the comma was part of the text of Scripture, no matter what some old Greek or Latin codices might say. Accordingly, their only criterion for judging whether a given manuscript reading was good or bad was the degree to which it conformed to the received canon of the Scripture, that is, the Latin Vulgate. Samunde was virtually the only delegate prepared to consider the possibility that the comma was not part of the biblical text. The responses given at the conference show that many of the delegates believed that the church had transmitted a biblical text that was essentially stable, and that the variants found in manuscripts were nothing more than deviations from this perfect text. It is no wonder then that they were so hostile towards a man who attributed more authority to aberrant readings found in isolated manuscripts than to the lapidary text handed down by the church through the ages.

Accordingly, Esteban de Almeida, Diego de Astudillo, Francisco de Castillo, Diego de Gouvea and Pedro Margallo judged that Erasmus had acted rashly in excluding the comma from his first edition. Should he persist in maintaining that it was not a part of the canon of Scripture now that he had been presented with good evidence to the contrary, he would stand under grave suspicion of heresy. Juan de Salamanca was of the opinion that there should be a general prohibition on selling or reading books lacking the comma. Gouvea proposed that anyone who maintained that the comma was not part of the canonical text of 1 Jn was to be burned along with their books. Pedro de Ciria was more lenient; Erasmus may have been rash in omitting the comma, but now that he had restored it, no more should be required of him. However, Quintana complained that Erasmus' stated reasons for restoring the comma showed an uncatholic spirit; Salamanca even claimed that these stated reasons placed him under suspicion of favouring the Arian cause. By contrast, Bishop Antonio de Guevera merely considered Erasmus' remarks about the comma ill-judged. To great men the matter was of no consequence, but to lesser men it was a scandal.

Some delegates found the exclusive focus on Jerome problematic. Samunde pointed out that the inquisitors relied simply on Jerome's word that some codices were corrupt. Erasmus had consulted many other fathers besides Jerome, and was thus in a position to speak with authority about the early attestation of the comma. And on what basis were the delegates to Valladolid to decide who was correct, Samunde asked pointedly, given that none of them had seen the manuscripts in question? Since they were bound to rely on others, they would be better to follow the judgement of Erasmus, who had seen these manuscripts, than the opinions of Lee, who had not. Cabrero and Gómez affirmed one of Erasmus' criteria for deciding the value of variants – the balance of the patristic witness – by pointing out that the comma was not cited by fathers such as Cyril, Bede or Augustine where one would have expected them to do so if they had known of it.

The question of the Scriptural canon also highlighted the sufficiency of Scripture to decide matters of faith. Astudillo, Castillo and Francisco de

Vitoria censured Erasmus' claim that what the Arians deny can only be demonstrated through reason. They maintained that the consubstantiality of the Father, Son and Holy Spirit may be demonstrated more than adequately through Scriptural testimonies such as the comma. Pedro de Lerma came to a similar conclusion. Fernando de Préjano asserted that the comma is entirely sufficient, shining forth like a lamp in a gloomy place (2 Pt 1:19), and Salamanca considered the comma totally clear to a person of the right disposition. Carranza had a more nuanced approach. He considered that some doctrines which might be disputed by the Arians, such as the divinity of Christ or his equality and consubstantiality with the Father, are clearly expressed in Scripture. But there are other doctrines which can only be proven by a combination of Scripture and the exercise of reason, such as the doctrine that the Holy Spirit is true God, of the same nature as the Father and Son, who proceeds from them both. Cabrero went even further, maintaining that since no single text in the Scriptures expresses the consubstantiality of the Father, Son and Spirit, the church has always acknowledged that a theology of the Trinity necessarily involves a complex of texts or even extra-Scriptural formulations.

Erasmus had argued that the difficulty of determining whether the comma refers to a unity of substance or agreement limits its utility in convincing heretics of the rightness of the orthodox position. Gómez and López de Béjar agreed with Erasmus that the meaning of the comma is obscure and liable to multiple meanings, and Matatigui concurred that is was therefore not much use in convincing heretics of their error. Gómez suggested that the fact that the *Glossa ordinaria* argued that the unity of the heavenly witnesses was one of testimony rather than essence was ample evidence that an orthodox writer could interpret this passage in such a way as might ostensibly be considered favourable to a heretical understanding. Samunde came to a similar conclusion. By contrast, Ciruelo argued that it was wrong to deny that the comma refers to anything but the unity of the divine essence, whatever the *Glossa ordinaria* might say.

Besides disagreeing about the meaning of the comma, the delegates were undecided about Erasmus' reasons for excising and then reintroducing it, and the significance and motivations of his actions. Several delegates – Cabrero, Carranza, Carrasco, Gómez, Lerma, Quintana and Virués – were prepared to believe that Erasmus had not found the comma in the manuscripts he had used to prepare the first two editions, but had solved the defect by restoring the comma to his text once he had seen such a manuscript. Alcaraz, López de Béjar and Pedro de Lerma pointed out that the presence of the comma in Erasmus' *Paraphrase* was sufficient evidence that he had come to accept its canonicity. Since Erasmus was not performing the task of a dogmatic theologian, but that of an interpreter and critic of the Scriptural text who merely intended to help scholars understand difficult passages of the Scripture, Virués did not believe that his omission of the comma constituted an attack on the doctrine of the Trinity. Others were unconvinced by Erasmus' reasons for preferring the readings in faulty Greek manuscripts to the better Latin ones. Gouvea asserted that Erasmus' reply to Lee revealed a depraved disposition. In such a grave matter, when the church's tradition was at stake, Erasmus should have kept quiet about the absence of the comma from his manuscripts until he had found more reliable ones, such as the three or four used by Ximénez for the reading of the comma in the Complutensian Polyglot. By contrast, Cabrero asserted that Erasmus would have been entitled to persist in excluding a verse attested in only one of his manuscripts, in favour of the seven that omitted it. And while Lopéz de Béjar was sympathetic to Erasmus' reliance on the Greek text, he still regretted his admission that his motive for including the comma in his third edition was ultimately self-serving. He therefore suggested that Erasmus should be asked to affirm unconditionally in the next edition of his *Annotationes* that the comma was an integral part of the text.

The diversity of opinion at Valladolid shows that Erasmus was not without supporters in Spain. Pedro de Vitoria wrote that although certain details of Erasmus' writings required correction, it should not be forgotten that he had brought incalculable benefits to the church through his efforts to revive both letters and knowledge of the Scriptures. The most comprehensive defence of Erasmus came from Cabrero, who praised Erasmus as a true and orthodox Christian, pious in his life and morals, who had rendered great services to Christendom as a whole, and to scholars in particular. Cabrero maintained that Erasmus' sincerity and orthodoxy were evident in his writings, and had been reported to Cabrero by many noble and learned Christians. Cabrero saw that criticism and faith were separate matters; Erasmus' denial of the canonicity of the comma did not mean that he did not believe in the Trinity or wished to promote Arianism. Indeed, he openly rejected Arius' ideas; to accuse such a man of Arianism was nothing short of culpable slander. While the conservative Préjano believed that Erasmus' excision of the comma on the basis of incorrect and suspicious books violated divine law and the determinations of the church, Cabrero and Virués noted that the church had never made a formal pronouncement on the canonicity of the comma. Cabrero even added that the Valladolid conference should not presume to decide what the church as a whole had not. While Quintana maintained that it was bold and erroneous to hold that the manuscripts lacking the comma preserved a less corrupt text than the codices consulted by Jerome, Cabrero stated that Erasmus did not defend corrupt codices, but merely amended them; furthermore, he had no reason to believe that the codices he had consulted were corrupt.

The next issue on the agenda was how to deal with Erasmus and his books. One disciplinary means open to the Inquisition was the selective correction or deletion of parts of books. Almeida, Juan de Arrieta, Francisco de Vitoria and Pedro de Victoria suggested that the text of Erasmus' annotation should be amended in future editions. Arrieta maintained that the reference to the absence of the comma in the Greek codices should be struck out. Almeida, Arrieta, López de Béjar and Pedro de Victoria suggested censoring Erasmus' statement that he added the comma simply to avoid deprive his enemies of the opportunity of criticising him. Almeida wished that Erasmus had said instead that he had acted from a desire to restore the sacred canon to completeness. Gouvea wanted to compel Erasmus to excise his opinion that the British codex had been adapted to the Latin reading, and to punish him if he resisted. Some other delegates, such as Cabrero, did not believe that any alteration of Erasmus' books was warranted.

The debates at Valladolid showed that even amongst a group of the most prominent theologians in Spain, there was still little appreciation of the issues involved in Erasmus' endeavour, such as the need to weigh the relative authority of different codices or textual traditions. These reports tacitly acknowledged the difficulties that arose in the absence of a stable biblical text to which all parties could refer. It is no coincidence that the question of the canon of Scripture would be addressed with such care – and answered with such blunt force – at Trent.

Plague struck Valladolid in August 1527, and the conference was dismissed before it had worked through any more than the first four articles. The commission did not make a final report, but Erasmus received a copy of the inquisitors' articles from Pedro Juan Olivar. In September 1527, Erasmus responded to Alfonso Manrique, Inquisitor General. Addressing the question of the comma, Erasmus argued that the failure of Cyril, Athanasius and Hilary to cite the comma against the Arians suggests that it was not present in their bibles. He had already replied to the arguments of Lee and Stunica, and was annoyed that the number of his critics was increasing. In any case, he had long since inserted the Latin reading into his Greek text, 'on the basis of one Greek codex alone which England supplied (though it is a recent one), and although the Greek codex in the Vatican library [GA 03] had what was in my texts'.[97] Erasmus' characterisation of Montfortianus as recent may hint at his suspicions about its origins, though it may be that he was simply comparing its relative newness with the antiquity of the Vatican codex.

Erasmus' full response to the articles of the Inquisition, *A defence against certain Spanish monks*, appeared in print in 1528. He objected that those who had drawn up the accusations at Valladolid had deliberately used prejudicial language by asserting that he had argued against the Trinity. As Erasmus pointed out, this accusation could not fail to raise horror and indignation, especially amongst the unlettered majority who fail to understand the issues at stake.

Erasmus was annoyed by the way his opinions had been misrepresented by the scholastic form of the inquisitors' articles, which paraphrased his words or combined statements from different places. 'The task of a legitimate inquisitor', he gnashed, 'is first to recite verbatim the words which he considers to have some suspicion of impiety, and then briefly to state what is found to be offensive in them.'[98] An accuser who immediately states his own opinion obliges himself to prove what he has asserted. Furthermore, no one is obliged to plead his own case simply because someone else has made an accusation against him. It was not only the scholastic method that Erasmus resented, but also those who accused him without a proper understanding of 'grammar', that is, of philology.

Erasmus dealt with the first accusation swiftly and cleanly: 'As far as the first item in this calumny is concerned, I nowhere defend corrupted codices knowingly, but transmit to Latin ears in good faith what I find in the Greek manuscripts. As far as I am concerned, I leave the reading in the Vulgate untouched. In my annotation I indicate which reading I consider genuine, submitting my judgement to the church, as I have always done.'[99]

Erasmus responded next to the charge that he had argued against the Trinity. His denial of the authenticity of the comma could not be construed as an argument against the Trinity, for one simple reason. The fact that the comma was never cited by the Greek fathers, even in their struggles against the Arians, is overwhelming evidence that it was not found in the text of the epistle with which they were familiar. The issue was not

[97] Erasmus, letter to Manrique, September [1527], *Epist.* 1877 (*Opus Epist.* 7:177).
[98] Erasmus 1528, 28; cf. *LB* IX:1030; cf. Rummel 1989, 2:93–94.
[99] Erasmus 1528, 28–29; cf. *LB* IX:1030.

whether the Father, Son and Spirit are of the same essence, but merely which reading – that in the Latin Vulgate or that in the Greek – faithfully reflected the Apostle's words. In the *Paraphrases* he had followed what was found in the Latin manuscripts; in the *Annotationes* he had indicated which reading he found more convincing on the basis of the Greek manuscripts, and gave a detailed explanation of his reasons for holding this opinion. Those who wished to know the details of his decision (he continued) should read his refutations of the criticisms of Lee, Stunica, the letter he wrote in defence of his reading at Jn 7:39 (published as an appendix to his 1527 edition of Chrysostom's *Martyrdom of Babyla*) (Erasmus 1527e) and his *Annotationes*, especially the most recent edition (1527).

However, Erasmus could not help touching upon at least some of the relevant issues. If the comma was missing from the Latin and Greek codices, he asks, from where did Jerome restore it? And if the comma was excised, who was responsible for this deed? The Arians? How could they corrupt all the codices of the orthodox? And besides, if the Arians had excised the comma from the bibles of their enemies, why did they not erase verses like Jn 10:30 ('the Father and I are one') while they were at it? What is more, if the Arians could argue forcefully that Jn 10:30 referred to a unity of will, they could say the same thing about the comma. And if the codices of the orthodox included this reading, why did Athanasius, Didymus, Gregory of Nazianzus, Chrysostom, Theophylact, Cyril, Ambrose, Hilary and Augustine all fail to cite it against the Arians? 'I do not know what these people are getting at,' Erasmus sighed in resignation, 'when they contend that this passage is necessary to prove that the three persons share the same nature.'[100] If this were the only passage from which this doctrine could be shown, then what were all those fathers doing who managed to make this point against the Arians without the help of the comma? 'Heaven forbid that we should force such an important dogma of the Catholic church into such straits that it would simply crumble if anyone could show that this passage did not faithfully reflect the Apostle's words.'[101] To those who complained that he ought to have avoided causing a scandal, Erasmus pointed out that he had not addressed his criticisms to the masses, but to scholars in their studies:

> I never discuss this passage without testifying to the truth of what people gather from that passage: that the Father, Son, and Holy Spirit share the very same essence, lest anyone should suspect any trace of heresy. And if

[100] Erasmus 1528, 31; cf. *LB* IX:1031.
[101] Erasmus 1528, 31; cf. *LB* IX:1031.

the slightest offence should arise from this, it comes from those who spin slander out of thin air, and drag into the open a question that ought to be discussed between scholars.[102]

As far as his criticisms of Jerome were concerned, Erasmus pointed out that he had always submitted his own judgements to the church, and that one Jerome does not make a whole church. In any case, the church should not immediately condemn someone for daring to question the soundness of a particular reading, given the great variety of readings found in the manuscripts. Such conversations have always gone on amongst scholars without any risk to the faith. Furthermore, the church has always had a sliding scale in matters of doctrine. It teaches some things as official doctrine; it considers other things as likely; it turns a blind eye to those things that are indifferent. Repeating an argument he had first made against Lee, Erasmus noted that the church has absorbed into its liturgy many biblical texts of questionable authority.

But more trouble was on its way. Among the opponents attracted by Lee and Stunica was Alberto Pio, prince of Carpi. In 1531, Pio published a series of criticisms of Erasmus' work, including his omission of the comma. Predictably, Pio relied on the authority of pseudo-Jerome's prologue to the Catholic Epistles, and accused Erasmus of rash impudence in daring to contradict the great father. Why doubt Jerome's word that the comma was deliberately removed, and thereby seek to diminish Jerome's authority? While Erasmus suggested that Jerome did not know what he was talking about, he himself unwittingly fostered Arian error. It was impossible for Erasmus to maintain that the bibles used by Cyril and Bede did not contain the comma. Perhaps they just omitted to comment on it. The comma was cited by Jerome and other fathers, and was found in the bibles used by the Catholic church; moreover, it fit well in the context of the epistle. If Erasmus maintained that the unity of the witness was one of testimony, the Arians would cite such a statement in support of their position. Pio then made a long and detailed excursus on the nature of unity, and the difference between the unity of the earthly witnesses and that of the heavenly witnesses. Wheat and snow are one in the sense that both are white, but they are of two distinct substances. Moreover, if the author of the epistle had believed that the witnesses were merely one in testimony, he would have said so. In any case, Pio said, words can be twisted to say almost anything, as the Arians did with Jesus' saying that he and the

---

[102] Erasmus 1528, 33; cf. *LB* IX:1031.

Father are one, and other similar passages. It is clear from the way John described Jesus in his gospel that he believed him to be *homousios* with the Father. In his epistle he affirmed this same belief to contradict Cerinthus and the Ebionites.[103] By the time Erasmus could respond, the elderly Pio was already dead, but he decided to reply anyway. Regarding the comma he merely remarked impatiently: 'On the triple witness I have replied as accurately as I can, and more than once, so it would be stupid to repeat that all.'[104]

In 1531 there appeared yet another critique of Erasmus' orthodoxy, this time from the theological faculty of Paris. The faculty particularly objected to Erasmus' translation of λόγος in Jn 1:1 and 1 Jn 5:7 as *sermo*, as well as the way his paraphrase of 1 Jn 5:7–8 implied that the unity of the three heavenly witnesses was merely one of testimony rather than one of essence. This, they suggested, gave some handle for a defence of the error of Arius.[105]

Erasmus' sarcastic defence went through two editions in 1532. He asserted that his paraphrase of the comma and the surrounding verses was perfectly orthodox, for it clearly expressed that there is only one nature in the three persons of the Trinity, and that they agree entirely amongst themselves. His paraphrase was in no way favourable to an Arian interpretation, for he clearly professed what Arius denies. Again he pointed out that the comma was not used by the orthodox apologists in their struggles against the Arians, either because their codices did not contain the verse, or because they believed that the unity of the heavenly witnesses was one of testimony rather than of nature, and thus inappropriate to their argument. Only in the time of Augustine did Latin theologians begin to cite the comma against the Arians. In any case, Erasmus points out that there is no law against interpreting Scripture in a sense different from Ambrose, Augustine or Jerome, as can be seen plainly from the works of modern theologians. The comma establishes the reliability of the witnesses by demonstrating their agreement, which arises from their shared nature. Nevertheless, the word 'one' does not necessarily mean 'one in nature,' but can also mean simply of one mind or heart. The comma was therefore not the failsafe weapon against heresy that some had claimed. If the church insisted that the comma proves the unity of the divine essence, the Arians would simply repudiate the authority of the church.[106]

---

[103] Pio 1531, 183v–184r. See Trapman 2002, 40–44, on Pio's assertion that Erasmus condoned lying.
[104] Erasmus 1531, 193 (*CW* 84:277).
[105] *Determinatio facultatis* 1531, C4r–v.
[106] Erasmus 1532, 182–183; cf. *CW* 82:147–148.

The dramatic opposition of Lee, Stunica, Pio and the Paris faculty might lead one to conclude that Catholic scholars inevitably disagreed with Erasmus' position on the comma, but this was not the case. The Dominican Tommaso de Vio Caetano (Cajetan), Luther's adversary at the Diet of Augsburg in 1518, agreed with Erasmus on the doubtful status of the comma: 'If these words belong to the text, they are applied to make manifest what was just said: namely, that the Spirit is truth. But I said, "*If* these words belong to the text," since they are not found in all the Greek codices, but only in some. We do not know how that diversity came about.'[107] Some took Cajetan's admission badly. Ambrosius Catharinus (1535) criticised Erasmus for calling into doubt what the church had accepted in its liturgical practice for so long, and accused him of striving after pointless and potentially heretical novelty. Catharinus also excoriated Cajetan for following Erasmus' example. To interfere with the textual integrity or interpretation of the comma was to invite a revival of Arianism.[108] In a second edition of his critique (1542), Catharinus noted pseudo-Jerome's opinion that the comma been omitted by careless translators.[109]

As usually happened, Erasmus had the last word. In the treatise *On the two kinds of martyrdom*, which he had passed off under the name of Cyprian, Erasmus included an oblique reference to Cyprian's Trinitarian interpretation of 1 Jn 5:8: 'Although these three are one, there is one God, who through the spirit, water, and blood declares his virtue and goodness to the human race; or they are called one because their testimony is entirely consistent, and nowhere self-contradictory; just as they who are joined by a common opinion are said to be one mind.'[110]

Summary

This chapter examined the New Testament edition of Erasmus and the opposition its appearance provoked. Objections to Erasmus' edition were motivated partly by fear that the changes he introduced to the familiar form of the biblical text, notably his excision of the Johannine comma, would sow doubts and error, and partly by personal animosity. Edward Lee implied that Erasmus was an incompetent editor, and suggested that his edition would open the door to a revival of Arianism. Erasmus was subsequently compelled to respond to the reproaches of a series of other critics,

[107] Cajetan 1531, 190r; cf. Bludau 1903a, 402–403.
[108] Catharinus 1535, 43–44.
[109] Catharinus 1542, 33; cf. Bludau 1903a, 403.
[110] Erasmus 1530, 510.

such as Jacobus Stunica, Noël Béda, a commission of theologians convened at Valladolid and Alberto Pio da Carpi. While preparing the third
edition of his New Testament, Erasmus was presented with a Greek New
Testament manuscript from England containing the comma. This manuscript, earlier owned by the Franciscan Francis Frowyk, later belonged to
Thomas More's protégé John Clement. It is likely that Clement presented
the book to Erasmus while he was studying under Vives at Leuven in 1521.
On the basis of this one manuscript, Erasmus included the comma in
his text, though his annotations on the passage make it clear that he suspected that the manuscript had been adapted to reflect the Latin Vulgate.

CHAPTER 2

The Johannine comma in sixteenth-century bibles after Erasmus

Even though Erasmus included the Johannine comma in his third, fourth and fifth editions of the New Testament (1522, 1527, 1535), it is clear from the comments cited in Chapter 1, and from the fact that he added material to his *Annotationes* on the comma until 1535, that he always considered it an intrusion. Some readers accepted Erasmus' reservations, while others assumed from the presence of the comma in the third, fourth and fifth editions of Erasmus' New Testament that he had finally become convinced of its genuineness. This divergence of opinion was reflected in the readings of the comma given in sixteenth-century bibles. Because of the nature of the material, this chapter is largely descriptive rather than analytical.

1.   The comma in sixteenth-century Greek editions

Of the Greek editions of the sixteenth and seventeenth centuries, the Aldine edition of 1518 generally follows Erasmus' first edition of 1516, augmented by additional details from an important codex in Venice (Biblioteca Marciana ms gr. Z. 10 (394), GA 209[eap]).[1] Consequently, Aldus' edition does not contain the comma. The comma is absent from the Greek editions of Nicolaus Gerbelius (Hagenau, 1521), based on Erasmus' 1519 edition, and consequently from that of Fabricius Köpfel (Strasbourg, 1524), based on Gerbelius' edition. Although Simon de Colines based his critical edition (Paris, 1534) principally on Erasmus' third edition and the Complutensian Polyglot, with further variants from manuscripts in Paris – many of which were later used by de Colines's son-in-law Robert Estienne the Elder – he deliberately omitted the comma.[2] The Basel printer Johannes Bebelius produced three editions (1524, 1531, 1535), based

---

[1] Hoskier 1929, 1:180.
[2] Bludau 1903a, 282.

largely on Erasmus' third edition; Bebelius (or rather his editor, Jacob Ceporinus) omitted the comma in his first two editions, but restored it in the third, perhaps for the same reasons as Erasmus himself. Bebelius' third edition formed the basis of Johannes Valderus' edition (Basel, 1536), which in turn served as parent for that of Melchior Sessa (Venice, 1538). Consequently, both Valderus and Sessa provide the comma.[3] The comma was also retained in the Greek editions of Robert Estienne the Elder (1546, 1549, 1550, 1551). Estienne based his great 1550 *editio regia* on Erasmus' fifth edition, and gave variants (though in an unsystematic and incomplete way) from the Complutensian edition and fourteen manuscripts in Paris.[4] Estienne marked off part of v. 7 between obelos and metobelos (thus: 'ἐν τῷ οὐρανῷ') to show that these words were not present in the seven manuscripts of the Catholic Epistles at his disposal. Nevertheless, his failure to register in the critical apparatus that the rest of the comma was not found in *any* of the manuscripts in the royal library in Paris subsequently led many later scholars to assume that it was. These included a number of editors, beginning with his son Robert Estienne the Younger, who produced an edition in 1569; Théodore de Bèze, who produced several editions between 1556 and 1598; Christophe Plantin, who published Montano's Antwerp Polyglot in 1571/1572;[5] Erasmus Schmidt and Zacharias Gerganos, who produced the Wittenberg edition of 1622, intended for distribution in the Greek east; the Leiden Elzeviers, who published three editions in 1624, 1633 and 1641; and John Mill (1707). Franciscus Lucas Brugensis pointed out in his notes on the text (1580) that none of the manuscripts in Paris contained the comma, and that the semicircular metobelos marking the end of the comma in Estienne's *editio regia* had clearly been put in the wrong place, but his comments were ignored.[6] It was not until later that the absence of v. 7 from Estienne's

---

[3] Hatch 1941.

[4] Krans 2006, 337–338, and Elliott 2009b, 391, identify the following manuscripts used by Robert Estienne the Elder for his *editio regia* (1550), augmenting the readings he took from the Complutensian Polyglot (which he designates as α') and from Erasmus: β' (GA D/05ᶜᵃ); γ' (GA 4ᵉ); δ' (GA 5ᵉᵃᵖ); ε' (GA 6ᵉᵃᵖ); ς' (GA 7ᵉ); ζ' (GA 8ᵉ); η' (GA L 019ᵉ); θ' (GA 38ᵉᵃᵖ); ι' (GA 2298ᵃᵖ); ια' (GA 8ᵃ 10ᴾ [lost]); ιβ' (GA 9ᵉ); ιγ' (GA 398ᵃᵖ); ιδ' (GA 120ᵉ); ιε' (GA 82ᵃᵖʳ); ις' (GA 3ʳ [lost]).

[5] Montano 1569–1572, 5.2:532–533. Montano gives the Greek text of 1 Jn 5:7–8 as it appears in the Complutensian edition. The Latin reading is also taken over from the Complutensian edition, with one change ('spiritus, aqua, & sanguis'). In the margin of the Latin Vulgate column, beside verse 8, Montano adds the phrase '& hi tres unum sunt'. In the Antwerp Polyglot, the comma is absent from the Syriac text and from the Latin translation of the Syriac.

[6] Lucas Brugensis 1580, 462: 'Inter omnes Parisiensium Graecos codices, ne vnus est qui dissideat; nisi, quòd, septem, duntaxat τὸ *in caelo* confodiant: si tamen semicirculus, lectionis designans terminum, suo loco sit collocatus.' Cf. Bludau 1903a, 284.

manuscripts was demonstrated definitively by Simon (1689), Le Long (1720) and Marsh (1795).

2. The comma in sixteenth-century Latin editions

Before Trent, printed Latin bibles were of three broad kinds. The first were basic editions with little engagement with textual issues. The next group showed the beginnings of an occupation with critical issues, such as the editions of Adrien Gémeau (Gumelli, 1504) and the oft-reprinted edition of Alberto da Castello (Castellanus, 1511). Da Castello's edition contained a short list of variant readings later used by both Erasmus and Estienne. The third group dealt with text-critical matters more extensively and contained some reworking of the text, such as the editions of Erasmus, Gobelinus Laridius and Estienne.[7]

Sixteenth-century editions of the Latin Vulgate, of whatever kind, almost always contained the comma, such as those of Gémeau, da Castello, Andreas Osiander (Nuremberg, 1522), Johannes Petreius (Nuremberg, 1527), Sante Pagnino (Lyon, 1527), Robert Estienne the Elder (Paris, 1528, 1532, 1534), Cajetan (Venice, 1530), Gobelinus Laridius (Cologne, 1530), Konrad Pellicanus (Zürich, 1532–1539), and Isidorus Clarius (Taddeo Cucchi; Venice, 1542). The editions of the Vulgate produced at Wittenberg by Paul Eber (1564) and Paul Crell (1574) omit the comma, consistent with the general suspicion towards this passage shown by the first two generations of Lutherans.[8] Behind some of these editions stands a perceptible engagement with Erasmus' editorial decisions. Konrad Pellicanus revised his initial opinion and omitted the comma from the 1543 Zürich Latin bible, in which Erasmus' text of the New Testament was reworked by Rudolf Walter. A marginal note states that the codices display a great variety of readings in v. 8. Pellicanus and Walter followed the shorter reading attested, for example, by Cyril and in virtually the same form in an ancient manuscript in Zürich. Finally, the note refers the reader to Erasmus' annotations on the passage.[9] In his separate commentary on the Catholic Epistles, Pellicanus remarked: 'The most diligent Erasmus gives ample discussion of the varying text amongst the Greeks and the Latins,

---

[7] Kaulen 1868, 358–373; Vaccari 1925–1929 (2nd ed.), 1:214–215. Delenus 1540, 211v, who reworked Erasmus' text, gave no indication of any doubts about the status of the comma. On the editions of Gémeau (1504) and Castello (1511), see de Jonge 1977. On Delenus, see de Jonge 1978a.

[8] Bludau 1903a, 289; Posset 1985, 248–251.

[9] Pellicanus 1543, NT:106r; *DM* 6124; Bludau 1903a, 286–287. VD16 distinguishes two different editions produced by Froschauer in 1543 (VD16 2618 and 2619); I used the latter.

both ancient and recent, as you can see in his *Annotationes*.'[10] In his Latin editions of 1540, 1543, 1545 and 1555, Estienne marked off the words *in caelo* to *in terra* with obeloi, suggesting that he harboured doubts about the authenticity of the passage, but did not want to strike it entirely.[11] Cucchi followed suit, but his comments are rather oblique: although he respected the opinions of those who would interpret the Greeks and Latins differently – he preferred not to mention Erasmus by name – he did not intend to modify his text accordingly. Estienne's last Latin New Testament, printed in Geneva in 1556/1557, contains the Vulgate text as well as a new translation and notes by Bèze, whose comments show that he was convinced that the comma belonged in the text. Although he acknowledged that the comma was not cited by Cyril, Augustine or Bede, Bèze claimed it as genuine, pointing to the evidence of pseudo-Jerome, Erasmus' Codex Britannicus, the Complutensian text and Estienne's previous editions, though noting that the reading is different in all these copies.[12] The comments of Pellicanus, Cucchi and Bèze show that any editor of the New Testament who took his job seriously had to engage with Erasmus' critical legacy, even if they disagreed with his conclusions. The editions of the Vulgate finally approved by the Roman Catholic church (*Biblia sacra Vulgatae editionis*), the poorly edited Sistina (1590) and its replacement, the Clementina (1592), were based on thirteenth-century manuscripts of the text-form of the bible common in Paris, which contained the comma.

Though most sixteenth-century printed editions of the Latin bible contained the comma, a small number followed the pre-1521 text of Erasmus' Latin translation, which excluded the comma. The editions published at Leuven (1519), Basel (1520, 1521) and Mainz (1520) all predate Erasmus' revision, but some that postdate it likewise exclude the comma, such as those produced at Wittenberg (1529) and Zürich (1543, 1544).

---

[10] Pellicanus 1539, 780; cf. Bludau 1903a, 286–288.

[11] Bludau 1903a, 282–283; Bludau does not mention the obeloi in Estienne's 1555 Latin edition, which likewise enclose the words *in caelo* to *in terra*.

[12] Bèze 1556, 318, revised slightly in the first Greek edition of Bèze 1565, 603: 'Nam tres sunt, &c. ὅτι τρεῖς εἰσιν, &c. Hic versiculus omnino mihi retinendus videtur. Explicat enim manifestè quod de sex testibus dixerat, tres seorsim caelo, tres terrae tribuens. Non legit tamen vetus interpres [i.e. the Latin Vulgate], nec Cyrillus, nec Augustinus, nec Beda; sed legit Hieronymus, legit Erasmus in Britannico codice, & in Complutensi editione. Legimus & nos in nonnullis Roberti nostri [*1565*: Roberti Stephani] veteribus libris. Non convenit tamen in omnibus inter istos codices. Nam Britannicus legit sine articulis πατήρ, λόγος, καὶ πνεῦμα. In nostris verò legebantur articuli, & praeterea etiam additum erat Sancti epitheton Spiritui, vt ab eo distingueretur cuius fit mentio in sequenti versiculo, quique in terra collocatur. – In caelo, ἐν τῷ οὐρανῷ: Hoc deerat in septem vetustis codicibus, sed tamen omnino videtur retinendum.' Cf. Bludau 1903a, 288; Heide 2006, 71 n. 132.

3.   Syriac and Arabic editions

Serious study of the Syriac Vulgate (Peshitta) in Western Europe only began in the middle of the sixteenth century. Discrepancies between this ancient translation and the Latin Vulgate caused concern in some quarters. Not only did this translation lack entire books (2 Pt, 2 Jn, 3 Jn, Jude, Rev), it also lacked the long ending of Mark, the *pericope de adultera* (Jn 7:53–8:11), and the Johannine comma. The Peshitta was first printed at Vienna in 1555, edited by the orientalists Johann Albrecht Widmannstetter and Claude Postel on the basis of a manuscript brought to the west by Moses of Mardin, a legate of the Jacobite Patriarch.[13] This text was reprinted in the Antwerp Polyglot (1568–1572), with a Latin translation by Guy Lefèvre de la Boderie (Fabricius).[14] On 16 August 1577, Juan de Mariana, appointed by the Spanish Inquisition as censor responsible for Scriptural publications, completed a report on the Polyglot. Amongst other criticisms, Mariana considered that the team of editors was too small for the task. The involvement of dubious characters such as Postel and Lefèvre de la Boderie rendered the entire enterprise suspect. Mariana believed that the committee sometimes departed further than necessary from the Vulgate. Moreover, the commentary quoted rabbinic literature more frequently than the church fathers.[15] Mariana criticised the Latin rendering of the Peshitta at several points. For example, he worried that the omission of the *pericope de adultera* and the comma from the Syriac text could be used by Antitrinitarians to argue that the Latin Vulgate was corrupt. Moreover, the omission of these passages from the Latin version undermined the Tridentine decree upholding the integrity of the biblical books included in the Latin Vulgate.[16] Despite these reservations, Mariana finally gave his approval for the edition.

When Immanuel Tremellius (*c.* 1510–1580), professor of Hebrew at the University of Heidelberg, published the second edition of the Syriac Peshitta in 1569 (with Latin translation), he refrained from inserting the comma into the text on the basis of its absence from the Syriac text – both the first printed edition and the manuscript available to him in Heidelberg – and 'from all the ancient Greek codices'. But to avoid a discrepancy of verse numbers between his Syriac text and those recently

---

[13] See Wilkinson 2007a.
[14] Wilkinson 2007b, 71.
[15] Wilkinson 2007b, 95–96.
[16] Mariana 1609, 72–73.

provided for the Greek text by Estienne, Tremellius provided a hypothetical rendering into Syriac, which remained however in a note.[17] In his polyglot New Testament (Nuremberg, 1599–1600), Elias Hutter moved Tremellius' hypothetical Syriac translation of the comma into the body text, though he placed it in parentheses. Hutter was evidently convinced of the genuineness of the comma. Citing the prologue to the Catholic Epistles, he condemned its omission from the German and Danish translations 'an egregious error that ought not to be passed over in silence nor excused on any account'.[18] Martin Trost, who produced an edition of the Syriac text of 1 Jn for use in schools in 1621, once again excised the comma.[19] However, on Hutter's authority, the comma was retained in the Syriac editions of Gutbier (Hamburg, 1664–1667) and Leusden and Schaaf (Leiden, 1709). However, Samuel Lee once again excluded the comma from his edition, published by the British and Foreign Bible Society in 1816.[20]

The exclusion of the comma from Samuel Lee's edition created a backlash that resulted in an edition produced by a team of Dominicans (1887–1891). This edition included the comma in a fresh translation from the Latin, without any indication that this reading did not appear in any of the manuscripts used for the edition. This edition had clear polemical motives, and was described by the patriarch of Babylon, Petrus Elias Abolyonan, as 'containing all the divine books in a perfect state, edited by the efforts of skilful critics and printed by Catholic presses'. The patriarch praised the Dominicans for doing away with editions prepared by Protestant scholars, 'in which there is clearly nothing of use to readers, which are defective, corrupted in many places by bad faith and overly subtle astuteness'.[21] The archbishop of Amid, Georgius Ebed-Jesus Khayyath,

---

[17] Tremellius 1569, 2:680v–681r; cf. Borger 1987, 281, with transcription of Tremellius' note.

[18] Hutter 1599–1600, 1:***r–v (commentary), 2:902–903 (text); cf. Borger 1987, 281–282.

[19] Trost 1621, 20.

[20] Gutbier 1664, 560 (text); Gutbier 1667, 43 (C6r in 'Notae' at the end of the volume); Leusden and Schaaf 1709, 597 (square brackets around 'in terra' only); Gwilliam 1905–1920, 2:64. Leusden 1670, 35–38, defended the comma as a 'splendid and very beautiful testimony for proving the Holy Trinity' (*Testimonium luculentum & pulcherrimum pro probanda S. S. Trinitate*). He explained the absence of the comma from the early translations (including the Syriac) by suggesting that these were made from corrupt Greek copies. Borger 1987, reprints the comments of Tremellius and Hutter. The Latin translation of the comma given by Tremellius is that of Beza, with one minor variant. Norton 1889, [footnote to 1 Jn 5:7, no page number], notes that the comma is also absent from *Novum Testamentum Syriacum, et Arabicum* 1703, representing the Syriac text used by the Maronites, as well as the editions of the Nestorians in India (ed. Samuel Lee 1816) and Kurdistan (1852, probably an error for Perkins' edition of 1846, *DM* 9029), though Norton included the comma in brackets in his translation both of the Syriac and the Greek text underlying the Revised Version of 1881. Further, see Bludau 1903b; Metzger 1977, 53.

[21] *Biblia sacra juxta versionem simplicem*, 1, approbation of Petrus Elias XII Abolyonan (unpaginated). On this edition and the approbations, see Borger 1987, 282.

was glad no longer to have to rely on editions 'issued by publishers attached to Protestant sects, which are in common use, though with great danger to our souls'.[22] Here too the comma had become an element in the struggle to assert the orthodoxy of a particular group to the exclusion of its rivals. Ignoring the polemical tone of the Dominican edition, Gwilliam excluded the comma once again from his edition, published by the British and Foreign Bible Society in 1905–1920. It is also excluded from the critical edition of Barbara Aland and Andreas Juckel (1986–2002).

Towards the end of the sixteenth century, Thomas Day of Cambridge translated the Arabic version of 1 Jn into Latin. His translation makes the absence of the comma from the Arabic text plain.[23] In his commentaries on the New Testament, the Dutch jurist and theologian Hugo Grotius (1583–1645) rejected the comma because it is absent from authoritative manuscripts such as Codex Alexandrinus (GA 02/A), as well as from the Syriac and Arabic versions. He suggested that the participle 'the witnessing ones' (μαρτυροῦντες) is a Hebraism, and remarked on the potential semantic difference between 'these three are one' and 'these three are unto one'.[24] From the sixteenth century onwards, the absence of the comma from the oriental versions was thus a factor of some importance in European discussions of the comma, even if few people were properly qualified to evaluate the evidence.

4. Lutheran reactions to the dispute over the comma

Erasmus' ambiguous stance over the comma led to a variety of responses amongst Lutheran critics. Luther used Erasmus' 1519 edition and annotations for his 1522 German translation of the New Testament. In addition to the fact that the comma was not present in the Greek text before him, he declined to include the comma on both textual and theological grounds.[25]

---

[22] *Biblia sacra juxta versionem simplicem* 1887–1891, 1, approbation of Georgius Ebed-Jesus Khayyath (unpaginated).

[23] Cambridge, Corpus Christi College ms 384.

[24] Grotius 1641–1650, 3:96–97. The collation of Codex Alexandrinus made for Grotius is now in Amsterdam, University Library ms III H 17[1]; see Mendes da Costa 1923, 20, n° 146; de Jonge 1984a, 109 n. 32.

[25] E. Abbott 1888, 458–463; Posset 1985. Metzger 1964, 450, wrote that the absence of the comma from Luther's translation was due to the fact that he used Erasmus' 1519 text. This is true for Luther's 1522 'September Testament', but he also declined to include the comma in later editions. In the margin of his copy of the 1527 edition of Erasmus' New Testament (Groningen University Library, HS 494), Luther did not make any note in the margin of the New Testament text beside the comma, but in the accompanying *Annotationes* (Erasmus 1527b, 696), he highlighted Erasmus' comments on Jerome.

This was only one of the many details that distinguished Luther's translations from earlier German versions. For example, the Low German bible published at Halberstadt in 1522 had been translated from the Latin Vulgate, and consequently included the comma.[26]

The influence of Luther's translation spread quickly, but was quickly overcome. While the comma was included in Dutch New Testaments based on the Latin Vulgate, such as those produced at Antwerp by Jan van Ghelen in 1524 and Willem Vorsterman in 1531, it was omitted from those based on Luther's version, such as those published by Christoffel van Ruremund in 1525 and c. 1526.[27] However, the Liesveldt bible (1542), which claimed to draw its authority both from the Greek and from the Latin Vulgate, includes the comma.[28] The widely used Protestant Dutch translation of the New Testament by Gillis van der Erven (1561) was based on the Greek text, but it also drew elements from the Liesveldt bible, including its inclusion of the comma.[29]

In 1527 Luther gave a series of lectures on the first letter of John, in which he stuck by his initial decision to reject the comma. It is clear that his opinions on this passage were determined largely by the judgement of Erasmus. Luther stated that Catholic apologists had added the comma clumsily to counter the Arians. Moreover, he added, the comma makes little sense: when we finally come to see God we will have no need of such witnesses. In heaven there is no need of testimony or faith; it is only here on earth that we need testimonies to God, but we have all the testimony we need in the Scriptures. Let us, he concluded, leave this text aside. 'I can make fun of this text easily, for there is no more inept passage in defence of the Trinity.'[30] Luther's suspicion of the comma is also reflected in more subtle ways, for example in the omission of the comma from

[26] *Biblia dudesch* 1522, IIIr: 'Und de geyst ys de daer betüghet dath christus ys de warheyt / wente dre synt de dar gheuen tüchenisse yn deme hymmele / de vader. dath wort / vnde de hyllighe gheyst / vnd düsse dre synt eyn.' Cf. Baumgarten 1748–1751, 7:390.
[27] The first volume in the only extant copy of Jan van Ghelen's five-volume New Testament of *c.* 1524 (Utrecht UB, D. oct. 1671 Rariora) lacks a title page. The comma is in the fourth volume, *Die kerstelijcke Epistelen, c.* 1524, c3r: '[...] Christus is die waerheyt. Want drie isser dye getugenisse geuen inden hemel die vader dat woort ende die heylige gheest ende dese drie sijn een. Ende drie sijnt die ghetughenisse gheuen opter aerden die gheest dat water ende dat bloet ende dese drie sijn een.' *Tnyeuwe Testament al gheel* 1531, Q4v: '[...] Christus is die waerheyt. Want drie zijnder die getuych gheuen in den hemel / die vader / twoort / ende die heylige geest / ende dese drie zijn een. Ende drie zijnder die getuych geuen inder aerde / die geest / ende twater / ende bloet / ende dese drie zijn een.' The comma is absent from *Dat heylich Euangelium* 1525, S5r, and from *Dat heylich Euangelium, c.* 1526, pp3r.
[28] *Den Bybel* 1542, SS5r.
[29] Van den Erven 1561, 90r. The Old Testament volume was published on 7 March 1562.
[30] *WA* 20:780–781, edited from two separate students' transcripts. Luther expressed himself in similar terms in his *Tischreden*, *WA TR* 48:688 (n° 7101); Koffmanne 1897; Posset 1985, 246–248. The

his 1542 German translation of *Against the law of the Turks* (*Contra legem Sarracenorum*) by the Dominican Ricoldus († 1320).[31]

The omission of the comma from Luther's translation of the New Testament occasioned a sharp rebuke from his former teacher Hieronymus Emser (1523), who argued that it would be positively harmful for the masses to read Luther's translation. In his comments on the comma, Emser cited the prologue to the Catholic epistles in its defence. Following this prologue, he suggested that the Greeks had 'stolen' the comma through their disregard for the Trinity. He also noted that while Luther was clearly following Erasmus' lead in making these omissions, he had failed to follow Erasmus' restoration of the verse in the 1522 edition. After all, Emser argued, Erasmus had never intended his first edition to be translated immediately into the vernacular, but submitted it first to the judgement of the learned.[32]

Luther's dogged opponent Johannes Cochlaeus used the Trinitarian symbolum *tres unum sunt* as the basis for crude satire. As he explained, the Trinity, in which 'these three are one', is a sublime theological mystery passing all understanding. Likewise, the seven-headed Luther, who combined the roles of preacher, church inspector, enthusiast, Barabbas, and more besides, was a mystery hitherto unknown to Christian, Jew or heathen. The title woodcut to Cochlaeus' book (Figure 2.1) satirically combines the image of the seven-headed beast of the Apocalypse with the mediaeval iconography of the three-faced or three-headed Trinity, seen for example in a thirteenth-century miniature of Abraham's encounter with the three men at Mamre (Gen 18:1–2), traditionally interpreted by Christian theologians as a vision of the Trinity (see Figure 2.2).[33]

Johannes Bugenhagen engaged with the comma in detail in his commentary on the book of Jonah (1550), remaining close to the position of Erasmus and Luther. Bugenhagen interpreted the earthly witnesses as divine signs in the church: the spirit is the ministry of preaching, in whom the Holy Spirit is manifest to the church; the water is baptism; and the blood is the eucharist. These witnesses are not mute, but give their testimony in the church, not simply within our own consciences, but audibly and visibly, in order to convert unbelievers.[34] These three

---

commentary on 1 Jn attributed to Luther by Walch in his edition (Luther 1739–1753, 9:1080–1251) is assigned to Agricola in *WA* 20:596.

[31] Ricoldus' text is in *LW* 53:367; Luther's translation is in *LW* 53:366.

[32] Emser 1523, 128v–129r.

[33] Cochlaeus 1529, (ijv).

[34] Bugenhagen 1550, d6v. A summary of Bugenhagen's position is in Posset 1985.

Figure 2.1. Title woodcut from Johannes Cochlaeus, *Septiceps Lutherus*
(Leipzig: Schumann, 1529). Bayerische Staatsbibliothek München, 4° Polem. 676.
Reproduced by kind permission.

witnesses in the church are 'unto one', that is, they agree in testifying that
Jesus is the Christ, the Son of God, who was sacrificed for us, who is our
justice and eternal life. Some, Bugenhagen noted, added another three
witnesses in heaven, though these heavenly witnesses have nothing to do

Figure 2.2. Abraham worships the Trinity. Cambridge, St John's College ms K26, 9r.
By permission of the Master and Fellows of St John's College, Cambridge.

with the point John is making here. Moreover, the addition of three heavenly witnesses would make six witnesses where John speaks only of three. Bugenhagen also pointed out that the phrases 'on earth' and 'in heaven' were not originally part of the text of the epistle, a circumstance that shows clearly that the heavenly witnesses were not part of John's original plan. Those who dared to add this text showed their audacity and lack of proper fear for God. While Jerome believed that these words could refute heretics, Bugenhagen argued they in fact strengthened the blasphemy of the Arians, against whom John struggled so hard in his gospel and in this epistle. (Bugenhagen, like everyone at the time, believed that the fourth gospel and the Johannine Epistles were written by the same person. He also believed that the beliefs held by the Arians already existed in the first century.) Indeed, Bugenhagen suggested that the comma was invented by Arians, for if the Father, Word and Holy Spirit were one in the same way as the spirit, water and blood are one, then the Arians would have won. To attribute such a blasphemy to John is to blaspheme the Son of God to whom John testified.[35] Bugenhagen made explicit reference to Erasmus' annotation on the comma, praising him for his industry and insight. He agreed with Erasmus that we would do better to strive for a closer walk with God than to speculate idly on the nature of the Trinity. In any case, what the Arians deny can only be demonstrated through logical argument, not by pointing to this or that verse in Scripture. Best of all is simply to remember Jesus' statement that God can only be known through him.[36] Bugenhagen also noted that of all the Greek manuscripts Erasmus had seen, the British codex was the only one containing the addition. Bugenhagen stated clearly what Erasmus had only hinted at obliquely: that the comma was invented for doctrinal ends by Jerome, who considered it a useful weapon against Arians. Bugenhagen urged his readers not to rely on this kind of beggarly evidence to confirm the equality of the three divine persons, something to which the writings of the prophets and the faith of Christians testify equally. Bugenhagen criticised Erasmus for losing his nerve and including the comma in his third edition, especially given his suspicion that the British codex was corrupt. By including this verse in his printed text, Erasmus had prepared the way for further textual corruption. For this reason, Bugenhagen urged printers and correctors issuing editions of the New Testament to omit the comma. Editors of the bible should safeguard the integrity of the text and honour

[35] Bugenhagen 1550, d7r–8v.
[36] Bugenhagen 1550, d8v–e1r.

the late Erasmus by refusing to allow a corruption of the text to be perpetuated in his name, since it had always been his desire that the text of
Scripture should be restored to its pristine form.[37]

5.   Zwinglian reactions to the dispute over the comma

Swiss Reformed theologians were also in two minds about the comma.
Zwingli declined to make any marginal comment next to the relevant passage in his personal copy of the 1519 Basel edition of Erasmus'
Annotationes (Zürich, Zentralbibliothek III M 5), which suggests that he
considered the comma a non-issue. In his commentary on 1 Jn, Zwingli
passed over the comma in silence.[38] And when Johannes Comandrus and
Nicolaus Balingius, pastor and schoolmaster respectively at Chur, wrote
to ask Zwingli how they were to interpret 1 Jn 5, his response omitted all
mention of the comma.[39]

Johannes Oecolampadius advised Erasmus when he was preparing the
first edition of the New Testament, and it is likely that they discussed the
comma. Accordingly, when Oecolampadius published his sermons on 1 Jn
(1524), he omitted the comma from the text without further comment.[40]

Heinrich Bullinger, Zwingli's successor at Zürich, suggested that any
agreement between the three persons of the Trinity as described in the
comma was one of witness rather than of essence. However, he maintained that this principle could be demonstrated more securely by other
Scriptural passages. Following Erasmus, Bullinger suggested that in 1 Jn
5:8, the water signifies heavenly doctrine, the blood redemption and the
spirit truth. The person who had originally made the allegorical leap to
interpret the earthly witnesses as types of the Trinity had misunderstood
the text. Furthermore, Bullinger followed Erasmus' judgement in the
Annotationes that this Trinitarian interpretation had begun as a marginal
gloss which a half-learned (*sciolus*) reader or scribe had integrated into the
text.[41] And when Johannes Cochlaeus cited the comma in his attack on
Bullinger's understanding of the doctrine of the Trinity, Bullinger declined
to respond to this detail, perhaps in order to avoid the issue of the canonicity of specific details of biblical books.[42]

---

[37] Bugenhagen 1550, e1r–2v.
[38] Zwingli 1581, 597–598; 1828–1842, 6.1:338; Posset 1985, 251.
[39] Oecolampadius and Zwingli 1536, 29v.
[40] Oecolampadius 1524, 87r–88r.
[41] Bullinger 1549, 103.
[42] Cochlaeus 1544, C3r; Bullinger 1544, 22r.

The rejection of the comma by the leading Zwinglian theologians led to its exclusion (or at least its typographical distinction) from German translations of the New Testament intended for use in Switzerland. The Swiss edition of Luther's translation, first printed by Froschauer at Zürich in 1529, gave the comma in small type, while the 1531 edition and those that followed gave it in parentheses. The Latin-German edition edited by Johannes Zwick and published at Zürich in 1535 omits the comma from the Latin text, but gives it in brackets in the German text. Rudolf Walter and Konrad Pellicanus omitted it altogether from the Latin *Versio Tigurina* (1543).[43]

6. English translations

The conflicted attitude towards the comma on the part of various Protestant parties is reflected in the English bible translations of the sixteenth and early seventeenth centuries. William Tyndale, who drew on the 1522 edition of Erasmus' New Testament and Luther's translation, gave the comma in the 1526 Worms edition of his New Testament translation without any typographical distinction.[44] Yet it seems that Tyndale harboured doubts about the passage. In his *Exposition of the fyrst Epistle of seynt Jhon* (1531), he included the comma in the text of the epistle, but in his commentary he avoided the issue of the Trinity, commenting exclusively on the sacraments of the water and the blood that bear witness to Christ.[45] In the revised edition of his New Testament (1534), Tyndale registered his reservations about the comma by placing it in parentheses and smaller type: '(For ther are thre which beare recorde in heauen / the father / the wordt / and the wholy goost. And these thre are one) For theare are thre which beare recorde (in erth:) the sprete / and water / and bloud: and these thre are one.' Myles Coverdale (1535) followed Tyndale's wording and his use of parentheses to mark off the comma, though he omitted the parentheses around the words 'in erth', perhaps in error. The 1539 translation of the New Testament, based on Erasmus' text, placed the comma in parentheses and small type.[46] The *Byble in Englyshe* (the 'Great Bible') of 1539 followed Tyndale's later practice of giving the comma in parentheses and small type. However, there are no distinguishing typographical marks

---

[43] Düsterdieck 1852–1856, 2:355–356; on the *Versio Tigurina*, see above, 58.
[44] Tyndale 1526, 298v.
[45] Tyndale 1531, G5r.
[46] Erasmus 1539, n8v.

in the Geneva Bible (1560), the Bishops' Bible (1568) or the Authorised Version (1611), which suggests a growing reluctance to call the authority of the comma into question. Cranmer's lectionary in the 1549 Book of Common Prayer (absorbed into later versions, including the 1662 Prayer Book) preserves 1 Jn 5:4–12 (including the comma) from the mediaeval lectionary as the epistle for the Lord's Supper on the octave of Easter. The Douay-Rheims version (1582) was translated from the Vulgate for Roman Catholic readers, and accordingly it includes the comma, though it is marked off with daggers. After the comma was included in the Authorised Version, its place in the English bible was secure until the eighteenth century, when alternative editions and translations again challenged its place in the text.[47]

Summary

In this descriptive chapter we examined the way in which Erasmus' inconsistent attitude towards the comma was reflected in sixteenth-century editions of the New Testament in Greek, Latin, Syriac, Arabic, German and English, and how the decision of later editors – whether Lutheran, Roman Catholic or Zwinglian – to include or exclude the comma invariably reflected theological developments within their respective theological traditions. These developments will be explored in more detail in the next chapter.

---

[47] See also Bludau 1922, 128–129.

CHAPTER 3

Raising the ghost of Arius: the Johannine comma and Trinitarian debate in the sixteenth century

Erasmus' initial exclusion and subsequent inclusion of the *comma Johanneum* in the text of the New Testament, one of his most controversial contributions to biblical scholarship, continued as the focus of critical and polemical attention through the sixteenth, seventeenth and eighteenth centuries.[1] While Antitrinitarians were virtually universal in their rejection of the comma, orthodox Protestants and Catholics were divided over its textual authority, and adapted their attitudes according to their purposes. But it is not enough simply to know which of a limited repertoire of arguments were adduced by any given author. Discussion of this question became increasingly more polemical over time. One must therefore be aware of the opponent – singular or plural, specific or general, real or imaginary, direct or indirect – against whom a particular argument is being advanced, and the reasons why. It is also important to remember that polemicists often have a number of motivations, arguments, opponents and purposes simultaneously, and that this plurality can sometimes cause apparent contradiction.[2]

Besides the fact that Erasmus had drawn attention to the issue of the comma, Antitrinitarians also drew on Erasmus for other details. Erasmus remarked that Jesus is rarely called God in the New Testament; the word 'God' without further precision invariably refers to the Father.[3] In his preface to Hilary's works, Erasmus also remarked that this author does not refer to the Holy Spirit as 'God', and noted that Jesus and the Spirit are rarely described as God in the New Testament. These observations would be picked up by many Antitrinitarian writers through the sixteenth

---

[1] The present discussion of the dispute over the status of the comma is not intended to be exhaustive, but merely highlights the most important contributions to the debate. More comprehensive, if somewhat uncritical, accounts of individual contributions to the debate are found in the articles of Bludau, listed in the bibliography.

[2] Frick 1995, 142–143.

[3] Erasmus 1516, 352 (annotation on Jn 1:1); *ASD* IX-2:124–130.

and seventeenth centuries.[4] For Stephen Nye, whose *Brief History of the Unitarians, called also Socinians,* sparked off the Trinitarian Controversy that would divide the Church of England for the next thirty years, Erasmus was one of those prominent scholars whose ostensible orthodoxy was merely a cloak to disguise their true Arian or Socinian identity, who 'have used much Caution in so expressing themselves, as not to lye too open to Exception, Envy, or a legal Prosecution'.[5] Accordingly, Nye cited Erasmus (alongside other critics such as Grotius and Courcelles) in his attempts to demolish the traditional interpretation of verses cited as evidence of the Trinity: Jn 1:15, Jn 3:13, Acts 2:28, Rom 9:5, 1 Jn 5:7–8 and Rev 1:17.[6] Edmund Calamy noted that objections to texts such as the comma were unknown 'till *Erasmus* rais'd a Dust, and began a Scruple, which others have taken no small Pleasure in increasing since'.[7] To Myles Davies (1716), Erasmus' role in preparing a highway in the desert for heretics was clear: 'upon *Erasmus's* doubts, the *Arians* and *Socinians* fram'd their Assertions and Asseverations: For the *Antitrinitarians* began upon certain doubtful Questions and Interpretations of *Erasmus,* whether such or such places of Scripture used against the *Arians* were well apply'd or no?'[8] According to Davies, Erasmus' teachings were not explicitly Arian, but his promotion of an aggressively inquisitive attitude towards the Scriptures would lead others into disastrous errors.[9]

At the other end of the scale stood Jean Le Clerc (1657–1736), professor at the Remonstrant seminary in Amsterdam and editor of Erasmus' works. Le Clerc was conscious that several of his own contemporaries found Erasmus' interest in the question of Christ's divinity suspicious: 'I know that there are some very erudite people who have said that Erasmus was a little too solicitous in collecting variant readings where Christ's divinity is discussed, and that he prepared the way for those who deny that divinity. For this reason they have desired to cast upon him the suspicion of closet-Arianism.' But Le Clerc argued that Erasmus' orthodoxy was evident in his apologetic works. 'And as far as those variant readings are concerned, if it is true what he says about the manuscripts and the

---

[4] Snobelen 2006, 118.

[5] Nye 1687, 30–31. Nye was refuted by Basset 1693, 154–158. Further, see Snobelen 2006, 126–127.

[6] Nye 1687, 59, 88, 90, 113, 118, 152, cit. Snobelen 2006, 127.

[7] Calamy 1722, 403.

[8] Davies 1716, 1:42.

[9] Davies 1716, 1:42–3. Further on the question of Erasmus and Arianism, see Martin Lydius, *Apologia pro Erasmo* (1606), ed. in *LB* X:1761–1780, esp. 1766–1767; Burigni 1757, 2:155, 530–533, cit. Pineau 1924, 266–267; Jortin 1808, 2:105, 125, 185–187, 216, 246, 250, 399–404, 411, 417, 428; Tracy 1981; Nijenhuis 1993, 259–260; Levine 1999, 43–45.

fathers, in whom many passages have different readings, that is no reason to chastise him.' In any case, the Scriptures contain more than enough clear evidence to refute Arians and other heterodox thinkers. Through his persistent criticism, Erasmus had shown which of these might be relied upon, and which were less secure.[10]

The debate over the question of Erasmus' alleged Arianism thus swung between two poles, represented by those who considered that Erasmus deliberately fomented doubt and heresy; and those who argued that his sole concern was to promote a pious and immediate engagement with the Scriptures, devoid of the claims of authority and the deceptions of those who profit from untruth.

The debates over the Trinity from the sixteenth to the eighteenth centuries had a number of effects. Orthodox theologians were forced to define their position strictly to avoid suspicion of heresy. This may have discouraged creative and potentially valuable developments in doctrine in the major denominations. On the other hand, those who had separated themselves from orthodoxy on such a central article of dogma were thus freed to ask a number of fruitful 'what if?' questions, not only in theology, but in philosophy, politics and even the natural sciences. Once it became clear that the Antitrinitarians were not going away, lawmakers and society at large had to find ways to deal with their presence. Would society try to expel them as a foreign body, carry on as though they were not there, tolerate them under sufferance or accept them openly?

1.   Miguel Servet

The scepticism of Miguel Servet (*c.* 1510–1553), the father of modern Antitrinitarianism, owes a discernible debt to Erasmus. As a young man, Servet acted as secretary to Juan de Quintana at the 1527 meeting at Valladolid, at which Erasmus' orthodoxy was examined. Soon after, Servet wrote his book *On the errors of the Trinity*. Julia Gauss and Carlos Gilly have characterised Servet's treatise as a reaction to Quintana's critique of Erasmus. Indeed, Servet consistently sides with Erasmus, following arguments from his *Annotationes* and citing from his translation. But if Servet received many initial impulses from Erasmus, he took them in more radical directions. For example, he adopted Erasmus' translation of Jn 7:39 ('the Holy Spirit did not yet exist'), but interpreted it not as an indication

---

[10] Le Clerc, preface to *LB* 6, *r–v. On Le Clerc as heir to Erasmus' philological method, see Asso 2004, esp. 111–112.

that the Apostles had not yet been empowered by the Holy Spirit, but as evidence that the Holy Spirit did not exist before being given to humans. Servet came to Basel in July 1530 to publish *On the errors of the Trinity* and perhaps to make contact with the elder scholar. When Servet discovered that Erasmus had left Basel, he followed him to Freiburg to present him with a copy of his book, but Erasmus refused to receive him.[11] Servet's eventual arrest, trial and execution in 1553 showed that questioning the doctrine of the Trinity in early modern Europe could draw the full force of the law down upon one's head.

While Servet learned much from Erasmus' *Annotationes*, he did not follow Erasmus in calling the authenticity of the comma into question. Instead he sought to work out an alternative theological position on the basis of the Scriptural texts that refer to the nature of the relationship between God and Jesus, whose status as 'great God' he maintained. Servet, drawing on the notion of the divine economy from Irenaeus and Tertullian, maintained that the Word is not a separate being, but an appearance or an economy. Until the incarnation, the Word was not begotten, merely uttered. The Word only became a separate being at the incarnation, and it is only at this point that we can talk of the Word as begotten. Since the pre-incarnate Word was not a being separate from God, it only makes sense to describe the incarnate Son as of one substance with the Father. Servet distinguished his position clearly from that of Arius, and blamed the metaphysical speculations of Arius and his followers for closing off fruitful paths of speculation. Servet's thought is closer to that of Marcellus or Photinus than to that of Arius, but is ultimately *sui generis*.[12]

In his first book, *On the errors of the Trinity* (1531), Servet discussed the Johannine comma in conjunction with Jn 10:30 and Jn 14:10. Servet noted that the neuter *unum* in Jn 10:30 refers to a unanimity and concord of wills, not a numerical singularity. He extended this conclusion to the comma, where *unum* likewise relates 'not to the nature of those three things, but to the faithfulness and the unity of their testimony' (*constat ibi agi non de natura illarum trium rerum, sed de fide et unitate testimonii*). Carlos Gilly has shown that Servet's wording here and the authorities he summoned in support (Cyprian and the *Glossa ordinaria*) are borrowed from Erasmus' *Annotationes*.[13]

---

[11] Bataillon 1937, 462; Gauss 1966, 417–434; Gilly 1985, 288; Bietenholz 2008, 35–39.

[12] Wiles 1996, 54–56; Bietenholz 2008, 33–39.

[13] Servet 1531, 22v–24v. Servet notes in the margin of 23v that Erasmus, like Origen (*Contra Celsum* VIII.12, *PG* 11:1534) also interprets *unum* in Jn 17:22 as a unity of wills (*Erasmus etiam in*

In his *Christianismi restitutio* (1553), Servet restated his argument that the Father communicated his deity only to the Son in an unmediated and corporeal way. From him the Holy and substantial Spirit (*halitus*) was given to others. The three heavenly witnesses bore witness to the unity of the deity, and the three earthly witnesses – the water, blood and spirit that issued from Jesus' body on the cross – showed that Jesus was not an incorporeal being, but a man who was moreover really the Son of God, a point that John continually emphasised.[14]

2. Philipp Melanchthon and the Lutheran turn towards the comma

While Luther and several other leading Lutherans of the first generation were sceptical (or at least reserved) about the comma, Servet's revival of Antitrinitarianism prompted Philipp Melanchthon and other Protestant theologians to clutch at all possible biblical evidence, including the comma, in their defence of Nicene orthodoxy. Yet their attitudes were by no means uniform.

Melanchthon dealt directly with Servet's *On the errors of the Trinity* in the 1535 revision of his *Loci theologici*, in a discussion of the doctrine of God. Melanchthon objected to Servet's discussion of the word *logos*, and believed that Servet either misunderstood or deliberately misquoted Irenaeus and Tertullian on this point.[15] Evidently as a direct consequence of his objections to Servet, Melanchthon cited the comma as one of the Scriptural witnesses to the Trinity, without further comment.[16] In the 1545 revision of his *Loci communes*, Melanchthon spoke out even more strongly against Servet.[17] Here he also made more of the comma as a valuable witness to the divine testimony:

> The expression *they bear testimony* is well said; [John] tells us about the way God reveals himself, that we should understand God as he reveals himself. God testifies about himself, who and what he is: the true God, creator of all things, who conserves and sustains them. And he testifies about his doctrine, about his will towards us, and affirms that there are three in heaven who have given this testimony.[18]

---

annotationibus ita exponit). This is the only explicit mention of Erasmus in the entire book. See Gilly 1985, 277–318, esp. 277–279; Gilly 2005, 326–327; Servet 2008, 220–227.
[14] Servet 1553, 22–23.
[15] Melanchthon 1535, c5v–6r; slightly different text in *CR* 21:359.
[16] Melanchthon 1535, d3v; *CR* 21:366.
[17] Melanchthon 1545, A8r; *CR* 21:614.
[18] Melanchthon 1545, D4r–v; *CR* 21:633.

Melanchthon does not state explicitly whether he considered the unity of
the heavenly witnesses as one of essence or testimony, though he seems to
imply the latter. This position would be taken up by Calvin.

Franz Posset (1985) suggested that Melanchthon departed from Luther's
position on the comma because he was not familiar with Luther's unpublished lectures on 1 Jn. But it seems rather that Melanchthon, faced with
the threat of Servet, grasped all weapons at hand, including the comma.
By 1534 Luther had concluded that Erasmus' comments about the divinity
of Christ had encouraged the Arians, by whom he clearly meant Servet,
and he wrote a long letter to Nicolaus von Amsdorf in early March 1534
in which he laid out his suspicions. Luther evidently showed this letter
to Melanchthon, who mentioned it in a letter to Joachim Camerarius,
before handing it on to the printer Hans Lufft, who printed it immediately. Erasmus did not reply in print, but claimed haughtily in a letter to
Melanchthon that it was hardly worth his while brushing off such baseless
criticism.[19]

Melanchthon's rehabilitation of the comma caught on quickly at
Wittenberg. Johannes Spangenberg based his catechism *Margarita theologica* (1540) on Melanchthon's *Loci*. Under the question: 'How do you prove
that there are three persons?' (*Vnde probas esse tres personas?*), Spangenberg
cited Mt 3:16–17, Mt 28:19, Jn 15:16, 1 Jn 5:7 and the Nicene creed.[20]
The Spanish Erasmian Francisco de Enzinas, a student at Wittenberg,
included the comma in his Castilian translation of the New Testament,
completed under Melanchthon's supervision and printed at Antwerp in
1543.[21] During the doctoral disputation of Georg Major and Johannes
Faber, over which Luther presided on 12 December 1544, Major cited only
three Scriptural passages under the head 'On the divinity of the essence'
(*De divinitate essentiae*): Jn 10:30, 17:11 and 1 Jn 5:7.[22] And in his doctoral
disputation, held at Wittenberg on 3 July 1545, Peter Herzog (Hegemon)
declared that the Scriptures contain many testimonies to the Trinity,
including Gen 1:26–27, Mt 3:16, Rom 11:36 and 1 Jn 5:7. In his response
to Herzog, even Luther quoted the comma.[23] Some of those who reha-
bilitated the comma did so on the flimsiest evidence. Jesper Rasmussen

---

[19] *WA Br* 7:27, 33–35; *CR* 2:709; *Opus epist.* 10:372, 11:44; cf. Gilly 1985, 288.
[20] Spangenberg 1540, 78.
[21] Enzinas 1543, 321r: 'Por que tres son los que dan testimonio en el çielo: El Padre, La Palabra, y el
Espirito sancto: Y estos tres son vna misma cosa. Tanbien son tres los que dan testimonio en la
tierra: El espirito, la agua, y la sangre: y estos tres son vno.' Further, see Gilly 1985, 326–328.
[22] *WA* 39.2:323–324.
[23] *WA* 39.2:382–384.

Brochmand (1585–1652), Lutheran bishop of Køge, defended the comma on the grounds that it was found in the Complutensian edition and in the 'very ancient' Codex Britannicus, 'praised to the uttermost degree by Erasmus'.[24]

In 1552, Lucas Lossius, a former student of Melanchthon and later rector of the Lutheran Gymnasium in Lüneburg, published a commentary on the epistles set down by in lectionary for all the Sundays and feast days of the year, giving the text of each lesson in the final form of Erasmus' Latin translation. For Quasimodogeniti Sunday (the octave of Easter), Lossius gives the reading 1 Jn 5:1–10, including the comma. (This reading remained in use in the Lutheran lectionary until the revised pericope book produced by the Eisenach Synod in 1897 amended the reading to 1 Jn 5:1–5 as a direct result of doubts about the genuineness of the comma.)[25] Lossius' commentary covered all bases, and frequently supplies a number of possible interpretations of any given word or passage. According to Lossius, the phrase *unum sunt* refers firstly to the ontological unity of the three persons of the Trinity, and secondly to the unity of their will and testimony to the divinity of Jesus. Lossius did not comment on the textual difficulties of the passage, but referred his readers to Erasmus' commentary for a 'different reading'. He also noted that Luther's translation varies from that which he had provided.[26]

The epistles in the Lutheran lectionary were also the subject of a work by the Wittenberg humanist and theologian Georg Oemler (1551), who translated them all into Latin hexameters. Oemler rendered 1 Jn 5:7–8 as follows:

> Quandoquidem tres sunt, qui testificantur in alto:
> Nempe Pater, Verbum, tum Spiritus ortus utroque:
> Atque hi tres unum simili sunt numine iuncti.
> Sic etiam tres sunt, qui testificantur in orbe:
> Spiritus, & fons uiuus aquae, sanguisque sacratus:
> Hi quoque tres unum concordi foedere perstant,
> Viribus occultis, & res operantur easdem.[27]

---

[24] Brochmand 1638, 37.

[25] Rietschel 1900–1909, 1:571.

[26] Lossius 1552, 159v–160r.

[27] Oemler 1551, 74: 'As there are three who testify above, namely the Father, the Word, and the Spirit who arises from both, and these three are one, joined by their shared godhead. Thus also there are three who testify on earth, the Spirit, the living fount of water, and the holy blood, and these three also consist in a bond of agreement, with hidden powers, and bring about the same effect.'

For Oemler, the unity of both sets of witness is of different kinds. The unity of the heavenly witnesses is one of shared divinity. The earthly witnesses, that is, the sacraments, are directed towards our salvation.

Once Protestant divines, reacting to the rise of Antitrinitarianism, began to defend the comma on doctrinal grounds, it also reappeared in their bibles. The parentheses marking off the comma in Swiss German bibles fell away in an edition of 1597. While some editions of Luther's translation continued to omit the comma (Wittenberg, 1607; Hamburg, 1596, 1619, 1620) or distinguished it through typographical means (Wittenberg, 1599), editions of Luther's translation which include the comma gradually appeared (Frankfurt, 1576; Wittenberg, 1596, 1597; Hamburg, 1596).[28] The growing acceptance of the comma in Lutheran circles left many traces. For example, when the castle church at Saalfeld, between Jena and Coburg, was renovated between 1707 and 1717, the comma was inscribed on the pulpit, suggesting a secondary reference to the liturgical triad of preaching, baptism and eucharist.[29]

3.   Jean Calvin and the non-essential comma

Jean Calvin (1509–1564), a generation younger than Luther, came to a different conclusion about the comma. It is likely that Calvin's attitude towards the comma was affected by his struggle against Servet, who was eventually burned at his instigation. Calvin's position was perhaps crystallised by the 1545 recension of Melanchthon's *Loci*, which he translated into French and published in 1546.[30] Accordingly, Calvin included the comma in his bible translation (1551), though with a marginal comment noting its absence in 'several copies'.[31] In his commentary on the Catholic Epistles (1551), Calvin wrote that the comma was absent in many sources, though he noted that 'Jerome' believed that the omission of this verse had come about through the malice of Latin translators. Because of the divergent readings in the Greek editions – that is, between those that derived from Erasmus' text, and those which followed the Complutensian Polyglot more closely – Calvin did not feel competent to judge the issue. Nevertheless, he did not believe that the comma interrupted the flow of the passage. Moreover, since he saw that the text was present in trustworthy codices – by which

---

[28] Düsterdieck 1852–1856, 2:355–356; Darlow and Moule 1903–1911, 2:497.
[29] Fleck 2007, 230.
[30] See the relevant passage in Melanchthon 1546, 51.
[31] Calvin 1551a, 905; cf. *CR* 85:616.

he evidently meant printed editions rather than manuscripts – he saw no reason to reject it. According to Calvin, the comma shows that 'God, in order to confirm our faith in Christ more fully, testifies in a threefold manner that we ought to agree with him.' Calvin thus concluded that this agreement is a unity of testimony, not one of essence, 'as if he were to say that the Father, his eternal Word [*sermo*] and the spirit equally approve of Christ, like the notes of a chord [*symphonia quaedam*]; and so several codices read "unto one" [εἰς ἕν]'. (In fact this reading [*Text und Texwert* 1/2G] is only attested in five extant manuscripts.) And even if one were to follow the reading ἕν εἰσιν, there is no doubt that the Father, Son and Spirit are being described as 'one' in the same sense as the blood, water and Spirit are said to be one in v. 8. As far as the double appearance of the Spirit is concerned, Calvin explained that the testimony of the Spirit mentioned in v. 7 is that given at the baptism of Jesus; that mentioned in v. 8 is that of the Spirit in our hearts, which remain on earth. For readers who rejected the authenticity of v. 7, Calvin also provided an interpretation of v. 8 as though the comma were not present.[32]

Reaction to Calvin's exegesis was mixed. Sebastian Castellio followed Calvin in including the comma in his Latin translation of the New Testament (1551). As in Calvin's French translation, the comma is enclosed in brackets, with a short acknowledgement that it is not found in some copies.[33] Théodore de Bèze also followed Calvin's lead, including the comma in his reworking of Erasmus' Latin translation (1556) and his Greek text (1565), though without any typographical distinction. Like Calvin, Bèze understood the agreement spoken of in v. 8 (and by implication that in v. 7) to refer to a unity of witness, not one of essence.[34] The comma was also cited by Heinrich Alting, a Calvinist theologian at Heidelberg, as evidence for the unity of the three persons in the Trinity.[35] Calvin's positive opinion of the comma was certainly responsible, directly or indirectly, for the fact that it was cited in the footnotes of the Westminster confession of faith (1647) and both the Larger and Shorter catechisms of the Presbyterian church (1649).[36]

---

[32] Calvin 1551b, 97–98.

[33] Castellio 1556, col. 1552. Bludau 1903a, 288–289, wrote that in the 1573 Basel edition of Castellio's translation (col. 361), only the words *in coelo* and *in terra* are bracketed. This is not correct; the brackets enclose the words from *in coelo* to *in terra*, just as in the earlier editions.

[34] Bèze 1565, 603–604.

[35] Alting 1646, 1:349–350.

[36] *The Confession of Faith, and the Larger and Shorter Catechisme* 1649, 10, 74–75, 158. On the printing of these documents, see Warfield 1901. The comma is also cited in earlier English catechisms, such as Egerton 1597, A5v, C7r–v; Browne 1613, 9; Mayer 1621, 19; cf. Dixon 2003, 12–13.

But not everyone was so positive about Calvin's exegesis. In his commentary on the Catholic Epistles, the Calvinist Benedictus Aretius († 1574) of Bern accepted the comma, but insisted (implicitly criticising Calvin) that the agreement of the three heavenly witnesses refers not merely their witness, but also to their essence. Aretius also argued that the Arians had attempted to expunge the comma from the Syriac text. But, he concluded, since this verse had been restored in 'all the corrected versions these days', the reader ought not give any importance to the absence of the comma from the Syriac version.[37] Aegidius Hunnius (1593), a fervent Lutheran who attempted to staunch the tide of Calvinism in Marburg, took Calvin's interpretation of 'that delightful testimony of John' as evidence of a 'Judaizing' tendency in his theology. Hunnius harboured no doubts about the authenticity of the comma, and suggested that Calvin's interpretation of the agreement of the witnesses as one of testimony opened a window not only to Judaism, but also to Arianism. Even if Calvin was not himself an Arian, Hunnius predicted that his arguments would be cited by Antitrinitarians in their polemics against the orthodox teaching on the Trinity. And as soon as one such concession was made, others would follow until the Arian flood drowned the whole world.[38] Calvin's orthodoxy was defended from Hunnius' charges by the irenic David Paraeus (1595).[39] But despite Paraeus' calls for calm, Hunnius' predictions turned out to have some foundation: the 1680 edition of the catechism that Johann Crell (1590–1633) wrote for the Socinian Academy at Raków contains an article on the spurious authority of the comma that resembles Calvin's exposition.[40]

The support given to the comma by Calvin and Bèze was later a source of considerable chagrin. In his lectures on the New Testament, published in 1870, William Kelly regretted that 'Beza, who ought to have known more of the manuscripts, follows in the wake of his leader. Such statements, I confess are inexplicable, save on the supposition both of strong prejudice and of surprising inattention to the facts of the case.'[41] But Kelly himself had failed to notice that Calvin and Bèze were both concerned to preserve orthodoxy from the attacks of Antitrinitarians. And within Calvinist discourse, the question of the comma was never far from the spectre of Arianism. In the annotations to the Dutch States' translation

---

[37] Aretius 1608, 257; cf. Bludau 1903a, 397.
[38] Hunnius 1593, 57–60.
[39] Further, see Pak 2009, 103–113.
[40] Crell 1680, 19.
[41] Kelly 1870, 338.

(*Statenvertaling*) of 1637, the comma is claimed – through creative stretching of the truth – as a genuine part of Scripture, and inextricably linked with the age-old struggle between orthodox and heretic.[42] According to the author of these notes, the unity of the three heavenly witnesses was one of both essence and testimony. The verse should thus be considered a 'very clear proof and testimony of the Trinity of persons in the unity of the divine essence'.[43]

4. The Johannine comma in post-Tridentine Catholicism

The work of humanists like Erasmus sharpened the question of textual authority to a point. Which of two possible sources of authority would be normative: the original Hebrew and Greek texts, or the tradition of exegesis of the Latin Vulgate handed down in the church? The former position came increasingly, though not exclusively, to be associated with the Protestant churches.[44] The Roman Catholic tendency towards the latter was crystallised on 8 April 1546, when the council of Trent declared in the decree *Insuper* that the 'old Latin Vulgate edition, which has come to be accepted through long use in the church', represented the authentic text of the bible.[45] As a result of increasing support for the comma among Roman Catholic scholars in the decades after Trent, the 1586 *Index expurgatorius* directed readers to delete the relevant paragraphs from their copies of Erasmus' *Annotationes*.[46]

Yet the Tridentine decree did not place critical questions concerning the Latin text on ice. In fact it stimulated a group of scholars at the University of Leuven in their efforts to determine the most accurate form of the text of the Latin Vulgate. In November 1547, the Leuven scholar Johannes Henten issued an edition of the Latin text, based on Estienne's editions of 1532 and 1540, with further readings added in the margin, collected from more than thirty Latin manuscripts and two incunable editions. Henten treated only the internal Latin tradition, not its relationship with other textual traditions. Besides its philological aspirations, Henten's work also

[42] *Biblia* 1637, NT:149v; English translation in Haak 1657, Kk4v. The translation of the comma in the *Statenvertaling* is as follows: 'Want dry zijnder die getuygen in den Hemel, de Vader, het Woort, ende de Heylige Geest: ende dese dry zijn een. Ende dry zijnder die getuygen op de aerde, de Geest, ende het water, ende het bloedt: ende die dry zijn tot een.'
[43] Haak 1657, Kk4v. Original text in *Biblia* 1637, NT:149v.
[44] Frick 1995, 151–152.
[45] *Canones et decreta* 1564, 31.
[46] *Index expurgatorius* 1586, 269; Coogan 1992, 110; Henderson 2007, 162–164 on Erasmus and the *Index*.

had a doctrinal purpose, and was supervised by the theologians Ruard Tapper and Peter de Corte. Henten marked off the comma with obeloi, and in a marginal note he remarked that the comma was absent from five of the Latin manuscripts he had consulted. However, these obeloi and the notes disappeared in a Flemish translation of Henten's edition, prepared by Claes van Winghe, a canon regular at Leuven, which appeared in 1548.[47]

In his critical comments on the New Testament (1555), the Franciscan Niklaas Zegers, professor of Scripture at Leuven, noted that the comma was not found in the Greek copies, and was lacking from many Latin ones. The only evidence for its authenticity was the prologue of 'Jerome' and the long usage of the Catholic church.[48]

Jan Hessels, professor of theology at Leuven, discussed the comma in his commentary on 1 Jn (1568). Hessels interpreted the unity of the heavenly witnesses as a unanimity of testimony to Jesus' status as Son of God. He noted that the Greek codices only contain v. 8, and that this reading reflects that found in some Latin fathers, such as Ambrose, Bede and Augustine. Hessels also noted that Erasmus had daringly excluded the prologue to the Catholic Epistles, the most important early witness to the authenticity of the passage, from his edition of Jerome's works. Hessels listed a number of Latin writers who cited the passage, such as pseudo-Hyginus, the author of *Against Varimadus*, Fulgentius, and pseudo-Athanasius. He also noted that the comma was transmitted in two Greek codices: Erasmus' British codex, and that on which the reading in the Complutensian Polyglot was presumed to have been based. Hessels also reported the readings from a number of old Latin codices in the libraries of St Peter's and St Gertrude's in Leuven.[49]

Another of the Leuven editors, Franciscus Lucas Brugensis (1580), compared the Latin readings with those in other textual traditions. Building on the work of Zegers, Lucas noted that the words are absent from many Greek codices (including those in Paris used by Estienne), the Syriac codices, from the Latins Augustine, Leo and Bede, and the Greeks Cyril and Oecumenius. The inversion of vv. 7 and 8 in some Latin manuscripts also indicated that the comma is textually unstable. In defence

---

[47] *Den gheheelen Bybel* 1548, N6v: 'Want drij isser die ghtuyghenis gheuen inden hemel. Die vader / dwoert / ende die heylighe gheest / ende dese drij sijn een. Ende drij esser die ghetuyughenis gheuen op deerde. Den gheest / dwater / ende tbloet / ende dese drij sijn een.' Further, see Darlow and Moule 1903–1911, 2:303. On the Leuven revisions, see François 2012, 237–243.

[48] Zegers 1555, 115r–116r.

[49] Hessels 1568, 106v–110v.

of the authenticity of the comma, Lucas noted that it occurs in many Latin manuscripts, in the Complutensian edition, and is also defended by the prologue to the Catholic Epistles by 'Jerome' and the letter by 'pope Hyginus'. (Lucas was evidently unaware that both documents are forgeries. The latter was a forgery based on pseudo-Athanasius' *Against Varimadus*, which first appears in a collection of ninth-century attributed to the fictional 'Isidorus Mercator'.)[50] Lucas followed a similar line in his printed comments (1603) on the official Roman text of the Vulgate as promulgated in the 1590 *Editio Sixtina* and its revision, the 1592 *Editio Clementina*, both of which included the comma.[51]

Some concluded from such findings that the Latin Vulgate, endorsed at Trent, was the most reliable textual form of the New Testament. The Spanish scholastic theologian Melchior Cano (c. 1509–1560) pointed out that the Latin Vulgate contains several passages – the story of the boys in the fiery furnace (Dan 3:24–90), Susanna (Dan 13 Vg), the *pericope de adultera* (Jn 7:53–8:11), the long ending of Mark (16:9–20) and the Johannine comma – which he believed had been omitted from the Greek and Hebrew texts through the negligence of scribes.[52] The Dominican Sixtus Senensis (1520–1569) quoted the letter attributed to Pope Hyginus as evidence that the comma was an original part of the text of Scripture, both in Greek and in Latin. He concluded triumphantly that this gave the lie to those who denied the originality of the passage, such as the Anabaptists and the followers of Servet.[53]

The Jesuit Benedetto Giustiniani was even more hostile to recent advances in philology. In his commentary on the Catholic Epistles (1621), Giustiniani wrote that although the comma was absent from many Greek and some Latin manuscripts, and was missing from the Syriac translation, not to mention from the works of many fathers who might have been expected to cite them, he was nevertheless scornful of the 'heretics and know-alls who report that one Greek manuscript reads "and these three are to one purpose [*ad unum*]" or "unto one" [*in unum*], as if they were conspiring precisely to the same end.'[54] Even if the Greek text says

[50] Pseudo-Hyginus, *De fide et reliquis causis*, included in *Isidori Mercatoris collectio decretalium*, PL 130:109; Thiele 1956–1969, 365.
[51] Lucas Brugensis 1580, 462. See also Lucas Brugensis 1603, 361; Bludau 1903a, 289–291.
[52] Cano 1563, 64; cf. Bludau 1903a, 405. Of course he was mistaken in the case of Dan 3:24–90 and Dan 13, which are transmitted in the Septuagint.
[53] Senensis 1566, 972; cf. Bludau 1903a, 404–405.
[54] Giustiniani 1621, 230 (the commentary on each of the letters is paginated separately). Giustiniani may be referring to the reading and note in Oecumenius 1545, 216r, whom he mentions at the beginning of the note.

'to one purpose', that does not actively *deny* the doctrine that the three persons of the Trinity are one in substance.[55] For Giustiniani, philological details were all very well, but such niceties should not be allowed to disturb the lapidary formulations of doctrine.

Many Catholic defenders of the comma wished to retain the comma because of its utility against Antitrinitarians. In his *Three books on the controversies of the Christian faith, against the latter-day heretics* (1586), Cardinal Roberto Bellarmino discussed the authority of various ancient versions of the biblical text. He did not place as much confidence in the Greek text as Protestant critics did, since it had been subject to a degree of corruption, both inadvertent and deliberate, despite the best efforts of Catholics to detect these corruptions and remove them from the text.[56] Bellarmino believed that some Greek codices lacked 'many parts of true Scripture', such as the story of the woman caught in adultery, the longer ending of Mark, and the 'most beautiful testimony of the Trinity', the Johannine comma.[57] Although Bellarmino was aware of Erasmus' work on the New Testament, he retained the comma as a weapon to confute the arguments of the Antitrinitarian Giorgio Biandrata (*c.* 1516–1588). Whereas Biandrata believed that the only father to quote the comma was 'Jerome' (that is, the prologue to the Catholic Epistles), Bellarmino pointed out that the comma was also cited by Hyginus, Cyprian, Ithacius, Athanasius, Fulgentius and Eugenius of Carthage. (Unfortunately for Bellarmino, some of these sources provide no clear reference to the comma, some were forged, and others were too late to provide an accurate indication of the genuineness of the passage.) Biandrata had objected that since the Spirit, water and blood are not one in essence, it makes no sense to argue by analogy that the Father, Word and Spirit are likewise one in essence. In reply, Bellarmino asserted that the readings in the Greek and Latin codices at this point are different: in v. 7, the Greek codices say that the Father, Son and Holy Spirit 'are one' (ἕν εἰσι), but in v. 8, that the Spirit, water, and blood are 'unto one' (εἰς τὸ ἕν εἰσιν), in other words they agree in their testimony to Christ. However, only three known manuscripts display this reading in the body text, and all three were copied between the sixteenth and the eighteenth centuries from printed editions.[58] Either Bellarmino

---

[55] Giustiniani 1621, 230.

[56] Bellarmino 1586, 103–104.

[57] Bellarmino 1586, 105. While the Protestant William Ames disagreed with Bellarmino's judgement on the reliability of Greek codices, he concurred that these three contested passages were genuine parts of Scripture; see Ames 1629, 20.

[58] GA 918, 2318, 2473; see K. Aland, Benduhn-Mertz and Mink 1987, 165, *Lesarten* [6, 6C].

had access to manuscripts that have since disappeared, or he was not telling the truth. His selective use of the philological evidence provided by Erasmus is also misleading, while his co-opting of those Latin fathers who merely provide an allegorical interpretation of 1 Jn 5:8 is deceptive. Moreover, Bellarmino's reliance on the decretal of pseudo-Hyginus was disingenuous.[59] However, Bellarmino's status within the church and his later canonisation gave his *Three books* particular prominence and authority, and they were reprinted into the eighteenth century.

Several counterreformation figures considered the attitude of the Protestant reformers towards the Johannine comma as a symptom of a broader problem of authority and doctrine in the schismatic churches. The Capuchin Lorenzo da Brindisi (1559–1619) wrote that Luther had excised the comma from the Scripture like the 'unfaithful translators' against whom Jerome had railed. 'God only knows what he thought about the Trinity', Lorenzo fretted.[60] According to Lorenzo, the Lutherans' rejection of the authority of councils kicked one of the legs out from under doctrine. For example, if the Lutherans refused to acknowledge the council of Nicaea, they were left with only Scripture to support the doctrine of the Trinity. And if they then got rid of the comma, they were rendered incapable of demonstrating the Trinity effectively from the Scriptures. 'For this reason we must conclude that either the Lutherans have no belief in the Trinity, or a very weak faith which they are entirely unable to defend against the new Arians and Antitrinitarians, who have no regard for councils.'[61] In short, Lorenzo concluded, 'Luther was an outstanding artificer in the adulteration of God's word. Inspired by the spirit of Satan, he dared to transfigure himself into a prophet of God and evangelist of Christ.'[62]

Other Roman Catholic apologists were either confused about the issues surrounding the comma, or unwilling to enter into controversy. In his *Annotationes decem in sacram scripturam* (1547), Pedro Antonio Beuter (*c.* 1495–*c.* 1555) advocated a historical and philological interpretation of Scripture. Citing Erasmus as his model, he suggested that readers should refer to the Hebrew and Greek text when the Latin is unclear. But despite this progressive approach, Beuter still cited the comma as the most important evidence in Scripture for the doctrine of the Trinity.[63] Benito Arias

[59] Bellarmino 1586, 306–307 (Cap. VI. De Christo. Lib. I. Cap. VI.). Further, see Bludau 1903a, 405; Coogan 1992, 111–113.
[60] Lorenzo da Brindisi 1928–1959, 2.1:448.
[61] Lorenzo da Brindisi 1928–1959, 2.3:270.
[62] Lorenzo da Brindisi 1928–1959, 2.3:126.
[63] Beuter 1547, 36v. On Beuter, see Tejero and Marcos 2008, 234, 239.

Montano, one of the editors of the Antwerp Polyglot, simply sidestepped the issue, though his evasion may have been a result of Juan de Mariana's intense scrutiny of the orthodoxy of Montano's edition.[64]

The growing doctrinal importance of the comma encouraged its use in the liturgy and liturgical music. The Tridentine breviary gave the comma as the capitulum at nones on Trinity Sunday.[65] It gave the responsory *Duo seraphim*, with its versicle *Tres sunt qui testimonium dant in caelo*, as the eighth responsory on the second to the sixth Sundays after Epiphany, on Trinity Sunday, and every Sunday from the third Sunday after Pentecost until the last Sunday before Advent.[66] The melody for the versicle uses a stereotyped opening formula found in about a dozen first-mode versicles, including one with a clear Scriptural and liturgical link: *Seraphim stabant super illud*, the versicle to the responsory at matins on the feast of All Saints (Figure 3.1).[67] In addition, the responsory *Duo seraphim/Tres sunt* was set more than four dozen times between 1583 and 1620, as polyphony and as continuo motets.[68] In the preface to the section of his 1567 German hymnbook containing hymns for the season of Trinity, the Roman Catholic hymnodist Johann Leisentrit exhorted his readers to avoid the errors of Arius and Sabellius. He indicated two passages in Scripture that reveal the mystery of the Trinity most clearly: the hand that wrote on the wall at Belshazzar's feast (Dan 5:5) – on the basis of Is 40:12, Leisentrit argued that it had three fingers, a figure of the Trinity – and the Johannine comma.[69]

5. Anabaptists, Erasmus and the comma

Some ideas put forward by the magisterial reformers and religious humanists were radicalised by Anabaptists, who often gave them a further social and collective dimension. Some Anabaptists rejected traditional dogmatic formulations of the essence of the divine persons and the relationship between them, though some, such as Roelof Martens, were dismissed from leadership roles when such speculations were considered to have gone too far.[70]

[64] Montano 1583, 342; Montano 1588, 25, 415.
[65] *Breviarium Romanum* 1568, 451.
[66] *Breviarium Romanum* 1568, 220.
[67] *Antiphonarium Romanum* 1596, 152v–153r.
[68] Kurtzman 1972, 426–432; Kurtzman 1999, 144–145; Cramer 1998.
[69] Leisentrit 1567, 188r–189r.
[70] Lech Szczucki, 'Antitrinitarianism', in *OER*.

Figure 3.1. 'Tres sunt qui testimonium dant', *Antiphonarium Romanum* (Venice: Giunta, 1596), 41v. Bayerische Staatsbibliothek München, Liturg. 22. Reproduced by kind permission.

Most of the earliest Anabaptists were not university-trained, and philological arguments about the status of the comma made little difference to them. In his 1530 commentary on the Apocalypse, the Anabaptist Melchior Hoffmann saw evidence of the Trinity in the story of the creation in Genesis, the episode of Abraham at Mamre (Gen 18:1–2), and the Johannine comma.[71] In about 1535, Hans Betz, one of the Anabaptists imprisoned at Passau, wrote the hymn *Herr Gott Vatter zu dir ich schrey*. This hymn was subsequently published in the collection *Etliche schöne Christliche Geseng* (1564), the basis of Amish hymnody in America. The second stanza reflects on the Johannine comma, and through the mnemonic power of song, the comma thus became further entrenched as a Scriptural witness for the Trinity:

> Die Dreyheit soltu wol verston /
>   wie sie Johannes zeiget an /
> Vatter / Wort / Geist thut nennen.
>   sie in dem Himmel Zeugen seyn /
> Die drey Namen dienen in ein /
>   jr solt es wol vernemmen.
> Deß Vatters Allmechtige krafft /
>   wird ersehen bein gschöfften /
> Die er durch das wort hat gemacht /
>   sein Geist alls thut bekrefften /
> Wann er sich deß würd underston /
>   den Geist in sich zu samlen /
> Müßt alls wider vergon.[72]

In the later sixteenth century, some Anabaptists became familiar with the doctrinal disputes arising from textual ambiguities in Scripture. One source of information was the work of the spiritualist writer Johannes Campanus, who maintained that while the Father and Son are of one essence, the Son is nevertheless subordinate to the Father. In his *Restitution of the divine and holy Scripture* (1532), Campanus pointed out that Erasmus had shown clearly that the comma was not written by John.[73] Accordingly, the comma was omitted in the Dutch Anabaptist translation of the bible published in 1560.[74]

[71] Hoffmann 1530, B6r.
[72] *Etliche schöne Christliche Geseng* 1564, 4 ('Das erst Lied mag gesungen werden ins Berners Thon / H. B.'): 'You should have a good understanding of the Trinity / as John reveals it, / calling them Father, Word, and Spirit, / who are witnesses in heaven. / The three names serve for one, / you should mark this well. / The almighty power of the Father / is seen in his creatures / which he made through his Word / and his Spirit strengthens all. / If he took it upon himself / to gather his Spirit within himself, / everything would pass again into nothingness.'
[73] Campanus 1532, a8r. Campanus may be relying on Franck 1531, 391r. Further, see Gilly 1985, 279; Lech Szczucki, 'Antitrinitarianism', in *OER*.
[74] *Dat nieuwe Testament* 1560, 94r: 'Want drie zijnder die daer getuychenisse geuen op Aerden / De Gheest / ende dat Water / ende dat Bloet / ende die drie zijn by malcanderen.'

On 10 May 1569, the Mennonite Anabaptist Hermann van Vlekwijk, a tailor, engaged in a disputation with the Franciscan Cornelis Adriaenssen at Bruges. The transcript of the disputation shows clearly how Erasmus' statements concerning the doctrine of the Trinity had begun to seem suspect in the light of the subsequent rise of Antitrinitarianism.[75] Indeed, Adriaenssen argued that Servet and Campanus had exposed Erasmus' latent Antitrinitarianism.[76] Vlekwijk maintained that he and his fellow believers based their theology exclusively on the Scriptures, but it seemed to Adriaenssen that the passages on which Vlekwijk drew, and the way in which he interpreted them, showed the influence of the 'devilish books of that damned Erasmus of Rotterdam'. For example, when Adriaenssen put it to Vlekwijk that the Scriptures speak of 'God the Father, of God the Son, and of God the Holy Ghost', Vlekwijk replied that they speak rather 'only of one God, and of the Son of the living God, and of the Holy Ghost'.[77] Adriaenssen accused Vlekwijk of following Erasmus' preface to the works of Hilary, where he wrote that this theologian had maintained that the Holy Spirit is never called God in the bible, and that we call the Spirit God when even the fathers hesitated to do so. Such statements, Adriaenssen asserted, show that Erasmus was a great enemy of the divinity of Christ.[78] Vlekwijk protested that he followed neither Erasmus nor Hilary, but only the bible, as they too had done.[79] When asked to clarify his position on the divinity of Christ, Vlekwijk explained that he and his fellows believed that Christ was 'divine and heavenly, but not of the earth' (cf. 1 Cor 15:47). This Word became flesh. They also believed that God was the Word, but did not understand thereby 'that the living God (whose Son Christ is) himself became flesh'. Adriaenssen cited Jn 10:30 and 14:9

---

[75] Trial record transcribed in Adriaenssen 1607–1608, 2:468–522. Extracts were later quoted in G. Brandt 1663, 647–656; English translations are from G. Brandt 1720–1723, 1:282–285, adapted to conform more closely to the original. Further, see Goldhill 2002, 31–32.

[76] Adriaenssen 1607–1608, 2:540: 'Ba ghy Catholijcken / wacht u doch voor die boose generatie der Erasmianen / want gheen snooder / argher / deurtrockender Ketters der weerelt dan die vervloecte Erasmianen / Servetianen / Campanisten ende andere Trinitarisen […].'

[77] Adriaenssen 1607–1608, 2:499: 'De heylighe Schriftueren en spreken nochtans maer van eenen Godt / ende vanden levenden Gods Sone / ende vanden heylighen Gheest.'

[78] Adriaenssen 1607–1608, 2:500: 'Ba maer dese ketterije light ghylieder en studeert inde duyvelsche boecken / van dien verdoemden Erasmus Roterodamus / die in sijn prefacie op de boecken van Sint Hilarius schrijft / dat S. Hilarius int eynde van sijn xij. boeck seyt / datten heyligen Geest nieuwers inde heylighe Schriftuere Godt wert ghenoemt / maer dat wy soo stoudt zijn ghewordan dat wy den heyligen Gheest derren Godt noemen / twelcke de oude Leeraers der Kercke niet en hebben derren doen. Ba dierghelijcken is dien boosen Erasmus oock alsoo grooten vyandt vande Godtheyt Christi.'

[79] Adriaenssen 1607–1608, 2:500: 'Wy en volghen Erasmum noch Hilarium niet / maer wy volgen de heylighe Schriftuere / ghelijck Hilarius ende Erasmus daer in doen.' Cf. 1 Cor 1:12, 3:4–6.

('Whoever has seen me has seen the Father') to demonstrate the unity of God the Father and Christ. In reply, Vlekwijk cited Jn 17:21, Acts 4:32, Gal 3:28 and Eph 5:31 to argue for their distinctness.[80] 'All this', Adriaenssen accused, 'have you sucked from the poisonous breasts of Erasmus'.[81] When asked how he interpreted Jn 14:9, Vlekwijk cited Jn 1:18, 6:46, 14:28 and Mk 13:32, from which one would naturally conclude that the Father was not incarnate.[82] When Adriaenssen accused Vlekwijk of denying that Christ, the second person of Trinity, became man, and of denying moreover that he was true God, Vlekwijk replied that he described Christ as the Son of the Living God (Mt 16:16) and the Lord, as the apostles had done.[83] Vlekwijk pointed out that Jesus is called a man at several points in the New Testament. In Acts 2:22, he is called a man attested by God with deeds of power, signs and wonders that God did through him. In Acts 17:31, he is described as a man by whom God will judge the world in righteousness. Adriaenssen dismissed these as 'the same trifling arguments that damned Erasmus uses in his little tract about prayer, and in his apology to Manrique'.[84] Vlekwijk defended himself by asserting that even if Christ's body was heavenly rather than earthly, he was truly the Son of God (1 Jn 5) and truly human (Rom 5).[85] Adriaenssen then cited what he considered the best Scriptural evidence of the consubstantial Trinity: the Johannine comma.[86] But Vlekwijk had often heard it said that Erasmus proved in his annotations on this passage that the comma was not present

---

[80] Adriaenssen 1607–1608, 2:501: 'Dat zy vere van ons / dat wy inde Godtheyt Christi niet en souden ghelooven dat hy Godlijck ende Hemels is / ende niet aerts en is / ghelijck ghylieder ghelooft / daerom worden wy van ulieder ghedoot. [...] Wy gelooven dattet Woort vleesch gheworden is / ghelijck Johannes int eerste Capittel van sijn Euangelium schrijft. [...] Wy ghelooven oock dat Godt het Woort was / maer wilt ghy dan daer wt verstaen / dat den levenden Godt (daer Christus den Sone van is) selven vleesch werdt / dat ware emmers seer techen alle de heylige Schriftuere.'
[81] Adriaenssen 1607–1608, 2:502: 'Sus sus / tis genoech gepreect / want dit hebdy al gesogen wt die venijnighe borsten van Erasmus.'
[82] Adriaenssen 1607–1608, 2:502–503: 'Waer wt genoech betoont [503] werdt / dat den Vader selven niet en ist vleesch gheworden.'
[83] Adriaenssen 1607–1608, 2:503: 'Ik noeme hem den Sone vanden levenden Godt / gelijck hem Petrus noemde / Matthei int 16. Capittel / ende den Heere / gelijck hem de Apostelen noemen.'
[84] Adriaenssen 1607–1608, 2:504: 'Ja [...] dit zijn al de selve argumentkens / die dien verdoemden Erasmus *In libello de modo orandi, & in Apologia ad Episcopum Hispalensem, Alphonsum Mauricum* [*sc.* Manricum] seyt.' Cf. G. Brandt 1663, 652.
[85] Adriaenssen 1607–1608, 2:504: 'En wilt doch aldus ongheregelt niet spreken / want Christus en is gheen duyvel / maer hy is den warachtigen sone Gods / ghelijck Johannes in sijn eerste Epistel int vijfde capittel schrijft. Ende hy is oock een warachtich mensche / ghelijck Paulus schrijft int 5. capittel aende Romeynen.'
[86] Adriaenssen 1607–1608, 2:505: 'Ba ghy Trinitaris / nu worde ick te peynsen dat S. Jan int <s>elfde capittel seydt: Drie isser die getuyghenisse gheven inden Hemel. Die Vader / het Woort / ende den heylighen Gheest / ende dese drie zijn een. Ba hier zijdy ter deghe int cot / armen Trinitaris als ghy sijt.'

in the Greek text, but had been inserted by the Roman Catholic church.[87] At last presented with evidence that the tailor had derived his errors from Erasmus, Adriaenssen addressed the secretary and clerk of the Inquisition:

> Gentlemen, what do you think about this? Am I to blame for opposing so often, in my Sermons, that wicked, that damned Antitrinitarian, Erasmus? For it is true, he does write so; nay what is worse, in his annotation on the fourth chapter of St Luke, he says, that a very great and strange corruption has crept into the holy Scriptures, in the Greek and Latin copies, that sometimes something is added and interpolated, and sometimes something is removed, left out and erased for the sake of the hereticks; and even that such marginal notes as had been occasionally made by one or another, were inserted into the Text itself. Well, my Lords, is that not a fine thing?[88]

Adriaenssen also railed against Erasmus' annotation on Rom 9:5, where he pointed out that the lack of punctuation in the Greek original resulted in an ambiguity: the passage could mean either that Christ is 'God over all, blessed for ever', or that Christ is 'over all, God be blessed for ever'. The former interpretation would constitute the sole instance in which Paul described Christ as God, but it is by no means clear that this is the correct interpretation. For drawing attention to the ambiguity of this and other doxologies, Erasmus was accused by several critics of sowing doubts about Christ's divinity.[89]

---

[87] Adriaenssen 1607–1608, 2:505: 'Ik heb dikmaels hooren seggen / dat Erasmus ulieder in sijn Annotationibus verwijt / dat ghy Papisten dese woorden daer aen gelapt hebt / ende datse inden Griexschen Text niet en staen / ghelijck ghylieder noch veel andere dinghen inde heylighe schriftuere af ende toe ghedaen hebt.' Cf. G. Brandt 1663, 653; G. Brandt 1720–1723, 1:284.

[88] Adriaenssen 1607–1608, 2:505–506: 'Ba mijn Heeren / wat dunckt [506] ulieder hier af / ba heb ick dan onghelijck / dat ic dien verdoemden Ketter / dien boosen Trinitarius Erasmus / in mijn sermoenen soo bijster te keer gae? want het is waer, sulcx schrijft hy. Ja dat noch arger is / ba hy heeft in *Annotationibus* opt vierde capittel van S. Lucas gaen schrijven datter een seer groote wonderlijcke verwoestinghe inde heylighe Schriftuere is gheraeckt / inde Griecxsche ende Latijnsche exemplaren / datter somtijts wat is toe gheschreven ende aenghelapt / ende datter somtijts wat is af gedaen / wtgelaten ende wtghecrapt om de Ketters wille. Ja ende tghene datter somtijts inde margine ende op de canten van d'een van d'ander gheschreven was / dat sulcx al inden Tecxt ghelapt is / ba mijn Heeren ist nit jent?' Cf. G. Brandt 1663, 653; G. Brandt 1720–1723, 1:284 (adapted).

[89] Adriaenssen 1607–1608, 2:506–507: 'Ba hy soude ons Catholijcken wel derren verwijten met sijnen hooftketter dien boosen Erasmum / dat wy int ix. capit. totten Romeynen / daer Paulus seyt: *Der welcker Vaderen zijn gheweest, daer Christus wt is nae den vleesche.* Dat wy daer oock aen gelapt hebben. *Die boven alle ist God gebenedijt inder eeuwicheyt, Amen.* Want dien vervloecten Erasmus schrijft dat hy aen dese clausel seer twijffelt. *Qui est benedictus in saecula, Amen.* Oft men soude dese woorden tot een dancksegginge Gods des Vaders aldus moeten bedieden ende verstaen. Christus &c. [507] die boven alle is. Godt zy ghebenedijt inde eeuwicheyt, Amen. Ofte anders twijffele ic seer (schrijft hy) datter dese Clausel aen ghelapt is / ghelijck ick in sommighe andere Texten noch bevinde / datse dierghelijcken clauselen tot bestuytinghe vande propoosten / daer aenghehanghen hebben / als *Tu autem Domine, &c. Gloria Patri & Filio, &c.*' Cf. *ASD* VI-7:224–231.

In a sermon delivered on 5 June 1569, Adriaenssen refuted Vlekwijk's claims, including his assertion that the comma had been interpolated into the text by the Roman Catholic church. Such calumny, he railed, was typical of the Erasmians' tendency to 'revile, ridicule and mock the Holy Trinity'.[90] As a result of Adriaenssen's harangue, Vlekwijk was seized and burned at the stake on 10 June 1569.

While vernacular literacy levels in the Southern Low Countries were quite high in the sixteenth century, it is worth considering where a tailor might have acquired such broad theological learning.[91] One possible source is sermons or Scriptural exposition during services and devotions, either in private or in groups. A likely source for many of the opinions expressed in the transcript of Vlekwijk's trial is Sebastian Franck's *Chronicle* (1531), published in Dutch translation in 1558, and reprinted in 1562, 1563, 1583 and 1595.[92] A comparison of Franck's *Chronicle* with the published trial record provides unexpected insights.

Sebastian Franck was a man of wide reading and independent thought. After ordination as a Catholic priest, he converted to Lutheranism, but soon broke from the magisterial reformation to develop an illuminist spirituality that conceived of the inner Word of God within each person as the source of religious truth and authority. Franck shared Erasmus' desire to cut away centuries of ignorance and sophistry, but when Franck's *Chronicle* was published, Erasmus was horrified that he had been associated with its anti-imperial undertone, offensive and potentially dangerous to Erasmus' patron Ferdinand I. Erasmus, seeing himself reflected in the distorting mirror of Franck's catalogue of heretics, must have recognised with shock that his attempts to defend his own orthodoxy over the previous decade had led in directions he had not foreseen. When Franck wrote to Erasmus in 1531 from prison, not to offer an apology, but 'to demand thanks for the great honour he has done me', Erasmus complained to

---

[90] Adriaenssen 1607–1608, 2:538–539: 'Ba maer ick mercte wel wt sijn woorden dat sy Herdoopers niewers anders wt heurlieder verdoemelijc en suygen tegen de H. Dryvuldich{eyt} / dan wt die duyvelsche mannen van dien vervloecten Erasmus / want dien Herman wiste my te verwijten dat Erasmus in sijn *Annotationibus* schrijft opt 5. cap. vande eerste Epistel Johan. dat ons moeder de H. Roomsche Kercke daer aen gelapt heeft dese woorden: *Drie isser die ghetuyghenisse gheven inden Hemel. Die Vader, het Woort, ende den heyligen Gheest, ende dese drie zijn een.* om dat sulcx inden Griecxschen text niet en staet. Ou / ba / hooren wy ooc dagelicx vande Erasmianen niet / alle [539] het schimpen / gecken ende spotten op de heylighe Dryvuldicheyt / die sy deur heurlieder vermaledijt backhuys versieren connen?'

[91] On literacy rates in the early modern Low Countries, see Spufford 1995.

[92] See Becker 1928; Van Gemert 1997; Bietenholz 2008, 31.

Martin Bucer that he allowed radicals like Franck say and print whatever they liked at Strasbourg.[93]

Franck's account of the history of religious thought in his *Chronicle* includes an account of the 'Roman heretics from Peter to Clement VII'. Amongst these, Franck devoted nine folio pages to Erasmus, presenting his 'heresy' as the attempt to restore Christianity to its pristine state. The first passage Franck quoted is an abbreviated extract from Erasmus' annotation on 1 Jn 5:7, which emphasises the futility of theological speculation on the inner workings of the Trinity.[94] Franck also cited Erasmus' report of Hilary of Poitiers's argument that the Son is truly God, despite the fact that in the gospels, only the Father is called true God, and the Holy Spirit is never described as God, or worthy of worship. As his sources, Franck named Erasmus' preface to his edition of Hilary and his devotional tract *Modus orandi deum*, precisely the works Adriaenssen identified as the source of Vlekwijk's opinion.[95] Adriaenssen's account

---

[93] *Opus epist.* 9:454; Bietenholz 2008, 30.

[94] Franck 1558, 86r: 'In zijn Annot. ouer dat v. Cap. des yersten Epist. Joan. verwerpt hy de sprueke: Drei zijnder die daer ghetuychenisse geuen inden Hemel / de Vader / dat woort ende de heylige Gheest / ende dese drie zijn eens / als den Text Joannis toegeset / die int Griecx niet en ist. Een weynich daer nae seyt hy breeder: Het waer profijtelic dat wy alle neersticheydt aenkeerden / dat wy eens met Godt werden: Want met spitsen ijuer ende oeffeninge te twisten / hoe de Sone van den Vader een onderscheydt heeft / ende van haer beyden de H. Gheest: warachtich dat de Arrianern verloochenen / en sie ic niet datment mach by brengen ende sluyten / dan met bewijselijcke Argumenten. Ten laetsten / nademael dese geheele plaetse duyster is / so en mach het niet veel dienstelijc zijn te becouten ende ouerwinnen de ketters.' German original in Franck 1531, 391r. In his account of Arius, Franck 1531, 342r, cites Erasmus' recycled citation of this passage from Erasmus 1528, 40.

[95] Franck 1558, 86v: 'Item alleen de Vader wert int Euangelio waerachtich Godt genoemt / So en hebben oock de Apostelen alderyerst Christum niet Godt genoemt: Want Paulus noemt den Vader altoos Godt / maer den Sone Heere. So is ooc in den Catechismo den Ouden voorghehouden / alleen de Vader Godt ghenoemt / ende anders noch de Soon / noch de H. Gheest. Soo heeft Petrus Jesum int beginsel der geheelder gemeynten gepredict / sonder eenighe ghedachtenisse der godlijcker naturen: So heet hem beyde / Petrus ende Paulus een man ende mensche. Hec in libello de modo orandi. Ende in Apologia ad Episcopum Hispalensem. [...] Item in de Voorreden ouer Hilarium / seyt Erasmus: De heylighe Hilarius int eynde van desen twelften Boeck / en dorfte niet met allen van den heylighen Gheest wt spreken / dan dat hi den Gheest Gods is: Hy en waer oock niet stout gheweest dat te spreken / waer hy het te voren niet in Paulo en hadde ghelesen. De heylighe Hilarius en schrijft nergens dat ick weet / dat men den H. Gheest sal aenbidden / ende en gheeft hem oock nerghens den Name Gods. Breeder aldaer: De Vader wert (verstaet hy Hilarium) dickwils Godt ghenoemt / Christus somtijdts menichmael: De heylighe Gheest / dat ic weet / nergens.' German original in Franck 1531, 392r. Franck's first source is Erasmus 1523b, aa6v: 'Pater frequentissime deus uocatur, filius aliquoties, spiritus sanctus nunquam. Atque haec dixerim, non ut in dubium uocem, quod nobis è diuinis literis patrum orthodoxorum tradidit autoritas, sed ut ostendam, quanta fuerit antiquis religio pronunciandi de rebus diuinis [...].' This passage is repeated in Erasmus 1531, 197, and Erasmus 1535c, aa6v. Franck's second source is Erasmus 1524, c6v: 'Eadem religione fuit sanctus Hilarius, qui post diuturnum silentium,

of Erasmus' annotation on Rom 9:5 also resembles Franck's summary.[96] Indeed, the correspondences between the words of both Vlekwijk and Adriaenssen on one side, and Franck's presentation of Erasmus' 'heresy' on the other, are so striking as to suggest that the text of the trial record published in Adriaenssen's biography (1607–1608) is not a verbatim transcript. Rather, it seems that Adriaenssen placed Erasmus' words, as presented in the Dutch translation of Franck's *Chronicle*, in Vlekwijk's mouth, to make the Anabaptist's statements square more closely with Erasmus' position. The published record of Vlekwijk's trial is thus to some extent a literary fiction.

6. East-central European Antitrinitarians of the later sixteenth and seventeenth centuries

The sixteenth century saw a variety of Antitrinitarian theologies emerge, especially in east-central Europe, as various individuals and groups reconceptualised Christianity on historical foundations, often drawing explicitly on Erasmus as inspiration. As a result of the fluidity and variety of these positions, orthodox apologists – whether Roman Catholic, Lutheran or Calvinist – were aiming at a moving target, and their arrows sometimes shot wide of the mark. The most vigorous and long-lasting Antitrinitarian systems arose from the spiritualist circle nurtured at Naples by Juan de Valdés.[97] At the Diet of Piotrków (1565), the Calvinist party used its political muscle to convince King Sigismund August of Poland and the other nobles to suppress Antitrinitarian belief. The king subsequently requested his secretary Andrzej Frycz Modrzewski, one of the foremost Polish humanists of his generation, to write up a summary of the theological positions presented, in order to find a compromise. The result, *Sylvae quatuor*, completed in 1565, mentions the comma on several occasions.

---

duodecim libris instantissime contendit, ut filium doceat esse uerum deum, quum solus pater dictus sit in Euangelio uerus deus: spiritum sanctum nusquam quod sciam audet pronunciare deum, nec adorandum profitetur, sed promerendum.' Cf. *Opus Epist.* 5:182.

[96] Franck 1558, 86r: 'Op de Spruecke Rom. ix. Wt welcken is Christus na den vleesch / die ouer alle dingen Godt is / ghebenedijt in eewicheyt / Amen / Seyt Erasmus: Hier mocht een te rugge grijpen / ende dese sprueke also onderscheyden / Christus / &cet. die daer is ouer alle dinck / Godt gebenedijt in eewicheyt / &c. Dat dese Clause eens dancseggenden is / te weten Pauli / dat hy Christum alsoo verheft / ende allen dingen heeft voorgeset. Aldaer seyt hy twijfelende aen dese clause: Welcke ghebenedijt is in eewicheyt. Ten sy dan dat dit stuck der reden daerby is gedaen / gelijc wy sommige andere vinden: Want dergelijcke clauselen werden in veel plaetsen om te voleynden ende de reden te sluyten / aengehangen geuonden / gelijck by ons een gebruyc is / aen onse Lessen of gebet te hangen / Tu autem Domine / &c. Gloria patri.' German original in Franck 1531, 391v; cf. Erasmus 1516, 439–440.

[97] Lech Szczucki, 'Antitrinitarianism', in *OER*.

Modrzewski cites the comma on the first page of his work, as part of his account of the orthodox conception of the Trinity.[98] The Trinity, Modrzewski continued, was revealed in the baptism of Jesus:

> O what theatre is this, how vast and magnificent, in which the Son of God is announced, and proven by the earthly descent of the Holy Spirit! What more outstanding or weighty testimony to the divine Trinity could exist? The Father speaks from the heavens; the Son is baptized in the Jordan; the Holy Spirit appears in the form of a dove. These things are one, as the apostle John says, for they testify to one thing. With one breath and will, they inaugurate the world's teacher and master, whom all would hear.[99]

But even when presenting the orthodox position, Modrzewski introduces doubt whether the unity of the three heavenly witnesses is one of testimony or essence. In summary, Modrzewski claimed to have demonstrated that there are three persons in the divine realm, as attested in Jn 10:30, 14:10 and 1 Jn 5:7–8. However, he noted that since the time of Arius to the present, there had been heated disagreement as to the nature of that unity.[100] Modrzewski acknowledged the exegetical discussions of the word *unum* in Jn 10:30, and suggested that the correct reading was perhaps *unus*. But there were theological problems with the passage as well. If we confess both the Father who generates and the Son who is generated to be God, do we not have two gods? If orthodox theologians distinguished the person of the Father from the person of the Son, but insisted that they are also the same in essence, then they already have three persons: Father, Son and the divine essence. When the Father generated the Son, did he make him a God? And what of the reciprocal relationship between them? If the Son received sonhood when he was generated, was the Father given fatherhood at that same moment?[101] As for the comma, that text on which the orthodox had relied so heavily in demonstrating the existence of the Trinity, Modrzewski pointed out that Erasmus, Calvin and Bèze had all argued that the unity of the three heavenly witnesses in this text, like that of the earthly witnesses, is one of testimony, not of essence. Modrzewski thus avoided the text-critical issue almost entirely in favour of exegetical concerns.[102] Modrzewski sent the manuscript of the *Sylvae* to Basel for publication, but it was intercepted and destroyed by a Polish Calvinist

---

[98] Modrzewski 1590, 1. Further, see Bludau 1904a, 280; Wilbur 1945–1952.
[99] Modrzewski 1590, 20–21.
[100] Modrzewski 1590, 22.
[101] Modrzewski 1590, 22–23.
[102] Modrzewski 1590, 32. See also Modrzewski 1590, 5, 263.

student, Krzystof Trecy (Trecius). However, Modrzewski had kept his notes, and rewrote the treatise, which circulated in manuscript until it was finally published at Raków in 1590, some years after his death.[103]

Following the formation, in 1563, of the so-called *ecclesia minor* by the Antitrinitarian Calvinists and Anabaptists in Poland, many orthodox Trinitarians attacked these 'Polish Brethren' as new Arians, Sabellians and Samosatians. In 1566, Johannes Wigand published his treatise *On God, against the new Arians recently arisen in Poland*. The biblical passages he cited as clear references to the Trinity form a predictable group: Gen 1:26–27, Gen 18:1–2, Mt 28:19, Jn 10:30 and 1 Jn 5:7–8, the last claimed as a clear testimony to the three in one, about which Wigand showed no discernible critical qualms.[104]

In reply, most Antitrinitarians pointed to Erasmus' critique of the one passage of Scripture that so many of their opponents claimed as their silver bullet. One of these was the Italian physician Giorgio Biandrata (*c.* 1516–1588), a founding member of the Antitrinitarian *ecclesia minor*. Biandrata had been charged by Isabella Jagiełło to work towards creating peace between the warring Lutherans and Calvinists in her realm, but in doing so he only managed to convert Ferenc Dávid, superintendent of the Calvinist church in Hungary, to an Antitrinitarian position. Biandrata advocated the rejection of the scholastic theology of the Trinity in favour of that of the earliest Christian theologians, such as Irenaeus, Tertullian and Hilary of Poitiers. He rejected the term 'Trinity' in favour of 'the three' in order to emphasise the separateness of Father, Son and Holy Spirit, and to allow for the subordination of the latter two to the Father.[105] In a work on the Trinity (*De falsa et vera unius Dei Patris, Filii, et Spiritus Sancti cognitione*), co-written with Dávid and published anonymously in 1567 or 1568, Biandrata declared that the first Christians had no doctrine of the Trinity, a conclusion reached earlier by Joachim of Fiore, Erasmus, Servet and Bernardino Ochino, a prominent Italian Franciscan who subsequently converted to Calvinism and then to Antitrinitarianism. According to Biandrata and Dávid, Erasmus' *Annotations on the New Testament* had revealed the extent to which the church had hoodwinked simple believers about the true nature of the faith. Erasmus' annotation on the Johannine comma in particular revealed the inconsistency of the fathers (notably Jerome) on this point.

[103] Wilbur 1945–1952, 2:325.
[104] Wigand 1566, 51, 53–54; cf. Bludau 1903a, 396.
[105] Lech Szczucki, 'Antitrinitarianism', in *OER*.

Erasmus had shown that the comma is absent from the best codices, 'but had been added by some enemy of the Arians'. He had also pointed out that the *Glossa ordinaria* interprets the unity of the witnesses as one of testimony rather than one of essence.[106] Although Biandrata and Dávid denied that Erasmus was an Arian, they believed that it was due to divine providence that he appeared on the scene when he did, to draw attention to the problematic status of the comma and to investigate the issue of God's unitary essence. Providence had likewise raised up men like Servet to continue Erasmus' project.[107]

Péter Melius Juhász, a senior pastor of the Reformed church in Hungary, convened a synod at Debrecen in 1567 to forge a united front against Antitrinitarianism. The following year, King János II Zsigmond Szapolyai of Hungary, who had employed Dávid as his chaplain and Biandrata as his personal physician, invited Melius to court to discuss the doctrines of the Trinity and Christ with them. In contrast to the theologians of the Antitrinitarian *ecclesia minor*, who maintained that 'the one God, the Father, Jehovah, is fount and wellspring of all essences, giving essence to all, the one God from whom all things flow, lacking nothing, from whom all things have their being and life', Melius argued that Jehovah is not merely the Father or fount of essence, but a common essence or nature in which reside three natures distinguished as three persons. These persons are in this essence, and the essence contains the persons.[108] Biandrata, relying on Erasmus, criticised Melius' reliance on the comma in his exposition of the Trinity. He maintained that the only father to defend the comma was the 'shameless Jerome', and that it was present only in the 'Spanish codex', that is, the Complutensian Polyglot, or perhaps the manuscripts on which it purported to be based.[109] And when Jesus said, 'My Father and I are one', a text traditionally used to interpret the comma, the word 'one' is neuter rather than masculine, which suggests a unity of witness rather than of essence. Biandrata thus came to much the same conclusion on this verse as Calvin and Bèze, even if he did not share their Trinitarian theology.[110]

In a defence of the orthodox doctrine of the Trinity against Biandrata and Ferenc Dávid, who had 'recalled the execrable Samosatian, Arian, Eunomian, and other heresies from Orcus and the Stygian swamp', the

[106] Biandrata and Dávid 1567, L2r–M1v. Further, see Bietenholz 2008, 42–46.
[107] Biandrata and Dávid 1567, E1v–2r, M1v, AA2r–v.
[108] Biandrata, *Demonstratio*, n. d., A2v.
[109] Dávid 1568, D4v–5r. Further, see Bludau 1903a, 405; Murdock 2011, 410–411.
[110] Biandrata, *Demonstratio*, n. d., C2v–3r.

Lutheran theologian Georg Major of Wittenberg (1569) cited the comma as one of eight New Testament passages that demonstrated the existence of the Trinity (Mt 3:13–17, 28:19; Jn 1:1, 1:14, 14:16, 15:26, 16:7, 1 Jn 5:7). In a co-written reply to Major, Biandrata and Dávid responded that anyone with eyes and a brain could see that the comma did not fit into the immediate context of the epistle. In any case, it was strange that Major should have given so little credit to Luther, who had rejected the passage. For further information, Biandrata and Dávid referred Major to Erasmus' judgement on this passage.[111]

In two of their joint publications (*De falsa et vera unius Dei cognitione* and *Refutatio scripti Georgii Maioris*), Biandrata and Dávid used the iconography of the Trinity as evidence of the incoherence of the doctrine and the idolatry into which its proponents had lapsed in their attempts to explain it. In many cases, Biandrata and Dávid identified the purported location of these visual representations, such as a church near Kraków or the palace of Clement VII in Rome. The appeal to real sources reveals how sensitive Antitrinitarians were to the ubiquity of imagery intended to illustrate the doctrine they opposed, as well as their intention to criticise specific representations rather than generic schemes. The eight woodcuts in the earlier book render iconographical conventions such as the three-headed or triple-faced Trinity; the three persons of the Trinity seated at a table as if for a meal; the iconography of the Father sending the Son to earth in the form of a baby; and the *Gnadenthron*, in which God the Father supports the crucified Jesus, surmounted by the dove of the Spirit. Dávid and Biandrata also attacked two schematic illustrations of the doctrine proposed by their religious opponents. First of these is a cruciform diagram devised by the radical theologian Francesco Stancaro, who had suggested that Jesus' role as mediator was restricted to his humanity, and whom Dávid had refuted in print. The other schematic image, a ring set with three jewels, had been proposed by Melius, whom Dávid and Biandrata debated in 1568. These images are complemented by texts drawn from Girolamo Cardano, and accounts of the 'Sabine Trinity' of Sanctus, Fidius and Semipater, excerpted from Flavio Biondo and Ovid.[112]

The woodcuts in the refutation of Georg Major introduce an element of satire. The first of these represents an image preserved at the cathedral in Kraków, and displayed each year on Trinity Sunday. It represents a

---

[111] Major 1569, 16v; Dávid 1569, N2r–v; cf. Bludau 1904a, 279.
[112] Biandrata and Dávid 1567, E3r–F4r (*De horrendis simulachris deum trinum et unum adumbranti-bus*); further, see Kís 2010.

monstrous anthropomorphic figure ('Ligaeus') sitting in majesty upon the starry firmament, endowed not only with three heads, but also with six hands and six feet (Figure 3.2). The second woodcut, the source of which is not identified, illustrates a female figure, Lycisca, holding an imperial orb and cross, and wearing the papal tiara and pallium, while her hair flies up in a triple plait from the back of her head (Figure 3.3). The third figure is a triple-faced deity, holding the *scutum fidei*, or shield of faith, a traditional representation drawing on Augustine's distinction between the three persons of the Trinity while maintaining their unity (Figure 3.4). The caption to this illustration states that it was taken from a book entitled *Officium beatae virginis*, allegedly printed at Rome in 1533. However, no trace of this edition could be found. This may suggest that these images were invented or adapted for satirical purposes.

The use of such images by Dávid and Biandrata was criticised by Péter Károlyi (Petrus Carolius) as a deliberate attempt to make the orthodox conception of the Trinity seem ridiculous.[113] Károlyi believed that the Scripture is full of evidence for the Trinity, first of all the comma, which Dávid had incorrectly dismissed as a forgery by Jerome or Athanasius.[114] Károlyi claimed that Erasmus had stated that the comma is attested in the writings of many early fathers. Károlyi also argued that it did not matter much whether the phrase 'these three are one' refers to a unity of nature or consent. Either way, the passage showed clearly that the Father, Son and Holy Spirit are one God bearing witness in heaven.[115] It was a feeble defence of the passage, and was soon contested by the Unitarian Johann Sommer (1540–1574). Sommer, who was influenced by Jacob Acontius' *Satanae Stratagemata* as well as by his own father-in-law, Ferenc Dávid, declared that the comma had crept surreptitiously into the text of the epistle, and therefore had no reason to be retained there.[116] By defending their ideas, the Unitarians gained legal recognition in Hungary in 1571, as well as the right to hold worship services.[117]

An original and subtle interpretation of the comma was made by Fausto Sozzini (Faustus Socinus, 1539–1604).[118] Sozzini, one of the most

---

[113] Károlyi 1571, 31.

[114] Károlyi 1571, 15.

[115] Károlyi 1571, 248.

[116] Sommer 1582, 155v–156r. See also Károlyi 1571, 248; Sommer 1583, 131r–v. Sommer's treatises were written in 1571–1572, and only published posthumously. Sommer was the first modern Antitrinitarian to attempt to explain the development of the doctrine of the Trinity through recourse to the history of philosophy. Further, see Pirnát 1961, 38–45.

[117] Bianchi 1985, 91

[118] My exposition of Sozzini draws on John C. Godbey, 'Sozzini, Fausto and Lelio', in *OER*; Lech Szczucki, 'Antitrinitarianism', in *OER*; Mortimer 2010; Lim 2013; Mortimer 2013.

LIBELLI MAIORIS.
Hoc Idolum extat in templo ad
Arcē Cracouienſem, quod quotan-
nis in Trinitatis feſto populo venerā
dum proponitur, A qua et nomen
ſuum polonicè ſortitū eſt rachos. *markocʒ*
TERTIVM IDOLVM.
HVIVS NOMEN.
LIGAEVS.

Figure 3.2. 'Ligaeus'. From Ferenc Dávid and Giorgio Biandrata, *Refutatio scripti Georgii Maioris* ([Cluj-Napoca]: [n. p.], 1569), H5r. Universitätsbibliothek Leipzig, Syst. Theol. 1956/1. Reproduced by kind permission.

prominent of the early Antitrinitarians, gave his name to one of its most characteristic forms, which combined Arius' subordination of Jesus with Sabellius' understanding of the Spirit not as a separate divine hypostasis, but as a personification of the spiritual gifts of the Father. Fausto was

REFVTATIO
SECVNDVM SYMV-
LACHRVM. HV-
IVS NOMEN,
LYCISCA.

Figure 3.3. 'Lycisca'. From Ferenc Dávid and Giorgio Biandrata, *Refutatio scripti Georgii Maioris* ([Cluj-Napoca]: [n. p.], 1569), H5v. Universitätsbibliothek Leipzig, Syst. Theol. 1956/1. Reproduced by kind permission.

influenced by a heterodox exposition of the Johannine prologue by his uncle Lelio Sozzini, who had suggested that ἐγένετο in Jn 1:14 means not 'the Word became flesh', but 'the Word *was* flesh'. The Word was thus not cosmological, but the historical man Jesus, predestined to be

Figure 3.4. 'Est, et non est'. From Ferenc Dávid and Giorgio Biandrata, *Refutatio scripti Georgii Maioris* ([Cluj-Napoca]: [n. p.], 1569), H6r. Universitätsbibliothek Leipzig, Syst. Theol. 1956/1. Reproduced by kind permission.

adopted as Son of God. As divine *sermo*, Christ expounded divine truth and preached the ideal of a society based on spiritual values. But Fausto also differed from his uncle in some details. Like Bernardino Ochino, Lelio believed that those who believe in Christ already possess eternal life, but Fausto held that belief gives us only the hope of eternal life. The Sozzini family was persecuted by the Inquisition on account of Lelio's heresy, and Fausto left Italy in 1561, travelling to Switzerland, Poland and Transylvania, where he met with the heterodox circles cultivated by his uncle. After returning to Italy in 1563, he found employment as secretary to duke Paolo Giordano Orsini. He maintained contact with Giorgio Biandrata and Ferenc Dávid in Transylvania, who published Lelio's treatise on the Johannine prologue in 1568, as part of one of their joint publications. In his treatise *On Jesus Christ the Saviour* (*De Iesu Christo Servatore*), written at Basel in 1578, Sozzini sketched his radical ideas on Jesus' nature and role. This important work circulated in manuscript, and was finally printed in 1594. Impressed by this work, Biandrata invited Sozzini to come to Cluj-Napoca (Kolozsvár) to help him bring his colleague Dávid back from a position he had taken in about 1575. Dávid had concluded that since Jesus is not divine, he is not worthy to receive worship or supplication. Biandrata considered this position (dubbed 'non-adorationism') as a relapse into Judaism. Unsuccessful in this attempt, Sozzini moved to Poland, where he associated with the Polish Brethren, defending their beliefs in debate against other radical groups. His defence of the authority of Scripture (*De sacrae scripturae auctoritate*), published anonymously in 1580, was praised by Protestants and Roman Catholics alike; biblicism would become a characteristic feature of his followers' thought. Until his death in 1604, Sozzini was the strongest force of coherence, both political and theological, in the Polish Antitrinitarian churches.

One distinctive feature of Sozzini's theology was his understanding of the atonement. He conceived of Jesus' death not a sacrificial and substitutionary propitiation for our sin, but as the result of his perfect obedience to God's will. Jesus was thus superior to the rest of humanity not in essence, but simply in degree. Socinian ethics thus focused not so much on Christ as on the individual's response to the divine commandments. Moreover, it emphasised not original sin as much as the possibility that perfectible humans might attain happiness. Sozzini justified this programme by making constant appeal to the beliefs common to Christians before the council of Nicaea. While Sozzini held to the orthodox view that humans receive knowledge of God from the twin streams of reason and revelation communicated by Scripture, he pointed out that neither of these streams speaks of a Trinity of three separate persons who are nonetheless united in one essence. Rather, the prevailing image of God in Scripture is that of the supreme and ontologically single law-giver.

If Christology had been the only radical feature of Socinian belief, that would have been enough to guarantee its condemnation. However, Socinian theology also touched upon issues of religion, natural law, freedom and human nature. First, Fausto Sozzini rejected the notions of predestination and absolute depravity, insisting that humans have freedom to do good or ill. God laid down certain commandments and promised eternal life to those who kept them. Without free will, we would have no way to obey the commandments of God, nor any reason to do so. Sozzini rejected Protestant objections that we carry out God's will with the help of divine grace. Unless we choose our actions freely, we can never be held responsible or judged for them, either by society or by God. For Sozzini, free will is thus a necessary precondition for both religion and law. Sozzini also taught that violence, even in self-defence, is contrary to divine law, and even insisted that Christians threatened by the Turkish advance should not offer violent resistance. He also taught that Christians were forbidden from rising up against their rulers, even when their religious liberties were threatened. Armed struggle was never the answer; those who resorted to bloodshed would forfeit their heavenly reward.

Sozzini's understanding of divine justice was intimately related to his view of human justice. He reasoned that anyone who suffers injury or offence earns the right to avenge himself, which he may exercise or remit at will. The same is true for God. Atonement takes place when God elects to remit his right to punish us. This understanding of atonement dispensed with the sacrificial model held by most theologians, both Roman Catholic and Protestant, who complained that it effectively denied that Jesus' death and resurrection had any significance. Sozzini's theory of rights spilled over into political philosophy. Sozzini and his follower Johann Crell posited that those who live in civil society lay aside their natural rights to revenge wrongs, in exchange for the greater benefits of peace and civil order. This abrogation of rights is an act of choice and will that cannot be revoked.

Sozzini examined the Johannine comma in his response to a series of lectures directed against the Antitrinitarians ('the new Samosatians'), given at the Jesuit college at Poznań in 1583. The seventeenth thesis defended in these lectures stated that although some words used by the church to describe God, such as 'Trinity', are not found in the bible, the concepts they describe are nevertheless implicit in Scripture. The Trinity is symbolised by the three men who visited Abraham at Mamre (Gen 18:1–2), in the description of God (Rev 1:8) as he 'who is and who was and who is to come', and in the Johannine comma.[119] In response, Sozzini pointed out that the comma is not found in the oldest Greek or Latin codices, nor in the Syriac translation, and was even recognised as spurious by the Leuven editors of the New Testament. In any case, the unity spoken of is clearly one of witness rather than agreement.[120]

In his commentary on 1 Jn, Sozzini dealt with both philological and exegetical aspects of the comma. In order to understand the entire passage, Sozzini suggested that it was necessary to account for the phrase 'in heaven' in v. 7. While the traditional interpretation assumed that there are two groups of witnesses testifying to Christ, one group in heaven and one on earth, Sozzini suggested instead that the three earthly witnesses testify to the existence of the Father, Word and Holy Spirit in heaven.[121] Furthermore, he suggested that the phrase 'and these three are one' (or 'in one') in v. 8 was not originally part of the reading, but once it had entered the text, it provided the mechanism for the invention of the comma.[122] This conclusion is not borne out by the manuscript evidence.

Sozzini's most extended treatment of the comma is found in his refutation of a treatise on the divinity of Christ and the Holy Spirit written by the Jesuit Jakub Wujek in 1590 against the latter-day Antitrinitarians such as Servet, Biandrata, Dávid and Sozzini. Sozzini noted that many of Wujek's arguments were drawn from Bellarmino's *Three books on the controversies of the Christian faith* (1586), and his refutations sometimes address Wujek, sometimes Bellarmino, sometimes both. Sozzini was not the only Antitrinitarian to take issue with Bellarmino. The Transylvanian Unitarian György Enyedi (1555–1597) criticised Bellarmino's defence of the comma as 'vain and deceptive'. According to Enyedi, only the most shameless or least well-informed disputant would deny that the comma is amongst the most dubious passages of Scripture cited in support of the doctrine of the Trinity. But even if the comma were genuine, Erasmus, Calvin, Bèze and others had shown that the unity of the three heavenly witnesses is one of testimony, not essence.[123]

In order to engage with Wujek's theological arguments, Sozzini at first accepted his assumption that the comma was present in the text. Wujek interpreted the comma with reference to Jn 10:30; controversially, Wujek

[119] *Assertio* XVII, repr. in Sozzini 1618, 67.
[120] Sozzini 1618, 69; cf. Bludau 1904a, 281.
[121] Sozzini 1614, 417–418. On an earlier response to Wujek's treatise by Marcin Czechowic, see Kawecka-Gryczowa 1974, 154.
[122] Sozzini 1614, 423.
[123] Enyedi [1598], 425–426; cf. Bludau 1904a, 279–280.

suggested that the unity of which Jesus speaks there is one of testimony, not one of essence. Wujek's first argument (borrowed from Bellarmino) was that the witness given by the two sets of witnesses in 1 Jn 5:7–8 must be complementary. If the earthly witnesses testify to Jesus' humanity, then the heavenly witnesses must testify to his divinity, as they did at his baptism and transfiguration.[124] However, Sozzini pointed out that Wujek had no warrant to assume that the testimony of the two sets of witnesses must be complementary.[125] Attempting to deduce Christ's divinity simply by assuming a contrast with the presumed content of the testimony of the earthly witnesses put the cart before the horse. Sozzini also pointed out that those occasions when Bellarmino imagined that the testimony of the three heavenly witnesses was revealed were not as clear as the Jesuit believed. For example, at the baptism of Jesus, the Father, and the Spirit testified, but the Word did not. On this occasion, the Father and Spirit testified to Jesus' status as Son of God, not to his divine essence and nature. According to Sozzini, Jesus' status as Son of God did not arise through generation from the essence of God, but through God's attribution of divine power and authority to the man Jesus.[126]

Bellarmino and Wujek interpreted the spirit, water and blood in 1 Jn 5:8 as a reference to the crucifixion. However, Sozzini argued that the 'spirit' in Scripture refers rather to the divine power spread abroad on earth to testify to Jesus' status as the Christ. Sozzini applied philological arguments to show that the spirit of v. 8 cannot be Jesus' dying breath. If one follows the Greek reading of 1 Jn 5:6 ('since the spirit is the truth'), it is clear that the spirit mentioned in v. 8 cannot be Jesus' dying breath. Conversely, if one follows the Latin reading of 1 Jn 5:6, according to which the Spirit testifies that Christ is the truth, it is equally clear that the spirit mentioned in v. 8 cannot be Jesus' dying breath.[127] Sozzini argued that the blood and water of v. 8 do not refer to the water and blood that issued from Jesus' side, since the author of the epistle here is not trying to establish Jesus' true humanity, but rather his status as the Christ, whose teaching is true and divine. Jesus is said to have come through water and blood (1 Jn 5:6). Sozzini therefore considered it unlikely that the water and blood mentioned in v. 8 referred to the water and blood from Jesus' side at his death, not at his coming. But if the blood must be referred to Jesus' death, the

---

[124] Sozzini 1624, 282–283. He is responding to Bellarmino 1586, 306–307; and Wujek 1590, 72–73. Bellarmino's arguments are examined above, 84–85.
[125] Sozzini 1624, 283.
[126] Sozzini 1624, 285–286.
[127] Sozzini 1624, 283–284.

water may refer to his purity of life and innocence, through which he 'came' along with the spirit, the divine force revealed through Christ's miracles, and through the miracles and martyrdom of his disciples.[128]

Bellarmino had distinguished the two sets of witnesses into two classes: human and created on one hand, and divine and uncreated on the other. Since the Word is included in the latter group, it must therefore be divine. However, Sozzini pointed out that this presented an insuperable difficulty: according to this scheme, the Spirit in the earthly group would be created. Sozzini was equally unconvinced by Bellarmino's suggestion that 'in heaven' and 'in earth' signify the nature of the testimony rather than its location. Had John meant this, he would have written, 'There are three in heaven (or on earth) who bear witness.'[129] Sozzini also made an interesting grammatical argument of his own. He noted that John used the present tense ('testify') rather than the past tense when speaking of both sets of witnesses. The divine testimony was given not only once, but continually through the testimony of the Spirit to the miracles wrought by God in the person of Jesus.[130]

To this point, Sozzini had been speaking as if the textual status of the comma was unproblematic, but in fact it had long been settled that the comma was an interpolation. Erasmus and the Leuven editors had shown that the passage is absent from the better Greek, Latin and Syriac manuscripts, and disrupted the sense of the context. Since this passage is so controverted, it can possess no decisive force in any argument.[131] Sozzini conceded that Bellarmino was right to have criticised Biandrata for claiming that 'Jerome' was the only Latin father to cite the comma, but he had still failed to prove the authenticity of the passage.

Unlike some other apologists, neither Bellarmino nor Wujek argued that the phrase 'these three are one' proves that the Son and the Spirit are of the same essence as God the Father, for they were aware that this argument could lead to the nonsensical conclusion that the Spirit, water and blood are also of one essence. Instead, Bellarmino and Wujek had argued from philological detail. Bellarmino stated that the words 'and these three are one' are absent from v. 8 in many Latin manuscripts. Wujek added that they were also missing from many Greek manuscripts. Bellarmino also mentioned that he had seen Greek manuscripts in which the earthly witnesses were said to be 'unto one' (εἰς τὸ ἕν), which suggests a unity of

---

[128] Sozzini 1624, 284–285.
[129] Sozzini 1624, 287–288.
[130] Sozzini 1624, 289.
[131] Sozzini 1624, 290.

testimony rather than will. Sozzini disputed these claims. Wujek's statement that the words 'and these three are one' are absent from v. 8 in many Greek manuscripts was doubtful, since Sozzini had 'no memory of any Greek copy that does not include these words, apart from the Spanish text that Erasmus mentions [that is, the Complutensian Polyglot]'. Sozzini also made a methodological point, warning that it is dangerous to give disproportionate credit to variants in the Latin tradition that contradicted the readings in the Greek and Syriac traditions. He also suggested (probably following Erasmus' *Annotationes*) that the word 'in' or 'unto' (εἰς) in the Greek text of v. 8 could be a Hebraism. If so, there would be no appreciable difference to the sense whether the passage read 'these three are one' or 'these three are *unto* one'. He concluded by warning his readers that 'what Bellarmino says about the variety of readings in the Greek manuscripts is not entirely true'.[132] Johannes Junius supported Wujek against Sozzini by arguing that the comma was found in the Complutensian edition and the editions of Estienne. He also dismissed Erasmus' arguments as based on an incomplete examination of the extant Greek manuscripts.[133]

The comma continued to cause disputes in the Protestant east. It was included in the Polish Protestant bible published at Brest (1563).[134] However, the prominent Polish-Byelorussian Antitrinitarian humanist Szymon Budny (*c.* 1530–1593) removed it from his 1572 revision.[135] Amongst radical critics, Budny was unusual in arguing that the Latin Vulgate is often more reliable than the current Greek text, for it was translated before the Greek text had been corrupted by careless or malicious scribes.[136] In his annotations on the passage, Budny remarks that he followed Erasmus, Luther, Bullinger and Zegers in rejecting the comma an addition to the text.[137] Budny's revision was praised by some, but many more accused him of undermining the authority of Scripture. In 1589 he issued a revision with an explanation of all his editorial decisions. The Lithuanian brethren forced him to make certain changes, though they

[132] Sozzini 1624, 291–292.
[133] J. Junius 1628, 229: 'Erasmus non dicit universaliter de omnibus.' Cf. Bludau 1904a, 282.
[134] *Biblia swięta* 1563, 2:133r: 'Abowiem trzey są którzy świadscżą na niebie / Ociec / Słowo / y Duch święty / a ci trzey iednoć są. A trzey są którzy świadscżą na ziemi / duch / y woda / y krew / a ći trzey na iedno się zgadzaią.'
[135] Budny 1572, R1v (cf. Budny 1574, BB8r): 'Gdysz trzey są świadscżą cy / duch / y woda / y krew / A trzey w iedno są.'
[136] Budny 1574, C3v–4r, cit. in Frick 1989, 93; Frick 1995, 140.
[137] Budny 1574, KK7r. See also Fleischmann 2006, 247–248; Fleischmann mistakenly stated that Budny's comment in the margin of the translation ('Łacin: ze Christus', Bb8r) refers to the comma, but it refers to the variant *Christus est veritas* in v. 6 found in many manuscripts of the Latin Vulgate.

promised to defend his choices in a number of instances, including 1 Cor 10:9, 1 Tim 3:16 and 1 Jn 5:7–8.[138] Jakub Wujek interpreted Budny's approach to the emendation of difficult passages as a challenge to the authority of Scripture, and censured many of his editorial choices, including his excision of the comma. Wujek claimed that his own rival Catholic translation of the New Testament (1593) was based on the Clementine Vulgate, but his rendering of the comma is clearly adapted from that in the Brest bible.[139] The Calvinist editors of the New Testament published at Gdańsk in 1606 also restored the comma, which they believed had been removed from the Greek text by Arians.[140]

Socinian suspicion of the comma was entrenched in the Racovian catechism, first published in Polish in 1605, and subsequently in German (1608), Latin (1609) and English (1652). The biblicism of the Socinians is evident in this document, which draws on many texts to demonstrate God's unity (Deut 6:4, 1 Cor 8:4–6, 1 Tim 2:5, Gal 3:20) and the proposition that this one God is the Father of our Lord Jesus Christ (Jn 17:3, 1 Cor 8:6, Eph 4:6). This catechism gives the impression of a real dialogue taking place in real time, in contrast to the simple question-and-response format of many orthodox catechisms, which dispense dogmatic verities in timeless formulations. 'You said a little before that the Lord Jesus is a man by nature', asks the questioner. 'Hath he not also a divine Nature?'[141] Unlike the catechumen in orthodox catechisms, who passively receives the catechist's instruction, the respondent in the Racovian catechism actively contributes to the determination of a doctrinally and historically sound understanding of the Scripture through dialogue. The Racovian catechism is also unusual in that the questioner often presents the orthodox position, while the respondent argues the Socinian perspective. The movement of ideas is thus not top-down, but is a dialogical process between two more equal parties, even if the outcome is a foregone conclusion in favour of the Socinian position. The rhetoric of the catechism thus relies both on humanist philosophical dialogues and on reformation dialogues between doctrinaire Catholic clergy and wily (and inevitably

---

[138] Budny 1589, e2v–3r; the translation of 1 Jn 5 is on Bb8r; further, see Frick 1989, 98–100, who inadvertently gives the reference as c2v–3r.

[139] Frick 1989, 145–147, citing Wujek 1593, 13–15. Wujek 1593, 826, translates the comma thus: 'Abowiem trzey są którzy świadcza ná niebie; Oćiec / Słowo / y Duch święty. á či trzey iedno są. A trzey są którzy świadcza ná žiemi; Duch / wodá / y krew / á či trzey iedno są.'

[140] *Nowy testament* 1606,):(5v, cit. Frick 1989, 230–231. According to Frick 1989, 234, the editors of the 1606 New Testament were somewhat reliant on Wujek. Further on this edition, see Pietkiewicz 2002, 296–303.

[141] *Catechesis ecclesiarum* 1609, 43; *The Racovian Catechisme* 1652, 28. Cf. Bludau 1904a, 283–284.

victorious) Protestant laymen. By promoting the conviction that those who appear heterodox know and understand the Scriptures better than their orthodox opponents, the Racovian catechism no doubt encouraged those who felt embattled in their religious position. The dialogue also primed its readers to respond to the questions they were likely to encounter when mixing in orthodox society, away from their sheltered communities.

The passages identified in the catechism as the chief supports for the doctrine of the Trinity, 'wherein mention is made of the Father, and the Son, and Holy Spirit', are Mt 28:19, 1 Cor 12:4–6 and 1 Jn 5:7–8. The respondent concedes that all three prove that the Father, Son and Holy Spirit exist, but points out that they 'do not demonstrate the Father, Sonne, and Holy Spirit to be three Persons in the one Divine Essence'. The catechism also lays out many of the historical and text-critical reasons for doubting the authenticity of the comma, from the lack of evidence in the Greek manuscripts and ancient translations to the doubts of orthodox critics such as Erasmus, Bèze, the Leuven editors, Luther and Bugenhagen. But even if the passage could be proven authentic, 'yet could it not be thence concluded, that there are three Persons in one Divinity'. The Father, Word and Spirit are no more separate persons than are the spirit, water and blood of the following verse. The only unity subsisting between them is a unity of testimony, not of essence.[142] For the Socinians, the comma, even if it were genuine, would not bolster Trinitarian theology any more than it would their own.

In 1614, Valentin Schmalz (Smalcius, 1572–1622), a German-Polish Socinian who contributed to the formulation of the Racovian catechism, engaged in a controversy over the comma with Hermann Ravensperger, subsequently foundation professor of theology at Groningen. Ravensperger denied that the comma was a human addition, arguing that the context demands the presence of the comma, and that 1 Jn 5:6 does not flow naturally to v. 8 without it. Ravensperger believed moreover that the comma had been removed from the text of Scripture by Arius. Schmalz replied that Ravensperger's assertions were based on an ignorance of the wording of the Greek text.[143]

Consistent with the Socinian reservations about the comma, Crell's edition of the bible (1630) marks it off with brackets. In his preface, Crell stated that the comma does not occur in the oldest manuscripts and

---

[142] *Catechesis ecclesiarum* 1609, 32–36; *The Racovian Catechisme* 1652, 20–24.
[143] Schmalz 1614, 49–50.

translations, was not mentioned by many Greek and Latin fathers, and was rejected by Luther and Bugenhagen as an interpolation.[144]

The comma was definitively rejected by Christoph Sand (1644–1680), an Arminian with Antitrinitarian leanings, in a twenty-page appendix to his *Paradoxical interpretations of the four gospels* (*Interpretationes Paradoxae quatuor evangeliorum*, 1669). 'These words are missing from an infinite number of Greek codices, and indeed from the very oldest, amongst which the first place is taken by the so-called Codex of St Thecla', that is, Codex Alexandrinus.[145] Sand reported that the comma was missing from the body text of the manuscript in the Franciscan monastery in Antwerp mentioned by Erasmus. He noted the absence of the comma from Codex Vaticanus and from the seven manuscripts Erasmus had consulted for his first edition of the New Testament. (Sand was evidently unaware that only three of the manuscripts used by Erasmus for the first edition contain the Catholic Epistles.)[146] He also noted with satisfaction that the comma was rejected by Luther, Bugenhagen and Naogeorgus. Sand, like John Selden and Richard Simon, concluded that the prologue to the Catholic Epistles, cited constantly by defenders of the comma, was not written by Jerome.[147] In a treatise on the Scriptural evidence for the doctrine of the Trinity, issued under the pseudonym Hermann Cingallus, Sand relied on Erasmus' *Annotationes* to argue that the comma had crept into the text from the margin. He also borrowed Calvin's argument that the original form of the comma in the Greek text refers to heavenly doctrine, redemption and truth rather than to the orthodox conception of the Trinity, a notion to which Sand was opposed.[148]

7.   The comma in the Eastern Orthodox churches

Beginning in the sixteenth century, the comma appeared in the Scriptures and liturgies of the eastern churches under western influence. In 1550 a Latin translation of a number of Ethiopic liturgies was printed along with a letter from Gelāwdēwōs (Claudius), emperor of Ethiopia, who had recently solicited aid from Pope Paul III. While the Ethiopic rubrics only

---

[144] Crell and Stegmann 1630, †8v–††1r, 849–850; Düsterdieck 1852–1856, 2:356; Bludau 1904a, 289–290, 299–300.

[145] Sand 1669, 376: 'His verbis carent infiniti codices *M.S. graeci*, & quidem vetustissimi, inter quos primum locum obtinet codex S. Theclae dictus [...].' On the designation 'Codex S. Theclae', see Grotius' *Annotations*; Gregory 1900–1909, 1:31; Bludau 1904a, 294–295.

[146] Sand 1669, 377.

[147] Sand 1669, 382–385.

[148] Sand 1678, 91–111.

give the references of the passages to be read, the Latin translation provides the full text of the readings. In the Latin version, the reading 1 Jn
5:5–13, intoned by the subdeacon, contains the comma, thus suggesting
misleadingly that the comma was contained in the Ethiopic text.[149] Even
more pointedly, when the St Thomas Christians of India, formerly allied
with the eastern Syrian church, united with the Roman Catholic church
at the council of Diamper (1599), they were officially obliged to 'amend'
their Syriac bibles, which excluded the comma, to make them consonant
with the Latin Vulgate.[150] This episode makes both the coercive and the
global aspects of the debate over the comma particularly clear.[151]

The comma also spread from the west to other traditions. It appears
in the Apostolos published at Venice in 1602 for use in the Greek east.[152]
Maximos Kallipolites (Bishop Maximus of Gallipoli) began translating
the New Testament from *koine* to modern Greek in 1629. He worked
from a recent printed edition, and his translation accordingly includes the
comma.[153]

In the seventeenth century, many Russian Orthodox clerics, while
wishing to legitimate their own church by emphasising its unbroken links
with Byzantium, nevertheless argued that many Greek texts had been
corrupted either by Greek heretics (an argument promoted by Szymon
Budny), or more recently by western (especially German) editors who prepared them for the press. Some, such as Sil'vestr Medvedev (1688), even
marshalled both arguments, apparently unconcerned that they are mutu-
ally contradictory: the first assumes that Greek texts are invariably corrupt,
while the second presupposes that they were reliable until corrupted by
western interference. Some Russians claimed that western scholars, having
plundered the libraries of Constantinople for manuscripts, had prepared
printed editions that supported their own heresies, and then destroyed
the originals.[154] Some even claimed that the authority previously enjoyed
by the Byzantine church had passed to Muscovy. While Ruthenian sacred
philology rested squarely on the study of Greek texts, these texts were usually read in editions produced by western humanists. Furthermore, the

---

[149] *Modus baptizandi* 1550, Cıv; Trumpp 1878, 161 (Ethiopic), 176 (German translation). Thanks to
Martin Heide for his assistance with the Ethiopic text.

[150] Geddes 1694, 134.

[151] On the turn to global history, see Hunt 2014.

[152] Pinelli 1602; Mill 1707, 742.

[153] Kallipolites 1638, 2:259r–v; his translation of 1 Jn 5:7–8 reads: "Ὅτι τρεῖς εἶναι ἐκεῖνοι ὅπου
μαρτυροῦσιν εἰς τὸν οὐρανόν, ὁ πατήρ, ὁ λόγος, καὶ τὸ ἅγιον πνεῦμα· καὶ ἐτοῦτοι οἱ τρεῖς
ἕνα εἶναι. Καὶ τρεῖς εἶναι ἐκεῖνοι ὅπου μαρτυροῦσιν εἰς τὴν γῆν, τὸ πνεῦμα, καὶ τὸ ὕδωρ, καὶ
τὸ αἷμα· καὶ οἱ τρεῖς εἰς τὸ ἕνα εἶναι.' Cf. Bludau 1915, 241.

[154] Frick 1995, 138–141.

appeal to the authority of the Greek sources, a rhetorical ploy designed to maintain the narrative of a continuity of Orthodoxy from Greece to Rus´, concealed the fact that Ruthenian scholars relied heavily on Polish translations as well as on the rhetorical strategies employed by Polish biblical scholars such as Budny and Wujek in their apologetic and polemical works. Western influence on eastern Orthodox scholars was also felt in the kinds of questions asked of the biblical text, and the attitude towards its textual problems. The preface to the 1623 Kiev edition of Chrysostom (based on the edition produced by Henry Savile at Eton between 1610 and 1612) contains a long textual note by Zaxarija Kopystens´kyj, who defended a textual interpolation at 1 Cor 8:6 (+ 'and one Holy Spirit, in whom are all things, and we in him') on the following grounds: (1) that the interpolation reflects correct doctrine; (2) that it was quoted by Greek theologians such as Gregory the Theologian, Basil the Great, John of Damascus and John Chrysostom; (3) that it is attested in Slavonic books, both manuscript and printed. Kopystens´kyj likewise remarked that the Johannine comma was received, namely by the Slavic Orthodox churches, even though it is not found in 'some' codices. As David Frick has remarked, 'Kopystens´kyj was clearly at pains to find "Greek" answers to these questions. But the questions themselves were "Latin".'[155]

The comma gradually gained a certain currency in the Slavonic churches as a result of the well-concealed appropriation of western attitudes to Scripture. It was quoted in the Orthodox Confession of the eastern church, drawn up in 1643 under the direction of Peter Mogilas, metropolitan of Kiev. This document, which distinguished the eastern position clearly from those of the Roman Catholic and Protestant churches, was adopted by the Graeco-Russian synod at Jassy (1643) and the synod of Jerusalem (1672). Ironically, the comma – quoted from Bèze's text – was deployed in the Confession as a weapon against the western doctrine of the *filioque*.[156] The comma was included in a Slavonic Apostolos printed in 1653, probably under the influence of Mogilas' Confession.[157]

Yet the place of the comma in the Slavonic text was by no means assured. One important episode marked the textual corpus used in the Russian Orthodox church: a textual reform undertaken in the 1650s at the command of Nikon, patriarch of Moscow (1605–1681), who had noted the presence of additions, deletions and alterations to the text of the Scripture. He therefore ordered that old Greek and Slavonic manuscripts should be

[155] Frick 1994, 76, 79–80.
[156] Schaff 1919, 2:275; the text is given in Kimmel 1843, 64–65, and Schaff 1919, 2:283–284.
[157] Porson 1790, xi–xii; Michaelis 1793–1801, 2,1:156.

brought from Mt Athos, Jerusalem and Constantinople, to compare their texts with those in circulation. This impulse to correct texts corrupted through ignorance or philological scrupulousness was essentially humanistic, but the enterprise was hampered by an incomplete grasp of the criteria by which the authority of any given source was to be judged. Nikon tried to excise the Johannine comma, but this attempt caused the conservative Solovki monks to complain of textual interference. By contrast, the triple alleluia, previously rejected in Russia as a western innovation, was 'restored' in the Nikonian reform. Simiaon Polatski praised the restoration of this passage, citing the Johannine comma in support.[158]

In 1780, Eugenius Bulgaris (1716–1806), former archbishop of Cherson, who had studied in Italy and had visited Germany and France, received an enquiry from Christian Friedrich Matthaei, a German who had recently been appointed professor of classics at Moscow. Matthaei asked Bulgaris about the quotation of the comma in the text of Bryennius, which Bulgaris had edited some years before. Bulgaris replied on 10 December 1780, confirming the presence of the comma in the manuscript of Bryennius. Bulgaris also showed considerable knowledge of the critical discussions of the passage in the west, from Erasmus to Mill. He was of the opinion that the Johannine comma was known to Tertullian and Cyprian; the presence of the comma in the African text of the Latin Vulgate was indicated by the fact that it was cited by the bishops who appeared before Hunneric.[159] As further evidence for the genuineness of the comma, Bulgaris noted the lack of grammatical coordination between the masculine τρεῖς μαρτυροῦντες and the three neuter nouns τὸ πνεῦμα, καὶ τὸ ὕδωρ, καὶ τὸ αἷμα. He remarked that although it is possible in Greek to agree masculine or feminine nouns with neuter adjectives or pronouns, the reverse was unusual; one would more normally expect τρία εἰσι τὰ μαρτυροῦντα ... καὶ τὰ τρία. Bulgaris seems then to be the first to have argued for the genuineness of the comma through the argument from grammar, but he advanced these arguments in the light of the critical controversies in the Latin world.[160] Matthaei was not won over by Bulgaris' arguments. He might have been convinced that the passage had dropped out of the Greek text through eye-skip if he had found at least the words 'in earth' (ἐν τῇ

[158] Frick 1995, 148–152.
[159] Tertullian, *Adversus Praxean* xxv.1, *CCSL* 2:1195 (cf. *CSEL* 47:267; *PL* 2:188); Cyprian of Carthage, *De catholicae ecclesiae unitate* 6, *CCSL* 3:254 (cf. *CSEL* 3.1:215; *PL* 4:503–504), Cyprian, *Epist.* 73.12, *CCSL* 3C:542–543 (cf. *CSEL* 3.2:786–787); Victor Vitensis, *Historia persecutionis Africanae provinciae*, *CSEL* 7:60 (cf. *PL* 58:227–228).
[160] An extract from the letter is reprinted in Matthaei 1782, LVI–LXII. On Bulgaris, see Tennent 1830, 2:292–295.

γῆ) in one manuscript, but to date he had not found this reading in any manuscript.[161]

More recently, the comma has crept into the biblical text used by the Greek Orthodox church. In 1904, Vasileios Antoniades published his Patriarchal Edition, based on about sixty manuscripts from the ninth to the sixteenth centuries. In his preface to the edition, Antoniades stated that the comma was unknown in the earlier Greek manuscript tradition and the works of the Greek fathers, but had been introduced gradually into the Latin Vulgate. He claimed to have retained the passage in his Greek text 'upon the opinion of the Holy Synod'.[162] Antoniades' textual instincts, like those of many before him, were trumped by theological and political concerns.

Summary

In this chapter we saw how the fears of Erasmus' opponents that his edition would foment heresy were not entirely groundless. Miguel Servet encountered Erasmus' theology at the conference at Valladolid in 1527, and would soon radicalise his Scriptural exegesis in his relentless interrogation of the orthodox conception of the Trinity. Philipp Melanchthon revised his chapter on the doctrine of God in his *Loci* in reaction to Servet's views. In his desperate desire to make use of every last piece of Scriptural evidence in defence of the orthodox doctrine of the Trinity, Melanchthon even quoted the comma, which Luther had previously excluded from his German bible and rejected in his lectures on 1 Jn. Melanchthon's rehabilitation of the comma led orthodox Lutherans and Calvinists from the second half of the sixteenth century onwards to hold an increasingly more positive view of its utility and even its authenticity. By contrast, Antitrinitarian theologians tended to reject the comma as one of the many means by which the Catholic church had distorted the primitive form of Christian belief, creating an erroneous conception of God from which not even the Protestant reformers could escape. At Trent, the Roman Catholic church enshrined the Latin Vulgate as its authoritative biblical text. This stimulated a good deal of text-critical work on the Vulgate, particularly at the University of Leuven. Although several Catholic biblical critics, such as Zegers and Lucas, had indicated the poor textual attestation of

[161] Matthaei 1782, 140.
[162] Antoniades 1904, ζ' (preface), 567. Antoniades' preface is translated into English in Rife 1933. The treatment of the comma in Modern Greek translations is treated fully by Vasileiadis 2013.

the comma, it was included in the official Roman Catholic editions of the Vulgate, the inaccurate *Sixtina* (1590) and its replacement, the *Clementina* (1592). At precisely this time, the responsory *Duo seraphim/Tres sunt* experienced a surge of popularity in polyphonic music. Under the combined influence of printed editions and political pressure from the west, the comma increasingly found its way into eastern Orthodox liturgical books and bibles.

CHAPTER 4

From Civil War to Enlightenment

During the seventeenth and eighteenth centuries, England was battered by several waves of religious struggle and social upheaval. The execution of Charles I destabilised the state and the Anglican church of which he was titular head. Under the Commonwealth, the number and variety of dissident religious groups exploded, and the government struggled to regulate religious belief and observance. Throughout the seventeenth century, toleration and its limits would thus become a pressing issue, which received philosophical consideration by such thinkers as Locke and Shaftesbury. In discussions of toleration, Erasmus was an ambivalent figure. While he often advocated an indulgent acceptance of a variety of non-essential religious beliefs in order to achieve that unity and concord that he considered the essence of Christianity, he never advocated the legal toleration of those who dissented from the official religious beliefs and practices of their territory.[1] Erasmus continued to play an important posthumous role in religious debate throughout this period on account of his promotion of biblical philology as a critique of dogmatics.[2]

Amongst the most controversial dissident movements in the seventeenth century was Socinianism, which first made its presence known in England in 1609, when a Latin translation of the Racovian catechism was published with a dedication to James I. But the king, far from embracing this new synthesis of Scripture and doctrine as the Socinians had hoped, was appalled, and ordered that the book should be burned. In the theological mix of mid seventeenth-century England, a bewildering variety of conceptions of the Trinity was proposed. Some maintained that the doctrine of the Trinity was 'a Popish tradition and a Doctrine of *Rome*', which had to be purged in a second reformation, a return to a more primitive form of Christianity. Others maintained that the Father, Son and Holy

---

[1] These two different notions of toleration are distinguished by Turchetti 1991.
[2] Snobelen 2006, 117–118.

Spirit are not separate persons, 'but only three Offices'. Others believed that 'there is but one Person in the Divine nature'. Such positions usually arose from heterodox Christologies. Some rejected traditional Christianity altogether in favour of an illuminist position, even cutting loose from the teaching of Jesus as recorded in the bible – which they rejected as a human document, incapable of revealing a divine God – in favour of the whisperings of the 'Christ formed in us, the deity united to our humanity'.[3]

Offensives against Antitrinitarians under the Commonwealth were part of a wider push to discipline blasphemy in all its forms. While some religious dissenters enjoyed a degree of toleration under the new regime, others, notably Antitrinitarians, were considered so blasphemous as to exclude them automatically from official toleration and clemency.[4] On 2 May 1648, the parliament passed *An ordinance for the punishing of blasphemies and heresies*, which condemned those who believed or taught

> that there is no God, or that God is not present in all places, doth not know and foreknow all things, or that he is not Almighty, that he is not perfectly Holy, or that he is not Eternall, or that the Father is not God, the Son is not God, or that the Holy Ghost is not God, or that they Three are not one eternall God: Or that shall in like manner maintaine and publish, that Christ is not God equall with the Father, or shall deny the Manhood of Christ, or that the Godhead and Manhood of Christ are severall Natures, or that the Humanity of Christ is pure and unspotted of all sinne; or that shall maintaine and publish, as aforesaid, That Christ did not Die, nor rise from the Dead, nor is ascended into Heaven bodily, or that shall deny his death is meritorious in the behalfe of Beleevers; or that shall maintaine and publish as aforesaid, That Jesus Christ is not the Sonne of God, or that the Holy Scripture [...] is not the Word of God, or that the Bodies of men shall not rise againe after they are dead, or that there is no day of Judgment after death.

Anyone found guilty of teaching or publicising such beliefs, who subsequently refused to recant, was to be executed without benefit of clergy.[5] Although the death penalty was never imposed under the terms of this ordinance, the threat was still perceived as real. It also reinforced the conviction – if anyone had ever doubted it – that religion and the state were not to be separated. However, such measures were only partially effective in preventing the publication of Socinian writings in Britain. In 1651, the London printer William Dugard published Samuel Przypkowski's

---

[3] T. Edwards 1646a, 18–21; cf. Dixon 2003, 37.
[4] Ruston 2005; Capp 2012, 87–92.
[5] *An Ordinance* 1648; cf. Lim 2012, 40–41.

edition of the Racovian catechism and biography of Fausto Sozzini, with a false Raków imprint. Dugard naively entered the work in the Stationers' Register on 13 November 1651, and was arrested on 27 January 1652. As a result of the ensuing investigation, Dugard requested on 29 January that the book be removed from the Register.[6] But within a matter of months, another London printer had released an English translation of the Racovian catechism, probably made by John Biddle, which appeared with a false Amsterdam imprint.[7] In response, parliament voted on 2 April 1652 that 'the Sheriffs of *London* and *Middlesex* be authorized and required to seize all the printed Copies of [...] *The Racovian Catechism*, whereso-ever they shall be found, and cause the same to be burnt [...]'.[8] Besides the Racovian catechism, English Antitrinitarians eagerly read the system-atic and apologetic treatises of their continental counterparts.

Conversion to Socinianism or Unitarianism often came after close study of the Scripture. It frequently presupposed a way of reading the text cut loose from the canons of interpretation developed within the church. Given the social stigma attaching to a repudiation of Trinitarianism, those who came to hold such a position out of religious scruples had to be sure that they had made the right decision. The following testimonial, published *c.* 1687, describes the intellectual and affective conversion of William Freke, an account comparable in its sense of conviction and mis-sion to anything by John Bunyan. In conversation, an acquaintance men-tioned to Freke that some people believed that the doctrine of the Trinity is not revealed in the New Testament, and is in fact an affront to the first commandment. Freke's initial reaction was violent rejection, but further consideration led him to a conversion of both head and heart. In London he looked for books that might resolve his doubts, but found none:

> whereupon resolving to know that by myself, which I could not by others, without either knowing of Arrianism, Socinianism, or Platonism, I took this following course: I took the New Testament, where I conceived this Truth was to be found reveal'd, if any where, and reading it with atten-tion I collected every Text relating to Father, Son, and Holy Ghost, into an Imperial Sheet of Paper; for neither liking giddy Tradition, nor the tricks of wresting single Texts, I thought that this could be the only way to find the Truth by, if any. Now God is my Witness, that when I did thus, I could not but fall into Arrianism; not that I then knew what Name my Opinion had; but some time after meeting with Books, I saw the difference of Arrianism

[6] Briscoe-Eyre 1913–1914, 1:383; Lewalski 2000, 632.
[7] McLachlan 1951, 191.
[8] *Racovian Catechism* 1652; *Votes of Parliament* 1652.

and Socinianism; and found that I was not singular in my Sentiments, but that the World had thought the same before me.[9]

Amongst the passages Freke gathered upon the sheet of imperial paper was of course the Johannine comma. His account of the passage neatly sidesteps the issue of authenticity, and deals exclusively with interpretation. In the comma Freke found no evidence of the consubstantiality of the three divine persons, only of a unity of purpose: 'without questioning the Authority of this place, what can we rationally mean by this Text; unless One in bearing Record, according as, 1 *Cor.* 3. 8. ["The one who plants and the one who waters have a common purpose, and each will receive wages according to the labor of each"] and the Context directs?'[10] Paul Best had reached the same conclusion as he languished in the Gatehouse at Westminster in 1647 on charges of heresy.[11] Freke's account of his gradual acceptance of Arianism as the native state of Christianity and the most natural reading of Scripture – and, even more importantly, the dawning realisation that he was not alone in holding this position – would prove a powerful tool in bolstering the image of Antitrinitarianism. Indeed, William Whiston (1667–1752) would cite Freke's 'very remarkable' account in his own defence against charges of promoting Antitrinitarian heresy in 1710.[12]

Self-study arising from dissatisfaction with conventional religion led others to similar conclusions. As a boy, Thomas Firmin found England

> involved in a Bloody Civil War, and the Church divided by several Schisms, as the state was distracted by different Factions. The Laity at that time looked upon themselves to be ill used by the Leaders of both Churches, who did not seem to contend for the purity of Religion, so much as they did who should have the Rod in their hands, to jerk the poor People that were under their Power, and as it is natural for Men to run out of one extream into another, they imagin'd a cheat put upon them, even where there was no reason to suspect one.[13]

Those who recognised that traditional interpretations of doctrinally significant texts were sometimes untenable, used all the resources of textual

[9] Freke, c. 1687, 11. The only surviving copy of this edition has no title page and thus no date; the title given in the bibliography is taken from the first page of text. Neither this edition nor the 1690 reprint appears in the Stationers' Register.
[10] Freke, c. 1687, 17.
[11] Best 1647, 4–5. Further on Best's biblical studies, including his use of Erasmus, see Snobelen 2006, 121–123.
[12] Whiston 1711b, 94–95.
[13] Anon. 1698a, 15.

scholarship to defend their beliefs against hostile enemies who sometimes had the power to ruin them.[14] After spending as much time in studying the work of biblical scholars such as Hugo Grotius and Richard Simon as his considerable commercial and charitable occupations allowed, Firmin arrived at essentially a Sabellian position.[15] Firmin's heretical career bears out Alister McGrath's identification of the most characteristic features of English religious life in the latter part of the seventeenth century. McGrath notes that biblical criticism undermined traditional confidence in the reliability and intelligibility of Scripture, while the Civil War had led to distrust of the claims of the church. The conjunction of these two tendencies led many to turn for certainty either to reason or to a 'religion of nature', both of which were less closely associated with traditional dogma. This tendency led to an increasing reliance on natural theology as an apologetic tool in English religious discourse.[16]

A critical attitude towards Scripture could lead to an even more pointed critique of the established church. In his *Considerations on the explications of the doctrine of the Trinity, occasioned by four sermons preached by his grace the Lord Arch-Bishop of Canterbury*, published anonymously in 1694, Stephen Nye accused the clergy of deceiving 'the (poor *gull'd*) English Reader' by neglecting to draw attention to dubious places in Scripture such as the comma, and by using a translation based on an inadequate Greek text.[17] Amongst those who replied to Nye's vigorous polemic was Edward Stillingfleet (1635–1699), bishop of Worcester.[18] Stillingfleet, a strident opponent of Unitarianism, was ambivalent about the role Erasmus had played in the question of the comma and the consequent revival of Arianism. But Stillingfleet only had a loose control over the facts. For example, he believed that the editors of the Complutensian bible had used Erasmus' Codex Britannicus, clearly unaware that the reading of the comma in these two sources is different.[19] He also asserted that Erasmus' ultimate decision to include the comma in the third edition of his text proved that he had come to accept its textual authority.[20] Stillingfleet also failed to address the theological issue raised by Nye, which played an

[14] See Snobelen 2006, 135–136.
[15] See Philip Dixon, 'Firmin, Thomas', in *ODNB*. Firmin knew Locke, and it may have been Locke who encouraged him to send Le Clerc a copy of Biddle's *The faith of one God* for review in the *Bibliothèque universelle*; see Le Clerc 1987–1997, 2:145, n° 228.
[16] McGrath 2011, 51.
[17] Nye 1694, 29. Cf. Nye 1687, 151–153, discussed in Bietenholz 2008, 178.
[18] Further, see Marshall 2000; Barry Till, 'Stillingfleet, Edward', in *ODNB*.
[19] Stillingfleet 1697, 162–163.
[20] Stillingfleet 1697, 166.

important role in Calvinist discussions of this passage: whether the unity of the three heavenly witnesses refers to their essence or to their testimony. Stillingfleet assured Nye that while certain propositions in Christianity might be incomprehensible, they are never '*Nonsense* and *Contradictions*'. As far as the mystery of the Trinity was concerned, this had never been imposed upon the church 'by Force or Interest'.[21] The inaccuracy and vagueness of Stillingfleet's account betrays the kind of complacent confidence in the textual stability of the received text, and lack of historical insight into the development of doctrine which radical critics like Nye wanted to upset. Nevertheless, the close association in many minds between textual scepticism and heterodoxy meant that a man like Stillingfleet perceived the symbolic importance of defending disputed passages such as the comma, no matter how cursorily. Despite his imprecise knowledge of the facts, Stillingfleet made a point of discussing the comma with each of those he intended to ordain, warning them that those who assented to the Anglican liturgy, in which the comma was cited, should not 'pretend to question its being Scripture'.[22]

Several attempts were made to regulate dissent on a state level. While the *Declaration for the liberty of Conscience*, proclaimed by James II on 4 April 1687, was intended to ease the condition of Roman Catholics in Britain, it had the unintended effect of authorising the publication of Antitrinitarian tracts.[23] The *Act of Toleration*, passed by the parliament under William and Mary in 1689, expressly excluded both Catholics and Antitrinitarians from its terms. However, the freedom of the press guaranteed by the new regime led to an upsurge in the production of heterodox literature. This caused a reaction amongst conservatives. In 1694, Gilbert Burnet wrote to Jean Le Clerc that many at Oxford were 'so much sharpned by the socinian books among us that they seem now rather to lean towards Calvinisme [...]. The insolence of the Socinians is like to spoil all and the high men among us hope to make that an Argument to destroy the Tolleration that it setled by law among us which the farre greater part of the Clergy doe detest.'[24] Opposition also came from outside the established church. In 1697, a group of dissenting ministers petitioned William III to ban the publication of Socinian books.[25] In 1698, parliament debated the *Act for the more*

---

[21] Stillingfleet 1697, 10–14.
[22] Binckes 1702, 91.
[23] Snobelen 2006, 125–126.
[24] Le Clerc 1987–1997, 2:137, n° 225.
[25] Colligan 1913, 45.

effectual Suppressing of Blasphemy and Profaneness, aimed against anyone raised as a Christian who denied 'any one of the Persons in the Holy Trinity to be God or shal assert or maintain there are more Gods than One or shal deny the Christian Religion to be true or the Holy Scriptures of the Old and New Testament to be of Divine Authority'. Those who opposed the bill appealed to the twin authority of Scripture and reason, arguing that their beliefs were 'drawn out of, grounded upon, and contained in Scriptures either expressly, or deduced by a true and Right Consequence'. Moreover, they argued for a limited separation of church and state, stating that it was contrary to custom that a parliamentary act or bill should be 'penn'd in a Scriptural Phrase, for a Parliament doth not draw up Articles of Faith'. Rather, the task of parliament was to confirm any bill only once it was satisfied that it was consonant with Scripture, and to lay down penalties for its breach. Supporters of the bill dismissed such objections as 'meer *Socinianism*,' and pointed out that the *Act of Toleration* was never 'intended for those who pull up by the very Root, and destroy the Fundamentals of Christianity'. Objectors to the bill suggested that it should be couched in more explicitly Scriptural terms, and directed simply against those who 'deny any of the Three that bear Record in Heaven, the Father, the Word, or the Holy Ghost to be God'. Many people, they pointed out, 'may Believe and Own the Father, Son, and Holy Ghost to be God, according to Holy Scripture, and yet Scruple the Term *Persons*, as Unscriptural; and thereby may be, by Invidious Informers, brought under Severe Suffering for a Circumstance of Words and Terms, when they Sincerely own the Substance in Terms of Holy Scripture'. Supporters of the bill rejected this plea as mere equivocation:

> But seeing the three, who bear Record in Heaven, are also in another Text call'd, the Father, the Son, and the Holy Ghost, *Matth*. 28. 19. in whose Name we are equally Baptized, why with the whole Christian Primitive Church, shall not we call them Persons, seeing we cannot be said to be Baptized in the Name of Things, but of Persons? They who do scruple to call them Persons, take the Son and the Holy Ghost for meer Attributes; whence 'tis plain enough, that the Dispute is not barely about Words and Terms, and that they do not own the Substance, but that under those Terms, they would shelter their Poison, therefore the true meaning must be explain'd.

Religious dissenters were also dangerous. Those who undermined the doctrine of the church endangered the state, ignoring the psalmist's injunction that 'except the Lord build the City, their labour is in vain that build it'. If Britain, growing to enjoy the feel of its new military and naval muscle, rejected God, it could rely on 'no Fleets, no Militia's or Armies' to save it from its enemies.[26] Laying down a doctrinally sound interpretation of ambivalent Scriptural passages as the Johannine comma thus became a matter of national security. Despite the arguments of the objectors, the bill passed into law on 30 March 1698.[27]

The status of the comma also played into disputes over the relationship of parliament and its ecclesiastical counterpart, convocation. In his commentary on the Thirty-Nine Articles of the Church of England (1699), Gilbert Burnet (1643–1715), latitudinarian bishop of Salisbury, argued that the requirement of subscribing to the strict and complex theology expressed in the Articles imposed an intolerable hardship on clergy. He suggested that one might assent to some doctrines, such as the mystery of the Trinity, without fully understanding them. Burnet rejected the comma as the most equivocal evidence for the doctrine of the Trinity in all Scripture. The doctrine had no need of such support, and could be proven 'whether that Passage is believed to be a part of the Canon, or not'.[28] Burnet had a detailed knowledge of the opinions of those who had previously written on the comma, and wherever he went during his three-year exile (1685–1688), whether Zürich, Basel, Geneva, Venice, Florence, Strasbourg or Rome, he had examined 'all the Antient Manuscripts of the New Testament, concerning that doubted passage of St John's Epistle', noting the variant readings of the comma and the presence or absence of the prologue to the Catholic Epistles.[29] The minuteness of Burnet's observations testifies to his conviction that the biblical scholar must be a historian and a philologist, obliged equally to use documents and to avoid exceeding the boundaries of what could be inferred from them.

After the publication of his *Exposition of the Thirty-Nine Articles*, the high-church party accused Burnet of sympathising with the Socinians, dissenters and freethinkers.[30] Some feared that Burnet's account of Christianity could lead equally to orthodox or heterodox conclusions, especially in matters of Christology. The high-church party therefore pushed for convocation to use its constitutional powers to settle the religious controversies of the time – rationalism, deism, Antitrinitarianism,

---

[26] Anon. 1698b, 1; Anon. 1698c, 1–2.

[27] *Statutes of the Realm* 1810–1828, 7:409; on the course of the parliamentary debate, see Graham 2008, 145–146.

[28] Burnet 1699, 40. Further, see Martin Greig, 'Burnet, Gilbert', in *ODNB*.

[29] Burnet 1686, 53–55.

[30] Further, see Greig 1994, who, mistakenly believing that Bincke's work was never published, used the extracts in London, BL Add. ms 4238, 53–59.

scholarly scepticism over the historicity and authorship of the bible – with a definitive doctrinal statement. Where Burnet suggested that the requirement that clergy subscribe to the Thirty-Nine Articles should be relaxed, his opponents reaffirmed the provisions in the Test Acts (1661, 1672 and 1678) prescribing that public office was only to be held by communicant Anglicans. Burnet's high-church opponents also complained that his *History of the Reformation of the Church of England* (1679–1681) compromised the church's independence. These ecclesiastical disputes were not simply internal, but also reflected broader political instabilities. The high-church party was dominant in the lower house of convocation, and aligned with the Tory party in parliament. The agitation of high-church activists like William Binckes and Francis Atterbury coincided with a crisis within the Whig party in parliament, with whom latitudinarians like Burnet were associated. Burnet's conviction that the reins of ecclesiastical power were held ultimately by the state was anathema to those like Atterbury who wished to see church governance remain in the hands of convocation.

In an anonymous broadside, William Binckes, prebendary of Lichfield, agitated for an official censure of Burnet's *Exposition*. Binckes deplored Burnet's account of his manuscript studies of the comma on the continent. In denying the authenticity of the comma, Burnet had trampled upon the sixth of the Thirty-Nine Articles, which lays down that the books of Scripture are to be accepted as canonical in every part. Moreover, he had showed contempt for the custom of the Church of England, which accepted the comma as part of its liturgy. He had also made room for heretics: what he had written about 'the Text of St. *John* under the first Article, the *Socinian* is certainly very much oblig'd to his Lordship for'. Furthermore, by elevating natural reason over revelation, Burnet had removed the principal means of distinguishing orthodox belief from the various heresies espoused by dissenters.[31] John Hoadly, Burnet's chaplain, wrote a defence in which he argued that the only way to break the stalemate between the established church and dissenters was for the church to relax the requirement of subscription. Responding to Binckes' denunciation of Burnet's conclusions on the comma, Hoadly satirically supposed that the bishop's enemies would have the sixth of the Thirty-Nine Articles altered to read as follows:

> Whoever says, that the Text in St. *John*'s *Epistle*, c. 5. 7. is not in the Manuscript at *Zurich*, or in those two at *Basil*, or at *Strasburg*, and thinks,

---

[31] Binckes 1702, 18–19, 56; further, see Gibson 2006a; and Tony Claydon, 'Binckes, William', in *ODNB*.

though there are considerable things urged to support its Authority, yet that it is safer to build upon sure and indisputable Grounds, favours *Socinians*, does not believe the Canonical Scriptures, and cannot honestly Subscribe to them.[32]

In order to forestall doubt about the ancient attestation of the comma, Edward Welchman included the passages from Tertullian and Cyprian widely believed to contain references to the comma in his 1713 patristic commentary on the Thirty-Nine Articles.[33]

The struggle to impose a uniform doctrine of the Trinity had several causes. John Bunyan spoke for many when he claimed that those who denied Jesus' equality with the Father undermined the doctrine of the atonement, thus gnawing away at hopes of salvation.[34] Many believed that the 'complicate errour of the Socinians sprung from Mahometism', thus associating an enemy within with an external foe whose military advance threatened Europe.[35] Early modern divines were convinced that personal piety and effective prayer depended upon a proper conception of God. If we are not to fall into wrong belief, we must know what kind of God we address, worship and obey. Recognising the actions of each of the persons of God in creating, redeeming and sanctifying us inspires us to love and fear God, and to imitate the Spirit who sanctifies us. Moreover, recognising the true nature of the Trinity saves us from common but mistaken conceptions of the divine, like those who 'conceiue GOD to be like *an old Man sitting in a chaire*: and the blessed *Trinitie* to be like that *tripartite Idoll*, which Papists haue painted in their Church-windowes', as Lewis Bayly put it.[36] And correct religious belief could only flow from correct beliefs about the Scriptures. This anxiety about correct belief is symptomatic of the normative power of documents such as the Thirty-Nine Articles. Those who doubted or repudiated such norms were treated as deviant, and thus liable to exclusion and punishment.

Over time, the contexts in which the status of the Johannine comma was discussed became more diverse. In the early period of the debate, much of the discussion took place in polemical works between Erasmus and his opponents. In the later sixteenth and seventeenth century, discussion moved to the field of critical and theological biblical commentary,

[32] Hoadly 1703, 57.
[33] Welchman 1713, 2 (article 1), 6 (article 5).
[34] Seager 2014.
[35] Leigh 1656, 9; cf. Cheynell 1650, 425; Leslie 1708, 28.
[36] Bayly 1613, 66; cf. Dixon 2003, 9.

most of it in Latin. This remained an important locus for debate, especially as dissenters such as Socinians used biblical commentary as a forum for justifying their theological positions through recourse to Scripture. Developments in biblical criticism from France and the Low Countries had an electrifying effect on religious discourse in England, and strengthened the first wave of Antitrinitarian thought. The importance of sacred philology as a location for the discussion of theological issues is illustrated in the discussions that arose in England in reaction to the work of Simon, Mill and Bentley. Radical English critics such as Whiston unwittingly provoked a revival of interest in biblical criticism in Germany under Semler and Griesbach, and German advances in turn fed back into English criticism in the nineteenth century.

As the seventeenth century advanced, the pulpit became more important as a locus of discussion. John Evelyn first heard a sermon against Socinianism in 1659, but makes no further note of another until 1679. However, references to anti-Socinian sermons become more frequent in Evelyn's diaries in the 1690s. Although it is difficult to derive a general trend from Evelyn's report of his own experiences, the fact that he mentions Socinianism more frequently in the 1690s than previously nevertheless suggests a increase in public awareness of Socinianism towards the end of the seventeenth century.[37] In the decades around 1700, many Protestant preachers delivered sermons dealing exclusively or in part with the comma, invariably from a theological perspective.[38] Typical is one delivered by William Howell at St Mary's Oxford on 13 May 1711. Howell asserted that while the doctrine of the Trinity 'may be abundantly Confirm'd from divers other plain texts of Scripture', the comma expressed the doctrine so clearly as to render other verses 'needless'. In fact, Howell would not have quoted any other passages beside the comma, 'had not our Adversaries rejected this, as foisted into the Sacred pages by the Trinitarian Patrons, because some copies of St. *John's* Epistle (bearing some face of Antiquity,) are found without it'.[39] Such a nonchalant dismissal of the hard-won conclusions of two centuries of scholarship betrays the disappointingly low

[37] Evelyn 1959, 13 February 1659, 15 June 1679, 19 July 1691, 19 May 1695, 2 July 1699, 26 May 1700; cit. Dixon 2003, 30–31.
[38] Patrick 1675; Howard 1700; Howell 1711; Boys 1716; Calamy 1722; Atkinson 1726; Wesley 1775, repr. 1776, 1783, 1784, 1789, 1792, 1803, 1805, 1812, 1813, 1816 and in further collected volumes; Burder 1805, repr. in collected volumes; Swift's sermon, analysed in the following text, is undated, but was first published in 1744.
[39] Howell 1711, 4–5.

intellectual level that could sometimes characterise sermons, even in centres of learning such as Oxford.

Although the sermon is ostensibly a monological genre, it could become dialogical when it provoked a response, either oral or written, from those who listened. A more obviously dialogical venue for discussing theological issues was personal correspondence. As the Republic of Letters expanded, correspondence dealing with various aspects of the debate over the comma criss-crossed Europe. In an age when some ostensibly private correspondence was written with an eye to potential publication, the line between private and public was easily crossed. In 1734, Thomas Dawson published a letter he had addressed to the Italian patristic scholar Scipione Maffei, in which he complained that English deists and freethinkers like Thomas Emlyn denied that the Latin bible text used by Cassiodorus contained the comma.[40] In order to refute their assertions, Dawson carefully examined the evidence from the Old Latin translation as recorded by such authors as Bede.[41]

The border between private and public was particularly permeable in the coffee-house, where conversations could be overheard and reported. Although Locke believed that 'Coffee-houses and Publick Tables are not proper Places for serious Discourses relating to the Most Important Truths', Charles Leslie complained in 1708 that he had 'heard *Socinianism* by Name Openly Defended in Publick *Coffee-Houses*, and the Persons own themselves to be *Socinians*, and no Notice taken!'[42] But sometimes notice was taken. When William Whiston was tried for promoting Arianism in 1710, he protested that 'Words spoken in private Conversation, or at a Coffee-house, or [written] in a private Letter', were not admissible in evidence.[43] And later, when John Simson, suspended from his chair in divinity at Glasgow in 1728 for alleged sympathies to Sabellianism, was pointed out at Hamlin's coffee-house in London, Whiston declined to speak to him, 'lest so small a Conversation should be a Foundation of a farther Accusation against him in his own Country'.[44] The openness of the coffee-house, which contributed so much to the formation of the public sphere, could be a double-edged sword when conversation was monitored

---

[40] Maffei had edited Cassiodorus' *Complexiones* in 1721.
[41] Dawson 1734; cf. Bede, *Super epistolas catholicas expositio, ad* 1 Jn 5:7–8, *CCSL* 121:321–322, ll. 84–111 (*PL* 93:114).
[42] Locke to William Molyneux, 27 May 1697, Locke 1976–1989, 6:132; Leslie 1708, 40.
[43] Whiston 1711–1712, 1:clvi.
[44] Whiston 1749–1750, 1:328.

and reported. And coffee-house discussion could easily become the means for the replication and hardening of hegemonic ideas and practices.[45]

Radical discussion of textual and theological issues also took place in closed circles. After Newton withdrew his *Historical Account of Two Notable Corruptions of the Scripture* (1 Jn 5:7–8 and 1 Tim 3:16) from publication at the last moment, he circulated it in manuscript and discussed its contents in a small group of his friends. After an incomplete copy was discovered after Newton's death, further copies were made, but the work remained unknown to the broader public until it was printed in 1754.

When Edward Gibbon inserted a short account of the Johannine comma in his *History* (1781), the issue flared up as never before. While George Travis' theologically motivated refutation of Gibbon was hobbled by Porson, Marsh and Pappelbaum, the reaction of the public, primed by pulpit oratory, was less predictable and uniform, and Travis found many supporters amongst the laity. Over the next half-century, literary journals ran dozens of book reviews, letters and articles concerning the comma, reflecting and stimulating further discussion within the public sphere. Those who contributed to such discussions employed reason, irony and even ridicule, lending the disputes of the late eighteenth century a pungency absent from previous polemic.

In Germany, the situation was a little different. Until the late eighteenth century, the status of the comma was discussed there primarily in formal disputations within (mainly Protestant) faculties of theology, held in Latin and thus restricted to a limited sphere. These disputations invariably defended the comma as genuine, or at least as theologically authentic.[46] In a 1619 disputation, Johann Gerhard argued that even if the comma is not genuine, it nevertheless expresses the same theological essence as other passages of undoubted canonicity, such as Mt 28:19. Dissertations written in conjunction with disputations tended to be short, and since they were aimed at establishing the candidate's mastery of orthodox theology and ability to weigh the many arguments already brought on both sides of the issue, they rarely broke new ground. The recursive nature of the discussion in Germany is illustrated by the fact that Gerhard's 1619 dissertation on the comma was reprinted in 1714, 1721, 1746 and 1747.

---

[45] Further, see Habermas 1989.
[46] Gerhard 1619, repr. 1714, 1721, 1746, 1747; Steuber 1640; Dorsche 1653; Reinhart 1666, repr. 1703; Dauderstadt 1674; Grabe 1675–1677, repr. 1717; Meinelff 1690; Kettner 1696; Wilhelmi 1715; Wagner 1740, repr. 1752; Rappolt 1745; Semler 1750; Pfeiffer 1743; Gerhard 1763; Pfeiffer 1764; Hofmann 1766; Jäger 1767; Pfeiffer, c. 1767–1772. By contrast, the comma was rejected as spurious by Maertens 1725, 3.

Sometimes academic debate spilled into the public sphere. Reviewing
the New Testament volume of the *Biblia pentapla* (1710–1712), which provided four parallel German translations and one in Dutch, Valentin Ernst
Löscher condemned the inclusion of a note on Luther's exclusion of the
comma, arguing that critics had established the authenticity of the passage
beyond any shadow of doubt. Behind Löscher's critique lurks the anxiety that the Pietist translator Johann Heinrich Reitz had let the genie out
of the academic bottle by alerting a vernacular readership to the disputes
over textual criticism.[47] In a vernacular defence of the divinity of Christ
(1714), Bartholomäus Kannegiesser argued that the Arians of the fourth
century had removed the comma from all the manuscripts they could get
their hands on, but Erasmus had managed to salvage the reading from a
'very ancient British codex'. However, latter-day Arians were trying once
again to undermine the authenticity and authority of the passage.[48]

As biblical scholarship advanced in Germany, especially at the hands
of scholars such as Johann David Michaelis (1717–1791), Johann Salomo
Semler (1725–1791) and Johann Jakob Griesbach (1745–1812), it became
increasingly more difficult to defend the comma. But consensus was not
reached overnight. When Semler first published his doubts about the genuineness of the comma in 1761, debate in Germany became so heated that
three disputations in quick succession had to counsel prudence and moderation.[49] However, Semler's fuller account of the issue (1764) more or
less settled the issue in Germany, and exchanges became less frequent and
more civil. By the 1780s, German philologists, historians, poets and peda-
gogues had managed to wrest the bible free of theology, while maintaining
its position as an important part of culture.[50] A defence of the comma by
Franz Anton Knittel (1785) and an exchange between Wilhelm Friedrich
Hezel and Griesbach in the 1790s were amongst the few extended treat-
ments of the subject in German to appear in the last third of the eighteenth
century. As a result, public discussion – and personal investment – in this
issue was less widespread in Germany than in Britain.

1.   The beginnings of the Socinian controversy in England

In summer 1645, the radical clergyman William Erbery (1604/5–1654)
stopped at Marlborough. The country was in the grip of the Civil War,

47 Löscher 1710, 617–617; cf. *Das Neue Testament* 1710, 799. Further, see Sheehan 2005, 57–58.
48 Kannegiesser 1714, 430–434.
49 Gerhard 1763; Hofmann 1766; Jäger 1767.
50 Sheehan 2005, 220.

crippled by political uncertainty and religious division. Erbery visited a 'house where commonly once a week many good people of that Town [met] together to confer and discourse of good things'. Here he 'declared his opinions, venting himself against Christ being God, affirming he was only man, pleading for universal Redemption, speaking against Baptism & all ministry', and accusing his audience 'that they knew not what to do without a man in black cloathes', a performance which caused considerable consternation in the assembly. When Erbery denied Jesus' divinity, some of those gathered cited passages of Scripture against him, including the Johannine comma, 'unto which Master *Erbury* replyed, it was not so in the Originall; but some of the people re-joyned they knew not the Originall, but they beleeved it was so; and however they were assured that he was the Sonne of God: Master *Erbury* objected again, those words were not in the Greek, but put in by some who were against the Arrians.'[51] The presentation of such ideas to people who by their own confession 'knew not the Originall' could hardly fail to arouse hostility; 'and so the meeting broke up, the people who met, being much offended at him'.[52] This vignette provides a dramatic picture of the uncertainty and anger that could be provoked when the most basic tenets of the bible and the Christian religion, the last refuge of a country torn apart by war, were challenged by those whose approach to Scripture had been fundamentally reoriented by the kind of biblical criticism begun by Erasmus and developed by radicals such as Sozzini.

Socinianism appealed to English Protestants in the confusion of the war. Like the Dutch Calvinist Jacobus Arminius, Sozzini maintained that humans have the freedom to cooperate with divine grace, and when they do, human nature and the material conditions of human life can be improved. The Socinian theory of non-resistance would also condition reactions to Socinianism during the English Civil War, as Sarah Mortimer has shown. In England, Socinian ideas refused to align neatly along previous doctrinal lines, and the presence of Socinianism thus made complex debates, such as those between Puritans and Laudians, even more so. This was partly because English Socinians were reacting both to the English religious scene and also to issues raging over the Channel, such as the Remonstrant debate.[53]

---

[51] T. Edwards 1646c, 89–90; further, see Stephen K. Roberts, 'Erbery [Erbury], William', in *ODNB*. Erbery's *Testament* lays out the kinds of arguments he will have presented to the people of Marlborough; see Erbery 1658, 119.

[52] T. Edwards 1646c, 90.

[53] Mortimer 2010, 206, 214–222, 236.

A shared appeal to Scripture as the canon for doctrine and belief united Socinians and orthodox Protestants. Yet from this one source they drew different results. In 1647, the Socinian John Biddle published a short tract in which he professed to lay out the evidence from Scripture that shows that the Holy Spirit is not God. The work was evidently popular, for it was reprinted the same year. Biddle's exposition of 1 Jn 5:7–8 shows the influence of the Racovian catechism; indeed, the English translation of the catechism which appeared in 1652 has been attributed to Biddle. He declined to discuss in detail 'the suspectednesse of this place, how it is not exant in the ancient Greek Coppies, nor in the Syriack Translation, nor in most ancient Books of the Latine Edition, and rejected by sundry Interpreters both Ancient and Mordern [sic]'. He denied that the unity of the heavenly witnesses was a 'union in Essence', 'since such an Exposition is not only contrary to common sence, but also to other places of the Scripture, wherein this kind of speaking prepetually [sic] signifyeth an union in consent and agreement'. His opinion that the phrase εἰς τὸ ἕν εἰσιν is a Hebraism is apparently derived from Erasmus' annotation on the comma.[54] In 1654, Biddle published a pair of his own catechisms, one for adults and a shorter one for children. In both, the responses consist exclusively of verses from the bible. Controversially, the word 'Trinity' does not occur at all in the longer catechism. However, in the children's catechism Biddle set out to show that 'God is not the whole Trinity, but one Person thereof,' for which he cited 1 Cor 12:4–6 and 2 Cor 13:13 as evidence.[55]

John Owen (1616–1683), dean of Christ Church and vice-chancellor of Oxford, condemned Biddle's catechisms as theologically inadequate. For Owen, Biddle was right to confess that there is but one God, but he had forgotten an important detail: 'that *there are Three that beare witnesse in Heaven, the Father, Word, and Spirit, and that these Three are one*'.[56] The Puritan Francis Cheynell (1608–1665) agreed that the comma was indispensible for proving both the equality and the distinctness of both these divine persons against the Socinians, who questioned the divinity of Christ and even the identity of the Holy Spirit as a distinct divine person.[57] For Owen, the Socinian understanding of Christ was self-contradictory, for it denied that he is fully divine in the same sense as God, yet maintained that

---

[54] Biddle 1647, 15. Biddle's assertion that the Complutensian bible reads εἰς τὸ ἕν εἰσιν in both vv. 7 and 8 is an error. Further on Biddle, see Snobelen 2006, 123–124.

[55] Biddle 1654b, 15–16.

[56] Owen 1655, 47.

[57] Cheynell 1650, 281. Further, see Reid 1811, 229; Roger Pooley, 'Cheynell, Francis', in *ODNB*.

he ought to be worshipped. The equality of Christ with God is revealed in the Johannine comma: 'So then is he to be worshiped.'[58] For Owen and Cheynell, the Johannine comma was *the* Scriptural proof text for demonstrating the perfect ontological unity of the three persons of the Trinity and the necessity of worshipping all three persons equally.

The Puritan hymnodist William Barton (*c.* 1598–1678) responded to Owen's call to worship the Trinity of three coequal persons with the following verses:

> Three witnesses there are above,
> > and all these three are one:
> The father, Son and sacred dove,
> > one Deity alone.
> The Living father sent the son,
> > who by the Father lives:
> And unto them that ask of him
> > the holy Ghost he gives.[59]

Barton interpreted those passages of Scripture in which Jesus refers to the Father and the Holy Spirit (such as Lk 11:13) as evidence for the essential unity of the three persons of the Trinity, a proposition most fully expressed by the comma. Casting this association into verses to be sung to well-known hymn tunes ensured that it would be remembered by the faithful. This is not to say that Puritan reaction to the comma was uniform. Despite his desire to confute Socinianism 'and to confirm the people in the Doctrine of the true Faith that Christ is God', Thomas Edwards was embarrassed by the strength of the critical arguments against the authenticity of the comma, and preferred to rely on other evidence: 'there are so many other places as that in 1 *John* 5. 20 *&c.* of which there can be no such questions, which prove Christ to be God.'[60]

Erbery's unsuccessful attempt to introduce Antitrinitarian ideas to Marlborough and the vigorous tracts against Socinianism by the Puritan divines show that the question of the textual authority of the comma had become a virtually indispensable part of the debates over the doctrine of the Trinity in mid- seventeenth-century England, though Edwards shows that Puritans were not always convinced by the evidence for its authenticity. Barton's hymn shows how orthodox clergy imprinted the comma firmly in the collective memory of the faithful by means of metre and melody.

---

[58] Owen 1655, 421–422.
[59] Barton 1659, 98, hymn XC; the original erroneously reads *fathers* in line 6. See also Dixon 2003, 20.
[60] T. Edwards 1646c, 90–92.

2. John Milton

Cheynell's fear that the seed of Socinianism had begun to spring up in England was borne out by the unpublished theological treatise *De doctrina Christiana* by John Milton (1608–1674). In this work, drafted during the Commonwealth, Milton characterised the orthodox doctrine of the Trinity as 'a mere verbal quibble, founded on the use of synonymous words, and cunningly dressed up in terms borrowed from the Greek to dazzle the eyes of novices'.[61] For Milton, it made no sense in metaphysics to say that Jesus and God were of one essence. Everything is distinguished from other things by its essence. If God has one hypostasis, he must have his own essence, which cannot be shared with or communicated to anything else. If the Son has his own hypostasis, he cannot also have the same essence as the Father. Those who insist that the Son has the same essence as the Father must conclude either that he is the same *ens* as the Father, or that he is no *ens* at all, a conclusion that 'strikes at the very foundation of the Christian religion'.[62] Milton suggested furthermore that those passages of Scripture normally cited to prove the essential unity of God and Jesus do no such thing. When Jesus says that he is one with the Father (Jn 10:30, 10:38, 14:10), he means that they have one will or purpose, not that they are of one essence. Furthermore, several sayings recorded in the fourth gospel suggest that Jesus considered himself both distinct from and subordinate to the Father (Jn 5:23, 5:35, 14:20–21, 14:28, 17:21). If it is true that there is only one God, then that God must be the Father. If the Son is also called God, he 'must have received the name and nature of Deity from God the Father, in conformity with his decree and will'.[63] Reason thus leads us to conclude that Jesus was ontologically subordinate to the Father. The radical Lawrence Clarkson (1615–1667) likewise declared that 'right Reason is the rule of Faith'. We are therefore obliged 'to beleeve the Scriptures, and the Doctrine of the Trinity, Incarnation, Resurrection, so far as we see them agreeable to reason, and no farther'.[64] But in such a world, what room was left for faith?

[61] Milton 1825b, 98; cf. Milton 1825a, 70. Milton's authorship of this treatise is established in Campbell et al. 2007; see esp. 98–101 on Milton's critique of Trinitarian belief.
[62] Milton 1825b, 99; cf. Milton 1825a, 70.
[63] Milton 1825b, 97; cf. Milton 1825a, 69.
[64] Lawrence Clarkson, *The Pilgrimage of Saints, by Church cast out, in Christ found seeking truth* (1646); no copies are known, but its arguments are recorded by T. Edwards 1646a, 19; see also Dixon 2003, 37.

Milton rejected appeals to the Johannine comma as evidence of the essential unity of the Father, Son and Holy Spirit. First, he pointed out that the comma, absent from the majority of Greek manuscripts as well as from the Arabic and Ethiopic versions, rests upon shaky textual foundations. Even assuming that the comma is genuine, the passage still does little to help the Trinitarian case. Both Erasmus and Bèze acknowledged that since the unity of water, blood and Spirit can only be one of witness, not essence, then the same must be the case for the heavenly witnesses, if indeed the comma is genuine at all.[65] Moreover, the testimony of the heavenly witnesses – that those who believe that Jesus is the anointed one, the Son of God, will overcome the world – leads naturally to a subordinationist position, since he who is anointed cannot be identical in essence or equal to him who does the anointing. 'Thus the very record that they bear is inconsistent with the essential unity of the witnesses, which is attempted to be deduced from the passage.'[66] If we accept that Jesus is not coessential with the Father or equal to him, then the comma raises yet another theological difficulty: who exactly are these heavenly witnesses? 'That they are three Gods, will not be admitted; therefore neither is it the one God, but one record or one testimony of three witnesses, which is implied. But he who is not coessential with God the Father, cannot be coequal with the Father.'[67] As Milton had already argued that the Spirit likewise cannot be equal to the Father, since the Spirit proceeds from the Father, 'it follows, therefore, that these three are not one in essence.'[68]

For Milton, the appearance of the Spirit amongst both the earthly and the heavenly witnesses was problematic: is this one Spirit or two? Elsewhere in the New Testament we hear that the Holy Spirit gives witness on earth, that is, in our hearts, but never in heaven. Likewise, Jesus (Jn 8:16, Jn 8:19) says that he bears witness to himself, and that the Father also bears witness to him, but nowhere in the Gospels does Jesus mention that the Spirit bears witness to him. 'Why then, in addition to two other perfectly competent witnesses, should the Spirit twice bear witness to the same thing? On the other hand, if it be another Spirit, we have here a new and unheard-of doctrine.' The theological difficulties arising from the double appearance of the Spirit confirmed Milton's conviction that the comma is an interpolation.

---

[65] Milton 1825b, 96; cf. Milton 1825a, 68.
[66] Milton 1825b, 170; cf. Milton 1825a, 122–123.
[67] Milton 1825b, 97; cf. Milton 1825a, 68.
[68] Milton 1825b, 171; cf. Milton 1825a, 123.

Milton brought his patient and sophisticated arguments against the comma as part of a larger argument for the fundamental instability of Trinitarian theology. 'There are besides other circumstances, which in the opinion of many render the passage suspicious; and yet it is on the authority of this text, almost exclusively, that the whole doctrine of the Trinity has been hastily adopted.'[69] Given the censure that such opinions would inevitably have brought down upon his head, it was prudent of Milton to have consigned this treatise to the bottom drawer.

3. Thomas Hobbes

In his *Leviathan* (1651), the political philosopher Thomas Hobbes (1588–1679) provided one of the most original interpretations of the Johannine comma yet offered. Hobbes made no reference to the critical controversy surrounding the comma, but employed the passage in his strikingly original interpretation of the three persons of the Trinity. His interpretation hung on his understanding of the word 'person', a critical issue in seventeenth-century discussions of both theology and politics.[70] In *Leviathan* I.14, Hobbes rejected the classic definition of person as an 'individual substance of a rational nature' (*naturae rationalis individua substantia*).[71] Rather, he based his definition of persons on the Roman notion of the *persona* as the mask worn by actors. As an advocate, wrote Cicero, 'I beare three Persons; my own, my Adversaries, and the Judges' (*De oratore* II.24.102). For Hobbes, then, a person is someone acting on their own behalf, or on behalf of another. This notion can be extended even to God, who has been 'personated' by three others in the course of human history:

> first, by *Moses*; who governed the Israelites, (that were not his, but Gods people,) not in his own name, with *Hoc Dicit Moses*; but in Gods Name, with *Hoc Dicit Dominus*. Secondly, by the son of man, his own Son our Blessed Saviour *Jesus Christ*, that came to reduce [that is, lead back] the Jewes, and induce [that is, lead in] all Nations into the Kingdom of his

---

[69] Milton 1825b, 171; cf. Milton 1825a, 123.
[70] Dixon 2003, 3; Skinner 2007.
[71] This definition is taken from Boethius, first cited by Peter Abaelard in *Theologia Christiana* III, written in the 1120s, *PL* 178:1258. Boethius' definition was subsequently applied by Simon of Tournai to individual human souls; ed. Schmaus 1932, 60. This definition became canonical in the later Middle Ages, but the way it was understood underwent substantial alteration, for example by Aquinas, *Summa theol.* III, q. XVI, a. 12. By returning to the forensic definition of *persona*, Hobbes recalled the original context of Abaelard's discussion, probably without knowing it.

Father; not as of himselfe, but as sent from his Father. And thirdly, by the Holy Ghost, or Comforter, speaking, and working in the Apostles: which Holy Ghost, was a Comforter that came not of himself; but was sent, and proceeded from them both.[72]

In his remarks on the Trinity (III.42), Hobbes extended this definition:

> God, who has been Represented (that is, Personated) thrice, may properly enough be said to be three Persons; though neither the word *Person*, nor *Trinity* be ascribed to him in the Bible. St. *John* indeed (1 Epist. 5.7.) saith, *There be three that bear witness in heaven, the Father, the Word, and the Holy Spirit; and these Three are One*: But this disagreeth not, but accordeth fitly with three Persons in the proper signification of Persons; which is, that which is Represented by another.

God, 'personated' as Father by Moses, is one person. God, as 'personated' by Jesus, is another person. God, as 'personated' by the apostles who had received the Holy Spirit and preached the risen Christ (Acts 1:21–22), and by the doctors of the church who derived their authority from the apostles, is yet a third person. These three persons bear witness that God has given us eternal life in his Son (1 Jn 5:11). The three earthly witnesses, 'that is to say, the graces of Gods Spirit, and the two Sacraments, Baptisme, and the Lords Supper', likewise agree in one testimony to assure believers of eternal life in the Son of man (1 Jn 5:10). However, Hobbes makes a fundamental distinction between the unity of the two sets of three witnesses. Those on earth are one merely in witness; they 'are not the same substance, though they give the same testimony'. However, the three heavenly witnesses are one in essence: 'But in the Trinity of Heaven, the Persons are the persons of one and the same God, though Represented in three different times and occasions,' that is, at Sinai in the time of Moses, in the Holy Land during the lifetime of Jesus and throughout the Roman empire in the early church. These persons are of course real humans, made of water and blood, as 1 Jn 5:6 has it. In conclusion, Hobbes remarks that the doctrine of the Trinity, 'as far as can be gathered directly from the Scripture', is that all three persons of God, as represented at various times by Moses, Jesus and the apostles, are all God. The reason why God is never spoken of in terms of personhood in the Old Testament is because this was not

---

[72] Hobbes 1651, 82. Lim 2012, 225, writes that according to Hobbes, 'it was Moses, Christ, and the Holy Spirit who comprised the Trinity.' This misunderstands Hobbes' basic definition of the person as an agent who represents someone else. Hobbes meant rather that Moses, Jesus and the Apostles 'personated' the Father, Son and Holy Spirit.

evident until he had been represented by a number of different men 'in ruling, or in directing under him'.[73]

Hobbes' conception of the Trinity was highly original. He was clearly unconcerned about steering towards Sabellian modalism, a position to which orthodox readers would object. His exegesis is consistently founded upon Scripture, and as such is fundamentally Protestant. It is also historical. Hobbes admitted that while the notions of 'person' and 'Trinity' do not occur in the Scriptures, they have nevertheless become part of Christian ways of thinking about God. Moreover, his exegesis of the comma was original. Most of those who accepted the comma as genuine related it to the immanent Trinity, that is, a way of conceiving of the Trinity which focuses exclusively on the relationship between the three persons within the godhead. By contrast, Hobbes related the comma to the economic Trinity, a way of understanding the Trinity in terms of the way the three divine persons reveal themselves to the created world, as recorded in the Old and New Testaments.

4.   Critique of the *textus receptus* and the shadow of heresy: Etienne de Courcelles and Jeremias Felbinger

The Elzevier editions of the Greek New Testament (1633 and 1641) present what has been dubbed the *textus receptus*. This text was based on the later editions of Erasmus, Robert Estienne and Bèze, which in turn drew on only a small number of relatively late manuscripts of the Byzantine text type. The *textus receptus* can thus make only a limited claim to represent the *Ausgangstext*.[74] The phrase *textus receptus* was not originally a theological term, but was used by early modern canon lawyers to designate a commonly accepted, and thus normative, form of a given legal text to which they could appeal in cases of dispute.[75] In his preface to the 1633 Elzevier edition, Daniel Heinsius first applied the term *textus receptus* to the text of the New Testament: 'Thus you have the text as received nowadays by everybody, in which we give nothing that has been altered

---

[73] Hobbes 1651, 268–269.
[74] As Wallace 2013, 723–724, points out, and Heide 2006, demonstrates in detail, the *textus receptus* departs from the Majority (or Byzantine) text in more than 1,800 places.
[75] For examples of the phrase in legal writing, see Du Moulin 1576, 13: 'Et haec veritas, quam nuper Papisticus [that is, a canon lawyer] quidam Volzius inuertere nisus est corrumpendo antiquum per quadringentos annos receptum textum.' Azpilcueta 1590, 2:616: 'Tum quia aut negandus est textus receptus ab omnibus Canonistis in d. §. leges .4. distin. aut concedendum, quod lex, quę à principio à nullis est recepta, non ligat [...].' Sánchez 1602–1605, 2:650: 'Qui textus quamuis sit ex quodam Archiepiscopo desumptus: at vsu Ecclesię quoad hoc tanquam textus receptus est.'

or corrupted.'[76] However, it took a century for this usage to catch on.[77] Protestant theologians invested the *textus receptus* with the same canonical status as their Catholic counterparts had given the Clementine Vulgate. The Greek text underlying the English Authorised Version and the Dutch *Statenvertaling* is essentially that later presented by Heinsius as the *textus receptus*, and the canonical status of those translations in their respective languages lent an even greater authority to the underlying form of the Greek text.

However, it was not long before the *textus receptus* came in for close scrutiny. A first impulse came in 1627, with the arrival in England of Codex Alexandrinus, which represented a different text-form from that familiar to that point. The extent of these differences became clear to the wider public when variants from Codex Alexandrinus were published in Walton's London Polyglot (1657).[78] This edition also contained variants from Codex Montfortianus, the manuscript from which Erasmus had drawn his reading of the comma. Sometime in the middle of the sixteenth century, Montfortianus had passed from the library of the Clements into the hands of William Chark († 1617), one of the most active Presbyterian controversialists of Elizabeth's reign.[79] He may have been a relative of Thomas Cark, gentleman of Llandysul in Cardiganshire, who in 1554 acted as Thomas Clement's sponsor for the prebends of Apesthorpe at York Minster, and Llanhennock at the collegiate church of Llanddewi Brefi in Monmouthshire.[80] If so, this could explain how the codex passed from the Clements to Chark. The codex subsequently passed into the possession of the Anglican priest Thomas Mountford (also Montforte, Mountforte), born *c.* 1547, who took his BD at Oxford in 1584, and his DD, also at Oxford, in 1588. Amongst the positions held by Mountford were chaplain to Ambrose Dudley, Earl of Warwick; canon of Westminster (1585); prebendary of St Paul's (1597); chaplain to Elizabeth I; vicar of St Martin-in-the-Fields (1602); vicar of St. Mary-at-Hill, Billingsgate (1606–1616); and rector of Tewin, Herts., where he died in 1633.[81]

---

[76] Heinsius, in Hoelzlin 1633, *2v: 'Textum ergo habes, nunc ab omnibus receptum: in quo nihil immutatum aut corruptum damus.' Further, see Metzger and Ehrman 2005, 149–152. De Jonge 1971, established that Heinsius wrote the preface to the 1633 edition; de Jonge 1978b, established that Hoelzlin edited the Greek text of the 1633 edition. The first Elzevier edition (1624) has no preface, and the editor of its Greek text is unknown.
[77] One of the first to use the term *textus receptus* after Heinsius was Wettstein 1730, 199–200.
[78] See Mandelbrote 2006.
[79] See *ASD* VI-4:58–62.
[80] Kew, National Archives E 334/4, 201r.
[81] Foster 1891–1892, 3:1043; Merritt 2005, 218–219, 311–312, 321, 331, 335, 338–339, 345–348; *ASD* VI-4:62–66.

Mountford lent the codex to Archbishop James Ussher (1581–1656), who was collecting variants of New Testament manuscripts with a view to publication.[82] In the spring of 1626, Ussher assembled a team of about three scholars at Cambridge, including Charles Chauncy and James White, to collate a number of biblical manuscripts. Ussher brought Montfortianus from London to collate it with three manuscripts at Cambridge: Codex Bezae (GA D^{ea}/05), an important manuscript from the fifth century which contains the gospels, Acts 1:1–22:29 and 3 Jn; Cambridge, Caius and Gonville College ms 403/412 (GA 59); and a manuscript owned by Henry Googe, the so-called Codex Googii (now lost).[83] Two slightly different copies of the resulting collation are extant.[84] They show that Ussher and his assistants did not collate all of Montfortianus, merely those books which are included in Codex Bezae (excluding 3 Jn), as well as a few selected readings from Rom 1. After returning to London, Ussher wrote to Samuel Ward in Cambridge on 30 June 1626, requesting him to 'intreat Mr Chancye to send hither Doctor Montfords Greek Testament MS: and whatever else he hath to send unto me [...]'.[85] It was not until Ussher later came to collect variant readings from Estienne's 1550 edition that he discovered, to his annoyance, that the earlier collation had not reached any further than 1 Jn 3:6.[86] The significance of Montfortianus was thus overlooked when its secret might have come to light.

When Ussher died in 1656, Montfortianus was still part of his collection, but it is not clear why: whether because he failed to return the manuscript, or because Mountford subsequently gave, sold or bequeathed the manuscript to him. However, Ussher was evidently unaware that the most controversial manuscript evidence for the comma, a passage he hailed as the most powerful Scriptural proof of the Trinity, nestled silently on his

---

[82] The following account of Ussher and Walton draws on *ASD* VI-4:43–45, 66–67; and Alan Ford, 'Ussher, James', in *ODNB*.

[83] On the now lost Codex Googii (Tischendorf 62^e), see Walton 1657, 6:1 (in the section entitled *Variantes lectiones Graecae Novi Testamenti*). Marsh erroneously identified this manuscript as Cambridge, University Library ms Kk.5.35; Tischendorf 1872–1894, 3:479; Gregory 1900–1909, 1:135, 143.

[84] Cambridge, Emmanuel College Cambridge ms 58, *olim* Cat. Mss. Angl. 119; Oxford, Bodleian Library ms Auct. T. 5. 30.

[85] Boran, 2015, 1:370, n° 210; Oxford, Bodleian Library ms Tanner 72, 142r–143v (original); Oxford, Bodleian Library ms Tanner 461 28r–v (copy); an incomplete text of the letter (omitting this passage) was printed in Ussher 1847–1864, 15:346. Thanks to Elizabethanne Boran for this reference.

[86] Oxford, Bodleian Library ms Auct. T. 5. 30, 370r: 'ὅτι πᾶς ὁ ἐν χριστῷ, etc.] Ista omnia, cum sequentibus sectionibus δ. ε. ϛ. ζ. in MS° nostro nusquàm comparent; nescio quo errore omissa.' The earlier collation ends on 358r.

own shelves.[87] After Ussher's death in 1656, his collection passed into the library of Trinity College, Dublin, where Codex Montfortianus continued to slumber for half a century without attracting notice.

Brian Walton included Ussher's collations in the London Polyglot, which appeared the year after Ussher's death. The codex appears in the list of Greek manuscripts under the siglum *Mont.* in honour of its former owner. In the apparatus, variants from Montfortianus are marked with the siglum *D*, as they had been in Ussher's collation.[88] But because Ussher's collation of Montfortianus was incomplete, the London Polyglot does not record variants from Montfortianus after Acts.[89] This lack was later deplored by Wettstein.[90] On the basis of the Greek inscription 'Jesus Mary Francis' on 198v, Walton conjectured correctly that Montfortianus' previous owner Froy [*sic*] was a Franciscan.[91] The London Polyglot gives the comma in the Latin and Greek texts (taken from the Antwerp Polyglot), but not in the Syriac, Ethiopic or Arabic texts. Of course Montfortianus is not mentioned as a textual witness to this controversial passage.[92] On the basis of the variants recorded in Walton's Polyglot, some seventeenth-century textual scholars, such as Thomas Marshall (1665), noted readings from Montfortianus in their own critical apparatus.[93]

In 1658, Etienne de Courcelles (Curcellaeus, 1586–1659), professor at the Remonstrant seminary in Amsterdam and friend of Descartes, edited a reprint of the *textus receptus*.[94] The impetus for his edition was probably provided by the appearance of the London Polyglot. In the preface, Courcelles complained that most earlier editions of the Greek New Testament, including those of the Elzeviers, presented a text whose smoothness, a figment of the editor's private judgements, gave the misleading impression of stability and reliability. However, he noted that

---

[87] Ussher 1645, 77–78.

[88] *ASD* VI-2:43.

[89] Dobbin 1854, 20–21.

[90] Wettstein 1730, 150: '[…] Codex Angl. XXXII. Montfortii dictus, qui totum N. T. continet, non nisi in Euangeliis & Actis cum editis collatus est, neglectis Epistoliis cum Apocalypsi […].' The description of Montfortianus in Wettstein 1730, 52, is based on Mill 1707, cxlviii, but adds a little new information.

[91] Oxford, Bodleian Library MS. Auct. T. 5, 15r, cit. earlier; cf. *ASD* VI-2:44 n. 36.

[92] Walton 1657, 5:922–923.

[93] Marshall notes two related variants from Montfortianus (Mk 12:25 and Lk 22:43) in the notes to his edition of the Anglo-Saxon Gospels: see Junius and Marshall 1665, 502, 505. The edition of Junius and Marshall, despite the scholarly plaudits it attracted, must have sold poorly, since in 1684 it was re-issued with a newly set first gathering (including a new title page with new date) to give the appearance of a new edition.

[94] On Courcelles' 1685 edition and the later editions based upon it, see Rump 1730, 279–280; Reuss 1872, 129–131; Jülicher 1906, 567; de Jonge 1980a, 24.

anyone who has worked with early manuscripts or the Scriptural citations of the fathers knew that the biblical text is in a bewildering state of flux. Variants are of different kinds. Some arose when copyists were careless or made misguided 'improvements'. But other variants, he continued, are more valuable. It was not the job of publishers, nor of the scholars who supervised print shops, to obtrude their own editorial preferences upon readers and sweep all other evidence under the carpet. (Courcelles, who had worked for the printer Jan Blaauw, spoke from experience.) Rather, they should present all the important variant readings in the margins, and give readers the chance to come to their own conclusions. 'It makes no difference how learned those men were, they did not have right – nor in my opinion did they want to arrogate this right to themselves – to prescribe to everyone else what they themselves judged good or bad.' In Courcelles' opinion, editors of the Scriptures must be as diligent as the editors of literary or legal texts in recording every detail, no matter how insignificant they might seem. No responsible publisher should release editions of the bible that lacked a critical apparatus.

Courcelles also complained that recent editors had failed to improve much on their textual models, which were already a century old. The editors of the Complutensian Polyglot failed to record any variant readings, which gave the misleading impression that all their manuscripts were in agreement, 'whereas it may easily be conjectured from those which one generally encounters that those who made the collations were presented with not inconsiderable variation'. Yet Plantin took this critically inadequate text as the basis for his *biblia regia*. Courcelles also criticised Estienne for failing to include all the variants present in the manuscripts he consulted. Bèze, Courcelles' former teacher, had become aware of this defect in Estienne's method when he reviewed his sources, yet even he withheld material from publication. Estienne sometimes followed readings from the Complutensian edition against the majority of his manuscripts he had consulted, even some which, to judge from his critical apparatus, seem not to have been attested in any of his manuscripts. Courcelles replied to those who feared that the presence of variant readings in an edition would undermine belief in the reliability of the Scripture, that instead they should hesitate before using a text *without* a critical apparatus, since they could never be sure how far to trust the editor's judgement. On the other hand, those who used an edition with a full critical apparatus could have some confidence that the correct reading lay somewhere amongst the variants, and that careful examination would distinguish good readings from bad. Those who feared that textual criticism of the bible would deprive

4. Critique of textus receptus, shadow of heresy

them of texts customarily used to combat heresy should be assured that
the central tenets of Christianity are attested so abundantly and variously
in Scripture that the rejection of one or other passage by critics made no
material difference to doctrine.[95] In line with this manifesto, Courcelles
provided variant readings and textual notes in the lower margin of his edition. To the side of the text he also provided extensive lists of parallel passages in Scripture. The Johannine comma appeared amongst the doubtful
passages, enclosed in square brackets. Courcelles noted that it is absent
from many ancient Greek and Latin codices, from the Syriac, Arabic and
Ethiopic versions, from the works of many of the fathers, and from many
old printed editions.[96]

For all Courcelles' good intentions, his edition was far from perfect.
Probably for reasons of space – his compact edition was printed in duo-
decimo – Courcelles did not identify the manuscripts from which his variant readings were drawn, and thus denied his readers the evidence they
needed to weigh the relative authority of the variants he presented. He
failed to exploit the variants from Codex Alexandrinus systematically.
About a hundred of the variants he records seem to be errors, since they
are not represented in any of the sources he used.[97] And his faith that the
original reading could always be found hiding somewhere amongst the
variants was as optimistic as the conviction that all those who used his
edition were equipped to judge the merits of any given variant. Courcelles
also failed to recognise the potential value of variants as evidence of shift-
ing nuances in doctrine. But despite these defects, Courcelles' critique of
the smooth, unrippled surface of earlier printed editions raised awareness
of the desirability of even a basic critical apparatus in pocket editions of
the New Testament. He had also drawn attention to the fact that the text
floating upon the sea of the apparatus is sometimes little more than an
emergency raft lashed together by an editor in extremis: take for example
the last five verses of Revelation in Erasmus' editions.

Courcelles' edition was used by the Silesian Jeremias Felbinger, living in exile in Amsterdam on account of his Socinian beliefs, as the
basis of his new German New Testament (1660).[98] Felbinger also translated Courcelles' footnotes, including the one on the comma.[99] Felbinger
complained in the preface that Protestant professors and preachers in

[95] Courcelles 1658, *2v–4v.
[96] Courcelles 1658, 307r.
[97] Fox 1954, 51–52.
[98] Felbinger 1660, 5; cf. Bludau 1904a, 300.
[99] Felbinger 1660, 660.

Germany, who would have been persecuted in Catholic territories, instead persecuted those amongst them whose beliefs differed from their own. Rather than embody the gentleness of their supposed master Jesus, they published venomous tracts against their opponents, threw them into prison, separated husbands from wives, and children from their parents. Such religious aggression was not fitting for Christians, who should simply believe, obey the salutiferous and reasonable teaching of Jesus Christ, and avoid controversy.[100]

Neither Courcelles nor Felbinger would escape criticism for long. In 1696, Nicolaus Richter defended a set of theses, under the presidency of Johann Gottlieb Möller, in which he accused Courcelles of promoting heresy by drawing attention to textual variants susceptible of a Socinian meaning. The principal errors of which he accused Courcelles were an aberrant conception of the divinity of the Son, of the satisfaction of Christ, and of the Trinity, a dogma not merely imposed by ecclesiastical authority, but revealed in Scriptural texts such as the Johannine comma. But in large part Richter found Courcelles guilty by association, since his edition had been used by the Socinian Felbinger.[101]

5. Richard Simon and the development of the historical-critical method

A more substantial advance in the study of the textual problem of the comma came with the *Critical History of the New Testament* (1689) by the French priest and orientalist Richard Simon (1638–1712). By emphasising the human contingencies of the composition and transmission of the bible, Simon intended to undermine Protestant belief in the self-sufficiency of Scripture, as emphasised by Simon's Calvinist antagonist Louis Cappel. Instead, an institution was needed that could provide an authoritative and binding interpretation of the text. That institution was of course the Roman Catholic church.[102] But Simon's radical conclusions, his prickly manner and his dismissive tone guaranteed that he would be opposed at every step.

Simon's studies of the Hebrew bible grew out of a historicised and increasingly sceptical approach to Scripture that developed through the seventeenth century.[103] In his influential treatise *On the theology of the*

---

[100] Felbinger 1660, 10–14.
[101] Richter 1696, 24–25, 27.
[102] Simon 1689a, *2r; 1689b, 1:A2r.
[103] My account of these developments draws on Popkin 1996.

gentiles (1641), Gerard Vossius showed that religion, or rather individual religions, had a history and a natural life cycle, and that different religions are genealogically related. Those who turned this insight to the study of the bible produced divergent results. Readers had long noted that the report of Moses' death at the end of Deuteronomy is problematic, given that he was supposed to have written the entirety of the Pentateuch. Some suggested that this account was added after Moses' death by Joshua or Samuel. In his *Leviathan*, Hobbes showed that other verses in the Pentateuch, such as Gen 12:6 and Num 21:14, pose the same problem, although he was content to conclude that Moses wrote everything that was otherwise attributed to him. In any case, Hobbes placed authority in textual questions in the hands of the commonwealth. For him, this meant the Church of England, not the rabble that had temporarily seized the reins of power. Isaac La Peyrère (1596–1677) sharpened this critique in his *Prae-Adamitae* (1655) by questioning the reliability of the biblical text as it has come down to us, a text that at times acknowledges that it was based on earlier sources now lost, and whose physical exemplars differ from each other in a myriad ways. The English Quaker Samuel Fisher (1605–1665), who cultivated contacts with Jewish communities on the continent, pointedly asked whether the Hebrew and Greek texts of the bible as they have come down to us are accurate, and whether either document, written by humans in time and circumscribed in a set canon, can be claimed as the Word of God. Fisher maintained that even if all the fallible physical copies were destroyed, the Word of God would still be available to believers through their inner spiritual light.

Baruch Spinoza, influenced by the Socinian insistence on the priority of reason in religious questions, built on the work of earlier Jewish writers such as Aben Ezra as well as more immediate predecessors like La Peyrère and possibly Fisher. He pointed out that the many difficulties that followed from the traditional attribution of the Pentateuch to Moses – Hobbes had only scratched the surface – led to the conclusion that this claim was untenable. Spinoza also denied that the Hebrew prophets had any access to knowledge beside what is available to anyone through reason and experience. They merely possessed a flair for presenting the products of their imagination. Instead, Spinoza maintained that study of the books of the bible must begin with close examination of the language and usage of their individual authors, the historical context in which they worked and the subsequent fate of each writing, such as the circumstances of its inclusion in the canon and any recension it may have undergone. Spinoza explained the law laid down in the bible as a relic of the historical circumstances in which it was formulated and of the characters of those who drew it up. This is not to say that Spinoza was an atheist. He asserted that a universal or divine moral law really exists, and that it is derived from rational principles. Historical study of the Scripture was one thing, he insisted, understanding the mind of God, that is, truth itself, is quite another. He rejected the illuminist position of those, such as the Quakers and other radical Protestants, who relied on an inner spiritual light as guide to interpretation, pointing out that it was incapable of rational demonstration. Nevertheless, he concluded that the teachers and scholars who determined the canon of Scripture must have had some idea of the Word of God as the standard by which books were either included or excluded from the canon. Indeed, he maintained that the bible can be called the Word of God insofar as it proclaims the divine law. Spinoza claimed that Jesus truly understood what God had revealed to him, and unfolded the divine moral law to his hearers. Like the Dutch Socinians with whom he associated, Spinoza seems to have considered Jesus as belonging to a different order from Moses or the Hebrew prophets, though he did not imply thereby that Jesus was divine. Spinoza was not a Christian in any conventional sense. Indeed, he confessed to his friend Henry Oldenbourg that was prepared to accept the historicity of the gospels – except for the account of the resurrection. Spinoza's uncomfortable conclusions, laid out in his *Tractatus theologico-politicus* (1670), not only destabilised the traditional view of biblical authorship, but also undermined the notion of the divine inspiration of Scripture and its truth claims. Many Jews and Christians alike therefore treated Spinoza's work with suspicion and hostility.[104]

The conflicts that arose from the work of Spinoza and Simon may be analysed through Michel Foucault's notion of the 'episteme', that is, an internally consistent mode of conceiving the world that determines which questions may conceivably be asked, and thus judged to be either true or false.[105] In the premodern episteme, in which critical thought was subordinated to a theological *a priori*, it was almost inconceivable to doubt the inspiration of Scripture, or even to conceive of it as a human text subject to the same rules of composition and transmission as any other. However, by disconnecting critical questions from theological ones, Spinoza and Simon created a context in which new questions could be asked and answered, such as the authorship of the Pentateuch or the inspiration of the prophets. But while Foucault argued that epistemes are discrete, one

---

[104] Israel 2012, argues that Spinoza's project was not inevitably secular; many of those who embraced Spinoza's work did not abandon religion.

[105] 'Le jeu de Michel Foucault' (1977), in Foucault 1994, 2:301.

yielding to the next following a sudden change of perception, I suggest that the episteme that existed before Spinoza and Simon never ended. Rather, their work fractured the hermeneutical consensus, leading to a situation in which two epistemes came to exist in parallel. One maintains an essentially premodern attitude towards Scripture, submitting judgement in textual matters to the ultimate criterion of doctrine, while the other has accepted, internalised and built upon the insights of Spinoza and Simon, using the tools of philology, history and sociology to illuminate the beginnings of Christianity. However, acknowledging the existence of a plurality of opinions does not force us to accept all opinions as equally valid. Insofar as exponents of the first approach fail to take account of historical and textual evidence, they render their own position incapable of verification. I suggest that many of the conflicts between academic biblical critics and conservative apologists arise out of a basic epistemological incompatibility.

Simon had already finished his *Critical History of the Old Testament* (1678) before he read the *Tractatus*, and he made only minor revisions in the light of Spinoza's book.[106] But if Simon disagreed with many details of Spinoza's arguments about revelation, he agreed with the philosopher's assumption that criticism must be independent of belief, and shared his conviction that the only way to reach the truth is through the exercise of critical reason.[107] Although the direct influence of Spinoza's work on Simon's *Critical History of the Old Testament* was minimal, Jacques-Bénigne Bossuet, tutor to the dauphin, was horrified by the apparent similarities of their approach and conclusions. Bossuet pressured the Oratorians to expel Simon from the order, and ordered that his book should be destroyed.[108] However, the work had been copied by the chaplain of the duchess of Mazarin, and the work was reprinted in Amsterdam from this copy.[109] After an English translation of the Amsterdam edition appeared in early 1682, John Evelyn complained to John Fell, bishop of Oxford, that this work had exposed 'not only the Protestant and whole Reformed Churches abroad, but (what ought to be dearer to us) the Church of England at home, which with them acknowledges the Holy Scriptures alone to be the canon and rule of faith; but which this bold man not only labours

---

[106] De Vet 1996, 86.

[107] Further, see Bernus 1869; Koselleck 1973, 87–89; Auvray 1974; Gibert 2010, 176–184. Reiser 2012, 158, overstates the matter when he claims that Simon was the only seventeenth-century scholar to investigate the problem of the comma.

[108] Lambe 1985; Champion 1999a, 40–41.

[109] Auvray 1974, 67; Locke's copy of one of the three 1680 Amsterdam editions is listed in Harrison and Laslett 1971, 233, n° 2673a.

to unsettle, but destroy'. The work was even more damaging because it was evidently written not by 'some daring wit, or young Lord Rochester revived', but by a sober, learned and judicious scholar whose opinions demanded to be taken seriously. Even Evelyn had to admit that Simon's book was 'a masterpiece in its kind'. As a result, the work had begun to enjoy considerable popularity and credit amongst students. The objectivity with which Simon approached his subject matter made it difficult to tell if he was 'a Papist, Socinian, or merely a Theist, or something of all three'. Evelyn was alarmed by Simon's claim that it is not possible to establish any 'doctrine or principles' upon the Scriptures, which left Protestant hermeneutics in a perilous situation. For this reason, Evelyn urged Fell to encourage the scholars of Oxford to unite in refuting the claims of both Simon and Spinoza.[110] Spinoza and Simon would both be attacked in sermons by Thomas Smith and Edward Stillingfleet.[111] Edmund Calamy regretted that Simon, 'with all his Skill was [...] as prejudic'd and canker'd a Writer, as any our Modern Times have afforded'.[112]

Simon spent the following years working on the textual history of the New Testament, 'in a small Hut surrounded with Books, without any Fire, [...] being us'd to fortifie himself against weather by several Caps upon his Head, a thick Robe, and a large leathern Girdle'.[113] Simon set out his findings on the comma in his *Critical History of the New Testament* (1689). After a thorough review of the manuscript evidence for the comma, Simon concluded that the Greeks, like the Latins, had a tradition of interpreting the water, Spirit and blood of 1 Jn 5:8 allegorically as a reference to the Trinity. He also argued that the prologue attributed to Jerome should no longer be assigned to the great father, but to an early epigone. Finally, he believed that some of Erasmus' conclusions about the textual status of the verse required revision. He criticised Erasmus for accusing the Greeks, after their reconciliation with the Roman church, of adapting the text of their bibles to conform to the Latin Vulgate. Moreover, he suggested that Erasmus' assessment of the manuscripts he used for his edition was imperfect.[114]

Simon also argued that previous scholars had not fully appreciated the complexities of the transmission of the comma in the Latin tradition.

---

[110] John Evelyn to John Fell, 19 March 1682, in Evelyn 1850–1857, 3:264–267; cf. Champion 1999a, 43.
[111] The latter is transcribed from Stillingfleet's shorthand in Reedy 1985, 145–155; on Smith's sermon, see below, 156–158.
[112] Calamy 1722, 461.
[113] Hearne 1885–1915, 1:179.
[114] Simon 1689a, *2v–3r; 1689b, 1:A2v.

Particularly culpable in this respect was an Oratorian of the previous generation, Denis Amelote. Charged by Louis XIV with creating an official French translation of the New Testament from the Vulgate, Amelote claimed to have inspected all the Greek manuscripts older than a thousand years in all Christendom, in order to make sure that they conformed to the Latin text.[115] Apart from the outrageous boldness of this claim, Simon pointed out the methodological naïveté of this position: the oldest manuscripts are not necessarily the best, especially if there is reason to believe that the text of their archetypes had been corrupted through inadvertence or deliberate scribal intervention.[116] Many of the details given by Amelote were also incorrect. While Erasmus stated that the comma was not attested in 'an ancient Greek manuscript in the Vatican', that is, Codex Vaticanus, Amelote claimed to have seen the comma in 'the oldest manuscript in that library'.[117] This claim was soon cited by others, such as David Martin and Richard Smalbroke, as evidence for the genuineness of the comma.

Simon examined six Greek manuscripts in the royal library in Paris and five in Colbert's library, but did not find the comma in any of them, either in the body of the text or in a marginal annotation. However, in some he found marginal annotations with various combinations of the symbolum 'one God, one divinity, the witness of God the Father and the Holy Ghost'. Simon believed that this symbolum attested to a Greek tradition of interpreting the three earthly witnesses of 1 Jn 5:8 as types of the persons of the Trinity. On this basis, he suggested that a scholium containing some form of this statement had been absorbed into the text in the Greek tradition and had subsequently given rise to the comma, even though he admitted that he could not find any Greek manuscripts in which this had happened. Nevertheless, he considered this a more likely explanation than Erasmus' theory that the reading of his Greek manuscript (namely, Montfortianus) had been altered to conform to the Latin Vulgate.[118]

---

[115] Amelote 1666–1670, ē9v–10r.

[116] Simon 1689b, 1:A2v; Simon 1689a, *2v.

[117] Amelote 1687–1688, 2:104: 'Elle manquoit, dit Erasme, dans un ancien MS. Grec du Vatican, (mais je la trouve au contraire dans le plus ancien de cette Bibliothèque.)'

[118] Simon 1689a, 203–204; Simon 1689b, 2:2–3. In the Royal library in Paris he inspected mss 1885 [now BnF ms Grec 216 = GA 605], 2247 [ms Grec 57 = GA 465], 2248 [ms Grec 56 = GA 337], 2870 [ms Grec 102 = GA 2298], 2871 [now BnF ms Grec 106 = GA 5, Estienne's ms δ'], 2872 [ms Grec 103 = GA 302]. In Colbert's library he inspected mss 871 [now BnF ms Grec 60 = GA 62], 2844 [now BnF ms Grec 14 = GA 33], 4785 [ms Grec 101 = GA 468], 6123 [ms Grec 104 = GA 601], 6584 [ms Grec 124 = GA 296]. He notes that in the margin of ms 2247 in the French royal library

A number of objections may be raised to Simon's hypothesis. First, Simon seems not to have recognised the phrase 'one divinity, one God' (μία θεότης, εἷς Θεός), which forms part of both the glosses he observed, as a citation from John Chrysostom's *In Johannem theologum*, expanded with a further theological gloss linking Chrysostom's words to 1 Jn 5:8.[119] The absence of any extant Greek manuscripts in which this gloss has slipped into the body text further undermines Simon's hypothesis. Furthermore, the textual discrepancies between the glosses he cites and the reading of the comma in the two Greek manuscripts in which it is attested (GA 61 and 629) are simply too great to permit of any simple explanation of how the former could have turned into the latter. Simon's theory ultimately fails to hold water.

Simon noted that the dispute over the comma was often associated with the question of Arianism.[120] Various scholars, driven by their own prejudices, imagined that the comma had arisen from deliberate tampering (whether addition or subtraction of text) perpetrated by a specific group (whether Catholics or Arians), but Simon remained unconvinced by such conjectures, preferring to explain the comma simply through carelessness on the part of scribes.[121] The accusation that a particular group has corrupted Scripture go back to the beginning of Christian apologetic, as seen for example in Justin's *Dialogue with Trypho* 71–73. Stunica had accused Erasmus of fomenting Arianism. The Catholic theologian Libert Froidmont argued that the ancient Arians had removed the comma from their bibles. Why is it then, Simon asked, that this verse is also absent from the text cited by Cyprian, who lived *before* Arius, and from the Syriac and other eastern versions? In any case, latter-day Arians gained nothing by pointing out that the comma is absent from the great majority of Greek manuscripts.[122] For Simon, as for Erasmus, any attempt to prove or disprove the doctrine of the Trinity on the basis of the comma alone was bound to fail. In fact, he saw that Lutheran apologists who cited the comma against the Socinians provided their opponents with the means to

---

[BnF ms Grec 57, 61v], next to verse 8a, is written: τουτέστι τὸ πνεῦμα τὸ ἅγιον καὶ ὁ πατὴρ καὶ αὐτὸς ἑαυτοῦ (*that is, the Holy Spirit and the Father, and He himself, his own*). Next to verse 8b in the same ms is written: τουτέστι μία θεότης εἷς Θεός (*that is, one godhead, one God*). In Colbert's ms 871 [BnF ms Grec 60] he found written in the margin: εἷς Θεὸς μία θεότης, μαρτυρία τοῦ Θεοῦ τοῦ πατρὸς καὶ τοῦ καὶ τοῦ ἁγίου πνεύματος (*one God, one divinity, the witness of God the Father and the Holy Ghost*). Further, see Bladau 1904b. A new translation of this chapter is now available in Simon 2013, 173–185.

119   Chrysostom 1834–1839, 8.2:785.
120   Simon 1689a, 206; Simon 1689b, 2:4.
121   Simon 1689a, 352–353; Simon 1689b, 2:123–124.
122   Simon 1689a, 215; Simon 1689b, 2:11; cf. Froidmont 1663, 657.

defeat them. Simon's examination of the verse was inconclusive, but his defence of orthodox Trinitarian belief was unwavering.[123]

Simon's account of Erasmus' decision to include the comma in the third edition of his Greek text contains the first traces of the persistent myth that Erasmus promised to include the comma in his edition of the New Testament if a single manuscript authority could be produced. As Henk Jan de Jonge has pointed out, this legend apparently arose from a misreading of Erasmus' response to Lee (1520). Erasmus was sure that no Greek manuscript contained the comma. Rather, he was defending himself against Lee's accusation of laziness and sloppy editing.[124] Simon's account bears the seed from which the myth of Erasmus' promise grew:

> In his *Response to Stunica*, Erasmus justified himself well enough by the authority of those Greek manuscripts he had read; yet he considered it acceptable to insert the Passage from St John in a new edition of his New Testament, contrary to the authority of all his manuscripts. He declares that he was only obliged to make this change on the authority of a Greek Copy he had seen in England, which he believed had been adapted on the basis of the Latin copies.[125]

According to Simon, Erasmus had been led astray by his belief that the Greek texts are invariably more authoritative than the Latin ones. (Had Simon read Erasmus' refutation of Lee's accusation that he considered the Greek texts as 'oracles', he would have come to a different conclusion.) Simon also makes the error of assuming that Erasmus saw the manuscript in England. In fact Erasmus visited England for the third and last time in 1517, before Lee and Stunica launched their attacks. Simon's talk of the obligation imposed upon him by seeing this British codex led in later accounts to the assumption of a promise and its fulfilment. According to some, Erasmus made his spurious promise to Stunica. However, the first time Erasmus addressed Stunica in print was in the *Apologia*, published in September 1521, three months after he had included the comma in an edition of his Latin translation of the New Testament.[126]

Amongst Simon's most important contributions to the debate over the comma was his assessment of the authorship of the prologue to the Catholic Epistles, about which John Selden and Christoph Sand

---

[123] Simon's position was shared by Jonathan Edwards, the Master of Jesus College, Oxford; see Jonathan Edwards 1698, 1:60–61, who relied on Poole 1669–1676, 4.2:1622–1626.

[124] *ASD* IX-4:323; de Jonge 1980b, 385.

[125] Simon 1689a, 205. I have adapted the faulty English translation from Simon 1689b, 2:3.

[126] De Jonge 1980b, 382–384; for one version of the myth in which the promise is made to Stunica, see Turner 1924, 23.

had already raised doubts. Simon criticised Erasmus for characterising Jerome (on the basis of the prologue to the Catholic Epistles) as 'violent, shameless and inconsistent'. (Simon's criticism of Erasmus is based solely upon the *Apology to Stunica*. In his refutation of Lee, Erasmus had defended Jerome's integrity.) Simon also bridled at Erasmus' implication that Jerome, in correcting the Old Latin translation without the authority of good Greek manuscripts, was guilty of forgery, or at least of gross presumption. Erasmus' accusations led Sozzini to suggest that Jerome, deceived by a small number of manuscripts containing the comma, concluded that those lacking the comma had been altered by heretics. But these accusations against Jerome arose from the mistaken assumption that he wrote the prologue to the Catholic Epistles. Had Erasmus examined the prologue more closely, he would have rejected it as spurious and would not have charged Jerome with forgery.[127]

Simon pointed out that in many of the earliest manuscripts of the Latin Vulgate, the prologue to the Catholic Epistles is not found with Jerome's authentic prefaces. Moreover, in the earliest copies that do contain the prologue – such as Charles the Bald's bible (now Paris, BnF ms lat. 1) – the name of the author is not given. Simon deduced that this prologue was written by a forger in imitation of Jerome's style, in order to supply prologues to those books for which Jerome had provided none, adding the name of the purported addressee, Eustochium, for an added touch of realism. The author of the prologue, perhaps ignorant of the Greek text, was nevertheless aware that some Latin manuscripts contain the comma and others do not, and mistakenly assumed that this discrepancy was due to the fault of bad translators. But the absence of the comma in some early bibles containing the prologue argued against Jerome's authorship of the prologue. 'This diversity of Copies is in my judgment an evident proof, that he did not compose that Preface to prefix it to the Canonical Epistles.'[128] The fact that many manuscripts containing the prologue include the comma only as a marginal addition, not to mention the lack of uniformity in the readings of the comma between the various manuscripts, 'makes it further manifest, that S. Jerome was not the true Author either of the Preface or Addition'.[129] Simon discussed the wild variety of readings in the oldest Latin manuscripts, which showed that this text was unstable, and had been interpolated in different ways by different hands.

[127] Simon 1689a, 206; Simon 1689b, 2:4.
[128] Simon 1689a, 209; Simon 1689b, 2:7.
[129] Simon 1689a, 210; Simon 1689b, 2:7.

Simon denied John Fell's assertion (1682) that Cyprian quoted the comma in *De unitate ecclesiae*.[130] If Augustine did not know the comma, it was reasonable to assume that his earlier compatriot was likewise unfamiliar with the text. Simon also suggested that the Trinitarian interpretation of the words 'these three are one' in the pseudonymous *Disputation of Athanasius against Arius at the Council of Nicaea* may have prompted scribes to insert the comma into the body text in some Greek manuscripts, which have since been lost. He found this explanation more plausible than Erasmus' suggestion that some Greek manuscripts had been corrected against Latin ones.[131]

However, since the presence or absence of the comma in the text of the epistle does not prove the existence or non-existence of the Trinity, Simon saw little point in arguing about it. He did not assume that those recent commentators who held that the unity of the heavenly witnesses refers to their testimony rather than their essence were secretly fomenting Arianism. He found it pointless to enumerate the editions and translations which did or did not include the comma, since most printed editions and translations could be traced to only a small number of editions actually based on manuscripts, such as the Complutensian Polyglot and Erasmus' editions. While Christoph Sand had made much of the fact that Luther excluded the comma from his translation, Simon did not think that he had done so because of the evidence of the Greek manuscripts. In any case, modern-day Lutherans did not follow his example. Rather, they claimed 'a thing they believed to be doubtful' as the Word of God. When Lutheran apologists quoted the comma against Antitrinitarians, they thus provided their opponents with 'the fairest occasion imaginable of Triumphing over them'.[132]

Yet after reading Sand, it was optimistic of Simon to conclude that 'I cannot imagin [*sic*] what advantage the *Antitrinitarians* can get against the Catholicks, upon this ground, that that passage is not found in the most part of the Greek manuscripts, nor those others of the Eastern Church, nor yet in the old Latin Copies.'[133] Few of Simon's readers were sufficiently experienced in the hermeneutical methods of the fathers to realise how pervasive their allegorical habit was. And even fewer of his readers had the *sang-froid* to follow his conclusion that it was only the authority of the

---

[130] Cyprian 1682, 109.
[131] Simon 1698a, 213–214; cf. *ASD* IX-2:259, l. 542.
[132] Simon 1689a, 216–217; Simon 1689b, 2:12–13.
[133] Simon 1689a, 214–215; Simon 1689b, 2:11.

church that obliged Christians to consider the comma as authentic. Most, whether Catholic or Protestant, still expected that such a central proof of the Trinity should rest on more secure foundations than these.[134]

In the *Critical History of the versions of the New Testament* (1690), Simon continued his discussion of the prologue to the Catholic Epistles. He noted that the number of prologues in the Latin bibles increased over time, and that Jerome's name was added to some prologues by later hands. He disagreed with the suggestion of Burnet ('neither a critic nor an able theologian') that the absence of the comma in some copies was due to 'the errour or omission of the Coppier'. The large number of manuscripts in which this verse does not appear would imply that this same error had been made more often than was credible. Simon also defended Erasmus from Burnet's criticism that he had omitted the prologue to the Catholic Epistles from his edition of Jerome's works. The real reason for this was simply that the prologue was not transmitted in the manuscripts of Jerome's collected writings, merely in some manuscripts of the Vulgate. Simon also pointed out that some mediaeval readers of the prologue concluded incorrectly that the Greek manuscripts were corrupt at this point, whereas the prologue claims that some Latin translations were incorrect.[135]

In response to Antoine Arnauld, Simon returned once more to the comma in his *Critical History of the Principal Commentators on the New Testament* (1693). Urban VIII (1623–1644) wished that the New Testament from the Antwerp Polyglot (based on the Complutensian text) should be improved through comparison with further manuscripts. Johannes Matthaeus Caryophyllus (*c.* 1566–*c.* 1635) accordingly collated twenty-two Greek manuscripts of the New Testament from the Barberini collection in Rome. Caryophyllus noted that the comma was absent from all eight manuscripts of the Catholic Epistles, but argued – in violation of the second of his own editorial principles – that the reading in both the Greek and Latin text of the Antwerp Polyglot should be retained on the strength of the purported citations in Cyprian, Fulgentius and Athanasius. Simon also suggested that the reading of the comma in Codex Britannicus was based on the Greek translation of the Acts of the fourth Lateran council. Here Simon also gave up his earlier theory that the comma had entered the Greek text from a marginal gloss. This error, he explained, arose because he trusted Bèze's testimony that he had seen the comma in some Greek

[134] Simon 1689a, 217; Simon 1689b, 2:13.
[135] Simon 1690, 99–121; cf. Burnet 1686, 53–54. Further, see Bludau 1904b, 36–38.

manuscripts, but now it was clear that this was not true.[136] Simon also criticised the New Testament paraphrase by François Titelmans (1543), which implied that the unity of the three persons was one not merely of testimony or will, but also one of essence.[137] Reviewing once again the poor manuscript attestation for the comma, Simon concluded that 'divine providence really must have failed the church, if this passage is as important as you [Arnauld] say'.[138]

Simon included the comma in his 1702 French translation of the Latin Vulgate New Testament, but in a footnote he questioned its authenticity, referring to Caryophyllus' failure to find it in any of the Barberini manuscripts at Rome.[139] In a vicious critique of Simon's translation, Bossuet accused Simon of disrespecting the declaration of the council of Trent and disregarding the evidence of Cyprian, Fulgentius and Victor Vitensis. He also insinuated that Simon's desire to banish the comma arose from closet Socinianism and misguided respect for the heretic Grotius.[140]

Simon returned to the comma once more in his final work on biblical criticism, published posthumously in 1730. Here he dismissed the account of Noël Alexandre (1710), who had tried to attribute its absence in 'many Greek manuscripts' to the negligence of scribes. Simon objected to Alexandre's implication that it was present in some copies, defying him to produce a single manuscript in support. Lest Alexandre should cite Amelote's report of a manuscript in the Vatican, Simon recalled Caryophyllus' report that the comma was absent from all the Barberini manuscripts. He also pilloried Alexandre's misrepresentation of Erasmus' Codex Britannicus as of 'venerable antiquity'. Erasmus actually believed that the codex was quite recent. As to Alexandre's assertion that only Socinians believed this passage to be an addition, Simon pointed out that Crell's edition actually includes the comma. In conclusion, Simon accused Alexandre of arguing 'according to false ideas on a matter about which he has practically no knowledge'. Simon's posthumous treatise appeared

---

[136] *Dissertation critique sur les principaux actes manuscrits*, appended to Simon 1693, 13–14, 80–99; cf. Poussines 1673, 460–461 (Caryophyllus' editorial principles), 522–523 (collation); Arnauld 1691, 3:341–369. Further, see Bludau 1904b, 38–39.

[137] Simon 1693, 565; cf. Titelmans 1543, 255v: 'Et hae tres personae tam substantia quam testimonio vnum sunt, testificantes concorditer, quod Christus sit verus filius Dei.'

[138] *Dissertation critique*, appended to Simon 1693, 94; cf. Bludau 1904b, 41–42.

[139] Simon 1702, 4:191; cf. Bludau 1904b, 42; Simon 2013, xxx–xxxi, 185 n. 39.

[140] Bossuet 1703, ix–xii, 185–190; cf. Bludau 1904b, 117. Simon's treatment of the comma was also refuted in print by Roger 1713, 99–119; Boucat 1766, 4:321–331; Maran 1746 161; and Wouters 1753–1758, 6:477–480.

with an appendix by Etienne Souciet, librarian of Louis-le-Grand, who attempted to refute Simon's arguments.[141]

Simon put the textual study of the New Testament on a firmer basis than ever before, and drew a number of important new conclusions about the comma. He insisted that any argument must be founded on the manuscripts. By reasoning from the manuscript evidence, Simon could show that the prologue to the Catholic Epistles was almost certainly not written by Jerome, and that the comma was either absent from the earliest manuscripts, added only later, or altered in other ways that showed that it was a foreign body. But many of Simon's readers, and not just the Protestant ones, were disquieted by his suggestion that much about the Scriptures is dependent on human contingency, and draws its authority solely from the magisterium of the church.

6. Thomas Smith

Since the publication of his *Histoire critique du Vieux Testament*, Richard Simon had enjoyed a reputation for critical acuity and boldness. Therefore, when his *Histoire critique du texte du Nouveau Testament* appeared in 1689, many readers, including Thomas Smith (1638–1710), snatched it eagerly from the booksellers' shelves. Smith had defended the genuineness of the *textus receptus* of the comma once before, in an appendix to a sermon published in 1675. After reading Simon's work, Smith felt compelled to write a more extensive defence of the comma, this time in Latin for a learned (and international) audience.[142] Smith observed with horror how Simon had exerted himself in 'expunging this most famous testimony of the most holy Trinity from the sacred writings'. While attracting for himself the reputation of an ingenious and subtle critic, Simon did not seem to care about the harm his critical conjectures might do to true piety by providing material to heretics, 'who strive to destroy the mysteries of the Christian faith through their dishonest perversity, under the shield of this new Enlightenment, or through subtlety of criticism'.[143] Smith maintained that the comma 'contains the chief mystery of the Christian religion, that of the most holy and indivisible Trinity, expressed in distinct words'. Although Smith admitted that the comma was absent from

---

[141] Simon 1730, 419–440, 575–628 (Souciet's notes); cf. Noël 1710, 213–214. See also Bludau 1904b, 114–116.

[142] On Smith, see Nichols 1812, 1:14–16.

[143] Smith 1690, 153–154. Bludau 1904b, 118, incorrectly states that this work was first printed in 1636.

many manuscripts, including Codex Alexandrinus, he regretted that
the poor textual record for the comma had led the 'arrogant enemies of
Christian doctrine' to assert that Catholics had inserted the comma into
the text against the author's intentions, and against the authority of the
most authentic texts. As representative of this position Smith cited Fausto
Sozzini, who wrote: 'It is clear that these words are forged, and were
stuffed into this passage by people who desired to defend their dogma of
the Trinity by whatever means possible.'[144]

Smith defended the attribution of the prologue to the Catholic Epistles
to Jerome, though he noted that 'Erasmus and Sozzini work hard to dis-
solve the strength and the bond of this testimony, by which they realise
that they are bound. They turn and twist this way and that; and lest they
should seem to be struck dumb, flatter themselves that this matter is to
be disentangled with untrustworthy and dishonest answers.'[145] Fausto
Sozzini had suggested in his commentary on the Johannine Epistles that
Jerome had chanced upon a copy containing the comma – perhaps even
several – and assuming that this reading was correct, complained that the
texts generally in use were corrupt. Smith characterised Sozzini's hypothesis as 'pure, vile calumny'. However, Smith's argument acknowledged tacitly that he was in a bind. To reject Jerome's authorship of the prologue
meant jettisoning a powerful piece of evidence for the authenticity of the
comma. To maintain Jerome's authorship of the prologue meant having to
having to consider the possibility that Jerome's version did not represent
the text as commonly accepted in his day, or – even worse – that Jerome
himself had interpolated the comma into the text.

One of the Antitrinitarians whom Smith took trouble to refute
was Christoph Sand. Smith dismissed Sand's suggestion that the logical flow of 1 Jn 5 runs more smoothly without the comma as 'vain and
frivolous'. He also rejected Sand's objection that the comma makes no
sense: 'Before what judge,' Sand had asked, 'might God stand as a witness?' Smith likewise rejected the suggestion, reported by Sand, that the
passage was inserted by Sabellians. Smith denied even more strenuously
the suggestion – which Sand adopted from Bugenhagen's *Commentary on
Jonah* – that the comma was introduced by Arians. And while Sand had
pointed out that the inversion of vv. 7 and 8 in many manuscripts seems
to indicate that the comma is an intrusion, Smith simply denied this suggestion, though he failed to provide any argument to the contrary.[146]

[144] Smith 1690, 125.
[145] Smith 1690, 139.
[146] Smith 1690, 148–150; Sand 1669, 381–382.

However, Smith did bring one new piece of evidence for the acceptance of the comma outside the western church. He cited the Orthodox Confession of Peter Mogilas (1654) as evidence that the comma was an established part of the eastern Scriptures and religious texts, evidently unaware that the reading of the comma in that document was taken from Bèze's text. Smith also made the startling claim that the evidence for the comma in both Latin and Greek manuscripts was so compelling that neither 'Erasmus, Sozzini, Sand nor Simon have called it into doubt'. For Smith, the only room for critical disagreement was the extent to which a given manuscript corresponded to the autograph.

Smith then drew on the principles of textual criticism to argue his case. (Some of these arguments, which appear to have been borrowed from Turrettin's disputation on the comma, would be repeated by yet others, such as Louis-Ellies Du Pin.)[147] While omissions are a common species of scribal error, additions are much less frequent, since they occur only through a conscious intention on the part of the scribe. Smith argued that the parallelism of vv. 7 and 8 could easily have led scribes to omit the heavenly witnesses through homeoteleuton. Smith then turned to the prologue to the Catholic Epistles. Where Simon had pointed out that many manuscripts transmit the prologue to the Catholic Epistles without Jerome's name, Smith asserted that an explicit ascription was unnecessary, since the authorship of the prologue was never in doubt. In response to Simon's point that some manuscripts containing the prologue do not include the comma in the text of the epistle, Smith argued that such codices could have been copied from mutilated originals. Simon had concluded from the presence of the comma in the margins of some manuscripts that the comma had originally crept into the text from the margin. By contrast, Smith believed that the presence of marginal additions showed that the scribes in such cases, suspecting that something was missing from the text but afraid to deviate from the original they were copying, might simply have included the text in the margins for safety's sake. Smith's lame attempt to refute Simon's arguments – relying in every case on what might have happened rather than on what demonstrably did – demonstrates how the misrepresentation of textual evidence often led to critically inadequate and ultimately unconvincing conclusions.

---

[147] Turrettin 1687, 94; cf. Turrettin 1679–1686, 1:283. Turretin's source is Walther 1654, 1347–1348. Du Pin 1699a, 2:226–227; Du Pin 1699b, 2:79.

7. Isaac Newton, 'a Bigot, a Fanatique, a Heretique'

While Simon was completing his *Histoire critique du texte du Nouveau Testament*, Isaac Newton (1642–1727) was undertaking a detailed examination of the authenticity of two of the same passages that had exercised Simon's attention: 1 Jn 5:7–8 and 1 Tim 3:16.[148] Newton considered 1 Tim 3:16 an interesting parallel case to the comma, for it showed that textual corruption of the Scriptures took place in the Greek tradition as well as the Latin. The *textus receptus* reads καὶ ὁμολογουμένως μέγα ἐστὶ τὸ τῆς εὐσεβείας μυστήριον· Θεός ἐφανερώθη ἐν σαρκί, translated in the Authorised Version as: 'And without controversy, great is is the mystery of godliness: God was manifest in the flesh.' Erasmus suggested that the reading Θεός had arisen from an optical confusion in the uncial manuscripts between the abbreviated *nomen sacrum* $\overline{\Theta\Sigma}$ (Θεός, 'God') and the relative pronoun ΟΣ ('who'), and even posited that the orthodox had corrupted this passage deliberately in their struggle against the Arians.[149] This double conclusion had some traction. While acknowledging that he was 'no textual critic', Luther acknowledged the critical disagreement over this issue in his lectures on 1 Tim (1528). Without naming Erasmus as his source, Luther noted Erasmus' suggestion that θεός was an anti-Arian corruption, and sided with Erasmus' conclusion that ὅς was the original reading.[150] These conclusions also appealed to Newton, who shared Erasmus' view that Christian doctrine had been subject to corruption over time, and that Athanasian orthodoxy had distorted the original Christian conception of God.[151]

---

[148] Newton, *An Historical Account of Two Notable Corruptions of the Scripture. In a Letter to a Friend*, in Newton 1779–1785, 5:495–531; 1959–1977, 3:83–109. Newton's autograph draft is in Oxford, New College ms 361.4, 2r–40v, now transcribed online: www.newtonproject.sussex.ac.uk. His notes are in Cambridge, King's College, Keynes ms 2, 20, also transcribed in the Newton Project. On the abortive publication, see King 1858, 231–234; Bourne 1876, 2:219–223; Bludau 1922, 210–212; Westfall 1980, 490–491.

[149] Erasmus 1516, 568: '*Quod manifestum est in carne.*) graece secus est, θεός ἐφανερώθη ἐν σαρκί, id est, deus manifestatus est in carne, & quae sequuntur, ad deum referenda sunt. Ambrosius & uulgatus interpres legerunt pro θεός ὅ, id est quod. Secus legunt Chrysostomus & Vulgarius [*sc.* Theophylactus], quos si sequi uolumus, genera participiorum mutanda sunt iustificatus, praedicatus, creditus, assumptus. Caeterum utra lectio sit uerior ambigo nonnihil. Offendit Laurentium quomodo mysterium dicatur assumptum in gloriam. At cur non magis offendit, quod deus dicitur iustificatus? Id quod ne in Christum quidem prima fronte satis congruit. Siquidem de Christo interpretatur Ambrosius. Mihi subolet, deum additum fuisse aduersus haereticos Arrianos.' Further on this passage, see Ehrman 1993, 77–78.

[150] *WA* 26:64. Luther did not make any note next to this passage his copy of Erasmus 1527b, 602–603 (Groningen University Library, HS 494).

[151] *Opus epist.* 5:176.

The requirements of Newton's college fellowship stipulated that he should take holy orders, although this requirement was waived by royal patent, obtained through the intervention of Isaac Barrow, master of Trinity College, on 27 April 1675.[152] Nevertheless, Newton's interest in theology, in particular in Antitrinitarianism, grew in the late 1670s and became critical in the 1680s, as he continued his study of the history of the early church. He had access to a large collection of heterodox writings owned by Isaac Barrow, and may have acquired some of Barrow's books when he died in 1677. At Trinity College, Cambridge, Newton could consult a number of heterodox titles in the college library. From 1689, when he became friends with John Locke, he had access to one of the largest collections of Socinian writings in England. After Locke's death in 1704, Newton had access to Antitrinitarian works in the library of his younger friend and fellow traveller Samuel Clarke (1675–1729). Clarke was chaplain to John Moore, successively bishop of Norwich and Ely, and warden of Moore's huge library, which contained nearly seventy Socinian works. Newton met the Transylvanian Unitarian Zsigmond Pálfi in 1701. In 1711 he met the Socinian Samuel Crell (1660–1747), grandson of Johann Crell and pastor of the church of the Polish Brethren. In 1726, Newton offered Samuel Crell financial support to publish a book on the prologue to the fourth gospel. Newton himself possessed at least ten Arian, Socinian and Unitarian works, including titles by John Biddle, Johann Crell, Samuel Crell, György Enyedi, Stanisław Lubienicki, Christoph Sand, Jonasz Szlichting and Fausto Sozzini, besides works by his followers Samuel Clarke and William Whiston, which were probably presented as gifts. From the Socinians, Newton inherited a strict biblicism and a strongly historical view of Christianity which privileged its 'primitive' apostolic form. Like many Antitrinitarians, Newton used philology and history to identify later doctrinal developments, which he rejected as dangerous innovations introduced under the influence of pagan philosophy. He considered such developments as the fruit of the human tendency to pervert true religion into idolatry. In particular, Newton identified the doctrine of the Trinity as a corruption of primitive Christianity that arose out of the dispute between Arius and Athanasius.

Newton's religious position refuses to fit neatly into known categories. According to Whiston, 'Sir *Isaac Newton* was so hearty for the baptists, as

---

[152] Westfall 1980, 310, stated that Newton began serious study of theology in the early 1670s, but Buchwald and Feingold 2012, 127–128, argue rather that his intensive theological study only began in the late 1670s.

well as for the *Eusebians* or *Arians*, that he sometimes suspected these two were the *two witnesses* in the *Revelation*.' Even though Newton occasionally expressed his disapproval of Socinianism, he held some recognisably Socinian positions. His close reading of Christoph Sand contributed to his increasing suspicion of the orthodox conception of the Trinity. Like the Socinians, Newton conceived of God the Father as a God of dominion; of Christ as God by office and not by nature; and of the unity that bound God and Jesus as one of will, not of essence or substance. However, he held to the Arian belief, distinct from that of the Socinians, that Christ existed before his incarnation. Like the Socinians, he rejected the belief in an eternal soul and the eternity of torment in hell, and even went beyond Socinian precedents in denying the existence of the devil and evil spirits. Newton held several distinctive beliefs inherited by the Socinians from their roots in Anabaptism, notably that only adult believers should be baptised, following a thorough catechesis. He shared the Socinians' commitment to the separation of church and state. He also shared their commitment to broad religious toleration, although this was tempered by his conviction that of the many religious perspectives on offer, only one was correct. It should also be noted that Newton's toleration did not extend to the Catholic church. He also espoused views fermenting within English Unitarianism in the decades around 1700, such as the view that God had sent Mohammed to the Arabs to reveal the one true God. He also shared the Unitarians' suspicion of the doctrine of the Incarnation.[153] Newton was aware of the differences between the varieties of Antitrinitarian belief, and was able to articulate their strengths and weaknesses. Whiston tells of a scholar at King's College, Cambridge who 'was at first inclinable to *Socinianism*, but upon a Conference with Mr. *Newton*, returned much more inclined to what has been of late called *Arianism*'.[154]

In one of his theological notebooks, Newton recorded a summary of his doctrine of God, in twelve articles. These articles show that Newton had moved away from conventional notions of the Trinity. For example, he makes no mention of the Holy Spirit, and espouses a distinctly subordinationist Christology. Newton begins by asserting the existence of 'one

---

[153] See Whiston 1727–1728, 2:1075; Whiston 1749–1750, 1:206 (Newton's support of Arian and Baptist positions); Iliffe 1999 (Newton's anti-Catholicism); Snobelen 1999, 383–390 (a careful comparison of Newton's beliefs and those of the Socinians and Unitarians), 404 (Newton and Crell); Snobelen 2005a, 248–251, 266–267, 294–295 (Newton, Pálfi and Crell), 252–255, 296–298 (Newton's heterodox library); Snobelen 2005b, 409; Buchwald and Feingold 2012, 433–434. On the distinctions between various Antitrinitarian groups in the later seventeenth century, see Mulsow 2005.

[154] Whiston 1730, 13. Wiles 1996, 93, claimed that Whiston was referring to himself, though this is not obvious from the context.

God the Father everliving, omnipresent, omniscient, almighty, the maker of heaven & earth'. Between this one God and humanity is one mediator, 'the Man Christ Jesus'. The Father communicates his own perfections to the Son, for example the quality of having life and knowledge within himself. Newton, who was fascinated by the notion of prophecy, emphasised that the Father 'communicates knowledge of future things to Jesus Christ', and to him alone. For this reason, Jesus' testimony is 'the Spirit of Prophesy & Jesus is the Word or Prophet of God'. The prophecies spoken by Jesus in the bible thus constitute divine oracles. The Father is distinct from the rest of creation in several respects. He is invisible, while the rest of creation is 'sometimes visible'. He is immoveable, and therefore every place is always entirely full of him; by contrast, all other beings can be moved 'from place to place'. The Father alone is due all worship, whether prayer, praise or thanksgiving; Christ's coming did not diminish the worship due to the Father. Prayers are most effective 'when directed to the father in the name of the son'. We are bound to thank the Father alone for creating us and blessing us with food, clothing and other benefits. Whenever we pray, we must direct our prayers to the Father in the name of Christ. We do not need to pray to Christ to intercede for us, since the Father himself will intercede if we pray to him aright. In stating that the first commandment forbids us from giving the worship due to the God of the Jews to angels or kings, though it does not forbid us from giving the name of God to angels or kings, Newton was presumably trying to find an explanation why Jesus was given the title of God in the early church. In conclusion, Newton glosses 1 Cor 8:6 by stating that 'we are to worship the father alone as God Almighty & Jesus alone as the Lord the Messiah the great King the Lamb of God who was slain & hath redeemed us with his blood [Rev 5:9] & made us kings & Priests [Rev 1:6].'[155] Of Jesus' redemptive or even exemplary role Newton makes no mention. Newton's unitarian vision of God thus has certain similarities to the views of Arius or Sozzini, but is identical with neither.

Newton's first extended engagement with the textual variants in the New Testament and the opinions of previous scholars like Erasmus and Grotius on particular details probably came through study of Walton's London Polyglot and Matthew Poole's synopsis of earlier biblical exegesis (1669–1676). This reading led him to the handful of debated passages which impinged on doctrine, including the Johannine comma. It is not

---

[155] Cambridge, King's College ms Keynes 8, 1r, transcribed online in The Newton Project. Cf. Pfizenmaier 1997a, 162–163.

unlikely that he discussed the matter with the biblical scholars John
Mill and John Covel, who had collected five Greek manuscripts of the
New Testament during his travels in the Ottoman Empire.[156] These men
were part of a scholarly coterie dedicated to the task of collecting variants for a new edition of the New Testament. Newton's association with
Mill went back to at least 1687, when Mill asked Covel to greet Newton,
John Montagu and Richard Laughton on his behalf.[157] In late 1693, Mill
visited Cambridge and spent time discussing Greek biblical manuscripts
with Newton. After the visit, Newton sent Mill his collation of the text
of Revelation, a central text in his obsession with prophecy, gathered
from the Complutensian Polyglot, Erasmus' *Novum instrumentum* (1516),
Codex Bezae and two manuscripts belonging to Covel, as well as a comparison with the oriental translations. Newton's letter to Mill shows how
seriously he took the tedious business of collating manuscripts. Before
sending his collations of Covel's manuscripts, he had them checked by
Richard Laughton, who 'found them right'. Newton's collation also
showed that Estienne had 'made several omissions & some other mistakes
in collating the Complutensian edition, tho' its probable that he collated
this edition with more diligence & accurateness then he did any of the
MSS'. At Mill's request, Newton also supplied a facsimile transcription of
a page of Codex Bezae, though he declined to do the same with Covel's
manuscripts, which 'were in such running hands that I could not imitate
them, nor did it seem worth the while the MSS being very new ones'.[158]
Though not formally trained in philology, Newton possessed the skill,
patience and intelligence to speak to professional textual critics as equals.

The course of Newton's initial reading and thinking on the comma may
be traced in one of his theological notebooks, written in the late 1680s.[159]
The notes are written with a number of different pens and inks, which

[156] These manuscripts are described by Mill 1707, CLXIII–CLXIV; and Uffenbach, in Mayor 1911, 148.
[157] Mill to Covel, 24 May 1687, London, BL Add. ms 22910, 256r. Further, see Iliffe 2016, chapter 11.
Thanks to Rob Iliffe for sharing this chapter in advance of publication.
[158] Mill to Newton, 7 November 1693, Cambridge, King's College Keynes ms 100; Newton to Mill,
29 January 1694, Oxford, Queen's College; Mill to Newton, 21 February 1694, London, Royal
Society Library, Miscellaneous Manuscripts 1/14; ed. in Newton 1959–1977, 3:289–290, 303–304,
305–307; Westfall 1980, 506. The current location of Newton's copy of Mill 1707, is unknown; see
Harrison 1978, 102, n° 204.
[159] Cambridge, King's College Keynes ms 2, 10r–v (originally 19r–v), transcribed online in The
Newton Project (checked by present author). See Smith 1675, 57–76, esp. 74–75 on Sand.
Further, see Iliffe 2016, chapter 11. Newton dog-eared the page of his copy of *The Holy Bible*
1660, Zz5r (Cambridge, Trinity College Adv.d.1.10) so that the corner of the relevant page
points to 1 Jn 5:7. This was his regular method of highlighting passages of interest; see Harrison
1978, 25.

indicates that Newton returned to these notes on several occasions, revising and adding new material as his investigations proceeded. The notebook includes references to Thomas Smith's *Sermon of the Credibility of the Mysteries of the Christian Religion* (1675), which contains an appendix dealing with the issue of the comma. It may even have been Smith's sermon that initially drew Newton's attention to Christoph Sand's discussion of the comma in the *Interpretationes paradoxae*, which would provide Newton with much of the material in this notebook. The comma is lacking from the great majority of Greek manuscripts, Newton notes, 'especially the ancienter as the Alexandrine sent to our king by Charles 1st by the patriarch of Constantinople & supposed to be written by that Thecla of whom Eusebius writes lib 8 hist as being martyred before the Councel of Nice, the capital letters tis wrote in & other signes arguing its great antiquity'. All these details are derived from Sand.[160] Sand had noted that the reading in Alexandrinus was followed by two manuscripts in Oxford.[161] Newton, perhaps recalling Smith's reference to the 'ancient Manuscript in the Archives of our *Colledg Library*', identified the two Oxford manuscripts provisionally as 'That of Magdalen Coll in Oxford [& in their publick library. Quaere?]'.[162] This *quaere* was apparently a reminder to search for further references. Probably after checking Fell's 1675 edition, or even after consulting Mill, Newton identified these manuscripts in an addendum further down the same page as 'that ancient MS. of Lincoln College in Oxford & those in Magdalen & New College'. Amongst the translations lacking the comma, Newton continued, were the 'Syriack Arabick & Aethiopick versions, which are very ancient'. This information is probably derived either from Sand, or from inspection of Walton's edition, where these eastern versions are supplied with Latin translations.[163] Newton named Sand explicitly as his source for

[160] Cambridge, King's College ms Keynes 2, 10r; cf. Sand 1669, 376: 'His verbis carent infiniti codices *MS. graeci*, & quidem vetustissimi, inter quos primum locum obtinet codex S. Theclae dictus, quia literis capitalibus ante annos 1400. ferè manu Theclae mulieris nobilis Aegyptiae, (cujus tanquam martyris meminit Eusebius in addit. Lib. V III. hist.) ante tempora Concilii Nicaeni I. exaratus fertur. Certum est plurima in eo admirandae vetustatis superesse vestigia. Dono missus hic codex Regi Angliae Carolo I. à Cyrillo Patriarchâ Constantinopolitano, hodieque in Bibliothecâ Regiâ Londini asservatur.' Further on Newton's reception of Sand, see Iliffe, forthcoming.
[161] Cambridge, King's College ms Keynes 2, 10r; cf. Sand 1669, 376: 'Codicem hunc (cujus autoritas ob antiquitatem potior est omnibus aliis multò recentiùs exaratis sive latinis, sive graecis,) sequuntur alia bina Msa Biblioth. Oxoniensis, quae etiam locum hunc non agnoscunt.'
[162] Cambridge, King's College ms Keynes 2, 10r; cf. Smith 1675, 58.
[163] Cambridge, King's College ms Keynes 2, 10r; cf. Sand 1669, 376: 'Deest quoque locus ille in *codicibus Syriacis*, (ut & in Mso Syriaco Bibliothecae Oxon: Arabicis, Aethiopicis).' At the time of his death, Newton possessed copies of Fell's 1675 edition, Walton's Polyglot, and Schaaf's 1709 Syriac/Latin diglot New Testament; see Harrison 1978, 102–103, n° 202, 216, 217. Newton progressively

information on the absence of the comma from a 400-year old Armenian codex.[164] The references to Erasmus in Sand, both direct and embedded within quotations from later authors, sent Newton back to Erasmus' published responses to Lee, Stunica and the Spanish monks, as well as his *Annotationes*.

Towards the end of his notes on the comma, Newton cited a passage from Smith's 1675 sermon which derided those scholars who 'adore' Codex Alexandrinus.[165] Smith mocked Sand's evaluation of this manuscript, concluding that it is 'not so antient, I believe, as is pretended, as if it had been wrote by the hand of Thecla'.[166] The fact that Newton recorded the jibe (and pointedly underlined it) suggests that he was affronted by Smith's cavalier attitude to the evidence of the manuscripts. Smith had also criticised Sand's conclusion that the context of 1 Jn 5 runs better without the imposition of the comma, as 'not only vain and frivolous, but very bold and immodest', tantamount to an accusation that the Holy Spirit should have spoken better Greek.[167] Newton, evidently irritated by Smith's tone, investigated some of his claims. Smith had written that '*R. Stephanus* in his Edition of the *N. T.* had the use of fifteen or sixteen old *Greek MSS.* above half of which retained it.' Newton, curious about the claims made about Estienne's manuscripts, asked his colleagues for further information. 'Dr Jo. Covell,' he subsequently added to his notes, 'shewed me an edition of the bible [in Greek] published at Paris A.C. 1515 with this title. Vet. et Nov. Bibliorum versio edit<a> a Roberto Stephano Paris. 1515.'[168] Newton evidently consulted with members of his immediate circle as he passed the outer reaches of orthodoxy, though it is not clear if they were aware where his investigations were leading him.

While reading around the subject of the comma, Newton consulted Gilbert Burnet's reports of manuscript readings in Germany and Switzerland, those reports that would cause such trouble for Burnet a decade later. He examined two Greek manuscripts belonging to Covel,

---

collected a list of the Greek manuscripts used by Estienne, Bèze and Ussher on the front flyleaf of his copy of Ἡ Παλαιά Διαθήκη 1653, now in Cambridge, Trinity College NQ.7.79. On the basis of these sources he concluded erroneously that Monfortianus contained only the gospels and Acts.

[164] Cambridge, King's College ms Keynes 2, 10r: 'Codex Armeniacus (inquit Sandius) ante 400 annos exaratus, quem vidi apud Episcopum Ecclesiae Armeniacae quae Amstelodami colligitur, locum illum non legit [Sand. Append. Interpr. Paradox.].' Cf. Sand 1669, 376–377.

[165] Cambridge, King's College ms Keynes 2, 10v; cf. Smith 1675, 66.

[166] Smith 1675, 57.

[167] Smith 1675, 74–75.

[168] Cambridge, King's College ms Keynes 2, 10v. No such edition could be traced, and the date is presumably an error.

from which he noted the variants at Rom 7:25, 1 Tim 3:16, 1 Jn 3:16, 1 Jn 5:6 and 1 Jn 5:7–8 which relate to the way God is named in Scripture.[169] On a loose scrap of paper he noted the absence of the comma from a number of printed editions: Nicolaus Gerbelius' edition of 1521, Fabricius Köpfel's edition of 1524, the Syriac edition of Guy Lefèvre de la Boderie (1584), a pocket Latin edition following the text of Henten (Antwerp, 1584), Fortunato Scacchi's edition of the Latin translation of the Syriac (Venice, 1609) and from the Arabic translation, which Newton presumably consulted in the London Polyglot.[170]

Newton evidently discussed biblical criticism with John Locke, who was well informed in recent religious thought. Amongst the heterodox literature in Locke's papers is a manuscript containing a partial English translation of Matthieu Souverain's bombshell *Platonism unveiled* (*Le Platonisme dévoilé*), in which he argued that Christianity had been corrupted early in its history by contact with pagan philosophy, particularly Platonism.[171] On the matter of the Johannine comma, Souverain suggested that Fulgentius had failed to recognise that Cyprian's apparent quotation of the Johannine comma was the result of allegorical interpretation. This allegorical manner of reading Scripture had led some of the fathers to equate the Johannine *logos* with Plato's second god.[172]

In 1690 Newton sent Locke *An Historical Account of Two Notable Corruptions of the Scripture*, the fruit of his investigations into the textual problems of 1 Jn 5:7–8 and 1 Tim 3:16. The self-consciously historical approach announced in the title of Newton's letter-treatise promised that the argumentation was not to be driven by doctrinal considerations, but by the empirical evidence of the extant documents. Newton protested to Locke that he intended to treat 'no article of faith, no point of discipline, nothing but a criticism concerning a text of scripture'.[173] Newton's motivation was also to an extent polemical and partisan. In his opening address he suggested that Locke, who had been constrained to flee to the Netherlands after being implicated in the anti-Catholic Rye House Plot of 1683, would appreciate the treatise all the more because of his opposition

---

[169] Cambridge, King's College ms Keynes 2, 51r. Newton searched Covel's manuscripts in vain for the variant τῷ θεῷ at 1 Jn 3:16. In fact this variant is not present in any manuscript. The variant he probably meant to search for was probably at 1 Jn 5:10, where the majority of Greek manuscripts have τῷ θεῷ, while a minority have τῷ υἱῷ, the reading underlying the Latin Vulgate ('filio').

[170] Jerusalem, National Library of Israel Yahuda ms 20, 5a.

[171] Oxford, Bodleian Library, ms Locke e. 17, 211–216; Snobelen 2005a, 267. On Locke, Newton and Socinianism, see Marshall 1994, 138–154, 289, 342–351, 366–367, 389–405, 415–430.

[172] Souverain 1700, 225–226.

[173] Newton 1959–1977, 3:83.

to 'the many abuses which they of the Roman church have put upon the world'. Indeed, the entire treatise presupposes that Newton and Locke were in basic agreement on a number of religious questions. Indeed, one of Newton's primary motivations in writing this treatise was to lay bare the ways in which the Catholic church had perverted the original message of Christianity by tampering with the text of Scripture.[174]

Newton's treatment of these two Scriptural cruces reflected his critical attitude towards traditional religion. Stephen Snobelen characterises Newton as intellectually disconnected from the content of the Church of England to which he professed outward allegiance, though 'by no means a deist, freethinker or anti-scripturalist'. Like all people with strong religious convictions, Newton was convinced of the rightness of his position, however radical it may have appeared to the masses. Newton's interest in both prophecy and the Scriptures sprang from his belief that these are the means that the elect use to discern the truth. Newton's 'remnant theology' was a relic of the Calvinism that had played such an important role in seventeenth-century English thought.[175] Newton's critical attitude towards the Church of England is consistent with Snobelen's suggestion that the *Historical Account* was intended as a contribution to the Trinitarian controversy that began with the publication of Nye's *History of the Unitarians* in 1687.[176]

Newton begins his *Historical Account* by noting that the spuriousness of the comma had previously been exposed by Erasmus, Luther, Bullinger, Grotius and other 'learned and quick-sighted men' who 'would not dissemble their knowledge'. Newton was clearly impressed by Erasmus' attitude of critical scepticism, and he takes over several broad arguments and many details from Erasmus' *Annotationes* and his reply to Lee. Despite the conclusions reached by scholars like Erasmus, many of Newton's contemporaries hung on to the comma as a defence against heresy. Newton considered such irrationality bordering on deceit unforgivable, especially in a Protestant: 'But whilst we exclaim against the pious frauds of the Roman church, & make it a part of our religion to detect & renounce all things of that kind: we must acknowledge it a greater crime in us to favour such practices, then in the Papists we so much blame on that account. For they act according to their religion but we contrary to our's.'[177] Yet Newton believed that Socinian critics who suggested that the relevant passage

[174] Iliffe 1999, 97–98; Iliffe 2006, 142.
[175] Snobelen 1999, 383, 389–390.
[176] Snobelen 2006, 128–129.
[177] Newton 1959–1977, 3:83.

from *De unitate* was corrupt had dealt 'too injuriously with Cyprian'. By contrast, Newton believed that the way Cyprian employed the phrase *tres unum sunt* suggested that the comma was not present in the Old Latin text in circulation during his lifetime.[178] In support of his contention, Newton mentions Eucherius' statement that many people interpreted the three earthly witnesses as types of the Trinity, and Facundus' account that Cyprian interpreted 1 Jn 5:8 in this way.[179] Newton even suggested that Cyprian's formulation 'the Father & Son & Holy Ghost' rather than the 'Father, the Word & the Holy Ghost', familiar from the later Latin Vulgate, showed that he was actually citing the baptismal formula given at the Great Commission (Mt 28:19), 'the place from whence they used at first to derive the Trinity'.[180]

From Cyprian, Newton worked backwards to Tertullian. The fact that Tertullian first gave a Trinitarian interpretation of the phrase *tres unum sunt* led Newton to suggest that this interpretation was 'invented by the Montanists for giving countenance to their Trinity. For Tertullian was a Montanist when he wrote this: & it is most likely that so corrupt & forct an interpretation had its' rise among a sect of men accustomed to make bold with the scriptures.' On Tertullian's authority, Newton suggested, this interpretation was subsequently adopted by Cyprian and other Latins.[181] Newton believed that the Trinitarian allegoresis of the earthly witnesses led a scribe (or several scribes) either to record this interpretation in the margin, 'whence it might afterwards creep into the text in transcribing', or to insert it into the text 'fraudulently'.[182]

As far as Newton knew, the earliest author who came under suspicion of inserting the comma deliberately was Jerome. While examining this accusation, Newton strikes a forensic pose. His interrogation of Jerome is simultaneously a summary of the ancient evidence for the comma. Like most of his contemporaries, Newton believed that Jerome wrote the prologue to the Catholic Epistles, and reintroduced into the Latin text a passage from the Greek which he believed had been omitted by 'unfaithful translators'. However, Jerome's admission that the comma was missing in the Latin text during his time 'cuts off all the authority of the present

---

[178] Newton 1959–1977, 3:84.
[179] Newton 1959–1977, 3:85; cf. Eucherius, *Liber formularum spiritalis intelligentiae* 9, *CSEL* 31:59; *Instructiones* I, *CSEL* 31:137–138; Facundus Hermianensis, *Pro defensione trium capitulorum concilii Chalcedonensis libri duodecim ad Justinianum imperatorem* I.3.8–13, *CCSL* 90A:12–14 (*PL* 67:535–536).
[180] Newton 1959–1977, 3:86.
[181] Newton 1959–1977, 3:86–87.
[182] Newton 1959–1977, 3:87–88.

Vulgar Latine for justifying it. And whilst he was accused by his contemporaries of falsifying the scriptures in inserting it, this accusation also confirms that he altered the public reading.' Jerome's insistence that the passage establishes the truth of Catholic doctrine renders it 'the more suspected'.[183] Newton could believe that Jerome was capable of such an alteration to the received Latin text. Anyone who has read Jerome's writings, Newton suggests, will have observed 'a strange liberty which he takes in asserting things'. Erasmus had characterised Jerome as 'frequently violent & impudent & often contrary to himself'.[184] Yet Newton was prepared to concede that in the present case, Jerome may have been 'imposed upon', or may simply have made a mistake. Nevertheless, Newton pointed out that those who accused Jerome of inserting the comma from a Greek text different from that commonly received in his time would 'overthrow the authority of his Version by making him depart from the received Greek'.[185] On the other hand, it would have been impossible for Jerome to have interpolated the comma on the basis of the Greek text, for all the evidence suggested that the Greeks had no knowledge of the comma. This conclusion is supported by the absence of the comma from other early translations from the Greek, such as the Arabic (which Newton consulted in Walton's Polyglot) and the Armenian (a detail Newton borrowed from Christoph Sand's *Interpretationes Paradoxae*), as well as its absence from the writings of the Greek and the early Latin fathers. Newton made heavy weather of Jerome. His difficulties sprang from the belief – as it would turn out, the mistaken belief – that Jerome had actually written the prologue to the Catholic Epistles. Even after reading Simon's book, Newton never seems to have dropped this misapprehension.

For Newton, the most compelling evidence against the proposition that the comma had originally been part of the Greek text was its demonstrable absence from the text during the time of the earliest fathers. Thomas Smith (1675) had challenged his readers to choose which of two explanations for this absence was more plausible: that the comma had been added by the orthodox 'without any necessity', or that that the comma had been removed by the Arians, notorious 'falsifiers of the sacred Records', who 'were so much concern'd to do it in defence of their private tenets and fancies, and especially to raze this Text, with which they were so oppressed, out of several Copies, from which by Transcripts it might easily

[183] Newton 1959–1977, 3:88.
[184] Newton 1959–1977, 3:89.
[185] Newton 1959–1977, 3:93.

be propagated into others'.[186] For Newton, the answer to Smith's question was clear:

> Yes truly those Arians were crafty Knaves that could conspire so cunningly and slyly all the world over at once [...] to get all men's books in their hands & correct them without being perceived: Ay & Conjurors too, to do it without leaving any blot or chasm in the books, whereby the knavery might be suspected & discovered; & to wipe even the memory of it out of all men's brains, so that neither Athanasius nor any body else could afterwards remember that they had ever seen it in their books before, & out of their own too so that when they turned to the consubstantial faith, as they generally did in the West soon after the death of Constantius, they could remember no more of it then any body else.

Such was the absurd conclusion obtruded upon those who asserted that the comma was an original part of the text. Those who inserted the comma into the text against the evidence of the manuscripts, as Newton believed Jerome to have done, revealed themselves as 'Falsaries by their own confession, & need no other confutation', unless they could prove that the comma had been removed from the text at an early stage 'by some better argument then that of pretense & clamour'.[187]

But having dismissed the comma as a later intrusion into the text, Newton had to explain how it arose. He suggested that this first happened 'by that abused authority of Cyprian [...], in the disputes with the ignorant Vandals to get some credit'. Moreover, he suggested that while the comma became established early in Africa, it did not become commonly accepted in Europe until the twelfth century or so. This error may be explained by the fact that many important texts from the early Middle Ages still remained unpublished and little known in Newton's time. Newton also pointed out that the evidence of the Latin bibles is ambiguous, since earlier manuscripts were corrected according to later recensions, causing a considerable variety amongst the texts in circulation: 'the old Latine has been so generally corrected that it is no where to be found sincere.'[188] In the case of the Johannine comma, the inconsistent application of these corrections – later strengthened by the misguided injunctions of Aquinas against the phrase *tres unum sunt* in 1 Jn 5:8 – led to an astonishing variety of different readings.

Using the notes he had taken when inspecting the early printed editions, Newton traced its gradual, but inconsistent, appearance in the

---

[186] Smith 1675, 58–59; this passage is discussed by Iliffe 2016, chapter 11.
[187] Newton 1959–1977, 3:93.
[188] Newton 1959–1977, 3:95.

Greek editions from the time of Erasmus onwards. Newton placed much of the blame for the confusion on Bèze, who maintained that the comma was read by Jerome, by Erasmus in the British codex and by the editors of the Complutensian edition, and that he himself had read it in 'several old books of our friend Estienne' (*in nonnullis Roberti nostri veteribus libris*). For Newton, such deliberately misleading language was reprehensible: 'Now to pull off the vizzard, I cannot but in the first place extreamely complain of Beza's want of modesty & caution in expressing himself.'[189] Newton showed that besides Estienne's printed editions, the only additional material available to Bèze comprised collations of two further manuscripts, though his words gave the impression that he had personally consulted more than two dozen manuscripts.[190] Newton also cleared up a persistent misapprehension about Estienne's edition. In the address to the reader in the 1550 New Testament, Estienne stated that he had used fifteen sources for his edition. The first was the Complutensian Polyglot, the second a collation of an old manuscript (Codex Bezae, later used by Bèze himself) sent to him by friends in Italy.[191] Since Estienne marked in the margin that the comma was absent from seven of his manuscripts, many readers assumed that it was present in the other eight. However, Newton pointed out that the Catholic Epistles were only transmitted in seven of Estienne's fifteen manuscripts. The comma was therefore absent from *all* his manuscripts. Newton noted furthermore that Estienne erroneously placed the closing metobelos after *in heaven* in v. 7 instead of after *on earth* in v. 8. Bèze, misled by Estienne's error, had mistakenly given the impression that the comma was attested in several of the Greek manuscripts used by Estienne.[192]

Having disposed of Estienne and Bèze, Newton concluded that the authority of the comma thus rests solely upon the authority of Erasmus' editions and the Complutensian Polyglot. 'But seeing Erasmus omitted it in his two first editions & inserted it unwillingly against the authority of his manuscripts in his three last, the authority of these three can be none at all.' Newton provided a short summary of Erasmus' exchange with Lee, and the appearance of Codex Britannicus:

> Hence notice was sent to Erasmus out of England that it was in a manuscript there; & thereupon to avoyd their calumnies (as he saith) he printed it in his following editions notwithstanding that he suspected that

---

[189] Newton 1959–1977, 3:98.
[190] On the manuscripts used by Bèze, see Krans 2006, 211–246.
[191] Estienne 1550, *2v: 'Secundo, exemplar vetustissimum, in Italia ab amicis collatum.'
[192] Newton 1959–1977, 3:99–100.

manuscript to be a new one corrected by the latine. But since upon enquiry
I cannot learn that they in England ever heard of any such manuscript but
from Erasmus, & since he was only told of such a manuscript in the time
of the controversy between him & Lee & never saw it himself: I cannot
forbear to suspect that it was nothing but a trick put upon him by some
of the Popish Clergy, to try if he would make good what he had offered
of printing the testimony of the three in heaven by the authority of any
one greek copy, & thereby to get it into his edition. Greek manuscripts of
the scriptures are things of value & do not use to be thrown away; & such
a manuscript for the testimony of the three in heaven would have made
a greater noise then the rest have done against it. Let those who have such a
manuscript at length tell us where it is.[193]

Newton noted Erasmus' suspicions that the British codex had been
adapted to conform to the readings in the Latin Vulgate. However,
Newton suspected either that the book never existed, or was the product
of 'some falsary of that age' who simply copied out the Epistles.[194] A few
pages later, Newton pointedly summarised the circumstances surrounding Erasmus' inclusion of the comma in his third edition of the New
Testament:

Erasmus who printed the triple testimony in heaven by that English MS,
never saw it, tells us it was a new one, suspected its sincerity & accused it
publickly in his writings on several occasions for several years together: and
yet his adversaries in England never answered his accusation, never endeavoured to satisfy him & the world about it, did not so much as let us know
where the record might be consulted for confuting him: but on the contrary when they had got the Trinity into his Edition, threw by their MS (if
they had one) as an Almanack out of date. And can such shuffling dealings
satisfy considering men?[195]

Newton's account of these events has a number of new turns. Newton
was convinced that the British codex was a deception masterminded by
the 'Popish clergy', a 'Phoenix' which 'once appeared to somebody somewhere in England but could never since be seen'.[196] Newton concluded
on this basis that Erasmus never saw this manuscript, but was only given
a report of its purported contents. Furthermore, Newton suggested even
more strongly than Richard Simon that Erasmus had 'offered' to Lee
that he would include the comma 'by the authority of any one Greek

[193] Newton 1959–1977, 3:100–101.
[194] Newton 1959–1977, 3:106.
[195] Newton 1959–1977, 3:109.
[196] Newton 1959–1977, 3:106.

copy'. These elements would become ingrained in the myths surrounding Erasmus' decision to include the comma in his Greek text.

Newton harboured similar suspicions about the authority of the reading in the Complutensian edition. While the edition was ostensibly based on manuscripts from the papal library, no such manuscripts containing the comma could later be found. Moreover, the marginal note in the Complutensian edition aroused Newton's suspicions. Admittedly, the annotation gave a justification for the reading in the Latin text:

> But this is not the main designe: for so the annotation should have been set in the margin of the Latin Version. It's being set in the margin of the Greek text shews that it's main designe is to justify the greek by the Latine thus rectified & confirmed. Now to make Thomas thus in a few words do all the work was very artificial, & in Spain where Thomas is of Apostolic authority might passe for a very judicious & substantial defence of the printed Greek: but to us Thomas Aquinas is no Apostle; we are seeking for the authority of greek manuscripts.[197]

More damning was the failure of Stunica and Erasmus' other Spanish critics to produce a manuscript supporting the reading. 'Neither could Sepulveda or the Spanish Moncks who next undertook the controversy find one greek manuscript which here made against Erasmus.'[198] Furthermore, the differences between the readings of the comma in the Complutensian Polyglot and Erasmus' Codex Britannicus argue that they do not rest on a genuine textual transmission: 'The differences are too great to spring from the bare errors of scribes & arise rather from the various translations of the place out of Latin into Greek by two several persons.'[199]

Newton concluded his critique by examining the context of the passage. He begins by giving a paraphrase of the entire passage, in the manner of Erasmus, interlarded with the text of the epistle. He maintained that the inclusion of the comma creates logical problems, for the presence of the heavenly witnesses is incomprehensible in the context:

> If their testimony be not given to men how does it prove to them the truth of Christs coming? If it be, how is the testimony in heaven distinguished from that on earth? Tis the same spirit which witnesses in heaven & in earth. If in both cases it witnesses to us men, wherein lies the difference between its witnessing in heaven & its witnessing in earth? If in the first case it does not witnesse to men, to whom does it witnesse, & to what purpose? & how does its witnessing make to the designe of John's discourse?

[197] Newton 1959–1977, 3:102.
[198] Newton 1959–1977, 3:103.
[199] Newton 1959–1977, 3:104.

For Newton, as for Milton in *De doctrina Christiana*, the inclusion of the comma, not least the double appearance of the Spirit, creates insuperable problems for the interpretation of the passage. 'Let them make good sense of it who are able: for my part I can make none.' Newton concluded by suggesting that his contemporaries' attachment to the comma sprang not from the love of truth or reason, but from the perverse attraction of mystery: 'Tis the temper of the hot and superstitious part of mankind in matters of religion ever to be fond of mysteries, & for that reason to like best what they understand least. Such men may use the Apostle John as they please: but I have that honour for him as to beleive he wrote good sense.'[200] The desire to discover the most parsimoniously simple explanation either of a text or of a natural phenomenon was a common thread in Newton's diverse intellectual pursuits, and a reflection of his abiding belief in divine orderliness.[201]

It is likely that Newton would have lost his position at Cambridge if his religious views had been more widely known.[202] He therefore planned that the *Historical Account* should be translated into French and published anonymously on the continent, perhaps recalling that the anonymous publication of Locke's *Letter on Toleration* in Latin (1689), albeit unintended, had to an extent shielded the author from negative consequences. Once Newton had gauged public reaction, he would decide whether to risk publishing the English original. On 14 November 1690, Newton sent the treatise to Locke. Locke replied the next day to confirm that he had received the work. Locke gave a fair copy of Newton's *Historical Account* to a friend who was travelling to Amsterdam around Christmas time, who was to pass it on to Jean Le Clerc with the request that he translate it into French or Latin, and arrange for its publication.[203]

Le Clerc was no friend to Socinianism. He stated that the Socinians, having refuted the 'chimeras' of the scholastic formulation of the Trinity, incorrectly believed that they had demolished the thing itself, but in this, he concluded, 'they were deeply mistaken'.[204] When Thomas Firmin sent

---

[200] Newton 1959–1977, 3:108.

[201] Snobelen 2001, 198–200.

[202] Further, see Westfall 1980, 318–319; Levine 1999, 200; Snobelen 1999; Champion 1999a; Champion 1999b; Iliffe 1999; Mandelbrote 2004; Snobelen 2005a; Iliffe 2006; Snobelen 2009.

[203] Locke 1976–1989, 4:164–165, n° 1338. Curiously, Locke wrote in a letter to Philippus van Limborch on 18 June 1691 (Locke 1976–1989, 4:277, n° 1398) that he had not heard from Le Clerc since he sent the papers in late December, which he found both surprising and worrying, for he considered Le Clerc otherwise to be a regular correspondent. However, he had endorsed Le Clerc's letter of 11 April 1691.

[204] Le Clerc 1987–1997, 2:145, n° 228.

Le Clerc a copy of the *Unitarian Tracts* of Biddle and Nye, the Swissman advised Locke to steer clear of this 'zelateur'.[205] Locke's decision to send Newton's treatise to Le Clerc thus suggests that he believed it to contain nothing that was technically unorthodox. But despite his ostensible orthodoxy, Le Clerc had an ambivalent reputation in England. In the early 1690s, Le Clerc was angling for a position at Oxford, but in November 1694, Gilbert Burnet sadly informed him that the suspicion of Socinianism that attached to his name had ruined his chances in England. According to Burnet, orthodox Anglicans concluded that the Socinians had 'endeavoured to reject the authority of all S. John's writings which is upon the matter to deny the whole New Testament; for if some books are rejected for which we have as good authority as for the rest, then all may be as well rejected. They study to make them pass for Cerinthus's works and thus they are serving the ends of the Atheists and are much supported by them.' Some in England even suspected that Le Clerc had been furnishing materials to these English Socinians.[206]

Le Clerc wrote back to Locke on 1 April 1691 to confirm that he considered the piece worth translating, but apologised that he had not yet had a chance to do so. In the meantime, he suggested that the author of the work should consult Simon's newly published *Histoire critique du texte du Nouveau Testament.* Given Le Clerc's own public disagreement with Simon over the question of Scriptural inspiration and Newton's violent antipathy towards the Catholic church, this recommendation indicates the impact that Simon's books had already begun to make on biblical studies.[207]

Newton took Le Clerc's advice, and read Simon's work carefully.[208] As Justin Champion has pointed out, Locke and Newton were amongst the few English readers who engaged constructively with Simon, however inimical his project appeared to Protestant sensibilities. Many others, such as Edward Stillingfleet, John Williams and Ofspring Blackhall, merely threw up their hands in horror at his challenge to religious certainties. But while Newton

---

[205] Locke 1976–1989, 4:354–355, n° 1446; Le Clerc 1987–1997, 2:66–68, n° 195; Locke 1976–1989, 4:433–436, n° 1486; Le Clerc 1987–1997, 2:69–74, n° 196.

[206] Le Clerc 1987–1997, 2:136, n° 225; Asso 2004, 92–94.

[207] Locke 1976–1989, 4:247–249, n° 1381; Le Clerc 1987–1997, 2:50–52, n° 187 (dates in old style).

[208] The catalogue of Newton's library, London, BL Add. ms 25424, 10r, lists the following works by Simon: 'Simon's Critical Enquiries London 1684 [Harrison 1978, n° 1514]; History of the Old Test: 3 books ib. 1682 [Harrison 1978, n° 1515; now Cambridge, Trinity College NQ.16.143]; History of the New Test: part 1. 2 ib. 1689 [Harrison 1978, n° 1516; Cambridge, Trinity College NQ.8.32].' See also London, BL Add. ms 25424, 18r: 'Lettres Choises [*sic*] de Simon (9) Amst. 1700 [Harrison 1978, n° 1517, Cambridge, Trinity College NQ.9.1].' Locke also owned a copy of Simon 1689a; see Harrison and Laslett 1971, 233, n° 2675–2676.

and Locke shared Simon's belief in the importance of a historical view of
the form of the text of Scripture, they disagreed with his conclusion that
interpretation was ultimately impossible.[209] When reading Simon's work,
Newton followed his habit of turning up the corners of the page to point
at passages he found significant. Having identified the most pertinent passages, he made a number of additions and corrections to his text. He noted
Simon's report that the comma was not found in any of the Greek manuscripts in the royal library at Paris or in Colbert's library. He also reported
the marginal annotations that Simon had found in some of these manuscripts, which indicated that the Greeks also had a tradition of applying
1 Jn 5:8 allegorically to the Trinity. (In his copy of Simon's book, Newton
dog-eared the page to point at this passage.) Newton also reported (again by
way of Simon) that the comma was absent in 'a certain version of the French
Church', about a thousand years old, which had been published by Mabillon
(namely, the lectionary of Luxeuil, Paris, BnF ms lat. 9427). (Newton had
likewise dog-eared this passage in Simon's book.) Newton also added further
details from Gilbert Burnet's descriptions of manuscripts in Zürich, Basel
and Strasbourg, to which he had referred only in passing in the first draft.
He also added details from his further reading of the ancient source material, such as the epistle of Pope Leo to Flavian against Eutyches.[210]

Newton sent these additions to Locke, and in a letter dated 30 June 1691
he expressed his excitement at the imminent appearance of his treatise.[211]
Locke wrote immediately to Le Clerc for news, but in his reply (21 July
1691) Le Clerc could only apologise that he still had not had time to translate the manuscript. However, he suggested that it be included in a larger
collection of dissertations, since 'a too-small book easily gets lost' (*un trop
petit livre se perd*).[212] Perhaps in order to give Le Clerc the chance to break
the back of the translation before burdening him further, Locke held back
from sending Newton's additions. He finally sent them in late 1691 or
early 1692, and Le Clerc duly integrated them in the translation.[213] But
by this stage Newton had cold feet, convinced that his authorship would

[209] Champion 1999b, 84–86, 92–93, 96.
[210] The following parts of Newton's text were inserted after Le Clerc had seen the draft: Newton
1959–1977, 3:87 ('For the Greeks ... insisted upon'), 90 ('Father Simon ... Monck'), 92 ('Epistle
of Pope Leo ... that Council'), 94 ('in the first Letter of his Travells,' 'kept at Strasburg ... St
Germans'), 100 ('And that this testimony ... Capital letters'), 115 ('And all this ... in the flesh'), 119
('Another report ... no more'), 120–121 ('I told you ... rashly corrected'); cf. Mabillon 1685, 476;
Simon 1689a, 211; Simon 1689b, 2:8.
[211] Locke 1976–1989, 4:288–290, n° 1405; Newton 1959–1977, 3:152–154, n° 365.
[212] Locke 1976–1989, 4:302–303, n° 1410; Le Clerc 1987–1997, 2:58–59, n° 191.
[213] Locke 1976–1989, 4:354–355, n° 1446; Le Clerc 1987–1997, 2:66–68, n° 195.

be recognised even in translation. It may be that the whiff of heresy that hung around Le Clerc's name in England made Newton wary of being associated with him. He hated being drawn into disputes, and his determination to share his religious views with only a small circle of adepts was motivated in part by his desire to avoid conflict.[214] It is also possible that he did not wish to break the second of the great commandments by undermining the faith of simple believers.[215] Moreover, the hostility provoked by Simon's work in England may have forewarned Newton that his own historicised reading of Scripture could elicit a similar response.[216] On 26 January 1692, Newton brusquely requested that Locke should return his papers.[217] When Locke told him that the translation was ready for the press, he wrote on 16 February 1692 to demand that publication be cancelled, offering to reimburse any expenses that Le Clerc had incurred.[218] On 1 April 1692 Le Clerc expressed his annoyance to Locke, assuring him that nobody would guess the author's identity.[219] But Newton's mind was made up. On 5 July 1692 Le Clerc informed Locke that he would keep the papers carefully awaiting further instructions.[220] Le Clerc evidently believed that the author of the *Historical Account* – whose identity was apparently still unknown to him – would recover from his jitters and agree to publish, for on 25 November he suggested to Locke that the author should read Richard Simon's latest work, the *Critical history of the principal commentators on the New Testament*, which contained further remarks on the Johannine comma.[221] Sixteen years later, in a review of John Mill's edition of the New Testament in the *Bibliothèque choisie* (1708), Le Clerc mentioned that he possessed a treatise in English on the textual history of the comma, sent to him many years earlier by Locke. He emphasised the work's importance, apparently hoping thereby to encourage its author to overcome his hesitation to publish.[222]

Newton had subscribed to Le Clerc's *Bibliothèque choisie* the year this review appeared, and in his copy, he turned down the corner of the page to

[214] Snobelen 1999, 390–391.
[215] Mandelbrote 1993, 287; Snobelen 1999, 389; Buchwald and Feingold 2012, 434.
[216] Champion 1999b, 96.
[217] Locke 1976–1989, 4:376, n° 1457.
[218] Locke 1976–1989, 4:387–388, n° 1465; Newton 1959–1977, 3:195–196, n° 384.
[219] Locke 1976–1989, 4:433–436, n° 1486; Le Clerc 1987–1997, 2:69–74, n° 196.
[220] Locke 1976–1989, 4:471–473, n° 1511; Le Clerc 1987–1997, 2:74–76, n° 197.
[221] Locke 1976–1989, 4:585–587, n° 1570; Le Clerc 1987–1997, 2:83–85, n° 201. Benjamin Furley mentioned the appearance of Simon's work in a letter to Locke dated from Rotterdam on 7 November 1692; Locke 1976–1989, 4:572, n° 1562.
[222] Le Clerc 1708, 319, 320, repr. in Mill 1710, **1r–3v.

point at Le Clerc's declaration that the *Historical Account* should be published.[223] Le Clerc's importunity evidently hit the mark, for Newton subsequently asked Hopton Haynes, one of his colleagues at the Royal Mint,
to translate the part of the *Historical Account* dealing with the comma
into Latin once again. Haynes was a man Newton could trust with his
religious secrets.[224] Richard Baron described Haynes as 'the most zealous
unitarian I ever knew', a judgement borne out by Haynes' *Causa Dei contra Novatores* (1747) and *Scripture Account of the Attributes and Worship
of God* (published posthumously in 1750). Baron reported some of the
theological opinions Newton had confided in Haynes: 'Sir *Isaac Newton*
did not believe our Lord's pre-existence, being a *Socinian*, as we call it, in
that article.' Indeed, Newton had predicted to Haynes that 'the time will
come, when the doctrine of the incarnation as commonly received, shall
be exploded as an absurdity equal to transubstantiation!' Baron was confident that Newton's opinions, however unorthodox, were well founded.
'No man,' he assured his readers, 'had searched the scriptures more than
Sir *Isaac Newton*, or understood them better.'[225]

The English text underlying Hayne's translation included the additions Newton had made after reading Simon's *Histoire critique*, as well as
a short coda. Newton corrected the translation at a number of points, and
took possession of the fair copy. On the frontispiece of the manuscript is
written '*Amstelaedami, Anno 1709*', which suggests that Newton intended
to have the translation published on the Continent immediately.[226] He
evidently wished to publish the translation anonymously, for when
William Whiston indiscreetly mentioned the impending publication in
conversation, Newton halted proceedings once again.[227] Within months

---

[223] Newton's copy of the *Bibliothèque choisie* for 1708 is now in Cambridge, Trinity College NQ.7.28;
dog-ear on 320. The *Bibliothèque choisie* appears in the catalogue of Newton's library, London,
BL Add. ms 25424, 17r; Harrison 1978, 176, n° 929. On Newton's renewed interest in theological
issues at this time, see Westfall 1980, 592–594.

[224] Haynes had written to Le Clerc in 1701 to discuss the interpretation of Rom 9:5; see Le Clerc
1987–1997, 2:363–365, n° 330; cf. Snobelen 1999, 402.

[225] Richard Baron, preface to Gordon 1763, 1:XVIII–XIX.

[226] Jerusalem, National Library of Israel Yahuda ms 20. The coda (95) reads: 'Cui latini recentio-
res plus aequo tribuentes, ausi sunt violare fidem tam graecorum, quam latinorum exemplarium:
cujus gravissimi sceleris utinam viri sapientes et ingenui paenitere tandem minus erubescant.' The
identity of the scribe is unknown. Comparison of this manuscript with autograph letters and
notes by Hopton Haynes (London, BL Add. ms 32415, 388r), Catherine Conduitt (London, BL
Add. ms 25424, 21v), John Conduitt (London, BL ms Sloane 4044, 183r), John Huggins (London,
BL Add. ms 25424, 21v), John Berriman (London, Lambeth Palace Library, Sion College ms ARC
L 40.2/E 39) and Jean Le Clerc (Copenhagen, Kongelige Bibliotek, Ms. Thott, n. 1208, lett. VII)
indicates that none of them was the scribe.

[227] London, Lambeth Palace Library, Sion College ms ARC L 40.2/E 39 (earlier shelfmarks: C.23, 16.6
and Ari 4 28), IV, cit. in the following text; cf. Mandelbrote 2004, 109–110. Newton returned to the

of Newton's death, William Whiston published the following account of these events, glossing over his own role in frustrating Newton's plans:

> He had early and throughly discovered that the Old Christian Faith, concerning the Trinity in particular, was then changed; that what has been long called *Arianism* is no other than Old uncorrupt *Christianity*; and that *Athanasius* was the grand and the very wicked Instrument of that Change. This was occasionally known to those few who were intimate with him all along; from whom, notwithstanding his prodigiously fearful, cautious, and suspicious Temper, he could not always conceal so important a Discovery. Nor need I now crave the Readers Belief of my Testimony in this Case. Sir *I. N.* has left not a few undeniable Testimonials of it behind him, Witness his MSS. Dissertations upon two of the famous New Testament Texts concern'd in that Controversy. 1 *Tim.* iii. 15 [that is, 16], and 1 *John* v. 7. both whose present Readings he took to be *Athanasian* Interpolations. Mr. *Le Clerke* mentions these *Dissertations* in his Epistle before Dr. *Kuster's* Edition of Dr. *Mill's Greek* Testament, without seeming to know their Author. He having received Copies of them from the famous Mr. *Lock*; and, I suppose, without any intimation that they were Sir *I. N.*'s. However, the Reader need not go so far as *Holland* for Satisfaction here, since these Dissertations were both put into *Latin* by a common Friend of Sir *I. N.*'s and mine, many Years ago, at Sir *I. N.*'s own desire; and, I suppose, with a design to have them then printed: tho' upon what occasion I can only guess, they were not printed at that time, and are now in the Hands of Sir *I. N.*'s Executors.[228]

subject in his draft *History of the Church*, written in the 1710s; Jerusalem, National Library of Israel Yahuda ms 15, 144r (transcr. Newton Project): 'Montanus for restraining their number to three gave them the name of Τριάς the Trinity. For I do not find that this name was used by any ancienter heretick. And his disciples erroneously pretended that baptism was performed in the name of this Trinity & that the spiritt the water & the blood in the first epistle of Iohn were symbols of this trinity.'

[228] Whiston 1727–1728, 2:1077–1078. One of the four copies of this book in London, BL (873.l.7) was owned and annotated by Whiston. The hand of the annotations matches that in a document signed by Whiston (Cambridge, University Library, National Maritime College ms 79/130.2); it also contains references to Whiston's works in the first person, such as a reference (2:1075) to Whiston's *Friendly Address to the Baptists* (1748). An annotation on 2:1077 identifies the 'common friend' who translated Newton's letter-treatise on the comma as 'Mr Hains'. Whiston 1727–1728, 2:1078, mentions further treatises on 'two other Texts which Sir *I. N.* believed the *Athanasians* had *Attempted* to corrupt, but were not able to carry their Point, which were intended to have been translated, and I suppose, published with the other two'. In the margin of London, BL 873.l.7, Whiston noted: 'But I have since heard they are preserv'd & are to be printed also.' This report of the translation of the *Historical Account* is repeated in Whiston 1736, 2–3. In his personal copy of that work (London, BL 873.l.19 (3)), Whiston likewise made an annotation identifying Haynes as the translator and noting that 'I have since heard they are preserv'd, and are to be printed also.' Whiston returned to the subject of the *Historical Account* nearly two decades later; see Whiston 1745–1746, 5:247, 321, 326, and esp. 322: 'The Editors also of the famous *Complutense* Edition have inserted it [the comma] in their Edition: But rather from *Thomas Aquinas*, whom they quote in the Margin, and the Vulgar *Latin*, than from any *Greek* Manuscript; as Sir *Isaac Newton* has fully shewn in his *Dissertation*, which I have read in Manuscript myself, from the Letters of the Editors

Any plan to publish the *Historical Account* directly after Newton's death was probably frustrated by the controversy that followed the posthumous appearance of his *Chronology of Ancient Kingdoms Amended* (1728).[229]

Newton's executors were reluctant to give out information about the contents of his unpublished papers. When Colin Maclaurin, who had discussed heterodox religious ideas with Newton, asked his trustees if anything relating to Samuel Clarke's theories about the Trinity had shown up amongst his papers, they told him that there was 'nothing they had seen as to that, or any other subject in Divinity'. This was a lie: the *Historical Account* is listed clearly in the rough catalogue of Newton's papers drawn up by Thomas Pellet in May 1727. When Maclaurin related their assurances to his friend Robert Wodrow, an orthodox Presbyterian, Wodrow was glad to hear this news, since he had heard rumours that Newton, Bishop John Moore, Samuel Clarke, and others had often met with others who favoured 'the revivall of Arrianisme in England'. Maclaurin's report gave Wodrow hope that these rumours were unfounded, for 'any small innuendos' made by a man of Newton's stature upon such subjects would be seized upon 'by multitudes'.[230] Soon after, when Whiston, ever indiscreet, revealed in print that it was Newton who had set him upon his Antitrinitarian course, Wodrow was aghast. Now Maclaurin admitted to Wodrow that Newton's religious sentiments were close to those of Samuel Clarke. Indeed, Maclaurin had heard Newton 'express himself pretty strongly upon the subordination of the Son to the Father, and say, that he did not see that the Fathers, for the first three or four centuries, had opinions the same with our modern doctrine of the Trinity'. According to

themselves.' See also Whiston 1745–1746, 5:329: 'We ought here to note, that Sr. *Isaac Newton* has written two Dissertations against the *second* and *fourth* of these corrupted Texts [1 Jn 5:7–8 and 1 Tim 3:16]; both which I have myself read, in Manuscript under his own Hand-Writing: And they are both mentioned by Monsieur *Le Clerk*, in his Preface to *Küster's* most excellent Edition of *Mills's Greek Testament*, as not knowing their Author. But he confesses, they both *deserve to be made publick*; (which I wish Sir *Isaac Newton's* Heir or Executor, the present Lord *Limmington* [John Wallop, husband of Kitty Conduitt], in whose Possession those and other original unpublished Writings of that great Man now are, would take Care of as soon as possible lest by some unhappy Accident they either perish, or be hereafter published from imperfect Copies, such as were those two which I read.) In those Texts Sir *Isaac* discovered, that the *Athanasians* had carried their Point, and had introduced their Interpolations into their common Text: which is the Case of the other three also. But he still observed, that there were *two* others which they attempted to corrupt, where they not could carry their Point; but failed of Success: Which were those two other Texts, that Sir Isaac meant, I could never learn [...].' Cf. Westfall 1980, 873; Snobelen 1999, 405, first drew attention to the marginal annotations in London, BL 873.l.7.

229 Mandelbrote 2004, 94.
230 Wodrow 1842–1843, 3:461–462. Conduitt's copy of Pellet's catalogue is in Cambridge, King's College Keynes ms 127a.5. On Pellet's catalogue and the Conduitts as trustees of Newton's papers, see Dry 2014, 10–21, 213.

Maclaurin, Newton was chary of discussing such matters, especially in the last years of his life.[231]

Newton's *Historical Account* of the Johannine comma was the most substantial to date. It sprang from his desire that the text of Scripture should be susceptible to proof and verifiability in the same way as experiments and hypotheses in the burgeoning natural sciences. Even though Newton halted publication of this work twice, he evidently shared its contents with a select circle: Samuel Clarke, Hopton Haynes, William Whiston and perhaps also Richard Bentley. The reactions of each depended on their different temperaments, their divergent conceptions of the boundaries between exoteric and esoteric religious knowledge, and their varying attitudes towards the necessity and means of bringing about a second reformation to a more primitive form of Christianity.[232] Newton's exposition also marked the beginning of a number of tenacious myths about Erasmus' encounter with the British codex, subsequently disseminated by Whiston and Thomas Emlyn. Once Newton's *Historical Account* was rediscovered and published in fragmentary form in 1754 and in a complete text in 1785, its impact increased substantially, working upon later critics such as Richard Porson.

8.   John Mill

The English critic John Mill (1644/45–1707), principal of St Edmund Hall, Oxford, could be a difficult man, described by some as 'craz'd & peevish', and of a notoriously 'Censorious Temper' towards the work of other scholars.[233] Nevertheless, his folio edition of the New Testament (1707), the culmination of some thirty years' work, built upon the foundations laid by the London Polyglot and John Fell's 1675 edition, was the most impressive work of biblical scholarship since Erasmus.[234] Certainly, the edition was not perfect. Mill confessed to Newton that it was 'not possible to observe every thing, nor yet to avoid errors in transcribing Lections out of my first book into my papers for the press, so as not sometimes to put one Copy for another, not to mention typographical blunders, and

---

[231] Wodrow 1842–1843, 4:59.

[232] Snobelen 1997.

[233] Hearne 1885–1915, 1:272.

[234] The article 'Mills, John', in Cross and Livingstone 1997, 1087, states: 'His correct name appears to have been "Mills", not (as commonly given) "Mill".' However, this form of his name, though occasionally attested, was rejected by Fox 1954, 5–6. Further, see Stuart Handley, 'Mill, John', in *ODNB*.

mistakes in correction'.[235] Besides examining manuscripts, Mill learned from Richard Simon that he should take account of Scriptural citations from the fathers.[236] But this was a massive task, one that not even Simon dared to undertake. Indeed, when Simon heard of Mill's work in 1706 from his visitor Miles Stapleton, 'he presently pull'd down 6 large Folios relating to the New Testament, being Collections of Lections, criticisms, &c. telling him that there were at least 100 Good MSS. he had made use of, which Dr Mill never either saw or had any Account of; and that if he presumed to publish his Book, he should rue the day that ever he undertook it.'[237] Given the consternation that Mill's edition generated, it was perhaps for the best that he died of a stroke within two weeks of its publication. The spread of reactions to Mill's edition, from wonder to apprehension to incomprehension, indicates that many considered this work comparable in importance to Newton's *Principia*: comprehensive, complex, difficult, but pregnant with the promise of laying bare the true kernel that lay under the surface phenomena.

The body text of Mill's edition is taken from Estienne's *editio regia* of 1550, with a few readings adopted from other editions, mainly those of the Elzeviers. Consequently, Mill's body text includes the Majority reading at 1 Tim 3:16 and the Johannine comma. After examining 1 Tim 3:16 in Codex Alexandrinus, Mill concluded that it had originally read $\Theta\Sigma$, and that a later hand had gone over the faint horizontal stroke of the Θ and added a stroke over the top with a darker ink, lest others should mistake the word for $O\Sigma$.[238] Mill's description of Erasmus' British codex expands on that in Ussher's manuscript collation, lent to him by James Tyrrell, Ussher's grandson.[239] However, it seems likely that Mill had inspected Montfortianus personally, for he adds a number of details not present in Ussher's description. First, he characterised the scribal hand of the body text as inaccurate. Second, he suggested that the marginal corrections and additions were added by Chark, whom he considered to have a beautiful script, though it is difficult to believe that such a description could be made of either the body text or the marginal annotations in Montfortianus. Mill noted that the text of Montfortianus diverges

---

[235] Newton 1959–1977, 3:305–306.
[236] Iliffe 2006, 140.
[237] Hearne 1885–1915, 1:179.
[238] Mill 1707, 624.
[239] Note in Oxford, Bodleian Library ms Auct. T. 5, 2r: 'Variantes Lectiones N. T. in hoc Libro comprehensas et ab Erudito Viro D. Iacobo Tirryl, clarissimi Armachanj Nepote, ante aliquot annos mecum peramicè communicatas, partim in Editionis meae N. T. corpore, partim in Appendice, fideliter exhibui. Oxon. Iun. 7. 1707. Joannes Mill.' Cf. *ASD* VI-4, 43.

significantly from the Majority text, and he registered more than 140 unusual readings in the gospels alone.[240] It seems that Mill did not work through the manuscript any further, probably assuming that the variants recorded in the London Polyglot would suffice for his purposes. However, as we have already noted, the collation prepared by (or for) Ussher did not include 1 Jn. As a consequence, Mill had no idea that Ussher's Codex Montfortianus was in fact Erasmus' Codex Britannicus.

Mill's note on the Johannine comma covers ten relentless folio pages of small type.[241] He enumerates the known manuscripts in which the comma is not found. He lists the fathers and councils, both Latin and Greek, that fail to cite the comma when one would expect them to do so. The only known manuscripts which exhibited the passage were Erasmus' British codex, the unidentified Vatican codex on which the editors of the Complutensian bible were presumed to have relied for their reading of the comma, and the manuscripts consulted by Estienne. (On this last point Mill evidently overlooked the objections of Lucas Brugensis and Simon.)[242] He also mentioned the Greek translation of the *acta* of the fourth Lateran council and a treatise on Roman Catholic theology by Emmanuel Calecas as Greek witnesses to this passage.[243] Mill concluded that the seeming citations in Tertullian, Cyprian and Augustine were merely allegorical readings of v. 8. He followed Simon in disputing the attribution of the prologue to the Catholic Epistles to Jerome. But just when the reader expects Mill to reject the comma, the critic declared that after weighing all the evidence he could see no evidence to excise the passage.[244] This note went unchanged in Ludolf Küster's revision of the late Mill's work, published in 1710.[245]

This strange conclusion, which seemed to undermine the promise held out by the edition as a whole, was nevertheless consistent with what

[240] Mill 1707, CXLVIII. Brown, in *ASD* IV-4:61 n. 95, asserts that it is 'abundantly clear that [Mill's] sole two sources of information [on Montfortianus] are Walton's Polyglot and Ussher's collation'. However, Mill's characterisation of the script of the body text as *minus accurata* and his comments on the presence of variant readings in the margins, not to mention his attempt to identify the scribe of these notes, suggests that he had seen the manuscript. Mill's comment on Mt 26:75, in which he refers to Ussher's collation rather than to the manuscript itself, could have been written some time after he had inspected the manuscript.

[241] Mill 1707, 738–749; Mill's remarks on the comma are reprinted in Burgess 1822, 11.

[242] Mill 1707, 742.

[243] The text of the Lateran Council's decision is in Denzinger 2001, 359–362, §§ 803–808, esp. 803. Emmanuel Calecas' *De fide et principiis catholicae fidei* is edited in Combefis 1672, 2:219C; repr. in *PG* 152:516B.

[244] Mill 1707, 749.

[245] Mill 1710, 586; Mill 1723, 586. The 1723 edition was a reissue made up of remaining copies of the 1710 edition, supplied with a new first gathering, including a new title page with the new date.

Thomas Hearne described as Mill's 'very wavering unsettled Principles'.[246] Mill's judgement on the comma was not without cost to his reputation. In a letter dated 18 September 1708, published in the *Bibliothèque choisi* as well as in the reissues of Mill's edition, Jean Le Clerc conceded that there was much to praise in Mill's treatment of the question of the comma, despite the conclusion. (Given Mill's opposition to the use of the writings of Locke and Le Clerc at Oxford, the tone of the review was notably generous.) Le Clerc was glad that Mill had rejected the attribution of the prologue to the Catholic Epistles to Jerome, as had Martianay and Pouget, editors of the recent Paris edition of Jerome (1693–1706). In fact, Le Clerc suspected that Mill had presented the evidence against the comma to make his opinion plain while maintaining a defence against potential criticism – in other words, by employing the same tactics as Erasmus himself:

> If Dr. Mill hath not concluded here like a judicious Critick, yet certainly he hath shown himself to be a candid and ingenuous Man, in producing the Arguments which effectually overturn his own Opinion; nor wou'd I impute it to his want of Judgment, in not yielding to the force of such Arguments, so much as to the Prejudice of a sort of Men, who are wont spitefully to reproach those who freely own the Truth; as if they favour'd I know not what Heresys, merely because they will not argue against 'em from corrupted Texts. Truly the best Men are sometimes under a necessity of giving way to the froward, which we must forgive.[247]

A review in the *Journal des Sçavans* likewise remarked that Mill's note on the Johannine comma exposed the tension between theological claims and philological facts.[248] By contrast, William Whiston (1711) flayed Mill for allowing his critical faculties to be led by *a priori* considerations of orthodoxy:

> In short, they who peruse the full Account of this Matter in Dr. *Mills*, and observe how much his *Premises*, however made too favourable by uncertain Suppositions, require him to reject this Verse, will wonder how his *Conclusion* comes to be for it; especially when he cannot come at that Conclusion without giving up the *Integrity* of almost all the original Copies and Versions of the New Testament for many centuries; only to support the Credit of one Text, which seems to favour some modern Opinions: whereas after all, the Reputation of it with him, as well as with every other considering Person, must be, at best, so *very weak*, as not to

---

[246] Hearne 1885–1915, 1:189.
[247] Le Clerc 1708, 320–321. English translation from Emlyn 1715, 54–55.
[248] Anon. 1708, 182–183; cf. Fox 1954, 83.

be able to *determine* their Opinions in any Point, in which they are not already satisfy'd from other Evidence; and so is even *to them* of very small Advantage or Consideration.[249]

Having been deprived of his chair at Cambridge for expressing unorthodox religious beliefs, Whiston should have known precisely why Mill had come to the conclusion he did, but he was nevertheless disappointed that Mill had not possessed the courage of his convictions. Whiston's associate Thomas Emlyn (1715) was equally aghast, describing Mill's judgement as

> a *suprizing Conclusion* in favour of *this Text,* so unsutable to *his Premises,* and against *all the Rules of Criticism;* in preferring *one* Copy to *all* the Copys besides; *one* Father to *all* the Fathers: nay rather, without *one* Copy, rejecting all the Manuscript Copys; and setting *one supposed,* at best but *dubious,* Testimony of *one* or *two Fathers,* against *all* the certain Evidences from *all* the Copys and *all* the Fathers for near 500 *Years.*[250]

Even at a remove of eighty years, Richard Porson could barely conceal his disgust: 'Mill, after fairly summing up the evidence on both sides, just as we should expect him to declare the verse spurious, is unaccountably transformed into a defender.'[251]

Yet Mill also found his champions. Le Clerc's review prompted the Lutheran cleric Friedrich Ernst Kettner (1671–1722) to publish an elaborate defence of Mill's conclusions in 1713. Kettner, who had published two books on the comma previously, including a refutation of the views of Christoph Sand, Richard Simon, Etienne de Courcelles and Le Clerc, argued that the comma had dropped out of the textual tradition soon after the composition of the letter, but had been providentially restored during the fifth century. Kettner could also bring an important new piece of evidence, communicated to him by Paul Ernst Jablonski, court preacher at Berlin: that the comma was attested in Codex Ravianus, allegedly bought in the east by Johannes Ravius and later sold to the royal library in Berlin.[252] But due to Kettner's implausible hypotheses, and to the quantity of nugatory and even contradictory arguments he brought forward in defence of the comma, his sprawling work ultimately collapsed under its own excessive weight.

---

[249] Whiston 1711–1712, 4:382.

[250] Emlyn 1715, 54.

[251] Porson 1790, v.

[252] Kettner 1713, 206, 210. The Berlin codex was mentioned by Saubert 1672, 61, and Le Long 1709b, 1:367, but without any mention of the comma. Jacob Tollius (1687) mentioned it as one of the noteworthy manuscripts of the electoral library; see Tollius 1700, 45.

9. William Whiston

William Whiston was the son, nephew and grandson of clergymen. His father Josiah, a Presbyterian, had conformed at the Restoration, but later regretted his capitulation. However, two uncles, likewise clergymen, refused to conform, and kept moderate dissenting chapels. The example of his penitent father and his steadfast uncles certainly imprinted in Whiston the importance of maintaining principles in the face of adversity. Entering Clare Hall in 1686, he was introduced into a world in which everything seemed in the process of being discovered anew. The dominant Cartesian world view was slowly yielding to a new vision of the universe as Newton's difficult ideas, comprehensible to only a few, promised to pull back the curtain and reveal the divine design behind all things. Through 'great Difficulty and Pains', Whiston set out to master Newton's writings, and was 'deeply and surprizingly affected' at the experience of encountering the 'amazing Truths' Newton had revealed, and the conclusions that could be derived from them. The development of Whiston's puritan religiosity at Cambridge was influenced by the pervasive presence of pietistic religious societies, which aimed to recover the simplicity of devotion believed to have characterised the primitive church. Whiston played an active role in the work of two such societies, the Society for the Promotion of Christian Knowledge (SPCK) and the Charity Schools. He associated primarily with Whigs and latitudinarians such as Richard Bentley, Francis Hare, Benjamin Hoadly and Samuel Clarke. In 1693 he was ordained as a priest by the latitudinarian bishop William Lloyd.[253]

Whiston met Newton in 1694 and cultivated his friendship for nearly two decades, first as his deputy as Lucasian professor of mathematics at Cambridge, and then as his successor. Although Whiston would later claim that Newton had taken him under his wing, Jed Buchwald and Mordechai Feingold have argued recently that the presumption of intimacy is largely the result of Whiston's own self-serving claims in print.[254] Indeed, it was not Newton who pushed for Whiston's appointment to the Lucasian chair, but Richard Bentley. In any case, Whiston was clearly awestruck by Newton. After promoting Newton's natural philosophy at Cambridge, Whiston came to share the heterodox religious views of Newton and Clarke in about 1704–1706. In 1711 Whiston described how a certain 'excellent friend' had told him and 'another

---

[253] Duffy 1976, 130–133.
[254] Buchwald and Feingold 2012, 331–352.

Person of great Eminence', presumably Clarke, that 'had it not been for the Church's farther Determination, he had been contented with the Arian Scheme'. Whiston's study of the apostolic fathers, prompted by his reading of Richard Brocklesby's *Gospel-Theism* (1706), led to a growing conviction that Athanasius' Trinitarian theology had corrupted primitive Christianity.[255] Whiston was a great talker, and he volubly espoused opinions in print and in coffee-houses which Newton only dared utter behind closed doors, and Clarke only in oblique terms.[256]

The desire to recover the pristine simplicity of the early church was not confined to a cabal of Newton's intimates, but was a fundamental impulse in the pietistic religious societies in which Whiston participated.[257] Indeed, Mill's explicit intention was to restore the New Testament text to its original and primitive state by laying bare to view all the errors in its transmission through time.[258] But Whiston's willingness to depart radically from the doctrinal norms of the church set him apart, as did his enthusiasm for early Christian apocrypha, whose existence seemed to threaten the self-evidence of the New Testament canon.[259] In 1708 Whiston sent a series of objections to the traditional conception of the Trinity to the archbishops of Canterbury and York, asking whether these doubts might best be discussed in convocation or in print. Both counselled prudence, but Whiston had the bit in his teeth. William Lloyd wrote on 30 July 1708 that he had heard that Whiston was working on an apologia for Socinianism. If these rumours were true, Lloyd warned that he would be forced to break off their friendship, 'For after that I cannot but look upon you as a Subverter of Souls, and as an Enemy to the Church of Christ.'[260] Whiston (26 August 1708) denied that he had any intention of 'going over to *Socinianism*: to which I have not the least Disposition, nor ever had in my Life'. However, he informed Lloyd that he had 'made an Extract of almost all the Texts of Scripture, and most ancient Testimonies relating to the Trinity and Incarnation, under their several Heads, and, without any Hypothesis at all of my own, have exactly followed those antient

---

[255] Whiston 1711–1712, I:IV–V, IX; Whiston 1727–1728, 2:1070–1071; Snobelen 1999, 402–403; Snobelen 2004.
[256] On 8 August 1710, Zacharias Uffenbach encountered Whiston at the Grecian Coffee-house in Cambridge; see Mayor 1911, 178–179.
[257] Duffy 1976, 132.
[258] Mill 1707, CLIII; cf. Sheehan 2005, 45.
[259] Sheehan 2005, 39–40, 42.
[260] Whiston 1711a, 21. Lloyd's fair copy of this correspondence between himself and Whiston is preserved in London, BL Add. ms 24197.

Testimonies'. It was his intention to publish these documents to promote rational and impartial discussion. 'If the common Doctrines disagree with those Texts and Testimonies, they ought certainly to be discarded. If they agree, my book will be an unanswerable Vindication of them. And it would make an honest Man amaz'd to see what Fears and Jelousies are conceiv'd from so fair and unexceptionable a Method as this is.' When he saw how the original form of Christianity had become altered through time, he could not hold his peace, 'lest I myself be condemned for my Silence and Hypocrisie another day'.[261] Lloyd (8 September 1708) tried to convince Whiston 'not to break the peace of the Church by writing against it'. In turn, Whiston replied (18 September 1708) that he had no intention to 'suppress or corrupt the ancient Books: to vouch spurious or suspected Authorities: [...] for fear of the imputation of *Arianism*'. Whiston asked Lloyd 'how the *Consubstantiality* and *Coequality* of the Holy Ghost to the Father and the Son' could be understood as anything but 'Popery', of which 'the Reformed Churches have not yet cast out all the Reliques'.[262] In response, Lloyd wrote (April 1709) that this doctrine is implicit in the form of baptism given by Jesus himself, as well as in several other passages in the New Testament, notably Jn 10:30 and the Johannine comma, cited by Tertullian, Cyprian and several other African fathers, as Mill had noted:

> It is evident that not only those Fathers themselves did not doubt but that St. *John* wrote those Words, but that neither did those that they wrote against, question it. For those Fathers did not only quote those Words, but they argued from them; which had been ridiculous if there had been any doubt of the Text. [...] This I take to be a sufficient Proof of the Unity of the Three Persons in the Divine Nature: and I think there needs no other Proof of their *Consubstantiality* and *Coequality*.[263]

Mill's critical commentary had evidently become a rich mine for disputants on both sides. In his reply (14 April 1709), Whiston characterised the comma as a 'gross *Interpolation*', and begged Lloyd to 'keep one Ear open for Antient Truth, and Genuine Christianity; and not, like your great Predecessor [Stillingfleet], run your self aground in the Defence of Modern Corruptions; which will soon appear utterly indefensible'.[264] Lloyd, exasperated by Whiston's refusal to heed his counsel and by the

---

[261] Whiston 1711a, 22–23.
[262] Whiston 1711a, 25, 27, 28.
[263] Whiston 1711a, 31–33.
[264] Whiston 1711a, 48–49.

imputation of dishonesty, broke off their correspondence. Whiston's desire to debate his ideas publicly was met with derision. After reading the correspondence between Whiston and Lloyd, Jonathan Swift satirically asked: 'pray, why might not poor Mr. *Whiston,* who denies the Divinity of Christ, be allow'd to come into the Lower House of Convocation, and convert the Clergy?'[265]

In the catechistical lectures that Whiston was giving at St Clement's Church in Cambridge at this time, he was accused of making assertions 'contrary to the Doctrine of the Church', and of omitting the invocation of the Holy Spirit and the Trinity in the litany. In his *Sermons and Essays,* published in August 1709, Whiston presented Arianism as the primitive form of Christian doctrine of God. Bishop Moore, who had presented Whiston for the lectureship, was informed of his protégé's aberrations, and John Covel, now vice-chancellor of the university, received a petition for Whiston's expulsion, but by 'the good Providence of God' the matter was dropped, at least for the time being.[266]

Even after this near-disgrace, Whiston had not quite used up his last reserves of goodwill. In mid-1710, the stewards of the Charity Schools and Parishes in Cambridge asked him to prepare an edition of Tate and Brady's metrical psalter. This work contained an orthodox versification of the *Gloria Patri* to be sung at the end of each psalm. According to Charles Wheatly, the Arians had attempted to change the earliest orthodox doxology, '*Glory to the only Father with the Son and the Holy Ghost*', to '*Glory be to the Father, by the Son, in the Holy Ghost*'. In response, the orthodox adopted the revised form '*Glory be to the Father, and to the Son, and to the Holy Ghost, now and ever world without end,*' and the western church added the phrase '*As it was in the beginning,* to shew that this was the Primitive Faith'.[267] Whiston baulked at the Trinitarian doxology given by Tate and Brady, arguing that the 'calling the Three Persons *One God,* or *the One God,* in any Doxologies is without all Example in our Publick Liturgy, [...] and came in only from the Poets to make up their Verses'. Whiston provided alternatives in which worship is offered to the Father alone. The stewards rejected Whiston's amendments, but he had 100 copies of his edition printed up for the private use of himself and 'some Friends, that might be willing to Glorify the Father *through* the

[265] Swift 1713, 8–9. Swift 1713, 14–15, writing satirically in the persona of Anthony Collins, refers directly to the correspondence between Whiston and Lloyd. Further, see Lynall 2012, 124–125.
[266] Whiston 1711a, 75–76; cf. Duffy 1976, 136.
[267] Wheatly 1710, 39. Further, see Helfling and Shattuck 2006, 136.

Son, *in* the Holy Spirit, according to the Original Appointment of the Apostles'.[268] With the return of two Tory MPs for Cambridge in the election of 5 October 1710, the political winds began to blow against Whigs like Whiston, and before the month was over, the university had begun formal proceedings against him, which led to a trial, banishment from Cambridge and ultimately dismissal from his professorial chair.[269] This was precisely the fate that Newton, discreet to the point of paranoia, had desired to avoid.

During this entire period, Whiston had been working out his ideas in a major tract, *Primitive Christianity Reviv'd*, which appeared in five volumes in 1711–1712, bearing a dedication to the archbishop of Canterbury and the convocation. In January 1709 he had sent a draft of the fourth volume (on the Trinity) to John Sharp, archbishop of York, by way of Clarke. Clarke declined to comment on the work, and Whiston accused him of 'plainly suppressing Conscience, and deserting the sacred Truths of God, out of worldly Considerations'.[270] Clarke had reason to be wary of associating too closely with Whiston. At his doctoral disputation, Henry James, regius professor of divinity, challenged Clarke to repudiate Whiston's ideas, and insinuated that his subscription to the Thirty-Nine Articles was insincere.[271]

At the conclusion of the chapter in *Primitive Christianity Reviv'd* which deals with the question whether '*God the Father*, the *Word*, or *Son of God*, and the *Holy Spirit*, are Beings, or Persons really and *numerically* distinct from each other', Whiston noted rhetorically that readers may wonder that he omitted to include the comma in his enumeration of the Scriptural evidence for the doctrine of the Trinity. 'But the plain reason is, that I believe 'tis certainly spurious, and inserted by some bold Transcribers from a marginal Gloss of the next Verse.' Whiston's eight arguments against the authenticity of the comma strongly resemble those presented in Newton's *Historical Account*.

Whiston considered it decisive that the comma is absent from the earliest biblical manuscripts, translations and commentators, 'excepting one inaccurate Citation in Cyprian'. The failure of the earliest fathers like Tertullian to quote the comma was 'one of the strongest Arguments against it in all Antiquity'.[272] It is true, Whiston added, that the comma

---

[268] Whiston 1711a, 109–113.
[269] Duffy 1976, 138.
[270] Whiston 1730, 16–17; Snobelen 1997, 164–165.
[271] Whiston 1730, 17–22; Duffy 1976, 136–137.
[272] Whiston 1711–1712, 4:379.

was quoted against the Arians at a later period, but such instances are met first in Africa, 'the Country where this Corruption was first made'. Only subsequently did the comma creep into texts in the West. 'And certainly no wonder, when it seem'd to support the *Orthodox Doctrine* beyond any other Text in the whole Bible.'[273]

Whiston noted that the 'strange Confusion' in the manuscript transmission betrays 'the greatest marks of Addition, Corruption, and Interpolation possible'.[274] Furthermore, he asserted that the verse was an allegorical interpretation, discernible in the writings of the African fathers up to Augustine. Like Newton, Whiston maintained that Facundus provides strong evidence that Cyprian's apparent quotation of the comma arose 'not as an original Text, but as a Gloss upon the Verse following'. And if the comma was an interpolation in Cyprian's text, it must be considered as such in the text of the epistle itself. Whiston also remarked that the comma is 'so singular and remarkable' that its sudden disappearance from the canonical Scriptures would certainly have caused comment, 'especially when it belong'd to one of the more undoubted Epistles, and not to any of those doubtful ones, which were a considerable time not so well known to a great part of the Church'.[275]

Whiston also argued that the comma fits badly into John's argument: that the water, blood and Spirit bear witness to Jesus as Saviour. Moreover, the presence of the Spirit amongst both the earthly and the heavenly witnesses 'reduces the six Witnesses propos'd, in reality to only five'. Whiston suggested that the inclusion of the Word amongst the three in heaven who witness to Jesus on earth implied that the Word and Jesus are two separate entities. But this would seem to make John into 'a *Cerinthian* Heretick, and to make *Christ* or the *Word*, and *Jesus* or the *Man*, to be two separate Beings', a notion which Irenaeus 'so earnestly cautions against'.[276] Whiston maintained a hostile position on the comma in a number of his subsequent works. In his edition of the Johannine Epistles, published in 1719 at Samuel Clarke's suggestion, Whiston omitted the comma from the text, and did not even mention it in his commentary.[277] He maintained this exclusion in his *Primitive New Testament* (1745).[278]

---

[273] Whiston 1711–1712, 4:381.
[274] Whiston 1711–1712, 4:379–380.
[275] Whiston 1711–1712, 4:380.
[276] Whiston 1711–1712, 4:380–381.
[277] Whiston 1719d, 68–70; on Clarke's role in instigating this commentary, see Whiston 1730, 100. Further, see Snobelen 2006, 134.
[278] Whiston 1745, O3r.

Whiston's attitude to Erasmus resembles that of Newton. He asserted that Erasmus 'was first oblig'd to insert [the comma] from a single *British* MS. which yet perhaps he never saw, and which has never appear'd since, in his third Edition of the *Greek* Testament; *ne cui foret ansa calumniandi*, or in plain *English, least he should be call'd an Arian*; as his Insertion was without the Authority of the rest of his ancient MSS. from which he had made his two former Editions'.[279] Whiston thus shared two unfounded ideas with both Newton and Thomas Emlyn: first, that Erasmus was under some obligation to include the comma; and second, that the British codex on which Erasmus claimed to have relied was a fiction. Only after running through all the evidence does Whiston voice his conclusion on the authenticity and value of the comma: 'As *to me*, 'tis, I confess, one of the plainest and most pernicious Corruptions or Interpolations that is now in the World; and built on such poor Evidence as in any other Case of meer Criticism, where *Orthodoxy* were not concern'd, would be look'd upon as perfectly inconsiderable.'[280] These similarities suggest strongly that Whiston had read Newton's *Historical Account*, and shared his conclusions.

However, Whiston's indiscretion, his extravagant prophetic claims, his love of public disputation in coffee-houses, his unguarded references to a nameless 'excellent friend' who communicated Arian views to him, and his publication of an unauthorised English translation of the theological sections of Newton's 'general scholium' to the second edition of the *Principia*, led to a decisive break with Newton.[281] Whiston, incapable of acknowledging his own contribution to his personal misfortunes, attributed the break to Newton's inability to bear contradiction:

> But he then perceiving that I could not do as his other darling friends did, that is, learn of him, without contradicting him, when I differed in opinion from him, he could not, in his old age, bear such contradiction; and so he was afraid of me the last thirteen years of his life. [...] He was of the most fearful, cautious, and suspicious temper that I ever knew.[282]

At his trial before convocation on charges of heresy in 1711, driven by the counter-revolutionary Tories Francis Atterbury and William Binckes, who had tried to bring down Gilbert Burnet a decade earlier, Whiston was acquitted. A second trial in the court of arches was ended by the

[279] Whiston 1711–1712, 4:381–382.

[280] Whiston 1711–1712, 4:382.

[281] The translation of the *Scholium generale* is in Whiston 1713, 29–31. Further, see Snobelen 1999, 412–415; Buchwald and Feingold 2012, 336–339; Snobelen 2004, 581–586, 591–592. The catalogue of Newton's library, London, BL Add. ms 25424, 13v, 15r (cf. Harrison 1978, n° 1729, 1734, 1737), contains Whiston's *Three essays, Primitive Christianity* and *Historical preface*, in which he referred to his 'excellent friend'.

[282] Whiston 1753, 250–251.

general amnesty extended to all pretended heretics by George I upon his accession in late 1714.[283] Whiston's subsequent attempt to promote his ideas through the establishment of a Society for Promoting Primitive Christianity and the Practice of Infant Baptism, where heterodox ideas could be discussed, and heterodox literature of all kinds could be read and purchased, had only a short life (1715–1717). Clarke and Newton declined to support the Society, evidently unwilling to associate too closely with such open heterodoxy.[284] As a result of his stubborn promotion of aberrant religious ideas, Whiston experienced frequent hostility within the Anglican church. Edward Welchman lamented that Whiston's 'Affection for *Arianism* had blinded his Eyes, and corrupted his Heart; so that either he could not, or would not, see the *clearest* Evidences that made for the *Catholick* Doctrine'.[285]

One embarrassing incident occurred during the service at St Andrew's Holborn on Trinity Sunday 1715. The epistle for the day was Col 1:13 ('He has rescued us from the power of darkness and transferred us into the kingdom of his beloved Son'). The assistant curate, Robert Lydal, took this as an opportunity to preach on the Trinity, a topic he found particularly apt because there was 'an *Arian* among his hearers, who ridiculously pretended to make Proselytes'. Lydal emphasised the Johannine comma as evidence of the Nicene doctrine of the Trinity, concluding, as Whiston recorded, 'with heavy Denunciations of Damnation, eternal Damnation in Hell-Fire, on me and my Proselytes'. It was an uncomfortable experience: 'no small Part of the Congregation did stare upon me, as they usually do upon such Occasions.' Whiston wrote a defence of his religious ideas, which he had printed and distributed to his fellow parishioners.[286] An even more dramatic event took place on 23 January 1719, when Whiston refused to stand during the Athanasian creed during a service at St Andrew's. The rector, the arch-Tory Henry Sacheverell, tried to have Whiston ejected, but Whiston refused to leave, and even resisted the efforts of some women to pull him bodily out of the church. Sacheverell stopped the service and retreated to the vestry, but 'Mr. *Whiston* continuing still in his Seat, and by sitting down plainly shewing that he waited for the remaining part of the Service as well as they,' Sacheverell had little choice but to continue through gritted teeth. Once again Whiston printed a defence of his actions, in which he objected to being branded as an

---

[283] Duffy 1976, 139–149. Neither Duffy nor I could find any other evidence for this amnesty.
[284] Duffy 1976, 149; Farrell 1981, 24–26, 280–281, 289; Force 1985, 19.
[285] Welchman 1721, 25.
[286] *The Layman's humble address* 1717, 31; Whiston 1749–1750, 1:241.

Arian by Sacheverell, preferring the label of '*Eusebian*, or such as had the odious Name of *Arian* unjustly given them by the *Athanasians*'. He later insisted that neither he nor Clarke ever supported 'gross' Arianism, that is, the polemical presentation provided by Athanasius, but such protestations did Whiston little good. By this time many of his neighbours considered him an 'Old Rogue' who had 'done a great deal of mischief', whose passive aggression was as irritating as his ideas were dangerous.[287] This episode prompted John Breval to write a satirical ballad, *The Church Scuffle*, to be sung to the tune of *A-begging we will go*. One stanza mocked Whiston's constant appeal to the bible to justify his radical revisions of doctrine:

> Alack! alack! that BOOK will prove
> Too strong, I plainly see,
> For ATHANASIUS and the *Church*,
> With all their *Mystery*!
> to St. Andrew's we will go, will go, will go, &c.[288]

The episode was still recalled with mirth decades later.[289] Whiston's attempts to set himself up as Newton's rival in natural philosophy and prophecy in the second and third decades of the eighteenth century likewise met with rebuffs, though a deep conviction of the correctness of his views kept Whiston from total humiliation.[290] However, his ideas proved decisive for a number of dissenters such as Thomas Chubb and John Jackson, even if they did not agree with him in every respect.[291] Although Whiston's position as a religious thinker in England was ambivalent, his work would later provoke significant realignment of the study of early Christian history in Germany.

10.   Samuel Clarke

Samuel Clarke, born to a mercantile family at Norwich in 1675, studied philosophy, mathematics, theology and classics at Gonville and Caius College, Cambridge.[292] He distinguished himself early, and in a disputation in 1695 he successfully defended a proposition drawn from Newton's *Principia*. When asked to translate Jacques Rohault's Cartesian textbook

---

[287] Whiston 1719c; Whiston 1730, 67. On the labels 'Arian' and 'Eusebian', see Wiles 1996, 5–6.
[288] Breval 1719, 3.
[289] Pennant 1790, 173.
[290] Snobelen 2004.
[291] Duffy 1976, 149.
[292] My account draws on John Cascoigne, 'Clarke, Samuel', in *ODNB*; Ferguson 1976; Reventlow 1985, 339–350; Pfizenmaier 1997a; Pfizenmaier 2009.

Traité de physique (1671), Clarke added notes explaining those points on which Newton provided a more satisfactory explanation. Clarke's Newtonian glosses on Rohault, in ever-expanding editions, contributed greatly to the dissemination of Newton's abstruse ideas amongst a broader public, and their gradual ascendency over Cartesianism. At Cambridge Clarke associated with Whiston, who passed on to him the position of chaplain to John Moore, bishop of Norwich, whose library provided ample material for Clarke's theological work.[293] In the early years of the new century, Clarke 'began to suspect, that the *Athanasian* Doctrine of the Trinity' was not the same as that of the earliest Christians. Whiston believed that Clarke was led to this conclusion by Newton, who 'knew it long before this time'.[294]

Soon after Newton left Cambridge in 1696, he took up residence in Jermyn St Westminster. In 1709 Clarke was appointed rector of St James' Westminster, Newton's parish church. Their previous association suggests that Newton may have used his influence to secure the appointment.[295] Newton and Clarke would influence each other's religious ideas deeply over the following years. In 1725 the Scottish minister Robert Wodrow reported that 'I am told that Dr Clerk is extremly intimat with Sir Isaack Neuton, and had much of what he published from him.' Wodrow had heard that the substance of Clarke's pamphlets against the deist Anthony Collins in 1707–1708 was 'all the fruit of his conversation with Sir Isaack'.[296] Whiston believed that Clarke and Newton were of the same opinion over the eternity and torments of hell.[297] He also noted that Clarke, to whom he referred enviously as Newton's 'bosom friend', 'used frequently to hear Sir *Isaac Newton* interpret Scripture Prophecies; to whose superior Authority, tho' so great a Man himself, he used entirely to submit'.[298] On 23 October 1730, a company of friends, including Viscount Percival and Arthur Onslow, Speaker of the House of Commons and a former member of Whiston's defunct Society for Promoting Primitive Christianity, met in a coffee-house, where the conversation turned to the recently deceased Isaac Newton and Samuel Clarke. Onslow remarked that 'Sir Isaac Newton and Dr. Clerk's opinion was that the great Antichrist is not a person, but the modern doctrine of the Trinity, *i.e.*, the vulgar manner

---

[293] See Schüller 2001.
[294] Whiston 1730, 12.
[295] See Whiston 1730, 17.
[296] Wodrow 1842–1843, 3:205; Snobelen 1999, 413.
[297] Whiston 1730, 98.
[298] Whiston 1730, 156; Whiston 1749–1750, 1:293.

of explaining that mystery.'[299] And Thomas Emlyn wrote that Clarke was 'very much affected with the wonderful evidence of St *John's* revelation, which relate to the Great Whore', that is, the Roman Catholic church, 'and intimated that Sir *Isaac Newton* had the same sentiments'.[300]

Clarke's early theological writings, including two series of Boyle lectures (1704 and 1705), stressed God's eternity, necessary self-existence, incomprehensibility, infinite omnipresence, uniqueness, intelligence, freedom, omnipotence, wisdom, goodness, justice and truth. Clarke's God intervenes in the world in acts of special providence and even occasionally in miracles. Clarke expressed the conviction that doctrine properly derived from Scripture is consonant with reason and conducive to personal morality, which he valued as more important than religious ritual. He emphasised the necessity of human free will for true religion. And although Clarke believed that natural theology could provide insight into the nature and attributes of God, he maintained that true religion was necessarily revealed. Clarke's deep engagement with Newton's work is clear from his axiomatic style of argumentation and his conviction that natural philosophy reveals the existence of an intelligent designer. The Newtonian theory of matter is also an important presupposition in Clarke's refutation of Henry Dodwell's view that the individual soul is created by direct divine intervention at baptism, and of Anthony Collins' assertion that thought is a material process. The influence of Newton's conception of God, as expressed in the general scholium, may also be seen in Clarke's insistence on God's transcendence and unity, which seemed to leave little room for a divine Word made flesh. Clarke's twin interests in natural philosophy and theology also reflected Newton's conviction that the investigation of God's presence in the phenomena of the physical world was an important part of the task of natural philosophy. In turn, Newton owned many books by Clarke, including his 1704 Boyle lectures, his *Reply to the Objections of Robert Nelson*, the first two editions of his *Scripture-doctrine of the Trinity* (1712, 1719), his sermons (1724), and the published correspondence with Leibniz.[301] Newton gloated maliciously that Clarke's defence of Newton's claim to have invented calculus 'had broke *Leibnitz's* Heart'.[302]

In 1712, Clarke published his *Scripture-doctrine of the Trinity*, in which he set out to interrogate the Scriptural foundation of the Athanasian creed

[299] Perceval 1920–1923, 1:113; cf. Force 1985, 19, 27 (on Onslow); Snobelen 1999, 413.
[300] Emlyn 1746, 2:487.
[301] London, BL Add. ms 25424, 13v–14v; Harrison 1978, 119–120, n° 388–393, 935, 1198, 1378–1390, 1625.
[302] Whiston 1730, 132.

by examining 1251 passages from the bible. With this exhaustive enumeration of Scriptural passages Clarke intended to ward off the potential criticism that his novel suggestions were merely the products of reason or speculation.[303] Clarke's assumption that a large base of information should yield a more certain outcome has certain analogies with Mill's legendary 30,000 variants. Clarke hoped that his work would help readers find their way through the labyrinth of potential error to which the learned apologists of the 1690s, notably William Sherlock and Robert South, had fallen prey:

> And it has been no small injury to Religion, in the midst of those Disputes; that as on the one hand, men by guarding unwarily against *Tritheism*, have often in the other extreme run into *Socinianism*, to the diminution of the Honour of the *Son* of God, and to the taking away the very Being of *the Holy Spirit*; so on the contrary, incautious Writers in their zeal against *Socinianism* and *Arianism*, have no less frequently laid themselves open to *Sabellianism* or *Tritheism*, by neglecting to maintain the Honour and Supremacy of the *Father*. The Design of the following Papers, is to show how This Evil may be prevented, and in what manner Both Extremes may rationally be avoided.[304]

Clarke based his arguments in large part on historical and philological reasoning. Like Newton and Whiston, Clarke believed that the original message of Christianity – and with it the true text of Scripture – had been perverted by the Roman Catholic church, and only partially restored in the Protestant reformation. He also insisted that Protestant doctrinal formulations such as the Thirty-Nine Articles should only be followed insofar as they can be shown to be consonant with Scripture. And the witness of Scripture, as he discovered, did not always say what it had long been presumed to say. Of all the Scriptural passages held to refer to the Trinity, Clarke dismissed the comma as the weakest, noting that it 'should not have too much stress laid upon it in any Controversy'.[305]

Clarke's theology of the Trinity, laid out in fifty-five propositions, is essentially unitarian.[306] He confessed a belief in God the Father, supreme

---

[303] Jackson 1714, 31; cf. Snobelen 2001, 201 n.136.
[304] S. Clarke 1712, c2r–v.
[305] S. Clarke 1712, 238.
[306] The articles are in S. Clarke 1712, A5r–a4r. There is an ongoing debate about the appropriate characterisation of Clarke's theology of the Trinity. Snobelen 2006, 132–133, characterised Clarke as near-Arian, while Pfizenmaier 1997a and 2009, argued that Clarke's theology of the Trinity was essentially orthodox, consonant with that of the 'Origenistic-Eusebian-Cappadocian trajectory of thought as it pointed toward both the Homoiousian and later Cappadocian positions'. Wiles 1999, questioned Pfizenmaier's definition of Arianism, which would exclude not only Clarke but

cause and fountain of all power, with whom the Son has existed from the beginning as a second divine person, and the Spirit of the Father and the Son, who has likewise existed from the beginning as a third divine person. The Father alone is 'Self-existent, Underived, Unoriginated, Independent; made of None, begotten of None, Proceeding from None' (§ V). In insisting that the Scripture nowhere declares 'the proper Metaphysical *Nature*, *Essence*, or *Substance*' of the divine persons, though it 'describes and distinguishes them always, by their *Personal Characters*, *Offices*, *Power* and *Attributes*' (§ IV), Clarke seemed to veer towards modalism. In insisting that the Father alone 'is in the highest, strict, and proper Sense, absolutely *Supreme over All*' (§ VII), he seemed to steer towards Arianism. There is more than a hint of subordinationism inherent in Clarke's insistence that divine authority is communicated to the Son from the Father (§ XXV), that the Son is 'evidently *Subordinate* to the *Father*, that *He derives* his *Being* and Attributes from the *Father*, the *Father* Nothing from *Him*' (§ XXXIV), and that the Spirit is similarly subordinate and derivative (§ XL). Clarke noted that the word '*God*, in Scripture, nowhere signifies the Person of the *Holy Ghost*' (§ XXXII). This observation had previously been made by Erasmus and Whiston.[307] The Holy Spirit, he continued, is subordinate not only to the Father but also to the Son (§ XLII). For these reasons, Clarke concluded, '*absolutely Supreme Honour* is due to the Person of the *Father* singly, as being Alone the *Supreme* Author of all Being and Power' (§ XLIII), and all '*Prayers and Praises* ought *primarily* or *ultimately* to be directed to the Person of the *Father*, as the *Original and Primary Author* of all Good' (§ XLIV). Any honours paid to Son or Spirit tend finally 'to the *Honour and Glory* of the *Father*', through whom the Son's work of redemption and the Spirit's work of sanctification are carried out (§ XLV). Prayer is thus made to the Father, 'in and by the *Guidance and Assistance of the Holy Spirit*, through the *Mediation of the Son*' (§ XLVI). The honour paid to Christ is 'not so much upon Account of his *metaphysical Essence* or *Substance*, and *abstract Attributes*; as of his *Actions* and *Attributes* relative to *Us*; his *Condescension* in becoming *Man*, who was the *Son of God*; his *Redeeming*, and *Interceding for*, us; his *Authority*, *Power*, *Dominion*, and *Sitting upon the Throne of God his Father*, as our *Lawgiver*, our *King*, our *Judge*, and our *God*' (§ LI). Clarke's non-adorationist stance

also Arius himself. He also questioned Pfizenmaier's argument that Newton became less inclined to Arianism over the course of his life. Snobelen 2001, proposed characterising Newton's theology of the Trinity as unitarian, a label that is also appropriate for Clarke. Further, see Snobelen 2006, 131–133.
[307] Erasmus 1523b, aa6v; Whiston 1711–1712, 4:361.

recalls that of Ferenc Dávid and Newton, who wrote in his twelve articles on religion that 'All the worship whether of prayer praise or thanks giving which was due to the father before the coming of Christ is still due to him. Christ came not to diminish the worship of his father. Prayers are most prevalent when directed to the father in the name of the son.'[308] It also resembles the second of Whiston's twenty-three articles of the primitive church: 'God the Father, and He *alone* is to be primarily Worshipp'd and Ador'd; or, in the most proper Sense, and in the highest Manner. He only being the Object of the Supreme Degree of such Divine Worship and Adoration, through Jesus Christ.'[309] Despite the subordinationism expressed in Clarke's articles, he explicitly rejected two of the Arian propositions condemned in the anathemas attached to the original form of the Nicene creed: that the Son was made out of nothing (ἐξ οὐκ ὄντων); and that there was a time when the Son did not yet exist (ὅτι ἦν ποτε ὅτε οὐκ ἦν). Clarke also condemned the notion that the Holy Spirit is not a person, but merely a 'power or operation of the Father' (§ XXII), the position taken by Sozzini.

Instead, Clarke's work presents the doctrine of 'the learned Eusebius, one of the ablest Men that were present at the Council of *Nice*', as 'the Unanimous Sense of the Catholick Church'.[310] Clarke's book may have been an attempt to save 'Eusebianism' from Whiston, who had proven himself a political liability. Whiston carped that Clarke had not gone far enough, and as a result their friendship cooled.[311] Despite Clarke's ostensible rejection of subordinationist heresies, the *Scripture-doctrine of the Trinity* immediately mired him in controversy.

In a letter dated 20 February 1713, the lawyer Roger North objected to Clarke's dismissal of the comma and his arrogant implication that 'the Christian church is much bound to you for your inclination to have uncovered such a desperate flaw.' North insisted that the comma expressed the metaphysical oneness of the 'three persons in unity', not merely an agreement of their wills, an interpretation he dismissed as human invention. For North, this unity entailed that all three persons were 'to be worshiped and adored'. Moreover, North accused Clarke of glossing over the textual problems with the verse. In North's memory, reports of Arian interference with New Testament manuscripts had become exaggerated,

[308] Cambridge, King's College Keynes ms 8, 1r, transcr. Newton Project.
[309] Whiston 1711–1712, 4:54.
[310] Clarke 1712, 89, 467.
[311] Whiston 1730, 66.

and he believed that evidence of their erasure of the comma was 'yet to be seen' in some copies. In his opinion, a fuller account of such issues would have given Clarke's readers 'somewhat more then your bare word to rely on in a caus of such consequence to the Christian faith and profession'. North suggested that Clarke should re-read Mill's note on the comma, or the apologies of Charles Leslie.[312]

In his reply, Clarke emphasised that the comma is 'a manifest interpolation (by accident I beleev of a coment creeping into the text rather then by any designe) it having never bin seen in one Greek copy in the world, nor ever bin quoted by any wrighter whatever either before or at the Arrian controversie'. Clarke informed North that he had been 'well acquainted' with Mill, but that the arguments he had adduced were 'very thin shaddows indeed' which he grasped at 'not without great diffidence'. Finally, Clarke warned North that 'If you would not be deceived, you must see with your owne, and not [with] other men's eyes.'

North was unconvinced by Clarke's dismissal of the comma: 'you cannot shuffle it off, no more then the Socinians before you have bin able to doe.' He also disputed Clarke's allegation that Mill's conclusions consisted in mere 'shaddow-catching and diffidence', since his report betrayed no such lack of confidence. North consulted the works of Bull and Hammond, and found that they too supported the genuineness of the comma. As to Clarke's advice to judge the evidence for himself, North admitted that he was 'dark as to Hebrew and Greek', but countered that 'Wee of the laity are comonly uncapable to judg crittically even of the evidences of our tradition, but must trust some persons.' The representations made by scholars and clergy in matters of faith were thus a pastoral matter in which they and the laity entered into a pact of authority and trust.[313]

Edward Wells, rector of Cotesbach in Leicestershire, who was at that time engaged in producing a new edition of the New Testament that would for the first time break with the *textus receptus*, did not keep his confutation of Clarke's work to private correspondence. Wells argued that

> altho' the Father, the Word, and the Holy Ghost, are said (1 *Joh.* 5. 7.) to be only *One*, not explicitly *One God*, or of the Same Divine Individual Essence; yet it will not follow [...] that I *confound and blend* the Ancient Writers with Scripture; because I look upon Their Testimonies to be a

[312] North to Clarke, 20 February 1713, London, BL Add. ms 32550, 2r, 5r, 6r, 17v, 24v, 31v, ed. Kassler 2014, 251, 255–256, 258–259, 277, 290, 302–303.

[313] Clarke's reply to North, and North's reply to that letter, were reported by North to George Hickes, 2 June 1713, London, BL Add. ms 32551, 35r–36v, ed. Kassler 2014, 304–308.

Sufficient Proof and Authority for believing Father, Son, and Holy Ghost, to be truly and properly One God, or of the Same Divine Individual Essence; or that this is the *True* sense, wherein St. *John* understood Them to be *One*.[314]

Clarke immediately refuted the textual basis of Well's defence of Trinitarianism. Erasmus, he noted, had shown that the comma, cited by none of the Greek fathers and missing from all extant Greek manuscripts of the bible, had entered the Greek text after the invention of printing, and had only received the appearance of good manuscript attestation by Estienne's error. The Latin attestation was equally sketchy. 'These things', Clarke continued,

> ought not, in justice and fairness, to be concealed from the World, by so citing the Text in a point of controversy, as if there *never* had been *any controversy* about it, and as if *all Primitive Writers* (who indeed never cite it at all) had agreed with you, both in the citation and in the interpretation of the words. You ought *at least* to have acknowledged the *dubiousness* of the Text.[315]

Moreover, Clarke accused Wells of misleading his readers by arguing from the ambiguity of the word 'one' in English, which may mean '*One God*, or *One Person*, or *One Nature*, or *One Essence*', where the Greek ἕν has none of this ambiguity. Moreover, Clarke rejected Wells' problematic definition of the Trinity as 'Three Persons of the same Divine INDIVIDUAL Essence', since the individual essence of any intelligent being is its personal essence, 'That by which a Person is that Individual Person which he is, and no Other.' Wells' definition of the Trinity, Clarke concluded, does not occur in Scripture, but was an 'Invention of the Schools, in latter Ages'.[316] Importing such later formulations violated the Protestant principle that '*Scripture only* is *Our Rule*.'[317]

Another challenge came from James Knight, who defended the comma and the doctrine it summarised, arguing that it was cited by both Tertullian and Cyprian, who interpreted it as referring to 'not a bare Unity of Testimony, but of *Substance*'.[318] In response, Clarke stressed that 'the natural signification of the words, *these three are One*, is, that they are *One agreeing*

[314] Wells 1713, 32; at 59, Wells also criticised Clarke for warning his readers not to be misled by the 'sound' of individual texts, that is, by their perceived literal meaning. We are not, for example, to conclude from St John's statement that 'these three are one', that they are not one.

[315] S. Clarke 1714a, 46. Further, see Snobelen 2006, 132.

[316] S. Clarke 1714a, 47.

[317] S. Clarke 1714a, 49.

[318] Knight 1714, 139. The only name that appears on the title page is that of Robert Nelson, who provided the introductory letter. The attribution of the body of this work to Knight was made by Herne 1720, 4–5; Snobelen 2001, 187, suggested that the author was Francis Gastrell.

Testimony. He also gave further details about the lack of manuscript author-ity for the comma. All the manuscript witnesses adduced by Mill were mis-takes. For a clarification of the lack of attestation of the comma in Estienne's manuscripts, he referred his readers to his earlier refutation of Wells. 'As to the *Manuscript in England*, it is only a Book mentioned by a *Foreigner*, but which no Man *in England* ever heard of. And *Erasmus* himself, who is the only person that mentions it, declares at the same time, that he did not believe there was any such thing.'[319] As to the Vatican manuscript alleged by Mill, Clarke pointed out that this was an error arising from a misreading of Stunica's first attack on Erasmus. Stunica had not cited any manuscript evi-dence for the comma against Erasmus, but only the purported evidence of the fathers. Moreover, 'an unprejudiced Reader would presently guess from the marginal Note in the very *Complutensian* Edition itself, that the Editors put in this Text upon the Authority of *St Thomas Aquinas*, who knew no Greek; and not from their *Vatican Manuscripts*.'[320] Clarke also cited Mill to support his statement that the comma was not present in the Scriptural text known to Tertullian and Cyprian.[321]

Knight disputed Clarke's assertions about the placement of the obeloi in Estienne's edition, and his suggestion that Erasmus' British codex was only a convenient fiction. Knight simply could not believe that Erasmus could have been 'either so *unsincere* as to insert a Passage upon the pre-tended Authority of a Manuscript, which he did not think was in being, that is, upon no Authority at all; or, so *weak*, as to own, at the same time, that there was no such Authority'.[322] Knight was also convinced that the Latin text used by Cyprian must have been based on a Greek text; for otherwise 'it is hard to tell, how it [that is, the comma] should get into the *Latin* Copies, if it had never been in the *Greek*.'[323]

In order to guard from such objections in the future, Clarke expanded his discussion of the comma in the second edition of his *Scripture-doctrine*, arguing that the passage makes much more sense without the comma. He also added a long footnote referring readers to Mill's note on the comma, and to the *A Full Inquiry into the Original Authority of That Text, 1 John V. 7* by Thomas Emlyn, whose anonymity he protected.[324]

---

[319] S. Clarke 1714b, 207.
[320] S. Clarke 1714b, 209.
[321] S. Clarke 1714b, 210–212.
[322] Knight 1715, 294.
[323] Knight 1715, 295.
[324] Clarke 1719, 206–207. Jackson 1716, 103, claimed not to know the identity of the author of the Emlyn 1715, but this was probably a ruse.

Clarke's assertion that Erasmus' British codex was a fiction and his conclusions about the circumstances surrounding the inclusion of the comma
in the Complutensian Polyglot recall Newton's *Historical Account*, which
(according to Whiston) Clarke knew.[325] These were not the only parallels
in the religious writings of Clarke and Newton. In 1714, Clarke wrote that
the word

> *God*, has in Scripture, and in all Books of *Morality* and *Religion*, a *rela-
> tive Signification*; and not, as in *metaphysical* Books, an *Absolute* One. As
> is evident from the *relative* Terms, which in *moral* Writings may always be
> joined with it. For instance: In the same manner as we say, *my* Father, *my*
> King, and the like; so it is proper also to say, *my* God, the God *of Israel*, the
> God *of the Universe*, and the like: Which Words are expressive of *Dominion*
> and *Government*.[326]

This proposition was praised by John Jackson, who pointed out that this
relative definition had implications for the nature of Christ's divinity.
Jackson noted that in the bible, 'the Son is not call'd *Jehova* at all, in his
own Person; or if He is, then the Name *Jehova* cannot mean so much as
necessary Self-Existence, but something which *may be Communicated*.'[327]
Others, such as Edward Welchman and Daniel Waterland, found the
proposition distinctly suspicious.[328] One sharp-eyed critic, the Calvinist
John Edwards, spotted that Clarke's argument was borrowed from the
treatise *On God and his attributes* (1630) by the Socinian Johann Crell.[329]
This treatise was reprinted in the *Bibliotheca fratrum Polonorum*, a copy of
which sat on Clarke's shelves.[330] Edwards also noticed that Newton had
run the same argument in the general scholium to the new edition of his
Principia, published in 1713.[331] Here Newton seemed to Edwards 'to lay
open his Heart and Mind, and to tell the World what Cause he espouses
at this Day, *viz.* The very same which Dr. *Clarke* and Mr. *Whiston* have
publickly asserted.'[332] These resemblances were not fortuitous, Edwards

---

[325] Newton 1959–1977, 3:100–102; Whiston 1730, 100.
[326] S. Clarke 1714b, 284; he emphasises this point at 290; cf. Snobelen 2001, 187.
[327] Jackson 1714, 11, 26–27, 30–31 (Clarke's reply), 32; cf. Snobelen 2001, 187.
[328] Welchman 1714, 13; Waterland 1719, 47–72.
[329] John Edwards 1714, 36; cf. J. Crell, in Völkel 1630, 101: '[…] vox *Dei* tum in Hebraeo, tum in
    Graeco, ejusmodi adjectionem amat, quâ relatio ad alios significatur, ut cùm Deus dicitur esse
    Deus hujus aut illius; […] Dei vox potestatis inprimis & imperii nomen est […].' Cf. Ferguson
    1976, 77–78; Snobelen 2001, 192–194.
[330] Snobelen 2001, 193–194.
[331] Newton 1713, 482.
[332] John Edwards 1714, 40. Further, see Stewart 1996, 132; Snobelen 2001, 192; Snobelen 2005a,
    277–280.

suggested, but arose from the fact that Newton and Clarke had 'conferr'd Notes together'. Indeed, Edwards intimated that 'it seems it was agreed upon, that Sir *Isaac* should appear in favour of those Notions which Dr. *Clarke* had publish'd.'[333] Edwards evidently considered Clarke the leader in this latest effort to corrupt the traditional doctrine of the Trinity, and Newton merely his follower.

Larry Stewart and Steven Snobelen have argued convincingly that Newton intended his scholium as a public identification with the theology outlined in Clarke's *Scripture-doctrine*. Clarke's argument here hinges on the proposition that 'God' is a relative word. This was not Clarke's invention, as Edwards realised. Newton's draft history of the church, written around this same time, presented this Antitrinitarian conception of God as the consensus position that emerged out of the struggles between the followers of Arius and Athanasius: 'the word God relates not to the metaphysical nature of God', that is, to his nature and essence, 'but to his dominion. It is a relative word & has relation to us as the servants of God.'[334] Edwards was probably right in identifying Crell as the immediate source, but in fact the notion appears *in nuce* in the Racovian catechism, where the word 'God' is defined as denoting 'him, who both in the heavens, and on the earth, doth so rule and exercise dominion over all, that he acknowledgeth no superior, and is so the Author and Principall of all things, as that he dependeth on none'. In an extended sense, the word 'God' is also used to designate 'him who hath some sublime dominion from that one God, and so is in some sort partaker of his Deity'.[335] This idea was current in Newton's circle even before the publication of the *Scripture-doctrine*. For example, Whiston cited it to convocation during his trial in 1711.[336]

It is suggested here that Newton's decision to attach himself publicly to Clarke's ostensibly less controversial exposition of the notion of the 'God of dominion' represents an attempt to reclaim this idea from Whiston. If so, then Whiston's inclusion of a translation of this passage from Newton's scholium in the *Three essays* of 1713 may be interpreted as Whiston's attempt to reclaim the idea once more, and to nullify Newton's attempt to distance himself from Whiston. Clarke took back the idea for Newton once again by citing it in a letter to Leibniz.[337] Whiston responded by

---

[333] John Edwards 1714, 36–37.
[334] Jerusalem, National Library of Israel Yahuda ms 15.7, 154r, transcr. Newton Project. Cf. Manuel 1974, 22; Stewart 1996, 131 (incorrectly referencing Yahuda ms 21); Snobelen 2001, 183–184.
[335] *The Racovian Catechisme* 1652, 19.
[336] Whiston 1711b, 71–72; cf. Snobelen 2001, 188.
[337] Clarke 1717, 50–51. Further, see Snobelen 2001, 174.

including the same passage (in John Maxwell's 1715 translation) on one of his astronomical broadsides, as an explanatory gloss on 'Mr. Whiston's scheme of the solar system'.[338] This conception of a 'God of dominion', which Newton had borrowed from the Socinian Crell, evidently proved irresistible to his followers, and a point on which they attempted publicly to forge – or break – alliances with each other.

In the suspected heretic Clarke, the Tory lower house of convocation saw a new opportunity to push for the requirement of conformity to the Thirty-Nine Articles, a concession that neither Whiston nor Clarke was prepared to make to gain further preferment. On 2 June 1714, the lower house complained to Archbishop Tenison that Clarke's *Scripture-doctrine* contained teachings contrary to the Anglican understanding of the Trinity, as laid out in the Thirty-Nine Articles, and tended 'to perplex the Minds of Men in the Solemn Act of Worship, [...] to the great Grief and Scandal of pious and sober-minded Christians'. The petition characterised Clarke's book as an attempt to undermine the Christian faith, to corrupt its worship and to subvert the unity of the church.[339] The bishops instructed the lower house to draw up an extract of those articles in Clarke's writings which it considered most offensive.[340] In response to the resulting document, Clarke sent Tenison a detailed defence on 26 June, pointing out that the document submitted by the lower house did not allege that he had misinterpreted or misapplied any of the hundreds of Scripture passages he had cited, nor that any of his fifty-five articles were 'false or erroneous'.[341] Nevertheless, the bishops urged Clarke to submit a formal declaration of his orthodox belief to convocation. He duly did so on 2 July, declaring that he did 'not intend to write any more concerning the Doctrine of the *Trinity* [...] contrary to the Doctrine of the Church of *England*'.[342] In a clarification, sent to the bishop of London on 5 July, Clarke said that he did not mean thereby to preclude himself from 'making any inoffensive Corrections in my former Books, if they shall come to

[338] Whiston, c. 1721, repr. Snobelen 2001, 190, fig. 4. Senex also published an variant edition of this undated broadside, which predicated the course of the solar eclipse of 1724, with the first line of the heading altered to *The Newtonian System of Sun, planets and comets* (Oxford, Museum of the History of Science, inv. 13601). It may be that Senex intended to broaden his market by producing charts that would appeal both to admirers of Newton and to those who attended Whiston's experimental demonstrations and lectures, but the implied equivalence of the systems of Newton and Whiston is nevertheless striking. The appearance of a review of the broadside entitled *The Newtonian System* in the *Acta eruditorum* for 1721, 362–364, provides a *terminus ante quem* for the broadsides. The c. 1723 dating given by Walters 1999, 3 and 21, must therefore be revised.
[339] Laurence 1714, 9–12.
[340] Laurence 1714, 15–16.
[341] Laurence 1714, 25–44.
[342] Laurence 1714, 46.

another Edition: or from vindicating myself from any Misrepresentations or Aspersions, which may possibly hereafter be cast upon me on the occasion of This Controversy'.[343] This careful, even evasive, promise allowed Clarke to issue a revised edition of the *Scripture-doctrine*. Behind the scenes, Clarke would encourage and assist others, such as John Jackson and Thomas Emlyn, to carry on his work. The house of bishops declared itself content with Clarke's undertaking, and resolved on 5 June 1714 not to proceed any further against him.[344] However, on 7 July the lower house declared itself unsatisfied with Clarke's statement, which contained no trace of any 'Recantation of the Heretical Assertions, and other offensive Passages' identified in Clarke's works.[345] By contrast, one of Clarke's supporters wrote to express his disappointment that he, under 'a *false* Notion of Peace', had abandoned his principles simply 'to stop the Rage of Persecution'.[346] Clarke replied that his official statement did not say anything different from his *Scripture-doctrine*, but was only intended to show 'that I did not in any of my Books teach (as had by Many been industriously reported) the Doctrine of *Arius*'.[347] Although Clarke expressed himself with meticulous care, perhaps conscious that this letter would be published, his express disavowal of Arianism to a supporter suggests that he at least did not believe that he had ever intended to overturn the traditional orthodoxy of the Church of England, but to return it to its true moorings. On the other hand, if we can trust the report of Hopton Haynes to Richard Baron, 'Sir *Isaac* much lamented Mr. *Clarke*'s embracing *Arianism*, which opinion he feared had been, and still would be, if maintained by learned men, a great obstruction to the progress of Christianity.'[348]

In the *Scripture-doctrine*, Clarke identified a number of details in the Anglican liturgy which he considered inconsistent with the primitive Christian conception of the Trinity.[349] As a consequence he set about to revise the Book of Common Prayer, striking out all the Trinitarian formulae so that prayers were directed exclusively to God the Father, and amending the doxology to 'Glory be to God, by Jesus Christ, through the

[343] Laurence 1714, 61–62.
[344] Laurence 1714, 63.
[345] Laurence 1714, 64.
[346] Laurence 1714, 51.
[347] Laurence 1714, 54–55.
[348] Richard Baron, preface to Gordon 1763, 1:XVIII. Wiles 1996, 76, warns that the information given by Whiston and Haynes has to be treated as partisan.
[349] Clarke 1712, 415–480.

heavenly assistance of the Holy Ghost.' He also excluded the Johannine comma from the epistle for the Sunday after Easter, and struck out the Nicene and Athanasian creeds, leaving only the Apostle's Creed. In 1718 Clarke edited a collection of *Select Psalms and Hymns* for use within the parish of St James, in which he subtly altered the doxologies given by Sternhold and Hopkins, which began 'To Father, Son, and Holy Ghost', to forms that better reflected his non-adorationist stance: 'To God, through Christ, his only Son', 'To Father, Son, with Holy Ghost', or 'With Son and Holy Ghost, / To God the Fath'r of Heav'n'.[350] Whiston, recalling his own attempt to do the same thing in 1710, hailed Clarke's introduction of the 'primitive' doxologies as one of his 'most Christian Attempts toward somewhat of Reformation, upon the Primitive Foot'.[351]

John Robinson, bishop of London, was disturbed by Clarke's breach of discipline. On 26 December 1718, he issued a letter to all clergy in the diocese in which he warned that 'Some Persons seduc'd, I fear by the strong Delusions of Pride and Self-conceit, have lately published new Forms of Doxology, entirely agreeable to those of some Ancient Hereticks, who impiously denied a Trinity of Persons in the Unity of the God-head.' The bishop forbade the use of these new forms, under pain of a fine.[352] Whiston wrote a sarcastic open letter to the bishop in response, in which he turned the tables by condemning the doxology in the Prayer Book as the real innovation, 'introduc'd by certain Hereticks in the fourth Century'. In a long appendix he provided a full account of all the doxologies in the New Testament and the patristic authors, pointing out in each case that worship and prayer are directed to God the Father.[353] Arthur Ashley Sykes ironically defended the doxologies of Paul and the other apostles from the charge of heresy.[354] On 11 March 1719, Whiston wrote to Robinson again, accusing him of privileging church tradition over the truth of religion. If the councils and canons of the Church of England should be allowed to trump the bible, Whiston argued, then

> we have no need to enquire into the ancient MSS. whether the pretended Verse, in St. *John's* first Epistle, concerning the *three that bear Record in Heaven*, or any other, be genuine or no, as Dr. *Mills*, and many others, have done; because, while it stands in the Church Bible, and is order'd by

[350] Clarke 1718, 9, 46, 50, 51. Further, see Colligan 1913, 41–42.
[351] Whiston 1730, 99.
[352] Robinson 1722, 11.
[353] Whiston 1719a, 4. This pamphlet, dated 17 January 1719, went through a second edition the same year.
[354] Sykes 1719a.

Authority to be read to the People, it is, it seems, true and authentick here, whether we suppose that St. *John* ever wrote it or not.

In such a case, the Church of England might as well dispense with Jesus' command to communicate in both bread and wine, or with Paul's injunction that the worship of God should not take place 'in an unknown tongue', and simply return to Roman Catholicism.[355] Whiston also disputed the claim that the Athanasians accused the Arians of changing the doxologies; rather, the Athanasians themselves introduced the new doxologies.[356] In response, Michel Mattaire published a short essay on the traditional form of the doxology, in which he lamented that freethinking had come so far that Clarke could alter the liturgy at whim, that Whiston's response to the bishop's warnings could be praised as 'the best thing he has yet writ', and that 'Two Divine Persons of the Trinity are robb'd of their Glory, and the Godhead is stript of its Unity.'[357] Clarke later entered all his intended changes to the Anglican liturgy in an interleaved copy of the Prayer Book. Shortly before he died, he urged Thomas Emlyn to preserve this book carefully.[358]

The doxology debate reflected two competing claims of fidelity to the usage of the ancient church: on one hand, claims made for the Prayer Book by traditionalists like Wheatly, and on the other hand the devotees of primitive Christianity like Whiston, Emlyn and (in a less radical form) Clarke. In its direct appeal to the documents of the early church, this debate represented a liturgical pendant to the issue of the Johannine comma, and played into wider debates within the English church, such as the Arian controversy and the debate over subscription to the Thirty-Nine Articles.

The work of Samuel Clarke thus represents an important attempt not merely to apply Newton's method to philosophy, but also to accommodate his religious ideas, hostile to 'corruptions' in text and doctrine, to the

[355] Whiston 1719b, 6.
[356] Whiston 1719b, 16–19.
[357] Mattaire 1718, iii–iv.
[358] Emlyn 1746, 2:494. Clarke's interleaved copy of 1724 edition of *The Book of Common Prayer* was presented to the British Museum by his son on 12 February 1768 (now London, BL C.24.B.21). Clarke's suggestions, described on the leaf facing C3r as 'Amendments humbly proposed to the Consideration of Those in Authority', follow the criticisms made earlier in the *Scripture-doctrine*. In the margin of the reading for the Sunday after Easter (G6v), Clarke places the Johannine comma in brackets and indicates that it should also be italicised. The Athanasian creed and the Trinitarian formulas of the Litany (D1v–2v) are excised. An abbreviated edition of *The Book of Common Prayer*, ostensibly according to Clarke's suggestions, was edited from this copy by Theophilus Lindsay in 1774. See also Sykes 1934, 386–390; Snobelen 1997, 163–164; Dixon 2003, 32–33.

teaching and liturgy of the Church of England. Clarke's rejection of the Johannine comma, one of the Scriptural trump-cards traditionally played by orthodox theologians in order to assert the essential unity of all three persons of the Trinity, was consistent with his attempt to redefine the doctrine of the Trinity on Scriptural grounds. It played a particular part in his efforts to defend Newton's suggestion that the word 'God' does not refer absolutely to a divine essence shared by Father, Son and Spirit, but is a relative term most properly applied to God the Father alone. Clarke's alignment with the Whigs and his royal patrons attracted the opposition of high-church Tories, who chafed at any deviation from the Thirty-Nine Articles, on which they insisted as the sole criterion of orthodoxy and the narrow gate to political eligibility. Clarke's manner of dealing with opposition was more shrewd and accommodating than that of Whiston, and as a result he maintained a respectable position within the church, even if his refusal to compromise on the matter of subscription to the Trinitarian sections of the Thirty-Nine Articles prevented him from accepting the preferment he otherwise would have enjoyed.

11.   Thomas Emlyn

Thomas Emlyn (1663–1741) was a Presbyterian minister from Lincolnshire who came to question the orthodox conception of the Trinity by discussing William Sherlock's *Vindication of the Trinity* (1690) with William Manning.[359] In 1702, Emlyn was tried, fined and imprisoned at Dublin on charges of blasphemy after expressing these doubts in his *Humble Inquiry into the Scripture-Account of Jesus Christ*. The judge presiding at Emlyn's trial warned that he should count himself lucky for the sentence of one year's imprisonment and a fine of £1000; in Spain or Portugal he would have been burned.[360]

After his release, Emlyn returned to England. He re-established contact with Whiston, whom he had met during the latter's time as rector of Lowestoft (1698–1702).[361] Emlyn read Clarke's first series of Boyle's lectures when they were published in 1705, and concluded from them that a man who held that 'it follows from his necessary existence, that God must of necessity be BUT ONE' could not be 'a right Athanasian'.[362]

---

[359] Alexander Gordon and H. J. McLachlan, 'Emlyn, Thomas,' in *ODNB*; Colligan 1913, 44.
[360] Emlyn 1719c, xxxii–xxxiii; Bludau 1922, 129–139; Gibson 2006b.
[361] Farrell 1981, 24–26.
[362] Emlyn 1746, 2:479; cf. Clarke 1705, 93–96. Further, see Wiles 1996, 118.

Emlyn delivered a letter to convocation on Whiston's behalf on 28 May 1711, a choice of messenger that Richard Smalbroke found a 'surprizing Piece of Conduct'.[363] Emlyn only met Clarke after the publication of the *Scripture-doctrine*. Although they were kindred spirits, Emlyn believed that Clarke could have gone further. By asserting that the divine power, knowledge and every other perfection was in the Son as well as in the Father, Clarke had endangered the absolute distinction between the '*unoriginate absolute first cause* of all, and all *derived* beings produced by his good pleasure'.[364] Like Whiston, Emlyn suffered persecution even in London. George Stonehouse, rector of Islington, 'most unjustly and irregularly refused the Communion' to Emlyn, who could not prevail upon the bishop of London to have the excommunication lifted.[365]

After Clarke was muzzled by convocation, he asked Whiston to write a detailed examination of Mill's conclusions on the Johannine comma. 'But', as Whiston would later explain,

> as we both knew that Sir *Isaac Newton* had written such a Dissertation already, and I was then engag'd in other Pursuits, I excused myself at that time; and we both agreed to recommend that Matter to Mr. *Emlyn*: which Work he undertook and performed with great Impartiality and Accuracy.[366]

Emlyn's *Full Inquiry into the Original Authority of that Text, 1 John V. 7* was published anonymously in 1715. In the dedication to Archbishop Thomas Tenison and convocation, Emlyn defended the importance of sacred philology. If classical philology, dedicated to 'the Trifles of a witty or wanton *Poet*, or a fabulous and remote *Historian*' is valuable, then biblical philology is even more so. By comparing manuscripts, ancient translations and patristic quotations, biblical philologists 'inform us certainly what is *original* and genuine, and what not, in any part of the Bible, more especially where some matter of great moment is concern'd'. The special status of the Scriptures makes it imperative that it should be free from 'all human spurious Additions'. However, as Francis Hare had noted in his satire *The Difficulties and Discouragements which attend the Study of the Scriptures*, philologists often avoided biblical criticism for fear of attracting accusations of impiety or heresy. Emlyn's proem was probably aimed at least in part at Bentley, whom Newton had criticised for fighting 'about

---

[363] Whiston 1711b, 31; Smalbroke 1711, 31–32. Further, see Duffy 1976, 143–144.
[364] Emlyn 1746, 2:480–482.
[365] Whiston 1749–1750, 1:252.
[366] Whiston 1730, 100; cf. Whiston 1736, 13.

a Playbook', that is, the text of Terence, while the Scriptures stood in need of gifted textual critics.[367]

While acknowledging that Mill had done inestimable service to learning and piety, Emlyn intended to show that his judgement on the comma was mistaken, in the hope that the convocation would 'rectify our Books, when the true Reading is found', even if it meant rejecting a text 'on which principally some important Branches of her *Creed* and *publick Offices* seem to be founded'. After all, there was no sense in searching for what is right, 'if we will still adhere to what is wrong'.[368] Emlyn applauded Mill's refusal to credit the improbable notion that the comma was erased by heretics, and his rejection of the prologue to the Catholic Epistles as the work of 'some *silly Rhapsodist* after Bede's time'. In favour of the authenticity of the comma, Mill could adduce the pseudo-Athanasian *Disputation against Arius*. But as Emlyn stated, it is unclear whether this passage refers to v. 7 or 8, and whether the pseudonymous author was from the eastern or western church.[369] Mill believed that the comma was present in the Armenian version, but Sand had shown that this was not the case. Mill placed confidence in the apparent quotations in the Latin fathers Tertullian, Cyprian, Victor Vitensis, Vigilius Tapsensis, Fulgentius and the author of the *Explication of the Faith*. However, Emlyn argued that Tertullian and Cyprian seem to be giving some 'mystical Interpretation' of 1 Jn 5:8, as Facundus believed. Victor Vitensis and the other witnesses lived too late to be of any authority in deciding the original form of the text. Mill also adduced several manuscripts that had since disappeared. Mill assumed that eight of Estienne's manuscripts contained the comma, but Simon had shown that this was an error. Mill presumed that the reading in the Complutensian bible was based on a Greek manuscript. This too was an erroneous presumption.[370] That left only one manuscript, the

> *British* Copy which *Erasmus* speaks of: who not finding one *Greek* Copy which had this Passage wou'd not put it into his first two Editions of the New Testament: but upon information of a Copy in *England* which had it, did, against the *Faith* of all his Copies, afterwards insert it; rather, as he confesses, to avoid the Reproach of others, than that he judg'd it to be of sufficient Authority.[371]

---

[367] Whiston 1730, 143.

[368] Emlyn 1715, 4, 19.

[369] Emlyn 1715, 10, 22–23; cf. *PG* 28:50: 'Πρὸς δὲ τούτοις πᾶσιν Ἰωάννης φάσκει· Καὶ οἱ τρεῖς τὸ ἕν εἰσιν.' Further, see Stockhausen 2010.

[370] Emlyn 1715, 23–26.

[371] Emlyn 1715, 30.

Emlyn suggested that Erasmus 'was moved' to include the comma 'against his own *free* Judgment [. . .] against the Evidence of all the other Manuscript *Greek* Copies'.[372] He also questioned the conclusions that earlier writers had based on the uncertain in the story: '*Simon* says *Erasmus* saw it: but where does *Erasmus* say so?'[373] Emlyn implied that Codex Britannicus was nothing but a convenient fiction, and that Erasmus had simply invented the reading:

> [W]ho ever saw this *British* Copy since, or that wou'd produce it? Dr. *Mill* does not tell us where it was, or that ever he heard more of it. Such rare Discoveries, so useful and grateful to the Publick, are not wont to be lost again, in so critical an Age. What! cannot all the Learned Men of our two Universities, nor our numerous Clergy, give us some account of it? Surely either there was no such Copy, or it is not for the purpose: else it had probably, long before this time, been produc'd. [. . .] Strange! that a *British* Copy is only to be mention'd by one beyond the Seas, while all *Britain*, and such an inquisitive *British* Critick as Dr. *Mill*, can know nothing more of it.[374]

Having dismissed Erasmus' British codex as a fiction, Emlyn believed that he had eliminated all the evidence that Mill could bring in favour of the comma.

Emlyn consequently enjoined the convocation to purge the text of Scripture of 'all such injurious Additions'. Any detail in the text of any classical author that was so poorly attested would have been deleted long since. The convocation should also consider the 'dreadful *Anathema*' against altering the Scripture (Rev 22:18). The twentieth of the Thirty-Nine Articles proclaims the church's role as witness and keeper of holy writ. It is thus 'a dismal thing to have it said to *your* Flocks, *Thus saith the Lord, when the Lord hath not spoken it*: and a hard task it is on him that reads *this* in the Church for St. *John*'s words, who doth not believe *it* to be such'. Emlyn thus pushed the issue of the comma directly into the dispute over subscription. The Church of England would be '*better* serv'd by disowning ingenuously what we find to be an *Error, even* tho it have long pass'd as current as *Truth*', even if some would denounce such an admission as 'Innovation' and cry out that 'Religion is subverted, that all is uncertain.' Such a '*false Notion of Peace*', Emlyn lamented, 'has often well nigh ruin'd Religion'. Finally, Emlyn pointed out that the doctrine of the Trinity depends purely on what is revealed in Scripture. It was, therefore,

---

[372] Emlyn 1715, 23.
[373] Emlyn 1715, 23, 31.
[374] Emlyn 1715, 30–31.

imperative that the church should warn believers 'not to be misled, by mistaking an unwarranted modern *Addition* for an *inspired Oracle*'.[375] Emlyn then comes to his point:

> I speak *this*, because I know not any *other* Text that *directly* or *clearly* says the *same* thing, *viz.* that *the Father, Word, and Spirit, are One*. They are not join'd in one Doxology, nor indeed do I find any given to the Holy Spirit in the New Testament, either jointly or separately; much less in the Spirit said to be one with the Father and the Son. I read of one Spirit, one Lord, one God and Father, Eph. 4. [Eph 4:6] but not that these Three are the One God. And if there be no other Text which says this, 'tis not the more likely to have been St. John's Saying here; but the more grievous to have it inserted by any who had not his Authority.[376]

Emlyn's impolitic admission that he was motivated by a suspicion of the traditional view of the Trinity made moderate churchmen suspicious of his purely text-critical arguments, and rendered it virtually impossible for the convocation to approve his suggestions.

There are striking similarities between Emlyn's conclusions and those of Newton. For example, Emlyn described the context of 1 Jn 5:6–8 in the absence of the comma as 'rather more smooth and easy', where Newton had described the same thing as 'good and easy'. Like Newton, Emlyn found it strange that 'the Spirit should be produc'd as another Witness *on Earth*, if it had been numbred before among the Witnesses *in Heaven*'. Emlyn's suspicions about the existence of Erasmus' Codex Britannicus also recall those of Newton. If Emlyn did see Newton's *Historical Account*, it was probably through the mediation of Clarke rather than through Whiston, who was estranged from Newton by this time. Although Emlyn was right to question the received narrative concerning Erasmus' inclusion of the comma in his third edition of the New Testament, and to separate critical judgement from considerations of orthodoxy, his suggestion that Erasmus faked a source was an albatross that would hang about his neck through the ensuing debate.

In a revised edition of his *Full Inquiry* (1717), Emlyn responded to those who suggested that he should take the edge off his conclusions. Emlyn dismissed those who objected that serious scholars had already 'given up' the comma, since the 'Bible is a *publick* Book, for the use of all,' which had to be translated and set forth for the unlearned 'free from all known Corruptions'. It was no use to say that the comma had been 'given up' by scholars 'while

---

[375] Emlyn 1715, 56–59, 67.
[376] Emlyn 1715, 68–69.

'tis read undistinguish'd in the Church, and urg'd from the Pulpit, in proof of a *fundamental* Point of Religion: and while Commentators still deliver it as their Opinion that 'tis genuine'. The comma would never be '*given up* fairly, till it be left out of our printed Copies'. While some argued that the comma should remain because it is consistent with the model of the Trinity that emerges from other biblical texts, Emlyn pointed out that the comma in fact does not express a specifically Nicene model of the Trinity. It might equally be cited by those who believed that the bible teaches that '*Three Infinite Minds*' or '*Three Infinite Modes*' are the three Persons, *Father, Son,* and *Holy Spirit.*' To those who believed that the comma should be included because Cyprian interpreted the three earthly witnesses as types of the three divine persons, Emlyn asked: 'Shall St. *Cyprian's* little Fancy be put into the Text? Is St. *Cyprian's* Authority as good as St. *John's?*' To those who blamed the abandonment of typographical means to mark off the comma as an interpolation on printers, Emlyn reminded the convocation of its duty to oversee 'the Sacred *Depositum* of the *Holy Scriptures,* that they be kept undepraved'. Besides, the fault lay not with the printers, but with the church which retained this spurious interpolation as part of the lectionary, employed it as the subject of sermons, and used it as proof 'even of what is accounted the most fundamental Article of the Christian Faith'.[377] While some, such as Samuel Clarke, Arthur Ashley Sykes and Hopton Haynes, considered that Emlyn had said the last word on the subject, it soon became clear that there was much more to be said.[378]

12. Jonathan Swift: satire in the service of orthodoxy

Jonathan Swift (1667–1745), dean of St Patrick's, Dublin, saw that Mill's conclusions about the comma had wider implications.[379] In his *Argument to prove that the abolishing of Christianity in England may, as things now stand, be attended with some inconveniences, and perhaps not produce those many good effects proposed thereby* (1708), Swift suggested that scholars like Mill had unwittingly fed doubts over the status of the comma and the doctrine of the Trinity amongst '*Atheists, Deists, Socinians, Anti-Trinitarians,* and other Sub-divisions of Free Thinkers'. Their ideas, received by readers ill-equipped to understand them, had enervated public morality:

> Free-Thinkers consider it [Christianity] as a Sort of Edifice, wherein all the
> Parts have such a mutual Dependence on each other, that if you happen to

[377] Emlyn 1717, 71–74.
[378] Clarke 1719, 206–207; Sykes 1719b, 141; Haynes 1747, 31 (contra Wilson 1747, 40).
[379] Further, see Clive Probyn, 'Swift, Jonathan', in *ODNB*; Damrosch 2013.

pull out one single Nail, the whole Fabrick must fall to the Ground. This
was happily exprest by him who had heard of a Text brought for Proof of
the Trinity, which in an antient Manuscript was differently read; he there-
upon immediately took the Hint, and by a sudden Deduction of a long
Sorites, most Logically concluded; Why, if it be as you say, I may safely
Whore and Drink on, and defy the Parson.[380]

Swift's characterisation of religious dissent as immoral and socially deviant
expresses something of the horror felt by those who feared that biblical
criticism could easily undermine virtue and subvert the social order. It
may also reflect Swift's dread of anarchy, a tendency he recognised within
himself.[381]

Swift expressed himself even more directly in a sermon given on Trinity
Sunday, for which he chose the Johannine comma as his text.[382] The sermon is not dated, but was probably written in the second decade of the
eighteenth century. In this sermon, Swift set out to show that the recent
flood of 'pestilent Books' attacking the doctrine of the Trinity proceeded
from two errors. The first error was misplaced Scripturalism. To those
who rejected the word 'Trinity' as unscriptural, Swift explained that it was
'a Term of Art invented in the earlier Times to express the Doctrine by
a single Word, for the sake of Brevity and Convenience'.[383] The second
error was a mistaken belief that an incomprehensible matters revealed in
Scripture can be explained through rational means.[384] Theologians and
philosophers had striven to understand the doctrine of the Trinity, but
the complexity of their arguments had 'multiplied Controversies to such
a Degree, as to beget Scruples that have perplexed the Minds of many
sober Christians, who otherwise could never have entertained them'.[385]
Following reason blindly could lead men into disaster:

Men of wicked Lives would be very glad there were no Truth in Christianity
at all; [...] If they can pick out any one single Article in the Christian
Religion which appears not agreeable to their own corrupted Reason, [...]
they presently conclude that the Truth of the whole Gospel must sink along
with that one Article.[386]

[380] Swift 1711, 176–179; Klauck 1991, 310.
[381] Damrosch 2013, 7, 142, 285, 403.
[382] The relevant passage from 1 Jn 5 was set down as the lectionary reading for the Sunday following Easter, not for Trinity Sunday, so the choice of text was a result of Swift's conscious decision.
[383] Swift 1744, 43. Of the three editions published by Dodsley in 1744, two contain thirty-two leaves in quarto. I used that in which the sermon on the Trinity begins on F1r. A third edition dated 1744 continues with another sixteen leaves (gatherings I–M), containing *The Difficulty of Knowing One's Self* and a catalogue of Dodsley's recent publications.
[384] Swift 1744, 60.
[385] Swift 1744, 45.
[386] Swift 1744, 42.

While conceding that 'every Man is bound to follow the Rules and Directions of that Measure of Reason which God hath given him,' Swift believed that in the Johannine comma, about which he himself harboured no perceptible doubt, 'God commandeth us to believe that there is a Union and there is a Distinction; but what that Union, or what that Distinction is, all Mankind are equally ignorant.'[387] While Antitrinitarians and freethinkers reviled such mysteries as 'Cant, Imposture, and Priest-craft', Swift countered that 'to declare against all Mysteries without Distinction or Exception, is to declare against the whole Tenor of the New Testament'.[388]

One of Swift's philosophical targets was probably the tract *Christianity not Mysterious* (1696) by the deist John Toland, to whom he referred directly in his satire on the abolition of Christianity, and on whom he wrote a lampoon in December 1711.[389] Toland had argued that the 'infallible Rule, or Ground of all right Perswasion, is *Evidence*; and it consists in the *exact Conformity of our Ideas or Thoughts with their Objects, or the Things we think upon.*'[390] Having established that 'what is evidently repugnant to clear and distinct Idea's, or to our common Notions, is contrary to Reason,' Toland set out to prove that 'the Doctrines of the Gospel, *if it be the Word of God*, cannot be irrational or incomprehensible.'[391] Toland considered it intellectually and morally reprehensible that the church asked believers 'to adore what we cannot comprehend'. Amongst these incomprehensible doctrines was the Trinity, from which not even the Socinians could free themselves.[392] Toland's work was widely perceived to promote unbelief, and attracted a flood of refutations. Gregory Lynall has argued that another target of Swift, a high-churchman in the matter of conformity, was the latitudinarian Whig Samuel Clarke.[393]

Swift proposed a double criterion for deciding whether a religious mystery is to be accepted. First, it must be expressed in Scripture. Second, it must not bestow advantage on those who preach it. In this regard the Protestant churches fare better than the Catholic church, which 'hath very much enriched herself by trading in Mysteries, for which they have not the least Authority from Scripture, and were fitted only to advance

---

[387] Swift 1744, 49.
[388] Swift 1744, 50.
[389] Swift 1756, 7:85–87 (*Toland's invitation to Dismal, to dine with the Calves-head Club*).
[390] Toland 1696, 16.
[391] Toland 1696, 23.
[392] Toland 1696, 24–25.
[393] Lynall 2012, 124–125.

their own temporal Wealth and Grandeur; such as *Transubstantiation, Worshipping of Images, Indulgences* for Sins, *Purgatory,* and *Masses* for the *Dead*'.[394] But while the enemies of the Protestant church 'charge us with the Errors and Corruptions of Popery, which all Protestants have thrown off near two hundred Years', the mystery of the Trinity holds out no such 'Prospect of Power, Pomp, or Wealth'. Furthermore, it had always formed part of the preaching of the Apostolic church.[395] The doctrine of the Trinity thus fulfils Swift's double criterion, for it is expressed in Scripture, notably the Johannine comma, and brings no material advantage to those who affirm it.

Swift drew a number of conclusions from these arguments. '*First*, It would be well, if People would not lay so much Weight on their own Reason in Matters of Religion, as to think everything impossible and absurd which they cannot conceive.' While early eighteenth-century Anglicans expected theological arguments to be reasonable, Swift believed that humans are fundamentally irrational, guided more often by emotion and self-interest than by reason: '*Reason* itself is true and just, but the *Reason* of every particular Man is weak and wavering, perpetually sway'd and turn'd by his Interests, his Passions, and his Vices.'[396] Further, Swift asserted that those who question religion invariably have dark ulterior motives: 'When Men are tempted to deny the Mysteries of Religion, let them examine and search into their own Hearts, whether they have not some favourite Sin which is of their Party in this Dispute, and which is equally contrary to other Commands of God in the Gospel.'[397] Indeed, Swift asserted that the recent revival of Arianism had arisen 'not out of a Zeal to Truth, but to give a Loose to Wickedness, by throwing off all Religion'.[398]

Swift encouraged his hearers to 'avoid reading those wicked Books written against this Doctrine, as dangerous and pernicious; so I think they may omit the Answers, as unnecessary'.[399] They should also avoid discussing the matter with those who busy themselves with such issues, lest they become 'Unbelievers upon Trust and at second Hand'.[400] Swift's closing remarks betray a certain diffidence not previously evident, a protestation

---

[394] Swift 1744, 50.
[395] Swift 1744, 50–51.
[396] Swift 1744, 57.
[397] Swift 1744, 57–58.
[398] Swift 1744, 44–45.
[399] Swift 1744, 60–61; further, see Lynall 2012, esp. 120–121, 125.
[400] Swift 1744, 61.

that its subject was one 'which probably I should not have chosen, if I had not been invited to it by the Occasion of this Season, appointed on Purpose to celebrate the Mysteries of the Trinity'.[401] Swift was happier to speak on ethical questions than on doctrinal ones, and the strain is evident in this sermon. Rather than discuss ineffable mysteries, Swift, who confessed his own incapacity to understand metaphysics, preferred to warn his hearers about the social and moral consequences which he feared would flow from the toleration of alternative doctrines.[402]

Swift was almost embarrassed by the requirement of expressing his religious convictions in public, and had an ambivalent attitude to his sermons, which he dismissed as 'the idlest, trifling stuff that ever was writ'.[403] While Swift burned most of his sermons, Dr Thomas Sheridan Sr asked him for the manuscripts of three, including that on the Trinity. In August 1744, Thomas Sheridan Jr, Swift's godson, sold Robert Dodsley the rights to publish Swift's sermons, letters and poems for £50. These three sermons clearly sold well. Dodsley published three editions in 1744, while George Faulkner reprinted the sermons at Dublin the same year.[404]

13.   Richard Bentley: between confidence and despair

In his youth, Richard Bentley, who would become the greatest textual critic of the eighteenth century, was part of the circle of John Mill, who encouraged him in his comparative studies of ancient Greek religion.[405] In the 1690s, Bentley established himself not only as a distinguished philologist, but also as a defender of orthodox Christianity against deists and 'atheists' who followed in Hobbes' train. He consulted Newton while working on the text of the astronomical poet Manilius, and used his theory of gravitation in his Boyle lectures (1692) to refute Epicurus' atomism. Bentley's maturation as a scholar reflected a simultaneous shift in apologetics from the historical to the textual, and in classical studies from the humanistic-aesthetic to the technically philological. While many seventeenth-century scholars sought to create huge synthetic histories of the classical world, with the ultimate purpose of demonstrating

[401] Swift 1744, 61.
[402] Mahoney 2009, 40–41.
[403] Swift 1794, 626.
[404] See H. H. Williams 1932, 34–35; Dodsley 1988, 80–81, 524; Parker 2009, 59.
[405] Monk 1833, esp. 1:122–125, 129, 149, 239, 287–289; Jebb 1899, 154–168; Bludau 1922, 204–206; Hugh de Quehen, 'Bentley, Richard', in *ODNB*; Sheehan 2005, 45–53; Metzger and Ehrman 2005, 154–157; Haugen 2011, esp. 187–210; Epp 2014.

the superiority of Christianity over its pagan rivals, the years around 1700 saw a turn towards philology, as orthodox Anglicans, Socinians and deists struggled to legitimate their various theological positions through recourse to texts. While a seventeenth-century scholar like Ralph Cudworth might try to determine the relationship between triadic structures in pagan philosophy and the Christian doctrine of the Trinity, his eighteenth-century descendants tended to concentrate their attention on the textual evidence for the Trinity. The mastery of increasingly complex philological techniques of dealing with textual transmission also served to set the professional critic apart from the half-schooled religious enthusiast.[406]

As we have already observed, Mill's New Testament, with its legendary 30,000 variant readings, had caused alarm. Daniel Whitby (1710) wrote: 'The vast quantity of various Readings collected by the Doctor, must of course make the Mind doubtful or suspicious, that nothing certain can be expected from Books, where there are various Readings in every Verse, and almost in every part of every Verse.'[407] Nevertheless, Whitby set out to show that only a small number of the variants collected by Mill (Mt 5:22, 6:13, 10:8, 11:23, 19:17; Lk 1:35, 2:22, 11:2, 11:4; Jn 1:3–4; Acts 8:37; Rom 1:32, 12:11; Gal 2:5; Eph 5:14; Heb 9:1) made any significant difference to the sense. Moreover, Whitby believed that in every case the reading of the *textus receptus* could be defended. With relief, Whitby cited Mill's judgement that the comma was the only textual variant in the New Testament that impinges to any appreciable degree on doctrine.[408] William Reeves (1709) was less sanguine, fearing that 'perhaps the various *Lections* in Dr. *Mills*'s late Edition of the New Testament, will in good time be urged by some *Criticks* against the Authority of the *Gospel*'.[409] Reeves did not have to wait long until his fears were realised. The deist Anthony Collins (1713) rejoiced in Mill's edition as a useful tool in exposing the 'Frauds [...] very common in all Books which are publish'd by *Priests* or *Priestly Men*'.[410]

Bentley saw that the New Testament had to be rescued from such ruinous doubts. In a published response to Collins (1713), Bentley argued that the number of variants did not mean that the text of the Scriptures was irreparably corrupt: 'If Religion therefore was true before, though such Various Readings were in being: it will be as true and consequently as

[406] Sheehan 2005, 46–47; Haugen 2011, 195–197.
[407] Whitby 1710, iii, translation from Collins 1713, 89.
[408] Whitby 1710, x.
[409] Reeves 1709, 1:xliii.
[410] Collins 1713, 96.

safe still, though every body sees them. Depend on't; no Truth, no matter of Fact fairly laid open, can ever subvert True Religion.'[411] Collins had
quoted the opinion of John Gregory (1646) to suggest that the huge number of variants meant that insisting on 'the miraculous conservation and
Incorruption' of the bible was a lost cause. Gregory pointed out that the
text of the Koran or of the classical authors showed less variation than
did the New Testament: there was 'no prophane Author whatsoever
(*caeteris paribus*) that has suffered so much at the hand of time' as the New
Testament. However, Collins cut short his quotation from Gregory before
he had come to his real point: that the sheer quantity of variants was a
boon to an editor who knew what to do with them:

> providence was shewed to be greater in these miscarriages (as we take them)
> then it could have beene in the absolute preservation. [...] These varieties
> of Readings in a few by-places doe the same office to the maine Scripture,
> as the variations of the Compasse to the whole Magnet of the Earth. The
> Mariner knowes so much the better for these how to steere his Course.[412]

Bentley denied Collins's insinuation that Scripture is unreliable, and
pointed out that Mill's alarming total of 30,000 variants was simply the
result of the large number of manuscripts he had used. If anything, this
total would only go up as more manuscripts were examined. Bentley
therefore hoped to still the panic caused by the appearance of Mill's edition, and to convince the public that the text of the New Testament was
'as firm as before'.[413] Making explicit reference to Gregory's statement on
the textual stability of the bible vis-à-vis the Koran or classical authors
(though apparently unaware that Gregory had emphasised the importance
of textual variations for the establishment of the text), Bentley stated
boldly that 'the *New Testament* has suffer'd *less injury by the hand of Time
than any Profane Author*'. He noted that critics who edited classical texts
had far fewer variants – and thus much less textual information – at their
disposal than editors of the New Testament, and were forced at times to
resort to critical conjecture. There was 'not One Antient Book besides
it [the New Testament] in the World, that with all the help of Various
Lections (be they 50000 if you will) does not stand in further want of
emendation by true Critic'. And there was no good edition of any ancient
text 'that has not inserted into the Text (though every Reader knows it

[411] R. Bentley 1713, 64.
[412] J. Gregory 1646, *2r–v; Collins 1713, 88.
[413] R. Bentley 1713, 64.

not) what no Manuscript vouches'.[414] By contrast, the editor of the New Testament had such a huge quantity of textual data that there was no need to resort to the expedient of conjecture.

Bentley therefore resolved to produce a new critical edition of the Greek New Testament, building upon Mill's data. Bentley believed that he could determine the form of the Greek text at various moments in time with greater accuracy by comparing it against the ancient translations, including the Latin Vulgate. For this reason he also set out to determine the earliest form of Jerome's Vulgate. However, Bentley's attitude to the Latin Vulgate was conflicted. In his notorious *Sermon upon Popery* (1715), Bentley expressed an opinion he shared with Newton: that the canonical status of the Latin Vulgate in the Roman Catholic church was evidence of the way that church had betrayed the heritage of primitive Christianity: 'Now can anything be more absurd, more shocking to common Sense, than [...] that such a Translation, I say, by a private unknown Person not pretending to Inspiration, should be rais'd and advanc'd above the Inspir'd *Greek*?'[415]

Bentley was assisted in the task of collating manuscripts by the young Swiss scholar Johann Jakob Wettstein; John Walker, who gathered variants from manuscripts in Paris; David Casley, a pioneer in palaeography and deputy librarian at the King's and Cottonian Libraries, who collected variants in Oxford; his nephew Thomas Bentley; and the German antiquarian Philipp von Stosch, who together with the Italian priests Mico and Rulotta collated Codex Vaticanus on Bentley's behalf.[416] But Bentley's methodology had its critics. Thomas Emlyn (1715) obliquely criticised Bentley's criteria for selecting manuscript witnesses as less satisfactory than those developed by Mill, who had 'dealt more fairly than our common unaccurate *Commentators*; who, without any Examination, talk roundly of *many*, the most antient and the best Copies, which have *these* Words, not knowing what they say: whereas he pretends but to *few*, and rather supposes and hopes, from some Hints in others, that they had such Copies, than knows of any himself'.[417] In March 1724, William Whiston

---

[414] R. Bentley 1713, 71.

[415] R. Bentley 1715, 10. These comments were censured by Middleton 1752, 2:328–329.

[416] Cambridge, Trinity College ms B.17.20, 83r, contains an unsigned collation of the readings of the comma from the twenty-five Latin bibles in the royal library in Paris. The collations Bentley commissioned at Rome were interrupted, as mentioned by an unknown correspondent of J. J. Wettstein, writing from Altorf on 25 April 1729; Amsterdam, Universiteitsbibliotheek ms J 101, 1r. Further, see Monk 1833, 2:239, 287–289; R. Bentley 1862, xx.

[417] Emlyn 1715, 36–37. Wettstein would likewise insist on the need to weigh the value of each manuscript source; see Sheehan 2005, 99–100.

revealed in a letter to William Paul that the 'common unaccurate com-
mentator' criticised by Emlyn was Bentley.[418]

That Emlyn should have made this comment in a treatise on the comma
suggests that Bentley's intention to omit the passage from his edition
was already known. It was certainly public knowledge by the following
year. On 20 December 1716, a correspondent (probably Joseph Craven,
later master of Sidney Sussex College) wrote to ask Bentley to confirm
the rumour. Craven believed it imperative that the comma should not
fall victim to the doubts of sceptics like Clarke. The argument of 1 Jn
5 – the testimony of the Father concerning the Son, and the gift of eternal life through his Son – simply demanded the presence of the comma.
Craven was of the opinion that it had been erased from the manuscripts
by the anti-Montanist Alogi. He could not, he concluded, 'foresee any
Objection from any side' to accepting the genuineness of the passage, 'but
Sabellianism'.[419]

In his reply to Craven, dated 1 January 1717, Bentley explained that his
operating premise was Jerome's claim to have corrected his revised translation against the Greek text. If Bentley could establish 'St. *Jerom*'s true
Latin', he could dismiss most of the variants recorded by Mill as textually
insignificant. He worked principally on Latin bibles and manuscripts of
the Latin fathers older than a thousand years, 'of which sort I have 20 now
in my Study, that one with another make 20000 years'. Bentley boldly
claimed that on the basis of the resulting text, he could lead readers 'out
of the Labyrinth of 60000 various Lections; (for St. *Jerom*'s Latin has as
many Varieties as the Greek) and to give the Text as it stood in the Best
Copies, in the Time of the Council of *Nice* [Nicaea], without the Error
of 50 Words'. Bentley intended to exclude conjectures and emendations,
allowing only readings attested in the biblical manuscripts and quotations of the fathers. This principle has an analogy in Newton's reluctance
to admit extravagant hypotheses in experimental philosophy where they
departed from the phenomena.[420] Bentley assured Craven – perhaps not
entirely truthfully – that he had not yet examined the manuscript evidence for the comma, and was therefore unable to say whether or not he
planned to include it. However, he assured Craven that 'in my proposed
Work, the Fate of that Verse will be a mere *Question of Fact*'. Although

---

[418] Whiston 1749–1750, 1:314, referencing the pagination of the reprint, in Emlyn's *Collection of
Tracts* (1719): 'Mr. *Emlyn* meant Dr. *Bentley* in his 331st Page, who read a very learned Lecture at
Cambridge, to prove 1 *Joh*. v. 7 to be spurious.'
[419] Craven 1717, 20.
[420] On Newton's use of this principle, see Snobelen 2001, 201.

Bentley was aware that the comma played an important role in contemporary religious debate, he was unconvinced of its apologetic utility: 'if the Fourth Century knew that Text, let it come in, in God's Name: But if that Age did not know it, then Arianism in its Height was beat down without the Help of that Verse: And let the *Fact* prove as it will, the *Doctrine* is unshaken.'[421]

Craven replied on 3 January 1717, annoyed that Bentley had not engaged with his elaborate arguments: 'You seem not to have read mine, which aspires to prove *not the Possibility, but the Certainty that St.* John *wrote the Text in Question* [...]. Either the Text is Genuin, or the whole Period from ver. 9 to ver. 16 inclusive, is Spurious.' As far as Craven was concerned, internal considerations trumped the evidence of manuscripts: '*the Authority of all* MSS, besides the Autographon is as best but *Conjecture*; whereas the Evidence I have alledged from the *Passage itself is Decisive.*'[422]

Bentley also received mail of a different tone. On 29 March 1717, a certain J. Shaw sent Bentley a copy of Emlyn's *Full Inquiry*, 'which has hitherto, & I believe wil for ever remain unanswerable'. Shaw hoped that Bentley would be swayed by Emlyn's arguments to omit the comma from his projected edition:

> The blessed Trinity require it at your hands, in vindication of their honor, & of the truth of those sacred oracles, they have graciously given, as the sole rule of doctrin for men, & which ought to be freed from a spurious interlineation foisted therein. Religion demands it, which has already but too much suffered, thro' such indirect, villanous, & pernicious practices; Al lerned men expect it, knowing your great abilities in critical learning, lastly, the souls of millions of mankind implore it from you, who have suffred & are daily suffring in doctrines relating to their eternal salvation.[423]

Shaw's impassioned oratory expresses the strength of feeling aroused by this issue, which was felt to bear directly on faith and the assurance of salvation.

After the death of Henry James, regius professor of divinity at Cambridge, on 15 March 1717, Bentley manoeuvred himself into the position of being one of only two viable candidates as James' successor. When the other candidate, Charles Ashton, bowed out, Bentley gave his

---

[421] R. Bentley to J. Craven, 1 Jan. 1717, in Craven 1717, 24–25, corrected against Bentley's manuscript, repr. in Bartholomew 1908, facing 20. Bentley's original letter, in the library of Sidney Sussex College, is endorsed 'University. Dr. Craven'. This suggests that Craven was Bentley's anonymous correspondent; see Bartholomew 1908, 20.

[422] Craven 1717, 26–28.

[423] Cambridge, Trinity College R.17.31; modern ed. in Bentley 1842, 1:531–532, n° 201.

probationary praelection on 1 May 1717 before a large audience. His theme was the authenticity of the Johannine comma. According to William Whiston, Bentley used Emlyn's treatise, though he doubtless avoided mentioning Emlyn's name.[424] The examiners were satisfied, and Bentley was formally elected on 2 May 1717.

Craven was not the only person anxious about Bentley's plan to edit the New Testament. At about the time of Bentley's election, an anonymous layman wrote to convocation to complain that the clergy had remained silent on the Antitrinitarian threat, and had failed to follow up the investigation into Samuel Clarke's orthodoxy. Laypeople were distressed when they attended a service led by a suspected Unitarian, uncertain 'what Danger we run of saying Amen to a corrupt and polluted Act of Prayer and Adoration'. When the presiding minister pronounced the Trinitarian doxology, the congregation could not be sure if he meant 'three Names of one Person, or three Persons of three Substances, or two Persons of two Substances, and one Attribute of one of those Persons'.[425] A number of 'impious, and even blasphemous Pamphlets' had appeared, notably Emlyn's *Full Inquiry into the Original Authority of That Text, 1 John V. 7*, and *The Supremacy of the Father*, written by the Salisbury glover Thomas Chubb, who argued that the comma 'is held to have little or no real Foundation in Antiquity, or even in the present *Greek* MSS. themselves'.[426] The layman had initially felt sure that some orthodox member of the clergy would refute Emlyn, 'but instead of that, we have of late been alarmed with Reports, that a very Learned Critick, a Member of the Lower-House, Dr. *Bentley*, Master of *Trinity*-College, being an Archdeacon, is upon an Edition of the *Greek* Testament, and intends to omit that Text, and we see nothing in Defence thereof, but a short Letter written on that Occasion to the Doctor, by a Layman'.[427]

Responding to the desire for a more public declaration of his method, Bentley laid out his editorial principles in a prospectus for the edition, released in 1720. His intention was to find a means to distinguish which

---

[424] Whiston 1730, 100–101. The text of this lecture is lost, although it was known to Porson at the end of the eighteenth century; Monk 1833, 2:11–19. Whiston 1736, 13, expressed his impatience that Bentley's lecture had never been published.

[425] *The Layman's humble address* 1717, 14–15.

[426] Chubb 1715, 99. Chubb 1715, 101, argued that even if the comma were genuine, it would not prove that the three persons of the Trinity did not exist in some hierarchical relationship, the position that Chubb himself held. Further on Chubb, see Sheehan 2005, 119.

[427] *The Layman's humble address* 1717, 18–19. The letter from the layman had not yet been published; the anonymous author's knowledge of the letter suggests that he was someone close to Craven, if not Craven himself.

of the 30,000 variants presented by Mill, 'all put upon equal Credit to the offence of many good Persons', were textually relevant. One way to verify the antiquity of a given variant was to look for its traces in the Syrian, Coptic, Gothic and Ethiopic translations. By employing these editorial principles scrupulously, Bentley believed that the number of significant textual difficulties could be reduced to about two hundred. In this way, readers would have 'under one View what the first Ages of the Church knew of the Text; and what has crept into any Copies since, is of no Value or Authority'. Moreover, his edition would not be swayed by the perspectives or requirements of any 'Sect or Party', but would 'serve the whole Christian name'.[428]

Bentley's prospectus was reviewed anonymously by an old enemy, the eminent classicist Conyers Middleton, a more weighty interlocutor than Craven. Middleton protested unconvincingly that his criticisms 'were not drawn from me by *Personal Spleen*, or *Envy* to the Author of the Proposals, but by a *Serious Conviction* that he has neither Talents nor Materials proper for the Work he has undertaken, and that *Religion* is much more likely to receive Detriment than Service from it'. Indeed, Middleton insinuated that Bentley's proposal was 'hastned out to serve quite *different Ends*, than those of *Common Christianity*'.[429] Middleton was unconvinced that the proposed edition offered any advance over Mill's edition, and suggested that Bentley, 'as ungrateful as unjust', intended merely to 'copy and transcribe' the textual data assembled by Mill rather than to establish his own text on the basis of new manuscript readings.[430] More seriously, Middleton believed that Bentley's failure to understand the nature and extent of Jerome's undertaking would lead him into methodological error: 'having formed his Design upon a Notion which is not true, [...] he will be apt to wrest and force both the *Greek and Latin* Texts, to make them answer, as well as he can, to his *Hypothesis*'.[431] Those foolish enough to subscribe to '*Bentley's* Bubble' could expect as little return on their investment as those burned in the recent collapse of the South Sea Company.[432]

Bentley defended his proposal in a response, also published anonymously. While Middleton had compared Bentley's proposed undertaking unfavourably with Mill's edition, Bentley damned his old master with faint praise. Worse still, he mistook his anonymous critic as John

---

[428] Bentley 1720, 1–2.
[429] Middleton 1752, 2:319.
[430] Middleton 1752, 2:323.
[431] Middleton 1752, 2:328.
[432] Middleton 1752, 2:337.

Colbatch, whom he described as an ignorant thief, a wretch of native stupidity, of low talents and vicious taste, a supercilious pedant, casuistic drudge, scribbler out of the dark, and many other choice insults.[433] Middleton published a further attack, this time under his own name, while Colbatch sued Bentley for libel.

Inevitably the debate over Bentley's edition touched upon the question of the comma. In his first reply to David Martin (1719), Emlyn predicted that Bentley's promised edition would set the question of the comma 'in a yet clearer Light'.[434] By contrast, Richard Smalbroke, bishop of Lichfield and Coventry, anonymously published an open letter to Bentley in which he defended the authenticity of the comma. His principal reasons were doctrinal rather than textual:

> But since this is a Text that has been frequently cited in Controversy against the *Unitarians* and others, as a Passage of Scripture that most expressly asserts Three Persons in the Divine Nature; and since both the *Greek* and *Latin* Churches now read this Passage, and have done so for many Ages, in a very solemn manner; and since in particular the Church of *England* has in her liturgy appointed the reading of this Passage [...] according to ancient Custom; [...] out of a just Regard to what has been so long reputed Part of the Word of God, its Authority ought to be examin'd with the most mature Deliberation, before it be either tacitly or avowedly given up as an indefensible Passage.[435]

Smalbroke was convinced that the reading of the comma in the Complutensian bible, 'not only the first, but the most Accurate edition' of the New Testament, had been drawn from 'that excellent *Vatican* MS. which was recommended, or rather prescribed, to the *Complutensian* Editors as the Ground-work of their Edition of the New Testament'.[436] Smalbroke's first argument was 'that the *Complutensian Greek* Testament, as soon as it appear'd in the World, was of that Authority, as to oblige *Erasmus*, Robert *Stephens*, and the other subsequent Editors of the New Testament, to accommodate their Text very much to that Edition'.[437] As a result of his respect for this edition, Erasmus 'seems to have been confirmed in the Genuineness of that Verse, since he continued it in his Fourth and Fifth Editions of the New Testament, that is, after he had

[433] Bentley 1721; Middleton 1752, 2:354.

[434] Emlyn 1719b, 12–13.

[435] Smalbroke 1722, 5–6. Like Newton, Smalbroke 1722, 27–28, moved towards expressing the myth of Erasmus's promise under the influence of Simon's language of obligation. Smalbroke's work was reprinted in 1815 and 1824, edited by Thomas Burgess.

[436] Smalbroke 1722, 7, 12.

[437] Smalbroke 1722, 7–9.

seen it in the *Complutensian* Edition, to which he paid a great Respect, and very much accommodated both those Editions'.[438] The fact that the reading in the Complutensian bible differs from that in any other source seemed to Smalbroke to prove its authenticity. Smalbroke drew further evidence for his conclusion from Amelote, who claimed to have seen the comma in the oldest manuscript in the Vatican:

> If this Testimony of F. *Amelote* be not true, he was certainly one of the most egregious Lyars in the World; and if it be true, there is an End put to our present Dispute: Since then no doubt this was the very MS. that was sent by P. *Leo* to C. *Ximenes* as the Standard of his Edition of the New Testament.[439]

Bentley declined to reply, but in 1752, César de Missy, chaplain of the French church at St James' in London, showed conclusively not only that Amelote's testimony was untrue, but also that Smalbroke was relying merely on David Martin's inflated report of Amelote's views. Amelote had said that he had found the comma in the oldest manuscript in the Vatican (*je la trouve [...] dans le plus ancien de cette Bibliothèque*), but had not named which one.[440] The only explanation was that Amelote, misinterpreting the apparatus of a critical edition, had mistakenly concluded that the reading was present in some manuscript in the Vatican. Martin, assuming that Amelote had seen the purported manuscript, gave a report of this 'discovery' in the Vatican more confident than Amelote's own vague formulation.[441] Yet, as the great German critic Johann David Michaelis remarked, Missy's tone was counter-productive: 'It cannot be denied, that La Croze and De Missy introduced so much satire and ridicule in their replies to Martin, that they diminished the confidence, which the public would otherwise have placed in their assertions.'[442]

Dogged by opposition and harassed by litigation, Bentley lost confidence in the project. By 1724, William Whiston reported that Bentley dared 'not now wholly omit it [the comma] in the Text of his Edition of the New Testament, which he has promised, but not yet performed'.[443] It is likely that the full collation of the readings from Codex Vaticanus, which Bentley received in 1729, led him to realise that the task he had undertaken was more complex than he had originally envisaged, and

[438] Smalbroke 1722, 10.
[439] Smalbroke 1722, 26.
[440] Amelote 1687–1688, 2:104.
[441] Missy 1752:203–205; cf. D. Martin 1721, 175; Semler 1764, 64–74.
[442] Michaelis 1802–1803, 2.1:295; cf. Michaelis 1788, 1:640.
[443] William Whiston to William Paul, 30 March 1724, repr. in Whiston 1749–1750, 1:314.

could not be completed according to the principles he had set himself. For example, his earlier resolve not to admit any 'conjectures or emendations' in the text was an impossible dream.[444] Although John Walker continued to collect variants on Bentley's behalf as late as 1732, the project was never completed.

14. David Martin and the rediscovery of Codex Montfortianus

Thomas Emlyn's *Full Inquiry* attracted international attention. It received a favourable review in the *Journal littéraire* of the Hague for 1716.[445] David Martin, Huguenot pastor of the Walloon church in Utrecht, told Paul Ernst Jablonski, who was now studying in Utrecht, that he intended to write a refutation of Emlyn, confident that he would 'enter the fray with new and hitherto unknown weapons, which he trusts cannot be met by any artful siege-engines'. On 31 December 1716, Jablonski informed Mathurin Veyssière La Croze (1661–1739), head of the royal library at Berlin, that he should expect to receive enquiries from Martin about the biblical manuscripts in his care, particularly Codex Ravianus.[446]

Martin had defended the comma as early as 1696. In the preface to 1 Jn in his translation of the New Testament, Martin alleged that the comma is a passage hateful to Antitrinitarians. While admitting that it was difficult to defend a passage so poorly attested in the manuscript sources, he asserted that the comma was found 'in a large number of manuscripts, which are even amongst the most ancient', and was quoted by a number of fathers before even the oldest extant manuscripts were copied.[447] Martin believed that since the comma was necessary for a rational belief in the Trinity, it should be defended by all means possible. 'If the Holy Spirit has plac'd it there, 'tis a crime to give it up to the audacious criticism of the enemies to the doctrine it contains; and I conceive nothing more injudicious [...] than to assert that this Text may well be dispens'd with [...] because we have many others in which the doctrine of the Trinity is clearly made good.'[448]

[444] Jebb 1899, 160–161. Krans 2006, provides an important conceptual framework for conjecture in the editing of the New Testament.
[445] D. Martin 1717, 8; D. Martin 1719a, 5; Anon. 1716.
[446] La Croze 1742–1746, 1:166; Berlin, Staatsbibliothek ms gr. fol. 1 and 2 (Wettstein ms 110).
[447] D. Martin 1707, 404–405; cf. Bludau 1922, 132.
[448] D. Martin 1721, 7; D. Martin 1722, 4.

Martin first defended the comma against Emlyn's attack in his *Deux dissertations critiques* (1717, English translation 1719).[449] Martin maintained that the comma was the most powerful evidence in Scripture to demonstrate the error of the Arians.[450] Given Erasmus' role in interrogating the comma, Martin attempted to determine his motivation and conclusions. For Martin, Erasmus was an ambiguous figure, for although he was a great scholar, he was also responsible for stirring up this unfortunate hornets' nest, since his investigations into the canonicity of many Christological passages in Scripture had been taken up by such men as Biandrata and Sozzini.[451] Yet they were not the only recent writers to question the comma: 'There's no *Socinian*, nor even *Arian*, has taken so much pains to decry this fam'd verse, as some of these Christian writers have done; and especially Mr. *Simon*.'[452]

Even though Erasmus had unwittingly contributed to the revival of Arianism, Martin still defended his 'uprightness and sincerity'. If he inserted the comma on the basis of his British codex alone, it was 'because he seems not to have been over-fond of the business himself, for he declares he did it purely *to guard against calumny*'.[453] Martin refuted Emlyn's suggestion that Erasmus invented the comma and covered his tracks through deliberate vagueness about the identity and whereabouts of Codex Britannicus.[454] Since the manuscript had since disappeared, Martin considered further speculation on its contents unproductive.[455] Even if Erasmus' British codex was lost, the comma had recently been discovered in Codex Ravianus.[456]

In January 1719, Emlyn reprinted his *Full Enquiry*, finally revealing his identity as its author, as well as *An Answer to Mr. Martin's Critical Dissertation on 1 John v. 7*.[457] Emlyn defended the character of Erasmus, 'the *Wonder* and *Glory* of his Age, and who laid the Foundations for After-Ages to build upon', complaining that it was 'very unfair and unjust to insinuate that I had *called in question the Veracity of this learned Man, two hundred Years after his Death*, when I never once suspected his Testimony in the least, and only said that I never found *he* gave any such

---

[449] The publication of the English translation was announced in *The Post Boy*, 10 January 1719.
[450] D. Martin 1722, 5–6.
[451] D. Martin 1719a, 3–4; D. Martin 1717, 4–5.
[452] Martin 1719a, 4–5.
[453] D. Martin 1719a, 72–73; Martin 1717, 133–134.
[454] D. Martin 1719a, 72; D. Martin 1717, 133.
[455] D. Martin 1719a, 73; D. Martin 1717, 134.
[456] D. Martin 1719a, 59; D. Martin 1717, 106.
[457] Publication of Emlyn 1719a, 1719b, and 1719c was announced *The Post Boy*, 24 January 1719.

Testimony'. If Erasmus said that he had seen the British codex, that was good enough for Emlyn, who considered Erasmus 'too great to use such Falsehood and Deceit'.[458] Emlyn recognised that Martin had shifted the focus of the debate to Erasmus' character, his trustworthiness, his motivation and his readiness to resort to pragmatic compromise. In this context, the myth of Erasmus' promise to Lee took on particular importance. But where Martin was prepared to let the question of Codex Britannicus drop, Emlyn was more tenacious: 'I think it does concern us greatly to know whether such a Manuscript be in being still, which was too remarkable to be lost in Obscurity, if it had once been taken notice of; and whether any one else ever saw it, since 'tis contested so much whether ever *Erasmus* saw it, or pretended to it.' Emlyn also accused Martin of making too much of Kettner's report of Codex Ravianus, and relying on a rumour that it contained the comma without having written to the library in Berlin for confirmation. By contrast, Emlyn had 'receiv'd Information from a very sure Hand, that *this Verse* is not in the Body of that Manuscript', but was added later in the margin. (Unfortunately for Emlyn, his source had given him inaccurate information.) Moreover, Emlyn's informant assured him that Codex Ravianus was 'not above 300 *Years* old'.[459] According to Emlyn, Martin had proposed to cure scepticism through a 'presuming Credulity'. But such complacency in important matters would not only prevent 'a severe Examination into Facts'. It would create a backlash as dissatisfaction about traditional claims grew.[460] The debate between Martin and Emlyn thus reflects basic differences in epistemological priorities. While Martin suggested that faith must be illuminated by reason, Emlyn maintained that biblical study had to conform to the objective scepticism emerging as a central feature of scientific method.

Martin's *Examination of Mr. Emlyn's Answer*, published simultaneously in French and English in July 1719, again addressed Emlyn's suggestion that Erasmus had merely invented the Codex Britannicus.[461] Martin pointed out that Erasmus wrote in his *Annotationes* that he had been sent a report by a friend (that is, Bombace) on the reading of the relevant passage in 1 Jn in an ancient manuscript in the Vatican. Erasmus' candour and healthy scepticism towards anything he had not seen with his own eyes argued against Emlyn's insinuation that the British codex was

---

[458] Emlyn 1719b, 24–25.
[459] Emlyn 1719b, 29–30.
[460] Emlyn 1719b, 25.
[461] The publication of D. Martin 1719a, 1719b and 1719c was announced in *The Post Boy* on 21 July, 23 July and 25 July 1719.

a will-o'-the-wisp, and that Erasmus had merely invented the reading of the comma.[462] Martin also refuted Emlyn's account of Codex Ravianus with information he had received from 'one of the King's Librarians' at Berlin, who informed him that the comma was 'in the Text of the *Greek Manuscript of the New Testament* in the King's Library at *Berlin*, but we can affirm nothing certain concerning its antiquity'.[463]

The exchange between Emlyn and Martin attracted attention from all over Europe. Samuel Crell mentioned it in a letter to La Croze.[464] Michel de la Roche covered the dispute in the *Bibliothèque angloise* and *Mémoires littéraires de la Grande Bretagne*, coming down on Emlyn's side. By contrast, a positive review of Martin's *Examen* appeared in the *Acta eruditorum* for 1720. Du Pin criticised Emlyn for doubting Estienne's competence and integrity, blaming the misplaced metobelos in the *editio regia* on his compositors.[465] Martin's *Deux dissertations* also came into the hands of the Parisian Oratorian Jacques Le Long, a noted biblical scholar. Once Le Long saw that Martin was publicly defending a number of errors, he wrote him an open letter dated 12 April 1720, which was published in the *Journal des Sçavans* on 6 May. Martin had assumed that all seventeen (actually fifteen) manuscripts inspected by Estienne contained the Catholic Epistles, and had been misled by Estienne's misplaced obeloi to the false conclusion that they all contained the comma. But Le Long pointed out that only seven of Estienne's manuscripts contained the Catholic Epistles, and none of these contained the comma. (Newton had made the same point in his unpublished *Historical Account*.) As far as Le Long was aware, only two Greek manuscripts contained the comma: the Codex Britannicus mentioned by Erasmus, and 'Codex Montfortius', a manuscript used for the London Polyglot and now held by the library of Trinity College, Dublin, which he took to be two distinct manuscripts.[466] Le Long had first learned of the Dublin manuscript in a letter dated 19 June 1708 from the French Huguenot refugee Jean Ycard, dean of Achonry in Ireland. Ycard's attention may have been drawn to the manuscript by a note on one of the front

---

[462] D. Martin 1719b, 125; D. Martin 1719c, 77.

[463] D. Martin 1719b, 165–166; D. Martin 1719c, 102.

[464] Samuel Crell to La Croze, 20 January 1718, in La Croze 1742–1746, 1:89–90; Bludau 1922, 138, misread the date of this letter as 1710. Crell published a study of 1 Jn 5 under the pseudonym 'J. Philalethe' in the *Bibliothèque angloise* for 1720.

[465] Du Pin, in Simon 1730, 576–580.

[466] Le Long 1720, 298–301. Le Long 1723, 1:172, repeated his opinion that Erasmus' Codex Britannicus and Codex Montfortianus were not the same book, arguing from the differences between Erasmus' transcription of the passage in the apology to Stunica and the reading of the comma in the Dublin manuscript.

flyleaves, made probably by Samuel Foley (1655–1695) while cataloguing the Dublin collection in about 1688.[467] Le Long had reported Ycard's discovery in his *Bibliotheca sacra* (1709), though he did not mention there that the Dublin manuscript contained the comma.[468] In a private letter to Louis Roger, dean of Bourges, Le Long wrote that Ycard had informed him of the presence of the comma in Montfortianus, but doubted that this manuscript was Erasmus' Codex Britannicus. Roger publicised this discovery in his treatise on the comma (1713), though it seems not to have been noticed by many readers, probably because neither Ycard, Le Long nor Roger had realised that the Dublin manuscript was Erasmus' Codex Britannicus.[469] In 1716 Christoph Matthäus Pfaff could still puzzle over what had become of Erasmus' British codex.[470] As late as 1722, Richard Smalbroke wrote that 'the *British Greek* MS. cited by *Erasmus* in Favour of this Text, and consulted by himself, is perish'd, or not now to be found'.[471]

By contrast, Le Long's open letter to Martin, thrown into a debate that was attracting international attention, electrified the learned public. Samuel Clarke asked John Evans, bishop of Meath, to request Ycard to send further information. Evans duly passed Ycard's reply (5 August 1720) on to Clarke, who then gave it to Emlyn.[472] Martin was mortified, incensed and excited in turns by Le Long's letter. He also wrote to Ycard for further details. On 21 August, he addressed an open letter to Le Long, which appeared in *L'Europe savante*. Martin argued that if the manuscripts cited by Le Long were indeed those used by Estienne, 'he would not be able to defend himself against the suggestion that he had acted in bad faith, and deceived the public'.[473] Le Long simply must have identified the wrong manuscripts. Nevertheless, Martin congratulated Le Long for announcing that the comma was attested in Codex Montfortianus, once used for the London Polyglot and now preserved in Dublin. By October, Martin had received from Ycard a precise transcript of the relevant passage from 1 Jn, certified as accurate by William Lewis, librarian of Trinity College, Dublin. Ycard followed this with details of the physical state of the manuscript and some of its unusual readings.[474]

---

[467] Dublin, Trinity College ms 30, 3r (in Foley's hand?): 'G. 97, Montfortius's Greek Testam. MS.'
[468] Le Long 1709a, 1:672; cf. Le Long 1709b, 1:372–373. On Ycard († 1733), see the brief notices in Hylton 2005, 122, 194.
[469] Roger 1713, 120–121.
[470] Pfaff 1716, 100.
[471] Smalbroke 1722, 7.
[472] Emlyn 1746, 2:270; Jortin 1760, 2:226.
[473] D. Martin 1720, 281.
[474] D. Martin 1720, 300–301; D. Martin 1722, 157–158.

In the meantime, La Croze asked a friend in Berlin to forward a letter to Martin, in which he reported politely that although many people had taken Codex Ravianus for an old manuscript, he had recognised it as a copy of the Complutensian bible, and thus of no independent critical value.[475] Soon after, La Croze received another enquiry about Ravianus from one of Emlyn's correspondents in Germany. In his reply to this letter, dated 31 December 1719, he expressed himself more freely:

> It seems very strange to me, that ever our Manuscript, a Book of no Authority at all, should be alledg'd in confirmation of a dubious Reading, since I have already discovered it to very many learned Men, and even to the Reverend Mr. *Martin* himself, that this Manuscript, tho much boasted of, and sold by a cunning Cheat for an antient Book, is but a late Transcript from the *Polyglot* of the *Complutensian* Edition; this I presently discerned, when as a Stranger only I view'd the King's Library, before I had any thoughts of settling at *Berlin*, and I then declared the same openly to *Hendreichius* now deceased: and ever since this Library has been committed to my Care, I have freely own'd it upon all Occasions without reserve; and the Reverend Mr. *Martin* knows it very well, who by my means has been informed of it.[476]

When a copy of this letter made it back to Martin, he claimed that La Croze had misrepresented the content of his letter to Martin, although the correspondence (published by Martin himself in 1721) show that this was not the case. In any case, La Croze had no interest in corresponding further with a man who disregarded his opinions and accused him of misrepresentation. When J. J. Wettstein asked La Croze about the correspondence in 1731, he simply responded: 'The good gentleman Mr Martin had no critical sense or merit. The respect that I believed myself due to pay to his age and character prevented me from replying to him. He would have done better to occupy himself with preaching.'[477]

Emlyn confuted Martin's fresh objections in *A Reply to Mr. Martin's Examination of the Answer to His Dissertation on 1 John 5. 7* (1720). Here Emlyn set about to remove some of the manuscript witnesses on which Martin had relied as foundations for the genuineness of the comma. He began with Codex Ravianus, which Martin had attempted to date at about 500 years old. Emlyn also corrected many of the errors Martin had

[475] Letter transcribed in D. Martin 1721, 203–204; translation in D. Martin 1722, 118.
[476] Letter transcribed and translated in Emlyn 1720, 9–12; extract in D. Martin 1722, 116. The publication of Emlyn 1720, was announced in *The Post Boy* on 24 March 1720.
[477] Extract from La Croze's letter to Wettstein published in Missy 1753, 90. See also Wettstein 1751–1752, 1:58–59; 2:723. Missy probably received a copy of La Croze's letter from Wettstein.

made concerning Estienne's sources, such as his exaggerated claim that
Estienne had found evidence of the comma in seventeen separate Greek
manuscripts.

Martin replied in a final tract, *The Genuineness of the Text of the First
Epistle of Saint John* [...] *Demonstrated by Proofs which are beyond all
Exception* (1721, English translation 1722). It is clear that Martin's ulti-
mate criterion for accepting the presence of the comma in the printed
editions, despite the textual differences between them, was the character
of the editors: 'A man of learning cannot be ignorant that the *Greek*
Editions of *Ximenes*, *Erasmus*, and *Stephens* were made from ancient
Manuscripts; and a man of candour cannot doubt of these Manuscripts
no more than if they were set before his eyes, unless he suspects *Ximenes*,
Erasmus, and *Stephens* to have been cheats and impostors.'[478] Emlyn's
scurrilous suggestion that Erasmus had simply invented the story of the
British codex to confound his enemies was a slander to which not even
Simon had sunk.[479] Fortunately, the means for vindicating Erasmus,
Ximénez and Estienne, and for proving that the comma was founded
on undeniable manuscript attestation, were in Martin's grasp. 'Divine
Providence, which visibly takes care to preserve in the Church the truth
of a Text so valuable for the doctrine it contains, has thrown into my
hands the extract of an ancient Greek Manuscript which I had no knowledge of [...].'[480] This, he claimed, was 'an authentick Piece never yet
produc'd, and which gives the finishing stroke to all the proofs urg'd for
the genuineness of this Text; and this is the extract of an ancient *Greek*
Manuscript of the New Testament found at *Dublin* in the University
Library'.[481]

Martin claimed as much credit for discovering the manuscript as he
could. Conveniently ignoring the fact that Jean Ycard had already written
to Le Long as early as 1708, Martin airily claimed: 'The Dissertation I had
wrote upon the disputed passage, was doubtless what did raise in him
[Ycard] the curiosity to see whether it [the comma] was in this Manuscript,
and he had the satisfaction to find it there.'[482] Martin made several observations about the manuscript, though some of these were incorrect, such

[478] D. Martin 1722, 156; cf. D. Martin 1721, 270.
[479] D. Martin 1722, 171; cf. D. Martin 1721, 296–297.
[480] D. Martin 1722, 157; cf. D. Martin 1721, 271.
[481] D. Martin 1722, A4r; cf. D. Martin 1721, *7r–v. The ms contains a note by Ycard, now bound in
       as 2r–v.
[482] D. Martin 1722, 160–161; cf. D. Martin 1721, 276.

as the erroneous identification of the writing material as parchment rather than paper. The presence of the prologues of Theophylact indicated to Martin that the book could not be older than the eleventh century, but he was inclined to place it as early as the end of that century. Martin misunderstood the note at the end of Mark, which stated that this gospel was written ten years after the resurrection of Jesus (ἐγράφη μετὰ χρόνους δέκα τῆς τοῦ χριστοῦ ἀναλήψεως, 87r), misconstruing it as meaning that the manuscript was written ten centuries after the resurrection, an error later derided by Wettstein and Semler.[483] Relying on the palaeographer Montfaucon (1708), Martin also cited the double dots over many of the ϊ and ϋ as evidence of great antiquity.[484] Martin also pointed out that the reading of the comma in Montfortianus is close to that given in the Greek translation of the *Acta* of the Fourth Lateran Council. But rather than taking this as evidence that the passage in Montfortianus had been translated from Latin, as had the *Acta*, he simply disputed Richard Simon's observation that those who translated the *Acta* sometimes translated passage of Scripture cited in the document from Latin rather than citing the Greek New Testament or Septuagint. 'The Manuscript of *Dublin* will finally ruin all these vain subterfuges invented against the *Greek* of the Council of *Latran*,' he crowed.[485]

Martin then compared the reading of the comma in Montfortianus with that from Erasmus' British codex, as quoted in the *Apologia to Stunica* and the *Annotationes*. Unfortunately he failed to check Erasmus' 1522 Greek New Testament, which gave a more accurate transcription. The apparent differences between the two readings – the omission of ἅγιον in v. 7 and of οἱ before μαρτυροῦντες in v. 8 – led Martin to the incorrect conclusion that the two manuscripts were not identical.[486] This conclusion had the happy result of apparently multiplying the manuscript evidence for the comma, thus seeming to bolster the case for its authenticity: '[T]he manuscript of *England*, whether it has been lost since the time of *Erasmus*, like an abundance of others, or that it subsists in some corner expos'd to the mercy of worms and damp, finds again its authority under that of the Manuscripts of *Ireland*, by the agreement that it has with it in the Text

[483] Wettstein 1751–1752, 1:52; Semler 1764, 56. See also the letter by William Doyle to John Wilson, Cambridge, Trinity College ms B.17.20, 147r.

[484] Montfaucon (1708), 33: 'Ab annis plus mille literae ϊ & ϋ, quando alteri vocali non junguntur, nec diphtongum efficiunt, punctis supernis notantur [...].'

[485] D. Martin 1722, 171–172; cf. D. Martin 1721, 294.

[486] D. Martin 1722, 173–174; cf. D. Martin 1721, 300–301.

of the three witnesses in Heaven, and this sacred Text thus receives from these two ancient Manuscripts combin'd together, a new proof of its being authentick.'[487] Martin ascribed the preservation of the comma in all these manuscripts to divine providence:

> These small variations in the Manuscripts of the *Greek* Editions seem to have been so order'd by Providence, to prevent the thought that some had been copied from the rest, and that one sole Manuscript had been the foundation of all three, or even that it had been a forg'd Manuscript.[488]

Given that the reading of the comma in Erasmus' British codex was demonstrably translated by the scribe from Latin, Martin's appeal to the powers of providence in preserving the comma was optimistic.

Martin's last tract also presented the first fully developed narration of the myth of Erasmus' promise to Lee. Martin presented Erasmus as torn between his belief in the comma's rightful place in the text and his frustration that this conviction was not borne out by the manuscript sources at his disposal. Having set up the story in such a way, Martin could present Erasmus' inclusion of the comma in the third edition of his Greek text not as a capitulation to pragmatism, but as the restoration of the reading he had always suspected to be correct:

> All this held his mind for some time in doubt betwixt these and the contrary reasons he had for believing the text genuine. Thus when *Ley* and *Stunica* had wrote against him upon his leaving it out of his two *Greek* Editions, he gives no other answer, but that he follow'd his Manuscripts closely, and that if they would shew him one which had the passage, he would streight put out another Edition, in which it should be inserted. Upon this he meets with a Manuscript in *England* where he finds this passage, and without hesitation or offering the least violence to himself, he gives it a place in his Edition. By this means he satisfies his conscience, and silences his calumniators, who spread abroad against him scandalous reports, as if he had meant to favour *Arianism* by suppressing so plain a Text.[489]

Martin's formulation of the myth of Erasmus' promise to Lee probably drew on Richard Simon's somewhat imprecise account of the story. Like Simon, Martin erroneously assumed that Erasmus saw the British codex in England. These errors were sown into the debate like weeds. Unfortunately Martin did not live long to savour what he believed to be his final victory, for he died soon after finishing the book. Many readers

---

[487] D. Martin 1722, 174; cf. D. Martin 1721, 301–302.
[488] D. Martin 1722, 81–82; cf. D. Martin 1721, 140.
[489] D. Martin 1722, 84; cf. D. Martin 1721, 144–145.

considered that the palm of victory went to Martin, and his arguments were repeated well into the nineteenth century.[490]

The beginning of the dispute between Martin and Emlyn coincided with a Trinitarian crisis within Nonconformist congregations in England. This crisis was catalysed by the publication of Whiston's tracts, Samuel Clarke's *Scripture-doctrine*, Emlyn's *Full Inquiry* and a pamphlet war between Daniel Whitby and Daniel Waterland over the nature of the divine persons. After reading such books, some Nonconformists in Exeter began to deny the equality of the Son with the Father. In 1718, Henry Atkins, minister of Puddington, was asked to preach on the satisfaction of Christ (1 Jn 2:2) and on the Johannine comma, in order to bring some clarity to his uncertain congregation. From Exeter, unrest spread through dissenting congregations throughout the country. A synod at Salters' Hall in London in 1719 discussed whether membership of a Nonconformist congregation should require adherence to a traditional Trinitarian confession, such as the first of the Thirty-Nine Articles or the sixth question of the Westminster catechism, or simply a declaration of belief in Scripture alone. Representatives of the latter position considered that documents such as the creeds were human inventions, and therefore had no necessary authority as tests of orthodoxy. Such claims could only be made for Scripture, understood as inspired and literally true. Thus a conservative view of Scripture was paired with the desire to uphold toleration and private judgement. The synod voted narrowly for the second requirement, though a majority of its members subsequently subscribed to articles of belief in the Trinity.[491]

In 1719 and 1720, the Nonconformist minister Edmund Calamy (1671–1732) preached a series of seventeen sermons on the Trinity at Salters' Hall, including four that dealt with the Johannine comma. Although Calamy rejected the requirement of subscription as contrary to the spirit of Nonconformism, he vigorously refuted 'that different Set of Notions concerning *Father, Son*, and *Holy Ghost*, which some would obtrude upon us, and which they applaud as much more rational and accountable'. By arguing that the Trinity could be demonstrated clearly from Scripture and reason, Calamy thus sought to bridge the two sides in the Salters' Hall dispute. According to Calamy, the ancient, protean and incoherent error of Arianism, driven by dark ulterior motives, had a modern face: 'I shall chiefly take Mr. *Emlyn* and Mr. *Whiston* for the Standards of this *New*

---

[490] Bludau 1922, 137.
[491] Colligan 1913, 43–67; the place of the comma in these debates is discussed by Freeman 2006.

Scheme.[492] Calamy considered it vital to defend the comma against the arguments of those who would dispute its legitimacy. 'If the text be genuine, the whole *Arian* Scheme is at once overthrown, and cannot stand before it: And upon that account we have the less reason to wonder that they that are in that Scheme, are so zealous against it, and so desirous to get rid of it.'[493] The terms of the debate had evidently shifted since the time when Erasmus could conclude that since the meaning of the comma is so obscure, it was 'not much use in refuting heretics'.[494]

In the interval between preaching his sermons and publishing them in 1722, Calamy had read Martin's final tract in the French edition. Calamy accepted Martin's argument that the slight differences between the text of Montfortianus and the text of the British codex reported by Erasmus in his apology to Stunica proved that they were different manuscripts.[495] Calamy also followed Martin in refuting Emlyn's suggestion that Erasmus had simply invented the story of the British codex to get the monkey off his back. Calamy knew that any judgement in this matter was going to reflect not merely on Erasmus' own character, but also on the status of the comma, since Emlyn had identified the existence of the Codex Britannicus as one of Mill's strongest arguments for the authenticity of the comma. 'And let Men quibble and cavil as long as they will, either there must have been some *British Copy*, that *Erasmus* could depend on, that had this Verse as he represents, or he that has hitherto been admir'd as a great Restorer of Learning, must come under the Imputation of being at once both weak and false; so that he cannot be depended on.'[496] Calamy, by affirming that Erasmus was indeed 'a Man of more Candor than most that are of his Communion', in a stroke saved the integrity of the comma, exonerated Erasmus from the suspicion of blame, and rescued the profession of biblical criticism from disrepute. However, by making the character of early editors into the primary criterion for the soundness of their editions, Martin and Calamy undermined the value of philological method. Moreover, Calamy's suggestion that Erasmus' honesty distinguished him from the majority of Roman Catholics shows how the myths that swirled around Erasmus' editorial decisions could be pressed into the service of confessional apologetic with little effort.[497] Emlyn bridled

---

[492] Calamy 1722, 289; cf. Wiles 1996, 139–140.
[493] Calamy 1722, 435.
[494] *ASD* IX-2:258.
[495] Calamy 1722, 469.
[496] Calamy 1722, 469.
[497] Calamy 1722, 464; Bludau 1922, 132.

at Calamy's appeal to character, and jibed that the preacher 'thought it the best Method to begin with Mens *Characters* rather than with their *Arguments*, and in effect to tell his People, that very good Men had been for the *Text*, and some very bad or indifferent ones against it'.[498]

In the 1731 collected edition of his tracts, Emlyn included a supplementary chapter on the readings in Codex Montfortianus, made on the basis of his own inspection of the manuscript in 1725. In the 1746 re-edition, Emlyn added the letters concerning Martin by Le Long and La Croze. But given that Martin was no longer alive to defend himself, Emlyn's insistence on having the final word was ill-judged.[499]

Despite the tawdry *ad hominem* attacks employed by both Martin and Emlyn, their exchanges raised the bar of argument and evidence in this debate. The rediscovery of Montfortianus in the course of this exchange raised a number of questions: the origin, age and textual authority of this manuscript, and its relationship to Erasmus' British codex. To those who believed that Erasmus' British codex and Montfortianus were different manuscripts, the discovery served to multiply the number of textual witnesses, and thus the likelihood that the comma was genuine. To those who accepted that Montfortianus was the manuscript used by Erasmus, or at least the source of an extract communicated to him, the existence of Montfortianus cleared Erasmus of the charge of fabricating the reading.

It soon became clear that a more detailed examination of Montfortianus was needed. John Wilson, a fellow of Trinity College Cambridge, made further enquiries on Bentley's behalf with Patrick Delany, chancellor of Christchurch Dublin and a friend of Swift. Delany sent a precise transcription of the page in question, but expressed his lack of sympathy for Bentley's project. He felt that the early printed editions of the New Testament should be accorded 'more weight than perhaps all the manuscripts now extant put together. No man that knows the characters of the early editors can doubt the credit of those manuscripts they published from.'[500] The argument from character, on which Martin had relied so heavily, evidently had a good deal of traction.

Bentley was unsatisfied with Delany's response, and in 1728 further enquiries were sent to the clergyman William Doyle. Doyle was deeply

---

[498] Emlyn 1719b, v; Emlyn 1746, 2:171, identified the 'Dr C—' to whom he had referred in 1719 as Calamy.

[499] Emlyn 1731, 2:161–164; Emlyn 1746, 2:273–299.

[500] Patrick Delany to Isaac Dalton, Dublin 24 January 1726, forwarded to Wilson and thence to Bentley; Cambridge, Trinity College ms B.17.20, 174r–175v. Delany later published a defence of the comma; see Delany 1766, 69–90.

interested in text-critical matters, and flattered to have been asked to contribute to Bentley's work. He sent three voluble letters describing the manuscript, as well as an accurate transcription of the passage containing the comma. Doyle also informed Wilson that Martin's account of the manuscript was inaccurate. The elderly and near-blind Jean Ycard had accompanied Doyle to the library, and informed him that Martin had 'very often not done him justice in misquoting and mistranslating the Latin Letter He sent Him on this Subject'. For example, whereas Ycard had told Martin that he believed Montfortianus to have been copied after the invention of printing, Martin cited him as stating that it was '5 or 6 hundred Years old'. Consequently, Doyle advised Wilson not to 'give much heed to any thing Mr. Martin there speaks about this Book at least Nothing contrary to the account I send you'. After examining the text of Montfortianus, Doyle noted that although the manuscript was written in a 'sad scrawling Hand', it contained many unusual and potentially valuable readings also attested in other early manuscripts such as Codex Alexandrinus. However, the division of the chapters after the Latin fashion indicated that it was copied by (or for) a western reader. Doyle warned that the collation of Montfortianus in the London Polyglot, taken over in Mill's edition, was incomplete and inaccurate, and suggested that Bentley should commission a new collation if he wished to cite its readings in his edition.[501]

In a third letter, Doyle provided further observations on the manuscript, including a drawing of the watermark of the paper. However, after comparing the hand of the manuscript to the plates in Montfaucon's *Palaeographia Graeca*, Doyle wondered now if Martin may have been right in dating Montfortianus quite early. Before signing off the letter, Doyle asked Wilson to try to arrange a posting for him in the Levant Company or some embassy in Turkey, 'for I have a violent Inclination to visit those Countrys intirely in order to discover MSS of the Bible, and to attain a perfect Knowledge of the Greek Church', which he believed would strengthen the Church of Ireland against the recrudescence of 'Popery'.[502] Doyle's request, though gauche, nevertheless reveals his awareness of the importance of biblical philology in the arms race between the churches.

Although interest in Montfortianus continued, it took some time before its text was studied intensively. John Jackson (1736) asserted

---

[501] Cambridge, Trinity College ms B.17.20, 145r–147v (6 August 1728); this letter refers to an earlier one which has not survived. Further, see Monk 1833, 2:286–289; Jebb 1899, 160.
[502] Cambridge, Trinity College ms B.17.20, 148r–149v (16 November 1728).

incorrectly that the comma was written in a different hand from the rest of the manuscript.[503] Having asked John Abernathy to make a precise copy of the relevant passage in Montfortianus, George Benson duly reported that it conformed to the reading in Erasmus' edition, and pointed out the inaccuracy of Jackson's report. Abernathy also sent a transcript to Joseph Wasse, the learned rector of Aynho in Northamptonshire, who expressed the opinion that the hand was no earlier than the thirteenth century.[504]

More pressing than the age of the manuscript was the question whether the comma was an original part of the Greek text or simply a translation from Latin. David Casley, perhaps echoing the opinion of Bentley, answered both questions crisply. Casley believed that the Dublin manuscript was identical to Erasmus' British codex, and declared that it had been copied not long before Erasmus saw it, probably 'translated or corrected from the Latin Vulgate'. Casley's ostensible uncertainty about the origins of the manuscript nevertheless revealed his suspicions. 'But how to account for this Verse's being first inserted, is the Difficulty,' Casley declared, 'and some hot Heads have not stuck to call it a grand Forgery.'[505]

15.   New editions of the New Testament: Wells, Mace, Bengel, Wettstein, Bowyer, Harwood

The eighteenth century saw the appearance of a number of editions and translations of the New Testament in which the comma was treated in several different ways. We shall examine six, prepared for different purposes and different audiences. While Wells' and Mace's work was quickly forgotten, Bengel's Pietist commentary worked upon later readers such as John Wesley. Wettstein's edition represented a considerable improvement on Mill's text, and was also connected with the rediscovery of Newton's *Historical Account*. The editions of Bowyer and Harwood mark a distinct move away from the *textus receptus*.

Edward Wells published an edition of the New Testament in eleven volumes between 1709 and 1719. While Mill had given the *textus receptus* as his body text, Wells used the variants recorded by Mill to improve the text in hundreds of places. He also gave a revision of the Authorised Version, 'render'd more Agreeable to the Original', an English paraphrase and annotations. Wells' work marks a move away from the general tendency of

---

[503]   J. Jackson 1736, 79.
[504]   Benson 1752, 28–29; Benson 1756, 639–640.
[505]   Casley 1734, XX–XXI.

English churchmen to insist on the Authorised Version as a way of keep-
ing lay doubts about the textual reliability of Scripture at bay.[506] Yet Wells
insisted that the text he presented did not pose any threat to doctrine.
For example, he asserted that the comma had inadvertently been left out
of the Greek text by an early scribe. However, it was clear that 'the present common Reading is nevertheless the true original Reading', since it
was preserved in the Latin translation, cited by Tertullian and Cyprian,
and was doctrinally consonant with Jn 10:30.[507] Such glib conclusions
did little to satisfy Emlyn, who criticised Wells for failing to engage with
the arguments Samuel Clarke had brought against the genuineness of the
comma.[508]

Another new edition of the Greek-English New Testament based on
Mill's work was published anonymously in 1729. Its editor, the Presbyterian
minister Daniel Mace, dedicated the work to Lord Chancellor Peter King,
author of an *Enquiry into the Constitution, Discipline, Unity and Worship
of the Primitive Church* (1691), who had defended Whiston in his trial
for heresy in 1713.[509] Mace was determined that religious belief should be
based on full and perfect understanding, and he inveighed against such
as 'pretend to believe they know not what, yet burn with enthusiastic
zeal they know not why'. Blind faith, Mace argued, 'far from being of the
nature of Religion, is an explicit abjuration of common sense and reason'.
According to Mace, religious understanding was first achieved as a result
of the reformation, which scattered the gloom of mediaeval ignorance,
and of its natural sequel, the enlightenment, which depended on 'free
inquiry, and dispassionate debate'.[510]

Although Mace based his text on Ludolf Küster's revision of Mill's
edition, he excluded the comma both from his Greek text and from the
parallel translation. Much of the substance of his explanatory footnote is
drawn from Mill.[511] Mace maintained that those who argue for the genuineness of this text against all the evidence imperil the reliability of the
biblical text: 'if this evidence is not sufficient to prove that the controverted text in St. John is spurious, by what evidence can it be proved that
any text in St. John is genuine?'[512]

---

[506] Sheehan 2005, 50–51.
[507] Wells 1709–1719, 5:124–125.
[508] Emlyn 1717, 72.
[509] Mandelbrote 2001, 40–41; Mandelbrote 2004, 95–96.
[510] Mace 1729, iv–v. Further on Mace, see McLachlan 1938/1939 and 1950.
[511] Mace 1729, 920–935.
[512] Mace 1729, 934; cf. Bludau 1922, 206–207.

Reaction to Mace's edition was mixed. One early reader commented that it had been produced by 'some one or more who seem to have set themselves down in the Seat of the Scorner, and to make it their Business to render the Authority of this Holy Book doubtful, and the Book it self as contemptible and ridiculous as they could to the *English* Reader'.[513] Once Mace's identity became clear, he was accused of promoting Unitarianism. His arbitrary selection of variants and conjectural readings were criticised by Leonard Twells (*c.* 1684–1742), who promised to vindicate the comma against Mace's 'partial representation of that matter'. Mace was also criticised by the biblical scholar Johann David Michaelis.[514]

The 1734 New Testament edition of Johann Albrecht Bengel (1687–1752) was a different production entirely. Bengel developed Bentley's insight that errors could be used systematically to distinguish good readings from bad ones. While Richard Simon sneered that the apparent instability of the biblical text was fatal to the principle of *sola scriptura*, Bengel's systematic exploitation of variants turned this apparent liability to profit. His method of judging the authority of individual manuscripts and then extracting their textual data as the basis for a reconstruction of the earliest text transformed the codices from theological or literary texts into non-literary documents, of limited worth in isolation but of great value when compared with other documents. Bengel's manner of presenting the resulting data was conservative. He retained the *textus receptus* as his body text, and gave significant variants in the margin, marked α (certainly correct) to ε (certainly incorrect) to indicate his judgement of their authenticity. Having laid out the evidence, Bengel thus left it to his readers to make of it what they would. The devotional tone of Bengel's accompanying commentary endeared it to many pietistic readers, including John Wesley.[515]

Bengel gave the matter of the comma considerable thought. On 14 March 1727, he complained to his friend Matthias Marthius that he wanted to bring out his edition soon, but still wished to wait until Bentley's edition had appeared, so that he might profit from his 'incomparable' critical apparatus. Bengel had heard a report that Jerome had prepared a Dalmatian translation of the Scriptures, and wondered if manuscripts of this translation might still be extant in the Balkans, for 'I would obviously like to know how he translated that famous passage,'

[513] Lewis 1731, 93.
[514] Bludau 1922, 206–208; McLachlan 1938/1939, 617–625.
[515] Further, see Sheehan 2005, 93–114, esp. 101–105.

the comma.[516] Marthius expressed his doubts about the existence of the
Dalmatian translation. He also mentioned that Le Clerc had noted that
the comma is not found in Codex Alexandrinus.[517] On 12 April 1728,
Bengel suggested to Marthius that Le Clerc's notes on the comma showed
an unhealthy desire to set textual critics and believers at each other's
throats.[518] On 21 December 1728 Bengel mentioned to Jeremias Friedrich
Reuß that he had spent almost the whole month working on the comma,
and was convinced that he could demonstrate its genuineness, although
he acknowledged that he would have to base his reading on the Latin
rather than the Greek textual tradition. He also suggested that the order
of vv. 7 and 8 should be reversed.[519] On 5 September 1729 Bengel wrote
confidently to Zacharias Conrad von Uffenbach that he had put an end
to the disagreements over this passage, and had thus removed one weapon
from the Antitrinitarians' arsenal. He also asked Uffenbach to check the
order of vv. 7 and 8 in manuscripts available to him.[520] On 19 September
1729 Bengel made a similar request to Philipp Jacob Crophius.[521]

Bengel presented the results of his investigation in the commentary to
his New Testament edition (1734). Having rejected Montfortianus as a
Latinising manuscript written after the invention of printing, he admitted
that the comma is not present in any Greek manuscript of any authority.[522] In the belief that both the Complutensian Polyglot and Erasmus'
Codex Britannicus (which he distinguished from Montfortianus) give καὶ
οἱ τρεῖς εἰς τὸ ἕν εἰσιν in reference to the heavenly witnesses (in fact, this
is not the reading in Montfortianus), Bengel suggested that the reading in
Codex Britannicus was taken from the Complutensian edition before its
publication, proposing that an agent of Catherine of Aragon brought the
materials from Alcalá to England.[523] Bengel noted that none of the Greek
fathers cite the comma, and that many Latin fathers omit the comma
when quoting the immediate context. Nevertheless, Bengel defended the
comma as an original part of the text, denying that it had arisen from
an allegorical gloss of v. 8. He also rejected the argument that the verse
had been removed by Arians, pointing out that it was apparently absent
from the text even before the birth of Arius. Rather, Bengel attributed

[516] Bengel to Matthias Marthius, 14 March 1727, in Bengel 2012, 522.
[517] Marthius to Bengel, 31 March 1727, in Bengel 2012, 525, 529.
[518] Bengel to Marthius, 12 April 1728, in Bengel 2012, 591.
[519] Bengel to Reuß, 21 December 1728, in Bengel 2012, 628.
[520] Bengel to Uffenfach, 5 September 1729, in Bengel 2012, 650.
[521] Bengel to Crophius, 19 September 1729, in Bengel 2012, 651.
[522] Bengel 1734, 749.
[523] Bengel 1734, 746.

the disappearance of the comma to the *disciplina arcani*, the practice of reserving the highest and holiest mysteries and ceremonies in the early church to the fully initiated. Isaac Casaubon had mounted a similar argument to explain why the early Christian authors were so taciturn about the Trinity.[524] Bengel suggested that the comma, a witness to the great mystery of the Trinity, was removed from copies of the Catholic Epistles read by the uninitiated. In time, these public copies supplanted those containing the fuller, esoteric text of the epistle.[525] In his *Gnomon Novi Testamenti* (1742), Bengel praised the comma as central to the meaning of the chapter, 'as the sun is in the universe, as the needle of a magnet, as the heart in the body'.[526] However, some conservative readers feared that Bengel, by conceding too much to modern criticism, had opened the door to doubt. One reviewer placed him amongst those who, 'under pretext of defending the three heavenly witnesses with moderation, defend them so gently, that a suspicious reader might doubt whether they defended them in earnest; *though God forbid that we should wish to insinuate any suspicion of Mr. Bengelius's orthodoxy*'.[527]

Bengel's conclusions were met with bemusement by the Swiss scholar Johann Jakob Wettstein (1693–1754).[528] Wettstein had begun collecting variant readings as a young man, and although he treasured Mill's edition, he soon became aware of its shortcomings. On a visit to England, Wettstein presented his preliminary findings to Bentley, thus providing an important initial impetus to Bentley's plan to edit the New Testament. While examining Codex Alexandrinus to check Mill's description, Wettstein noted two details about the reading of 1 Tim 3:16: first, that the horizontal bar of the first E of the word EYΣEBEIAN (1 Tim 6:3) showed through the leaf when the page was held up to the light, making the OΣ look like ΘΣ; second, he could confirm Mill's observation that the bar over O̅Σ̅ was added by a later hand.[529] After Wettstein returned to Basel, his friend Johann Ludwig Frey encouraged him to read Samuel Clarke's *Scripture-doctrine of the Trinity*.[530] Wettstein developed an increasingly critical attitude towards several textual difficulties in the New Testament, including

[524] See Haugen 2011, 197–198.
[525] Bengel 1734, 765.
[526] Bengel 1742, 1061.
[527] Anon. 1753, 133; the translation is from Porson 1790, 18–19.
[528] Wettstein 1751–1752, 2:727.
[529] Wettstein 1751–1752, 1:20–22; Hulbert-Powell 1938, 23. Unfortunately the reading of 1 Tim 3:16 in Codex Alexandrinus (120r) has now been obscured by dirty fingers. However, the stroke over the word is quite clearly in a different ink.
[530] Wettstein 1751–1752, 1:191.

the Johannine comma and 1 Tim 3:16, and became ever more aware of the relationship between critical and doctrinal questions.[531] He differed increasingly with Bentley on methodological issues, including Bentley's reliance on the Latin text, and in 1721, he decided to prepare his own edition on the basis of Codex Alexandrinus.[532]

Wettstein was not always an easy person. By 1728 Frey, tired of Wettstein's arrogance, broke off their friendship and accused Wettstein of using textual criticism to promote Socinianism. Wettstein was consequently tried by a committee of the Basel clergy, which found that his projected edition indeed smacked of Socinianism and libertinism. In the opinion of the committee, readings in Semler's favoured source, Codex Alexandrinus, such as its omission of the comma, could be understood in such a way as to compromise Christ's divinity and thus undermine the Christian order.[533] A letter was produced in evidence at the trial, in which Wettstein was reported to have told two students of his intention to exclude the comma from his edition as an interpolation.[534] Wettstein pointed out that Erasmus had likewise been reviled for daring to challenge the hitherto familiar form of the biblical text.[535] But his enemies were resolved, and in 1730 he was dismissed from his post as deacon at St Leonhard's in Basel. Wettstein moved to Amsterdam, where he was appointed as successor to Jean Le Clerc at the Remonstrant seminary.

By 1735, Le Clerc was incapacitated by illness, and his library was auctioned off by Wettstein's relatives, the Amsterdam publishers and booksellers Jakob Wettstein and William George Smith.[536] After Le Clerc died in 1736, his letters were given to Wettstein, who was to hand them over to the Remonstrant seminary. Amongst this correspondence, Wettstein found

---

[531] Wettstein 1751–1752, 1:192.

[532] Hulbert-Powell 1938, 35. A letter from Jean-Daniel Scherpflin to J. J. Wettstein on 28 June 1729 (Amsterdam, Universiteitsbibliotheek ms J 77), IV, indicates that some believed that Wettstein's edition would outclass that of Bentley: 'Enfin je vous avoüe franchement, que je fais plus de compte sur votre travail que sur celui de Bentlei. Quelques fois j'ai admiré l'habileté de cet homme là, quelques fois j'etois surpris de son ignorance. Minimus saepe in maximis, Maximus plerumque in minimis. Sed haec inter nos.' Scherpflin also mentioned that Thomas Bentley was still occupied in Rome: 'Comme le jeune Bentlei s'est saisi probablement pour le présent du vieux MS. du Vatican, dont vous souhaiteriés une collation, on aura peut-être de la peine a en tirer quelque chose jusqu'à ce qu'il aura achevé ses variantes.' Scherpflin also offered to act as Wettstein's intermediary with Giovanni Vignoli, Vatican librarian.

[533] *Acta oder Handlungen* 1730, XX (on the comma), XIII–XIV (on 1 Tim 3:16 in Codex Alexandrinus). Cf. Hulbert-Powell 1938, 52, 56–57.

[534] *Acta oder Handlungen* 1730, 305.

[535] *Acta oder Handlungen* 1730, LIV.

[536] Wettstein and Smith 1735; Le Clerc's correspondence does not appear in the auction catalogue. Cf. Mandelbrote 2004, 108.

Locke's fair copy of Newton's *Historical Account*. Wettstein was impressed by Newton's engagement with the sources and almost mathematical reasoning. Since several pages had been lost from the beginning and the end of the manuscript, Wettstein asked his second cousin, Johann Caspar Wettstein, librarian to the Princess of Wales, to find a complete manuscript in England.[537] On 17 August 1736, Johann Caspar Wettstein sent an enquiry to Hopton Haynes, who informed him that the original was probably in the possession of John Conduitt, husband of Catherine Conduitt, Newton's niece and heir, whom Newton had appointed as one of his executors. Haynes also added that he had translated the work into Latin at Newton's request, and that Newton had simply been waiting for the right moment to publish the translation.[538] Johann Jakob Wettstein asked the Conduitts several times for a copy of Newton's original manuscript, but without success.[539]

It may have been Wettstein's importunity that prompted Catherine Conduitt to add a codicil to her will on 26 January 1737, in which she provided for the publication of Newton's papers on biblical studies and church history, so that 'the labour and sincere search of so good a xtian and so great a Genius, may not be lost to the world'. Conduitt intended to publish these manuscripts 'if God grant me life, but as I may be snatched away before I can have leisure to undertake so great a work towards publishing of which I design to ask the help of Learned men, I will, and appoint, and ordain, that my Executor do lay all the tracts relating to divinity before Dr Sykes, and in hopes he will prepare them for the press.' Conduitt, concerned to maintain control over Newton's legacy, insisted that 'the papers must be carefully kept, that no copys may be taken, and printed'. Her husband John Conduitt had offered a bond of £2000 to Newton's seven nearest living relatives – who had little interest in the papers apart from their potential to generate profit – which they might claim if 'any accident' should come to the manuscripts. Not even the intended editor, the Antitrinitarian Arthur Ashley Sykes (*c.* 1684–1756),

---

[537] Wettstein 1751–1752, 1:185. J. J. Wettstein was in frequent contact with his relatives, the booksellers Smith and Jacob Wettstein, who carried letters between him and Caspar Wettstein in London; see Amsterdam, Universiteitsbibliotheek mss A168a, A 170.

[538] H. Haynes to J. C. Wettstein, 17 August 1736, London, BL Add. ms 32415, 388r: 'The MSS. Copies, to which you refer in your Letter to me dated this day, are, as I suppose, in the hands of Mr Conduit, one of the Executors of Sr Isaac Newton; together with my Latin version; which many yeares agoe I undertook, at the desire of Sr Isaac. Mr Conduit is now out of Town, but is expected about Mich[ael]mas next; he lives near St George's Church by Hanovor [*sic*] Square. I know Sr Isaac intended them for the Press, and only waited for a good opportunity. Had the MSS. been in my power, I would readily have Favoured you with them, to compleat the other imperfect Copies which you mention.' Cf. Snobelen 1999, 405; Mandelbrote 2004, 108.

[539] Wettstein 1751–1752, 1:185, cit. earlier.

was permitted to remove the papers from the Conduitts' house. However, both John and Catherine Conduitt were dead by 1739, and the papers passed to their only child, Catherine, or Kitty, wife of John Wallop, later Lord Lymington.[540]

News of the discovery of Newton's manuscript travelled quickly. Samuel Crell ordered a copy immediately, and on 28 September 1736 he sent news of its existence to William Whiston Jr, the son of Newton's former protégé, attributing the loss of the pages at either end to Le Clerc's negligence.[541] William Whiston Sr also ordered a copy of the Amsterdam manuscript, and in a letter of 20 April 1738 to John Depee, he noted insouciantly: 'it is so very doubtful whether the true old reading [of 1 Tim 3:16] had the word *God* or not. I have now by me a dissertation of Sir *Isaac Newton's*, to disprove that reading. And upon its perusal, I cannot say, whether the word written by St. Paul, were Θεός, or Λόγος, or Χριστός, or ὅ: which last all the Latin copies suppose.'[542]

Encouraged by the orthodox Trinitarian Daniel Waterland (1683–1740), master of Magdalene College Cambridge, the Anglican clergyman John Berriman (1691–1768) discussed the textual difficulties surrounding 1 Tim 3:16 in his 1737–1738 Moyer lectures, delivered at St Paul's cathedral. In 1738, the London merchant Peter Dobrée informed Berriman that he had seen a copy of a treatise on this passage, made from a manuscript in Amsterdam. When John Kippax, fellow of Clare Hall, Cambridge, was leaving for Holland, Berriman asked him to make a copy of this manuscript. Berriman transcribed Kippax's copy of Newton's treatment of 1 Tim 3:16 in full, and made extracts from his account of the comma. Berriman was not entirely sure who had written these twin treatises, but aware that 'common Fame both in England & Holland' identified them as the work of Newton, he asked Rev. Alexander Chalmers, a relative of Catherine Conduitt, if any such treatises on biblical criticism had survived in Newton's papers. Chalmers confirmed that there had, but

[540] Oxford, New College ms 361.4, 139r (codicil to Catherine Conduitt's will); Gloucester, Gloucestershire Archives D678/1 Z4/1–3 (wills of John and Catherine Conduitt, and of their daughter Catherine Wallop). Cf. Brewster 1855, 2:341–342; Mandelbrote 2004, 103; Dry 2014, 28.

[541] Samuel Crell to Whiston Jr, Leicestershire Record Office, Conant MSS, DG11/DE.730/2 letter 123A, cit. Snobelen 2005b, 407–408 n. 134: '[…] adeo a Clerici negligenter habitas ut prioris initium alterius finis desit'. A copy of the copy ordered by Samuel Crell is extant in Leiden, Universiteitsbibliotheek ms Semin. Remonstr. Bibl. 12. Cf. Mandelbrote 2004, 108; Snobelen 2005a, 250 n. 48; Snobelen 2005b, 408 n. 135.

[542] Whiston 1749–1750, 1:365; Snobelen 1999, 405 n. 195. It is clear from the references in Whiston's *Athanasian forgeries* (1736) that he knew that Newton had treated of 1 Tim 3:16 and 1 Jn 5:7–8, though the lack of more concrete detail suggests that he had not yet seen the manuscript; Whiston 1736, 13.

regretted to say that 'the Copies, which were got abroad, were interpolated & corrupted'. Berriman also questioned Whiston, who confirmed that Newton had written on the Johannine comma and 1 Tim 3:16, and confessed to Berriman that Haynes' translations of these works 'would have been printed, if he had not blabb'd it out, that Sr Isaac was the Author of them'. But even after satisfying himself of the authorship of these works, Berriman was unimpressed by their argumentation: 'It is very remarkable, that the same Authorities which are allowd to be good in the one [treatise], are reckond bad in the other; & they are represented as valid or invalid according as they make for, or against, the point the Author had in view.'[543] Berriman accused Newton of inconsistency, condemning the early Catholic theologians and praising the Arians for the same reasons: 'To say the Catholicks were honester men than the Hereticks, & cannot be so easily convicted, as they may be, of corruption & prevarication in such matters, might perhaps be reckond partiality: but surely, it will be allowd, that Hereticks were as cunning & able to contrive & carry on Forgeries as the Catholicks; & it ought to pass for equal & fair dealing on both sides, that neither be condemnd without sufficient Evidence.'[544] Nevertheless, Berriman realised that Newton's treatise could lead readers into error, and laid down strict conditions for access to the transcript he deposited in the library of Sion College in London. On the cover he wrote that the copy was to be 'perusd, by those that desire it, in the presence of the Librarian: but not to be lent out, without leave from the President, Deans & Assistants for the time being, & upon sufficient caution & security, to be punctually & faithfully returned, in a short time'.[545] This was a book that required close surveillance. In the published version of his Moyer lectures (1741), Berriman added a short discussion of the 'anonymous' treatise on 1 Tim 3:16. However, Berriman revealed nothing about its location or its presumed author, whom he criticised for relying on a Latin translation of Nestorius rather than consulting the Greek (this cavil is unfair – Newton cites the relevant passage in Greek and in Latin translation), and

---

[543] London, Lambeth Palace Library, Sion College ms ARC L 40.2/E 39 (Berriman's transcript of the treatise on 1 Tim 3:16; earlier shelfmarks: C.23, 16.6 and Ari 4 28), 1r–v. A reference in the margin to *Mr. Whiston's Sacred history of the Old and New Testament* 1745–1746, gives a *terminus post quem* for Berriman's report. The publication of the treatise in 1754 gives a likely *terminus ante quem*; it would have made little sense for him to deposit this manuscript under such strict conditions if the work was widely available in print. Berriman's marginal comments in his personal copy of Berriman 1741 (London, BL 1017.k.17), 117, 165, 167, repeat some of the same information as the report in the Sion College manuscript. Cf. Mandelbrote 2004, 109–110.

[544] London, Lambeth Palace Library, Sion College ms ARC L 40.2/E 39, 11v.

[545] London, Lambeth Palace Library, Sion College ms ARC L 40.2/E 39, note on the front cover, signed by Berriman.

for assuming that the bilingual Cassian wrote his tract *On the incarnation of Christ, against Nestorius*, in Greek rather than in Latin.[546]

On 26 March 1741, Berriman sent his published lectures to Wettstein. In a cover note he thanked Wettstein for the information he had provided to Kippax at Amsterdam, and asked him to confirm whether he had in fact discovered 'upon a narrower inspection' of the reading of 1 Tim 3:16 in Codex Alexandrinus, 'the Traces of the old Line in the Letter Θ', as he had reported in his book.[547] Amongst other codicological questions, Berriman asked Wettstein 'what grounds you have for placing the Montfort MS in the 16th Century', requested details of manuscripts in which Wettstein had found the doxology at Mt 6:13, and enquired about the reading of 1 Tim 3:16 in the Greek and Arabic lectionaries he had collated.[548]

Wettstein politely answered each of Berriman's questions and commented on a number of passages in his book. He begged to differ with Martin's assessment of Montfortianus, echoing the judgement of La Croze, who described Martin as an eloquent preacher but a poor critic. Since Wettstein had not seen the manuscript, he had to rely on the description in Walton's Polyglot and Le Long's open letter to Martin. However, he mentioned that the manuscript was written on paper, not parchment, as Martin claimed. Furthermore, he noted that the presence of the Latin chapter divisions, introduced in the thirteenth century, indicates that it cannot have been written before that time. Finally, he pointed out that the manuscript omits the words 'and these three are one' in v. 8, an alteration often observed in Latin manuscripts following the censure of Aquinas, but never in the Greek tradition.[549] All these features suggested that the manuscript was written by a western scribe. Since few western scholars knew Greek before the middle of the fifteenth century, it was likely that the manuscript was written after this time. Those who dated the manuscript to the tenth to the twelfth centuries had failed to consider the evidence correctly.[550] Wettstein also noted that he had never seen a single codex that

---

[546] Berriman 1741, 167–172; cf. Newton 1959–1977, 3:111–113.

[547] Berriman 1741, 155.

[548] J. Berriman to J. J. Wettstein, 26 March 1741, Basel, Öffentliche Bibliothek der Universität, ms Ki. Ar. 154, 6. Berriman also notes that having finally read Le Long 1720, he was compelled to retract some of the comments he made in Berriman 1741, 61–62. Cf. Mandelbrote 2004, 109.

[549] This omission is observed only in the Latinising manuscripts GA 61 and 326; see K. Aland, Benduhn-Mertz and Mink 1987, 165.

[550] Undated draft of J. J. Wettstein's reply to Berriman, Basel, Öffentliche Bibliothek der Universität, ms Ki. Ar. 154, 8, 14r: 'De codice Montfortii sententiam Martini non moror, fuit ille quidem facundus Gallus orator, sed Criticus parum peritus. Cum Codicem ipsum, qui in Hibernia latet, non inspexissem, conjecturis agendum fuit.'

contained the comma as it customarily appeared in the printed editions. Furthermore, the reading of the comma in Montfortianus bore distinct signs of having been translated from Latin, such as the lack of articles before Father, Word and Holy Spirit.[551]

Berriman's second letter to Wettstein, dated 20 July 1741, was in turns ingratiating and defensive. He claimed that he had relied on Kippax's report of his conversation with Wettstein, and blamed Kippax for failing to pass Berriman's inquiries on to Wettstein before his lectures went to press. Berriman did not hesitate to disagree with Wettstein on many details: 'I dare say you would not chuse to have others misled by your Authority in any thing wherein you are mistaken, whoever you have followed in such mistake.' However, he confessed himself 'very well pleasd with what you have said of the Inscription at the End of St Marks Gospel in the Montfort MS however different from the Account I had given from Mr Martin: and what you have said concerning the Age of the MS inclines me to think it not older than the 13th or perhaps the 14th Century, tho I can't with you bring it down to the 16th'. Furthermore, he promised to consider what Wettstein had written about Codex Alexandrinus and the comma. Probably in order to clarify his own conclusions about the Johannine comma and the prologue to the Catholic Epistles, Berriman asked Wettstein whether he believed that 'Jerom revisd the Epistles & the rest of the New Test. as well as the Gospels.' For Berriman, the reading of 1 Tim 3:16, like that of the comma, was of more than philological interest, 'because Socinians Arians &c have endeavourd so much to overthrow it'.[552]

Even after this annoying exchange with Berriman, the reading of 1 Tim 3:16 continued to engage Wettstein's attention. On 24 February 1748 he mentioned to Johann Caspar Wettstein that he had been asked to write a study on this question, but intended to decline the invitation, giving the excuse that the notes on this passage, which he was working up for his New Testament edition, were not yet in order. But lest he make any error in this delicate matter, he asked his cousin to re-examine the passage in

[551] Basel, Öffentliche Bibliothek der Universität, ms Ki. Ar. 154, 8, 14r: 'Ne unus quidem codex Graecus MS reperiri potuit, qui locum I Io. V. exhibet, ut nunc vulgo editum est. Codex iste Montfortii Codex, praeter insignem omissionem verborum καὶ οἱ τρεῖς ἐν τὸ ἕν εἰσιν, articulos omnes omisit, quod magnam suspicionem habet verba πατήρ καὶ λόγος τό πνεῦμα non ex antiquiore Codice Graeco profluisse, sed ex versione Latina, quae articulis caret, imperite satis in Graecam conversa fuisse [...].' Cf. Berriman 1741, 50.

[552] J. Berriman to J. J. Wettstein, 20 July 1741, Basel, Öffentliche Bibliothek der Universität, ms Ki. Ar. 154, 7. Cf. Berriman 1741, 120–128.

Codex Alexandrinus to verify his earlier hypothesis about the intervention of a second hand.[553]

When Wettstein's edition finally appeared in 1751–1752, a seven-page footnote made his doubts about the authenticity of the comma plain.[554] In his six-page note on 1 Tim 3:16, Wettstein referred to Newton's *Historical Account*, so traduced by Berriman.[555] Wettstein drew on patristic, rabbinic and classical sources to provide readers with a biblical text as close as possible to the autographs, and the means to understand it in its ancient context. He also wished to promote a better knowledge of the manuscript sources of the Scriptures. Condemning the ignorance of many clergy of the textual history of their own Scriptures, he relates hearing a preacher insist that the Johannine comma was found in Codex Bezae – but that manuscript does not contain 1 Jn.[556]

Wettstein never gave up his search for a complete manuscript of Newton's *Historical Account*. In 1747, Haynes too expressed the hope that Newton's 'short Discourse upon the pretended Text of St. *John*', still 'in the Hands of a *noble Lord*', would 'be published in convenient Time'.[557] In 1752, Johann Caspar Wettstein reported from London that he had not heard any further news from Samuel Koenig in Berlin, who was evidently making a search for Newton's manuscript amongst his contacts on the Wettsteins' behalf.[558]

In 1754, an edition of Newton's *Historical Account* was printed at London from a copy of the Amsterdam manuscript. In place of the pages lost from the start of the work, the editor reprinted a reconstruction supplied by the scribe who copied the manuscript.[559] César de Missy's abbreviated French

[553] J. J. Wettstein to J. C. Wettstein, Amsterdam, 24 February 1748, Universiteitbibliotheek ms J 97, 1r: 'Mr Rathlef m'a écrit, qu'il fera tout à ma satisfaction. Je lui ai communiqué la découverte de OΣ qui lui fait plaisir. Je crois même qu'il me veut défoncer [?] en écrivant une dissertation là-dessus car il me prie de lui fournir tous ce que j'ai à dire sur ce passage; je m'en excuserai sur ce que mes papiers ne sont pas encore en ordre. À propos du MS d'Alexandrie, je suis dans l'embarras par rapport à quelques passages, sur lesquels ma collation n'est pas d'accord avec celle des autres [...]. Item au passage 1 Tim. III.16 s'il y a au-dessus de l'OΣ une ligne, et au cas qu'elle y soit, comme je le crois, si la ligne sure le est de la seconde main et du nouvel ancre [*sic*]?' Cf. Mandelbrote 2004, 108.
[554] Wettstein 1751–1752, 2:721–727. Cf. Hulbert-Powell 1938, 247–248.
[555] Wettstein 1751–1752, 2:335 (notes on 1 Tim 3:16).
[556] Wettstein 1751–1752, 1:7. Cf. Hulbert-Powell 1938, 99.
[557] Haynes 1747, 31.
[558] J. C. Wettstein to J. J. Wettstein, London, 10 March 1752, Amsterdam, Universiteitbibliotheek ms A 168a, 2r: 'Et enfin pour fureter après les Dissert. de Newtonne – Je n'ay point de nouvelles encore de Prof. Koenig.' Cf. Mandelbrote 2004, 108.
[559] Newton 1754a. The 1734 edition *Two letters to Mr Clarke*, mentioned in King 1858, 2:231, is a ghost. The editor of the 1754 edition did not identify himself. He stated that the Amsterdam manuscript was in the hand of Locke and was amongst the papers of Le Clerc, but this information could

translation of this edition was published in the *Journal Britannique* for 1754.[560] In reaction to the publication of Newton's *Historical Account*, John Mawer, a client of the late Daniel Waterland, published a series of letters he had exchanged in 1738–1739 with an unnamed correspondent, discussing the manuscript readings of 1 Tim 3:16 and the comma in the eastern versions. The edition appeared without introduction or commentary, but Mawer was clearly pleased that he had come to the same conclusions as the great Newton.[561]

In 1755, perhaps in reaction to the publication of the fragment of the *Historical Account* the previous year, the Wallops handed Newton's papers over to Sykes for editing, but he died before he could do anything with them. After Kitty Wallop's death, the papers passed to Jeffery Ekins, later dean of Carlisle, one of the executors of her will.[562] When Samuel Horsley inspected the papers in Ekins' care while preparing a five-volume edition of Newton's works, published with the support of the Royal Society, he found the manuscript of the *Historical Account* amongst them. Ekins lent the manuscript to Horsley on the condition that it be returned as soon as it was copied. On 26 January 1779 Horsley apologised to Ekins that he had not yet done so, but promised to return the letter by way of Lord Carlisle. He also assured Ekins that he would not publish any part of the papers without his consent.[563] Horsley wrote to Ekins again on 29 August 1780 to apologise that 'for want of an intelligent transcriber', he had been constrained to copy the

---

have been taken from Wettstein 1751–1752, 1:185. The footnote on 13–14 indicates that the edition was printed on the basis of a second-generation manuscript. That Wettstein himself was not the editor of the 1754 edition may be inferred from the editor's belief that Le Clerc lodged the letter in the library of the Remonstrant seminary, whereas Wettstein states clearly that he deposited the manuscript along with Le Clerc's other correspondence in that library after his predecessor's death.

[560] Newton 1754b. Letters from Missy to J. J. Wettstein are in Amsterdam, Universiteitsbibliotheek ms A 158, Q 97. Ms Q 97a comprises Missy's detailed collation of Codex Leicestrensis, intended to replace the faulty collation in Mill's edition; it was delivered to J. J. Wettstein by his cousin J. C. Wettstein. Ms Q 97c is a single half-sheet containing 1 Jn 5:4–9a, transcribed in capitals from 'an Old Manuscript in the Vatican Library, supposed to be written about the Beginning of the 8th Century', with a further note in pencil that this note had been 'Given me by Mr Phelps'. Missy found the note in a book he had bought at the auction of the library of Michel Mattaire, and was of the opinion that the pencil annotation was in Mattaire's hand.

[561] Mawer 1758, 24; cf. Mandelbrote 2004, 109. It is possible that Mawer's unnamed correspondent was Berriman. Mawer 1758, 31–32, mentions that his correspondent had recorded the readings in a Syriac New Testament manuscript owned by a 'Mr. R—'. This may be the same Syriac manuscript mentioned by Berriman 1741, 282, 305, in possession of 'the Reverend Mr. [Glocester] Ridley, the very worthy Minister of Poplar'. Mawer 1758, 31, notes that this manuscript apparently contained the same translation as had been published by Pocock and Le Dieu; Berriman 1741, 279, likewise refers to Pocock and Le Dieu. Further on Ridley, see Dodsley 1988, 89.

[562] Mandelbrote 2004, 103–105; Dry 2014, 28.

[563] Oxford, New College ms 361.4, 142r–143v.

manuscript himself. Aside from the *Historical Account* of the comma and 1
Tim 3:16, he had also copied a third letter, dealing with further textual corruptions in the New Testament.[564] While the *Historical Account* appeared in
the fifth volume of Horsley's edition of Newton's works (1785), the third letter did not, either because it was censored by Ekins, or simply because it
is less detailed and coherent than the *Historical Account*. Horsley's purpose
in publishing Newton's theological works was to remove an arrow from the
Antitrinitarians' quiver by exposing Newton's alleged weaknesses as a textual critic and exegete.[565] However, Horsley's intention backfired when the
Historical Account was taken up eagerly by Nonconformists. Horsley's edition of the work was reprinted in a collection of Quaker tracts (1803), bringing it to the attention of a reading public who could not afford Horsley's
five-volume edition. It appeared again in a collection of tracts published in
1823 for the benefit of American Unitarians, reissued in 1841 as a separate
volume.[566] Newton's denial of the authenticity of the comma was noted by
radicals like Joseph Priestley.[567] However, those who attempted to sanitise
Newton's image in the nineteenth century dismissed his studies of Scripture
as peripheral, or simply as senile delusions, while deploying his natural theology against unbelievers.[568]

In the wake of Wettstein's Greek New Testament, two subsequent editions departed even further from the *textus receptus*. In 1763, the learned
London printer William Bowyer used Wettstein's commentary to reconstruct the earliest discernible form of the text. Bowyer included the
comma, but in brackets.[569] In 1776, the Nonconformist minister Edward
Harwood also used Wettstein's edition to create a Greek text based closely
on Codex Bezae (GA D^{ea}/05) and Codex Claromontanus (GA D^p/06),
employing Codex Alexandrinus (which he considered inferior) where
the others were defective. Harwood's preface attests to his intense piety
and sincerity. In his method and his results, Harwood foreshadowed
Lachmann. Harwood excluded the comma entirely, and covered the gap
by rearranging the text in vv. 6–8. In a footnote, he glossed εἰς τὸ ἕν in

---

[564] An early fair copy, not in Newton's hand, is in Oxford, New College ms 361.4, 49r–68r; Newton
deals with Mt 19:17, 24:6; Lk 19:41, 22:43–44; Jn 4:24, 19:40; Acts 13:41, 20:28; Rom 9:5, 15:32; 1
Cor 10:9; Eph 3:9, 3:14; Phil 3:3, 4:13; 2 Thess 1:9; 2 Pt 3:18; 1 Jn 2:14, 3:16, 4:3; 5:20; Jude 4, 5; Rev
1:11. This letter is edited in Newton 1959–1977, 3:129–142; a fourth letter is in Newton 1959–1977,
3:144–146.
[565] Mandelbrote 2004, 104–105.
[566] Matthews 1802–1803, 2:182–254; Sparks 1823–1826, 2:235–320; Newton 1841.
[567] Priestley 1785, 37–38.
[568] Mandelbrote 2004, 110–111.
[569] Bowyer 1763, 2:429; further, see Metzger and Ehrman 2005, 162; Epp 2014, 43.

v. 8 as meaning 'these three witnesses unite to attest one truth, namely, that Jesus is the Messiah'.[570]

16. Johann Salomo Semler

Johann Salomo Semler, professor at Halle, was one of the pioneers of the historical-critical method of biblical scholarship. By uncoupling the study of the bible from theological concerns and considering it in historical terms, Semler redefined theology as a *Wissenschaft*. He challenged the prevailing belief in the divine inspiration of Scripture by treating it as subject to the same forces of composition, transmission and interpretation as any other literary work. Semler steered an orthodox Lutheran middle course between the subjective, ahistorical approach to Scripture promoted by the Pietists, and the rejection of revealed religion by deists and freethinkers. In Semler's hands, history became a way to interrogate orthodoxy in light of the intellectual and cultural needs of the mid-eighteenth century. Despite his desire to separate the historical study of the bible from dogmatic presuppositions, Semler maintained that faith must remain the fundamental basis for understanding religious questions. His work on the varieties of early Christian belief also led him to a conviction of the importance of religious pluralism. In combining philology and history with an undogmatic, ethically based faith, he tempered Lutheran orthodoxy with the tradition of Christian humanism exemplified by Erasmus. However, this combination proved unstable, and led to a recurrence of subjectivism.[571]

In 1748, Semler's teacher Siegmund Jakob Baumgarten launched his *Reports from a library in Halle* (*Nachrichten von einer Hallischen Bibliothek*), which introduced readers to significant theological literature from Spinoza onwards. This series also introduced German critics to the English deist controversy, even after the storm had more or less blown itself out. Baumgarten enlisted the help of his students, including Semler, to write some of the articles.[572] It was Baumgarten's intention that this series would expose recent critiques of revealed religion as groundless. But by exposing his readers to sophisticated critiques of traditional orthodoxy, Baumgarten inadvertently piqued interest in heterodoxy. Through Baumgarten's rear-guard action, Semler first came to read Pierre Bayle and

---

[570] Harwood 1776, 2:210; further, see Metzger and Ehrman 2005, 163; Epp 2014, 44. On Harwood's English translation, see Sheehan 2005, 118–119.

[571] My summary draws on Hornig 1996; and Carlsson 2006.

[572] Semler 1772, 26–27.

Richard Simon. For the fourth volume of the *Nachrichten* (1749), Semler reviewed Whiston's *Primitive Christianity Reviv'd* (1711–1712).[573]

In his master's thesis (1750), the young Semler sought not only to defend the traditional reading of 1 Tim 3:16 and 1 Jn 5:7–8 against Whiston's criticisms, but also to disarm his critical principles more generally. Semler's erudition was evident even in this early work, as was his unshakeable belief that doctrinal orthodoxy was to be discovered through historical investigation.[574] Thirty years later, he remembered with embarrassment how he had been congratulated for defending the orthodox reading of these passages so successfully. 'But at that time,' he later cringed, 'criticism of the ancient text of the New Testament in Germany was actually still in its infancy, and try as I may, I was not in a position to escape from my error of judgement.'[575] Semler even sent his dissertation to Whiston, either in the hope of changing his mind or gaining his approval. Although Whiston's reply was friendly, Semler realised later how painfully obvious his own ignorance of the material must have seemed to the old man. In his reply, Whiston even made excuses on Semler's behalf: he could not be blamed for having come to such conclusions, since German criticism had not yet attained sufficient sophistication to see over the old horizons. Whiston also expressed his hope that providence might reveal new manuscripts to reveal the deception of the Athanasian party. Semler, objective as always, knew that even such discoveries could only help Whiston indirectly, because the old man's expertise in Greek was quite limited. However, Semler also realised that the discovery of the ancient redactions of the New Testament had fulfilled Whiston's hopes.[576] As Semler investigated the issues more deeply, he saw that his earlier conclusions had to be discarded. Only gradually did he manage to distinguish between theological metaphysics and real history. It also took him a long time to break free of the old hermeneutical methods by which even Whiston had been limited.[577] He also concluded that it was pointless to insist on a given position simply because he had once affirmed it to be true.[578]

---

[573] Semler 1749; Hornig 1996, 233–234; Carlsson 2006, 97–99. Like Carlsson, I attribute this review tentatively to Semler, on the basis of a comment in his *Lebensbeschreibung* 1781–1782, 1:118: 'Weil ich Whistons englische Schriften zeither gelesen, und theils darüber Recensionen gemacht hatte [...].'

[574] Semler 1750, 55–60; further, see Carlsson 2006, 107–109, whom I follow.

[575] Semler 1781–1782, 1:118.

[576] Semler 1772, 88–89; Semler 1781–1782, 1:118–120; Hornig 1996, 225, 233–235; Carlsson 2006, 108–109.

[577] Semler 1781–1782, 1:120.

[578] Semler 1781–1782, 2:372–373.

In the second volume of his textbook of hermeneutics (1761), Semler discussed the comma in the light of his distinction between internal and external circumstances of textual composition. The inner circumstances of the composition of 1 Jn – the fact that it was written to people who had to choose between Judaism and Christianity – would be unmistakable even if the letter were incomplete. However, the internal circumstances do not allow us to determine its external circumstances, such as the precise number of words or the exact wording. It is thus hermeneutically invalid to argue that the comma *must* be a part of the epistle because its contents demand its presence.[579]

Semler expounded these conclusions more fully in four consecutive issues of the *Wöchentliche Hallische Anzeigen* in November and December 1762. He complained that too many of his colleagues considered theology a fixed and unchangeable body of knowledge that could be assimilated entirely just by reading a few reference books. Consequently, many beliefs were perpetuated on trust, without being verified against the historical sources. Semler used the jumble of erroneous beliefs surrounding the comma to illustrate this problem, and hoped that this would spur his colleagues to investigate the textual basis of other articles of dogma. As an example of the problems of tradition, he cited Johann Gerhard, one of the most prominent Lutheran scholastics of the early seventeenth century, who named the Antwerp codex mentioned by Erasmus as evidence for the textual attestation of the comma, whereas this codex was in fact a Latin codex of Bede, in which the comma had been added recently in the margin.[580] These articles drew Semler into a long controversy with the Hamburg pastor Johann Melchior Goeze over the textual value of the Complutensian bible. In 1764 Semler published the first of two volumes of *Historical and Critical Collections on so-called Proof-texts in Dogmatics*, the result of his study of the way the fathers used Scripture to develop and articulate their theological positions. The first volume of the *Collections* dealt with the thorny problem of the Johannine comma. Semler confessed in the preface that his previous statements on the comma had brought upon him 'all kinds of evil slander, public and private suspicion and reproach'.[581] Semler admitted that he had been wrong to condemn Whiston in his master's disputation.[582] Indeed, he hoped that readers

[579] Semler 1760–1769, 2:184–185; cf. Carlsson 2006, 360.
[580] Semler 1762, 762–767; J. Gerhard 1610–1619, 1:369.
[581] Semler 1764, *Vorrede*, 7–8.
[582] Semler 1750, *Vorrede*, 55–60.

would take his conclusions even more seriously when they saw that he had the courage to admit that he had been wrong.[583] But Semler, careful to avoid any suspicion of Socinianism, insisted that 'one can correctly, edifyingly and faithfully hold and declare the entire doctrine of God as Father, Son and Spirit, even if one does not consider this passage as genuine, or the way it is normally interpreted as hermeneutically justifiable'.[584]

Semler considered the comma as one of the most controversial passages in the bible. Conflicts over its status had arisen because of the mismatch between its perceived doctrinal utility and its poor textual attestation.[585] He acknowledged that the verse is problematic in many ways. Its meaning is not at all clear. The fathers who most strenuously defended the doctrine it was supposed to prove failed to cite it. It is poorly attested in the earliest biblical manuscripts of all traditions. Semler thus found it surprising that the comma should have found such willing defenders in the preceding two centuries. Recalling Erasmus' struggle against Lee, he noted that many of his contemporaries likewise used the appearance of piety to bring into disrepute those who served religion through their learning.[586]

As a result of Semler's criticisms, scholarly opinion in Germany moved against the comma. In 1785 Franz Anton Knittel published a treatise defending the authenticity of the passage, but a reviewer found it astonishing that a defence of the comma should have come 'in our time from a German critic'. The issues had been covered so comprehensively in recent debates that the case seemed quite closed, at least until new evidence should appear. Despite his promises, Knittel had failed to produce any such evidence.[587]

17.   Johann Jacob Griesbach

The task of collating and evaluating the New Testament manuscripts was continued by Johann Jacob Griesbach, whose edition appeared in 1775–1777. In the preface, Griesbach explained that he had begun with the *textus receptus*, but wherever he had revised the text on the basis of manuscript evidence, he had marked any such changes in the footnotes, signalling substitutions with small type, either in the body text or in the inner

---

[583] Semler 1764, *Vorrede*, 8.
[584] Semler 1764, *Vorrede*, 13.
[585] Semler 1764, 10.
[586] Semler 1764, 43–44.
[587] Anon. 1785, 229.

margin. He refused to admit conjectural emendations, but only admitted readings that were attested in the manuscripts or in quotations from
the fathers. Variant readings were given in order of probability. Words or
phrases that Griesbach believed should be added or removed were indicated with a complex system of typographical symbols. Words or passages
that were to be excised were removed from the text and placed in the margin below the text, and the place where the excision had been made was
marked with a dagger. Words or passages which Griesbach considered less
certain remained in the text, but were marked with other symbols.

About the comma Griesbach had no hesitation: he excised it and placed
it in the margin with a dagger, providing an eleven-page footnote justifying his choice. In his opinion, special pleading for the comma threatened
the legitimacy of textual criticism:

> If witnesses so few in number, so doubtful, so suspicious and so recent,
> and arguments so frivolous were sufficient to demonstrate the legitimacy of
> any reading, even in the teeth of such weighty evidence and so many argu-
> ments, there would no longer be any criterion of truth or falsehood left at
> all in the business of criticism, and the entire text of the New Testament
> would be left on a very unsure and dubious footing.[588]

Griesbach came to a similar conclusion on the *pericope de adultera*.

In 1794, Griesbach published a lengthy reply to a defence of the comma
addressed to him the previous year by Wilhelm Friedrich Hezel, professor of oriental languages at Giessen. Griesbach treated his colleague's letter not as a declaration of war, but as an invitation to a mutual search
for the truth. In his reply, Griesbach considered Montfortianus in some
detail, and though he recognised that it contained traces of an old text
type, these readings were only of value when they agreed with the early
codices. The unique readings in Montfortianus, such as the comma, were
essentially of no value in establishing the authorial text. Indeed, Griesbach
found some readings in the manuscript so puzzling that he could almost
believe that the scribe had used a defective Greek original, and simply
translated from the Latin Vulgate as best he could when he could not read
his archetype.[589] In 1806, Griesbach laid out his arguments in more detail
(this time in Latin for an international readership) in an appendix to the
second edition of his Greek New Testament.[590]

---

[588] Griesbach 1775–1777, 2:236.
[589] Griesbach 1794, 12–14.
[590] Griesbach, *Diatribe in locum I Ioann. 5, 7. 8*, Appendix to vol. 2 of Griesbach 1796–1806.

18. John Wesley: the appeal to pietism

The competing opinions on the status of the comma continued to cause anxiety amongst the faithful, who were increasingly unsure what they should believe. In his *Explanatory Notes upon the New Testament* (1755), John Wesley deferred to Bengel's conclusions on the comma. He also implicitly contradicted Calvin by giving a comprehensive interpretation of the comma that included an ontological unity: '[Father, Son, and Holy Spirit] are one in Essence, in Knowledge, in Will, and in their Testimony.'[591]

The comma was part of the lectionary reading for the octave of Easter in *The Book of Common Prayer*, and was retained in Wesley's Methodist revision, *The Sunday Service* (1784). Wesley was occasionally called to preach on this text, as is recorded on Trinity Sunday 1760, during a visit to Ireland.[592] Wesley travelled to Ireland again in April 1775 to inspect the congregations he had visited two years previously. He was asked to preach on the comma at Cork on Sunday 7 May. He recorded in his journal that the 'congregation was exceeding large; but abundantly larger in the evening. I never saw the house so crowded before. It was much the same the next evening'.[593]

Wesley noted in a preface to the printed transcript of the sermon that he did not have any books to consult on his journey, nor any time to read.[594] Although we might be suspicious of this claim, the sermon ostensibly represents the stock of arguments Wesley could draw from his memory. The lack of learned detail and the sensitivity to the pastoral implications of the issue are unusual. Wesley drew a distinction between religion and opinion. It is possible, he believed, to hold right opinions but be irreligious, or to be truly religious while holding wrong opinions. Simply witness the many 'real inward Christians' in the Roman Catholic church, despite the 'heap of erroneous Opinions' they hold, or the many good Calvinists who

[591] Wesley 1755, 663.
[592] Wesley 1784, 72; Wesley 1909–1916, 4:391.
[593] Wesley 1909–1916, 6:58–62. Wesley left Cork on 9 May, arriving the next day at Limerick. Wesley's preface states that he had been urged to publish the sermon at Cork, but there is no evidence of such an edition. Wesley's sermon was published at Dublin in 1775, and at London in 1776. (Some later editions bear a note on the title page stating that the book was not to be sold, but given away free.) An undated edition was published at Limerick by J. Ferrar; given that Wesley travelled directly from Cork to Limerick, it is possible that the undated Limerick edition predates the Dublin edition. However, I follow the 1775 Dublin edition, which is the earliest securely datable edition.
[594] Wesley 1775, 5.

nevertheless hold to the doctrine of absolute predestination, Wesley's particular bugaboo. The only honest conclusion to be drawn from this observation is that 'there are ten thousand mistakes, which may consist with real Religion'. Although Wesley insisted on the existence of a hierarchy of truths, he shied away from the term '*fundamental* Truths', since there was such disagreement over the number and nature of such fundamentals. However, amongst those doctrines with 'a close connexion with vital Religion' is that expressed in the Johannine comma. Wesley denied that it is important to believe one particular explication of these words, and said that no one person can understand all the implications. As Jonathan Swift wrote in his sermon on the Trinity, all those who have attempted to do so have lost their way and 'hurt the cause, which they intended to promote'. Wesley even had his scruples about subscribing to the Athanasian creed, until he realised that the anathema pronounced upon those who reject this formulation applies only to those who know the truth and reject it, and that the creed requires adherence only to the substance of the doctrine it promotes, not to its philosophical illustrations. Perhaps suspecting that his congregation included some Unitarians, he stated that he 'dare not insist upon any one's using the word *Trinity*, or *Person*. I use them myself without any scruple, because I know of none better: But if any man has any scruple concerning them, who shall constrain him to use them? I cannot.' As an illustration of the evils to which an insistence on such matter can lead, he mentioned that the 'merciful John Calvin' had burned Servet for asserting that although he believed that the Father, Son and Holy Spirit were all God, nevertheless he hesitated to use the words 'Trinity' and 'persons', since they were not found in the bible. By contrast, Wesley would insist only that his hearers embrace the words of the comma 'as they lie in the text'.

Wesley was aware of the critical difficulties attending the comma, but maintained its authenticity. He noted that although Bengel, 'the most pious, the most judicious, and the most laborious, of all the modern Commentators on the new Testament', was initially sceptical about the authenticity of the comma, he became convinced of its genuineness by three considerations:

> 1. That tho' it is wanting in many Copies, yet it is found in more, and those, Copies of the greatest authority. 2. That it is cited by a whole train of ancient Writers, from the time of St *John* to that of *Constantine*. This argument is conclusive: for they could not have cited it, had it not then been in the sacred Canon. 3. That we can easily account for its being after that time wanting in many Copies, when we remember, that *Constantine*'s Successor

was a zealous Arian, who used every means to promote his bad cause, to spread Arianism throughout the Empire: In particular, the erasing this text out of as many Copies as fell into his hands.[595]

Even though Wesley did not have a copy of Bengel's commentary to hand, his presentation of Bengel's position on the comma was misleading. What Bengel in fact said was that the number of Greek codices containing the Epistles is rather small. Advocates of the authenticity of the verse therefore had to rely on the witness of the Latin translation, which Bengel praised as 'very ancient and very faithful'. A large number of fathers from Africa, Spain, Gaul and Italy had used this translation over an unbroken period of time, despite the temptation to make their reading agree with that of the Arians.[596] Those who heard Wesley's sermon in Cork or subsequently read the printed version received an incorrect impression of the reasons that Bengel had put forward in favour of the verse.

Wesley then dealt with the Antitrinitarians' objection that the church required them to accept mysteries they could not comprehend. Wesley denied that Christianity required anyone to believe mysteries, and pointed out that in any case, everyone believes many things they cannot understand. We believe that light, the sun, air or earth exist, but we cannot fully grasp their nature or properties. If we believed only what we can fully comprehend, we would be forced to give up our belief in all these natural things. Wesley's argument here recalls one element of the deist controversy, which sought to clarify the epistemological basis of religious faith:

> [...] as strange as it may seem, in requiring you to believe, *There are three that bear record in Heaven, the Father, the Word, and the Holy Ghost; and these three are one:* You are not required to believe any Mystery. Nay, that great and good man, Dr. *Peter Browne*, sometime Bishop of *Cork*, has proved at large, that the Bible does not require you to believe any mystery at all. The Bible barely requires you, to believe such *facts*, nor the manner of them. Now the Mystery does not lie in the *fact*, but altogether in the *manner*.[597]

Wesley's references to the Irish prelates Browne and Swift were evidently calculated to appeal to the patriotism of his audience. Peter Browne, a high-church Tory, had responded to Toland in *A Letter in Answer to a Booke, intituled, Christianity not Mysterious* (1697). Browne agreed with Toland's thesis that 'nothing in the Gospel is contrary to Reason, or above

---

[595] Wesley 1775, 14.
[596] Bengel 1742, 1066.
[597] Wesley 1775, 23–24.

it', and acknowledged that 'the Revelations of God are in a way suitable to those powers of knowledge we have, and he requires us to believe nothing, but what is just and reasonable'. However, he found Toland's epistemology, which drew elements from both Descartes and Locke, problematic.[598] Browne pointed out that we do not always have access to clear and distinct ideas. He used the example of a blind man to show that knowledge and belief cannot always arise from the kind of empirical experience that Toland required as the basis for true knowledge:

> For upon his Principles it were a thing utterly impossible for any Man that was born Blind, to believe there is such a thing as *Light*, upon the testimony either of *God* or *Man*. For without the use of *one* of his *Eyes* at least, he's so far from having any clear and distinct Idea of it, that he cou'd have no Idea at all of it as it is in it self; and therefore must never believe that there is such a thing.[599]

According to Browne, mysteries of religion thus rely on two sources of knowledge: first, '*Something that we do comprehend fully*, and Secondly, *Something that we have no notion at all of.* As to this latter part of it, it is wholly exempted from the disquisition of Reason, and Faith alone can reach it, for our Reason fails us where we have no Idea's.'[600] Browne asserted that the revelations of supernatural things in the gospels 'have better proofs of their *Divinity* than any other whatsoever', and that the doctrines they contain agree 'to our common Notions, that if I use my *Reason* with the same *impartiality* in these that I do in other things, I must give my assent to them'.[601] One example of such supernatural revelation was the doctrine of the Trinity, revealed particularly by the Johannine comma:

> From whence, and from many other passages in the Scriptures, I find that there is a *Distinction* made in the Godhead, under these three names of *Father*, *Son*, and *Holy Ghost*, which the *Church* hath exprest, altogether by the word *Trinity*, and singly by the word *Person*. And I think these terms proper enough, to express all that we know of the *Mystery*.[602]

Browne admitted frankly that the bible provides few details of the doctrine. It describes neither the manner nor the nature of the distinction between the persons, only that 'the Son was begotten, and that the Holy Ghost comes from the Father and the Son'. He declared that the formula

---

[598] Browne 1697, 48.
[599] Browne 1697, 44.
[600] Browne 1697, 46–47.
[601] Browne 1697, 56–57.
[602] Browne 1697, 58.

for baptism provided by Jesus in the great commission shows that there is 'something more than a meer *Nominal Distinction*' between the persons of the Trinity, otherwise Jesus simply would have told his disciples to baptise in the name of God. He also concluded from the Scriptural witness that there are not simply three '*distinct different Spirits*, for then there must be *three Gods*', a proposition he rejected as contrary both to reason and Scripture. In the Scriptures, each of the three divine persons is named separately, but also described jointly as God, and accordingly paid divine honours and worship. Browne admitted that 'I have not the least knowledge how strict this *Union* is, nor how great the *Distinction*. It is as much beyond my *Reason*, as the *Glory* of God is beyond my *Sight*.' Browne was thus prepared to declare against the 'insolent' Toland that 'I thus *adore what I cannot comprehend*.' Moreover, his acceptance of this doctrine was not '*precarious* and *implicite*, or any *easie blind Credulity*; but is founded upon *clear* and *distinct Idea's*'.[603] By stripping the doctrine of the Trinity down to its bare bones, Browne presented the doctrine in such a way that could allow of a Socinian interpretation of the Scriptural witness to the Trinity, but he evidently wished to win the minimum of assent from his readers before making more specific claims. Browne also suggested a basic hermeneutic procedure to readers faced with a Scriptural text 'wherein a *Mystery* is reveal'd'. First, they should ensure that they understand the meaning of the Words properly. Second, they must make sure that the words do not contain any contradiction. Third, they ought to satisfy themselves of the evidence that the revelations come from God. Any reader who followed this procedure would soon discover if the mystery in the text was reasonable.[604]

In a footnote, Browne made a number of interesting comments about the Johannine comma. He considered that even if the passage was not cited by the early councils, even if it is not found in many ancient codices, even if it was not an original part of the text of the epistle, 'it is however a good Argument for the Doctrine of the *Trinity*'. And even if it began as a marginal gloss that was inserted by the orthodox or expunged by the Arians, then it can still be said to represent the opinion of 'the most Ancient and Primitive Christians who put this Comment to the Text'. And the manuscript evidence, Browne asserted, is not as bad as critics pretended: 'Though it be not in *some* Copies, yet it is in others, and those

---

[603] Browne 1697, 56–60.
[604] Browne 1697, 61.

very ancient.' Moreover, he claimed that it was cited by Cyprian, before the Arian controversy began. But most important of all, the proposition it expresses is consistent with that contained in the other Scriptural passages relating to the Trinity.[605]

Wesley's extensive use of Browne gives the sermon a slightly archaic feel, since he was reviving issues from the deist controversy of eighty years earlier. Although Wesley read Browne's 1728 critique of Locke, *The Procedure, Extent, and Limits of the Human Understanding* soon after its publication, there is no evidence that he knew Browne's refutation of Toland before his visit to Cork in 1775.[606] Despite his protestation that he did not have any books to consult, his extensive use of Browne's argumentation suggests that he had read the book not long before preaching this sermon. Wesley drew in particular on Browne's argument that we ought to believe statements in the bible if they are consonant with reason, as well as on his distinction between the fact of a mystery (which we should accept if it passes the triple test of comprehensibility, non-contradiction and divine origin) and the manner in which such a mystery is brought about, which we cannot understand and are thus not obliged to believe. The bible says that God spoke light into existence, and there was light. 'I believe it,' Wesley declares, 'I believe the plain fact: There is no mystery at all in this. The mystery lies in the manner of it. But of this I believe nothing at all; nor does God require it of me.'[607] The same may be said of propositions such as: 'the Word became flesh,' or 'there are three that bear record in heaven.' Although Wesley accepted these statements as true, he admitted that he did not understand how they came about, and thus considered himself free of any obligation to hold any particular beliefs about the manner in which these mysteries came about. 'But would it not be absurd in me, to deny the fact, because I do not understand the manner? That is, to reject *what GOD has revealed*, because I do not comprehend *what he has not revealed?*' Browne's argument for the reasonability of accepting revealed religion thus provided an important foundation for Wesley's understanding of the relationship between knowledge and faith. Having established the reasonability of accepting the mystery revealed by the Johannine comma, Wesley argued that it was only natural to honour the Son as equal to the Father. For Wesley, 'The knowledge of the three-one GOD is

---

[605] Browne 1697, 57–58 (footnote).
[606] Wesley 1975–1983, 25:271.
[607] Wesley 1775, 24–25.

interwoven with all true Christian faith; with all vital religion.' And faith in the Trinity is intimately connected with salvation:

> But I know not how any one can be a Christian Believer, 'till he *hath* (as St. *John* speaks) *the witness in himself:* 'till *the Spirit of* GOD *witnesses with his spirit, that he is a child of GOD:* that is, in effect, 'till GOD the Holy Ghost witnesses that GOD the Father has accepted him, thro' the merits of GOD the Son; and having this witness, he honours the Son, and the blessed Spirit, *even as he honours the Father.*[608]

For Wesley, the experience of accepting the witness of the Spirit that we are saved and accepted as children of God through the merits of Jesus leads naturally to the worship of all three persons of the Trinity equally: 'Therefore I do not see how it is possible for any to have vital Religion, who denies that these three are one.'[609]

Despite its problems, notably its exaggeration of Bengel's claims for the authenticity of the comma, Wesley's sermon on the Trinity was prized by Methodists, especially for its forceful advocacy of belief in the Trinity as the only reasonable response to the experience of being saved. It was reprinted ten times on both sides of the Atlantic (1776, 1783, 1784, 1789, 1792, 1803, 1805, 1812, 1813 and 1816) before being included in the many editions of Wesley's collected sermons, and would be cited often when Methodists expounded the doctrine of the Trinity.[610]

19. Edward Gibbon, George Travis, Georg Gottlieb Pappelbaum, Richard Porson and Herbert Marsh

After discovering Montesquieu as a student at Lausanne, Edward Gibbon (1737–1794) developed a philosophical historiography that dealt for the first time in English with the idea of historical progress. English historiography between Camden and Gibbon had generally been of a literary and dully antiquarian type generally devoid of strong philosophical conviction. As a result, most English critics failed to see past Gibbon's peculiar literary style to recognise his revolutionary historiographical approach. The Scottish Enlightenment was more open to new currents in continental thought, and Gibbon's work was consequently received with greater acclaim at Edinburgh than in London. Gibbon's ostensible hostility to

---

[608] Wesley 1775, 29.

[609] Wesley 1775, 30.

[610] See for example Crowther 1815, 170–175, which consists largely of a paraphrase of the sermon; Ward 1815, 18; Exley 1818, 53.

religion was not simply bigotry, such as he deplored in Voltaire. Rather, it proceeded from his insight that ideas and beliefs, including religion, are intimately related to social institutions and political systems, and that these inevitably contribute to social progress or decline. Gibbon posited that the institutionalisation of Christianity contributed to the decline of the Roman Empire by exaggerating its worst features: the centralism of its administration, its monopolistic control of wealth, and its tendency to smother autonomous thought. By promoting 'patience and pusillanimity', Christianity discouraged civic action, which Gibbon considered essential to a healthy and progressive society. This is not to say that the church contributed nothing to European civilisation: Gibbon praised Christian resistance to the cruelty of the arena, and the efforts of generations of monks to preserve classical texts. But the suggestion that Christianity could contribute to the decline of a civilisation idolised by Europeans since the fifteenth century left a bitter taste in the mouths of many of Gibbon's English readers.[611]

Although Gibbon was not blind to Erasmus' faults, he admired his learning, which was 'all real, and founded on the accurate perusal of the antient authors', and his genius, 'which could see through the vain subtleties of the schools, revive the laws of criticism, treat every subject with eloquence and delicacy'.[612] Joseph Levine characterised Gibbon's treatment of the Johannine comma as the apotheosis of Erasmus' discovery that the bible is not merely a stock of theological arguments, but a historical text – indeed, the most important historical witness to Jesus, our highest moral exemplar – whose layers can be laid bare by patient and systematic examination.[613] Gibbon's account forms part of his analysis of the gradual ascendancy of the orthodox position over that of the Arians, in the third volume of his *History of the Decline and Fall of the Roman Empire* (1781):

> The [...] orthodox theologians were tempted, by the assurance of impunity, to compose fictions, which must be stigmatized with the epithets of fraud and forgery. They ascribed their own polemical works to the most venerable names of Christian antiquity [...]. Even the Scriptures themselves were profaned by their rash and sacrilegious hands. The memorable text, which asserts the unity of the THREE who bear witness in heaven, is condemned by the universal silence of the orthodox fathers, ancient versions, and authentic manuscripts. It was first alleged by the Catholic bishops whom Hunneric summoned to the conference of Carthage. An

[611] Momigliano 1954; Trevor-Roper 1976.
[612] Gibbon 1796, 2:74–75. Cf. Momigliano 1954, 454.
[613] Levine 1999, 25–31, 157–170.

allegorical interpretation, in the form, perhaps, of a marginal note, invaded the text of the Latin Bibles, which were renewed and corrected in a dark period of ten centuries. After the invention of printing, the editors of the Greek Testament yielded to their own prejudices, or those of the times; and the pious fraud, which was embraced with equal zeal at Rome and at Geneva, has been infinitely multiplied in every country and every language of modern Europe. The example of fraud must excite suspicion; and the specious miracles by which the African Catholics have defended the truth and justice of their cause, may be ascribed, with more reason, to their own industry, than to the visible protection of Heaven.[614]

In a footnote, Gibbon became more specific:

The three witnesses have been established in our Greek Testaments by the prudence of Erasmus; the honest bigotry of the Complutensian editors; the typographical fraud, or error, of Robert Stephens in the placing of a crotchet [that is, a metobelos]; and the deliberate falsehood, or strange mis-representation, of Theodore Beza.[615]

For Gibbon, whose entire method depended on intensive engagement with the original sources, the absence of Greek manuscripts attesting the comma – as demonstrated by Simon, Mill, Wettstein, Emlyn and Missy – was fatal. Montfortianus and Ravianus were 'unworthy to form an exception' to this conclusion.[616] Gibbon lamented that personal priorities had too often prevented scholars from seeing the problem clearly: 'In 1689, the papist Simon strove to be free; in 1707, the protestant Mill wished to be a slave; in 1751, the Arminian Wetstein used the liberty of his times, and of his sect.'[617] If Gibbon intended to provoke a reaction amongst the believ-ers of his own day, to puncture the inflated piety and hypocrisy of the established church, he was spectacularly successful.

Gibbon's characterisation of the comma as a confidence trick perpet-uated over the course of centuries prompted the Anglican clergyman George Travis to defend its authenticity a series of letters published in the *Gentleman's Magazine* in 1782.[618] According to a contemporary admirer, Travis had 'little of the *stiffness* of a churchman about him, [...] presiding one day with propriety and ability at the head of a canal committee, the next superintending the sale of a lot of oxen, and the third, collecting, in his library, arguments in support of the doctrine of the Trinity'. However,

---

[614] Gibbon 1776–1788, 3:543–545.
[615] Gibbon 1776–1788, 3:545 n. 119.
[616] Gibbon 1776–1788, 3:544 n. 115.
[617] Gibbon 1776–1788, 3:544 n. 114.
[618] See Hugh de Quehen, 'Travis, George', in *ODNB*.

in vindicating the comma, he had taken up a task 'for which he was by no means qualified'.[619] Travis' letters against Gibbon, and two more explaining his position in more depth, appeared in book form in 1784. According to a critique of Travis' book in *The English Review*, there were not 'many controversies that have had a greater eclat'.[620] Moreover, this exchange showed that in the eighteenth century, even lay readers expected empirical evidence for whatever they were asked to believe, and were unwilling to take important conclusions on trust: 'no doubt every one would be apt to feel a decided preference for the testimony of his senses. The evidence of Valla, Stephens and Beza can never be put upon a par with it; because on this side there is a previous question, that of their veracity [...].'[621] Travis released a revised edition of his book in 1785, after reading Newton and Griesbach.

In his account of the manuscript evidence for the comma, Travis was prone to optimistic exaggeration. According to his tally, the comma was attested in thirty-one of the eighty-one manuscripts of the Catholic Epistles known to him, namely the seven used by Valla, sixteen used by Estienne, Erasmus' Codex Britannicus, Codex Montfortianus, Stunica's Codex Rhodiensis, Codex Ravianus in Berlin and four lectionaries collated by Wettstein.[622] Travis wrote to the library at Trinity College, Dublin for further information about Montfortianus, and reprinted a report sent by the College librarian.[623] He also wrote to Johann Friedrich Zöllner, a Lutheran clergyman in Berlin, for information about Codex Ravianus.[624]

Gibbon's ambiguous reference to Erasmus' 'prudence' in eventually including the comma in his text drew attention to the Dutchman's motivations. Travis had his own ideas: 'In whatever light we view the conduct of Erasmus, it betrays, at least, great weakness.' If the comma was missing from all the manuscripts on which he based the text of his first two editions, 'he ought not to have restored it, in his third edition, upon the authority of a single MS only'.[625] Travis chose to ignore Erasmus' protestation that he had included the verse only to avoid further slander, preferring to attribute his actions to darker motives. While Emlyn believed that

[619] Anon. 1797c, 240.
[620] Anon. 1785a, 167.
[621] Anon. 1785a, 168.
[622] Travis 1785, 18–19, 282 (Valla), 116–138 (Estienne), 138–149 (Erasmus), 149–159 (Montfortianus), 159–171 (Ravianus), 282–283 (Rhodiensis and Wettstein's mss 44, 48, 51, 57, 58).
[623] Travis 1785, 150–153.
[624] A response from Zöllner to Travis, dated 25 Mary 1785, is reprinted in Travis 1794, 67–73.
[625] Travis 1785, 8.

Erasmus had simply invented the British codex and its purported reading of the comma, Travis suggested that Erasmus actually had a number of manuscripts containing the comma, 'which he was not, however, ingenuous enough to acknowledge', hiding them from view in order to conceal the truth of the matter. There could only be one motive for such behaviour: '*Erasmus* was secretly inclined to *Arianism*: a circumstance, which rendered him, by no means, *an indifferent* editor of this *fifth* chapter of St. *John*.' In concealing 'his *true* motives of action', his conduct was '*grossly disingenuous*, and unworthy'.[626]

In 1785, the Lutheran clergyman and critic Georg Gottlieb Pappelbaum published a study of Codex Ravianus. He had first been prompted to investigate the Catholic Epistles and Apocalypse in this manuscript in 1769 after reading Michaelis' description of his attempt to verify – and if necessary, to contradict – La Croze's conclusion that the codex was essentially a transcript of the Complutensian bible. Michaelis' method and his frankness about his own failure to falsify La Croze's finding suggests the incipient impact of scientific method on biblical study. When Pappelbaum heard of Travis' exaggerated claims about the manuscript attestation of the comma from Johann Friedrich Zöllner, he decided that it was time to set his investigations in order.[627] He also addressed a letter to Travis, dated 1 December 1785, to vindicate La Croze and Wettstein against Travis' libels, and to give a summary of his own method and results. He had discovered that the text of Codex Ravianus agreed with the Complutensian edition to a remarkable degree, including a number of typographical errors peculiar to that edition. Where it did differ, the variation was due either to error, ignorance or a deliberate attempt to conceal the origin of the text. He noted that Johannes Saubert's collation of the text of Matthew in Ravianus (1672) was unreliable, and had led Travis into a number of errors. He corrected a number of Travis' mistakes concerning variant readings in Codex Ravianus, and refuted his erroneous assertion that the Complutensian Polyglot includes the doxology at Mt 6:13. He noted that Travis had made two errors in his description of the comma in the Complutensian Polyglot and Codex Ravianus. He also chided Travis for a number of misleading statements about the manuscripts described by Wettstein. Finally, of the thirty-one manuscripts alleged by Travis to contain the comma, Pappelbaum pointed out that this passage is only found in two: Montfortianus and Ravianus. On the same day, Zöllner also wrote

---

[626] Travis 1785, 9.
[627] Michaelis 1765–1766, I:XVIII–XXII, 671–675; Pappelbaum 1785, v–x.

to advise Travis not to make any more unadvised statements about the Berlin codex.[628] Since Travis declined to respond to Pappelbaum's letter, Michaelis stated that he would publish it if he could obtain the author's permission.[629]

Travis' book was lambasted on the continent. The Helmstedt theologians Heinrich Philipp Konrad Henke and Paul Jacob Bruns dismissed it as 'this child of his diligence, or rather this abortion, with a vast body, but no brain'.[630] By contrast, Travis' work was widely praised by conservatives in England as a welcome counterweight to Gibbon's godless scepticism. As a reward for his defence of the faith, Travis was made first prebendary (1783) and then archdeacon of Chester (1786).[631] Travis' letters show clearly that the debate over the comma was not simply about the bible, but about social cohesion and a breakdown of consensus. Travis accused Gibbon of promoting the corrosive scepticism of Toland, Spinoza, Rousseau and Voltaire, and challenged him to make his philosophical standpoint clear to his readers, lest they 'confound, in you, modern Deism with ancient Polytheism, or either of them with Atheism'.[632] In an attempt to flush out the quarry, one of Travis' partisans even resorted to *ad hominem* attack in a published review of Gibbon's work:

> It is notorious that Gibbon was a professed infidel. Among his friends he was accustomed to ridicule religion, and all its appendages, in a most indecent manner. But he confined not his cavils and sarcasms within the circle of his intimate acquaintance. The writer of this article is well acquainted with several persons – a lady in particular – whom Gibbon, in violation of all the rules of good-breeding, attacked on the subject of their faith, the very first time he had an opportunity of conversing with them. It was by sneers and inuendos that he conducted the assault. The historian scoffed much at the lady's hopes of a resurrection.[633]

According to this reviewer, Christian history can only be treated by faithful Christians; piety is a necessary precondition of learning.

Although Gibbon dismissed Travis as destitute of 'learning, judgement, and humanity', he abstained from entering into the debate that exploded in the press.[634] Despite his personal dislike of Gibbon, Richard

---

[628] Pappelbaum 1796, 188–206.

[629] Porson 1790, XIV; Pappelbaum 1796, IX.

[630] Henke and Bruns 1786, 386; transl. from Porson 1790, XV.

[631] For a typically positive judgement of Travis' defence of the comma, see Hawkins 1787, 188.

[632] Travis 1785, 471.

[633] Anon. 1795, 380.

[634] Gibbon 1796, 1:171.

Porson, later regius professor of Greek at Cambridge, took up the lance in his *Letters to Mr. Archdeacon Travis.*[635] The *Letters* were first published under the pseudonym 'Cantabrigiensis' in the *Gentlemen's Magazine* in 1788–1789. In 1790 a revised text was published as a book, under Porson's real name.[636] In these acute letters, miniature masterpieces of criticism and prose style, Porson, not quite thirty years old, poured out blistering torrents of scorn on the unfortunate Travis.[637]

Like Gibbon, Porson was judged even by his friends to have been 'without the protection of early, vigorous, and permanent piety'.[638] Thomas Rennell, canon of Winchester, dryly remarked that Porson's refutation of Travis was 'just such a book as the devil would write, if he could hold a pen'.[639] Porson found the doctrine of the Trinity incomprehensible: '*Porson* was walking with a Trinitarian friend; they had been speaking of the Trinity; a buggy came by with three men in it; "There," says he, "is an illustration of the Trinity;" "No," said his friend Porson, "you must shew me one man in *three* buggies, if you can." '[640] But Porson's disdain for the doctrine of the Trinity was indiscriminate. When asked his opinion of Socinianism, Porson replied: 'If the New Testament is to determine the question, and words have any meaning, the Socinians are wrong.'[641] He was motivated to spend so much time refuting Travis not by any concern for theological orthodoxy, but by a desire to clear textual criticism of patent errors.[642] It is also hard to escape the impression that Porson enjoyed breaking lance upon lance on Travis: 'To peruse such a mass of falsehood and sophistry; and to write remarks upon it, without sometimes giving way to laughter, and sometimes to indignation, was, to me at least, impossible.'[643]

Porson owned and admired Newton's treatise on the comma.[644] Just as Newton's intensive studies of theology were catalysed, at least in part, by the looming stipulation that he be ordained as an Anglican priest, the

[635] See Geoffrey V. Morson, 'Porson, Richard,' in *ODNB*.
[636] Publication was announced in *The Gazetteer and New Daily Advertiser*, 5 July 1790, 1.
[637] Porson owned copies of Travis 1784 and 1785. Two copies of Porson 1790, are in the library of Trinity College, Cambridge (adv.c3.70 and adv.c3.71), the latter of which belonged to Porson; Naiditch 2011, n° 1402, 1404, 1769, 1770.
[638] Pye-Smith 1810, 164.
[639] Rogers 1856, 303.
[640] E. H. Barker 1852, 2:2; transmission of the anecdote is attributed to a 'Mr Rodd', probably the bookseller Thomas Rodd; see Naiditch 2011, 33.
[641] Anon. 1826, 99.
[642] Clarke 1937, 27.
[643] Porson 1790, XXIII.
[644] Naiditch 2011, 215.

theological reflection evident in Porson's letters to Travis apparently arose from precisely the same requirement of his fellowship at Trinity College. Porson's response to Travis revealed that the dispute had as much to do with religious anxieties as with philological niceties. For example, Travis had concluded that Erasmus must have been an Arian because he rejected the comma, and believed that this religious error impaired Erasmus' ability to present the evidence honestly. Porson dismissed Travis' accusation that Erasmus tended towards Arianism: 'instead of accounting for his conduct from his natural timidity, and the violent clamours of his enemies, you make it spring from sheer Arianism, villainy and hypocrisy.'[645] Such arguments were not only nonsensical; they made it impossible to reach fair conclusions: 'For it is a maxim with you, Sir, that all Arians are wholly possessed by the devil, and that it is impossible for them "to quote fairly, to argue candidly, and to speak truly," (p. 127. 374.); while the orthodox may say what they please, and their bare word is taken without farther inquiry.'[646]

On the question of Erasmus and Codex Montfortianus, Porson had his own ideas. He surmised that Erasmus' excuse to Lee had occasioned a hunt for a Greek manuscript containing the comma, which eventually turned up such a manuscript in England.[647] Porson maintained that 'Erasmus never saw the Codex Britannicus, but had only an extract from it,' but his sole grounds for coming to this conclusion is that Erasmus did not return to England after 1517. He failed to consider the possibility that someone brought the manuscript to Erasmus.[648] In any case, Porson's judgement on the status of Montfortianus was unambiguous:

> [Montfortianus] was probably written about the year 1520, and interpolated in this place for the purpose of deceiving Erasmus. This hypothesis will explain how it so suddenly appeared when it was wanted, and how it disappeared as suddenly after having atchieved the glorious exploit for which it was destined. It might have been hazardous to expose its tender and infantine form to barbarous critics. They would perhaps have thrown brutal aspersions upon its character, from which it might never have recovered. The freshness of the ink and materials might then have led to a detection of the imposture; but time would gradually render such an event less probable in itself, and less hurtful in its consequences.[649]

[645] Porson 1790, 118.
[646] Porson 1790, 2–3.
[647] Porson 1790, 112.
[648] Porson 1790, 112–115.
[649] Porson 1790, 117.

Porson rejected Travis' insinuation that Erasmus possessed – but concealed – a large number of Greek manuscripts containing the comma:

> Inquisitive people will say, how happens it that none of these MSS. now remain, except the Dublin copy, which Wetstein is so cruel as to attribute to the sixteenth century [...?] But the answer is easy. They are lost. Either they have been burned, or have been eaten by the worms, or been gnawed in pieces by the rats, or been rotted with the damps, or been destroyed by those pestilent fellows the Arians; which was very feasible; for they had only to get into their power all the MSS. of the New Testament in the world, and to mutilate or destroy those which contained *un des plus beaux passages dans l'Ecriture Sainte*. Or, if all these possibilities should fail, the devil may play his part in the drama to great advantage. For it is a fact of which Beza positively assures us, that the devil has been tampering with the text, I Tim. III. 16; and that Erasmus lent him an helping hand.[650]

Despite the brilliance of Porson's refutation of Travis' arguments, he too made some errors. He deployed the legend of Erasmus' promise, even though he knew (and quoted) the relevant passage from Erasmus' defence against Lee's *Annotationes*.[651]

Gibbon was glad that he did not have to soil his hands with a reply to Travis' 'brutal insolence'. He praised Porson's reply as 'the most acute and accurate piece of criticism which has appeared since the days of Bentley', and gleefully rejoiced that 'the wretched Travis still smarts under the lash of the merciless Porson'.[652] Porson's work was also praised in the *Allgemeine Literatur-Zeitung* as 'one of the most learned and thorough works of biblical criticism that we have received from England in recent years'.[653] Yet many English readers, especially lay ones, were still inclined to give the palm to Travis. According to the lawyer William Bolland:

> On Greek, no longer Porson founds his fame,
> Since the divine has taught the sceptic shame;
> Though tauntingly, his bitter logic prest,
> Yet Travis conquers by the heavenly text.[654]

---

[650] Porson 1790, 22–23. Cf. Bèze 1565, 463 (*ad* 1 Tim 3:16). The French quotation is from Martin 1717, *21. Porson owned Martin 1717, 1719a and 1721; see Naiditch 2011, 197–198. Porson's tone is perhaps influenced by a passage in Newton 1959–1977, 3:93, cit. above, 170.

[651] Porson 1790, 111: 'Erasmus said, in his answer to Lee, that if he had found a single Greek manuscript containing the three heavenly witnesses, he would have inserted them in his text.'

[652] Gibbon 1796, 1:159.

[653] Anon. 1791, 197.

[654] Bolland 1800, 50.

And if book sales are any measure of success, Travis trounced Porson. 'I got but £30 for my labours,' Porson boasted ironically, 'but I have the consolation of thinking that my publisher *lost* money by the speculation.'[655] And Gibbon was realistic enough to see that even Porson's brilliant 'strictures' were insufficient to sway public opinion: 'prejudice is blind, authority is deaf, and our vulgar bibles will ever be polluted by this spurious text.'[656]

Porson's letters set off a reaction against Travis in learned circles that sometimes threatened to get out of hand. The Cambridge biblical critic Thomas Kipling, editor of Codex Bezae, gave a mock oration in defence of Travis 'in a ludicrous, but classical style', which exposed the archdeacon to 'the laughter and contempt of the assembly'. But Porson found this performance regrettable:

> however I may be delighted with the matter, the tendency, and the effect of my learned ally's oration, I must not be so partial to the failings of a friend, as to conceal my displeasure at the air of levity and banter which visibly ran through the whole harangue. It neither suited the gravity of his character, the dignity of his office, the solemnity of the occasion, nor the sanctity of the subject.[657]

Porson also received fan mail from admirers such as John Pope, tutor in the *belles-lettres* and classical literature at the New College Hackney.[658]

The next significant contribution to the debate was made by Herbert Marsh (1757–1839), a Cambridge graduate whose three-year stay in Göttingen and Weimar exposed him to recent developments in German biblical criticism, such as Reimarus' critique of the notion of biblical inspiration.[659] While in Germany, Marsh translated the fourth edition of Michaelis' *Introduction to the New Testament*, one of the monuments of late eighteenth-century New Testament criticism, augmenting it with notes that introduced English readers to recent German biblical criticism. In one of his notes, Marsh identified Cambridge, University Library ms Kk 6.4 (GA 398[ap]) as Estienne's lost codex ιγ'. Significantly, Marsh noted that this manuscript lacks the comma. In a third edition of his letters against Gibbon (1794), Travis dismissed Marsh's arguments, but passed over Porson's book in complete silence, an astonishing omission contemporary observers did not fail to notice.[660]

---

[655] E. H. Barker 1852, 2:32–33; Luard 1857, 139.
[656] Gibbon 1796, 1:160.
[657] Porson 1867, 26.
[658] Pope 1792, 340–348; Porson 1867, 54–60.
[659] See Robert K. Forrest, 'Marsh, Herbert', in *ODNB*. Porson owned a copy of Marsh 1795; see Naiditch 2011, 195–196.
[660] *The Oracle and Public Advertiser*, 10 April 1794, 2.

Marsh replied with a collection of seven letters (1795), in which he carefully laid out the mistakes in Travis' collations of the Paris manuscripts. He also included an extract from Pappelbaum's study of Codex Ravianus. Finally, Marsh included an account of the readings in Estienne's codex ιγ´. Marsh was theologically orthodox, and certainly no friend to deism or Socinianism, but it annoyed him that defenders of orthodoxy such as Travis too often relied on inadequate evidence and reasoning. Marsh's criticisms of Travis went straight to the heart of the matter and, as William Orme (1830) would later write, 'supplied every thing that was wanting to complete the discomfiture and disgrace of the unfortunate Archdeacon'.[661]

But perhaps not quite. In the intervening decade, Georg Gottlieb Pappelbaum had worked through the Pauline letters in Ravianus, and had determined that those details that deviate from the Complutensian Polyglot are taken from Estienne's third edition of the Greek New Testament. When Pappelbaum read the third edition of Travis' letters, he was incensed to discover that the English cleric had not made any of the revisions he had suggested in his letter of 1785. In an appendix to his publication of his latest findings, Pappelbaum included an annotated transcript of his letter, thus exposing Travis to further embarrassment.

Summary

This chapter examined the place of the Johannine comma in the disputes over Trinitarian theology in England between the Civil War and the fallout from Gibbon's *History*, one of the crowning achievements of English Enlightenment scholarship. In the turmoil of the mid-seventeenth century, radicals who dismissed the doctrine of the Trinity as an innovation often emphasised the textual reasons for rejecting the comma. By contrast, religious conservatives tended to defend the comma as a powerful Scriptural proof for the doctrine of the Trinity, and thus of the theological and ecclesiastical status quo. John Milton rejected the biblical and theological bases for the doctrine of the Trinity in an unpublished manuscript. Thomas Hobbes cited the comma in his exploration of the ways in which God the Father, Son and Spirit were 'personated' in history by Moses, Jesus and the Apostles. The second half of the seventeenth century saw a renewal of interest in biblical philology and consequent critique of the *textus receptus*. The London Polyglot was soon followed by the pocket Greek edition of Etienne de Courcelles, translated into German

---

[661] 'Criticus' 1830, 94.

by Jeremias Felbinger. But the efforts of Courcelles and Felbinger failed to realise their ambitions, and both were accused of using philology to promote heresy. In his monumental *Histoire critique du texte du Nouveau Testament* (1689), Richard Simon demonstrated that the prologue to the Catholic Epistles, one of the texts traditionally considered as one of the most potent pieces of evidence in support of the comma, was not written by Jerome. He noted the absence of the comma from Greek manuscripts of the bible in the royal library at Paris and in the library of Colbert. He also suggested that glosses in some of these Greek bibles gave evidence of Trinitarian allegoresis of 1 Jn 5:8 in the Greek church.

The appearance of Simon's work coincided with two related disputes in the Anglican church in the wake of the Glorious Revolution: the debate over subscription to the Thirty-Nine Articles, considered by low-church Whigs as a stumbling block to the integration of Nonconformists; and the Trinitarian controversy. The question of the comma was examined in the light of these disputes by Isaac Newton and several members of his circle: John Mill, William Whiston, Samuel Clarke, Thomas Emlyn and Richard Bentley. Newton addressed a *Historical Account* of two contested passages in the New Testament (1 Jn 5:7–8 and 1 Tim 3:16) to John Locke. After examining the textual evidence, Newton concluded that the readings of these passages in the *textus receptus* were the result of the doctrinal corruption of the church since the time of Athanasius. While some of Newton's colleagues, such as Mill and Bentley, maintained an orthodox theological position, others, such as Clarke and especially Whiston, were censured by convocation for their criticism of traditional Trinitarian belief, and criticised by high-church Tories such as Daniel Waterland and Jonathan Swift. Mill's great 1707 critical edition of the New Testament was a powerful stimulus to biblical philology in the early eighteenth century, though the shortcomings of the edition, arising mainly from inaccurate or incomplete collations of manuscripts, led scholars such as Bentley, Bengel and Wettstein to undertake improved editions. Inevitably, each of these scholars ran up against the question of the comma, still considered by many as a touchstone of orthodox Trinitarian belief. Bengel's defence of the comma was welcomed in orthodox circles, and cited with approval by John Wesley. In 1736 an incomplete copy of Newton's unpublished *Historical Account* came into Wettstein's hands, and the ensuing search for a complete manuscript and the publication of Newton's treatise excited renewed interest in the question of the comma and its relationship to orthodoxy. A belated reception of Whiston's work in Germany contributed to a wave of interest in biblical philology there, as well as a realisation that biblical studies could only advance if historical questions were kept distinct from doctrinal considerations. When Edward Gibbon rejected the Johannine comma as a textual aberration, he was attacked by the conservative clergyman George Travis. Travis' arguments were in turn exposed as inaccurate and misjudged by Richard Porson, Georg Gottlieb Pappelbaum and Herbert Marsh.

CHAPTER 5

The Johannine comma in the
long nineteenth century

The Gibbon-Travis-Porson-Pappelbaum-Marsh dispute rumbled through the scholarly literature and gentlemen's magazines for decades. During this time, the textual authority of Codex Montfortianus, the manuscript from which Erasmus had taken the controversial passage, was subject to renewed attention. In the continuing dispute over the comma, the anxieties that had motivated Lee, Standish and Stunica again came to the fore: namely, the fear that biblical criticism would bring down the church and its doctrines by opening the wicket gate to Socinianism, deism and ultimately atheism. But the dispute was as much about culture and civilisation as it was about erudition and philological precision. In Britain, the bible, and notably the Authorised Version, had taken on the status of a cultural text as much as a religious one, the cornerstone of civilisation.[1] Fault lines in the text of the bible represented cracks in the foundations of society. The status of the comma, one of the few textual cruces considered by early-modern critics to impinge directly upon doctrine, rarely lost its power to fascinate. In a published account of his travels through Germany, Switzerland and Italy in 1791–1792, Robert Gray (1762–1834), who had followed the controversy between Porson and Travis attentively, described a visit to the monastery library at St Gallen, reporting on the readings of the comma found in the Latin manuscripts there.[2] And the comma rode on the back of the Authorised Version into the territories conquered by the British Empire. When the New Testament from the Authorised Version was translated into Bengali in 1839, the comma was included. Curiously, it was placed in parentheses in the Bengali text, but not in the English text on the facing page.[3]

The venues for discussing the comma changed over time. Sermon literature remained popular, and Wesley's sermon on the Trinity was reprinted

---

[1] Mandelbrote 2001, 37–40; Sheehan 2005, 241–258.
[2] Gray 1794, 95–97.
[3] *Dharmapustaker Antabhag* 1839, 2:524–525.

separately many times until 1816, after which time it was included in collected editions of his sermons. In 1805 it was joined by another sermon by George Burder, printed separately and then included in his oft-reprinted *Village Sermons*. When clergy wanted to expatiate for longer than a sermon would bear, they sometimes resorted to public lectures.[4] In the United States, Unitarian ministers such as Frederick Farley and Henry Ware published sermons, open letters and tracts disputing the genuineness of the comma as part of a defence of the Unitarian position.[5] Theological polemic, sometimes disguised as criticism, thus continued to play an important role.

In the previous chapter we saw how the legend of Erasmus' showdown with Edward Lee took on a life of its own, sprouting apocryphal details which were frequently used to misrepresent the authenticity of the comma as well as Erasmus' attitude towards it. Variations on the legend, invented by Simon, developed by Newton and Martin, and publicised by Porson, were used in later debates to depict Erasmus the conservative, Erasmus the radical, Erasmus the honest scholar, Erasmus the coward, Erasmus the good Catholic or Erasmus the proto-Socinian. Every possible variation was employed in the debates over the status of this difficult passage of Scripture. The popularity of the legend was certainly due the fact that it could be deployed so deftly and flexibly in the debates amongst Anglicans, Unitarians and Catholics that took place in nineteenth-century England. Because the story was not anchored to a definite textual source, it could take on virtually any number of possible variations. The story's lack of determinacy may in fact go some way towards explaining its appeal.

Erasmus' final decision to include the comma in his edition seemed to be vindicated in 1823, when Johann Martin Augustin Scholz published his discovery of a second Greek New Testament manuscript containing the comma (Vatican, BAV ms Ottob. gr. 298, GA 629[ap], known as Codex Ottobonianus). Defenders of the comma leapt at the discovery as further proof of the authenticity of the reading.[6] However, Scholz was of the opinion that this reading was one of the many Latinising alterations

---

[4] For example, the Rev. J. R. Beard gave a lecture on the comma at the Unitarian Meeting House, Greengate, Salford, on 1 April 1832; see *The Manchester Guardian*, 10 March 1832, 1. On 6 November 1856, the Rev. Dr. John Cumming delivered a ninety-minute lecture on the revision of the bible at the Caledonian Church on Holloway Road in London, expounding the case against the comma in some detail; see *The Observer*, 9 November 1856, 8.

[5] Farley 1845; Ware 1849, 243–248.

[6] This discovery was hailed by Evanson 1829, xvi, but 'Clemens Anglicanus' 1829, 31, rejected the comma as an interpolation, noting that 'the Codex Ottobonianus is of an exceedingly inferior order to the Codex Montfortianus.'

to the Greek text made by the scribe.[7] This manuscript thus stood under the same suspicion as Montfortianus, of containing a Greek text had simply been altered to conform to the Latin Vulgate. But even in those disposed to believe in the genuineness of the comma, the appearance of a manuscript reading so different from any yet known caused as much discomfort as elation: 'though I would willingly defend the text', wrote one correspondent to Thomas Burgess in 1830, 'I do not know what is to be defended.'[8]

Thomas Burgess (1756–1837), bishop of St David's (1803–1825) and Salisbury (1825–1837), a staunch enemy of Unitarianism, undertook a sustained defence of the comma through the 1820s and 1830s. He began with *A Vindication of 1 John v. 7. from the objections of M. Griesbach* (1821, repr. 1823). This work excited considerable interest (mainly negative) in literary and learned journals such as *The British Review* and the *Quarterly Review*, and involved Burgess in public controversy with Thomas Turton, Lucasian professor of mathematics and subsequently regius professor of divinity at Cambridge, who defended the late Porson against Burgess' disparagements. It also drew Burgess into a dispute with Thomas Benyon, archdeacon of Cardigan. Burgess also edited two book-length florilegia containing defences of the comma by earlier scholars. The first was in Latin, and contained the remarks of Mill, Wettstein, Bengel and Auguste Sabatier, pioneer in the study of the Old Latin translation. The other was in English, and gathered up the remarks of bishops Thomas Barlow and Richard Smalbroke, the correspondence between Craven and Bentley, extracts from Martin's writings against Emlyn, notes by Hammond and Whitby, as well as Adam Clarke's account of Codex Montfortianus. In 1831 Burgess even accused David Brewster, Newton's learned biographer, of injuring Newton's memory by restating the contents of the *Historical Account* without noting that the scientist had 'deliberately and anxiously suppressed' this writing. Brewster curtly replied that he had analysed the

---

[7] Scholz 1823, 105; Scholz 1830–1836, 2:152–153. The Greek reading of 1 Jn 5:6–8 in the manuscript (on 105v) is unique and reflects precisely the reading of the parallel Latin text. The reading ὁ χριστὸς εἰσὶν ἡ ἀλήθεια in v. 6 provides strong evidence that this entire passage has been altered to fit the Latin reading. The Greek column reads: '[...] ὅτι ὁ χριστὸς εἰσὶν ἡ ἀλήθεια. Ὅτι τρεῖς εἰσὶν οἱ μαρτυροῦντες ἀπὸ τοῦ οὐρανοῦ· πατήρ· λόγος καὶ πνεῦμα ἅγιον· καὶ οἱ τρεῖς εἰς τὸ ἕν εἰσί. καὶ τρεῖς εἰσὶν οἱ μαρτυροῦντες ἀπὸ τῆς γῆς, τὸ πνεῦμα τὸ ὕδωρ καὶ τὸ αἷμα. Εἰ τὴν μαρτυρίαν [...].' The parallel Latin text reads: '[...] quoniam christus est ueritas. Quia tres sunt qui testimonium dant in celo. pater. uerbum & spiritus sanctus et hij tres unum sunt. Et tres sunt qui testimonium dant in terra. spiritus aqua et sanguis. Si testimonium hominum [...].' See Capecelatro 1893, 161, for a description of the manuscript.

[8] E. Burton to Thomas Burgess, Oxford, 10 June 1830; Oxford, Bodleian Library ms Engl. Lett. c. 133, 193r–v.

relevant events 'more fully than it is done by your Lordship, or any other author whatever'. He also repudiated Burgess' claim that Newton had deliberately and anxiously suppressed the *Historical Account*. That Newton made no attempt to recover the letters, and kept the draft amongst his papers rather than destroying it, argued against the conclusion that he intended to suppress the work entirely. Rather, he was simply waiting for an opportune moment to publish. But Burgess was not to be put off, and consigned his criticisms of Brewster to print.[9] Meanwhile, Burgess had enlisted the assistance of Nicholas Wiseman in Rome, who made a precise tracing of the reading of the comma in Codex Ottobonianus, which served as the template for an engraving. In return, Burgess arranged for Wiseman's election as fellow of the Royal Society of Literature.[10] In 1835 Burgess published *An introduction to the controversy on the disputed verse of St. John, as revived by Mr. Gibbon*, and in 1837 published three open letters to Scholz, excoriating him for excising the comma from his edition of the Greek New Testament (1830–1836) and for casting doubt on the passage in his notes.

But Burgess and his fellows were fighting an uphill battle. In a critique of William Alleyn Evanson's introduction to his translation of Knittel's work on the comma (1827), Thomas Turton remarked that if the comma could not be 'maintained on the common principles by which other texts are established, that circumstance is of itself a strong indication that the verse is spurious'.[11] The defence of the comma was becoming increasingly less tenable as new manuscripts appeared, as data on known New Testament manuscripts increased in detail, and as critical techniques were refined. In the first edition of his influential *Introduction to the Critical Study and Knowledge of the Holy Scriptures* (1818), Thomas Hartwell Horne expressed a tentative confidence in the authenticity of the comma, but by the sixth edition (1828), he had rejected any internal evidence that seemed to support the authenticity of the verse in view of the overwhelming external evidence to the contrary.[12] A comprehensive account of the history of the debate by 'Criticus' (the Scottish Congregationalist

---

[9] Brewster 1831, 274–276; Brewster to Burgess, 5 December 1831, Oxford, Bodleian Library ms Engl. Lett. c. 133, 131r–135v; Burgess 1832, 79–87. Brewster 1855, 2:335, would later have the pleasure of writing that Burgess' publications on the comma were characterised by 'a boldness of assumption, and a severity of intolerance, unworthy of a Christian divine'. Cf. Mandelbrote 2004, 110–111.

[10] Wiseman's letters to Burgess are in Oxford, Bodleian Library ms Engl. Lett. c. 139, 76r–81v. Wiseman published on the subject of the comma in 1835.

[11] 'Clemens Anglicanus' 1829, 5.

[12] Horne 1828, 4:485; 'Criticus' 1830, 257–260.

minister William Orme) appeared in 1830.[13] Orme's account remained popular, and was reprinted at New York (1866) and Boston (1867, 1869, 1872, 1875, 1883), edited by the prominent Unitarian biblical scholar Ezra Abbot, who extended Orme's account up to his own time. The attention attracted by the excision of the comma from the *textus receptus*, which was slowly being dismantled by the critics, indicates the strong feelings this issue aroused, especially among Protestants. The critical issues were often secondary to the perceived implications of the excision. Some feared that it would undermine the integrity, and thus the credibility, of Scripture more broadly, thus opening the door to heresy or unbelief. Others saw in the excision of the comma one step towards the restoration of the original form of the text, on which a more authentic and less dogmatic Christianity might be built. The Revised Version of 1881, for all its stylistic awkwardness, responded to this hope.[14]

Just when the issue seemed to have blown itself out in Protestant circles, it flared up again in France, as two divergent tendencies within Catholic scholarship came into conflict: on one hand, a revival of Thomist dogmatics, which affirmed the authority of the Vulgate as promulgated at Trent; and on the other, a renewed interest in text-critical matters. The intensive researches into the textual history of the Vulgate by Jean-Pierre Paulin Martin and Samuel Berger stimulated a debate which became so heated that the Vatican felt it necessary to release a decree in 1897 to rein in speculation about the history of the comma. However, detailed investigation of the question during the first three decades of the twentieth century by two conservative Catholic clergymen, Karl Künstle and August Bludau, led finally to the repeal of the decree in 1927.

1. The scientific study of Codex Montfortianus

After its rediscovery and deployment in the dispute between Martin and Emlyn, Montfortianus attracted occasional interest. In 1760, John Jortin concluded in his *Life of Erasmus* that Montfortianus was identical to Erasmus' British codex.[15] The German critic Paul Jacob Bruns asked William Newcome (1729–1800), bishop of Waterford and Lismore, to examine the manuscript, and Bruns duly reported Newcome's findings in the *Repertorium für biblische und morgenländische Litteratur* in

---

[13] Alexander Gordon and Anne Pimlott Baker, 'Orme, William', in *ODNB*.
[14] Thuesen 1996.
[15] Jortin 1760, 2:226.

1778, supplying a copperplate facsimile of the reading of the comma in Montfortianus. Newcome reported that the manuscript was written on paper, though of such a kind as might be mistaken for parchment. Although Bruns believed that Montfortianus was probably Erasmus' British codex, others disagreed, usually with the intention of multiplying the textual witnesses to the comma. Newcome collated the three Johannine Epistles, Jude and a part of Revelation in Montfortianus, picking up where Ussher and his assistants had left off. On the basis of this collation John Pope concluded that Montfortianus was 'modern and of no authority', and that its reading of the Johannine comma had been translated from the Latin Vulgate 'in a most clumsy and bungling manner'. Meanwhile, the famous eccentric John ('Jacky') Barrett (1753/54–1821) of Trinity College was preparing a more complete collation of the biblical manuscripts at Dublin, including Montfortianus.[16]

At the request of Heinrich Eberhard Gottlob Paulus, professor of theology at Jena, Herbert Marsh ordered a precise transcript of the text of 1 Jn from Montfortianus. Rather than a transcript, the librarian at Trinity College sent Marsh a collation of the manuscript against the edition of Wettstein, probably that prepared earlier by Newcome. Paulus published his conclusions on this information in 1794. On the basis of the double dots over the ï and ü and the various Latinising features of the manuscript, Paulus dated the manuscript to the fifteenth century. From the collation he extracted all the unusual readings in 1 Jn and their concordances with other known Greek manuscripts and the Latin Vulgate. Paulus noted striking resemblances between the readings in Montfortianus and GA 326, but the published collation of GA 326 in Wettstein's edition was not sufficiently complete or accurate to allow him to conclude that it was the parent manuscript of Montfortianus. He also proposed that where Montfortianus corresponded to the Latin Vulgate against all other Greek manuscripts known at that time, the scribe had almost certainly altered the reading found in his *Vorlage*.[17]

In the third edition of his letters against Gibbon (1794), Travis provided a copper engraving of the passage from Montfortianus, apparently unaware of the work done by Newcome, Bruns and Paulus in the meantime.[18] On the basis of the engraved facsimiles published by Bruns and Travis, the Jena professor Franz Carl Alter concluded that the scribe

---

[16] Pope 1792, 349–350; H. T. Welch, 'Barrett, John [Jacky]', in *ODNB*.
[17] Paulus 1794.
[18] Travis 1794, facing 282.

was not a native Greek speaker, and had lived in the sixteenth century, though Alter was misled by Erasmus' transcriptional errors in the *Apology to Stunica* to the conclusion that Montfortianus was not Erasmus' Codex Britannicus.[19] After examining Montfortianus in 1790, the Methodist minister Adam Clarke (1762–1832) also had an engraved printing plate made of the passage containing the comma, which was verified by Barrett. This plate was printed in a pamphlet reporting on Clarke's examination of the manuscript (1805), and again in his *Concise View of the Succession of Sacred Literature* (1807). Yet another printing plate was cut for Thomas Hartwell Horne's *Introduction to the Critical Study and Knowledge of the Holy Scriptures* (1818), one of the most frequently reprinted and widely used textbooks on biblical criticism in English in the nineteenth century.[20] Clarke followed Martin in dating the manuscript to the thirteenth century, a conclusion seized upon by Thomas Burgess.[21] Readers were now in the position to see for themselves that the comma was part of the body text of the manuscript, and to draw their own conclusions from that fact.

Barrett's edition of the biblical manuscripts at Dublin appeared in 1801, with an appendix containing a collation of those parts of Montfortianus that had not been included in the London Polyglot (in essence Romans to Revelation), along with speculations on the provenance of the manuscript. Barrett's edition probably integrated Newcome's earlier work. Barrett noted the close correspondence between Montfortianus and Oxford, Lincoln College ms gr. 82 (GA 326).[22] As a result of this intensified scholarly attention, Montfortianus appeared regularly in nineteenth-century tourist guides of Dublin as a must-see.[23] Amongst those who came to inspect the manuscript was William Alleyn Evanson, who published an annotated translation of Knittel's 1785 defence of the comma in 1829.[24] But as a result of constant handling and examination by candlelight, the page containing the comma became quite soiled, and the glazing became more visible than elsewhere. 'We often hear', quipped one Irish bishop, 'that the text of the Three Heavenly Witnesses is a *gloss*; and any one that will go into the College Library may see as much for himself.'[25]

[19] Alter 1796, 179–183.
[20] Horne 1818, 2.2:118; A. Clarke 1833, 254; A. Clarke 1836, 1972.
[21] See, for example, Anon. 1821, 220, who concurs with Burgess 1821, 12, in positing an earlier date for Montfortianus.
[22] Barrett 1801, 1–2.
[23] Gamble 1811, 24; McGregor 1821, 204; Wright 1825, 17; 'X. D.,' 1841, 341.
[24] Knittel 1829, 95.
[25] Cit. Scrivener 1861, 149.

Yet Barrett's edition still failed to answer some lingering questions. Orlando Thomas Dobbin (1807–1890) therefore undertook a more detailed study of Codex Montfortianus, which duly appeared in 1854. Dobbin included a full collation of the textual variants in the gospels and Acts (excluded from Barrett's edition), and a full account of the manuscript basis for the Johannine comma, with which he intended to put an end to speculation over its textual legitimacy. Dobbin's examination of Montfortianus led him to conclude that the manuscript was written by three or four different scribes; and that the gospels were copied from GA 56 and 58, and Acts and the Epistles from GA 326. On this evidence he dated Montfortianus confidently to the sixteenth century. Regarding the Johannine comma, which he considered 'neither genuine, nor of any importance in dogmatical theology', and whose Greek expression 'manifestly betrays a translation from the Latin', Dobbin continued: 'by this single testimony the verse must stand or fall. [...] It is wanting in the Lincoln College Codex [GA 326]; – therefore its presence in the Monfort ms. is an arbitrary and unauthorised interpolation.'[26] Dobbin asserted – though without tendering any proof – that the Epistles in Montfortianus were written 'before the Erasmian controversy began'. On this basis he found no reason to conclude that the scribe had mischievous motives in inserting the comma:

> Let a moderate share of Greek scholarship be combined with a high veneration for the Latin Vulgate, and a desire to complete what is evidently a tentative text throughout, – one designed for private edification, and not for sale, – and this supposition meets all the phenomena of the case; the existence of the reading in our Codex is accounted for, and the fair fame of the author is untarnished.[27]

However, Dobbin's exoneration of the scribe was not universally accepted. A. G. Little, who accepted James Rendel Harris' theory that Montfortianus had been written by the Franciscan William Roye, characterised the production of the manuscript as 'a disreputable episode'.[28]

Dobbin also disposed of many of the other claims made about Montfortianus. He refuted the opinions of Adam Clarke and Thomas Burgess, who had claimed a great antiquity for the codex on the basis of its script. He also dismissed their argument that the textual differences between Montfortianus on the one hand and the Complutensian edition and Erasmus' text on the other proved that Montfortianus must

---

[26] Dobbin 1854, 6, 9, 57, 61.
[27] Dobbin 1854, 61–62.
[28] Little 1943, 142. On Harris' theory, see Chapter 1.6 above, 37–38.

predate the age of printing.[29] Although Dobbin was aware that his work would be controversial, he was glad to have brought clarity to an issue that had lain in such doubt. Dobbin protested all along that his motives were pious: 'We have always held as indisputable, that there is as serious damage done to the sacred oracles by the retention of doubtful Scripture in the Inspired Volume, as by the exclusion of the true.'[30] But far from being killed off by the evidence brought by Dobbin, the comma and its associated myths continued to be employed for confessional purposes of all kinds.

2. Erasmus and English Unitarianism

The situation of English Unitarians around 1800 was still difficult. In 1779, the terms of the 1689 *Act of Toleration* had been broadened to permit adherence to Scripture 'as commonly received among Protestant Churches' rather than to the Thirty-Nine Articles, but this provision still effectively excluded Antitrinitarians, who lobbied for total equality under the law. In an afterword to a 1784 reprint of the trial record of Herman van Vlekwijk, the minister Joshua Toulmin – who started as a Presbyterian, subsequently became a Baptist and ended as a Unitarian – complained that English law was 'still very heavy' against those who believed that God the Father is '*the one*, or *only God*', and that Jesus is 'inferior to Almighty God'.[31] As a result of mounting pressure, parliament passed the *Doctrine of the Trinity Act* (commonly known as the *Unitarian Relief Act*, 1813), which repealed three previous laws that discriminated against Antitrinitarians.[32] Nevertheless, Unitarians were still subject to discrimination of various kinds.

Scepticism towards the comma was still widely considered, rightly or wrongly, as good reason to suspect an individual of Unitarian leanings. This was certainly the case for Hannah Barnard, who joined a Unitarian congregation after being expelled from the Society of Friends. When asked her opinion of the comma, Barnard declared: 'I felt not the least hesitation in saying I believed it to be a corrupt interpolation, for the very purpose of establishing the absurd and pernicious doctrine of the Trinity in Unity, some ages after the first promulgation of the gospel.'[33] But while

[29] Dobbin 1854, 5.
[30] Dobbin 1854, 62.
[31] Toulmin 1784, 18–24. The trial record was extracted from G. Brandt 1720–1723. Toulmin mentions that the trial record shows how 'the writings of *Erasmus* prepared the minds of men' to accept the primitive Unitarianism of Christianity.
[32] Maclear 1995, 189.
[33] 'Christicola' 1802, 16; Maxey 1989, 73.

Unitarians were inclined to conclude that the Johannine comma was a spurious interpolation, they were also in the frustrating position of knowing that many of their opponents still clung to the passage as evidence of the Trinity.

The growing confidence of English Unitarians in the early nineteenth century was reflected in an increasing number of their publications. In 1818, the Presbyterian (later Unitarian) minister Thomas Rees (1777–1864) published an annotated English translation of the Racovian catechism, a work previously burned in England in 1609 and 1652. Rees was scathing on the comma, which he characterised as

> convicted, upon evidence the most ample and demonstrative, of shameless effrontery, fraud, and imposture; and condemned, without benefit of clergy, to excision and everlasting infamy. In death, indeed, it has not been wholly abandoned: some pious friends still pursue its ghost, and fondly clasp the airy nothing to their doting breasts. But their grief is unavailing.[34]

Two Unitarian versions of the New Testament, based on the translation of William Newcome, appeared in 1807 and 1808 respectively. The 1807 edition was edited by Timothy Brown, the 1808 edition by Thomas Belsham, though both appeared anonymously. In a discourse delivered at a Unitarian meeting at Bristol in 1800, Belsham had emphasised that readers ought to be apprised of the current conclusions over critical difficulties such as the comma, which are 'easily comprehended', even though the process of reaching those conclusions was 'most tedious and difficult'.[35] The two editions were subject to a joint critique in *The Eclectic Review* in 1809, probably written by Rev. John Pye-Smith of Homerton College, a Congregationalist seminary in Hackney.[36] Pye-Smith praised the exclusion of the comma from the 1808 New Testament, which follows Newcome here without alteration. (Brown's abbreviated New Testament does not contain the Catholic Epistles.)[37] However, Pye-Smith believed that other details of Belsham's edition, such as the translation of Jn 1:1 ('and the Word was *a* god'), promoted a theological position unacceptable to the majority of orthodox Christians.[38]

---

[34] Rees 1818, 43. On Rees, see Alexander Gordon and R. K. Webb, 'Rees, Thomas,' in *ODNB*.

[35] Belsham 1800, 7.

[36] In identifying the anonymous author as Pye-Smith I follow Orme 1830, 139. In identifying the editors of the 1807 and 1808 editions as Timothy Brown and Belsham respectively, I follow Paul 2003, 26–27, 78, 174.

[37] Pye-Smith 1809a, 248; cf. *The New Testament* 1808, 563.

[38] Pye-Smith 1809a, 335–343. As far as I could determine, the English translation 'the Word was a God' was first argued by Nye 1692, 24: 'Our Opposers themselves will not deny, because every

A certain 'J. Pharez' disagreed with Pye-Smith's conclusions, and sent him transcripts from Martin's *Examination of Emlyn's Answer*, but Pye-Smith merely referred Pharez to Porson's *Letters to Travis*.[39] Offended by what he took as a snub, Pharez published a pamphlet containing the extracts from Martin's tract as well as his own thoughts on the issue. Pharez' work was applauded by the popular readership. One reviewer calling himself 'Scrutator' remarked that 'this is a subject in which the people are interested, who have neither the opportunity, the time, nor the talent, to search MSS. for themselves.' This is an important point. It would be easy to imagine that this debate was conducted merely between archdeacons, bishops and Oxbridge dons, while the readers of smart literary magazines applauded politely from the sidelines. But there was clearly a cloud of witnesses, the 'plain folks' to whom Scrutator addressed himself, who took these issues equally seriously, even if they did not have the time or expertise to follow every detail of the debate. Many of these plain folks were no doubt women, whose effective exclusion from the public sphere rendered their contributions to the debate over the comma almost inaudible. An author like Scrutator permits us to view the debate from a different perspective, one stripped of the elegant sophistication of Porson or Marsh: 'What description of characters ever have disputed, and still do dispute the authenticity of this passage? To this question I answer, Arians and Socinians!' The comma, Scrutator insisted, was 'a barrier they must destroy before they can be quite happy in robbing CHRIST of his DEITY; and since we know this, I beg leave to be suspicious of the men, and their communications'. Scrutator's loathing was almost boundless; for him, 'Arians and Socinians are a race of miscreants that infests God's earth; like vermin of the dunghill, they are exhaled by the sun – bask in its beams; yet, while they exist by the warmth of that luminary, say, "O how I hate thy beams."'[40] Scrutator was also suspicious of the Unitarians' program of social improvement and their emphasis on the importance of individual happiness, which he feared would corrode morality and enervate the social order.[41]

Novice in Grammar knows it, that the original words should have been thus rendred, The WORD was with *the* God, and the WORD was *a* God. We claim this Translation as absolutely necessary for clearing the meaning of the Evangelist in this place.' It was immediately denounced as a Socinian intrusion by Chauncy 1693, 38.

[39] Pye-Smith 1809b, 392.

[40] 'Scrutator' 1809, 229. 'Scrutator' may have been John Loveday Jr, who wrote articles against Gibbon in the *Gentleman's Magazine* 1778, one of which appeared under this pseudonym; see McCloy 1933, 76. The end of the passage cited is a quotation from Milton, *Paradise Lost* IV.37.

[41] 'Scrutator' 1809, 230–231.

The Unitarian Robert Blackley Drummond discussed Erasmus' role in the dispute over the comma in his 1873 biography. Drummond believed that Erasmus' omission of the comma in the first two editions of his New Testament exemplified his 'courage and honesty'.[42] Drummond pinned responsibility for the production of Montfortianus on Lee, whose character was such as to have ventured such a 'pious fraud'. He recorded Erasmus' doubts about the passage (which was, according to Drummond, communicated to him in a letter), and portrayed Erasmus' decision to include the comma as a pragmatic concession made to avoid further conflict.[43] Drummond's narration implies that the comma has no place in the text, and that readers who accepted the comma as a genuine part of Scripture capitulated to untruth for the sake of irrational dogma.

The battle over the comma reached into all parts of English society. In 1834, Francis Close (1797–1882), Anglican rector of Cheltenham and proponent of evangelical education, complained that the Unitarian minister Samuel Wood, rector of the school in Harp Alley (Fleet Street), run by the British and Foreign School Society, was promoting heresy to his pupils. Until this time, the Society had expressed its satisfaction with the standards at Harp Alley.[44] But as a result of Close's complaint, Wood was summoned to appear before the House of Commons in August 1834. Wood gave a full statement of his position of the relationship between religion and education. He made sure not to give preferential bias to the beliefs of any denomination.[45] Wood confirmed that the Authorised Version was used in the school, but noted with pride that the students were informed of the findings of critics such as Griesbach. Although the comma was set down in the Scripture lessons used at the Society's school at Borough Road, Wood considered himself conscience-bound to inform his students of the critical disagreements over its authenticity. If the prescribed lesson for the day should happen to be 1 Jn 5, 'I should say distinctly to the boys, "This [the comma] is no part of Scripture, and ought not to have been inserted here."'[46] Although Wood was cleared of the charge of promoting heresy, Close pursued the matter for some years.[47]

---

[42] Drummond 1873, 1:313, 318.
[43] Drummond 1873, 1:333–335.
[44] Anon. 1833, 62.
[45] *Report from Select Committee* 1834, 159.
[46] *Report from Select Committee* 1834, 160. For the Scripture lessons of the British and Foreign Bible Society, see Allen 1820, 64. Dunn 1839, 254, reports that 1 Jn 5:7 was one of the passages cited to him by a student from the Borough Road School when he was asked to name 'some part of the scriptures that applies to doctrine'.
[47] See Close 1839.

3. Erasmus and the Johannine comma in the struggle for Catholic emancipation

Besides toleration of Nonconformists like Unitarians, the most urgent issue in nineteenth-century English religious politics was Catholic emancipation. Although Catholics and Unitarians were worlds apart theologically, the Unitarian push for toleration worked in favour of Catholic struggles for legal recognition. The Papists Act (1778) permitted Roman Catholics to purchase and inherit land in Great Britain. Under the provisions of the Roman Catholic Relief Act (1791) Catholics could exercise their religion freely and set up Catholic schools, as well as enter the legal profession. After the repeal of the Test Acts in 1829, Roman Catholics were again permitted to hold public office in the United Kingdom. The vacuum created by the removal of legal discrimination from Unitarians and Roman Catholics was soon filled by new categories of deviants, who were often conceived in medicalised terms: the insane, the feeble-minded, the pathologically criminal, the morally degenerate, the drunkard and members of inferior races, categories put on an ostensibly scientific footing in works such as Cesare Lombroso's *Criminal Man* (*L'uomo delinquente*, 1876).

A favourite topos in anti-Catholic rhetoric of the nineteenth century was the depiction of the Church of Rome as the enemy of intellectual freedom and integrity. This theme emerges in several early nineteenth-century accounts of Erasmus' dispute with Lee. According to Herbert Marsh, Erasmus' omission of the comma 'gave great offence to the members of the church of Rome, whose oracle was the Vulgate'.[48] Marsh promoted the misconception that Erasmus had never seen Montfortianus, but merely received a transcript of the passage.[49] Marsh's narrative implies that Erasmus was the victim of a confidence trick perpetrated by the Catholic authorities. This insinuation was consistent with Marsh's belief that 'the Church of Rome not only carries its Authority further, than is necessary for its own preservation, but that its authority is exercised in such a manner, as to extinguish the right of private judgment in its own members, and to trample on the rights of all other Churches'.[50]

But the story of Erasmus' purported promise to Lee could also be used by Roman Catholic apologists. Charles Butler, a Roman Catholic lawyer and amateur biblical critic, gave a different spin to the story as part

---

[48] Michaelis 1793–1801, 4:437–438; this is a reworking of a longer note in Marsh 1795, XXI–XXIII.
[49] Marsh 1812–1823, 6:24.
[50] Marsh 1816, 177–200.

of his defence of the veracity of the comma. Rather than painting Lee
and Stunica as devious or doltish, Butler emphasised their piety and reputation, and by implication the authority of the Roman Catholic church
and the integrity of its processes. Stunica's failure to produce the Rhodian
manuscript was saved by the appearance of Montfortianus, about which
Butler harboured no doubts. Erasmus, compliant and cooperative to the
last, submitted to the authority of the church, and cheerfully included the
comma in all subsequent editions of his New Testament.[51]

4.   Critical advances: Lachmann and Tischendorf

The philologist Karl Lachmann, who had developed a method for establishing the text of Old High German sagas, turned his attention to the
New Testament in the late 1820s. He departed from the recension theory of Wettstein, Bengel and Griesbach, and rather than trying to recover
the original authorial text, he set about instead to reconstruct the text of
the New Testament as it existed in the fourth century. In fact Lachmann,
in sidestepping the troublesome concept of an 'original text', was conceptually close to the methods of the Institut für Neutestamentliche
Textforschung at the University of Münster, which likewise aims to establish the *Ausgangstext* of the transmission.[52] Lachmann set out his method
in an article published in 1830.[53] Like Bentley, who intended to retrieve
'the true Exemplar of *Origen*, which was the Standard to the most Learned
of the *Fathers*, at the time of the Council of *Nice* and two Centuries after',
Lachmann employed an approach that was synchronic rather than dia-
chronic.[54] His method was to work on the basis of a small number of the
oldest manuscripts, without trying to account for readings in later ones.
He gave his manuscripts equal weighting, though when required to choose
between conflicting readings he considered external evidence such as the
Latin Vulgate or Scriptural citations in the works of Irenaeus and Origen.
Although he did not consciously employ Griesbach's recensional groups,
the manuscripts he used happened to come from Griesbach's Alexandrian
group. Lachmann's edition broke decisively with the *textus receptus*. Since
his text was based entirely on early manuscripts, the comma does not

---

[51] Butler 1807, 2:257–258.
[52] Epp 1999; B. Aland 2003; Elliott 2009a.
[53] His method is set out in Lachmann 1830 and 1835. Further, see Tregelles 1854, 97–115;
Timpanaro 2005.
[54] Bentley 1721, 3–4.

appear in the body text, nor even in the critical apparatus.[55] However, his method struck some as arbitrary and restrictive. Reviewers complained of the lack of a proper preface, in lieu of which readers were simply referred to Lachmann's 1830 article. Moreover, the fact that his edition was useful only to a small coterie of critics, not the general run of students who needed a uniform text for their studies, meant that it did not receive the attention it deserved until his readings were integrated into the critical apparatus of later editions.[56]

In 1841, Constantin von Tischendorf published an edition of the Greek New Testament in some ways even more radical than that of Lachmann, even if it drew on a wider manuscript base. Tischendorf excluded many controversial passages, but explained his editorial choices in the apparatus. Tischendorf excised the comma from the body text and marked it as an addition in the *textus receptus*.[57] The edition was immediately acclaimed, and the Parisian publisher Firmin Didot entered into negotiations with Tischendorf for a reprint. However, conservative elements within the French clergy wished to block publication. Tischendorf knew that it would have been hopeless to expect the Roman Catholic clergy to treasure the Protestant *textus receptus* higher than the Latin Vulgate. In consultation with Jean Nicolas Jager, professor at the Sorbonne, Tischendorf conceived the idea of publishing a diglot edition, with the Latin Vulgate accompanied by a Greek text that reflected the readings of the Latin, but drawn wherever possible from Greek manuscripts. Accordingly, this edition includes features typical of the Clementine Vulgate, including the comma, although the absence of this passage from the Greek manuscripts is signalled in the apparatus in the appendix. Tischendorf hoped that this edition, published in 1842 with a dedication to Denis-Auguste Affre, archbishop of Paris, would encourage the study of the Greek New Testament amongst Roman Catholic students, who would move on to better editions once they had acquired a taste for the Greek text.[58] Tischendorf's French critics were apparently satisfied, and Didot released Tischendorf's critical text the same year, with a revised apparatus in the appendix.[59] Tischendorf knew that the diglot edition would attract negative press in Germany, and he published a sheepish defence of his recent editions in the *New*

---

[55] Lachmann 1831, 297, 487.
[56] Gregory 1900–1909, 2:966–972; Horne 1835–1836, 2:18, had not seen Lachmann's 1830 article, and had difficulty understanding his method.
[57] Tischendorf 1841, 615–616.
[58] Tischendorf 1842b, 380–381; appendix (*lectiones variantes*), 32–33.
[59] Tischendorf 1842a, 495; *lectiones variantes*, 80.

Jena General Journal of Literature in April 1843, warding off potential criticism by arguing that if the text he had established was not perfect, it was
in any case better than the *textus receptus*. Moreover, he pointed out that
he had laid bare doubtful readings, such as the comma, in the critical
apparatus.[60] Despite the carping of scholars – Caspar René Gregory could
scarcely believe that Tischendorf had even contemplated such a project –
the diglot edition received personal plaudits from Pope Gregory XVI.[61]

The techniques perfected by nineteenth-century philologists like
Tischendorf for studying genealogical relationships between textual
sources had a surprising parallel in Darwin's theory of evolution. Darwin's
techniques for tracing the descent of species through homologies and analogies were analogous to those used by textual critics, who used the minute
changes from one copy of a given text to another to reconstruct genealogical trees of extant texts and even 'missing links' whose existence, form and
even location was suggested by the extant evidence. Nineteenth-century
philologists used similar techniques to trace the development of families
of languages. These similarities were not lost on Darwin.[62]

5.   Renewed defence of the *textus receptus*

Advances in biblical philology in the late eighteenth and nineteenth
centuries caused considerable anxiety, especially when textual questions
seemed to impinge on doctrine. Such anxieties prompted conservatives
to put their case in ever more strident terms, and increasingly to insist
on notions such as inerrancy, which had played little role in earlier attitudes to Scripture.[63] Frederick Nolan (1815) feared that the work of critics like Griesbach had undermined doctrine by threatening the textual
integrity of passages such as Jn 7:53–8:11 (the woman caught in adultery),
Acts 20:28 (the command to the bishops), 1 Tim 3:16 and the Johannine
comma. Nolan therefore set about to prove the inspiration, and thus the
accuracy, of the *textus receptus*. His view of inspiration was far from sim-
plistic. He considered that an insistence on the 'literal identity between
the present copies of the inspired text, and the original edition' was 'a
vulgar errour' and 'repugnant to reason'. On the other hand, he maintained that belief in the doctrinal integrity of the bible is 'necessary to the

---

[60] Tischendorf 1843, esp. 328.
[61] Tischendorf 1859, 1:CXXVI.
[62] Dennett 1995, 136–138.
[63] Mandelbrote 2001, 35–37.

conviction of our faith'.[64] In his judgement, the efforts of biblical critics had not brought us any closer to God's word. Instead, they were 'so far from having established the integrity of any particular text, that they have unsettled the foundation on which the entire canon is rested'.[65]

Nolan believed that the text of the bible had become compromised especially during the persecutions of Diocletian, when many manuscripts were destroyed, and at the hands of Eusebius, whose recension was 'peculiarly accommodated to the opinions of the Arians'.[66] In Nolan's view, biblical criticism should aim to restore the Greek text to the pristine state it had enjoyed before these two periods of confusion. The passages threatened by the slashing of Griesbach's pen would then emerge as original constituent parts of the Greek text, and the *textus receptus*, which Nolan considered to represent this original 'Vulgar Greek' text most closely, could be used to defend doctrine against modern-day heretics and rationalist critics. The response to Nolan's work was mixed. One reviewer crowed that it had 'given an effectual check to Socinian insolence'.[67] By contrast, Samuel Prideaux Tregelles characterised Nolan's manner of argumentation as 'peculiarly repulsive and uncandid'.[68]

By the middle of the nineteenth century, England had fallen well behind Germany in cutting-edge biblical philology. Tregelles was one of the few English critics of international reputation, and even he never held a university position. In 1860 there appeared a distillation of recent continental biblical scholarship for Anglophone readers, modestly titled *Essays and Reviews* (1860). The program of this collection is encapsulated in Benjamin Jowett's dictum: 'Interpret the Scripture like any other book.'[69] The collection immediately set off a heated controversy between conservatives and moderns. Charles Forster, preacher at Canterbury cathedral, published a defence of the *textus receptus* in 1867.[70] Forster was particularly perturbed by the rejection of the comma by 'progressives'. He identified Richard Simon as the fountainhead of critical opposition to this passage, and blamed Porson for bringing the issue to the attention of a wider public. Their arguments had weighed heavily on Forster's heart for some thirty-six years, but he had finally been motivated to write a defence

---

[64] Nolan 1815, VII.
[65] Nolan 1815, VIII.
[66] Nolan 1815, 28.
[67] Anon. 1816, 23.
[68] Tregelles, in Horne 1856, 93.
[69] Jowett 1860, 377. Further, see Sheehan 2005, 251–252.
[70] Forster 1867, 1–2.

when he saw the 'mutilated text' of Wordsworth's Greek Testament (1866), which excised the comma on the authority of Griesbach, Scholz, Lachmann and Tischendorf. But Forster warned that Wordsworth's 'very learned, and very elaborate, edition' was jeopardised by 'a false first principle of Scripture criticism', namely 'the rejection of a common Textus Receptus'. According to Forster, any departure from this *textus receptus* 'makes every man, at once, the manufacturer of his own Bible, and the dictator of that Bible as the standard for all others'. For Forster, there was only one answer: 'as the rejection of the Textus Receptus is the sole cause of the evil, so the restoration of the Textus Receptus is its only remedy'. Biblical scholarship based on critical editions risked exposing tender consciences to 'the sport of every novelty-loving scholastic speculatist'.[71] But by this time, critics like Forster were swimming against the tide.

6.   Westcott, Hort and the Revised Version

The most thoroughgoing revisions to the Greek text of the New Testament undertaken in the Anglophone world of the late nineteenth century were due in large part to two men: Brooke Foss Westcott (1825–1901) and Fenton John Anthony Hort (1828–1892). These two scholars worked together for some twenty-eight years to construct a Greek text of the New Testament based on the advances of earlier scholars such as Tischendorf and Tregelles. Westcott and Hort distinguished the families of texts proposed by Bengel into further divisions, and proposed two new ideas: first, that the Syrian text (the basis of the Byzantine text) had been subject to two separate recensions; and that there existed a pre-recensional text close to that written by the original authors.[72]

Such advances in the study of the Greek text, alongside the proliferation of sectarian translations in the nineteenth century, led to a general conviction of the desirability of a non-denominational revision of the Authorised Version.[73] The committee for the revision, headed by Westcott and Hort, decided that it would not construct a new Greek text upon which to base its revision. However, wherever they considered that recent textual scholarship had established a better reading than that presumed to have been used for the Authorised Version, and that such an improved

---

[71] Forster 1867, vii–xii; C. Wordsworth 1866, 2:123.
[72] Gregory 1900–1909, 2:917–921.
[73] See Thuesen 1996.

reading would materially alter the English translation, they added it to a list of variants to be used in the revision.

John Burgon (1813–1888), the conservative dean of Chichester, vigorously opposed the methodology of Westcott and Hort. Burgon favoured the Majority (Byzantine) text, though his attitude towards the *textus receptus* was less than enthusiastic: 'we do not, by any means, claim perfection for the Received Text. We entertain no extravagant notions on this subject. Again and again we shall have occasion to point out [...] that the *Textus Receptus* needs correction.'[74] Burgon's principal objection to the revision was the editorial methodology adopted by the committee, 'the new German system', which he felt gave disproportionate weight to minority readings; and the way in which the committee structure failed to do justice to the opinions of those dissenters, like Frederick H. A. Scrivener (1813–1891), who wanted to stay closer to the Majority Text. It is worth noting that Burgon never objected publicly to the excision of the comma by the revision committee.[75] Indeed, he quoted with approval Griesbach's warning that those who defend the comma undermine the entire project of textual criticism.[76] In contrast to Burgon's rather refined position, the revision prompted a less nuanced popular defence of the *textus receptus* as the basis of several revered national versions, such as the Authorised Version and the Dutch States Version (*Statenvertaling*), which conservatives in Britain, America and the Netherlands hailed not merely as repositories of true doctrine, but also as hallowed cultural documents, a 'priceless treasure which was bequeathed to them by the piety and wisdom of their fathers'.[77]

Anglican reaction of the Revised Version was generally positive. In a sermon given on 5 June 1881 at Collyhurst, James Fraser, bishop of Manchester, declared that there was 'not one single article of the Christian Creed, either the Apostles' Creed, the Nicene, or that of St. Athanasius, in the slightest degree affected' by alterations to critically suspect passages such as the *pericope de adultera*, the ending of Mark, Luke's rendering of the Lord's Prayer, or the Johannine comma.[78] At the Church Congress at Newcastle-on-Tyne, held on 8 October 1881, Joseph Lightfoot, bishop of Durham, remarked that the continued presence of the comma in the

[74] Burgon 1883, 21 n. 2; Wallace 2013, 713–714; G. Martin Murphy, 'Burgon, John William', in *ODNB*.
[75] Wallace 2013, 714.
[76] Burgon 1883, 483; White 2009, 103–104.
[77] Burgon 1883, 232.
[78] *The Huddersfield Daily Chronicle* 4318 (7 June 1881), 4.

Authorised Version was a stumbling block to the ordinary reader, as *The Times* reported:

> People would discover accidentally that it had no authority whatever. Some popular – perhaps Secularist – lecturer, or he knew not who, would tell them so, and they would jump to the conclusion that the great doctrines which appeared in the passage rested upon it, and therefore fell to the ground. The sooner they swept away such a passage as that the better for them all. (Cheers.)[79]

A reviewer in *The Times* praised the excision of verses such as the comma: 'It has long been felt as a weakness in our version that unquestionable errors of this kind exist in its text, and it will be a great practical gain to get rid of them.'[80] By contrast, the revision received a blistering critique in the *Dublin Review*:

> The Revisers have left out the whole verse in 1 John v. 7, 8, without one word of explanation. Surely no one but a textual critic could be capable of such a deed. [...] But textual critics are like book-worms – devoid of light and conscience, following the blind instincts of their nature, they will make holes in the most sacred of books.[81]

The reviewer also pointed out that the atomisation of the biblical text by critics put strain on the Protestant principle of *sola scriptura*. If *scriptura* is no longer assured, what happens to confidence in doctrine? The reviewer also feared for the social impact of criticism. The editors of the Revised Version had suggested that the best way to convert the working classes was to present them with a trustworthy text of the bible that they could understand. 'Heaven help the poor working man,' shrilled the reviewer, 'if his sole hope of salvation lies in the new Gospel of Textual Criticism!'[82] What the working classes needed was a church that could interpret the bible to them with confidence and love. The only church competent to do that was the Roman Catholic church. 'Scripture is powerless without the Church as the witness to its inspiration, the safeguard of its integrity, and the exponent of its meaning. And it will now be clear to all men which is the true Church, the real Mother to whom the Bible of right belongs. Nor will it need Solomon's wisdom to see that the so-called Church which heartlessly gives up the helpless child to be cut in pieces by textual critics cannot be the true Mother.'[83] This attitude was typical of a conservative

[79] Anon. 1881c, 10.
[80] Anon. 1881a, 4.
[81] Anon. 1881b, 141.
[82] Anon. 1881b, 144.
[83] Anon. 1881b, 144.

stream within the Roman Catholic church, but it would not be long before that church was likewise rent by critical disputes.

The work of the textual scholar Frederick Henry Ambrose Scrivener illustrates the still-powerful gravitational pull of the Authorised Version in the nineteenth century. Scrivener's expertise in biblical studies was considerable, and he did valuable work on important early manuscripts like Codex Bezae. He published two different editions of the New Testament. The first presents the text of Estienne's 1550 edition, with variants given from Bèze, the *textus receptus*, Lachmann, Tischendorf and Tregelles. It went through four printings. In 1876 Scrivener completed his integration of Tregelles' variants, and updated Tischendorf's variants from the latter's eighth edition (1869/1872). In 1886 he added the variants from Westcott and Hort, and the Greek text upon which the Revised Version was supposed to be founded. The last edition of Scrivener's text of Estienne was published by Eberhard Nestle in 1906.[84] Scrivener devoted the last years of his life to another edition, a reconstruction of the Greek text presumed to underlie the Authorised Version. This edition was founded largely on Beza's text of 1598, which was in Scrivener's opinion 'more likely than any other to be in the hands of King James's revisers, and to be accepted by them as the best standard within their reach'. Where the Authorised Version seemed not to reflect Bèze's text, Scrivener surmised that the translators had used the reading from other printed editions of the Greek text, some of which he could identify, or from variants given in Bèze's critical notes. In certain cases he could show that the translators of the Authorised Version simply wanted to retain Tyndale's wording, or followed the Latin Vulgate rather than any known Greek reading.[85] Scrivener gave his reconstruction as the body text. Where the editors of the Revised Version had chosen different readings, he gave the text in smaller type and footnoted the variant adopted by the revisers. One such section was the Johannine comma.[86] A slightly revised edition was published in 1894, after Scrivener's death.[87] This 1894 edition remains the authorised Greek text of

---

[84] Scrivener 1859 (*DM* 4888; repr. 1861, 1862, 1864, 1865, 1867, 1868, 1870, 1871, 1873, 1875); Scrivener 1876 (repr. 1877, 1878, 1881, 1883, 1886); Scrivener 1886 (repr. 1900, 1902); Scrivener 1906 (*DM* 4955); see also Darlow and Moule 1903–1911, 2:660, 666, 673. Further, see E. C. Marchant and D. C. Parker, 'Scrivener, Frederick Henry Ambrose', in *ODNB*.

[85] Scrivener 1881, VII–IX.

[86] Scrivener 1881, V–VI, 594.

[87] Scrivener 1894a, 594; in this new edition, the discrepancies between the presumed Greek text of the Authorised Version and the variants adopted by the revisers are not set in smaller type, but in spaced lettering.

conservative groups such as the Trinitarian Bible Society.[88] The inclusion of the comma in Scrivener's 1881/1894 edition of the Greek text underlying the Authorised Version has lent the verse a spurious authority, even if Scrivener considered that the authenticity of the comma could 'no longer be maintained by any one whose judgement ought to have weight'.[89]

7.   The Johannine comma and the Catholic modernist crisis

During the last third of the nineteenth century, conflicting priorities brought about massive changes within the Roman Catholic church. On one hand, some Catholics wished to come to terms with the social, intellectual and religious challenges of the day, such as Darwinism, text-critical issues and the 'historical Jesus' movement. Others wanted to fend off 'Americanism' and 'the illusions of a Kantianism and of a Protestantism absolutely devoid of any true Christian principle'.[90] During his long incumbency (1878–1903), Pope Leo XIII rode the rough waves of this modernist crisis, but not always with success. In his encyclical *Providentissimus* (1893), he attempted to clarify the Catholic approach towards the study of Scripture. This document was aimed specifically against Protestants and rationalists, who denied revelation and inspiration, dismissing Scripture as a congeries of feeble lies, and biblical prophecy either as 'predictions' recorded after the fact, or simply as natural phenomena. However, this document also encouraged critical study of the biblical texts in Hebrew and Greek, so long as it was carried out in a faithful spirit. This led to a tentative bloom of historical-critical study amongst Catholic scholars, especially in France. However, the same period was also a high water mark for Catholic dogmatics, especially under the influence of the prevailing Neo-Thomism. Influential dogmatists like Giovanni Perrone were of the opinion that Catholic exegetes only needed to know enough about biblical criticism to defend the truths of the faith.[91] It was only a matter of time until the interests of traditional dogmatists and historical modernists would come into conflict.

One issue that precipitated this conflict was the authenticity of the comma. The Austrian Jesuit (and later cardinal) Johann Baptist Franzelin (1816–1886), professor of dogmatics at the Roman College, who

---

[88]   www.tbsbibles.org/basis/doctrine-of-holy-scripture, accessed 1 January 2016.
[89]   Scrivener 1894b, 401.
[90]   Jules Didiot to Charles Maignen, 17 June 1898, trans. in Gibson 1899, 787.
[91]   Turvasi 1979, 15–16.

contributed to the formulation of the doctrine of papal infallibility, considered the question of the comma in his treatise on the Trinity (1869).[92] Franzelin maintained that the church has been charged with the task of guarding over Scripture, assisted by the Holy Spirit. For this reason the council of Trent commanded that all those books 'customarily read in the Catholic church and included in the ancient Latin Vulgate version' were to be accepted as canonical. Not simply was each book of Scripture considered canonical, but also every detail of its text. Anyone who taught otherwise was by definition anathema.[93] Franzelin believed that the genuineness of the comma could be proven on theological grounds, and guaranteed by the authority of the church:

> According to the Catholic principles that it is the task of the church, with the assistance of the Holy Spirit, to guard the sacred Scriptures as public instruments of revelation, and to distinguish them from human texts, the passage 1 Jn 5:7 ought to be considered genuine. As concerns the manner of conservation, there exist documents which go towards showing the immemorial antiquity of this reading, and these constitute a historical defence sufficient for legitimate judges to determine that the text has an apostolic origin. Moreover, those documents produced to the contrary do not prove that it is an interpolation, although they do reveal that when codices were being copied, the omission of the text was more or less widespread even in antiquity.[94]

When put in these terms, it seemed only reasonable that the church should protect this fragment of the Scriptures over which it had been commissioned to watch. Franzelin's position was motivated not merely by a doctrinal *a priori*, but also by a certain denominational chauvinism. Since Protestant critics had repudiated the authority of the church as custodian and interpreter of the word of God, Franzelin imagined them 'blown about by every wind of doctrine, unable to understand the Catholic method instituted by Christ from his economy, and unable to rely on its assistance as long as they are in the grip of their fundamental error'.[95] A similarly positive attitude towards the comma influenced those who drew up the liturgy for the feast of the Most Precious Blood (1 July), introduced into the Roman calendar in 1849, in which the pericope 1 Jn 5:5–8, including the comma, is used as the versicle to the gradual, *Hic est qui venit per aquam.*[96]

---

[92] Franzelin 1869, 38–90; on Franzelin's role in Vatican I, see Lio 1986.
[93] Franzelin 1869, 42.
[94] Franzelin 1869, 38.
[95] Franzelin 1869, 38.
[96] *Graduale sacrosanctae Romanae ecclesiae*, 537–538; *Liber Usualis*, 1533–1534.

Amongst the Catholic biblical critics who took a historical, even quantitative view of the question was Jean-Pierre Paulin Martin. The fifth volume of Martin's *Introduction to the textual criticism of the New Testament*, based on lectures given at the École supérieure de théologie at Paris in 1885–1886, contains a detailed account of many hundreds of variant manuscript readings of the comma which he had collected over three decades. Despite his confessed affection for the verse as a neat summary of the doctrine of the Trinity, this evidence convinced Martin that the comma was an allegorical interpolation. As far as he was concerned, the question was still open, since the church had never officially declared the comma to be absolutely authentic, even if such a conclusion might be inferred from the Tridentine pronouncement on the integrity of the Latin Vulgate. However, Martin pointed out that the church had never maintained that the Latin Vulgate was anything more than an imperfect rendering of the perfect Word of God, or that the printed editions of the Vulgate were anything more than an imperfect record of Jerome's imperfect version. Nevertheless, Martin conceded that if the church were to pronounce in favour of the comma, its members would be obliged to accept this decision, even if it ran contrary to their own personal inclinations.[97]

Martin's summary of his conclusions, published in the *Revue des sciences ecclésiastiques* in 1887, set off a spasm of controversy, and a number of rebuttals were submitted to the *Revue*. The first came from Pierre Rambouillet, vicar at Saint-Philippe-du-Roule, an enemy of modernism, who argued that the Arians, 'heretics as cunning as they were daring', had corrupted the text of 1 Jn.[98] The second was from Auguste-François Manoury, who defended the comma as authentic in his commentary on the Catholic Epistles (1888). Manoury challenged Martin's position that the Greek manuscripts present the authentic text of the Scriptures, and that the failure of the Greek fathers to cite the comma in their polemics against the Arians suggested that it was not present in their bibles. A third refutation came from Jean-Michel-Alfred Vacant, a student of the decrees of Vatican I. The fourth came from Jules Didiot, who condemned Martin's desire to downgrade to the rank of pseudepigrapha those passages present in the Vulgate but not in the Hebrew bible or the earliest Greek manuscripts of the New Testament – the Song of the Three Young Men and the story of Susanna in Daniel, the woman caught in adultery in John, the longer ending of Mark, or the Johannine comma – as a violation of the

---

[97] J.-P. P. Martin 1887, 100.
[98] On Rambouillet, see Montclos 1996, 217–218.

decree of the council of Trent. Martin's error, Didiot suggested, arose from his failure to distinguish *partes* of the Scripture from *particulae*. What is worse, Didiot chafed, if the church cut itself loose from the Vulgate and had recourse only to the Hebrew text of the Old Testament, it might be compelled to cede to the rabbis in its exegesis.[99] Martin defended his position in a series of replies, likewise published in the *Revue*.

The controversy in France created unrest elsewhere as well. In a lecture delivered before the General conference of the Silesian Lutheran Union at Liegnitz on 12 October 1892, Wilhelm Kölling eulogised the comma as 'a precious and genuine pearl of the canon' and a 'masterpiece of the heavenly inspirer', which had been removed from the text in the interests of promoting heresy.[100] The lecture went down badly. Emil Schürer lamented that Kölling's lecture threatened a retrograde reformation back to the seventeenth century.[101] Eberhard Nestle characterised such attempted defences of the comma by Protestants as of 'pathological interest'.[102]

As a result of the controversy over the comma, the Congregation of the Inquisition submitted it to investigation, with the aim of making a definitive pronouncement. These discussions were guided by the recent encyclical *Providentissimus*, which pronounced that scholars should only admit to the presence of scribal errors in the biblical manuscripts when the evidence was unambiguous. But in the case of the comma, textual evidence was trumped by considerations of doctrine. As the Italian modernist Giovanni Genocchi complained bitterly, the result of the discussion was a forgone conclusion: 'A syllogism was made, taking Franzelin's thesis as a base. Every dogmatic text of the Vulgate is authentic. Atqui. Ergo. But it is not in the Greek codices. Respondeo: if it is not there, it must be. Look more closely and you will find it.'[103] Accordingly, on 13 January 1897, the Congregation voted that it was not safe or even permissible to call the genuineness of the comma into doubt.[104] The decision of the Congregation was ratified two days later by Pope Leo XIII.

This decision unleashed a dispute over its meaning and implications. Some argued that it meant that the text was 'really written by St John, or rather dictated, and was therefore originally located in his epistle, not inserted in some later century'. Others read the declaration as an

[99] Didiot 1890, 207–210.
[100] Kölling 1893, 3, 17.
[101] Schürer 1894, 110; cf. C. R. Gregory 1907, 131.
[102] Nestle 1899, 260.
[103] Genocchi to Umberto Fracassini, professor of Scripture at Perugia, 24 May 1903, trans. in Turvasi 1979, 16.
[104] Denzinger 2001, 997, § 3681.

admission that the comma was not part of the Greek text of the epistle, though its place in the authentic Vulgate rendered it useful for use in dogmatic arguments.[105] The modernist Louis Duchesne was bitterly opposed to the decision, and made his displeasure known, at least amongst friends.[106] The modernist priest and biblical scholar Alfred Loisy wrote to Eudoxe Irénée Mignot, bishop of Fréjus, on 11 February 1897, suggesting that the journalist Émile Dillon, now resident in the United Kingdom, should be asked to write a piece about 'the church's thought-police' for the *Nineteenth Century*. Mignot suggested that it would be tactically smarter to publish something in the French press, since the *Nineteenth Century* did not have many readers in France or at Rome.[107] Loisy considered the Congregation's decision 'une gaffe monumentale', which proved that the decisions of the Holy Office were indeed 'très faillibles'.[108] Mignot drafted a letter to Leo XIII, pointing out that the pronouncement on the comma was redundant, a 'décision de luxe', since the doctrine of the Trinity does not depend on this one passage. Moreover, the decree was dangerous, since the Congregation risked seeming both fallible and foolish as soon as a Catholic scholar should prove that the comma is an interpolation. The decree also gave non-Catholic scholars even more reason to conclude that Roman Catholic scholarship had fallen embarrassingly behind recent advances in biblical criticism. The church, concluded the bishop, ought to leave scholars a certain liberty, if only to give them the means to defend it against its adversaries. However, it is not clear if the letter was ever sent.[109]

The report on the Congregation's decision in *The Tablet*, the British Catholic weekly, on 8 May 1897, provoked an angry letter from Baron Friedrich von Hügel, a leader of the Catholic modernist movement in England, printed in *The Tablet* on 5 June 1897.[110] The Catholic convert William Gibson, Baron Ashbourne, suggested that two recent decrees – that on the comma, and that which granted Thomism an exclusive place of privilege over other philosophical systems – were symptomatic of the Vatican's desire 'to consolidate the system, to ensure unity of teaching, and to silence all discordant notes'.[111]

The French Jesuit Joseph Brucker declared that even though he personally believed that the authenticity of the comma could be defended, he

[105] Hetzenauer 1900, 198.
[106] O'Connell 1994, 168.
[107] A. Loisy to Mignot, 11 February 1897, cit. Sardella 2004, 297.
[108] A. Loisy to Mignot, 17 April 1897, ed. in Bécamel 1968, 260, cit. Sardella 2004, 297.
[109] Cit. Sardella 2004, 298.
[110] Anon. 1897a; von Hügel 1897.
[111] Gibson 1899, 785.

did not see, 'even after the declaration of the Holy Office, that Catholic exegetes should be obliged to consider it certain'. However, given that the inauthenticity of the comma had not been proven definitively, it was best not to reject it, for fear of losing a precious fragment of revelation. In such a state of uncertainty, the best course was to maintain the passage, at least provisionally.[112] The American Paulist father William Sullivan character-ised Brucker's statement as typical of 'many similar interpretations con-trived by Catholic theologians to extricate themselves from the evidently uncomfortable position in which the Inquisition has placed them'.[113]

By contrast, some Catholic scholars rejoiced at the decree. The Austrian Capuchin Michael Hetzenauer argued that the Congregation's deci-sion had spread 'a very welcome light over the whole involved question'. However, Hetzenauer's understanding of the implications of the decrees of Trent and Vatican I were questioned by more than one reviewer.[114] Joseph Pohle, professor of dogmatic theology at Breslau, likewise applauded the Commission's decision.[115]

As Loisy and Mignot feared, the decision attracted criticism from out-side the Catholic church. The prominent Protestant textual critic Caspar René Gregory found it astonishing that the Congregation, which con-tained many learned men, had nevertheless 'permitted itself to be advised on a textual question by men ignorant of, or incapable of judging of, the text-critical work of the last fifty years'. He also regretted that this 'ill-advised, warped decision' forced scholars to prevaricate and equivocate for fear of running up against the authority of the Congregation.[116] Such critique from outside the Catholic church caused considerable resentment within.[117]

The form of the decree led to disagreement over its implications. Decisions of the Congregation were intended merely to direct scholars how to avoid error, and as such were disciplinary rather than doctrinal. As the editors of *The Tablet* explained to their readers, a decision made by the Congregation that a given proposition may not safely be taught did not

> foreclose research upon the opinion, nor would it even prevent the author, or those who are like-minded, from accumulating and strengthening the

---

[112] Brucker 1900, 403.

[113] Sullivan 1906–1907, 178–179.

[114] Hetzenauer 1900, 187–206, at 206. Hetzenauer first published his views in the *Katholische Kirchenzeitung* (Salzburg) in 1898 and 1899, with particular reference to the decision of the Congregation. His conclusions were opposed by 'Vindex' 1899; and Gregory 1907, 133.

[115] Pohle 1915, 33–34.

[116] Gregory 1907, 132, 137.

[117] Anon. 1897b.

evidence which might go to support it. But it would prevent the minds of the faithful at large from being misled or troubled, or disedified by having this new opinion put before them as if it were part and parcel of the safe and authorized public teaching, covered by the sanction of the Church.[118]

It was also pointed out that the pope's ratification of the Congregation's decision was made *in forma communi* rather than *in forma solemni*. Since it lacked the delegated power of papal infallibility, it could not preclude further investigation.[119] Such distinctions could be confusing or even meaningless to those unfamiliar with the structures of authority and discipline within the Catholic church. For C. R. Gregory, this distinction seemed 'very much like saying something, but says nothing at all'.[120] Cardinal Vaughan assured Wilfrid Ward, editor of the *Dublin Review*, that the decision was 'not intended to close the discussion on the authenticity of that text. The field of Biblical Criticism is not touched by this decree.'[121] Gregory noted with acerbic irony, 'It is hard to see what else is touched by the decree, yet we may well rejoice at this assurance that biblical criticism at all events, is not.'[122]

Leo XIII was succeeded in 1903 by the conservative Pius X. One of his first acts was to approve the Pontifical Biblical Commission founded by Leo XIII at the end of his life. Amongst the consultants were some modernists, including Genocchi, who immediately set about lobbying to have the Congregation's decree on the comma overturned. 'That', Genocchi wrote to his friend Umberto Fracassini, 'would be a triumph of the Commission'. Accordingly, Genocchi was charged to investigate whether Franzelin's thesis was consonant with the decree of Trent. Although the Commission agreed unanimously that the 1897 decree should be rejected, implementation of this decision was frustrated by the intervention of the conservative antimodernist Thomist Louis Billot. Genocchi lamented the defeat as 'a second Galileo case'.[123]

It was a difficult situation. As Teófilo Ayuso Marazuela was later to explain, many Catholic biblical scholars felt forced onto the horns of a dilemma: were they to follow the Tridentine decree and uphold the integrity of the Vulgate, or to respect the evidence offered by all the other

---

[118] Anon. 1897b, 921.
[119] Pohle 1915, 33; further, see Fries 1996, 608–609.
[120] Gregory 1907, 137.
[121] *The Guardian* (Church of England journal), 9 June 1897, 27; 16 June 1897, 26; Gregory 1907, 132.
[122] Gregory 1907, 133.
[123] Turvasi 1979, 16–17; Fogarty 2013, 253.

documents of the early church? Would they be forced to turn their back on history and research to remain faithful sons of the church, or abandon the faith to follow the dictates of criticism? But there was a way out. Ayuso realised that investigating the earliest textual forms of the Vulgate was a way to remain faithful to the Tridentine decree. 'And just like that,' he concluded, 'the critical problem disappears. What is more, the dogmatic problem disappears.'[124]

August Bludau, professor at Münster and subsequently Roman Catholic bishop of Ermland (East Prussia), was of the same mind. In 1902, he published an article on the beginnings of the dispute over the genuineness of the comma in the sixteenth century. The article began with explicit reference to the 1897 decision, and lamented the fact that the exertions of so many learned men had not managed to reach any consensus on the question of the comma. The issue would continue to occupy Bludau for the following twenty-five years, and resulted in a dozen articles which remain useful for their thoroughness, if not for any great critical insight.

In 1905, Karl Künstle, professor at Freiburg im Breisgau, published one of the most important books yet to appear on the origins of the comma, issued with the imprimatur of Thomas Nörber, archbishop of Freiburg. But the imprimatur was bought at a price. Even though Künstle's findings confirmed that the comma was not a genuine part of the Scripture, he emphasised that his results did not contradict the 1897 decree, affirming that the comma, even if not an original part of the Johannine epistle, nevertheless 'contains a dogmatically powerful proof for the Trinitarian conception of God in the spirit of John the Evangelist'.[125]

Künstle's book caused some unease. The Benedictine Laurent Janssens suggested that Künstle's protestations betrayed a certain anxiety about the conclusions to which his investigations had led him. Janssens regretted that Künstle felt compelled to try to circumvent the decree, which, he emphasised, had only disciplinary force anyway.[126] Künstle's weasel-words were also criticised by Caspar René Gregory.[127] William Sullivan concluded from the appearance of Künstle's book that 'however the words of the Inquisition be understood, refined away, or evaded, at all events they leave criticism with a free field in the examination of this text'. In the year since the appearance of his book, Künstle's work had 'met with no ecclesiastical

[124] Ayuso 1947–1948, 98–99.
[125] Künstle 1905, 56.
[126] Janssens 1906, 118.
[127] Gregory 1907, 137.

censure, and is not likely even to provoke a serious reply'.[128] In an editorial for the *Expository Times* in November 1906, the Presbyterian minister James Hastings expressed his disquiet at Sullivan's remarks. 'It may be,' he warned, 'that the Church of Rome can afford to make decrees and ignore them, but no Church on earth can afford to drive its students more than once or twice to such intellectual and moral makeshifts.'[129]

Hastings' comments on Künstle's book and on the Biblical Commission's reactionary statement on the authorship of the Pentateuch (27 June 1906) provoked two published responses: one from Jacques Chevalier in Paris, and another from an anonymous correspondent in Rome. Chevalier explained patiently that the decisions of the Congregation and the Commission were not made principally to fetter scientific investigation, but out of pastoral concern for unlettered believers who might be confused by the investigations of scholars. 'It is not,' Chevalier explained, 'always advisable to proclaim to the Church at large what is thought and said in the secret of the Cabinet.' A religious fact is not like a scientific fact, but 'has a direct connexion with our moral life', governing our conduct. We must not therefore think of such questions 'in a purely intellectual way'.[130] Künstle's book illustrated the 'double aspect' of any religious question:

> The general public who do not read the works of critics will continue to live in peace, while Catholic scholars will continue to examine texts in a scientific way without being at all eager to disturb the minds of the mass of worshippers, who all the while take part in the same worship and have the same beliefs as they, although not so definite, and resting upon different grounds.[131]

This attitude, considered pastorally sensitive from the Catholic perspective, seemed both paternalistic and duplicitous to Protestant readers. But the principle of Scriptural inerrancy and the rejection of biblical criticism, fast becoming widespread in conservative Evangelical circles at this same time, was simply another way of avoiding the doubts that engagement with critical issues could stir up.

By contrast, the anonymous letter from Rome expressed the author's anger that Hastings should have presumed to comment on the internal workings of the Catholic church:

> Suffice it to say that the Holy Church is the best interpreter of her own decrees. Who can be surprised if the Holy Seat should consider that the

---

[128] Sullivan 1906–1907, 179.
[129] Hastings 1906–1907, 55.
[130] Chevalier 1906–1907, 235–236.
[131] Chevalier 1906–1907, 236.

time has come to permit Catholic scholars all latitude on this question now that it has been better illuminated? Or speaking more precisely, if Rome permits the problem of the comma Johanneum to be treated now with the liberty of a Karl Künstle, who would not rejoice? In England you do not rescind laws; you simply make new ones.[132]

Indeed, the author of the letter remarked that even if Protestants were unwilling to grant that Rome was correct in all matters of doctrine, they must nevertheless admit that by defending Christianity against its enemies, the Catholic church had shown itself as an impenetrable fortress preserving Scripture, the sole basis for Protestant doctrine. In conclusion, the author characterised the decision of the Congregation as 'not simply a luminous act, but rather a providential act in defence of Christianity'.[133]

Despite the apparent freedom exercised by the priest Künstle and the bishop Bludau, some early twentieth-century Catholic biblical scholars felt compelled to soft-pedal the textual difficulties of the comma. In 1907, Friedrich Brandscheidt reissued an unchanged reprint of his 1893 edition of the Greek New Testament, which included the comma without any comment or sign of doubt. Caspar René Gregory lamented 'that a theologian could in the twentieth century still be found so devoid of critical insight' as to include the comma in an edition of the bible.[134] However, Gregory failed to appreciate the tremendous pressures felt by Roman Catholic biblical scholars, especially in light of the disgrace of Alfred Loisy, and the statements issued by the Vatican in 1907, *Lamentabili sane exitu* and *Pascendi dominici gregis*, which required all Catholic teachers, priests and bishops to forswear modernism.

An important contribution to the debate came with the publication of a detailed study of the development of the doctrine of the Trinity by Jules Lebreton, professor at the Institut catholique in Paris. Lebreton argued that the comma was an interpolation, and pointed out that Franzelin failed to understanding the patristic evidence regarding the comma. The Tridentine decree upholding the integrity of the Vulgate did not apply to the comma, since scholars like Jean-Pierre Paulin Martin, Berger and Künstle had demonstrated that it was not an original part of the Vulgate. The official approval of Künstle's work showed that the church had no real intention of stopping investigation of the comma and other controversial passages like it.[135]

---

[132] Anon. 1906–1907, 381.
[133] Anon. 1906–1907, 381–382.
[134] Gregory 1907, 310–311.
[135] Lebreton 1919, 1:599–606.

The work of Künstle, Bludau and Lebreton eventually led the Congregation to revisit its earlier decision. On 2 July 1927, it explained that the decree of 1897 was simply intended to rein in the audacity of private scholars who claimed for themselves the right to make pronouncements whether or not the comma should be rejected or called into doubt merely on the basis of their own judgement. The Congregation did not wish to prevent Catholic writers from investigating the issue or even from reaching a negative result. It simply insisted that the arguments on both sides be weighed carefully and discussed with requisite gravity. However, scholars had to abide by the judgement of the church entrusted by Christ with the twin tasks of interpreting Scripture and preserving it faithfully. Those who drafted the 1927 decision were careful to point out that this proclamation was in effect little more than a restatement of the authority of the church over the judgement of individuals.[136] Commenting on the decision, M. de Jonghe emphasised that the purpose of this new decree was to make it clear that a judgement over the authenticity of the comma was not merely a critical question, but also a religious one. As such, only the church has the power and the right to decide whether or not this text, or any other, is divinely inspired. Those who observed this right of the church, who declared their intention to uphold the judgement of the church and who took due consideration of the gravity of the matter were not to be condemned for holding the comma as inauthentic.[137]

This decision, while ostensibly conservative, was to have unexpected consequences. At Vatican II, Cardinal Julius Döpfner used the Congregation's 1927 ruling on the comma as evidence that theologians were permitted to continue their research even when the ordinary non-infallible magisterium had made a declaration on a particular doctrine. The definitive text that issued from this discussion at the Council suggests that since our will has priority over our intellect, the believer assents to a given doctrine through faith rather than through understanding.[138] This position is surprisingly close to that of the Puritan Ralph Venning, who wrote: 'The Scripture saith, that one is three, and three are one. 1 *Ioh.* 5. 7. *How can reason think this true?* and yet 'tis true; for God who is truth, and speaks nothing but truth, saith 'tis so';[139] or that of the Baptist Elder John Leland, who declared: 'That there are *three* that bare

---

[136] Denzinger 2001, 997, § 3682 (2 June 1927).
[137] De Jonghe 1927, 455.
[138] Naud 1996, 31–32; Figueiredo 2001, 219–220.
[139] Venning 1652, 39.

record in heaven, and that these *three* are *one*, I believe, because God has said it; but I cannot understand it.'[140]

Reaction to the 1927 statement was mixed. Bover (1943) and Merk (1944) felt free to excise the comma from their editions of the Greek New Testament.[141] But in a footnote to his English translation of the Vulgate (1950), Ronald Knox remarked equivocally: 'This verse does not occur in any good Greek manuscripts. But the Latin manuscripts may have preserved the true text.'[142] However, by 1969, when the Württembergische Bibelanstalt published its critical edition of the Vulgate under the joint direction of Roman Catholic and Protestant scholars, the critical consensus finally decided against the Johannine comma, and it was relegated to the critical apparatus.[143] The present-day 'official' Roman-Catholic bible in Latin, the *Nova Vulgata* (1979), reflects the Greek text of the Nestle-Aland edition, and thus excludes the Johannine comma. After more than four and a half centuries, Erasmus' initial judgement on the Johannine comma was finally vindicated.

Summary

In this chapter we traced three principal themes. First, we saw how the development of modern techniques of philology and codicology led the majority of professional biblical critics to treat the textual transmission of Scripture in essentially the same as that of any literary text, whatever other claims might be made about its content. Second, we saw how the professionalisation of biblical criticism excited alarm and resentment in those who feared that questioning the textual stability of the *textus receptus* would lead inevitably to the erosion of doctrine, morality and the authority of the church. Third, we saw the ways in which the historical narrative of Erasmus' initial rejection and subsequent acceptance of the comma was used by partisans on several sides as an element in their histories of persecution, with the ultimate purpose of lobbying for toleration. While most of these disputes played out in the Protestant context, the issue of the Johannine comma later played an important role in the modernist crisis that gripped the Roman Catholic church in the decades around 1900.

[140] Leland 1845, 732.
[141] Ayuso 1947–1948, 88.
[142] Knox 1950a, 256; Meehan 1986, 12.
[143] Metzger 1977, 351.

Conclusion

The hostility generated by the Johannine comma over the past 500 years shows how much has been invested in these few words by those afraid that the divine essence itself might be lost forever if the textual vessel of the comma should be broken. The extent and acrimony of the debate becomes more comprehensible when we realise what is tied up in the issue. For Erasmus, his reputation and integrity as a scholar were at stake. If this had been damaged, Erasmus knew that his mission of reform could be seriously impeded. Lee and Stunica maintained that the preservation of every jot and tittle of Scripture was the only way to ensure the stability of the church, its doctrine and its authority. Luther and many of his early followers were convinced by Erasmus' arguments against the authenticity of the comma. By contrast, Calvin and his followers tended to accept the comma but reduce its theological significance. Antitrinitarians almost universally argued against the authenticity of the comma, though many unwittingly accepted thereby their opponents' assumption that establishing the authenticity of the comma would amount to providing substantive proof of the validity of Trinitarian doctrine. More recent religious conservatives have treated a defence of the comma as the keystone in the preservation of the *textus receptus* and the Authorised Version, which in turn forms the basis of a conservative social program.

The growth of biblical philology in the eighteenth century, to which Erasmus had given an important initial impetus, coincided with the rise of deism, Unitarianism and the Enlightenment. These factors conspired against traditional faith in favour of a religion that aimed at reason and humanity, as well as a historical and critical attitude towards the sources of religious faith and institutions. For agnostic humanists like Gibbon or Porson, the rejection of the comma was an important symbolic gesture in their general critique of religion and the church. For Anglican apologists, the preservation of the comma was one means to preserve the established church's claim to authority in matters of Scripture, while the legend of Erasmus' promise to Lee could be used to refute both Unitarians and Roman Catholics, thus excluding them from participation in the political arena. For these minority groups, the issue at stake was public recognition of the validity of their belief and consequently their political enfranchisement.

The myth of Erasmus' promise to restore the Johannine comma arose not merely through a misunderstanding of his reply to Lee, as Henk Jan de Jonge rightly suggested, but also because it provided a convenient focus for religious tensions and anxieties of all kinds. The myth was first publicised by David Martin, who drew on Richard Simon's slightly loose account of Erasmus' exchanges with Edward Lee. Through the eighteenth and nineteenth centuries, the myth of Erasmus' promise appeared in many different versions and contexts. The fact that the myth could not be referred back to any text in Erasmus' *œuvre* meant that it could be adapted easily to many different purposes. Depending on how it was told, the myth could be used to exemplify Erasmus' honour, his scholarly integrity, his pragmatism, or his weakness in the face of authority. It could be used as evidence that Erasmus came to accept the comma, or that he rejected it as an interpolation from the Latin Vulgate with no real claim to be included in the Greek text. It could be used as a stick to beat the Roman Catholic church, or a rock on which to build it up. It could be used as evidence that Christian doctrine rests on sufficiently strong foundations that it does not rely on any one text for its claim to truth. It could be employed as evidence of the providential preservation of the *textus receptus*, or of the Unitarianism of primitive Christianity. For sceptics like Gibbon or Porson, the presence of the comma within the biblical text was simply one more reason to despair of the reliability of Scripture and the arbitrariness of ecclesiastical structures.

One of the most surprising things about the Johannine comma is its resilience. A century ago, Adolf Jülicher could opine: 'We make far too much fuss about the Johannine comma; it is only a harmless parasite in the body of the Holy Scripture.'[1] But Jülicher was wrong if he thought the fight was over. Over the past half-century, the defence of the comma has become a rallying-cry against 'liberal' textual criticism. For example, D. A. Waite, president of the conservative Dean Burgon Society, published an article in 1979 which claimed that the comma is transmitted in

---

[1] Jülicher 1905, 935.

twenty manuscripts, and that Greek scholars, 'who should know better', had supplied him with 'false information' to the contrary.[2] Now dozens of fundamentalist websites peddle similar misinformation on the textual status of the comma, reviving arguments decisively refuted decades – if not centuries – ago. Influential fundamentalists like Waite, Edward F. Hills, Jack Moorman and Peter Ruckman have spread misconceptions about the aims and achievements of biblical criticism, suggesting that the critical rejection of the comma is part of a conspiracy to deceive the honest bible believer. Underlying this position is the fear that biblical scholarship will inevitably erode faith and morals.

This is nothing new. Discussions of the comma have invariably been drawn into wider discussions of toleration and social order. In the sixteenth to the nineteenth centuries, the debate was driven by fear of the perceived threat of Socinians, Unitarians, Roman Catholics or modernists. Today this anxiety has been replaced by the fear that Christianity is under attack from science and liberal humanism. Some who believe that empirical science is incompatible with a literal understanding of Scripture have sought to replace it with 'biblical' views of nature such as Creation Science or Intelligent Design. Some who believe that abandoning old certainties about the bible is the first step on the road to Babylon take up arms against the hydra of secular humanism. One internet blogger has claimed that the omission of the Johannine comma from modern critical editions has been driven by 'deceitful' textual scholars, 'lying homosexuals, homosexual sympathizers, abortion supporters, feminazis, socialists, and Christ denying apostates'.[3] The question of the comma is thus not merely a dusty chapter in the annals of biblical scholarship, but a microcosm of the cultural and religious conflicts in which we find ourselves right now.

[2] Waite 1979, 2.
[3] http://av1611.com/kjbp/ridiculous-kjv-bible-corrections/1-John-5-7-Scams.html (accessed 1 January 2016).

Translation of Erasmus' annotations on the Johannine comma (1516–1535)

This translation of Erasmus' two annotations on the Johannine comma is based on the fifth edition of 1535, collated with all the preceding editions (1516, 1519, 1522 and 1527). The text is cumulative; nothing was removed from these two annotations in successive editions apart from some minor rephrasing in the annotation on the phrase *Et hi tres unum sunt* in v. 8. The Latin text and a full commentary are given in *ASD* VI-10, 540–552.

There are three that bear witness in heaven.) [*1516*: In the Greek manuscript text[1] I find only this about the threefold testimony: Ὅτι τρεῖς εἰσιν οἱ μαρτυροῦντες, τὸ πνεῦμα καὶ τὸ ὕδωρ, καὶ τὸ αἷμα, that is: 'For there are three that bear witness, the Spirit, and the water, and the blood.'] [*1522*: In his prologue to the Catholic epistles, St Jerome suspects that this passage was corrupted by Latin translators, and that several of them had omitted the testimony of the Father, Son and Holy Spirit.[2] Yet Cyril, in the second-last chapter of book XIIII of the work he calls *On the treasure*, cites this passage in conformity with our edition:[3] 'Again,' he said, 'John states in the same epistle, "Who is it that conquers the world but the one who believes that Jesus is the Son of God? This is the one who came by water and blood and Spirit,[4] Jesus Christ, not with the water only but with the water and the blood. And the Spirit is the one that testifies, for the Spirit is the truth. There are three that testify: the Spirit,

---

[1] *In graeco codice.* The singular form *codice* led Lee to suggest that Erasmus only had the authority of one manuscript for his omission of the comma, a suggestion that angered Erasmus (*ASD* IX-4:326). In the *Responsio ad Annotationes Lei novas* (*ASD* IX-4:323), Erasmus changed this phrase to *In graecis codicibus*, but in the *Annotationes* he left it in the singular. By contrast, Brown (*ASD* VI-4:483) suggested that Erasmus was perhaps alluding to a particular manuscript he had used in England.

[2] Pseudo-Jerome, *Prologue to the Catholic epistles*, PL 29:825–831.

[3] That is, in accordance with Erasmus' New Testament text of 1516 and 1519. Erasmus used Cyril in the Latin translation of George of Trebizond; see *CW* 46:229–230; *ASD* VI-10:541.

[4] Cyril's reading of 1 Jn 5:6, which includes 'and spirit', is attested in some New Testament manuscripts. It probably reflects a desire to harmonise this passage with v. 8; see K. Aland, Benduhn-Mertz and Mink 1987, 161, *Lesarten* [4, 4B].

the water, and the blood, and these three agree. If we receive human testimony, the testimony of God is greater, etc."⁵ This is what Cyril says, a man who is – unless I am mistaken – orthodox. And since he is fighting here against Arians, and piles up against them many testimonies from the holy Scriptures, it is unlikely that he would have omitted that weapon by which they might be vanquished so completely, if he had either known of it, or believed that it was written by the Apostle.] [*1535*: For Cyril infers that the Holy Spirit is God not from what is subjoined – 'and these three are one' – but from what follows: 'If we receive human testimony, the testimony of God is greater,' which refers to the Spirit, who was mentioned previously.⁶] [*1522*: Now although Bede gives an accurate and lengthy exposition of the triple witness on the earth in his careful commentary on this passage, he made no mention of the testimony of the Father, Son and Spirit in heaven. And this was not a man utterly devoid of linguistic skill or diligence in examining ancient manuscripts. Indeed, he does not even add the words 'on earth',] [*1527*: at least not in the manuscript version of his work,] [*1522*: but reads simply: 'There are three that bear witness.'⁷ In a manuscript supplied to me from the Franciscan library at Antwerp, there was an annotation about the testimony of the Father, Word and Spirit added in the margin, but it was in a rather recent hand, such that it was clear that it had been added by some learned fellow who did not want this phrase to be omitted.]⁸ [*1535*: Seeing that there is no mention of the Father, Son and Spirit, not even in the edition of Josse Bade, Bede followed the example of Augustine. Though he leaves no stone unturned⁹ in his books against Maximinus the Arian to demonstrate from the canonical Scriptures that the Holy Spirit is God, and that all three persons are of the same substance, nevertheless Augustine does not adduce this testimony, even though he cites the context several times elsewhere, especially in *Against Maximinus* III.22, where he argued that the Spirit, blood and water are to be understood as standing for the Father, Son and Holy Spirit. There he puts forward and then forcefully proves the principle that nothing can be called one except what is of the same substance.

⁵ *PG* 75:616A-B. This argument has been taken over from *Responsio ad Annotationes Lei novas, ASD* IX-4:324–325.
⁶ 1 Jn 5:6.
⁷ *CCSL* 121, 321–322, ll. 84–111 (cf. *PL* 93:114b–d). This section on Bede has been taken over from *Responsio ad Annotationes Lei novas, ASD* IX-4:325.
⁸ This discussion of the Antwerp manuscript has been taken over from Erasmus' *Apologia ad Annotationes Stunicae, ASD* IX-2:254. This was a manuscript of Bede's commentary, as may be seen from Erasmus' annotations on Acts 1:14 and 1 Pt 2:2; cf. Semler 1762, 766; *ASD* IX-10:543.
⁹ Erasmus, *Adag.* 330, *ASD* II-1:429–430.

If this principle is as true as he wishes it to appear, then this would be a prize-winning passage for proving that not only the Son is of the same substance with the Father, but so is the Holy Spirit. It is therefore quite clear that Augustine did not read this passage in his manuscripts, for if he had read it but did not adduce it, he might have appeared to collude with the enemy, but this was nowhere his practice.]

[*1522*: But the authority of Jerome is brought forcefully against us, which I should certainly not wish to disparage, although he is frequently violent and shameless, fickle and inconsistent. However, I do not quite understand what Jerome means at this point.[10] I shall record his words: 'But just as I corrected the evangelists some time ago according to the rule of truth, likewise I have with God's help restored these [the Catholic epistles] to their proper order: the first of them is the one of James, then two of Peter, three of John, and one of Jude. If the letters were rendered faithfully by translators into Latin just as their authors composed them, they would not cause the reader confusion, nor would the differences between their wording give rise to contention, especially in that place where we read the statement about the unity of the Trinity, in the first letter of John. It has come to our notice that especially at that point, unfaithful translators have gone far astray from the truth of the faith, for in their edition they give just the words for three [witnesses], namely water, blood, and spirit, but omitting the testimony of the Father, the Word, and the Spirit, by which the Catholic faith is very greatly strengthened, and proof is tendered of the single substance of divinity shared by Father, Son, and Holy Spirit.'[11] We have repeated Jerome's words to this point, from which it is clear that Jerome was not complaining about Greek codices, simply about those who translated the Greek into Latin. But precisely that which Jerome complains was omitted is now absent from the Greek manuscripts, whereas it is present in the Latin manuscripts, though not all of them. But from where does Jerome correct the error of the translators? Clearly, from the Greek manuscripts. But they either had what we have translated, or another reading. If they had another reading that agreed with the Latin [Vulgate] version, what criterion did he have to show which of the two readings is more correct, or which written by the Apostle, especially since what he reproaches was the reading in the public usage of the church at that time? If this were not the case, I cannot see how the following passage

[10] Erasmus made similar comments about Jerome in his *Responsio ad Annotationes Lei novas, ASD* IX-4:323.
[11] These words were cited against Erasmus by Lee; see Erasmus 1520, 200.

Appendix

fits: 'But Eustochium, virgin of Christ, by asking me so eagerly about the reliability of the Scriptures, you expose me in my old age to considerable risk of being torn by the teeth of those who envy me, who call me a forger and a corrupter of the Holy Scriptures.' Who would have called him a forger, unless he had changed the public reading?[12]

So if Cyril amongst the Greeks read what the Greek codices have now, and if Augustine and Bede amongst the Latins read only this, or both readings, I do not understand what kind of argument Jerome can bring to show that the reading he transmits to us is genuine. Perhaps someone will say, 'This was an effective weapon against the Arians.' But first, since it is certain that at an earlier stage, the reading was different both in the Greek and in the Latin traditions, this weapon will be worthless against them, since they doubtless claimed indiscriminately for themselves whichever reading served their cause. But just supposing that the reading were not in dispute, since what is said about the testimony of the water, blood and Spirit being one refers not to an identity of nature, but to an agreement in testimony, do we really think that the Arians would be so stupid as not to apply the same interpretation to the Father, the Word and the Spirit here, especially since orthodox writers give this same interpretation to a similar passage in the gospels, since Augustine does not reject this interpretation in his diatribe *Against the Arian Maximinus*, and even more since an inter-linear fragment of the *Glossa ordinaria* interprets this very passage in the same way? '[The three] are one', says the *Glossa*, 'that is: testifying about the same thing'.[13] Deluding ourselves with explanations like that does not amount to strengthening the faith, but rendering it suspect. Perhaps it would be better to occupy ourselves in pious studies with the aim of being united with God, than to engage in overly subtle arguments about how the Son is distinguished from the Father, and how the Spirit differs from both. I for one do not see how the position rejected by the Arians[14] can be demonstrated except through the exercise of reason. But finally, since this entire passage is obscure, it does not have much power to refute heretics. But we have responded to our calumniator [that is, Lee] on this matter rather fully with an *Apologia*.

One thing I shall add: though my dear Stunica so often boasts of his Rhodian codex, to which he attributes such authority, he has strangely

---

[12] This argument was taken over from Erasmus' *Responsio ad Annotationes Lei novas*, ASD IX-4:324, and (in large part verbatim) *Apologia ad Annotationes Stunicae*, ASD IX-2:254–256.

[13] *Glossa ordinaria* 1603, 1414; the interlinear gloss actually says: 'Vnus Deus de eadem re testantes.' On Erasmus and the *Glossa ordinaria*, see de Jonge 1975.

[14] That is, the orthodox view of the Trinity.

not adduced it as an oracle here, especially since it almost agrees with our [Latin] codices so well that it might seem to be a 'Lesbian straight-edge'.[15]

But to return to my subject, lest I should keep anything hidden, there has been found in England one single Greek manuscript in which occurs what is lacking in the commonly-accepted texts. It is written as follows: Ὅτι τρεῖς εἰσιν οἱ μαρτυροῦντες ἐν τῷ οὐρανῷ, πατήρ, λόγος καὶ πνεῦμα, καὶ οὗτοι οἱ τρεῖς ἕν εἰσιν. Καὶ τρεῖς εἰσιν μαρτυροῦντες ἐν τῇ γῇ, πνεῦμα, ὕδωρ, καὶ αἷμα. Εἰ τὴν μαρτυρίαν τῶν ἀνθρώπων ....[16] However, I am not sure if it is an accident that the phrase 'and these three are unto one', which is found in our Greek manuscripts, is not repeated at this point [that is, in v. 8].[17] I therefore restored from this British codex what was said to be lacking in our editions, lest anyone should have any handle to blame me unjustly.[18] However, I suspect that this codex was adapted to agree with the manuscripts of the Latins.[19]

I have consulted two extraordinarily old manuscripts in the library of St Donatian at Bruges. Neither had the testimony of the Father, Word and Spirit. One of them did not even have the phrase 'on earth', but only, 'There are three that bear witness: the Spirit, the water, and the blood.'[20]]

[*1527*: In both copies at Constance, after the testimony of the water, blood and Spirit was added the testimony of the Father, Word and Spirit, with these words: 'Likewise in heaven there are three, the Father, Word, and Spirit, and the three are one.' Neither the words 'give testimony' nor the pronoun 'these' were added.

In a copy I consulted at the public library of the University of Basel, the testimony of the Spirit, water and blood does not occur.

Additionally, Paolo Bombace, a learned and honest man, made a literal transcription of this passage at my request from a very ancient codex in

[15] Erasmus, *Adag.* 493, *ASD* II-1:563–564.

[16] This information on the reading in the British codex was first given in Erasmus 1521b, qiv (cf. *ASD* IX-2:258), where Erasmus (or the compositor) in his haste made three errors recording the manuscript reading. See above, 29.

[17] Erasmus was evidently aware, even before seeing the Complutensian bible, that Aquinas suggested that the phrase 'and these three are one' was added to v. 8 by Arians to make it seem that their unity was only one of testimony or intention, not one of essence; as a result, this phrase was subsequently omitted from many Latin bibles. The omission of this phrase in the Greek text of the British codex made Erasmus suspect its authenticity. See above, 22, 24, 29.

[18] Despite what has been asserted since Le Long (1720), this statement is true. In his 1522 edition, Erasmus spliced the Johannine comma as it appears in Montfortianus (up to the word πνεῦμα in verse 8) into the reading he had given in his 1516/1519 text. Erasmus, *Adag.* 304, *ASD* II-1:411–412.

[19] The preceding discussion (from 'So if Cyril amongst the Greeks' to here) is adapted from Erasmus' *Apologia ad Annotationes Stunicae, ASD* IX-2:256–258; cf. *ASD* VI-10:545.

[20] The Bruges codices are first mentioned in Erasmus' *Apologia ad Annotationes Stunicae, ASD* IX-2:256. De Jonge, *ASD* IX-2:257, notes that this passage refers to a visit to Bruges in August 1521. This passage was written in September 1521.

the Vatican Library, in which there is no mention of the testimony of the Father, Word and Spirit.[21] (If the authority of antiquity impresses you, the book was extremely old; if you are impressed by the authority of the Pope, it is his library from which this witness was sought.)

The Aldine edition agrees with this reading. It is not entirely clear what Lorenzo [Valla] read.[22]

In the meantime the Spanish edition [that is, the Complutensian Polyglot] was brought to me, which conflicted with all the rest, for it reads as follows: Ὅτι τρεῖς εἰσιν οἱ μαρτυροῦντες ἐν τῷ οὐρανῷ, ὁ πατήρ, καὶ ὁ λόγος, καὶ τὸ ἅγιον πνεῦμα, καὶ οἱ τρεῖς εἰς τὸ ἕν εἰσι. Καὶ τρεῖς εἰσιν οἱ μαρτυροῦντες ἐπὶ τῆς γῆς, τὸ πνεῦμα, καὶ τὸ ὕδωρ, καὶ τὸ αἷμα. First of all, the exemplar which the Spanish have followed, which, if I am not mistaken, they obtained from the very same library,[23] differs from the British codex in this respect: that here the articles are added – ὁ πατήρ, ὁ λόγος, τὸ πνεῦμα – which were not given in the British codex. Second, where the British codex had οὗτοι οἱ τρεῖς, the Spanish exemplar had simply καὶ οἱ τρεῖς. There is a similar discrepancy with the Spirit, the water and the blood [in v. 8]. Furthermore, where the British codex had ἕν εἰσι, the Spanish edition gives εἰς τὸ ἕν εἰσι. Finally, where the British codex added καὶ οἱ τρεῖς εἰς τὸ ἕν εἰσι to the earthly witnesses as well, this phrase was not added in the Spanish edition, at least not here.[24] I am quite certain that the phrase εἰς τὸ ἕν is a Hebraism.[25] 'I shall be as a father towards him' cannot mean anything but 'I shall be his father.'[26]

---

[21] The information on the Vatican codex inspected by Bombace (GA ms B/03) is mentioned in Erasmus' *Apologia ad Annotationes Stunicae, ASD* IX-2:256. De Jonge, *ASD* IX-2:257, notes that Bombace's letter (*Epist.* 1213) was dated 18 June 1521.

[22] Lee had argued that if this variant was so important, it would have been mentioned by Valla, who had seen seven codices of the Greek text; see Erasmus 1520, 200–201. In his reply to Lee (*ASD* IX-4:323, 326), Erasmus points out that Valla was a fallible human, and that he himself had seen more than Valla's seven codices, all of them lacking the comma.

[23] That is, from the Vatican library, repository of codex B, which Erasmus has just mentioned.

[24] Erasmus made an error in comparing the readings of Montfortianus and the Complutensian edition. Just like the Complutensian edition, Montfortianus lacks the phrase καὶ οἱ τρεῖς εἰς τὸ ἕν εἰσιν in 1 Jn 5:8, as Erasmus had already remarked in the *Apologia ad Annotationes Stunicae* (*ASD* IX-2:258) and his comments in the 1522 *Annotationes*, just a few lines above. This inconsistency can be explained by the fact that these observations were written at different times. By the time Erasmus saw the Complutensian edition, Clement had taken Codex Montfortianus to Italy. By 1527 Erasmus had evidently forgotten that the phrase καὶ οἱ τρεῖς εἰς τὸ ἕν εἰσιν in his text was carried over from the 1516 and 1519 edition. This should not be taken as evidence that Montfortianus and the Codex Britannicus are different manuscripts, merely as proof that even Erasmus sometimes made mistakes.

[25] Erasmus seems to suggest that the reading in Montfortianus, which contains this apparent Hebraism, looks more trustworthy than that in the Complutensian edition, which lacks it.

[26] 2 Sam 7:14 (Vulg.).

Now, the Spanish edition had added a scholium from the decretals, attributed to St Thomas. It declares that in the testimony of the Spirit, the water and the blood in carefully-copied codices, the phrase 'and these three are one' is not added, and that it seems that this was added by those who favoured the Arian teaching. For if it were added here, it could only be interpreted as referring to the consensus of their testimony, for Spirit, water and blood cannot be said to be one in nature. From this it would follow that the previous iteration of the phrase 'and these three are one', relating to the Father, Son and Holy Spirit, could be understood as relating to the consensus of their love and witness. Now, with these words John asserted that the essence of the Father, the Son and the Holy Spirit is the same. In the first place, what they infer is very true: that the nature of the Father, the Son and the Holy Spirit is the same, most simple and indivisible. If this were not the case, the Son would not truly be born from the Father, nor would the Holy Spirit truly proceed from the Father and the Son, at any rate not as God from the substance of God.

In summary then, it is clear that this phrase relates to the reliability of testimony, not to the substance of persons. For if this word 'one' in many other places means 'agreement' rather than 'the unity of an individual', what is so strange in our interpreting it here in a similar way? How often do we read in either the Old or New Testament 'one heart', 'one spirit and soul', 'one voice', 'one mind', when this signifies agreement and mutual love? Since this literary trope is so common in the Scriptures, what prevents us from interpreting it in the same way here? In Jn 10[:30], the Lord says: 'The Father and I are one.'[27] How will an Arian be vanquished by this evidence, unless you can convince him that the word 'one' in the Scriptures can only mean 'things that are of the same substance'? Now, since the Scriptures provide numerous passages which indicate that this phrase can be understood as referring to consent or mutual love, this passage will be able to confirm the opinion of an orthodox person, but I cannot see how successful it will be in checking the stubbornness of the heretic. However, it can be inferred with a high degree of likelihood that Christ is speaking there of the concord he has with the Father, since he is not responding to what he had said about his being one with the Father, but to the fact that he called God his Father, and was thus, remarkably enough, calling himself the Son of God. And in Jn 17[:11] he says, 'Holy Father, protect them in your name whom you have given me, so that they may be one, as we are one.' And again [Jn 17:21] he says, 'that they may

27 Cf. *ASD* IX-4:327.

all be one; as you, Father, are in me and I am in you, may they also be in us.'[28] This entire passage deals with the consensus of love and witness, and whether we like it or not,[29] we are compelled to interpret that word 'one' in a different way when it is referring to us from when it is referring to the divine persons. Therefore, this passage does not constrain us, unless the authority of the orthodox fathers and ecclesiastical requirement should compel us by teaching that this passage cannot be interpreted any other way. For it is pious always to submit our thinking to the judgement of the church as soon as we have heard it make a clear statement. But in the meantime it is not wicked to investigate the truth, though without causing contention, as God reveals different things to different people.

But to return to the business of this reading, the evidence we have recalled here shows clearly that the Greek and Latin codices disagree. In my opinion it makes little difference which reading you embrace. For as to what Thomas says about the passage being added by heretics, first of all he does not affirm it; he simply states, 'It is said that ....' Otherwise, the Catholic church throughout the entire world would embrace what had been adulterated by heretics.

It will torture the grammarians that the Spirit, water and blood are modified by the phrases 'there are three' and 'these are one', for the particular reason that the words 'Spirit', 'water' and 'blood' are grammatically neuter in Greek. But the Apostle pays more regard to the sense than to the words, and for three witnesses, as if they were three people, he has supplied three things: Spirit, water and blood. You use the same manner of speaking if you say: 'The building is a witness to the kind of builder you are.']

And these three are one.) [*1516*: The word 'these' is redundant] [*1519*: except as far as the translator added it to make the meaning plain.] [*1516*: And it should not be 'one', but 'unto one',] [*1527*: εἰς τὸ ἕν, as in some manuscripts.]

---

[28] Cf. *ASD* IX-4:327–328.
[29] Erasmus, *Adag.* 245, *ASD* II-1:358–359; *Adag.* 1682, *ASD* II-4:137–138.

Bibliography

Abbot, Ezra. *The Authorship of the Fourth Gospel.* Ed. J. H. Thayer. Boston: Ellis, 1888.

Abbott, Thomas Kingsmill. 'Note on the Codex Montfortianus.' *Hermathena* 7 (1893): 203.

Catalogue of the Manuscripts in the Library of Trinity College, Dublin. Dublin: Hodges, Figgis, & Co., 1900.

Acta oder Handlungen, betreffend die Irrthümer und anstößige Lehren H[errn] J[ohann] J[akob] W[etsteins] gewesenen Diac. Leonh. enthaltend. Basel: Decker, 1730.

Adriaenssen, Cornelis. *Historie van B. Cornelis Adriaensen van Dordrecht/ Minrebroeder binnen der Stadt van Brugghe.* The second volume has the title: *Het tweede boeck, vande sermoenen.* 2 vols. Amsterdam: Cornelis Claesz and Albert Bouwmeester, 1607–1608.

Aland, Barbara. 'Der textkritische und textgeschichtliche Nutzen früher Papyri, demonstriert am Johannesevangelium.' In *Recent Developments in Textual Criticism.* Ed. Wim Weren and Dietrich-Alex Koch. Assen: Van Gorcum, 2003: 19–39.

Aland, Barbara, Kurt Aland, Gerd Mink, Holger Strutwolf and Klaus Wachtel, ed. *Novum Testamentum Graecum, Editio Critica Maior IV: Catholic Letters.* Stuttgart: Deutsche Bibelgesellschaft, 1997–2006; rev. ed. 2013.

Aland, Barbara, and Andreas Juckel, ed. *Das Neue Testament in syrischer Überlieferung.* 4 vols. Berlin: De Gruyter, 1986–2002.

Aland, Kurt, and Barbara Aland. *The Text of the New Testament.* Trans. Erroll F. Rhodes. 2nd ed. Grand Rapids: Eerdmans, 1995.

Aland, Kurt, Annette Benduhn-Mertz and Gerd Mink, ed. *Text und Textwert der griechischen Handschriften des Neuen Testaments. Die Katholischen Briefe.* 3 vols. Berlin: De Gruyter, 1987.

Aland, Kurt, Michael Welte, Beate Köster and Klaus Junack. *Kurzgefaßte Liste der griechischen Handschriften des Neuen Testaments.* 2nd ed. Berlin: De Gruyter, 1994.

Alexandre, Noël. *Commentarius litteralis et moralis in omnes epistolas Sancti Pauli Apostoli, et in VII. epistolas catholicas.* Rouen: Herault and Le Boucher, 1710.

Allen, William, ed. *Scripture Lessons, for Schools on the British System of Mutual Instruction.* London: British and Foreign School Society, 1820.

Alter, Franz Carl. 'Philologische Bemerkungen aus Briefen von Herrn Prof. Alter.' *Memorabilien* 8 (1796): 179–220.

Alting, Heinrich. *Scriptorum theologicorum Heidelbergensium tomi.* 3 vols. Amsterdam: Jansson, 1646.

Theologia elenctica nova. Amsterdam: Jansson, 1654.

Amelote, Denis, trans. *Le Nouveau Testament de Nostre Seigneur Jesus-Christ.* 3 vols. Paris: Muguet, 1666–1670.

Le Nouveau Testament de Nostre Seigneur Jesus-Christ. 2 vols. Paris: Muguet, 1687–1688.

Ames, William. *Bellarminus enervatus.* Amsterdam: Jansson, 1629.

Anon. *The Charitable Samaritan: or, a Short and Impartial Account of that Eminent, and Publick-spirited Citizen Mr. Tho. Firmin.* London: [n. p.], 1698a.

Some Considerations upon the Bill for the more Effectual Suppressing Blasphemy and Prophaness. [London]: [n. p.], [1698b].

The Considerations upon the Bill for the more Effectual Suppressing of Blasphemy and Prophaneness, Animadverted. [London]: [n. p.], [1698c].

Review of Mill 1707. *Journal des Sçavans* 41 (July–September 1708): 163–183.

Review of Emlyn 1715. *Journal littéraire* 8 (1716): 57–67.

Review of Martin 1719b. *Acta eruditorum* 1720: 357–363.

'Mémoire envoyé à l'Auteur du Journal Britannique, au sujet des Lettres de Mr. de Missy sur le passage des trois témoins célestes.' *Journal Britannique* 10 (1753): 127–134.

Review of Travis 1785. *The English Review* 5 (1785a): 167–177.

Review of Knittel 1785. *Allgemeine Literatur-Zeitung* 131 (1785b): 229–231.

Review of Porson 1790. *Allgemeine Literatur-Zeitung* 289 (1791): 196–200.

Review of Travis 1794. *The English Review* 24 (1795): 378–380.

Review of Pappelbaum 1796. *Neue allgemeine deutsche Bibliothek* 33 (1797a): 115–120.

Review of Pappelbaum 1796. *The Monthly Review* 22 (1797b): 493–497.

'Deaths in and near London.' *The Monthly Magazine, and British Register, for 1797. From January to June, inclusive* 3 (1797c): 238–240.

Review of Nolan 1815. *The British Critic* 5 (1816): 1–24.

Review of Burgess 1821. *The British Review* 18 (1821): 219–235.

Review of Burgess 1823. *The Quarterly Review* 33 (1826): 64–104.

'British and Foreign School Society.' *The Quarterly Journal of Education* 5 (1833): 52–71.

'The Revised Version.' *The Times,* 17 May 1881a: 4.

'The Revision of the New Testament.' *The Dublin Review,* 3rd series, 6 (1881b): 127–144.

'The Church Congress.' *The Times,* 8 October 1881c: 10.

'Notes.' *The Tablet* 89, n° 2974 (8 May 1897a): 728.

'The Decree of the Holy Office on the Authenticity of 1 John, V. 7.' *The Tablet* 89, n° 2979 (12 June 1897b): 921–922.

'La Commission Biblique.' *The Expository Times* 18 (1906–1907): 381–382.

Antiphonarium Romanum. Venice: Giunta, 1596.

Antoniades, Vasileios, ed. Ἡ Καινή Διαθήκη. Istanbul: Patriarchal Printer, 1904 [1907].

Aquinas, Thomas. *Opuscula selecta*. 3 vols. Paris: Lethielleux, 1881.

Summa Theologiae. Ed. Thomas Gilby and T. C. O'Brien. 61 vols. London: Blackfriars, 1964–1981.

Aretius, Benedictus. *Commentarii in Epistolas canonicas*. [Bern]: Jean Le Preux, 1608.

Arnauld, Antoine. *Difficultez proposées à Mr. Steyaert*. 9 parts in 4 vols. Cologne: Le Grand, 1691.

Asso, Cecilia. *La teologia e la grammatica. La controversia tra Erasmo ed Edward Lee*. Florence: Olschki, 1993.

'*Erasmus redivivus*. Alcune osservazioni sulla filologia neotestamentaria di Jean Le Clerc.' In *Vico nella storia della filologia*. Ed. Silvia Caianello and Amadeu Viana. Naples: Alfredo Guida, 2004: 79–115.

Atkin, Nicholas, and Frank Tallett. *Priests, Prelates and People. A History of European Catholicism since 1750*. Oxford: Oxford University Press, 2003.

Atkinson, John. *The Father, the Word, or (Son) and the Holy Ghost, the one true God together with the necessity of believing it*. London: Cox, 1726.

Auvray, Paul. *Richard Simon, 1638–1712. Étude bio-bibliographique avec des textes inédits*. Paris: PUF, 1974.

Avilés, Miguel. *Erasmo y la Inquisición*. Madrid: Fundación Universitaria Española, 1980.

Ayuso Marazuela, Teófilo. 'Nuevo estudio sobre el Comma Johanneum.' *Biblica* 28 (1947): 83–112, 216–235; 29 (1948): 52–76.

Azpilcueta, Martín de. *Consiliorum sive responsorum libri quinque*. 2 vols. Rome: Tornieri, 1590.

Bainton, R. H. *Erasmus of Christendom*. London: Collins, 1970.

Bang, Willy. 'Acta Anglo-Lovaniensia: John Heywood und sein Kreis.' *Englische Studien* 38 (1907): 234–250.

Barker, Edmund Henry. *Literary Anecdotes and Contemporary Reminiscences of Professor Porson and Others*. 2 vols. London: Smith, 1852.

Barmann, Larence F. *Baron Friedrich von Hügel and the Modernist Crisis in England*. Cambridge: Cambridge University Press, 1972.

Barrett, John. *Evangelium secundum Matthaeum ex codice rescripto in bibliotheca Collegii SSae. Trinitatis juxta Dublin*. Dublin: Mercier, 1801.

Bartholomew, Augustus Theodore. *Richard Bentley, D.D. A bibliography of his works*. Cambridge: Bowes and Bowes, 1908.

Barton, William. *A Century of Select Hymns. Collected Out of Scripture*. London: 'T. R.' and Francis Tyson for Francis Eglesfield and Thomas Underhill, 1659.

Basset, William. *An Answer to the Brief History of the Unitarians, Called Also Socinians*. London: Everingham, 1693.

Bataillon, Marcel. *Erasme en Espagne*. Paris: Droz, 1937.

Bateson, Mary, ed. *Grace Book B. Part I*. Cambridge: Cambridge University Press, 1903.

Bauer, Walter. *Rechtgläubigkeit und Ketzerei im ältesten Christentum*. Tübingen: Mohr (Siebeck), 1934.

Orthodoxy and Heresy in Earliest Christianity. Ed. and trans. Robert A. Kraft and Gerhard Kroedel. Philadelphia: Fortress Press, 1971.

Baumgarten, Siegmund Jakob. *Nachrichten von einer hallischen Bibliothek.* 8 vols. Halle: Gebauer, 1748–1751.

Bayly, Lewis. *The Practise of Pietie.* London: Hodgets, 1613.

Bécamel, Marcel. 'Autres lettres de Loisy à Mgr. Mignot.' *Bulletin de littérature ecclésiastique* 69 (1968): 241–268.

Becker, Bruno. 'Nederlandsche vertalingen van Sebastiaan Franck's geschriften.' *Nederlandsch Archief voor Kerkgeschiedenis,* n. s. 21 (1928): 149–160.

Béda, Noël. *Annotationum [...] in Iacobum Fabrum Stapulensem libri duo: et in Desiderium Erasmum Roterodamum liber unus.* Paris: Bade, 1526.

Bellarmino, Roberto. *Disputationes de controversiis Christianae fidei.* Ingolstadt: Sartorius, 1586.

Belsham, Thomas. *Freedom of Enquiry, and Zeal in the Diffusion of Christian Truth, Asserted and Recommended in a Discourse Delivered at Bristol, July 9, 1800.* London: Woodfall, 1800.

— ed. *The New Testament, in an Improved Version, upon the Basis of Archbishop Newcome's New Translation: with a Corrected Text, and Notes Critical and Explanatory.* London: Taylor, 1808.

Beltrán de Heredia, Vicente. *Cartulario de la universidad de Salamanca.* 6 vols. Salamanca: Universidad de Salamanca, 1970–1973.

'Ben David' [John Jones]. 'Letters to the Editor.' *The Monthly Repository of Theology and General Literature* 20 (1825), 533–534; 21 (1826): 15–20, 91–94, 146–152, 214–221, 274–280, 318–322, 468–473.

Bengel, Johann Albrecht, ed. Ἡ Καινὴ Διαθήκη. *Novum Testamentum graecum.* Tübingen: Cotta, 1734.

— *Gnomon Novi Testamenti.* Tübingen: Schramm, 1742.

— *Apparatus criticus ad novum testamentum.* 2nd ed. Tübingen: Cotta, 1763.

— *Briefwechsel: Briefe 1723–1731.* Ed. Dieter Ising. Göttingen: Vandenhoeck & Ruprecht, 2012.

Benson, George. *Dissertatio de Loco 1. Joh. V. com VII.* Halle: Bauer, 1752.

— *A Paraphrase and Notes on the Seven (Commonly Called) Catholic Epistles [...] Attempted in Imitation of Mr. Locke's Manner.* London: Waugh and Fenner, 1756.

Bentley, Jerry H. 'Erasmus, Jean Le Clerc, and the Principle of the Harder Reading.' *Renaissance Quarterly* 31 (1978): 309–321.

— 'New Light on the Editing of the Complutensian New Testament.' *Bibliothèque d'Humanisme et Renaissance* 42 (1980): 145–156.

— *Humanists and Holy Writ.* Princeton: Princeton University Press, 1983.

Bentley, Richard. *Remarks upon a late Discourse of Free-Thinking.* London: Morphew, 1713.

— *A Sermon upon Popery.* Cambridge: Cambridge University Press, 1715.

— Ἡ Καινὴ Διαθήκη *Graece. Novum Testamentum versionis Vulgatae, per S^{tum} Hieronymum ad vetusta Exemplaria Graeca castigatae & exactae. [...] Proposals for Printing.* [London]: [Knapton], [1720].

Dr Bentley's Proposals For Printing a New Edition of the Greek Testament and St. Hierom's Latin Version. With a Full Answer to all the Remarks of a Late Pamphleteer. London: Knapton, 1721.

Correspondence. Ed. John Wordsworth and Christopher Wordsworth. 2 vols. London: Murray, 1842.

Bentleii Critica Sacra. Ed. Arthur Ayres Ellis. Cambridge: Deighton, Bell & Co., 1862.

Berger, Samuel. *Histoire de la Vulgate pendant les premiers siècles du moyen age.* Paris: Hachette, 1893.

Bernard-Maître, Henri. 'Lettres d'Henri Bremond à Alfred Loisy.' *Bulletin de littérature ecclésiastique* 69 (1968): 3–24, 161–184, 269–289; 70 (1969): 44–56.

Bernus, Auguste. *Richard Simon et son Histoire critique du Vieux Testament.* Lausanne: Bridel, 1869.

Berriman, John. Θεὸς ἐφανερώθη ἐν σαρκί. *Or, a Critical Dissertation upon 1 Tim. iii. 16. Wherein Rules are Laid Down to Distinguish, in Various Readings, which is Genuine.* London: Innys and Nourse, 1741.

Best, Paul. *Mysteries Discovered, or, a Mercuriall Picture Pointing Out the Way from Babylon to the Holy City.* [London]: [n. p.], 1647.

Beuter, Pedro Antonio. *Annotationes Decem ad Sacram Scripturam.* Valencia: Mey, 1547.

Bèze, Théodore de, ed. and trans. *Novum D. N. Iesu Christi Testamentum Latine iam olim à Veteri interprete, nunc denuò à Theodoro Beza versum: cum eiusdem annotationibus, in quibus ratio interpretationis redditur.* Geneva: Robert Estienne, 1556.

Iesu Christi D. N. Nouum testamentum, siue Nouum foedus. Cuius Graeco textui respondent interpretationes duae: vna, vetus: alter, noua, Theodori Bezae, diligenter ab eo recognita. Geneva: Henri Estienne, 1565.

The New Testament of Our Lord Iesus Christ, Translated Out of Greeke by Theod Beza: With briefe Summaries and expositions [...]. Englished by L. Tomson. 1599. London: Deputies of Christopher Barker, 1599.

Bianchi, Daniela. 'Some Sources for a History of English Socinianism: A Bibliography of 17th Century English Socinian Writings.' *Topoi* 4 (1985): 91–120.

Biandrata, Giorgio and Ferenc Dávid. *De falsa et vera unius Dei Patris, Filii, et Spiritus Sancti cognitione, libri duo.* Alba Iulia [Gyulafehérvár]: [n. p.], [1567].

Demonstratio falsitatis doctrinae Petri Melii, & reliquorum Sophistarum. Alba Iulia [Gyulafehérvár]: [n. p.], [n. d.].

The Bible and Holy Scriptures conteyned in the Olde and Newe Testament. Geneva: Hall, 1560.

Biblia Das ist / Die gantze heilige Schrifft / Teutsch. Frankfurt/Main: Egenolff for Adam Lonicer, 1576.

Biblia Das ist / Die gantze heilige Schrifft / Deudsch. Wittenberg: Lehman, 1596.

Biblia, Dat is: De gantsche H. Schrifture. Leiden: Paulus Aertsz van Ravensteyn, 1637.

Biblia dudesch. Halberstadt: Lorenz Stuchs, 1522.

Biblia. Hebraea, Chaldaea, Graeca & Latina. Paris: Estienne, 1540.

Biblia sacra juxta versionem simplicem quae dicitur Peschitta. Mosul: Typis Fratrum Praedicatorum, 1887–1891.

Biblia sacra Vulgatae editionis tribus tomis distincta. Rome: Typographia Apostolica Vaticana, 1590.

Biblia sacra Vulgatae editionis. Rome: Typographia Apostolica Vaticana, 1592.

Biblīa sirēch knigy vetkhago i novago zavĕta po jazykŭ slovenskŭ. Ostroh: Ivan Fedorov, 1581.

Biblia swięta, tho iest, Księgi Starego y Nowego Zakonu. [II:] *Księgi Nowego Testamentu.* Brześć Litewski: Mikołaj Radziwiłł Czarny, 1563.

Biddle, John. *Twelve arguments drawn out of the Scripture, wherein the commonly received opinion touching the deity of the Holy Spirit, is clearly and fully refuted.* [London]: [n. p.], 1647.

A Twofold Catechism. London: J. Cottrel for R. Moone, 1654a.

A Brief Scripture-Catechism for Children. London: J. Cottrel for R. Moone, 1654b.

Bietenholz, Peter G. *Encounters with a Radical Erasmus.* Toronto: Toronto University Press, 2008.

Bikhchandani, Sushil, David Hirshleifer and Ivo Welch. 'A Theory of Fads, Fashion, Custom, and Cultural Change as Informational Cascades.' *Journal of Political Economy* 100 (1992): 992–1026.

[Binckes, William.] *A Prefatory Discourse to an Examination of a Late Book, Entituled an Exposition of the Thirty Nine Articles of the Church of England, by Gilbert, Bishop of Sarum.* London: Clavell, 1702.

Bludau, August. *Die beiden ersten Erasmus-Ausgaben des Neuen Testaments und ihre Gegner.* Freiburg i. B.: Herder, 1902a.

'Der Beginn der Kontroverse über die Aechtheit des Comma Johanneum (1 Joh. 5, 7. 8.) im 16. Jahrhundert.' *Der Katholik* 82 (1902b): 25–51, 151–175.

'Das Comma Johanneum im 16. Jahrhundert.' *Biblische Zeitschrift* 1 (1903a): 280–302, 378–407.

'Das Comma Johanneum (1. Joh. 5, 7) in den orientalischen Übersetzungen und Bibeldrucken.' *Oriens Christianus* 3 (1903b): 126–147.

'Das Comma Johanneum (1 Joh. 5, 7) in den Schriften der Antitrinitarier und Sozinianer des 16. und 17. Jahrhunderts.' *Biblische Zeitschrift* 2 (1904a): 275–300.

'Richard Simon und das Comma Johanneum.' *Der Katholik* 84 (1904b): 29–42, 114–122.

'Das Comma Johanneum bei den Griechen.' *Biblische Zeitschrift* 13 (1915): 26–50, 130–162, 222–243.

'Das Comma Johanneum (1. Joh. 5, 7) in dem Glaubensbekenntnis von Karthago vom Jahre 484.' *Theologie und Glaube* 11 (1919a): 9–15.

'Der hl. Augustinus und 1 Joh. 5,7–8.' *Theologie und Glaube* 11 (1919b): 379–386.

'Das Comma Johanneum bei Tertullian und Cyprian.' *Theologische Quartalschrift* 101 (1920): 1–28.

'Der Prolog des Pseudohieronymus zu den katholischen Briefen.' *Biblische Zeitschrift* 15 (1921): 15–34, 125–137.

'The Comma Johanneum in the Writings of English Critics of the Eighteenth Century.' *Irish Theological Quarterly* 17 (1922): 128–139, 201–218.

'Das Comma Johanneum 1. Joh. 5, 7 bei Eucherius und Cassiodor.' *Theologie und Glaube* 19 (1927): 149–155, 418.

Bolland, William. *The Campaign.* London: Bensley, 1800.

The Book of Common Prayer, and Administration of the Sacraments. London: Baskett, 1724.

Boran, Elizabethanne, ed. *The Correspondence of James Ussher, Archbishop of Armagh 1600–1656.* 3 vols. Dublin: Irish Manuscript Commission, 2015.

Borger, Rykle. 'Das Comma Johanneum in der Peschitta.' *Novum Testamentum* 29 (1987): 280–284.

Bossuet, Jacques-Bénigne. *Seconde instruction: sur les passages particuliers de la version du Nouveau Testament, imprimée à Trévoux en l'année M.DCC.II.* Paris: Anisson, 1703.

Boucat, Antoine. *Theologia patrum scholastico-dogmatica, sed maxime positiva.* Venice: Ghirardi, 1766.

Bourne, Henry Richard Fox. *The Life of John Locke.* 2 vols. New York: Harper, 1876.

Bowyer, William, ed. *Novum Testamentum Graecum, ad fidem Graecorum solum Codicum MSS. nunc primum expressum.* 2 vols. London: Bowyer, 1763.

Boyle, Marjorie O'Rourke. 'Reopening the Conversation on Translating Jn 1,1.' *Vigiliae Christianae* 31 (1977): 161–168.

Boys, James. *A Practical Exposition upon the Thirty-Nine Articles of the Church of England.* London: Caldecott, 1716.

Brandscheidt, Friedrich, ed. *Novum Testamentum Graece et Latine.* Freiburg i. B.: Herder, 1893. 2nd ed., 1901. 3rd ed., 1906–1907.

Brandt, Geeraert. *Verhaal van de Reformatie, in en ontrent de Nederlanden.* Amsterdam: Rieuwertsz, 1663.

The History of the Reformation and Other Ecclesiastical Transactions in and about the Low-Countries. Trans. John Chamberlayne. 3 vols. London: Wood for Childe, 1720–1723.

Brandt, Pierre-Yves. 'Manuscrits grecs utilisés par Erasme pour son édition du *Novum Instrumentum* de 1516.' *Theologische Zeitschrift* 54 (1998): 120–124.

[Breval, John]. *The Church Scuffle: or, News from St. Andrew's: A Ballad. To the Tune of a Begging We Will Go, &c. Written by Mr. Joseph Gay.* London: Currl, 1719.

Breviarium Romanum, Ex Decreto Sacrosancti Concilij Tridentini restitutum. Rome: Paolo Manuzio, 1568.

Brewer, J. S., et al., ed. *Letters and Papers, Foreign and Domestic, of the Reign of Henry VIII.* 21 vols. London: Longman, 1862–1908.

Brewster, David. *The Life of Sir Isaac Newton.* London: Murray, 1831.

Memoirs of the Life, Writings, and Discoveries of Sir Isaac Newton. 2 vols. Edinburgh: Constable, 1855.

Briquet, C. M. *Les filigranes. Dictionnaire historique des marques du papier dès leur apparition vers 1282 jusqu'en 1600.* 4 vols. Paris: Picard, 1907.

Briscoe-Eyre, George Edward, ed. *A Transcript of the Registers of the Worshipful Company of Stationers, from 1640–1708* A.D. 3 vols. London: Company of Stationers, 1913–1914.

Brochmand, Jesper Rasmussen. *Universae theologiae systema, tomus I.* Ulm: Kühne for Görlin, 1638.

Brocklesby, Richard. *An Explication of the Gospel-Theism and the Divinity of the Christian Religion.* London: Heptinstall, 1706.

Brown, Andrew J. 'The Date of Erasmus' Latin Translation of the New Testament.' *Transactions of the Cambridge Bibliographical Society* 8 (1984): 351–380.

Brown, Keith Duncan. 'The Franciscan Observants in England, 1482–1559.' Diss. Oxford, 1986.

[Brown, Timothy, ed.]. *A New Testament; or the New Covenant according to Luke, Paul, and John. Published in Conformity to the Plan of the Late Rev. Edward Evanson, A. M.* London: Taylor for Phillips, 1807.

Browne, Gregory. *An Introduction to Pietie and Humanitie.* London: E. A[llde] for Edmund Weaver, 1613.

Browne, Peter. *A Letter in Answer to a Booke, Intituled, Christianity Not Mysterious.* London: Clavell, 1697.

The Procedure, Extent, and Limits of the Human Understanding. London: Innys, 1728.

[Browne, Simon]. *A Sober and Charitable Disquisition Concerning the Importance of the Doctrine of the Trinity.* London: Gray, 1732.

Bruce, Frederick Fyvie. *The Book of Acts.* Rev. ed. The New International Commentary on the New Testament. Grand Rapids: Eerdmans, 1988.

Brucker, Joseph. Review of *Novum Testamentum Vulgatae Editionis.* Ed. Michael Hetzenauer. *Études publiées par des Pères de la Compagnie de Jésus* 82 (1900): 402–403.

Bruns, Paul Jacob. 'Zu 1 Joh. V, 7.' *Repertorium für biblische und morgenländische Litteratur* 3 (1778): 258–260.

Bryennius, Joseph. Ἰωσὴφ Μοναχοῦ τοῦ Βρυεννίου τὰ Εὑρεθέντα ἀξιώσει τοῦ Ὑψηλοτάτου καὶ εὐσεβεστάτου πρώην ἡγεμόνος Μολδοβλαχίας Κυρίου Κυρίου Γρηγορίου Ἀλεξάνδρου Γκίκα Βοεβόδα δι' ἐπιμελείας Εὐγενίου διακόνου τοῦ Βουλγάρεως ἤδη τὸ πρῶτον τύποις ἐκδοθέντα. 2 vols. Leipzig: Breitkopf, 1786.

Buchwald, Jed Z. and Mordechai Feingold. *Newton and the Origin of Civilization.* Princeton: Princeton University Press, 2012.

Budny, Szymon, trans. *Biblia. To iest / księgi starego y nowego przymierza / znowu z języka Ebreyskiego, Greckiego, Łacińskiego / na polski przełożone.* Nieśwież: Daniel z Łęczycy and Maciej Kawęczyński, 1572.

Nowy Testament znowu przełożony. Łosk: [Daniel z Łęczycy for] Kiszka, 1574.

Nowy Testament w tłum. S. Budnego. [Łosk]: [Bolemowski for Kiszka], [1589].

Bugenhagen, Johannes. *Ionas propheta expositus in tertio capite.* Wittenberg: Creutzer, 1550.

Bullinger, Heinrich. *Brevis* ἀντιβολὴ *sive responsio secunda Heinrychi Bullingeri ad maledicam implicitamque Ioannis Cochlaei de Scripturae & ecclesiae authoritate replicam.* Zürich: Froschauer, 1544.

In omnes apostolicas epistolas, divi videlicet Pauli XIIII. et VII. canonicas, commentarii. Zürich: Froschauer, 1549.

Burder, George. *The Doctrine of the Trinity. A Sermon.* Hartford: Lincoln and Gleason, 1805.

Burgess, Thomas. *A Vindication of 1 John v. 7. from the objections of M. Griesbach.* London: Rivington, 1821.

ed. *Adnotationes Milli, Auctae et Correctae ex Prolegomenis suis, Wetstenii, Bengelii, et Sabaterii, ad 1. Joann. V. 7.* St Davids: Evans, 1822.

A Vindication of 1 John v. 7. 2nd ed. London: Rivington, 1823.

A Selection of Tracts and Observations on 1 John v. 7. London: Rivington, 1824.

A letter to the clergy of the diocese of St. David's on a passage of the second Symbolum Antiochenum of the fourth century as an evidence of the authenticity of 1 John v. 7. London: Rivington, 1825.

A letter to the Reverend Thomas Benyon, Archdeacon of Cardigan: in reply to A Vindication of the Literary Character of Professor Porson by Crito Cantabrigiensis; and in further Proof of the Authenticity of 1 John, v. 7. Salisbury: Brodie, 1829.

Remarks on the General Tenour of the New Testament, Regarding the Nature and Dignity of Jesus Christ. 2nd ed. Salisbury: Brodie, 1832.

An introduction to the controversy on the disputed verse of St. John, as revived by Mr. Gibbon: to which is added, Christian theocracy; or, a second letter to Mrs. Joanna Baillie, on the doctrine of the Trinity. Salisbury: Brodie, 1835.

Three letters to the Rev. Dr. Scholz, editor of a new edition of the Greek Testament, Lips., 1836, on the contents of his note, on 1 John, v., 7 in his edition of the Greek Testament. Southampton: King, 1837.

Burgon, John William. *The Revision Revised.* London: Murray, 1883.

Burigni, Jean Lévesque de. *Vie d'Erasme.* 2 vols. Paris: De Bure, 1757.

Burnet, Gilbert. *The History of the Reformation of the Church of England.* 2 vols. London: Chiswell, 1679–1681.

Some Letters. Containing, An Account of What Seemed Most Remarkable in Switzerland, Italy, &c. Rotterdam: Acher, 1686.

An Exposition of the Thirty-Nine Articles of the Church of England. London: Chiswell, 1699.

Butler, Charles. *Horae Biblicae.* 2nd ed. London: White, 1807.

The Byble in Englyshe. [London]: Grafton and Whitchurch, 1539.

Cajetan, Tommaso de Vio. *Epistolae Pauli et aliorum apostolorum ad graecam veritatem castigatae.* Venice: Giunta, 1531.

Calamy, Edmund. *Thirteen Sermons Concerning the Doctrine of the Trinity. Preach'd at the Merchant's-Lecture, at Salter's-Hall. Together with a Vindication of that Celebrated Text, 1 John v. 7. from being Spurious; and an Explication of it, upon the Supposition of its being Genuine.* London: Clark, 1722.

Calvin, Jean, trans. *Le Nouveau Testament.* Geneva: Riveriz, 1551a.

Commentarii in Epistolas Canonicas, Vnam Petri. Vnam Ioannis. Vnam Iacobi. *Petri alteram. Iudae vnam.* Geneva: Jean Crispin, 1551b.

Campanus, Johannes. *Göttlicher und heiliger Schrifft, vor vilen jaren verdunck-elt, und durch unheylsame leer und Lerer (auß Gottes zůlassung) verfinstert, Restitution und besserung.* [Strasbourg]: [Cammerlander], 1532.

Campbell, Gordon, Thomas N. Corns, John K. Hale and Fiona J. Tweedie. *Milton and the Manuscript of* De Doctrina Christiana. Cambridge: Cambridge University Press, 2007.

Cano, Melchior. *De locis theologicis libri duodecim.* Salamanca: Gastius, 1563.

Canones et decreta, sacrosancti oecumenici, & generalis concilij Tridentini. Alcalá: Robles, 1564.

Capecelatro, Alfonso. *Codices Manuscripti Graeci Ottoboniani.* Rome: Typographeum Vaticanum, 1893.

Capp, Bernard. *England's Culture Wars: Puritan Reformation and Its Enemies in the Interregnum, 1649–1660.* Oxford: Oxford University Press, 2012.

Cappel, Louis. *Critica sacra, sive de variis quae in sacris Veteris Testamenti libris occurrunt lectionibus libri six.* Paris: Cramoisy, 1650.

Carlsson, Eric Wilhelm. 'Johann Salomo Semler, the German Enlightenment, and Protestant theology's historical turn.' Diss. Wisconsin-Madison, 2006.

Casley, David. *A Catalogue of the Manuscripts of the King's Library.* London: Casley, 1734.

Cass, Frederick Charles. *South Mimms.* London: Nichols, 1877.

Cassiodorus, Flavius Magnus Aurelius. *Complexiones in Epistolas et Acta Apostolorum et Apocalypsin.* Ed. Scipione Maffei. Florence: Manni, 1721.

Castellio, Sebastian, trans. *Biblia, interprete Sebastiano Castalione.* Basel: Oporinus, 1556.

Biblia Sacra ex Sebastiani Castalionis postrema recognitione. Basel: Peter Perna, 1573.

Castello, Alberto da, ed. *Biblia cum concordantijs veteris et noui testamenti & sacrorum canonum: nec non & additione in marginibus varietatis diuersorum textuum.* Venice: Giunta, 1511.

Catechesis ecclesiarum quae in Regno Poloniae, & magno Ducatu Lithuaniae, & aliis ad istud Regnum pertinentibus Provinciis, affirmant, neminem alium, praeter Patrem Domini nostri Jesu Christi, esse illum unum Deum Israëlis. Raków: [Sternacius], 1609.

Catharinus, Ambrosius. *Annotationes [...] in excerpta quaedam de commentarijs Reuerendissimi Cardinalis Caietani S. Xisti, dogmata.* Paris: Simon de Colines, 1535.

Annotationes in Commentaria Caietani denuò multò locupletiores & castigatiores redditae. Lyon: Bonhomme, 1542.

Champion, Justin A. I. 'Père Richard Simon and English Biblical Criticism, 1680–1700.' In *Everything Connects.* Ed. James E. Force and David S. Katz. Leiden: Brill, 1999a: 37–61.

'"Acceptable to Inquisitive Men": Some Simonian Contexts for Newton's Biblical Criticism, 1680–1692.' In Force and Popkin 1999b: 77–96.

Chauncy, Isaac. *A Rejoynder to Mr. Daniel Williams His Reply to the First Part of Neomianism Unmaskt*. London: Barnard, 1693.

Chevalier, Jacques. 'The Biblical Commission.' *The Expository Times* 18 (1906–1907): 235–237.

Cheynell, Francis. *Chillingworthi novissima. Or, the Sicknesse, Heresy, Death, and Buriall of William Chillingworth*. London: Gellibrand, 1644.

The Divine Trinunity of the Father, Son, and Holy Spirit. London: Gellibrand, 1650.

'Christicola' [John Bevans, Jr.], ed. *Some Tracts Relating to the Controversy Between Hannah Barnard and the Society of Friends*. London: Darton and Harvey, 1802.

Chrysostom, Johannes. Τοῦ ἐν Ἁγίοις Πατρὸς ἡμῶν Ἰωάννου Ἀρχιεπισκόπου Κωνσταντινουπόλεως τοῦ Χρυσοστόμου τῶν Εὑρισκομένων. Ed. Henry Savile. 3 vols. Eton: Norton, 1610–1612.

Chrysostom, John. *Opera omnia quae exstant*. 13 vols. Paris: Gaume, 1834–1839.

Chubb, Thomas. *The Supremacy of the Father Asserted*. London: Roberts, 1715.

Clarke, Adam. *Observations on the Text of the Three Divine Witnesses: accompanied with a Plate containing two very correct Facsimiles of I John, Chap. V. Ver. 7, 8 and 9, as they stand in the first edition of the New Testament, printed at Complutum, 1514, and in the Codex Montfortii, a Manuscript marked G. 97, in the Library of Trinity College, Dublin*. Manchester: R. & W. Dean, 1805.

An Account of the Religious, and Literary Life of Adam Clarke. 2 vols. London: Clarke, 1833.

ed. *The Holy Bible, containing the Old and New Testaments*. London: Tegg, 1836.

Clarke, Martin Lowther. *Richard Porson: A Biographical Essay*. Cambridge: Cambridge University Press, 1937.

Clarke, Samuel. *A Demonstration of the Being and Attributes of God: more particularly in Answer to Mr. Hobbs, Spinoza, and their Followers*. London: Botham, 1705.

A Discourse concerning the Unchangeable Obligations of Natural Religion, and the Truth and Certainty of the Christian Revelation. London: Botham, 1706.

The Scripture-Doctrine of the Trinity. London: Knapton, 1712.

A Letter to the Reverend Dr Wells. London: Knapton, 1714a.

A Reply to the Objections of Robert Nelson, Esq; and of an anonymous Author, against Dr Clarke's Scripture-Doctrine of the Trinity. London: Knapton, 1714b.

A Collection of Papers, which passed between the late Learned Mr. Leibnitz, and Dr. Clarke, in the Years 1715 and 1716. Relating to the Principles of Natural Philosophy and Religion. London: Knapton, 1717.

[ed.] *Select Psalms and Hymns for the Use of the Parish-Church, and Chappels belonging to the Parish of St. James's Westminster. With Proper Tunes in three Parts*. London: Pearson, 1718.

The Scripture-Doctrine of the Trinity. 2nd ed. London: Wilkins for Knapton, 1719.

The Book of Common Prayer Reformed according to the Plan of the late Dr. Samuel Clarke. London: J. Johnson, 1774.

'Clemens Anglicanus' [Thomas Turton]. *Remarks upon Mr. Evanson's preface to his translation of Knittel's New Criticisms on I John, v. 7*. Cambridge: Smith for Deighton, 1829.

Close, Francis. 'The British and Foreign School Society.' *The Standard*, 30 April 1839: 4.

Coates, Alan. *English Medieval Books*. Oxford: Oxford University Press, 1999.

Cochlaeus, Johannes. *Septiceps Lutherus, ubique sibi, suis scriptis contrarius*. Leipzig: Schumann, 1529.

—— *Replica brevis Iohannis Cochlaei, aduersus prolixam responsionem Henrici Bullingeri de scripturae & ecclesiae authoritate*. Ingolstadt: Weissenhorn, 1544.

Colines, Simon de, ed. Ἡ Καινὴ Διαθήκη. Paris: de Colines, 1534. *DM* 4608.

Colligan, J. Hay. *The Arian Movement in England*. Manchester: Manchester University Press, 1913.

Collins, Anthony. *A Discourse of Free-Thinking, Occasion'd by The Rise and Growth of a Sect call'd Free-Thinkers*. London: [n. p.], 1713.

Combefis, François, ed. *Bibliothecae graecorum patrum auctarium novissimum*. 2 vols. Paris: Hotot, 1672.

The Confession of Faith, and the Larger and Shorter Catechisme, First agreed upon by the Assembly of Divines at Westminster. And now appointed by the General Assembly of the Kirk of Scotland. Edinburgh: Gedeon Lithgow, 1649.

Coogan, Robert. *Erasmus, Lee and the Correction of the Vulgate: The Shaking of the Foundations*. Geneva: Droz, 1992.

Cooper, Charles Henry and Thompson Cooper. *Athenae Cantabrigienses. Volume I: 1500–1585*. Cambridge: Deighton, Bell & Co, 1858.

Cornwall, N. E. 'The genuineness of I. John, v. 7: proved by neglected witnesses.' *The American Church Review* 29 (1877): 509–528.

Courcelles [Curcellaeus], Etienne de, ed. Ἡ Καινὴ Διαθήκη. *Novum Testamentum. Editio nova: In qua diligentius quàm unquam antea variantes lectiones tam ex manuscriptis quàm impressis codicibus collectae, & parallela Scripturae loca annotata sunt*. Amsterdam: Elzevier, 1658.

Coverdale, Myles, trans. *Biblia The Bible / that is, the holy Scripture of the Olde and New Testament*. [Antwerp]: [M. de Keyser], 1535.

—— *The Byble which is all the holy Scripture: in whych are contayned the Olde and Newe Testament*. [Antwerp]: Crom, 1537.

Coxe, H. O. *Codicum Manuscriptorum Bibliothecae Bodleianae pars prima*. Oxford: Oxford University Press, 1853.

Cramer, Eugene Casjen. *Tomás Luis de Victoria: a guide to research*. London: Routledge, 1998.

[Craven, Joseph.] *Two letters to the reverend Dr. Bentley, Master of Trinity-College in Cambridge, concerning his intended edition of the Greek Testament*. London: Morphew, 1717.

Crehan, F. J. 'The Bible in the Roman Catholic Church from Trent to the Present Day.' In *The Cambridge History of the Bible. The West from the Reformation to the Present Day*. Ed. S. L. Greenslade. Cambridge: Cambridge University Press, 1963: 199–237.

[Crell, Johann and Joachim Stegmann, trans.] *Das Newe Testament, Das ist / Alle Bücher des newen Bundes / welchen Gott durch Christum mit den menschen gemacht hat / Trewlich aus dem Griechischen ins Teutsche versetzet.* Raków: [Sternacius], 1630.

Crell, Johann. *Catechesis ecclesiarum Polonicarum.* Stauropolis [Amsterdam]: Eulogetus Philalethes [Christiaan Petzold?], 1680.

'Criticus' [William Orme]. *Memoir of the Controversy Respecting the Three Heavenly Witnesses, 1 John v. 7.* London: Holdsworth and Ball, 1830.

'Crito Cantabrigiensis' [Thomas Turton]. *A vindication of the Literary Character of the late Professor Porson from the Animadversions of the Right Reverend Thomas Burgess.* Cambridge: Smith for Deighton, 1827.

Cross, Frank Leslie and Elizabeth A. Livingstone, ed. *The Oxford Dictionary of the Christian Church.* 3rd edition. Oxford: Oxford University Press, 1997.

Crowther, Jonathan. *A Portraiture of Methodism.* London: Edwards, 1815.

Curley, Edwin. 'Hobbes and the Cause of Religious Toleration.' In *The Cambridge Companion to Hobbes's Leviathan.* Ed. Patricia Springborg. Cambridge: Cambridge University Press, 2007: 309–336.

Cyprian of Carthage. *Opera.* Ed. John Fell. Oxford: Sheldonian Theatre, 1682.

Czechowic, Marcin. *Wuiek, To iest / krotki odpis / na pisanie X. Jakuba Wuyka z Wągrowca / Theologa Societatis Iesu / o Bostwie syna Bożego / y ducha ś.* Kraków: Rodecki, 1590.

Damrosch, Leo. *Jonathan Swift: His Life and His World.* New Haven, CT: Yale University Press, 2013.

Darlow, Thomas Herbert and Horace Frederick Moule. *Historical Catalogue of the Printed Editions of the Holy Scripture in the Library of the British and Foreign Bible Society [DM].* 2 vols. London: Bible House, 1903–1911.

Das Neue Testament / Oder: Der Neue Bund / Welchen GOtt Durch JEsum CHristum Mit Uns Menschen gemachet [. . .]. Wandsbek: Holle, 1710.

Dat heylich Euangelium, dat leuende woort gods wtghesproken door onsen salichmaker Jesum Christum. [Antwerp]: [Christoffel van Ruremund], 26 September 1525.

Dat heylich Euangelium dat leuende woort Godts wtghesproken door onsen salichmaker Jesum Christum. Antwerp: Christoffel van Ruremund, [c. 1526].

Dat nieuwe Testament ons Heeren Iesu Christi. Emden: Biestkens, 1560.

Dauderstadt, Caspar Christophorus. *Dissertatio theologica inauguralis ad Cap. I.I. Joh. Epist. V. 7.* Jena: Samuel Krebs, [1674].

Dávid, Ferenc, ed. *Brevis enarratio disputationis Albanae de Deo trino et Christo duplici coram Serenissimo Principe, & tota ecclesia decem diebus habita.* Alba Iulia: Widow of Raphael Hoffhalter, 1568.

Dávid, Ferenc and Giorgio Biandrata. *Refutatio scripti Georgii Maioris, in quo Deum trinum in personis, et unum in Essentia: Vnicum deinde eius Filium in persona, & duplicem in naturis, ex lacunis Antichristi probare conatus est.* [Cluj-Napoca]: [n. p.], 1569.

Davies, Myles. *Athenae Britannicae: or, a Critical History of the Oxford and Cambridge Writers and Writings, with those of the Dissenters and Romanists.* London: Davies, 1716.

Davis, Virginia. *Clergy in London in the Late Middle Ages. A Register of Clergy Ordained in the Diocese of London Based on Episcopal Ordination Lists, 1361–1539* [Database]. London: University of London Centre for Metropolitan History, 2000.

Dawson, Thomas. *Disceptatio epistolaris de coelestibus testimoniis 1 Joh. v. 7. in qua ex binis Manuscriptis Eximiis, Indubio evincitur* αὐθεντία *istius versiculi.* London: Wilcox, 1734.

De Bruyne, Donatien. *Les Fragments de Freising (épîtres de S. Paul et épitres catholiques).* Rome: Biblioteca Apostolica Vaticana, 1921.

De Jonge, Henk Jan. *Daniel Heinsius and the Textus Receptus of the New Testament.* Leiden: Brill, 1971.

'Erasmus und die *Glossa ordinaria* zum Neuen Testament.' *Nederlands Archief voor Kerkgeschiedenis* 56 (1975): 51–77.

'À propos des premiers apparats critiques dans la Bible latine imprimée.' *Nederlands Archief voor Kerkgeschiedenis* N. S. 57 (1977): 145–147.

'Caro in Spiritum. Delenus en zijn uitlegging van Joh. 6:51.' In *De Geest in het geding.* Ed. I. B. Horst, A. F. de Jong and D. Visser. Alphen aan den Rijn: Tjeenk Willink, 1978a: 145–168.

'Jeremias Hoelzlin: Editor of the 'Textus Receptus' Printed by the Elzeviers Leiden 1633.' In *Miscellanea Neotestamentica I.* Ed. T. Baarda, A. F. J. Klijn and W. C. van Unnik. Leiden: Brill, 1978b: 105–128.

De bestudering van het Nieuwe Testament aan de Noordnederlandse universiteiten en het Remonstrants Seminarie van 1575 tot 1700. Amsterdam: Noord-Hollandse Uitgevers Maatschappij, 1980a.

'Erasmus and the *comma Johanneum.*' *Ephemerides Theologicae Lovanienses* 56 (1980b): 381–389.

'Hugo Grotius: exégète du Nouveau Testament.' In *The World of Hugo Grotius (1583–1648)*, intro. by R. Feenstra. Amsterdam/Maarsen: APA Holland University Press, 1984a: 97–115.

'Novum Testamentum a nobis versum: the essence of Erasmus' edition of the New Testament.' *Journal of Theological Studies* N. S. 35 (1984b): 394–413.

'The Date and Purpose of Erasmus' *Castigatio Novi Testamenti*: A Note on the Origins of the *Novum Instrumentum.*' In *The Uses of Greek and Latin.* Ed. A. C. Dionisotti, A. Grafton and J. Kraye. London: Warburg Institute, 1988a: 97–110.

'Wann ist Erasmus' Übersetzung des Neuen Testaments entstanden?' In *Erasmus of Rotterdam. The Man and the Scholar.* Ed. J. Sperna Weiland and W. T. M. Frijhoff. Leiden: Brill, 1988b: 151–157.

'Comma Johanneum.' In *Religion in Geschichte und Gegenwart.* Ed. H. D. Betz et al. 4th ed. Tübingen: Mohr (Siebeck), 1999, 2:429.

De Jonghe, M. 'Declaratio circa decretum de authentia 1 Jo., V, 7.' *Collationes Brugenses* 27 (1927): 452–455.

De la Roche, Michel. Review of Emlyn 1719b. *Bibliothèque angloise* 5 (1720): 281–320.

Review of Martin 1719b and Emlyn 1720. *Mémoires litéraires de la Grande Bretagne* 3 (1720): 1–6.

Delany, Patrick. *Eighteen Discourses and Dissertations.* London: Johnston, 1766.

Delenus, Walterus, trans. *Novum Testamentum Latinum.* London: John Mayler, 1540.

Delitzsch, Franz. *Studien zur Entstehungsgeschichte der Polyglottenbibel des Cardinals Ximenes.* Leipzig: Edelmann, 1871.

Den Bybel met groter neersticheyt ghecorrigeert. Antwerp: Jacob van Liesveldt, 1542.

Den gheheelen Bybel / Inhoudende het oude ende nieuwe Testament. Leuven: Bartholomeus van Grave, 1548. *DM* 3287.

Dennett, Daniel. *Darwin's Dangerous Idea. Evolution and the Meanings of Life.* New York: Simon & Schuster, 1995.

Denzinger, Heinrich. *Enchiridion symbolorum definitionum et declarationum de rebus fidei et morum. Kompendium der Glaubensbekenntnisse und kirchlichen Lehrentscheidungen.* Trans. Helmut Hoping and Peter Hünermann. 39th ed. Freiburg i. B.: Herder, 2001.

De Rossi, Johannes Franciscus Bernardus Maria. *De tribus in caelo testibus, Patre, Verbo et Spiritu Sancto, qui tres unum sunt, I. Ep. Joan. Cap. V. V̇. 7. Dissertatio Adversus Samuelem Crellium, aliosque.* Venice: Occhi, 1755.

Determinatio facultatis theologicae in Schola Parisiensi super quamplurimis assertionibus D. Erasmi Roterodami. Paris: Badius Ascensius, 1531.

De Vet, Jan. 'In Search of Spinoza in the *Histoire des Ouvrages des Savans*.' In *Disguised and overt Spinozism around 1700.* Ed. Wiep van Bunge and Wim Klever. Leiden: Brill, 1996: 83–101.

De Vocht, Henry. *Monumenta Humanistica Lovaniensia. Texts and Studies about Louvain Humanists in the First Half of the XVth Century.* Leuven: Uystpruyst, 1934.

―――. *History of the Foundation and the Rise of the Collegium Trilingue Lovaniense 1517–1550.* 4 vols. Humanistica Lovaniensia 10–13. Leuven: Bibliothèque de l'Université, 1951–1955.

Dharmapustaker Antabhag. The New Testament of Our Lord and Saviour Jesus Christ, in Bengali and English. 2 vols. London: British and Foreign Bible Society, 1839.

Didiot, Jules. 'Commentaire traditionnel de la IVᵉ session du Concile de Trente.' *Revue des sciences ecclésiastiques* 62 (1890): 193–226, 385–400.

Die kerstelijcke Epistelen ende leeringhen der eerwaerdigher apostelen. Antwerp: Van Ghelen, [1524].

Dionisotti, A. C. 'On the Greek Studies of Robert Grosseteste.' In *The Uses of Greek and Latin.* Ed. A. C. Dionisotti, A. Grafton and J. Kraye. London: Warburg Institute, 1988: 19–39.

Dixon, Philip. *'Nice and Hot Disputes': The Doctrine of the Trinity in the Seventeenth Century.* London: T & T Clark, 2003.

Dobbin, Orlando Thomas. *The Codex Montfortianus.* London: Bagster, 1854.

Dodds, Gregory D. *Exploiting Erasmus: The Erasmian Legacy and Religious Change in Early Modern England.* Toronto: Toronto University Press, 2009.

Dodsley, Robert. *The Correspondence of Robert Dodsley, 1733–1764.* Ed. James E. Tierney. Cambridge: Cambridge University Press, 1988.

Dorsche, Johann Georg. *Dissertatio theologica de spiritu, aqua et sanguine in terra tribus testibus pro Christo Dei filio, ex I. Johan. cap. V. vers. IIX. sive de verbo et duobus Nov. Test. sacramentis.* Frankfurt/Main: Fischer, 1653.

Drummond, Robert Blackley. *Erasmus, His Life and Character as Shown in His Correspondence and Works.* 2 vols. London: Smith, Elder & Co, 1873.

Dry, Sarah. *The Newton Papers.* Oxford: Oxford University Press, 2014.

Düsterdieck, Friedrich Hermann Christian. *Die drei johanneischen Briefe.* 2 vols. Göttingen: Dieterich, 1852–1856.

Duffy, Eamon. ' "Whiston's Affair": The Trials of a Primitive Christian 1709–1714.' *The Journal of Ecclesiastical History* 27 (1976): 129–150.

Du Moulin [Molinaeus], Charles. *Commentarii in Parisienses totius Galliae supremi Parlamenti consuetudines.* Lausanne: François Le Preux, 1576.

Dunn, Henry. *Principles of Teaching.* 3rd ed. London: Sunday-School Union, 1839.

Du Pin, Louis-Ellies. *Dissertation préliminaire ou prolégomènes sur la bible.* 2 vols. Paris: A. Pralard, 1699a.

A Compleat History of the Canon and Writers, of the Books of the Old and New Testament. 2 vols. London: H. Rhodes, 1699b.

Edwards, John. *Some Thoughts Concerning the Several Causes and Occasions of Atheism, Especially in the Present Age. With Some Brief Reflections on Socinianism: and on a Late Book.* London: Robinson, 1695.

Some Brief Critical Remarks on Dr. Clarke's Last Papers. London: Burleigh, 1714.

Edwards, Jonathan. *A Preservative against Socinianism. First Part.* 3rd ed. Oxford: Clements, 1698.

Edwards, Thomas. *Gangraena: or a Catalogue and Discovery of Many of the Errours, Heresies, Blasphemies and Pernicious Practices of the Sectaries of This Time, Vented and Acted in England in These Last Four Years.* London: Ralph Smith, 1646a.

The Second Part of Gangraena. London: Ralph Smith, 1646b.

The Third Part of Gangraena. London: Ralph Smith, 1646c.

Egerton, Stephen. *A Briefe Methode of Catechising.* 5th ed. London: R. F. for Robert Dexter, 1597.

Ehrman, Bart D. *The Orthodox Corruption of Scripture.* New York: Oxford University Press, 1993.

Elliott, J. Keith. Review of Greenlee 2008. *Review of Biblical Literature* 11 (2009a): 538–543.

'Manuscripts Cited by Stephanus.' *New Testament Studies* 55 (2009b): 390–395.

'The Text of the New Testament.' In *A History of Biblical Interpretation. Vol. 2: The Medieval through the Reformation Periods.* Ed. Alan J. Hauser and Duane F. Watson. Grand Rapids: Eerdmans, 2009c: 227–253.

Emden, Alfred B. *A Biographical Register of the University of Cambridge to 1500.* Cambridge: Cambridge University Press, 1963.

A Biographical Register of the University of Oxford, A. D. 1501 to 1540. Oxford: Oxford University Press, 1974.

Emlyn, Thomas. *An Humble Inquiry into the Scripture-Account of Jesus Christ: or, a Short Argument Concerning His Deity and Glory, According to the Gospel.* [London?]: [n. p.], 1702.

A Full Inquiry into the Original Authority of That Text, 1 John V. 7. There are Three That bear Record in Heaven. London: Baker, 1715.

A Full Inquiry into the Original Authority of That Text, 1 John V. 7. 2nd ed. London: Harrison and Dodd, 1717.

A Full Inquiry into the Original Authority of That Text, 1 John V. 7. 3rd ed. London: Darby, 1719a.

An Answer to Mr. Martin's Critical Dissertation on 1 John v. 7. London: Darby, 1719b.

A True Narrative of the Proceedings of the Dissenting Ministers of Dublin against Mr. Thomas Emlyn. London: Darby, 1719c.

A Reply to Mr. Martin's Examination of the Answer to His Dissertation on 1 John 5. 7. London: Darby, 1720.

A Collection of Tracts, Relating to the Deity, Worship, and Satisfaction of the Lord Jesus Christ. 2nd ed. 2 vols. London: [n. p.], 1731.

The Works of Mr. Thomas Emlyn. 3 vols. 4th ed. London: Noon and Whiston, 1746.

Emser, Hieronymus. *Auß was gründ vnnd vrsach Luthers dolmatschung / vber das nawe testament / dem gemeinen man billich vorbotten worden sey.* Leipzig: Stöckel, 1523.

Enyedi, György. *Explicationes locorum Veteris & Novi Testamenti, ex quibus Trinitatis dogma stabiliri solet.* [Cluj-Napoca]: [Heltai], [1598].

Enzinas, Francisco de, trans. *El nuevo testamento de nuestro Redemptor y Salvador Iesu Christo.* Antwerp: Mierdmans, 1543.

Epp, Eldon Jay. 'The Multivalence of the Term "Original Text" in New Testament Textual Criticism.' *The Harvard Theological Review* 92 (1999): 245–281.

'In the Beginning was the New Testament Text, but Which Text?' In *Texts and Traditions.* Ed. Peter Doble and Jeffrey Kloha. Leiden: Brill, 2014: 35–70.

Erasmus, Desiderius, ed. *Novum instrumentum omne.* Basel: Froben, 1516.

ed. *Omnia opera divi Eusebii Hieronymi Stridonensis.* 10 vols. Basel: Froben and Amerbach, 1516–1520.

ed. *Novum testamentum omne.* Basel: Froben, March 1519a.

Des. Erasmi Roterodami in Novum Testamentum ab eodem denuo recognitum, Annotationes. Basel: Froben, 1519b.

Ratio seu methodus compendio peruéniendi ad veram theologiam. Mainz: Schöffer, May 1519c.

Responsio ad annotationes Lei nouas. Basel: Froben, 21 July 1520.

ed. *Novum Testamentum omne.* Basel: Froben, 14 June 1521a.

D. Erasmi Roterodami Apologia respondens ad ea quae Iacobus Lopis Stunica taxauerat in prima duntaxat noui Testamenti aeditione. Leuven: Dirk Martens, 1521b.

ed. *Novum Testamentum omne, tertio iam ac diligentius ab Erasmo Roterodamo recognitum.* Basel: Froben, February 1522a.

Des. Erasmi Roterodami in Novum Testamentum ab eodem tertio recognitum, Annotationes. Basel: Froben, 1522b.

Tomus secundus continens Paraphrasim D. Erasmi Rot. In omneis epistolas apostolicas. Basel: Froben, 1523a.

ed. *Diui Hilarii Pictauorum episcopi lucubrationes per Erasmum Roterodamum non mediocribus sudoribus emendatae.* Basel: Froben, 1523b.

Modus orandi Deum. Basel: Froben, 1524.

ed. *Novum Testamentum, ex Erasmi Roterodami recognitione, iam quartum.* Basel: Froben, March 1527a.

Des. Erasmi Roterodami in Novum Testamentum Annotationes, ab ipso iam quartum recognitae. Basel: Froben, 1527b.

Prologus supputationis errorum in censuris Bedae. Basel: Froben, March 1527c.

Supputationes errorum in censuris Natalis Bedae. Basel: Froben, March 1527d.

Io. Frob. Studioso Lectori S. D. Tria noua dabit hic libellus, Epistolam Erasmi, de modestia profitendi linguas [. . .]. Basel: Froben, August 1527e.

Apologia aduersus articulos aliquot per monachos quosdam in Hispanijs, exhibitos. Basel: Froben, 1528.

ed. *Divi Caecilii Cypriani episcopi Carthaginensis et martyris opera iam quartum accuratiori uigilantia à mendis repurgata, per Des. Erasmum Roterod. Accessit liber eiusdem apprimè pius ad Fortunatum De duplici martyrio, antehac nunquàm excusus.* Basel: Froben, 1530.

Apologia adversus rhapsodias calumniosarum querimoniarum Alberti Pij. Basel: Froben, 1531.

Declarationes Des. Erasmi Roterodami, ad Censuras Lutetiae uulgatas sub nomine Facultatis Theologiae Parisiensis. Basel: Froben, September 1532.

ed. *Novum Testamentum iam quintum accuratissima cura recognitum à Des. Erasmo Roter.* Basel: Froben and Episcopius, March 1535a.

Des. Erasmi Roterodami in Novum Testamentum Annotationes, ab ipso autore iam quintum sic recognitae, ac locupletatae, ut propemodum nouum opus uideri possit. Basel: Froben and Episcopius, March 1535b; fascimile in Reeve and Screech, 1990 and 1993.

ed. *D. Hilarii Pictavorum episcopi lucubrationes quotquot extant.* Basel: Froben, 1535c.

The newe testament in Englyshe translated after the texte of Master Erasmus of Roterodame in Anno. 1539. London: Grafton and Whitchurch, 1539.

Ausgewählte Werke. Ed. Hajo Holborn and Annemarie Holborn. Munich: Beck, 1933.

Controversies: Apologia qua respondet invectivis Lei; Responsio ad annotationes Lei. Collected Works of Erasmus 72. Ed. Jane E. Phillips. Trans. Erika Rummel. Toronto: Toronto University Press, 2005.

Erbery, William. *The Testimony of William Erbery.* London: Calvert, 1658.

Estienne, Robert, ed. Τῆς Καινῆς Διαθήκης ἅπαντα. Paris: Robert Estienne, 1550. *DM* 4622.

Etliche schöne Christliche Geseng / wie sie in der Gefengkniß zu Passaw im Schloß von den Schweitzer Brüdern durch Gottes gnad geticht vnd gesungen worden. [n. p.]: [n. p.], 1564.

Evelyn, John. *Diary and Correspondence.* Ed. William Bray. 2nd ed. 4 vols. London: Colburn, 1850–1857.

Diary. Ed. E. S. De Beer. London: Oxford University Press, 1959.

Exley, Thomas. *Reply to Mr. Watson's Remarks on the Eternal Sonship of Christ.* London: Butterworth, 1818.

Farley, Frederick A. *Grounds for Rejecting the Text of the Three Heavenly Witnesses; 1 John, V, 7.* Boston: Munroe for the American Unitarian Association, 1845.

 Unitarianism Defined: The Scripture Doctrine of the Father, Son and Holy Ghost. Boston: Walker, Wise & Co, 1860.

Farrell, Maureen. *William Whiston.* New York: Arno Press, 1981.

Felbinger, Jeremias, trans. *Das Neue Testament / Treulich aus dem Grichischen ins Deutsche übersetzet.* Amsterdam: Christoph Cunrad, 1660.

Fell, John, ed. Τῆς Καινῆς Διαθήκης ἅπαντα. *Novi Testamenti Libri Omnes. Accesserunt Parallela Scripturae Loca, nec non Variantes Lectiones ex plus 100 MSS. Codicibus, et Antiquis Versionibus Collectae.* Oxford: Sheldonian Theatre, 1675. *DM* 4711.

Ferguson, James P. *Dr. Samuel Clarke, an Eighteenth-Century Heretic.* London: Roundwood Press, 1976.

Figueiredo, Anthony J. *The Magisterium-Theology Relationship.* Rome: Editrice Pontificia Università Gregoriana, 2001.

Firmin, Thomas. *Some Proposals for the Imploying of the Poor, Especially in and about the City of London.* London: Aylmer, 1681.

Fischer, Bonifatius. *Lateinische Bibelhandschriften im frühen Mittelalter.* Freiburg: Herder, 1985.

Fisher, Samuel. *Rusticus ad Academicos in Exercitationibus Expostulatoriis, Apologeticis quatuor. The Rustick's Alarm to the Rabbies.* London: Wilson, 1660.

Fleck, Niels. 'Die allegorisch-emblematischen Bildprogramme in Schloß und Schloßkirche Saalfeld.' *Marburger Jahrbuch für Kunstwissenschaft* 34 (2007): 217–249.

Fleischmann, Stefan. *Szymon Budny.* Cologne: Böhlau, 2006.

Fogarty, Gerald. 'The Catholic Church and Historical Criticism of the Old Testament.' In *Hebrew Bible/Old Testament: The History of Its Interpretation. III/1: The Nineteenth Century.* Ed. Magne Saebø. Göttingen: Vandenhoeck & Ruprecht, 2013: 244–261.

Force, James E. *William Whiston, Honest Newtonian.* Cambridge: Cambridge University Press, 1985.

Force, James E. and Richard H. Popkin, ed. *Newton and Religion: Context, Nature, and Influence.* Dordrecht: Kluwer, 1999.

Forster, Charles. *A New Plea for the Authenticity of the Text of the Three Heavenly Witnesses.* Cambridge: Deighton, Bell and Co., 1867.

Foster, Joseph. *Alumni Oxonienses.* 4 vols. Oxford: Parker, 1891–1892.

Foucault, Michel. *Dits et écrits.* Ed. Daniel Defert and François Ewald. 2 vols. Paris: Gallimard, 1994.

Fowler, Thomas. *The History of Corpus Christi College.* Oxford: Oxford Historical Society, 1893.

Fox, Adam. *John Mill and Richard Bentley.* Oxford: Basil Blackwell, 1954.

François, Wim. 'Augustine and the Golden Age of Biblical Scholarship in Louvain (1550–1650).' In *Shaping the Bible in the Reformation*. Ed. Bruce Gordon and Matthew McClean. Leiden: Brill, 2012: 235–289.

Franck, Sebastian. *Chronica, Zeytbůch vnd geschychtbibell*. Strasbourg: Balthasar Beck, 1531.

    Chronica, Tytboeck ende gheschiet bibel. [Emden]: [Willem Gailliart], 1558.

Franzelin, Johann Baptist. *Tractatus de Deo trino secundum personas*. Rome: Sacra congregatio de propaganda fide, 1869.

Freeman, Curtis W. 'God in Three Persons: Baptist Unitarianism and the Trinity.' *Perspectives in Religious Studies* 33 (2006): 323–344.

[Freke, William]. *A Vindication of the Unitarians*. [London]: [n. p.], [*c*. 1687].

Frick, David A. *Polish Sacred Philology in the Reformation and the Counter-Reformation*. Berkeley: University of California Press, 1989.

    'The Uses of Authority and the Authority of Use: Philological Praise and Blame in Early Modern Rus´.' *Harvard Ukrainian Studies* 18 (1994): 76–93.

    'Sailing to Byzantium: Greek Texts and the Establishment of Authority in Early Modern Muscovy.' *Harvard Ukrainian Studies* 19 (1995): 138–157.

Fries, Heinrich. *Fundamental Theology*. Trans. Robert J. Daly. Washington, DC: Catholic University of America Press, 1996.

Froidmont, Libert. *Commentaria in omnes B. Pauli Apostoli, et septem canonicas aliorum apostolorum epistolas*. Leuven: Nempaeus, 1663.

Gamble, John. *Sketches of History, Politics and Manners Taken in Dublin*. London: Cradock, 1811.

Gamillscheg, Ernst and Dieter Harlfinger. *Repertorium der griechischen Kopisten, 800–1600. 1. Teil: Handschriften aus Bibliotheken Großbritanniens*. 3 vols. Vienna: Verlag der Österreichischen Akademie der Wissenschaften, 1981.

    Repertorium der griechischen Kopisten, 800–1600. 2. Teil: Handschriften aus Bibliotheken Frankreichs. 3 vols. Vienna: Verlag der Österreichischen Akademie der Wissenschaften, 1989.

Gauss, Julia. 'Der junge Michael Servet.' *Zwingliana* 12 (1966): 410–459.

Gaza, Theodore of. *In hoc volumine haec insunt. Introductivae grammatices libri quatuor*. Venice: Aldus, 1495.

Geddes, Michael. *The History of the Church of Malabar*. London: Smith and Walford, 1694.

Gémeau [Gumelli], Adrien, ed. *Biblia cum pleno apparatu summariorum concordantiarum*. Paris: Tielman Kerver for Jean Petit, 1504.

Gerbelius, Nicolaus, ed. *Nouum Testamentum Graece*. Hagenau: Anshelm, 1521. DM 4598.

Gerhard, David Gottfried. *Dictum Ioanneum 1. Ep. V. 7. Ab exceptionibus recentissimis summorum quorundam virorum modeste vindicatum*. Breslau: J. E. Meyer, 1763.

Gerhard, Johann. *Loci theologici cum pro adstruenda veritate, tum pro destruenda quorumvis contradicentium falsitate per Theses nervosè, solidè & copiosè explicati*. 6 vols. Jena: Steinmann, 1610–1619.

    Disputationis Theologicae Ex dicto Apostolico I. Joh. 5. v. 7 [...] Orationem [...] habebit. Jena: Steinmann, 1619.

Dissertatio Theologica bipartita ex dicto apostolico 1. Joh. v, 7. [...]. Jena: Marggraf, 1714.

Commentatio uberior in dictum Johanneum 1. Joh. V, 7. de tribus in coelo testibus: Von denen dreyen Zeugen im Himmel, ob argumenti dignitatem, atque tractationis praestantiam luci publicae vindicata. Jena: Marggraf, 1721.

Commentatio qua dictum Johanneum de tribus testibus in coelo sive Von den Dreyen Zeugen im Himmel, 1. Epistol. V, 7. fuse enarratur atque explicatur. Jena: Marggraf, 1746.

Commentatio qua dictum Johanneum de tribus testibus in coelo sive Von den Dreyen Zeugen im Himmel, 1. Epistol. V, 7. fuse enarratur atque explicatur. Jena: Marggraf, 1747.

Gibbon, Edward. *History of the Decline and Fall of the Roman Empire.* 6 vols. London: Strahan and Cadell, 1776–1788.

Miscellaneous Works. 2 vols. London: Strahan, Cadell and Davies, 1796.

Gibert, Pierre. *L'invention critique de la Bible, XVe–XVIIIe siècle.* Paris: Gallimard, 2010.

Gibson, William, Baron Ashbourne. 'An Outburst of Activity in the Roman Congregations.' *The Nineteenth Century* 45 (1899): 785–794.

Gibson, William. 'Brother of the More Famous Ben: The Theology of Archbishop John Hoadly.' *Anglican and Episcopal History* 75 (2006a): 401–422.

'The Persecution of Thomas Emlyn, 1703–05.' *A Journal of Church and State* 48 (2006b): 525–539.

Gilly, Carlos. *Spanien und der Basler Buchdruck bis 1600.* Basel: Helbing & Lichtenhahn, 1985.

'Erasmo, la Reforma radical y los heterodoxos radicales españoles.' In *Les lletres hispàniques als segles XVI, XVII i XVIII.* Ed. Tomàs Martínez Romero. Castelló de la Plana: Publicacions de la Universitat Jaume I, 2005: 225–376.

Giustiniani, Benedetto. *In omnes canonicas Epistolas Explanationes.* Lyon: Cavellat, 1621.

Glossa ordinaria. In *Biblia sacra cum glossa ordinaria iam ante quidem à Strabo Fulgensi collecta.* 6 vols. Venice: Giunta, 1603.

Goldhill, Simon. *Who Needs Greek? Contests in the Cultural History of Hellenism.* Cambridge: Cambridge University Press, 2002.

Gordon, Thomas. *A Cordial for Low Spirits.* 3rd ed. 3 vols. London: Wilson and Fell, 1763.

Grabe, Martin Silvester. *Programma de Canonica auctoritate Dicti I. Joh. V, 7.* 5 vols. Königsberg: Reusner, 1675–1677.

Graduale sacrosanctae Romanae ecclesiae. Paris: Desclée, 1952.

Grafton, Anthony. *Forgers and Critics.* London: Collins & Brown, 1990.

Graham, Michael F. *The Blasphemies of Thomas Aikenhead: Boundaries of Belief on the Eve of the Enlightenment.* Edinburgh: Edinburgh University Press, 2008.

Gray, Robert. *Letters During the Course of a Tour through Germany, Switzerland and Italy.* London: Rivington, 1794.

Greenlee, Jacob Harold. *The Text of the New Testament.* Peabody, Mass.: Hendrickson, 2008.

Gregory, Caspar René. *Textkritik des Neuen Testamentes.* 3 vols. Leipzig: Hinrichs, 1900–1909.

'Critical note: 1 John 5:7, 8.' *The American Journal of Theology* 11 (1907): 131–138.

Gregory, John. *Notes and Observations upon Some Passages of Scripture.* Oxford: H. Hall for E. Forrest Jr., 1646.

Greiff, A. 'Die drei Zeugen in 1 Joh. 5:7f.' *Theologische Quartalschrift* 114 (1933): 465–480.

Greig, Martin. 'Heresy Hunt: Gilbert Burnet and the Convocation Controversy of 1701.' *The Historical Journal* 37 (1994): 569–592.

Griesbach, Johann Jakob. *Novum Testamentum Graece.* 2 vols. Halle: Curtius, 1775–1777.
Symbolae criticae ad supplendas et corrigendas variarum N. T. lectionum collectiones. 2 vols. Halle: Curtius, 1785–1793.
Bemerkungen über des Herrn Geheimen Regierungsraths Hezel Vertheidigung der Aechtheit der Stelle 1 Joh. 5, 7. Giessen: Heyer, 1794.
Novum Testamentum Graece. 2nd ed. 2 vols. Halle: Curtius, 1796–1806.

Grotius, Hugo. *Annotationes in Novum Testamentum.* 3 vols. Paris: Pelé (vols. 1–2), Pepingué and Maucroy (vol. 3), 1641–1650.

Gryson, Roger. *Altlateinische Handschriften.* 2 vols. Freiburg: Herder, 1999–2004.

Guilday, Peter. 'The English Catholic Refugees at Louvain, 1559–1575 (Vatican Library, MS. Regina, 2020, f. 445–446).' In *Mélanges d'histoire offerts à Charles Moeller.* Leuven: Bureaux du Recueil, 1914: 2:175–189.

Gustavson, Royston. 'Competitive Strategy Dynamics in the German Music Publishing Industry 1530–1550.' In *NiveauNischeNimbus: 500 Jahre Musikdruck nördlich der Alpen.* Ed. Birgit Lodes. Wiener Forum für ältere Musikgeschichte 3. Tutzing: Schneider, 2010: 185–210.

Gutbier, Aegidius. *Novum Domini nostri Jesu Christi testamentum Syriace.* Hamburg: Gutbier, 1664.
Lexicon Syriacum, continens omnes N. T. Syriaci dictiones et particulas. Hamburg: Gutbier, 1667.

Gwilliam, G. H., ed. *The New Testament in Syriac.* 2 vols. London: British and Foreign Bible Society, 1905–1920.

Gwynn, John, ed. *Liber Ardmachanus. The Book of Armagh.* Dublin: Hodges Figgis & Co, 1913.

Haak, Theodore, trans. *The Dutch Annotations upon the Whole Bible.* London: Henry Hills for John Rothwell, Joshua Kirton and Richard Tomlins, 1657. *DM* 518.

Habermas, Jürgen. *The Structural Transformation of the Public Sphere.* Trans. Thomas Burger and Frederick Lawrence. Cambridge, MA: MIT Press, 1989.

Hallyn, Fernand. 'Le fictif, le vrai et le faux.' In *Le topos du manuscrit trouvé.* Ed. Jan Herman, Fernard Hallyn and Kris Peeters. Leuven: Peeters, 1999: 489–506.

Hamilton, Adam. *The Chronicle of the English Augustinian Canonesses Regular of the Lateran, at St. Monica's in Louvain (now at St. Augustine's Priory, Newton Abbot, Devon) 1548–1644.* 2 vols. Edinburgh: Sands, 1904–1906.

[Hare, Francis.] *The Difficulties and Discouragements Which Attend the Study of the Scriptures in the Way of Private Judgment.* London: Baker, 1714.

Harrington, Daniel J. 'The Reception of Walter Bauer's *Orthodoxy and Heresy in Earliest Christianity* During the Last Decade.' *The Harvard Theological Review* 73 (1980): 289–298.

Harris, James Rendel. *The Origin of the Leicester Codex of the New Testament.* London: Clay, 1887.

Harrison, John and Peter Laslett. *The Library of John Locke.* 2nd ed. Oxford: Oxford University Press, 1971.

Harrison, John. *The Library of Isaac Newton.* Cambridge: Cambridge University Press, 1978.

Harwood, Edward ed. Ἡ Καινὴ Διαθήκη. *The New Testament, Collated with the Most Approved Manuscripts, with Select Notes in English.* 2 vols. London: Cornish, 1776. *DM* 4762.

Hastings, James. 'Notes of Recent Exposition.' *The Expository Times* 18 (1906–1907): 49–57.

Hatch, William H. P. 'An Early Edition of the New Testament in Greek.' *The Harvard Theological Review* 34 (1941): 69–78.

Haugen, Kristine Louise. *Richard Bentley: Poetry and Enlightenment.* Cambridge, MA: Harvard University Press, 2011.

Hawkins, William. *Discourses on Scripture Mysteries.* Oxford: Clarendon Press, 1787.

[Haynes, Hopton.] *Causa Dei contra Novatores: or, the Religion of the Bible and the Religion of the Pulpit compared.* London: Noone, 1747.

The Scripture Account of the Attributes and Worship of God and of the Character and Offices of Jesus Christ. London: Noone, 1750.

Hearne, Thomas. *Remarks and Collections.* Ed. C. E. Doble et al. 10 vols. Oxford: Oxford Historical Society, 1885–1915.

Heide, Martin. *Der einzig wahre Bibeltext? Erasmus von Rotterdam und die Frage nach dem Urtext.* 5th ed. Nuremberg: Verlag für Theologie und Religionswissenschaft, 2006.

Ἡ Καινὴ Διαθήκη. *Novum Testamentum. Ex Regiis aliisque optimis editionibus cum cura expressum.* Leiden: Elzevier, 1624.

Helfling, Charles and Cynthia L. Shattuck. *The Oxford Guide to the Book of Common Prayer.* Oxford: Oxford University Press, 2006.

Henderson, Judith Rice. 'Humanism and the Humanities: Erasmus' *Opus de conscribendis epistolis* in Sixteenth-Century Schools.' In *Letter-writing Manuals and Instruction from Antiquity to the Present.* Ed. Carol Poster and Linda C. Mitchell. Columbia: University of South Carolina Press, 2007: 141–177.

Henke, Heinrich Philipp Konrad and Paul Jacob Bruns. Review of Travis 1784. *Annales Literarii* May 1786: 385–394.

Henten, Johannes, ed. *Biblia ad vetustissima exemplaria nunc recens castigata.* Leuven: Bartholomaeus van Grave, November 1547. *DM* 6129.

Novum Jesu Christi Testamentum. Quid in hac editione, à theologis Lovaniensibus, sit praestitum, sequenti praefatione indicatur. Antwerp: Plantin, 1584.

[Herne, Thomas.] *An Account of All the Considerable Books and Pamphlets That Have Been Wrote on Either Side in the Controversy Concerning the Trinity, since the Year MDCCXII.* London: Knapton, 1720.

Hessayon, Ariel and Nicholas Keene, ed. *Scripture and Scholarship in Early Modern England*. Aldershot: Ashgate, 2006.

Hessels, Jan. *In primam B. Ioannis Apostoli et Evangelistae canonicam epistolam absolutissimus commentarius*. Leuven: Bogaert, 1568.

Hetzenauer, Michael. *Wesen und Principien der Bibelkritik auf katholischer Grundlage*. Innsbruck: Wagner'sche Universitäts-Buchhandlung, 1900.

Hezel, Wilhelm Friedrich. *Ueber die Aechtheit der Stelle Johannis (1 Joh. v. 7), Drey sind die da zeugen im Himmel, etc. aus Gründen der höhern Kritik*. Giessen: Heyer, 1793.

Hilgert, Earle. 'Johann Froben and the Basel University Scholars, 1513–1523.' *The Library Quarterly* 41 (1971): 141–169.

Hills, Edward F. *The King James Version Defended*. 4th ed. Des Moines, IA: Christian Research Press, 1984.

[Hoadly, John.] *A Defence of the Right Reverend the Lord Bishop of Sarum. In Answer to a Book, Entituled, A Prefatory Discourse to an Examination of the Bishop of Sarum's Exposition of the XXXIX Articles of the Church of England, &c*. London: Baldwin, 1703.

Hobbes, Thomas. *Leviathan or the Matter, Forme and Power of a Commonwealth Ecclesiastical and Civil*. London: A. Crooke, 1651.

Hoelzlin, Jeremias, ed. Ἡ Καινὴ Διαθήκη. *Novum Testamentum*. Leiden: Elzevier, 1633.

Hoffmann, Melchior. *Außlegung der heimlichen Offenbarung Joannis des heyligen Apostels vnnd Euangelisten*. Strasbourg: Balthasar Beck, 1530.

Hofmann, Carl Gottlob. *De prudentia in disquisitione* αὐθεντίας *dicti Ioannei 1. Io. V, 7. observanda*. Wittenberg: Dürr, 1766.

The Holy Bible, Conteyning the Old Testament, and the New. London: R. Barker, 1611.

The Holy Bible, Containing the Old Testament and the New. London: Hills and Field, 1660.

Homza, Lu Ann. 'Erasmus as Hero, or Heretic? Spanish Humanism and the Valladolid Assembly of 1527.' *RQ* 50 (1997): 78–118.

Religious Authority in the Spanish Renaissance. Baltimore: Johns Hopkins University Press, 2000.

Horne, Thomas H. *An Introduction to the Critical Study and Knowledge of the Holy Scriptures*. London: Cadell and Davies, 1818.

Introduction. 2nd ed. London: Cadell and Davies, 1821.

Introduction. 4th ed. Philadelphia: Littell, 1825.

Introduction. 6th ed. London: Cadell, 1828.

Introduction. 7th ed. Philadelphia: Desilver, Thomas & Co., 1835–1836.

Introduction. 10th ed. London: Longman, 1856.

Hornig, Gottfried. *Johann Salomo Semler. Studien zu Leben und Werk des Hallenser Aufklärungstheologen*. Tübingen: Niemeyer, 1996.

Hoskier, Herman Charles. *Concerning the Text of the Apocalypse*. 2 vols. London: Quaritch, 1929.

Hottinger, Johann Heinrich. *Bibliothecarius quadripartitus*. Zürich: Stauffacher, 1664.

Howard, John. *The Trinity Asserted. A sermon preach'd before the Lord-Mayor and aldermen of the City of London, at the cathedral church of St. Paul, upon Trinity-Sunday, Anno Dom. 1700.* London: Lawrence, 1700.

Howell, William. *The Doctrine of the Trinity prov'd from Scripture. A sermon preach'd before the University of Oxford, at St. Mary's, on Sunday, May 13. 1711.* Oxford: Peisley for Knapton, Clements and Morphew, 1711.

Hügel, Friedrich von. 'The Comma Johanneum.' *The Tablet* 89, nº 2978 (5 June 1897): 896–897.

Hulbert-Powell, C. L. *John James Wettstein 1693–1754.* London: SPCK, 1938.

Hunnius, Aegidius. *Calvinus Iudaizans.* Wittenberg: Welach, 1593.

Hunt, Lynn. *Writing History in the Global Era.* New York: Norton, 2014.

Hunwick, Andrew trans. *Richard Simon: Critical History of the Text of the New Testament.* New Testament Tools, Studies, and Documents 43. Leiden: Brill, 2013.

Hutter, Elias, ed. *Novum Testamentum Domini nostri Iesu Christi.* 2 vols. Nuremberg: [Dietrich], 1599–1600.

Hylton, Raymond. *Ireland's Huguenots and Their Refuge, 1662–1745: An Unlikely Haven.* Brighton: Sussex Academic Press, 2005.

Ibenthal, Lorenz Jakob. *Erweis daß die Worte I. Joh. V. 7. 8. göttlichen Ursprunges.* Hamburg: Reuß, 1772.

IJsewijn, Jozef, G. Tournoy, D. Sacré, Line IJsewijn-Jacobs, M. Verweij and M. Mund-Dopchie. 'Litterae ad Craneveldium Balduinianae. A Preliminary Edition. 4. Letters 86–116.' *Humanistica Lovaniensia* 44 (1995): 1–78.

Iliffe, Rob. 'Those "Whose Business It Is To Cavill": Newton's Anti-Catholicism.' In Force and Popkin 1999: 97–119.

'Friendly Criticism: Richard Simon, John Locke, Isaac Newton and the *Johannine Comma*.' In Hessayon and Keene 2006: 137–157.

Priest of Nature: The Religious Worlds of Isaac Newton. Oxford: Oxford University Press, 2016.

Index expurgatorius librorum qui hoc seculo prodierunt. Lyon: Mareschall, 1586.

'Inspector.' 'Sabellian, or Unitarian Controversy. Letter XI.' *The Antijacobin Review and True Churchman's Magazine* 50 (1816): 495–513.

Israel, Jonathan. 'Spinoza and the Religious Radical Enlightenment.' In *The Intellectual Consequences of Religious Heterodoxy, 1600–1750.* Ed. Sarah Mortimer and John Robertson. Leiden: Brill, 2012: 181–203.

Ives, Eric William. *The Common Lawyers of Pre-Reformation England.* Cambridge: Cambridge University Press, 1983.

Jackson, John. *Three Letters to Dr Clarke, from a Clergyman of the Church of England; Concerning His Scripture-Doctrine of the Trinity.* London: Baker, 1714.

A Collection of Queries. Wherein the Most Material Objections from Scripture, Reason, and Antiquity, Which Have as Yet Been Alleged Against Dr Clarke's Scripture-Doctrine of the Trinity, and the Defenses of It, Are Proposed and Answered. London: Knapton, 1716.

Memoirs of the Life and Writings of Dr. Waterland. London: Noon, 1736.

Jackson, W. A., F. S. Ferguson and Katharine F. Pantzer. *A Short-Title Catalogue of Books Printed in England, Scotland, & Ireland and of English Books Printed*

Abroad 1475–1640. First compiled by A. W. Pollard and G. R. Redgrave. 2nd ed. London: Bibliographical Society, 1986.

Jäger, Karl Friedrich. *De moderatione theologica in probanda vel non probanda Trinitate ex dicto 1 Joh. V. 7: dissertatio inauguralis*. Tübingen: Sigmund, 1767.

Janssens, Laurent. Review of Künstle 1905a. *Revue bénédictine* 23 (1906): 117–119.

Jebb, R. C. *Bentley*. New York: Harper, 1899.

Jerome of Stridon. *Sancti Eusebii Hieronymi Stridonensis presbyteri Divina bibliotheca antehac inedita*. Ed. Jean Martianay and Antoine Pouget. 5 vols. Paris: Roulland and Anisson, 1693–1706.

Jortin, John. *The Life of Erasmus*. 2 vols. London: Whiston & White, 1760.

The Life of Erasmus. 2 vols. 2nd ed. London: Taylor, 1808.

Jowett, Benjamin. 'On the Interpretation of Scripture.' In *Essays and Reviews*. Ed. John William Parker. London: Parker, 1860: 330–433.

Jülicher, Adolf. Review of Künstle 1905a. *Göttingische gelehrte Anzeigen* 167 (1905): 930–935.

Einleitung in das Neue Testament. 5th ed. Tübingen: Mohr (Siebeck), 1906.

Junius, Franciscus and Thomas Marshall, ed. *Quatuor D. N. Jesu Christi euangeliorum Versiones perantiquae duae, Gothica scil. & Anglo-Saxonica*. Dordrecht: Typis et sumptibus Junianis excudebant Henricus et Joannes Essaei, urbis typographi ordinarii, 1665.

Quatuor D. N. Jesu Christi euangeliorum Versiones. Amsterdam: Apud Janssonio-Waesbergios, 1684.

Junius, Johannes. *Examen responsionis Fausti Socini, ad Librum Jacobi Wieki, de Divinitate Filij Dei & Spiritus Sancti*. Amsterdam: Henricus Laurentius, 1628.

Kallipolites, Maximos, trans. Ἡ Καινὴ Διαθήκη τοῦ Κυρίου ἡμῶν Ἰησοῦ Χριστοῦ δίγλωττος. 2 vols. Geneva: Heirs of Pierre Aubert, 1638.

Kannegiesser, Bartholomäus. *Kern und Safft der erbaulichen Schrifft des [...] D. Philipp Jacob Speners Vertheidigung des Zeugnisses von der ewigen GOttheit JEsu CHristi*. Erfurt: Engelhardt, 1714.

Károlyi, Péter. *Brevis, erudita, et perspicua explicatio orthodoxae fidei de vno vero Deo, Patre, Filio & Spiritu sancto, aduersus blasphemos Georgij Blandratae, & Francisci Dauidis errores*. Wittenberg: Schleich and Schöne, 1571.

Kassler, Jamie C. *Seeking Truth: Roger North's Notes on Newton and Correspondence with Samuel Clarke c. 1704–1713*. Farnham: Ashgate, 2014.

Kaulen, Franz. *Geschichte der Vulgata*. Mainz: Kirchheim, 1868.

Kawecka-Gryczowa, Alodia. *Les imprimeurs des antitrinitaires polonais Rodecki et Sternacki*. Geneva: Droz, 1974.

Kell, Edmund. *Unitarians, Not Socinians. An Appeal to the Good Sense and Candour of Professing Christians, Against the Improper Use of the Term 'Socinian'*. 2nd ed. London: Hunter, 1830.

Kelly, William. *Lectures Introductory to the Study of the Acts, the Catholic Epistles, and the Revelation*. London: Broom, 1870.

Kettner, Friedrich Ernst. *Insignis ac Celeberrimi De SS. Trinitate Loci, qui 1. Joh. V. 7. extat, divina autoritas sensus et usus Dissertatione Theologica demonstratus*. Leipzig: Heinrich Richter for the heirs of Friedrich Lanckisius, 1696.

Vindiciae novae dicti vexatissimi: De tribus in coelo testibus I. Joh. V, v. 7. Oppositae Christophori Sandii interpretationibus paradoxis, Richardi Simonii historiae criticae Novi Testamenti, Stephani Curcellaei, Johannis Clerici et quibusdam monachorum Benedictorum objectionibus recentissimis. Delitzsch: Vogelgesang, [c. 1702].

Historia dicti Johannei de sanctissima Trinitate 1. Joh. Cap. V. vers. 7. per multa secula omissi, seculo v. *restituti, et exeunte seculo* xvi. *in versionem vernaculam recepti.* Frankfurt and Leipzig: Calvisius, 1713.

Kimmel, Ernst Julius. *Libri symbolici ecclesiae orientalis.* Jena: Hochhausen, 1843.

[King, Peter.] *An Enquiry into the Constitution, Discipline, Unity & Worship, of the Primitive Church.* London: Robinson, 1691.

The Life and Letters of John Locke. 2nd ed. London: Bohn, 1858.

Kís, Tímea. '"Olyan Istent ... hordoznak a lelkükben, amilyent meg is festettek." Illusztrációk két 16. századi antitrinitárius kiadványban.' In *Ars perennis.* Ed. Anna Szerkesztette Tüskés. Budapest: CentrArt Egyesület, 2010: 71–80.

Klauck, Hans-Josef. *Der erste Johannesbrief.* Evangelisch-Katholischer Kommentar zum Neuen Testament XXIII/1. Zürich: Benzinger, 1991.

[Knight, James]. *The Scripture Doctrine of the Most Holy and Undivided Trinity Vindicated from the Misinterpretations of Dr. Clarke. To Which Is Prefixed a Letter to the Reverend Doctor, by Robert Nelson, Esq.* 2nd ed. London: Smith, 1714.

The True Scripture Doctrine of the Most Holy and Undivided Trinity, Continued and Vindicated From the Misinterpretations of Dr. Clarke. In Answer to his Reply. By the Author of the Scripture-Doctrine. Published and Recommended by Robert Nelson, Esq. London: Smith, 1715.

Knittel, Franz Anton. *Neue Kritiken über den berühmten Spruch: Drey sind, die da zeugen im Himmel, der Vater, das Wort und der heilige Geist; und diese drey sind eins.* Braunschweig: Meyer, 1785.

New criticisms on the celebrated text, 1 John V. 7. 'For there are three that bear record in heaven, the Father, the Word, and the Holy Ghost; and these three are one.' Trans. William Alleyn Evanson. London: Rivington, 1829.

Knox, Ronald A. *The Holy Bible: A Translation from the Latin Vulgate in the Light of the Hebrew and Greek Originals.* New York: Sheed & Ward, 1950a.

Kölling, Wilhelm. *Die Echtheit von 1. Joh. 5, 7.* Breslau: Dülfer, 1893.

Köpfel, Fabricius, ed. *Nouum Testamentum Graece.* Strasbourg: Köpfel, 1524. DM 4600.

Koffmanne, Georg. 'Ist Luther Verfasser einer Schrift, welche das Komma Johanneum behandelt?' In *Theologische Studien Herrn Wirkl. Oberkonsistorialrath Professor D. Bernhard Weiss [...] dargebracht.* Göttingen: Vandenhoeck & Ruprecht, 1897: 30–51.

Kortholt, Christian. *De variis scripturae editionibus tractatus theologico-historico-philologicus.* Kiel: Richelius, 1686.

Koselleck, Reinhart. *Kritik und Krise.* Frankfurt/Main: Suhrkamp, 1973.

Krans, Jan. *Beyond What Is Written: Erasmus and Beza as Conjectural Critics of the New Testament.* Leiden: Brill, 2006.

Kraye, Jill. 'Erasmus and the Canonization of Aristotle: The Letter to John More.' In *England and the Continental Renaissance*. Ed. Edward Chaney and Peter Mack. Woodbridge: Boydell, 1990: 37–52.

Künstle, Karl. *Das Comma Ioanneum. Auf seine Herkunft untersucht.* Freiburg i. B.: Herder, 1905.

Kurtzman, Jeffrey G. 'The Monteverdi Vespers of 1610 and Their Relationship with Italian Sacred Music of the Early Seventeenth Century.' Diss. Illinois, 1972.

The Monteverdi Vespers of 1610: Music, Context, Performance. Oxford: Oxford University Press, 1999.

Lachmann, Karl. 'Rechenschaft über seine Ausgabe des Neuen Testaments.' *Theologische Studien und Kritiken* 3 (1830): 817–845.

Novum Testamentum graece. Berlin: Reimer, 1831.

'De ordine narrationum in evangeliis synopticis.' *Theologische Studien und Kritiken* 8 (1835): 570–590.

La Croze, Maturin Veyssière. *Thesaurus epistolicus Lacrozianus.* 3 vols. Leipzig: Gleditsch, 1742–1746.

Lambe, Patrick J. 'Biblical Criticism and Censorship in Ancien Régime France: The Case of Richard Simon.' *The Harvard Theological Review* 78 (1985): 149–177.

La Peyrère, Isaac. *Prae-Adamitae.* [Amsterdam]: [Elzevier], 1655.

Laridius, Gobelinus, ed. *Biblia iuxta divi Hieronymi Stridonensis tralationem.* Cologne: Cervicornus for Hittorp, 1530.

Laurence, John, ed. *An Apology for Dr Clarke. Containing an Account of the Late Proceedings in Convocation Upon His Writings Concerning the Trinity.* London: Burleigh, 1714.

The Layman's Humble Address to the Bishops and Clergy in Convocation Assembled, Concerning an Attempt to Subvert the Christian Faith, Lately Made by Sam. Clarke, D.D. and Also of Some Dangerous Opinions That Perplex the Minds of Pious People, Lately Advanced by the Bishop of Bangor, Mr. Whiston, and Others. London: Rivington, 1717.

Lebreton, Jules. *Les origines du dogme de la Trinité.* 5th ed. Paris: Beauchesne, 1919.

Lechat, Robert. *Les refugiés anglais dans les Pays-Bas espagnols durant le règne d'Elisabeth, 1558–1603.* Leuven: Roulers, 1914.

Le Clerc, Jean. 'Lettre latine, sur l'édition du N. T. par Mr. Mill.' *Bibliothèque choisie* 16 (1708): 311–342.

Epistolario. Ed. Maria Grazia Sina and Mario Sina. 4 vols. Florence: Olschki, 1987–1997.

Lee, Edward. *Annotationes Edoardi Leei in Annotationes Novi Testamenti Desiderii Erasmi.* Paris: De Gourmont, [January/February 1520a].

Annotationes Edoardi Leei in Annotationes Novi Testamenti Desiderii Erasmi. Basel: Froben, May 1520b.

Lee, John A. L. 'Dimitrios Doukas and the Accentuation of the New Testament Text of the Complutensian Polyglot.' *Novum Testamentum* 47 (2005): 250–290.

Lee, Samuel, ed. *Novum Testamentum Syriace.* London: British and Foreign Bible Society, 1816. *DM* 8979.

Lefèvre de la Boderie, Guy, ed. דיתיקא הדתא. ʾΗ Καινὴ Διαθήκη. *Nouum Iesu Christi D. N. Testamentum*. Paris: Benenatus, 1584. *DM* 6174.

Lefèvre d'Étaples, Jacques. *Commentarii in Epistolas Catholicas*. Basel: Cratander, 1527.

Leigh, Edward. *A Treatise of Religion & Learning, and of Religious and Learned Men*. London: Adams, 1656.

Leisentrit, Johann. *Geistliche Lieder vnd Psalmen / der alten Apostolischer recht vnd warglaubiger Christlicher Kirchen*. Bautzen: Wolrab, 1567.

Leland, John. *The Writings of the Late Elder John Leland*. New York: Wood, 1845.

Le Long, Jacques. *Bibliotheca sacra*. 2 vols. Paris: Pralard, 1709a.

——— *Bibliotheca sacra*. Ed. Christian Friedrich Boerner. 2 vols. Leipzig: Gleditsch, 1709b.

——— 'Lettre du Pere le Long à Monsieur Martin, Ministre d'Utreck. De Paris, ce 12. Avril 1720.' *Journal des Sçavans* 1720: 298–303.

——— *Bibliotheca sacra*. 2nd ed. 2 vols. Paris: Montalant, 1723.

Lente, Willem Johan. *Het leven en werken van Johan Jakob Wettstein*. Leiden: Adriani, 1902.

Leslie, Charles. *The Socinian Controversy Discuss'd*. London: Strahan, 1708.

Leusden, Johannes. *Philologus Hebraeo-Graecus Generalis*. Utrecht: Smijtegelt, 1670.

Leusden, Johannes and Karel Schaaf, ed. *Novum Domini Nostri Jesu Christi Testamentum Syriacum, cum versione Latina*. Leiden: Müller, Boutesteyn and Luchtmans, 1709.

Levine, Joseph M. *The Autonomy of History: Truth and Method from Erasmus to Gibbon*. Chicago: Chicago University Press, 1999.

Lewalski, Barbara K. *The Life of John Milton*. Oxford: Blackwell, 2000.

Lewis, John, ed. *The New Testament of Our Lord and Saviour Jesus Christ, Translated Out of the Latin Vulgat by John Wiclif*. London: Page and Mount, 1731.

Liber Usualis. Paris: Desclée, 1961.

Lim, Paul Chang-Ha. *Mystery Unveiled: The Crisis of the Trinity in Early Modern England*. Oxford: Oxford University Press, 2012.

——— Review of Mortimer 2010. *The Journal of Ecclesiastical History* 74 (2013): 855–857.

Lio, Ermenegildo. *Humanae vitae e infallibilità: Paolo VI, il Concilio e Giovanni Paolo II*. Rome: Libreria Editrice Vaticana, 1986.

Little, Andrew George. *Franciscan Papers, Lists, and Documents*. Manchester: Manchester University Press, 1943.

Locke, John. *The Correspondence of John Locke*. Ed. E. S. de Beer. 8 vols. Oxford: Clarendon Press, 1976–1989.

[Löscher, Valentin Ernst]. Review of *Das Neue Testament* (Wandsbek: Holle, 1710). *Unschuldige Nachrichten von alten und neuen theologischen Sachen* 10 (1710): 615–618.

Lombroso, Cesare. *L'uomo delinquente*. Turin: Hoepli, 1876.

Long, Thomas. *Apostolical Communion in the Church of England*. 2nd ed. Exeter: Farley, 1703.

Longland, John. *Tres conciones*. [London]: Pynson [and Redman], [c. 1528–1532].

Lorenzo da Brindisi. *Opera omnia*. 11 vols. Padua: Officina typographica Seminarii, 1928–1959.

Lossius, Lucas. *Annotationes scholasticae in epistolas dominicales*. Frankfurt/Main: Egenolph, 1552.

Luard, H. R. 'Porson.' *Cambridge Essays* 3 (1857): 125–171.

Lucas Brugensis, Franciscus. *Notationes in sacra biblia, quibus, variantia discrepantibus exemplaribus loca, summo studio discutiuntur*. Antwerp: Plantin, 1580.

Romanae correctionis in latinis bibliis editionis vulgatae, iussu Sixti V. Pont. Max. recognitis, loca insigniora. Antwerp: Plantin, 1603.

Lupton, Joseph Hirst. *A Life of John Colet*. London: Bell, 1909.

Luther, Martin, trans. *Das Newe Testament Deutzsch*. Wittenberg: Lotter, 1522.

Biblia: das ist: Die gantze Heilige Schrifft. Wittenberg: Luft, 1545.

D. Martin Luthers sämtliche Schriften. Ed. Johann Georg Walch. 24 vols. Halle: Gebauer, 1739–1753.

Lyell, James P. *Cardinal Ximenes: Statesman, Ecclesiastic, Soldier and Man of Letters*. London: Grafton, 1919.

Lynall, Gregory. *Swift and Science: The Satire, Politics, and Theology of Natural Knowledge, 1690–1730*. Basingstoke: Palgrave, 2012.

Mabillon, Jean. *De liturgia gallicana libri III*. Paris: Martin and Boudot, 1685.

[Mace, Daniel, ed. and trans.]. *The New Testament in Greek and English*. 2 vols. London: Roberts, 1729.

Maclear, J. F. *Church and State in the Modern Age*. Oxford: Oxford University Press, 1995.

Maertens, Heinrich Richard. *De tribus in terra testibus ad 1. Joh. V, 8*. Helmstedt: Buchholz, 1725.

Mahoney, Robert. 'Certainty and Irony in Swift: Faith and the Indeterminate.' In *Swift as Priest and Satirist*. Ed. Todd C. Parker. Cranbury, NJ: Associated University Presses, 2009: 37–57.

Major, Georg. *Commonefactio B. Georgii Maioris, ad Ecclesiam Catholicam, Orthodoxam, de fugiendis et execrandis blasphemijs Samosatenicis, Arianis, Eunomianis, et alijs, quae hoc tempore à Francisco Dauidis, et quodam Italo Georgio Blandrata, et nonnullis alijs, ab Orco et Stygia palude reuocantur, et paßim sparguntur*. Wittenberg: Lufft, 1569.

Mandelbrote, Scott. '"A Duty of the Greatest Moment": Isaac Newton and the Writing of Biblical Criticism.' *The British Journal for the History of Science* 26 (1993): 281–302.

'The English Bible and its Readers in the Eighteenth Century.' In *Books and their Readers in Eighteenth-Century England*. Ed. Isabel Rivers. London: Continuum, 2001: 35–78.

'Eighteenth-Century Reactions to Newton's Anti-Trinitarianism.' In *Newton and Newtonianism, New Studies*. Ed. James E. Force and Sarah Hutton. Dordrecht: Kluwer, 2004: 93–111.

'English Scholarship and the Greek Text of the Old Testament, 1620–1720: The Impact of Codex Alexandrinus.' In Hessayon and Keene 2006: 74–93.

Mangan, John Joseph. *Life, Character and Influence of Desiderius Erasmus of Rotterdam*. 2 vols. New York: Macmillan, 1927.

Manoury, Auguste-François. *Commentaire sur les Épîtres catholiques de S. Jacques, S. Pierre, S. Jean et S. Jude.* Paris: Bloud et Barral, 1888.

'Le verset des trois témoins célestes.' *Revue des sciences ecclésiastiques* 59 (1889): 289–297.

Manuel, Frank E. *The Religion of Isaac Newton.* Oxford: Oxford University Press, 1974.

Maran, Prudent. *Divinitas Domini Nostri Jesu Christi, manifesta in scripturis et traditione.* Paris: Collombat, 1746.

Mariana, Juan de. *Tractatus VII.* Cologne: Hieratus, 1609.

Marsh, Herbert. *Letters to Mr. Archdeacon Travis.* Leipzig: Solbrig, 1795.

A Course of Lectures, Containing a Description and Systematic Arrangement of the Several Branches of Divinity. 7 vols. Cambridge: Hilliard and Smith, 1812–1823.

A Comparative View of the Churches of England and Rome. London: Rivington, 1816.

Marshall, John. *John Locke: Resistance, Religion and Responsibility.* Cambridge: Cambridge University Press, 1994.

'Locke, Socinianism, "Socinianism", and Unitarianism.' In *English Philosophy in the Age of Locke.* Ed. Michael Alexander Stewart. Oxford: Oxford University Press, 2000: 111–182.

Martin, David. *Le Nouveau Testament, de nôtre Seigneur Jesus-Christ.* Utrecht: Halma, 1696.

La Sainte Bible qui contient le Vieux et le Nouveau Testament. 2 vols. Amsterdam: Desbordes, 1707.

Deux dissertations critiques: La premiere sur le verset 7. du ch. 5 de la I. Epist. de S. Jean; Il y en a trois au Ciel, &c. Dans laquelle on prouve l'authenticité de ce texte; La seconde sur le passage de Joseph touchant Jésus-Christ, où l'on fait voir que ce passage n'est point supposé. Utrecht: Van der Water, 1717.

A Critical Dissertation upon the Seventh Verse of the Fifth Chapter of St John's First Epistle, There Are Three, That Bear Record in Heaven, &c. Wherein the Authentickness of This Text Is Fully Prov'd Against the Objections of Mr. Simon and the Modern Arians. London: Innys, 1719a.

Examen de la Réponse de Mr. Emlyn à la Dissertation Critique sur le Verset 7. du Chap. 5. de la 1 Epître de St. Jean. Il y en a trois, qui rendent témoignage dans le Ciel. London: Innys, 1719b.

An Examination of Mr. Emlyn's Answer to the Dissertation upon the Seventh Verse of the Fifth Chapter of the First Epistle of St. John, for There are Three That Bear Record in Heaven, the Father, the Word, and the Holy Ghost: and These Three Are One. London: Innys, 1719c.

'Réponse de M. Martin, Ministre d'Utrecht à la Lettre de P. Le Long de L'Oratoire de Paris, dattée du 12. Avril 1720.' *L'Europe savante* 12 (1720): 279–301.

La Vérité du Texte de la 1. Epistre de saint Jean, ch. 5, vs. 7. Car il y en a trois au Ciel, &c. Démontrée par des preuves qui sont au dessus de toute exception, prises des témoignages de l'Eglise Latine, & de l'Eglise Grecque, & en particulier d'un Manuscrit Grec du N. Testament, trouvé en Irlande. Utrecht: Broedelet, 1721.

The Genuineness of the Text of the First Epistle of Saint John. Chap. v. V. 7. There Are Three in Heaven, &c. Demonstrated by Proofs Which Are Beyond All Exception, Taken from the Testimonies of the Greek and Latin Churches, and Particularly from a Greek MS. of the New Testament, Found in Ireland. London: Innys, 1722.

Martin, Jean-Pierre Paulin. *Introduction à la critique textuelle du Nouveau Testament.* 6 vols. Paris: Leclerc, 1884–1886.

'Le verset des trois témoins célestes, I Jean, V. 7, et la critique biblique contemporaine.' *Revue des sciences ecclésiastiques* 56 (1887): 97–129, 193–223.

'Les trois témoins célestes.' *La controverse et le contemporain*, n. s. 13 (1888): 408–425.

'Le verset des trois témoins célestes est-il authentique?' *Revue des sciences ecclésiastiques* 59 (1889a): 97–140, 209–243, 385–389.

'Un dernier mot sur le verset des trois témoins célestes.' *Revue des sciences ecclésiastiques* 60 (1889b): 538–560.

Masch, Andreas Gottlieb. *Bibliotheca sacra.* 5 vols. Halle: Gebauer, 1778–1790.

Mattaire, Michel. *A Short Essay or Dissertation Upon the Doxology of the Church of England.* London: Bowyer, 1718.

Matthaei, Christian Friedrich, ed. *SS. apostolorum septem epistolae catholicae ad codd. mss. Mosqq.* Riga: Hartknochen, 1782.

Matthews, William, ed. *The Recorder: Being a Collection of Tracts and Disquisitions, Chiefly Relative to the Modern State and Principles of the People Called Quakers.* 2 vols. Bath: Crutwell for Matthews, 1802–1803.

[Mawer, John.] *Letters in answer to some queries sent to the Author, concerning the genuine Reading of the Greek Text, I Tim. iii. 16. ΘΕΟΣ ἐφανερώθη ἐν σαρκί. GOD was manifest in the Flesh. Now first published on Occasion of Sir Isaac Newton's Two Letters to Mr. Le Clerc, lately published.* York: Ward, 1758.

Maxey, David W. 'New Light on Hannah Barnard, a Quaker "Heretic".' *Quaker History* 78 (1989): 61–86.

Mayer, John. *The English Catechisme.* London: Marriot, 1621.

Mayer, Thomas F. and Courtney B. Walters. *The Correspondence of Reginald Pole. Volume 4. A Biographical Companion: The British Isles.* Aldershot: Ashgate, 2008.

Maynard, Michael. *A History of the Debate Over 1 John 5:7–8.* Tempe, AZ: Comma Publications, 1995.

Mayor, J. E. B., ed. *Cambridge under Queen Anne.* Cambridge: Cambridge Antiquarian Society, 1911.

McCloy, Shelby Thomas. *Gibbon's Antagonism to Christianity.* London: Ayer, 1933.

McConica, James. 'The Rise of the Undergraduate College.' In *The History of the University of Oxford, vol. 3: The Collegiate University.* Ed. James McConica. Oxford: Oxford University Press, 1986: 1–68.

McDonald, Grantley Robert. 'Raising the Ghost of Arius. Erasmus, the Johannine Comma and Religious Difference in Early Modern Europe.' Diss. Leiden, 2011.

'Thomas More, John Clement and the Palatine Anthology.' *Bibliothèque d'Humanisme et Renaissance* 75 (2013): 259–270.

McGrath, Alister E. *Darwinism and the Divine. Evolutionary Thought and Natural Theology.* Chichester: Wiley-Blackwell, 2011.

McGregor, John James. *New Picture of Dublin.* Dublin: Archer, 1821.

McLachlan, Herbert. 'An Almost Forgotten Pioneer in New Testament Criticism.' *Hibbert Journal* 37 (1938/1939): 617–625.

'Daniel Mace (d. 1758), a Pioneer in New Testament Criticism.' In idem, *Essays and Addresses.* Manchester: Manchester University Press, 1950: 230–247.

McLachlan, H. John. *Socinianism in Seventeenth-Century England.* Oxford: Oxford University Press, 1951.

Meehan, Thomas More. 'John 19:32–25 and 1 John 5:6–8: A Study in the History of Interpretation.' Diss. Drew University, 1986.

Meinelff, Johann Christoph. *Vindicatio Testimonii, Trium testium in coelo, 1. Joh. V. commate 7. Qvod genuina Divinitus inspiratae atque Canonicae Scripturae Particula sit, non adjecta ab aliis, sed ab ipso Johanne Apostolo scripta ac relicta: Adversus Christophorum Sandium potissimum instituta [...] Sub Praesidio [...] Gothofridi Wegneri [...] examini submittit, Joh. Christoph. Meinelffus.* Frankfurt/Oder: Wegner, 1690.

Melanchthon, Philipp. *Loci theologici recens collecti & recogniti.* Wittenberg: Klug, 1535.

Loci theologici recens recogniti. Wittenberg: Seitz, 1545.

La somme de théologie, ou lieux communs, reueuz & augmentez pour la dernière foys, par M. Philippe Melancthon. Trans. Jean Calvin. [Geneva]: [Jean Girard], 1546.

Opera quae supersunt omnia. Ed. C. G. Bretschneider and H. E. Bindseil. 28 vols. Halle and Braunschweig: Schwetschke, 1834–1860.

Mendes da Costa, M. B. and J. Berg. *Catalogus der Handschriften VII. De Handschriften, Krachtens Bruikleencontract in de Universiteitsbibliotheek berustende. Eerste gedeelte: De handschriften van de Remonstrantsche Kerk [...]. De handschriften van het Evangelisch-Luthersche Seminarium.* Amsterdam: Stadsdrukkerij, 1923.

Mercati, Giovanni. 'Sopra Giovanni Clement e i suoi manoscritti.' *La Bibliofilia* 28 (1926): 81–99.

Merriam, Thomas. 'John Clement, His Identity, and His Marshfoot House in Essex.' *Moreana* 25 (1988): 145–152.

Merritt, J. F. *The Social World of Early Modern Westminster.* Manchester: Manchester University Press, 2005.

Metzger, Bruce M. 1964. Review of *The Cambridge History of the Bible: The West from the Reformation to the Present Day.* Ed. S. L. Greenslade (Cambridge: Cambridge University Press, 1963). *Journal of Biblical Literature* 83 (1964): 448–450.

1977. *The Early Versions of the New Testament: Their Origin, Transmission, and Limitations.* Oxford: Oxford University Press, 1977.

Metzger, Bruce M. and Bart D. Ehrman. *The Text of the New Testament: Its Transmission, Corruption and Restoration*. 4th ed. Oxford: Oxford University Press, 2005.

Michaelis, J. D. *Einleitung in die göttlichen Schriften des Neuen Bundes*. 2nd ed. 2 vols. Göttingen: Vandenhoeck, 1765–1766.

Einleitung in die göttlichen Schriften des Neuen Bundes. 3rd ed. 2 vols. Göttingen: Vandenhoeck & Ruprecht, 1777.

Einleitung in die göttlichen Schriften des Neuen Bundes. 4th ed. 2 vols. Göttingen: Vandenhoeck & Ruprecht, 1788.

Introduction to the New Testament, trans. and augmented by H. Marsh. 4 vols. Cambridge: Archdeacon for Rivington, 1793–1801.

Introduction to the New Testament, trans. and augmented by H. Marsh. 2nd ed. 4 vols. Cambridge: Archdeacon for Rivington, 1802–1803.

Introduction to the New Testament, trans. and augmented by H. Marsh. 4th ed. 4 vols. London: Rivington, 1823.

[Middleton, Conyers.] *Remarks, Paragraph by Paragraph, upon the Proposals Lately Publish'd by Richard Bentley, for a New Edition of the Greek Testament and Latin Version*. London: Roberts, [1721].

Some Farther Remarks, Paragraph by Paragraph, upon Proposals Lately Publish'd for a New Edition of a Greek and Latin Testament by Richard Bentley, Containing a Full Answer to the Editor's Late Defence of His Said Proposals as Well as to All His Objections There Made Against My Former Remarks. London: Bickerton, 1721.

The Miscellaneous Works. 4 vols. London: Manby, 1752.

Mill, John, ed. Ἡ Καινὴ Διαθήκη. *Novum Testamentum. Cum lectionibus variantibus MSS Exemplarium, Versionum, Editionum, SS Patrum et Scriptorum Ecclesiasticorum; & in easdem Notis*. Oxford: Sheldonian Theatre, 1707.

Novum Testamentum graecum. 2nd ed. Ed. Ludolf Küster. Rotterdam: Fritsch and Böhm, 1710.

Novum Testamentum graecum. 2nd ed. Ed. Ludolf Küster. Leipzig: Gleditsch, 1723.

Milton, John. *De doctrina Christiana*. Ed. Charles R. Sumner. Cambridge: Cambridge University Press, 1825a.

A Treatise on Christian Doctrine. Trans. Charles R. Sumner. Cambridge: Cambridge University Press, 1825b.

Minnich, Nelson H. and W. W. Meissner. 'The Character of Erasmus.' *The American Historical Review* 83 (1978): 598–624.

Missy, César de. 'Lettre de Mr. de Missy sur le MS. du Vatican cité par le P. Amelote, en faveur du passage des trois Témoins célestes.' *Journal Britannique* 8 (1752): 194–211.

'Seconde Lettre de Mr. de Missy sur le MS du Vatican cité par le P. Amelote, en faveur du passage des trois Témoins célestes.' *Journal Britannique* 8 (1752): 274–296.

'Troisième Lettre de Missy sur le MS. du Vatican cité par le P. Amelote, en faveur du passage des trois Témoins célestes.' *Journal Britannique* 9 (1752): 44–66.

'Lettre de Mr. de Missy sur tout ce qui a été écrit contre lui en faveur de Mr. Martin: & principalement sur le Mémoire inséré dans l'avant-dernier volume de ce Journal.' *Journal Britannique* 11 (1753): 66–98.

'Lettre de M. de Missy à l'Auteur du Journal sur l'Article suivant.' *Journal Britannique* 15 (1754): 148–151.

Modrzewski, Andrzej Frycz. *Sylvae quatuor.* [Raków]: [Sternacius], 1590.

Modus baptizandi, preces et benedictiones, quibus ecclesia Aethiopum utitur. Leuven: Verhasselt, 1550.

Momigliano, Arnaldo. 'Gibbon's Contribution to Historical Method.' *Historia: Zeitschrift für Alte Geschichte* 2 (1954): 450–463.

Monk, James Henry. *The Life of Richard Bentley.* 2 vols. 2nd ed. London: Rivington, 1833.

Montano, Benito Arias, ed. *Biblia sacra Hebraice, Chaldaice, Graece, & Latine.* 8 vols. Antwerp: Plantin, 1569–1572.

ed. *Novum Testamentum graece, cum vulgata interpretatione latina graeci contextus lineis inserta.* Antwerp: Plantin, 1583.

Elucidationes in omnia sanctorum apostolorum scripta. Eiusdem in S. Ioannis Apostoli et Evangelistae Apocalypsin. Antwerp: Plantin, 1588.

Montclos, Xavier de. 'Le Ralliement: intentions de Léon XIII et réactions françaises.' In *Monseigneur d'Hulst fondateur de l'Institut catholique de Paris.* Ed. Francesco Beretta. Paris: Beauchesne, 1996.

Montfaucon, Bernard de. *Palaeographia Graeca.* Paris: Guérin, 1708.

Moorman, Jack A. *When the KJV Departs from the 'Majority' Text. A New Twist in the Continuing Attack on the Authorized Version.* Collingswood, NJ: Bible for Today, 1988.

Moorman, John R. H. *The Grey Friars in Cambridge, 1225–1538.* Cambridge: Cambridge University Press, 1952.

Mortimer, Sarah. *Reason and Religion in the English Revolution. The Challenge of Socinianism.* Cambridge: Cambridge University Press, 2010.

'Freedom, Virtue and Socinian Heterodoxy.' In *Freedom and the Construction of Europe.* Ed. Quentin Skinner and Martin Van Gelderen. Cambridge: Cambridge University Press, 2013: 1: 77–93.

Mulsow, Martin. 'The "New Socinians". Intertextuality and Cultural Exchange in Late Socinianism.' In *Socinianism and Arminianism: Antitrinitarians, Calvinists and Cultural Exchange in Seventeenth-Century Europe.* Ed. Martin Mulsow and Jan Rohls. Leiden: Brill, 2005: 49–78.

Murdock, Graeme. 'Multiconfessionalism in Transylvania.' In *A Companion to Multiconfessionalism in the Early Modern World.* Ed. Thomas Max Safley. Leiden: Brill, 2011: 393–416.

Murr, Christoph Theophilus von. *Memorabilia bibliothecarum publicarum Norimbergensium et Vniversitatis Altdorfinae.* 3 vols. Nuremberg: Hoesch, 1786–1791.

Naiditch, Paul G. *The Library of Richard Porson.* Bloomington, IN: Xlibris, 2011.

Naogeorgus, Thomas. *In primam D. Ioannis Epistolam annotationes, qui vice pro-lixi commentarii esse possunt.* Frankfurt/Main: Braubach, 1544.

Naud, André. *Un aggiornamento et son éclipse: la liberté de la pensée dans la foi et dans l'Église à Vatican II et aujourd'hui.* Montréal: Les Editions Fides, 1996.

Nestle, Eberhard. *Einführung in das Griechische Neue Testament.* 2nd ed. Göttingen: Vandenhoeck & Ruprecht, 1899.

———. *Introduction to the Textual Criticism of the Greek New Testament.* Trans. William Edie. London: Williams and Norgate, 1901.

The New Testament of Iesus Christ, Translated Faithfully into English, Out of the Authentical Latin. Reims: Fogny, 1582.

A New Testament; or, the New Covenant According to Luke, Paul and John. Published in Conformity to the Plan of the Late Rev. Edward Evanson. London: Taylor for Phillips, 1807.

The New Testament of Our Lord and Saviour Jesus Christ, Translated Out of the Greek: Being the Version Set Forth A.D. 1611, Compared with the Most Ancient Authorities and Revised, A.D. 1881. Oxford: Oxford University Press, 1881.

Newcome, William. *An Attempt toward Revising Our English Translation of the Greek Scriptures, or the New Covenant of Jesus Christ: and Toward Illustrating the Sense by Philological and Explanatory Notes.* 2 vols. Dublin: Exshaw, 1796.

Newton, Isaac. *Philosophiae naturalis principia mathematica.* 2nd ed. Cambridge: [Crownfield], 1713.

———. *The Chronology of Ancient Kingdoms Amended.* London: Tonson, Osborn and Longman, 1728.

———. *Two Letters of Sir Isaac Newton to Mr. Le Clerc, Late Divinity Professor of the Remonstrants in Holland. The Former Containing a Dissertation upon the Reading of the Greek Text, 1 John, v. 7. The Latter Upon That of 1 Timothy, iii. 16. Published from authentick MSS in the Library of the Remonstrants in Holland.* London: Payne, 1754a.

———. 'Traduction libre [by César de Missy] de la Lettre du Chevalier Newton sur le passage des trois Témoins célestes, 1 Jean, V, 7 & 8.' *Journal Britannique* 15 (1754b): 151–190.

———. *Opera quae extant omnia.* Ed. Samuel Horsley. 5 vols. London: Nichols, 1779–1785.

———. *An Historical Account of Two Notable Corruptions of Scripture: in a Letter to a Friend.* London: Green, 1841.

———. *The Correspondence of Sir Isaac Newton.* Ed. H. W. Turnbull et al. 7 vols. Cambridge: Cambridge University Press, 1959–1977.

Nichols, John, ed. *Literary Anecdotes of the Eighteenth Century.* 6 vols. London: Nichols, 1812.

Nijenhuis, Willem. 'Riskante Toleranz. Martinus Lydius' "Apologia pro Erasmo".' *Zwingliana* 19 (1993): 245–261.

Nolan, Frederick. *An Inquiry into the Integrity of the Greek Vulgate or Received Text of the New Testament.* London: Rivington, 1815.

Norton, William. *A Translation, in English Daily Used, of the Peshito-Syriac Text, and of the Received Greek Text, of Hebrews, James, 1 Peter, and 1 John.* London: Bloom, 1889.

Nova vulgata bibliorum sacrorum editio. Rome: Libreria Editrice Vaticana, 1979.

Novum Testamentum Syriacum, et Arabicum. 2 vols. Rome: Sacra congregatio de propaganda fide, 1703. *DM* 8968.

Nowy Testament Pana Naszego Jezusa Chrystusa z Greckiego na polski Język z pilnością przełożony. Gdańsk: Drukowano v Wdowy Guilhelma Guilmothana, 1606.

[Nye, Stephen]. *A Brief History of the Unitarians, Called Also Socinians. In Four Letters, Written to a Friend.* [Bristol]: [Kienton], 1687.

—— *An Accurate Examination of the Principal Texts Usually Alleged for the Divinity of Our Saviour; and for the Satisfaction by Him Made to the Justice of God, for the Sins of Men.* London: [n. p.], 1692.

—— *Considerations on the Explications of the Doctrine of the Trinity.* [London]: [n. p.], 1694.

O'Connell, Marvin Richard. *Critics on Trial: An Introduction to the Catholic Modernist Crisis.* Washington, DC: Catholic University of America Press, 1994.

Oecolampadius, Johannes. *In epistolam Ioannis apostoli catholicam primam, Ioannis Oecolampadii demegoriae, hoc est, homiliae una & viginti.* Nuremberg: J. Petreius, 1524.

Oecolampadius, Johannes and Huldrych Zwingli. *Epistolarum libri quatuor, praecipua cum religionis à Christo nobis traditae capita, tum ecclesiasticae administrationis officia [...] exprimentes.* Basel: Thomas Platter and Balthasar Lasius, 1536.

Oecumenius. *Enarrationes vetustissimorum theologorum, in Acta quidem Apostolorum et in omnes D. Pauli ac Catholicas epistolas ab Oecumenio: in Apocalypsim verò, ab Aretha Caesareae Cappadociae episcopo magna cura collectae.* Trans. Johannes Henten. Antwerp: Steelsius, 1545.

Oemler, Georg. *Epistolae, quae dominicis atque Festis diebus in Ecclesia, ueteri more proponi solent, Heroico carmine, ceu prius Euangelia, à Georgio Aemylio redditae.* Basel: Oporinus, 1551.

An Ordinance of the Lords and Commons Assembled in Parliament, for the Punishing of Blasphemies and Heresies: With the Severall Penalties Therein Expressed. Die Martis, 2 Maii 1648. London: John Wright, 1648.

Owen, John. *Vindiciae Evangelicae or The Mystery of the Gospell vindicated, and Socinianisme Examined, in the Consideration, and Confutation of a Catechisme, Called a Scripture Catechisme, Written by J. Biddle, M.A., and the Catechisme of Valentinus Smalcius, Commonly Called the Racovian Catechisme.* Oxford: Lichfield, 1655.

Oxford Dictionary of National Biography [ODNB]. Ed. H. C. G. Matthew and Brian Howard Harrison. 60 vols. Oxford: Oxford University Press, 2004.

Pabel, Hilmar M. 'Credit, Paratexts, and the Editorial Strategies in Erasmus of Rotterdam's Editions of Jerome.' In *Cognition and the Book.* Ed. K. A. E. Enenkel and Wolfgang Neuber. Leiden: Brill, 2005: 217–256.

Paget, James Carleton and Joachim Schaper, ed. *The New Cambridge History of the Bible: From the Beginnings to 600*. Cambridge: Cambridge University Press, 2013.

Pak, G. Sujin. *The Judaizing Calvin: Sixteenth-Century Debates over the Messianic Psalms*. Oxford: Oxford University Press, 2009.

Ἡ Παλαιά Διαθήκη. London: R. Daniel, 1653.

Pappelbaum, Georg Gottlieb. *Untersuchung der Rauischen griechischen Handschrift des Neuen Testaments*. Berlin: Maurer, 1785.

    Codicis manuscripti N. T. Graeci Raviani in bibliotheca regia Berolinensi publica asservati Examen. Berlin: Wegener for Himburg, 1796.

Parker, David C. 'The New Testament Text and Versions.' In Paget and Schaper 2013: 412–454.

Parker, Todd C. '"The Idlest Trifling Stuff That Ever Was Writ", or, Why Swift Hated His Sermons.' In *Swift as Priest and Satirist*. Ed. Todd C. Parker. Cranbury, NJ: Associated University Presses, 2009: 58–71.

Patrick, Simon. *The Witnesses to Christianity; or, The Certainty of Our Faith and Hope: In a Discourse upon 1 S. John v. 7, 8*. London: Royston, 1675.

Paul, William E. *English Language Bible Translators*. Jefferson, NC: McFarland, 2003.

Paulus, Heinrich Eberhard Gottlob. 'Kritische Vergleichung des Codex Montfortianus im 1. Br. des Joh. mit Anmerkungen.' *Memorabilien* 6 (1794): 14–31.

Payne, J. B. 'Toward the Hermeneutics of Erasmus.' In *Scrinium Erasmianum*. Ed. J. Coppens. Leiden: Brill, 1969–1970: 2:13–49.

Pellicanus, Konrad. *In omnes apostolicas epistolas, Pauli, Petri, Iacobi, Ioannis et Iudae D. Chuonradi Pellicani [. . .] Commentarij*. Zürich: Froschauer, 1539.

    Biblia sacrosancta Testamenti Veteris & Noui, [. . .] translata in sermonem Latinum. Zürich: Froschauer, 1543.

Pennant, Thomas. *Of London*. London: Faulder, 1790.

Perceval, John. *Diary of Viscount Percival Afterwards First Earl of Egmont*. 3 vols. London: HMSO, 1920–1923.

Pfaff, Christoph Matthäus. *Dissertatio critica de genuinis librorum Novi Testamenti lectionibus*. Leiden: Boutesteyn, 1716.

Pfeiffer, Joachim Ehrenfried. *De tribus testibus in terris, ad I. Johann. V. 5. 8.* Jena: Heller, 1743.

    Differentia spiritus in terra cum aqua et sanguine testantis a spiritu teste caelesti ex 1. Joh. V, 8. proposita. Erlangen: Camerarius, 1764.

    Triada testium in caelo qui unum sunt ut I. Joh. V, 7, legitur contra D. Bensonium vindicat. Erlangen: Camerarius, [c. 1767–1772].

Pfizenmaier, Thomas C. *The Trinitarian Theology of Dr. Samuel Clarke (1675–1729): Context, Sources, and Controversy*. Leiden: Brill, 1997a.

    'Was Isaac Newton an Arian?' *Journal of the History of Ideas* 58 (1997b): 57–80.

    'Why the Third Fell Out: Trinitarian Dissent.' In *Religion, Politics and Dissent, 1660–1832*. Ed. Robert D. Cornwall and William Gibson. Aldershot: Ashgate, 2009: 17–33.

'Pharez, J.' *The Critique in the Eclectic Review, on 1 John v. 7. Confuted by Martin's Examination of Emlyn's Answer; to Which Is Added an Appendix, Containing Remarks on Mr. Porson's Letters to Archdeacon Travis, Concerning the Three Heavenly Witnesses.* London: Ogle, Hamilton, Button, 1809.

'Philalethe, J.' [Samuel Crell]. 'Explication de trois Passages de la Sainte Écriture, savoir Gen. III.17. & IV. 15. & 1 Jean V. 8.' *Bibliothèque angloise* 7 (1720): 248–284.

Pietkiewicz, Rajmund. 'Pismo Święte w języku polskim w latach 1518–1638: sytuacja wyznaniowa w Polsce a rozwój edytorstwa biblijnego.' Diss. Wrocław, 2002.

Pineau, J.-B. *Erasme: sa pensée religieuse.* Paris: PUF, 1924.

Pinelli, Antonio the Elder, ed. Ἀπόστολος. Venice: Antonio Pinelli the Elder, 1602.

Pirnát, Antal. *Die Ideologie der siebenbürger Antitrinitarier in der 1570er Jahren.* Trans. Edith Roth. Budapest: Akadémiai Kiadó, 1961.

Pio, Alberto. *Tres & viginti libri in locos lucubrationum variarum D. Erasmi Roterodami.* Paris: Bade, 1531.

Pohle, Joseph. *The Divine Trinity.* Trans. Arthur Preuss. 2nd ed. St Louis: Herder, 1915.

Polanus von Polansdorff, Amandus. *Das gantz Newe Testament vnsers Herren Jesu Christi [. . .] Mit den besten getruckten / vnnd auff Pergament geschribenen alten Griechischen Exemplaren collationiert / vnd mit allen trewen vbersehen.* Basel: [n. p.], 1603.

Syntagma theologiae christianae. Hanau: Wechel, 1609.

Poole, Matthew. *Synopsis criticorum.* 4 vols in 5. London: Flesher and Roycroft for Smith, 1669–1676.

Pope, John. *Observations on the Miraculous Conception and the Testimonies of Ignatius and Justin Martyr on That Subject.* London: Johnson, 1792.

Popkin, Richard H. 'Newton as a Biblical Scholar.' In *Essays on the Context, Nature and Influence of Isaac Newton's Theology.* Ed. James E. Force and Richard H. Popkin. Dordrecht: Kluwer, 1990: 103–118.

'Spinoza and Biblical Scholarship.' In *The Cambridge Companion to Spinoza.* Ed. Don Garrett. Cambridge: Cambridge University Press, 1996: 383–407.

Porson, Richard. *Letters to Mr. Archdeacon Travis in Answer to His Defence of the Three Heavenly Witnesses, 1 John V. 7.* London: Egerton, 1790.

The Correspondence of Richard Porson. Ed. Henry Richards Luard. Cambridge: Cambridge University Press, 1867.

Posset, Franz. 'John Bugenhagen and the Comma Johanneum.' *Concordia Theological Quarterly* 49 (1985): 245–252.

Poussines, Pierre. *Catena graecorum patrum in evangelium secundum Marcum.* Rome: Michael Hercules at the Barberini Press, 1673.

[Priestley, Joseph]. *A Familiar Illustration of Certain Passages of Scripture Relating to the Power of Man to Do the Will of God, Original Sin, Election and Reprobation, The Divinity of Christ, and Atonement for Sin by the Death of Christ. By a Lover of the Gospel.* London: Johnson, 1785.

Przypkowski, Samuel. *Catechesis ecclesiarum quae in Regno Poloniae, & magno Ducatu Lithuaniae, & aliis ad istud Regnum pertinentibus provinciis, affirmant, Neminem alium praeter Patrem Domini nostri Iesu Christi, esse illum unum Deum Israëlis: Hominem autem illum Iesum Nazarenum, qui ex Virgine natus est, nec alium, praeter aut ante ipsum, Dei Filium unigenitum & agnoscunt & confitentur. Cui accedit Fausti Socini Senensis vita. Et Dissertatio Operibus suis ab Equite Polono praemissa. Cum Catalogo Operum ejusdem Fausti Socini.* Raków [London]: [William Dugard], 1651.

Pseudo-Athanasius. *Enarratio pseudo-Athanasiana in Symbolum.* Ed. Giuseppe Bianchini. Verona: Berno, 1732.

[Pye-Smith, John.]. Review of Brown 1807 and Belsham 1808. *The Eclectic Review* 5 (1809a): 24–39, 236–251, 329–346.

'Correspondence.' *The Eclectic Review* 5 (1809b): 392.

Review of 'Pharez' 1809. *The Eclectic Review* 6 (1810): 61–71, 155–164.

Quentin, Henri. *Mémoire sur l'établissement du texte de la Vulgate. Ière partie. Octateuque.* Rome: Desclée, 1922.

The Racovian Catechisme. Amsterdam: Brooer Janz, 1652.

Rambouillet, Pierre. 'L'authenticité du verset des trois témoins célestes.' *Revue des sciences ecclésiastiques* 58 (1888): 230–244.

Ranke, Ernst. *Codex Fuldensis.* Marburg: Elwert, 1868.

Rappolt, Johann Jakob. *Dissertatio academica, de authoritate canonica dicti Johannis I. Epist. V. 7. de tribus in coelo testibus.* Tübingen: Widow of Roebel, 1745.

Reader, Thomas. *The Three Witnesses in Heaven: Or the Divine Inspiration of I. John v. 7. Proved from the Scripture Itself.* Taunton: Norris, 1791.

Reed, A. W. 'John Clement and His Books.' *The Library*, Fourth Series, 6 (1926): 329–339.

Reedy, Gerard. *The Bible and Reason: Anglicans and Scripture in Late Seventeenth-Century England.* Philadelphia: University of Pennsylvania Press, 1985.

Rees, Thomas, trans. *The Racovian Catechism.* London: Longman, 1818.

Reeve, Anne and Michael A. Screech. *Erasmus' Annotations on the New Testament: Acts, Romans, I and II Corinthians.* Leiden: Brill, 1990.

Erasmus' Annotations on the New Testament: Galatians to the Apocalypse. Leiden: Brill, 1993.

Reeves, William, ed. and trans. *The Apologies of Justin Martyr, Tertullian, and Minutius Felix.* 2 vols. London: W. B. for Churchill, 1709.

Reid, James. *Memoirs of the Lives and Writings of Those Eminent Divines, Who Convened in the Famous Assembly at Westminster, in the Seventeenth Century.* London: Young, 1811.

Reinhart, Elias Sigismund. *Dissertatio Praeliminaris ad intimiora, cum Deo dieque penetralia Socinianae & Socinianizantis scholae, Hoc potissimum exhibitura nunc Argumentum: etiamsi dictitasset nunquam Spiritus S. Certissimam Illam Canonis Graeci Particulam 1. Joh. V, 7: Tres In Celis Unum Sunt; Eandem tamen Concludendi Vim contineri iam in Illustrissimo pariter Commate Matth. XXVIII. vers. 19: Baptizate In Nomen Patris, Filii & Spiritus S.* Leipzig: Wittigau, 1666.

Reiser, Marius. 'Theologie und Kritik. Richard Simon und das Comma Johanneum.' *Studien zum Neuen Testament und seiner Umwelt, Serie A (Aufsätze)* 37 (2012): 151–165.

Report from Select Committee on the State of Education; With the Minutes of Evidence, and Index. Ordered, by the House of Commons, to be Printed, 7 August 1834. [London]: [n. p.], 1834.

Reuss, Eduard. *Bibliotheca Novi Testamenti Graeci.* Halle: Schwetschke, 1872.

Reventlow, Henning, Graf. *The Authority of the Bible and the Rise of the Modern World.* Trans. John Bowden. Philadelphia: Fortress Press, 1985.

Rex, Richard. 'Lady Margaret Beaufort and her Professorship, 1502–1559.' In *Lady Margaret Beaufort and Her Professors of Divinity at Cambridge, 1502–1649.* Ed. Patrick Collinson. Cambridge: Cambridge University Press, 2003: 19–56.

Richter, Nicolaus. *Stephanum Curcellaeum, in editione originali Novi Testamenti textus, variantium lectionum, et parallelorum Scripturae locorum, additamentis vestita, ut Socinizantem [...] praeside [...] Joh. Gotlieb Möllero [...] adumbrare instituet.* Rostock: Richelius, 1696.

Ridpath, George. *An appeal to the Word of God for the Trinity in Unity, or the Godhead of the Father, Son, and Holy Ghost; as asserted in the first article of the Church of England, and the fifth and sixth answers of the Assemblys Catechism, prov'd to be the Scripture-Doctrine of the Trinity. With arguments in Defence of the Controverted Text, 1 John V. 7. of our Translation of Philip. ii. 5, 6, and of Scripture Cousequences [sic].* London: Tookey for Bell and Popping, 1719.

Rietschel, Georg. *Lehrbuch der Liturgik.* 2 vols. Berlin: Reuther & Reichard, 1900–1909.

Rife, John M. 'The Antoniades Greek Testament.' In *Prolegomena to the Study of the Lectionary Text of the Gospels.* Ed. E. C. Colwell and D. W. Riddle. Chicago: Chicago University Press, 1933: 57–66.

Robertson, Archibald and Alfred Plummer, *A Critical and Exegetical Commentary on The First Epistle of St Paul to the Corinthians.* 2nd ed. Edinburgh: T. & T. Clark, 1914.

[Robinson, John.] *A Letter from the Lord Bishop of London, to the Incumbents of All Churches and Chappels in His Diocess, Concerning Their Not Using Any New Forms of Doxology, and the Reading the Common-Prayer at Least Once a Month.* London: Motte for Roberts; 2nd ed. Dublin: Sadlier, 1722.

Roffey, Simon. *The Medieval Chantry Chapel: An Archaeology.* Woodbridge: Boydell, 2007.

Roger, Louis. *Dissertationes duae critico-theologicae: I^a De his Joannis Evangelistae verbis: Tres sunt qui testimonium dant in coelo, &c. adversùs Socinianos, nuperosque Criticos. II^a. De Isaiae Prophetiâ: Ecce Virgo concipiet & pariet, & contra Judaeos.* Paris: Girin, 1713.

Rogers, Samuel. *Recollections of the Table-talk of Samuel Rogers. To Which Is Added Porsoniana.* New York: Appleton, 1856.

Ruckman, Peter S. *The Christian's Handbook of Manuscript Evidence.* Pensacola: Pensacola Bible Press, 1973.

Rummel, Erika. *Erasmus' Annotations on the New Testament: From Philologist to Theologian.* Toronto: Toronto University Press, 1986.

——— *Erasmus and His Catholic Critics.* 2 vols. Nieuwkoop: De Graaf, 1989.

Rump, Justus Wessel. *Commentatio critica ad libros Novi Testamenti in genere.* Leipzig: Haeredes Friderici Lanckisii, 1730.

Ruston, Alan. 'English Approaches to Socinianism.' In Szczucki 2005: 423–433.

Sánchez, Tomás. *Disputationes de sancto matrimonii sacramento.* Madrid: Ludovicus Sánchez, 1602–1605.

Sand, Christoph. *Interpretationes Paradoxae quatuor evangeliorum: Quibus affixa est dissertatio de Verbo.* 'Cosmopolis' [Amsterdam]: 'Apud Libertum Pacificum', 1669.

——— *Scriptura S. Trinitatis Revelatrix, Authore Hermanno Cingalio.* Gouda: Jacobus de Graef, 1678.

Sander, Nicholas. *De visibili monarchia ecclesiae, libri octo.* Leuven: Reynerus Velpius for John Fowler, 1571.

Sardella, Louis-Pierre. *Mgr Eudoxe Irénée Mignot (1842–1918): un évêque français au temps du modernisme.* Paris: Éditions du Cerf, 2004.

Saubert, Johannes. *Variae lectiones textus graeci evangelii S. Matthaei.* Helmstedt: Müller, 1672.

Scacchi, Fortunato, ed. *Sacra Biblia Vulgata Editione, translat. ex Hebraeo Sanctis Pagnini, Transl. Romana ex Septuag. & Chaldaicae Paraphrasis Transl. congesta Fratris Fortunati Fanensis Ordinis Erem. S. Augustini Studio & labore.* Venice: Pinelli, 1609.

Schaff, Philip. *Bibliotheca Symbolica Ecclesiae Universalis. The Creeds of Christendom with a History and Critical Notes.* 3 vols. New York: Harper, 1919.

Sherlock, William. *A Vindication of the Doctrine of the Holy and Ever Blessed Trinity, and the Incarnation of the Son of God. Occasioned by the Brief Notes on the Creed of St. Athanasius, and the Brief History of the Unitarians, or Socinians, and Containing an Answer to Both.* London: Rogers, 1690.

Schmalz [Smalcius], Valentinus. *Refutatio thesium, De Sacrosancta unitate Divinae essentiae, & in eadem Sacrosancta personarum Trinitate, a Iacobo Schoppero SS. Theologiae Doctore & professore primario Altorfii anno 1613 propositarum. Cui addita est responsio ad ea, quae Hermannus Ravenspergerus S. Th: Doctor, in Gymnasio Steinfurtensi praeter haec attulit, in scripto, cui titulum fecit: SS. Mysterium unitatis essentiae divinae in personarum Trinitate, duabus sectionibus per Theses & exegeses explicatum, &c.* Raków: Sternacius, 1614.

Schmaus, M. 'Die Texte der Trinitätslehre in den Sententiae des Simon von Tournai.' *Recherches de théologie ancienne et médiévale* 4 (1932): 59–72; 187–198; 294–307.

Schmidt, Erasmus and Zacharias Gerganos, ed. Ἡ Καινὴ Διαθήκη Ἰησοῦ Χριστοῦ. Wittenberg: August Boreck, 1622.

Scholz, Johann Martin Augustin. *Biblisch-kritische Reise in Frankreich, der Schweitz, Italien, Palästina und im Archipel.* Leipzig: F. Fleischer, 1823.

——— ed. *Novum Testamentum graece.* 2 vols. Leipzig: F. Fleischer, 1830–1836.

Schüller, Volkmar. 'Samuel Clarke's annotations in Jacques Rohault's *Traité de Physique*, and How They Contributed to Popularising Newton's Physics.' In *Between Leibniz, Newton, and Kant: Philosophy and Science in the Eighteenth Century*. Ed. Wolfgang Lefèvre. Dordrecht: Kluwer, 2001: 95–110.

Schürer, Emil. Review of Kölling 1893. *Theologische Literaturzeitung* 9 (1894): 109–110.

Scrivener, Frederick Henry Ambrose, ed. Ἡ Καινὴ Διαθήκη. *Novum Testamentum textûs Stephanici A. D. 1550. Accedunt variae lectiones editionum Bezae, Elzeviri, Lachmanni, Tischenendorfii, Tregellesii*. Cambridge: Deighton, Bell & Co., 1859.

A Plain Introduction to the Criticism of the New Testament. London: Deighton, Bell & Co., 1861.

ed. Ἡ Καινὴ Διαθήκη. *Novum Testamentum textûs Stephanici* A.D. *1550*. Cambridge: Deighton, Bell & Co., 1876.

The New Testament in the Original Greek According to the Text Followed in the Authorised Version Together with the Variations Adopted in the Revised Version. Cambridge: Cambridge University Press, 1881.

ed. Ἡ Καινὴ Διαθήκη. *Novum Testamentum textûs Stephanici* A.D. *1550*. Cambridge: Deighton, Bell & Co., 1886.

ed. *The New Testament in the Original Greek According to the Text Followed in the Authorised Version Together with the Variations Adopted in the Revised Version*. 2nd ed. Cambridge: Cambridge University Press, 1894a.

A Plain Introduction to the Criticism of the New Testament, 4th ed. 2 vols. London: Bell, 1894b.

ed. Ἡ Καινὴ Διαθήκη. *Novum Testamentum textûs Stephanici, [...] curante F. H. A. Scrivener. [...] Editio quarta ab Eb. Nestle correcta*. London: Bell, 1906.

'Scrutator.' Review of Pharez 1809. *The Watchman, or Theological Inspector* 1 (1809): 225–237.

Seager, Nicholas. 'John Bunyan and Socinianism.' *The Journal of Ecclesiastical History* 65 (2014): 580–600.

Seidel Menchi, Silvana. 'Un'opera misconosciuta di Erasmo? Il trattato pseudo-ciprianico *De duplici martyrio.' Rivista storica italiana* 90 (1978): 709–743.

Selden, John. *De Synedriis & Praefecturis Iuridicis veterum Ebraeorum liber secundus*. London: Flesher, 1653.

[Semler, Johann Salomo.] Review of Whiston 1711–1712. *Nachrichten von einer hallischen Bibliothek* 4 (1749): 237–254.

Vindiciae plurium praecipuarum lectionum codicis graeci Novi Testamenti adversus Guilielmum Whiston Anglum atque ab eo latas leges criticas. Halle: Gebauer, 1750.

Vorbereitung zur theologischen Hermenevtik, zu weiterer Beförderung des Fleisses angehender Gottesgelerten. 4 vols in 3. Halle: Hemmerde, 1760–1769.

'Anmerkung über die lange Fortdauer mancher irrigen Meinungen, über die Stelle 1 Joh. 5, 7.' *Wöchentliche Hallische Anzeigen vom Jahr 1762*, 48:761–769; 49:777–782; 50:793–802; 51:809–820.

D. Joh. Sal. Semlers historische und kritische Sammlungen über die so genannten Beweisstellen in der Dogmatik. Erstes Stück. über 1 Joh. 5, 7. Halle: Hemmerde, 1764.

Zum Andenken einer würdigen Frau, Frauen Christina Magdal. Philipp. Semlerin gebornen Döbnerin. Halle: Hendel, 1772.

Lebensbeschreibung. Halle: [Schwetschke], 1781–1782.

Senensis, Sixtus. *Bibliotheca sancta.* Venice: Franciscus Franciscius, 1566.

Servet, Miguel. *De Trinitatis erroribus libri septem.* [Hagenau]: [Secerius], 1531.

Christianismi restitutio. [Vienne]: [Arnollat], 1553.

Sept livres sur les erreurs de la Trinité. Ed. and trans. Rolande-Michelle Bénin and Marie-Louise Gicquel. Paris: Honoré Champion, 2008.

Sheehan, Jonathan. *The Enlightenment Bible: Translation, Scholarship, Culture.* Princeton: Princeton University Press, 2005.

Sherlock, William. *An Apology for Writing against Socinians.* London: Rogers, 1693.

Simon, Richard. [*Histoire critique du Vieux Testament.*] Paris: Billaine, 1678.

A Critical History of the Old Testament. Trans. Henry Dickinson. London: Davis, 1682.

Histoire critique du texte du Nouveau Testament. Rotterdam: Leers, 1689a.

Critical History of the Text of the New Testament. London: Taylor, 1689b.

Histoire critique des versions du Nouveau Testament. Rotterdam: Leers, 1690.

Histoire critique des principaux commentateurs du Nouveau Testament. Rotterdam: Leers, 1693 [1692].

Simon, Richard, trans. *Le Nouveau Testament de nôtre Seigneur Jesus-Christ.* 4 vols. Trevoux: Ganeau, 1702.

Simon, Richard. *Critique de la bibliothèque des auteurs ecclésiastiques et des prolegomènes de la bible, publiez par M. Elies Du-Pin.* 2 vols. Paris: Ganeau, 1730.

Critical History of the Text of the New Testament. Trans. Andrew Hunwick. New Testament Tools, Studies, and Documents 43. Leiden: Brill, 2013.

Skinner, Quentin. 'Hobbes on Persons, Authors and Representatives.' In *The Cambridge Companion to Hobbes's Leviathan.* Ed. Patricia Springborg. Cambridge: Cambridge University Press, 2007: 157–180.

[Smalbroke, Richard.] *Reflections on the Conduct of Mr. Whiston, in His Revival of the Arian Heresy.* London: Childe, 1711.

An Enquiry into the Authority of the Primitive Complutensian Edition of the New Testament, as Principally Founded on the Most Ancient Vatican Manuscript; Together with Some Research after That Manuscript. In order to decide the Dispute about 1 John v. 7. In a Letter to the Reverend Mr. Archdeacon Bentley, Master of Trinity-College in Cambridge. London: J. Nicks, 1722.

Smith, Thomas. *A Sermon of the Credibility of the Mysteries of the Christian Religion.* London: Roycroft, 1675.

Miscellanea, In quibus continentur Responsio ad nuperas D. Simonii in libro super fide Graecorum de dogmate Transsubstantiationis cavillationes. Dissertatio, in qua Integritas & αὐθεντία istius celeberrimi loci 1. Epist. S. Joannis, cap. V. vers. 7. vindicatur. Defensio superioris Dissertationis contra exceptiones

D. *Simonii in Criticâ historiâ novi Testamenti. Commentarius in secundam S. Petri Apostoli Epistolam.* London: S. Smith, 1690.

Snobelen, Stephen D. 'Caution, Conscience and the Newtonian Reformation: The Public and Private Heresies of Newton, Clarke and Whiston.' *Enlightenment and Dissent* 16 (1997): 151–183.

'Isaac Newton, Heretic: The Strategies of a Nicodemite.' *The British Journal for the History of Science* 32 (1999): 381–419.

'"God of Gods, and Lord of Lords": The Theology of Isaac Newton's General Scholium to the *Principia*.' *Osiris*, 2nd Series, 16 (2001): 169–208.

'William Whiston, Isaac Newton and the Crisis of Publicity.' *Studies in the History and Philosophy of Science* 35 (2004): 573–603.

'Isaac Newton, Socinianism and the "One Supreme God".' In *Socinianism and Arminianism: Antitrinitarians, Calvinists and Cultural Exchange in Seventeenth-Century Europe*. Ed. Martin Mulsow and Jan Rohls. Leiden: Brill, 2005a: 241–293.

'Socinianism and Newtonianism: The Case of William Whiston.' In Szczucki 2005b: 373–413.

'"To Us There Is But One God, the Father": Antitrinitarian Textual Criticism in Seventeenth- and Eighteenth-Century England.' In Hessayon and Keene 2006: 116–136.

'Isaac Newton, Heresy Laws and the Persecution of Dissent.' *Enlightenment and Dissent* 25 (2009): 204–259.

Sommer, Johann. *Refutatio scripti Petri Carolii editi Wittebergae.* Ingolstadt [Kraków]: Ravisius, 1582.

Tractatus aliquot Christianae religionis. Ed. Matthias Vehe-Glirius (Theodosius Schimberg). Ingolstadt [Kraków]: [Rodecki], 1583.

Sotheby's. *Books from the John Rylands University Library of Manchester. Day of Sale: Thursday 14th April 1988.* London: Sotheby's, 1988.

Libri, stampe e disegni: lunedì, 27 giugno 2005. Milan: Sotheby's, 2005.

Souverain, Matthieu. *Le Platonisme dévoilé.* Cologne [Amsterdam]: Pierre Marteau [Sebastiaan Petzold], 1700.

Sozzini, Fausto. *Commentarius in epistolam Iohannis apostoli primam.* Raków: Sternacius, 1614.

Assertiones theologicae de trino et uno deo, Adversus novos Samosatenicos. 3rd ed. Raków: Sternacius, 1618.

Responsio ad libellum Iacobi Wuieki Iesuitae Polonicè editum De Divinitate Filii Dei, & Spiritus sancti. Raków: Sternacius, 1624.

Opera. 2 vols. 'Irenopolis' [Amsterdam]: [n. p.], 1656.

Spangenberg, Johannes. *Margarita theologia.* Leipzig: Blum, 1540.

Sparks, Jared, ed. *A Collection of Essays and Tracts in Theology.* 6 vols. Boston: Everett, 1823–1826.

'Sir Isaac Newton's History of the Text of the Three Heavenly Witnesses.' *The Unitarian Miscellany and Christian Monitor* 5 (1824): 292–310.

Spinoza, Baruch. *Tractatus Theologico-Politicus.* Hamburg [Amsterdam]: Heinrich Künrath [Israel de Paul for Jan Rieuwertsz], 1670.

Spufford, Margaret. 'Literacy, Trade and Religion in the Commercial Centres of Europe.' In *A Miracle Mirrored: The Dutch Republic in European Perspective.* Ed. Karel Davids and Jan Lucassen. Cambridge: Cambridge University Press, 1995: 229–283.

Statutes of the Realm. [London]: [Eyre and Strahan], 1810–1828.

Steuber, Johannes. *Exegesis dicti 1 Jo. V, 7. Tres sunt, qui testimonium perhibent in coelo.* Marburg: Chemlin, 1640.

Stewart, Larry. 'Seeing Through the *Scholium*: Religion and Reading Newton in the Eighteenth Century.' *History of Science* 34 (1996): 123–165.

Stillingfleet, Edward. *A Discourse in Vindication of the Doctrine of the Trinity.* 2nd ed. London: Henry Mortlock, 1697.

Stockhausen, Anette von. 'Die pseud-athanasianische *Disputatio contra Arium.* Eine Auseinandersetzung mit "arianischer" Theologie in Dialogform.' In *Von Arius zum Athanasianum. Studien zur Edition der 'Athanasius Werke'.* Ed. Anette von Stockhausen and Hanns Christof Brennecke. Berlin: De Gruyter, 2010: 133–155.

Stunica, Jacobus Lopis [Diego Lopez de Zúñiga]. *Annotationes Iacobi Lopidis Stunicae contra Erasmum Roterodamum in defensionem tralationis novi testamenti.* Alcalá: Arnald Guillén de Brocar, 1520.

Sullivan, William L. 'The Three Heavenly Witnesses.' *The New York Review* 2 (1906–1907): 175–188.

Swift, Jonathan. *Miscellanies in Prose and Verse.* London: Morphew, 1711.

    Mr. C—ns's Discourse of Free-Thinking, Put into Plain English, by Way of Abstract, for the Use of the Poor. By a Friend of the Author. London: Morphew, 1713.

    Three Sermons: I. On Mutual Subjection. II. On Conscience. III. On the Trinity. London: Dodsley, 1744.

    The Works of Dr Jonathan Swift. 8 vols. Edinburgh and Glasgow: Kincaid and Donaldson, 1756.

    'Original Letters of Dean Swift to Dr Windar.' *The Gentleman's Magazine* 44 (1794): 625–626.

[Sykes, Arthur Ashley.] *An Humble Apology for St. Paul, and the Other Apostles; or, a Vindication of Them and Their Doxologies from the Charge of Heresy. By Cornelius Paets.* London: Roberts, 1719a.

    A Modest Plea for the Baptismal and Scripture-Notion of the Trinity. Wherein the Schemes of the Reverend Dr Bennet and Dr Clarke Are Compared. London: Knapton, 1719b.

Sykes, Norman. *Church and State in England in the XVIIIth Century.* Cambridge: Cambridge University Press, 1934.

Szczucki, Lech, ed. *Faustus Socinus and His Heritage.* Kraków: Polish Academy of Arts and Sciences, 2005.

Tejero, Emilia Fernández and Natalio Fernández Marcos. 'Scriptural Interpretation in Renaissance Spain.' In *Hebrew Bible-Old Testament. The History of its Interpretation. II: From the Renaissance to the Enlightenment.* Ed. Magne Saebø. Göttingen: Vandenhoeck & Ruprecht, 2008: 231–253.

Tennent, James Emerson. *The History of Modern Greece*. 2 vols. London: Colburn and Bentley, 1830.

Text und Textwert. *Text und Textwert der griechischen Handschriften des Neuen Testaments*. Ed. Kurt Aland *et al*. Berlin: De Gruyter, 1987–2013.

Thiele, Walter, ed. *Vetus Latina: die Reste der altlateinischen Bibel 26/1, Epistulae Catholicae*. Freiburg i. B.: Herder, 1956–1969.

Thuesen, Peter Johannes. 'Some Scripture Is Inspired by God: Late-Nineteenth-Century Protestants and the Demise of a Common Bible.' *Church History* 65 (1996): 609–623.

Timpanaro, Sebastiano. *The Genesis of Lachmann's Method*. Ed. and trans. Glenn W. Most. Chicago: Chicago University Press, 2005.

Tischendorf, Constantin von, ed. *Novum Testamentum Graece*. Leipzig: Köhler, 1841.

Novum Testamentum graece. Ad antiquos testes. Paris: Didot, 1842a.

Ἡ Καινὴ Διαθήκη. *Novum Testamentum graece et latine. In antiquis testibus textum versionis vulgatae latinae indagavit lectioneque variantes Stephani et Griesbachii notavit V. S. Venerabili Jager in consilium adhibito Constantinus Tischendorf*. Paris: Didot, 1842b.

'Theologie.' *Neue Jenaische allgemeine Literatur-Zeitung* 2 (1843): 326–334.

Novum Testamentum latine interprete Hieronymo. Ex celeberrimo codice Amiatino omnium et antiquissimo et praestantissimo. Leipzig: Avenarius, 1850.

Novum Testamentum graece. Ad antiquos testes. 7th ed. 2 vols. Leipzig: Winter, 1859.

Novum Testamentum graece. Ad antiquissimos testes. 8th ed. Leipzig: Hinrichs, 1872–1894.

Titelmans, François. *In omnes epistolas apostolicas [...] Elucidatio, una cum Textu suo loco ad marginem translato*. Paris: [n. p.], 1543.

Tnyeuwe Testament al geheel. Antwerp: Forsterman, 1531.

Toland, John. *Christianity Not Mysterious, or, A Treatise Shewing, That There Is Nothing in the Gospel Contrary to Reason, Nor Above It: And That No Christian Doctrine Can Be Properly Call'd a Mystery*. London: [n. p.], 1696.

Tollius, Jacob. *Epistolae itinerariae*. Ed. H. C. Henninius. Amsterdam: Halm for van Oosterwijk, 1700.

Toulmin, Joshua, ed. *A Dialogue between a Dutch Protestant, and a Franciscan Friar of Dort*. London: J. Johnson, 1784.

Tournoy, Gilbert, Jan Roegiers and Christiaan Coppens, ed. *Vives te Leuven*. Leuven: Leuven University Press, 1993.

Tracy, James D. 'Erasmus and the Arians: Remarks on the *Consensus Ecclesiae*.' *The Catholic Historical Review* 67 (1981): 1–10.

Trapman, Johannes. 'Erasmus on Lying and Simulation.' In *On the Edge of Truth and Honesty*. Ed. Toon van Houdt, Jan L. de Jong, Zoran Kwak, Marijke Spies and Marc van Vaeck. Leiden: Brill, 2002: 33–46.

Travis, George. *Letters to Edward Gibbon [...] In Defence of the Authenticity of the Seventh Verse, of the Fifth Chapter, of the First Epistle of St. John*. London: Rivington, 1784.

Letters to Edward Gibbon. 2nd ed. London: Rivington, 1785.

Letters to Edward Gibbon. 3rd ed. London: Rivington, 1794.

Tregelles, Samuel Prideaux. *The Book of Revelation in Greek.* London: Bagster, 1844.

An Account of the Printed Text of the Greek New Testament. London: Bagster, 1854.

Tremellius, Immanuel, ed. and trans. Ἡ Καινὴ Διαθήκη. *Testamentum novum.* דיתיקא חדתא. *Est autem interpretatio Syriaca Noui Testamenti, Hebraeis typis descripta, plerisque etiam locis emendata. Eadem latino sermone reddita.* Geneva: H. Estienne, 1569.

Trevor-Roper, Hugh R. 'Gibbon and the Publication of The Decline and Fall of the Roman Empire 1776–1976.' *Journal of Law and Economics* 19 (1976): 489–505.

Triglandus, Jacobus. *Disputatio theologica de tribus in coelo testibus.* 5 parts. Leiden: Elzevier, 1693–1696.

Trost, Martin, ed. *Divi Johannis apostoli et evangelistae epistola catholica prima Syriace.* Köthen: [Fürstliche Druckerei], 1621.

Trumpp, Ernst. 'Das Taufbuch der Aethiopischen Kirche. Aethiopisch und Deutsch.' *Abhandlungen der philosophisch-philologischen Classe der Königlich Bayerischen Akademie der Wissenschaften* 14 no. 3 (1878): 147–183.

Turchetti, Mario. 'Une question mal posée: Érasme et la tolérance. L'idée de sygkatabasis.' *Bibliothèque d'Humanisme et Renaissance* 53 (1991): 379–395.

Turnbull, Joseph. *The Seven Epistles of James, Peter, John and June, and the Revelation, Translated from the Original Greek; with Critical Notes, and a Dissertation on the Authenticity of I John V. 7, 8, Respecting the Three Heavenly Witnesses.* London: Bagster, 1858.

Turner, Cuthbert Hamilton. *The Early Printed Editions of the Greek Testament.* Oxford: Oxford University Press, 1924.

Turrettin, François. *Institutio theologiae elencticae.* 3 vols. Geneva: Samuel de Tournes, 1679–1686.

De necessaria secessione nostra ab Ecclesia romana, et Impossibili cum Eâ syncretismo, disputationes. 2nd ed. Geneva: Samuel de Tournes, 1687.

Turvasi, Francesco. *The Condemnation of Alfred Loisy and the Historical Method.* Rome: Edizioni di Storia e Letteratura, 1979.

Twells, Leonard. *A Critical Examination of the Late New Text and Version of the New Testament.* 3 vols. London: Gosling, 1731–1732.

Tyndale, William. *The Newe Testamente.* [Worms]: [Peter Schoeffer], 1526.

The Exposition of the Fyrst Epistle of Seynt Jhon with a Prologge Before It. [Antwerp]: [De Keyser], September 1531.

trans. *The newe Testament / dylygently corrected and compared with the Greke by Willyam Tindale.* [Antwerp]: [De Keyser], November 1534.

trans. *The New Testament Yet Once Again Corrected by William Tyndale.* Antwerp: De Keyser for van der Haghen, 1535.

Ussher, James. *A Body of Divinitie.* London: M. F. for Thomas Downes and George Badger, 1645.

The Whole Works. Ed. Charles Richard Elrington (vols. 1–15) and J. H. Todd (vols. 15–16). Dublin: Hodges and Smith, 1847–1864.

Vacant, Jean-Michel-Alfred. 'Revue theologique.' *La controverse et le contemporain*, n. s. 13 (1888): 125–141, 426–445.

Vaccari, Alberto. *Institutiones Biblicae scholis accomodatae*. 3 vols. Rome: Pontificio Istituto Biblico, 1925–1929.

Van der Erven, Gillis, trans. *Het nieuwe Testament, dat is, het nievve verbont onses Heeren Iesu Christi, In Nederduytsch na der Grieckscher waerheyt ouergheset*. [Emden]: [Van der Erven], 1561.

Van Gemert, Guillaume. 'Die niederländischen Texte Sebastian Francks.' In *Editionsdesiderate zur Frühen Neuzeit*. Ed. H.-G. Roloff. 2 vols. Amsterdam: Rodopi, 1997: 669–685.

Van Poll-van de Lisdonk, Miekske. 'Erasmus' Annotations on 1. Cor. 15, 51: "We shall indeed all rise" or "We shall not all sleep".' In *Ultima Aetas. Time, Tense and Transience in the Ancient World*. Ed. Caroline Kroon and Daan den Hengst. Amsterdam: VU Press, 2000: 163–174.

Vasileiadis, Pavlos D. 'Comma Johanneum (1 John 5:7, 8): A Study on Its Interpolation and Removal from the Biblical Text.' MTheol thesis, Aristotle University of Thessaloniki, 2013.

Venning, Ralph. *Mysteries and Revelations*. London: Rothwell, 1652.

'Vindex.' 'Zur Frage von der Authenticität der Vulgata.' *Historisch-politische Blätter für das katholische Deutschland* 124 (1899): 102–114.

Völkel, Johann. *De vera religione libri quinque: quibus praefixus est Iohannis Crellii Franci liber De deo et eius attributis, ita ut unum cum illis opus constituat*. Raków: Sternacius, 1630.

Vossius, Gerard. *De theologia gentili et physiologia christiana; sive de origine ac progressu idololatriae*. 3 vols. Amsterdam: Blaauw, 1641.

Votes of Parliament Touching the Book Commonly Called the Racovian Catechism. London: John Field, 1652.

Wagner, Johann Ehrenfried. *Integritas commatis VII. cap. V. primae Ioannis epistolae ab impugnationibus novatoris cujusdam denuo vindicata*. Chemnitz: Stoessel, 1740.

Waite, D. A. 'Most Frequent Questions We've Been Asked: What Is the Evidence Supporting 1 John 5:7?' *The Dean Burgon News* 1/5 (1979): 1–3.

Wallace, Daniel B. 'The Majority Text Theory: History, Methods, and Critique.' In *The Text of the New Testament in Contemporary Research*. Ed. Bart D. Ehrman and Michael W. Holmes. 2nd ed. Leiden: Brill, 2013: 711–744.

Walters, Alice N. 'Ephemeral Events: English Broadsides of Early Eighteenth-Century Solar Eclipses.' *History of Science* 37 (1999): 1–43.

Walther, Michael. *Harmonia Biblica*. 7th ed. Nuremberg: Endter, 1654.

Walton, Brian, ed. *Biblia sacra polyglotta*. 6 vols. London: Roycroft, 1657.

Ward, Valentine. *A Brief Statement of Facts, Designed for the Information of Those Who from Good Motives Enquire, What Are These Methodists?* 2nd ed. Edinburgh: Stewart for Nichols and Blanshard, 1815.

Ware, Henry. *Prose Works*. Ed. Chandler Robbins. London: Simms and McIntyre, 1849.

Warfield, Benjamin B. *The Printing of the Westminster Confession*. Philadelphia: MacCalla, 1901.

Waterland, Daniel. *A Vindication of Christ's Divinity: Being a Defense of Some Queries, Relating to Dr. Clarke's Scheme of the H. Trinity*. Cambridge: Crownfield, 1719.

[Welchman, Edward.] *Concentus veterum, sive appendix ad [IX. articulos Ecclesiae Anglicanae*. Oxford: Sheldonian Theatre, 1713.

Dr. Clarke's Scripture Doctrine of the Trinity Examined. Oxford: Lichfield, 1714.

A Conference with an Arian, Occasion'd by Mr. Whiston's Reply to the Right Honourable the Earl of Nottingham. Oxford: Lichfield, 1721.

Wells, Edward. *An Help for the More Easy and Clear Understanding of the Holy Scriptures*. 11 vols. Oxford: Sheldonian Theatre. 1709–1719.

Remarks on Dr Clarke's Introduction to His Scripture-doctrin of the Trinity. Oxford: Peisley, 1713.

Wenkebach, Ernst August. *John Clement: ein englischer Humanist und Arzt des sechzehnten Jahrhunderts*. Leipzig: Barth, 1925.

Wesley, John. *Explanatory Notes upon the New Testament*. London: Bowyer, 1755.

A Sermon on 1st John, v. 7. Dublin: William Kidd for William Whitestone, 1775.

The Sunday Service of the Methodists in North America. With Other Occasional Services. London: [n. p.], 1784.

The Journal of the Rev. John Wesley. Ed. Nehemiah Curnock and John Telford. 8 vols. London: Kelly, 1909–1916.

Works of John Wesley. 34 vols. Oxford: Clarendon Press, 1975–1983.

Westcott, B. F. *The Epistles of St. John*, 3rd ed. Cambridge: Macmillan, 1892.

Westfall, Richard S. *Never at Rest: A Biography of Isaac Newton*. Cambridge: Cambridge University Press, 1980.

'Newton's Theological Manuscripts.' In *Contemporary Newtonian Research*. Ed. Zev Bechler. Dordrecht: Reidel, 1982: 129–143.

Wettstein, Jakob and George Smith. *Catalogus librorum [...] Joannis Clerici*. Amsterdam: Wettstein and Smith, 1735.

Wettstein, Johann Jakob. *Prolegomena ad Novi Testamenti Graeci editionem accuratissimam*. Amsterdam: Wetstein and Smith, 1730.

Novum Testamentum Graecum. 2 vols. Amsterdam: Dommer, 1751–1752.

Wheatly, Charles. *The Church of England Man's Companion*. Oxford: Sheldonian Theatre, 1710.

Whiston, William. *New Theory of the Earth*. London: Roberts for Tooke, 1696.

Sermons and Essays upon Several Subjects. London: Tooke, 1709.

An Historical Preface to Primitive Christianity Reviv'd. London: Whiston, 1711a.

An Account of the Convocation's Proceedings with Relation to Mr. Whiston. London: Whiston, 1711b.

Primitive Christianity Reviv'd. 5 vols. London: Whiston, 1711–1712.

Three Essays. London: Whiston, 1713.

Mr. Whiston's Letter of Thanks to the Right Reverend the Lord Bishop of London, for His Late Letter to His Clergy against the Use of New Forms of Doxology. London: Senex, 1719a.

Mr. Whiston's Second Letter to the Right Reverend the Lord Bishop of London, Concerning the Primitive Doxologies. 2nd ed. London: Senex, 1719b.

Mr. Whiston's Account of Dr. Sacheverell's Proceedings in Order to Exclude Him from St. Andrew's Church in Holborn. London: Senex, 1719c.

A Commentary on the Three Catholick Epistoles of St. John. London: Senex, 1719d.

Mr Whiston's Scheme of the Solar System Epitomis'd. To Which Is Annex'd. A Translation of Part of Ye General Scholium at Ye Second Edition of Sir Isaac Newton's Principia Concerning God. London: Senex, c. 1721.

A Collection of Authentick Records Belonging to the Old and New Testament. 2 vols. London: Whiston, 1727–1728.

Historical Memoirs of the Life of Dr. Samuel Clarke. 2nd ed. London: Gyles, 1730.

Athanasian Forgeries, Impositions, and Interpolations. London: Noon, 1736.

trans. *Mr. Whiston's Primitive New Testament.* Stamford and London: Whiston, 1745.

Sacred History of the Old and New Testament. 6 vols. London: Whiston, 1745–1746.

Memoirs of the Life and Writings of Mr. William Whiston. 3 vols. London: Whiston and Bishop, 1749–1750.

Whitby, Daniel. *Examen Variantium Lectionum Johannis Millii, S. T. P. in Novum Testamentum.* London: Bowyer, 1710.

White, James R. *The King James Only Controversy: Can You Trust the Modern Translations?* 2nd ed. Minneapolis: Bethany House, 2009.

Widmannstetter, Johann Albrecht and Claude Postel, ed. *Liber sacrosancti evangelii de Iesu Christo Domino & Deo nostro.* Vienna: Michael Zimmerman, 1555.

Wigand, Johannes. *De Deo, contra Arianos novos, nuper in Polonia exortos.* [Frankfurt/Main]: Peter Braubach, 1566.

Wilbur, Earl Morse. *A History of Unitarianism.* 2 vols. Cambridge, MA: Harvard University Press, 1945–1952.

Wiles, Maurice. *Archetypal Heresy: Arianism Through the Centuries.* Oxford: Oxford University Press, 1996.

Review of Pfizenmaier 1997. *The Journal of Ecclesiastical History* 50 (1999): 389–390.

Wilhelmi, Peter Sigmund. *Dissertationum-theologicarum octava de genuitate loci 1. Ioh. v. 7.* Bern: Officina typographica Reipublicae Bernensis, 1715.

Wilkinson, Robert J. *Orientalism, Aramaic and Kabbalah in the Catholic Reformation. The First Printing of the Syriac New Testament.* Leiden: Brill, 2007a.

The Kabbalistic Scholars of the Antwerp Polyglot Bible. Leiden: Brill, 2007b.

Williams, Harold H. *Dean Swift's Library.* Cambridge: Cambridge University Press, 1932.

Williams, Rowan D. *Arius: Heresy and Tradition.* London: Darton, 1987.

Wilson, Samuel. *The Deity and Satisfaction of Christ Asserted.* London: Ward, 1747.

Wiseman, Nicholas Patrick. *Two Letters on Some Parts of the Controversy Concerning 1. John V. 7.* Rome: Salviucci, 1835.

Wodrow, Robert. *Analecta.* 4 vols. Edinburgh: Maitland Club, 1842–1843.

Wolf, Johann Christian. *Cura philologica et critica.* 5 vols. Basel: Christ, 1741.

Wordsworth, Christopher, ed. *The New Testament of Our Lord and Saviour Jesus Christ.* 2 vols. London: Rivington, 1866.

Wordsworth, John, Henry J. White and H. F. D. Sparks, ed. *Nouum Testamentum Domini nostri Iesu Christi latine secundum editionem Sancti Hieronymi ad codicum manuscriptorum fidem.* 3 vols. Oxford: Clarendon Press, 1889–1954.

Wouters, Martinus. *Dilucidatio selectarum S. Scripturae quaestionum.* 6 vols. Leuven: Van Overbeke, 1753–1758.

Wright, George N. *An Historical Guide to the City of Dublin.* London: Baldwin, 1825.

Wujek, Jakub. *O Bóstwie syna Bożego y ducha świętego.* Kraków: Piotrkowczyk, 1590.

Nowy Testament Pana naszego Iesusa Christusa. Z nowu z Laćińskiego y z Gręckiego na Polskie. Kraków: Piotrkowczyk, 1593.

'X. D.' 'Trinity College Library.' *The Irish Penny Journal* 24 April 1841: 340–342.

Zegers, Niklaas. *Epanorthotes. Castigationes in Novum Testamentum.* Cologne: Birckmann, 1555.

Zwick, Johannes, ed. *Novum Testamentum omne latina versione, oppositum aeditioni uulgari siue Germanice, in usus studiosorum uulgatum. Das gantz Neüw Testament zu Teütsch dem Latinen entgägen gesetzt.* Zürich: Froschauer, 1535.

Zwingli, Huldrych. *In plerosque Novi Testamenti libros, quorum elenchum post Praefationem & Indicem reperies, Annotationes ex ipsius ore exceptae per Leonem Iudae.* Zürich: Froschauer, 1581.

Opera. Ed. Melchior Schuler and Johann Schulthess. 8 vols. Zürich: Schulthess, 1828–1842.

Index